PATENTED

PATENTED

1,000 DESIGN PATENTS

THOMAS
RINALDI

The revelation that inspired this book is my own belated appreciation of design patents as tools for identifying the designers of seemingly innumerable manufactured objects. As a student of architectural history, I knew well the thrill of unearthing forgotten design authorships for historic buildings, especially when the mystery architect turned out to be an eminent name. Despite my longstanding interest in industrial design, however, I shrugged off the design origins of most manufactured goods as simply unknowable, lost in corporate archives that I had no hope of ever laying eyes on.

Of course, there are those landmark works of design whose authorship is widely known: Henry Dreyfuss's model 500 telephone for the Bell System, for example, or famous chairs by the Eameses that figure prominently in museum collections. As time went on, I occasionally found other resources that went further: catalogs for industrial design exhibitions at important museums, or back issues of trade journals whose pages yielded attributions for everything from cars to cocktail shakers. But these offered a flashlight in a graveyard approach at best.

By the early 2010s, I found myself stumbling on ever more U.S. patent images in the odd internet searches that filled my idle hours. As one unfamiliar with patent documents, their technical looking drawings and paragraphs of ponderous text didn't hold my interest, at first. Eventually I understood that I was looking at two different types of patent documents. Utility patents are those typically invoked in our vernacular use of the term "patent." Generally speaking, they protect inventions — the way things work. Design patents are something different. Their job is to document and protect an object's appearance.

The U.S. government began issuing utility patents in 1790. Utility patents typically involve numerous detailed drawings with key tags that refer to lengthy accompanying text. Design patents came later, in 1842. They can quickly be spotted by the prefix "D" in their patent numbers. Utility patents outnumber design patents by about ten to one. While utility patents identify the individuals responsible for how something works, design patents name their designers (called "inventors" in patent parlance) and often their commissioning manufacturers (referred to as "assignees").

With this knowledge in hand, I realized that all those PDFs I'd been turning up were the tip of an archival iceberg that represented a design historian's El Dorado, a proverbial rabbit hole of unfathomable depth. I took the plunge.

1,000 DESIGN PATENTS

This book is based on the exploration of two ideas that can vastly inform our perspective on the designed world we inhabit. The first is the existence of an invaluable yet underutilized historical resource in the form of nearly one million design patents issued by the U.S. Patent Office (USPO, later USPTO, to include Trademarks) since 1842. The second, predicated upon the first, is that using these documents to identify the design provenance of seemingly inconsequential objects allows us to broaden our concept of design to include mundane items as expressions of human creativity in a way that has been generally reserved for higher art forms up until now.

The 1,000 design patents in this book are shortlisted from a pool of more than 750,000 issued from 1900 to the present. Starting the survey at the dawn of the twentieth century, the book focuses on an era in which developments such as the introduction of electricity for domestic use revolutionized the character of consumer goods. While the United States is not the only nation to have established a legal apparatus for documenting and protecting works of design, the USPTO's archive of design patents is unique for its scope, consistency and accessibility, making it the ideal subject for study. As the USPTO imposes no citizenship or residency requisites on who can apply for a patent, its archive includes works by inventors from all over the world. This is reflected in the selections featured in the book.

The patents included here are presented in simple chronological sequence. This is to emphasize the way different kinds of objects relate to one another, and the idea that their stylistic evolution is based on technical developments and creative processes that transcend typology. In addition to basic information such as inventor, assignee and relevant dates, a series of directories in the back of the book include PTO classification codes and a helpful typological taxonomy for each patent.

Beyond offering an interesting catalog of designs from the last twelve decades, this book seeks to spotlight some of the most important designers many of us have never heard of — prolific figures like Jean Reinecke and Charles Harrison — thus introducing readers to names that are largely unknown, though their work is familiar to many of us. The book should inspire readers to dig deeper by using online patent databases and other research tools to further explore the legacy of these designers and others like them. It should promote the notion that the creative approach of industrial designers is manifest across the different types of things they design, how that approach evolves over time, and how trajectories of creative output overlap between successive generations of designers — in short, how relationships exist between these different things we make, and how even the contrasts between them can be seen as responses to common themes that continue to steer their ongoing evolution.

ORIGINS OF DESIGN PATENTS

Although the story of design patents is closely intertwined with that of industrial design, in fact design patents predate the emergence of industrial design as an organized professional discipline by nearly a century. What's more, design patents are issued for works whose provenance belongs to other disciplines, such as fashion or graphic design. Their legal mandate is to guarantee designers the proprietary use of their work for a set period of time. While the legislation governing their issuance and enforcement has been revised through the years, the basic function of design patents has remained basically the same since 1842.

As a modern legal concept, patents came out of the Industrial Revolution in England during the seventeenth and eighteenth centuries. One year after enacting its new Constitution, the U.S. government adopted patents into its own legal system with the Patent Act in 1790. Borrowing from English precedent, the idea was not simply to guarantee fair treatment for inventors: the system sought to stimulate technological development by rewarding competitive innovation while at the same time making new inventions a matter of public record so that inventors could build on each other's work.

By the nineteenth century, advances in industrial processes such as casting, stamping, weaving, and cutting had given rise to mass production. This reality carried with it certain aesthetic implications. While manufacturers availed themselves of these innovations to produce more goods at lower cost, consumer expectations demanded that the manufactured origins of these goods not overly cheapen their appearance. At the same time, other technical developments enabled the application of decorative patterns that, used judiciously, could help manufacturers conceal the industrial processes employed in making their goods while adding decorative flair to lend their products consumer appeal in a competitive marketplace.

Thus by the 1830s American manufacturers saw real monetary value in design for mass-produced goods. But existing patent law in the United States, intended to protect how things worked rather than how they looked, proved ill suited to protect product design. So manufacturers (notably Jordan L. Mott, owner of a New York ironworks) began lobbying for a new type of legal protection to defend against "design piracy." Their efforts culminated in what became known as the Design Patent Act of 1842, a federal law that, like its predecessor, took cues from England as a precedent.

The Patent Office issued just fourteen design patents in the law's first year. These included designs for a typeface, a candelabrum, cast iron stoves, and a bathtub, a "corpse preserver," and a decorative pattern for an oilcloth floor covering. As initially crafted, design patents proved to be something of a blunt instrument. With the volume of mass-produced goods steadily rising, the shortcomings of the original statute forced a major re-writing of the legislation in what came to be known as the Patent Act of 1902. Rather than set forth specific lists of patentable objects as had been done previously, the Patent Office thenceforth operated on the basis of a one-size-fits-all statute to protect "any new, original, and ornamental design for an article of manufacture."

PATENT DRAWINGS

The PTO's standards for design patent drawings have remained consistent since the nineteenth century. Photographs have sometimes been allowed as substitutions for drawings, and in recent years the agency has accepted color images and 3-D renderings, but the overwhelming majority of patents are illustrated in the same line drawings that have a character of their own. That character owes in large part to the need for all patent drawings to withstand reproduction at reduced scale in periodically issued gazettes, which was how the PTO historically met its public dissemination mandate. With drawing standards set forth in a document known as the Manual of Patent Examining Procedure (MPEP), this enforced consistency also levels the playing field so that patent examiners can make apples-to-apples comparisons when evaluating new applications.

Design patent drawings are similar to those for utility patents, but are generally simpler, illustrating their subjects in plan, elevation, and sometimes perspective views, occasionally with the aid of section details. The MPEP establishes graphic conventions such as the use of diagonal lines to represent transparent surfaces. Dashed or broken lines indicate parts of the object that are helpful for context but are not included in what is being protected in that specific patent. The artists who create patent drawings do so on a contractual basis. While some patent artists are able to lend their drawings a unique style that sets them apart, even within a system of a standardized graphic conventions, frustratingly, the artists who create them are nowhere named in the patent documents themselves.

DESIGN FOR INDUSTRY

That the character of design patent documents has remained so consistent for so long is especially noteworthy given how dramatically the world outside the PTO has changed since 1842. Not least among those changes is the emergence of industrial design as a widely recognized professional discipline in the 1930s. Historians debate whether this development was cause or consequence of the complete stylistic revolution in product design that took place in those years. However, it seems hardly coincidental that the number of design patents issued during this period more than doubled from a yearly average of approximately 3,000 in 1930 to a high of nearly 6,500 in 1941, before plummeting afterwards with the onset of World War II. This statistic would not again exceed 6,000 until 1989.

That sustained slump may reflect a certain skepticism on the part of some industrial designers. "Many of our designs are patented and assigned to our clients, but designs, like ideas, are difficult to protect," wrote Henry Dreyfuss in 1955.[1] "A design patent is worth little more than the paper it is printed on," remarked J. Gordon Lippincott a decade earlier, "except perhaps for a doubtful degree of scare value."[2] Yet despite these misgivings, designers still actively sought design patents: Dreyfuss alone was granted more than 300 throughout his career.

In the twenty-first century, any lingering doubts shadowing the efficacy of design patents appear to have been laid to rest by the 2016 U.S. Supreme Court decision Apple v. Samsung, in which Apple was awarded nearly $400 million on the basis of design patents for various aspects of the company's iPhone, first introduced in 2007. This decision came down in the midst of a surge in annual issuance statistics for both design and utility patents. From 6,092 design patents issued in 1989, that figure grew to nearly 30,000 by the time of the Supreme Court's Apple v. Samsung decision, and then jumped to nearly 35,000 by the close of the decade. The USPTO has issued more design patents in the first two decades of the twenty-first century than it did during the entire 157-year history of design patents before that.

PATENTS AS TOOLS FOR DESIGN HISTORIANS

As the value of design patents for their intended purpose has been appraised and reappraised, their importance as a resource for design historians went largely overlooked until recently. Although publication had always been part of their mandate, accessing and searching patent documents remained primarily the domain of patent agents,

examiners and attorneys before digitization. The advent
of searchable electronic databases for U.S. patents made
available by Google Patents (beginning in 2006) and other
online platforms has made these previously obscure documents far easier to find. This newfound accessibility has
made design patents an invaluable resource for historians
of industrial design.

That said, it must be noted that design patents are not
without their limitations as a documentary record. Patent
applications are made on a voluntary basis: some of the most
important figures in design history have not a single patent
to their name, and many iconic designs were simply never patented. Some corporate patrons meanwhile seem to have not
bothered with design patents as a matter of policy. While
the Zenith Radio Corporation aggressively sought patents
for its products in the decades after World War II, one finds
not a single design patent issued to the Radio Corporation
of America during the same period.

Furthermore, the various infrastructures of the U.S.
patent system have not always been equally accessible
to all. Women and people of color remain problematically
underrepresented in industrial design to this day. In writing on the economic fallout of racial injustice in the United
States, academic economist Lisa Cook of Michigan State
University found that "extrajudicial killings and loss of
personal security depressed patent activity among blacks
by more than 15 per cent annually between 1882 and 1940."[3]
The documentary record patents provide must be understood with this in mind.

Recent decades have seen design patent activity grow
at a staggering pace, particularly in the wake of Apple v.
Samsung. Indicative of increased economic globalization,
more nations around the world have codified their own systems for design protection. These governmental agencies
cooperate through the World Intellectual Property Orga-
nization, a United Nations agency formed in 1967. With
intellectual property infrastructures in the United States
and elsewhere now recording design activity to a greater
degree than ever before, one imagines that these records
will be an even stronger resource for the design historians
of tomorrow.

When I was ten years old, my parents and I took a family vacation to Detroit, Michigan. One of our agenda items during that trip was a visit to the Henry Ford Museum. The museum has made a point of collecting examples of various things that aren't typically thought of as museum pieces. The collection includes cars, of course, but I still remember my excitement to find things like giant steam engines that had once powered entire factories; one of Ford's early tri-motor airplanes; and an elaborate neon sign that had advertised a Holiday Inn before being displaced by subsequent generations of corporate branding.

In one area, the museum displayed various types of ordinary household objects like radios, toasters, and vacuum cleaners. The curators arranged these items in chronological sequence to emphasize their evolution over time. This exhibit made an impression that resonates with me still. Already by that age, I had realized a budding fascination with old things. Like many of us, I still find myself drawn to ordinary objects left over from years past. However, the chemistry of that attraction goes largely unexplored. In the pages that follow, design patents for selected typologies, such as kitchen appliances, mobile telephones, and televisions, have been gathered and arranged in chronological sequence to spotlight their specific developmental trajectories. Like the displays I saw in my youth at the Henry Ford Museum, these evolutionary case studies help shed light on the science behind our sensory response to aesthetic distinctions between products of different eras.

It is an incidental quirk of the past few hundred years that the things we make are of such different character from one generation to the next. Case studies such as these help illustrate the notion that stylistic evolution is not simply a reflection of changing tastes, but also a consequence of innovations in material science (from wood, to metals, to Bakelite, to modern plastics, for example), and developments in production techniques that cut manufacturing costs while facilitating increased volumes of production. The interplay of these processes continuously renders old things visibly different from their newer counterparts.

Very often, objects whose design is clearly of a different time take on an appeal that transcends their usefulness.

But not all products reach a state of retro-chic maturity at the same rate. What governs the timing of the watershed moment when yesterday's trash becomes tomorrow's treasure is perhaps as much a question for psychologists as it is for design practitioners or antiquarians. Some typologies hit a sort of developmental stasis at which point their design changes less over decades than it once did from year to year. This is certainly the case for automobiles, whose stylistic development progressed at a staggering pace through the mid-twentieth century before slowing dramatically by century's end. Once this kind of visual parity is reached, age alone seems to be less of an appeal. Is it a coincidence that cars made after the 1970s seldom turn up at antique car shows, even though they are now comfortably old enough to meet the typical 25-year minimum age requirement for entry?

Technological developments meanwhile not only render stylistic changes among items of given typologies; they sometimes create whole new typologies (while also rendering other typologies extinct). Mobile telephones, for example, began their evolution as a spin-off from traditional landline units, then evolved rapidly through the 1980s and 90s, appropriating adjunct functions along the way. By the first decade of the twenty-first century, they had not only eviscerated the primacy of their parent typology, but also subsumed the short-lived trajectories of hand-held computers and portable audio players, and even that of consumer point-and-shoot cameras.

Beyond past-versus-present distinctions of material, style, or function, the appeal of old things depends also on a scarcity that can only be acquired through attrition. For each typology, there is an awkward in-between age when being outdated seems only a handicap. Try giving away a big-screen television from the 1990s, for instance. Or imagine the emotional trauma of a front-row style blogger caught brandishing a two-year-old iPhone. This is the danger zone, the age at which anything is fair game for the landfill (or the e-waste recycle bin).

But for those objects lucky enough to survive this treacherous period, there comes a time when age is an asset. Once it becomes clear that most examples of a given typology have disappeared, the few that survive take on a unique ability to provide contrast by standing out from that which is current. Almost anything old can become appealing once it's rare enough, no matter how ordinary or unimpressive it may have been in its own time. Together, these forces of scarcity together with age-accrued aesthetic distinction can lend appeal to an unreliable old car, a broken iPod or an alarm clock whose sole functional virtue is being right twice a day. Pre-smartphone-era flip phones seem not to have hit their stride as collectors' items yet, but it's probably just a matter of time.

As for current trends in design evolution, one can only wonder what the future holds for such products as smartphones or flat screen televisions whose design trajectories have reached type-forms so static that stylistic differences between models are nuanced to the extreme. It is noteworthy that the apparent sameness of these items seems not to have dissuaded their makers from pursuing design patents, which as noted previously are now issued in greater numbers than ever before. Where these threads go from here may be determined by technological developments that change the function of these products as much as by any trend of fashion or material innovation. As years pass and the dust settles on today's array of consumer goods to reveal which designs will take their place among the classics, these very words will endure their own period of being awkwardly out of date, before, with any luck, aging gracefully to a point where they too offer a reflection of their time in a way that is meaningful, or at least amusing, to future readers.

PATENT NO. USD 41,725
GRANTED AUGUST 29,1911

PATENT NO. USD 80,628
GRANTED MARCH 4,1930

PATENT NO. USD 85,916
GRANTED JANUARY 5,1932

PATENT NO. USD 91,054
GRANTED NOVEMBER 21,1933

PATENT NO. USD 114,262
GRANTED APRIL 11,1939

PATENT NO. USD 122,316
GRANTED SEPTEMBER 3,1940

PATENT NO. USD 131,802
GRANTED MARCH 31,1942

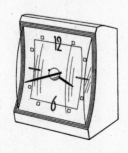

PATENT NO. USD 146,322
GRANTED FEBRUARY 4,1947

PATENT NO. USD 162,523
GRANTED MARCH 20,1951

PATENT NO. USD 186,529
GRANTED NOVEMBER 3, 1959

PATENT NO. USD 196,525
GRANTED OCTOBER 8, 1963

PATENT NO. USD 201,895
GRANTED AUGUST 10, 1965

PATENT NO. USD 228,791
GRANTED OCTOBER 23, 1973

PATENT NO. USD 239,091
GRANTED MARCH 9, 1976

PATENT NO. USD 255,876
GRANTED JULY 15, 1980

PATENT NO. USD 311,141
GRANTED OCTOBER 9, 1990

PATENT NO. USD 602,380
GRANTED OCTOBER 20, 2009

PATENT NO. USD 845,149
GRANTED APRIL 9, 2019

PATENT NO. USD 33,041
GRANTED JULY 31, 1900

PATENT NO. USD 38,028
GRANTED MAY 22, 1906

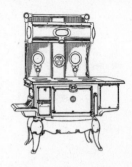

PATENT NO. USD 42,802
GRANTED JULY 16, 1912

PATENT NO. USD 54,479
GRANTED FEBRUARY 10, 1920

PATENT NO. USD 82,851
GRANTED DECEMBER 16, 1930

PATENT NO. USD 90,108
GRANTED JUNE 13, 1933

PATENT NO. USD 95,268
GRANTED APRIL 16, 1935

PATENT NO. USD 99,048
GRANTED MARCH 24, 1936

PATENT NO. USD 99,438
GRANTED APRIL 28, 1936

PATENT NO. USD 100,221
GRANTED JUNE 30, 1936

PATENT NO. USD 124,847
GRANTED JANUARY 28, 1941

PATENT NO. USD 150,516
GRANTED AUGUST 10, 1948

PATENT NO. USD 161,648
GRANTED JANUARY 16, 1951

PATENT NO. USD 175,847
GRANTED OCTOBER 18, 1955

PATENT NO. USD 200,890
GRANTED APRIL 13, 1965

PATENT NO. USD 242,836
GRANTED DECEMBER 28, 1976

PATENT NO. USD 314,305
GRANTED FEBRUARY 5, 1991

PATENT NO. USD 685,602
GRANTED JULY 9, 2013

PATENT NO. USD 31,369
GRANTED AUGUST 8,1899

PATENT NO. USD 70,930
GRANTED AUGUST 24,1926

PATENT NO. USD 84,642
GRANTED JULY 14,1931

PATENT NO. USD 104,259
GRANTED APRIL 27,1937

PATENT NO. USD 133,051
GRANTED JULY 14,1942

PATENT NO. USD 157,406
GRANTED FEBRUARY 21,1950

PATENT NO. USD 164,114
GRANTED JULY 31,1951

PATENT NO. USD 182,029
GRANTED FEBRUARY 4,1958

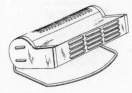

PATENT NO. USD 217,459
GRANTED MAY 5,1970

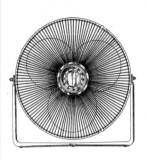

PATENT NO. USD 240,231
GRANTED JUNE 8,1976

PATENT NO. USD 270,941
GRANTED OCTOBER 11,1983

PATENT NO. USD 291,486
GRANTED AUGUST 18,1987

PATENT NO. USD 309,944
GRANTED AUGUST 14,1990

PATENT NO. USD 359,116
GRANTED JUNE 6,1995

PATENT NO. USD 458,673
GRANTED JUNE 11, 2002

PATENT NO. USD 511,017
GRANTED OCTOBER 25,2005

PATENT NO. USD 538,921
GRANTED MARCH 20,2007

PATENT NO. USD 729,375
GRANTED MAY 12,2015

PATENT NO. USD 33,286
GRANTED OCTOBER 2, 1900

PATENT NO. USD 46,277
GRANTED AUGUST 18, 1914

PATENT NO. USD 75,732
GRANTED JULY 10, 1928

PATENT NO. USD 83,800
GRANTED MARCH 31, 1931

PATENT NO. USD 101,495
GRANTED OCTOBER 6, 1936

PATENT NO. USD 114,093
GRANTED APRIL 4, 1939

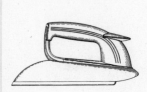

PATENT NO. USD 154,278
GRANTED JUNE 28, 1949

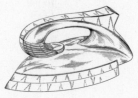

PATENT NO. USD 158,295
GRANTED APRIL 25, 1950

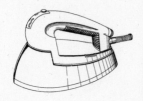

PATENT NO. USD 165,909
GRANTED FEBRUARY 12, 1952

PATENT NO. USD 176,977
GRANTED FEBRUARY 28,1956

PATENT NO. USD 186,907
GRANTED DECEMBER 22,1959

PATENT NO. USD 196,746
GRANTED OCTOBER 29,1963

PATENT NO. USD 230,458
GRANTED FEBRUARY 26,1974

PATENT NO. USD 285,737
GRANTED SEPTEMBER 16,1986

PATENT NO. USD 487,832
GRANTED MARCH 23,2004

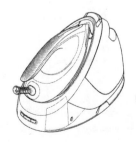

PATENT NO. USD 550,915
GRANTED SEPTEMBER 11,2007

PATENT NO. USD 739,630
GRANTED SEPTEMBER 22,2015

PATENT NO. USD 838,424
GRANTED JANUARY 15,2019

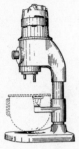

PATENT NO. USD 73,464
GRANTED SEPTEMBER 20, 1927

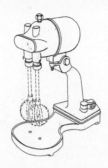

PATENT NO. USD 83,410
GRANTED FEBRUARY 17, 1931

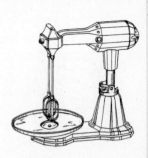

PATENT NO. USD 90,794
GRANTED OCTOBER 3, 1933

PATENT NO. USD 95,352
GRANTED APRIL 23, 1935

PATENT NO. USD 102,148
GRANTED DECEMBER 1, 1936

PATENT NO. USD 132,968
GRANTED JULY 7, 1942

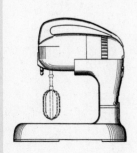

PATENT NO. USD 158,835
GRANTED JUNE 6, 1950

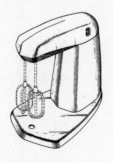

PATENT NO. USD 170,130
GRANTED AUGUST 4, 1953

PATENT NO. USD 194,473
GRANTED JANUARY 29, 1963

PATENT NO. USD 210,682
GRANTED APRIL 2, 1968

PATENT NO. USD 242,109
GRANTED NOVEMBER 2, 1976

PATENT NO. USD 255,760
GRANTED JULY 8, 1980

PATENT NO. USD 286,258
GRANTED OCTOBER 21, 1986

PATENT NO. USD 387,610
GRANTED DECEMBER 16, 1997

PATENT NO. USD 395,572
GRANTED JUNE 30, 1998

PATENT NO. USD 533,021
GRANTED DECEMBER 5, 2006

PATENT NO. USD 633,334
GRANTED MARCH 1, 2011

PATENT NO. USD 868,531
GRANTED DECEMBER 3, 2019

PATENT NO. USD 234,605
GRANTED MARCH 25,1975

PATENT NO. USD 269,873
GRANTED JULY 26,1983

PATENT NO. USD 289,044
GRANTED MARCH 31,1987

PATENT NO. USD 289,896
GRANTED MAY 19,1987

PATENT NO. USD 305,427
GRANTED JANUARY 9,1990

PATENT NO. USD 319,053
GRANTED AUGUST 13,1991

PATENT NO. USD 334,568
GRANTED APRIL 6,1993

PATENT NO. USD 359,734
GRANTED JUNE 27,1995

PATENT NO. USD 382,873
GRANTED AUGUST 26,1997

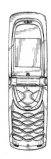

PATENT NO. USD 392,285
GRANTED MARCH 17, 1998

PATENT NO. USD 443,866
GRANTED JUNE 19, 2001

PATENT NO. USD 456,375
GRANTED APRIL 30, 2002

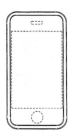

PATENT NO. USD 500,750
GRANTED JANUARY 11, 2005

PATENT NO. USD 558,756
GRANTED JANUARY 1, 2008

PATENT NO. USD 599,794
GRANTED SEPTEMBER 8, 2009

PATENT NO. USD 626,929
GRANTED NOVEMBER 9, 2010

PATENT NO. USD 777,699
GRANTED JANUARY 31, 2017

PATENT NO. USD 793,986
GRANTED AUGUST 8, 2017

PATENT NO. USD 81,846
GRANTED AUGUST 19,1930

PATENT NO. USD 88,997
GRANTED JANUARY 10,1933

PATENT NO. USD 99,737
GRANTED MAY 19,1936

PATENT NO. USD 105,126
GRANTED JUNE 29,1937

PATENT NO. USD 109,710
GRANTED MAY 17,1938

PATENT NO. USD 137,990
GRANTED MAY 30,1944

PATENT NO. USD 171,067
GRANTED DECEMBER 8,1953

PATENT NO. USD 183,106
GRANTED JUNE 24,1958

PATENT NO. USD 197,533
GRANTED FEBRUARY 18,1964

PATENT NO. USD 210,689
GRANTED APRIL 2, 1968

PATENT NO. USD 220,127
GRANTED MARCH 9, 1971

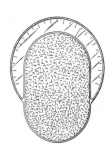

PATENT NO. USD 224,443
GRANTED JULY 25, 1972

PATENT NO. USD 289,386
GRANTED APRIL 21, 1987

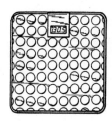

PATENT NO. USD 313,765
GRANTED JANUARY 15, 1991

PATENT NO. USD 505,874
GRANTED JUNE 7, 2005

PATENT NO. USD 538,190
GRANTED MARCH 13, 2007

PATENT NO. USD 551,580
GRANTED SEPTEMBER 25, 2007

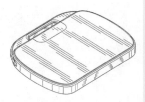

PATENT NO. USD 653,571
GRANTED FEBRUARY 7, 2012

PATENT NO. USD 152,266
GRANTED JANUARY 4, 1949

PATENT NO. USD 158,618
GRANTED MAY 16, 1950

PATENT NO. USD 174,076
GRANTED FEBRUARY 22, 1955

PATENT NO. USD 183,782
GRANTED OCTOBER 21, 1958

PATENT NO. USD 185,282
GRANTED MAY 26, 1959

PATENT NO. USD 194,628
GRANTED FEBRUARY 19, 1963

PATENT NO. USD 205,194
GRANTED JULY 5, 1966

PATENT NO. USD 224,346
GRANTED JULY 18, 1972

PATENT NO. USD 226,329
GRANTED FEBRUARY 13, 1973

PATENT NO. USD 227,701
GRANTED JULY 10,1973

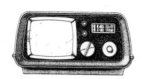

PATENT NO. USD 232,258
GRANTED JULY 30,1974

PATENT NO. USD 238,511
GRANTED JANUARY 20,1976

PATENT NO. USD 252,395
GRANTED JULY 17,1979

PATENT NO. USD 272,908
GRANTED MARCH 6,1984

PATENT NO. USD 275,855
GRANTED OCTOBER 9,1984

PATENT NO. USD 394,089
GRANTED MAY 5,1998

PATENT NO. USD 519,117
GRANTED APRIL 18,2006

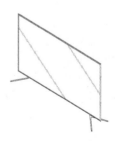

PATENT NO. USD 735,153
GRANTED JULY 28,2015

PATENT NO. USD 72,495
GRANTED APRIL 19,1927

PATENT NO. USD 78,504
GRANTED MAY 14,1929

PATENT NO. USD 86,804
GRANTED APRIL 19,1932

PATENT NO. USD 91,978
GRANTED APRIL 17,1934

PATENT NO. USD 93,903
GRANTED NOVEMBER 20,1934

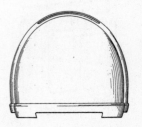

PATENT NO. USD 107,552
GRANTED DECEMBER 21,1937

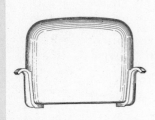

PATENT NO. USD 153,901
GRANTED MAY 24,1949

PATENT NO. USD 161,266
GRANTED DECEMBER 19,1950

PATENT NO. USD 183,808
GRANTED OCTOBER 28,1958

PATENT NO. USD 189,440
GRANTED DECEMBER 13,1960

PATENT NO. USD 203,527
GRANTED JANUARY 18,1966

PATENT NO. USD 226,242
GRANTED JANUARY 30,1973

PATENT NO. USD 287,808
GRANTED JANUARY 20,1987

PATENT NO. USD 338,368
GRANTED AUGUST 17, 1993

PATENT NO. USD 362,992
GRANTED OCTOBER 10,1995

PATENT NO. USD 505,584
GRANTED MAY 31,2005

PATENT NO. USD 796,248
GRANTED SEPTEMBER 5,2017

PATENT NO. USD 876,872
GRANTED MARCH 3,2020

PATENT NO. USD 95,451
GRANTED APRIL 30,1935

PATENT NO. USD 99,888
GRANTED JUNE 2,1936

PATENT NO. USD 105,228
GRANTED JULY 6,1937

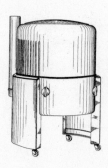

PATENT NO. USD 119,543
GRANTED MARCH 19,1940

PATENT NO. USD 145,543
GRANTED SEPTEMBER 3,1946

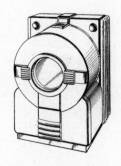

PATENT NO. USD 153,920
GRANTED MAY 31,1949

PATENT NO. USD 169,351
GRANTED APRIL 21,1953

PATENT NO. USD 173,655
GRANTED DECEMBER 14,1954

PATENT NO. USD 177,010
GRANTED MARCH 6,1956

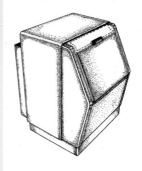

PATENT NO. USD 193,066
GRANTED JUNE 19,1962

PATENT NO. USD 211,601
GRANTED JULY 2,1968

PATENT NO. USD 292,629
GRANTED NOVEMBER 3,1987

PATENT NO. USD 360,501
GRANTED JULY 18,1995

PATENT NO. USD 446,891
GRANTED AUGUST 21,2001

PATENT NO. USD 465,622
GRANTED NOVEMBER 12,2002

PATENT NO. USD 527,150
GRANTED AUGUST 22,2006

PATENT NO. USD 554,307
GRANTED OCTOBER 30,2007

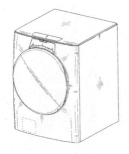

PATENT NO. USD 773,755
GRANTED DECEMBER 6,2016

One thousand design patents might seem like a generous allowance.
Yet the designs included here constitute a tiny fraction — something approaching one-one-thousandth — of the pool from which
they were selected. Capping the list at 1,000 therefore made the
selection process something of a gruelling undertaking. These
paragraphs outline what the reader will and will not find among the
selections, and why.

Design patents are issued for a broad range of products. While
most of these fall under the umbrella of what is generally considered
industrial design, some do not. For the purposes of this book,
works whose provenance belongs to well-defined disciplines other
than industrial and product design — such as fashion and graphic
design — have been foregone to allow the focus to remain on works
of industrial design.

In addition, the selection features many designs that are
universally owned, used, and loved in homes, offices, and towns
across the world, from the tiny to the gigantic, providing a
synthesis of product design through the objects the majority
of us use every day at home, at work, out and about in towns and
cities, and while traveling at home and abroad.

In each of the 1,000 patents presented on the following pages,
readers will generally see the first page of the original patent
document, reproduced in its entirety to give the flavor of the
original patent as an archival artefact. In some cases, pages
other than the first page have been selected in order to feature
a particular drawing that best conveys the design. On every page,
readers will also find key information about each patent including
the name of the designer (or "inventor" in patent parlance),
manufacturer ("assignee"), the name of the design, the date the
patent was filed, the date it was granted, and the patent number.
In addition to this key information, at the back of the book, three
directories – by type, by inventor, and by assignee – give readers
alternative ways of understanding this particular selection of
design patents, as well as providing a fascinating insight into what
was patented, who patented them, and for whom, over the last
120 years.

TITLE: BILLIARD-TABLE
INVENTOR: DANIEL W. DELANEY
ASSIGNEE: ALFRED B. MARX & GEORGE E. MARX

PATENT NUMBER: USD 32,835
PATENT FILED: APRIL 19, 1900
PATENT GRANTED: JUNE 12, 1900

DESIGN.

No. 32,835.

Patented June 12, 1900.

D. W. DELANEY.
BILLIARD TABLE.

(Application filed Apr. 19, 1900.)

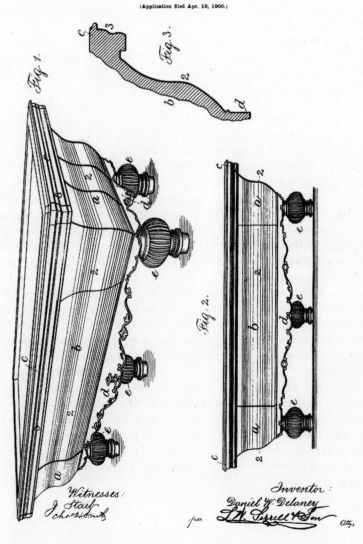

Witnesses:
J. Staib
Chas H. Smith

Inventor:
Daniel W. Delaney
per L. M. Ferrell & Son
Attys.

TITLE: SAD IRON
INVENTOR: GEORGE H. DIPPO
ASSIGNEE: FERRO-STEEL COMPANY

PATENT NUMBER: USD 33,286
PATENT FILED: MARCH 28, 1900
PATENT GRANTED: OCTOBER 2, 1900

DESIGN.

No. 33,286.

Patented Oct. 2, 1900.

G. H. DIPPO.
SAD IRON.
(Application filed Mar. 28, 1900.)

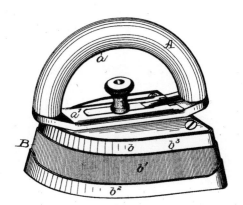

WITNESSES:
J.C. Turner
N. Emerich.

INVENTOR.
BY G. H. Dippo,
J. D. Fay
ATTORNEY.

41

TITLE: CREAM WHIPPER
INVENTOR: PEARL F. FELL
ASSIGNEE: NONE

PATENT NUMBER: USD 34,098
PATENT FILED: JANUARY 14, 1901
PATENT GRANTED: FEBRUARY 19, 1901

DESIGN.

No. 34,098.

Patented Feb. 19, 1901.

P. F. FELL.
CREAM WHIPPER.
(Application filed Jan. 14, 1901.)

Witnesses:
J. P. Appleman
E. E. Potter.

Inventor
Pearl F. Fell.
By
N. C. Evert & Co.
Att'ys.

TITLE: TELEPHONE TRANSMITTER BOX
INVENTOR: RICHARD M. EATON
ASSIGNEE: NOVELTY ELECTRIC COMPANY

PATENT NUMBER: USD 35,266
PATENT FILED: SEPTEMBER 23, 1901
PATENT GRANTED: NOVEMBER 5, 1901

DESIGN.

No. 35,266.

Patented Nov. 5, 1901.

R. M. EATON.
TELEPHONE TRANSMITTER BOX.
(Application filed Sept. 23, 1901.)

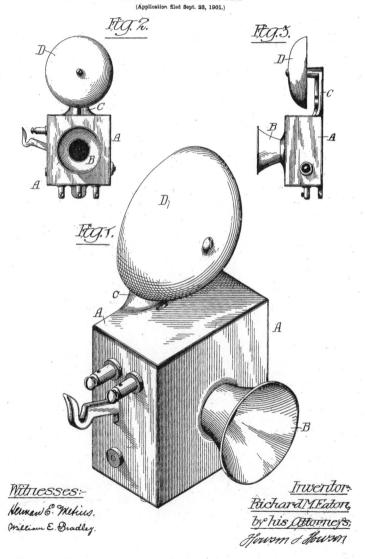

Fig. 2.

Fig. 3.

Fig. 1.

Witnesses:-
Herman E. Metius.
William E. Bradley.

Inventor:
Richard M. Eaton,
by his Attorneys,
Howson & Howson

TITLE: CASH REGISTER CABINET OR CASING
INVENTOR: LEOPOLD JACOBI
ASSIGNEE: NATIONAL CASH REGISTER COMPANY

PATENT NUMBER: USD 36,767
PATENT FILED: OCTOBER 14, 1903
PATENT GRANTED: FEBRUARY 2, 1904

DESIGN.

No. 36,767.

PATENTED FEB. 2, 1904.

L. JACOBI.
CASH REGISTER CABINET OR CASING.
APPLICATION FILED OCT. 14, 1903.

Witnesses
W. W. Cartle
John J. Ungváry

Inventor
Leopold Jacobi
by Frank Parker Davis
+ J. B. Hayward *Attorneys*

TITLE: TEA OR COFFEE POT OR SIMILAR ARTICLE
INVENTOR: ALBERT STEFFIN
ASSIGNEE: PAIRPOINT CORPORATION

PATENT NUMBER: USD 37,008
PATENT FILED: APRIL 4, 1904
PATENT GRANTED: JUNE 28, 1904

DESIGN.

No. 37,008.

PATENTED JUNE 28, 1904.

A. STEFFIN.

TEA OR COFFEE POT OR SIMILAR ARTICLE.

APPLICATION FILED APR. 4, 1904.

Witnesses
James F. Duhamil
BE Stickney

By

Inventor
Albert Steffin
Attorney
A Bull Malcomson

45

TITLE: BATH TUB
INVENTOR: WILLIAM H. LLOYD
ASSIGNEE: CRANE COMPANY

PATENT NUMBER: USD 37,257
PATENT FILED: MARCH 9, 1904
PATENT GRANTED: DECEMBER 6, 1904

DESIGN

No. 37,257.

PATENTED DEC. 6, 1904.

W. H. LLOYD.
BATH TUB.
APPLICATION FILED MAR. 9, 1904.

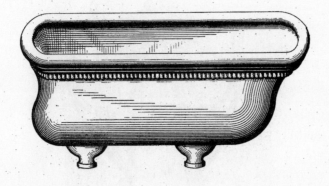

Witnesses:
F. E. Gaither.
Archworth Martin

Inventor:
William H. Lloyd,
By Paul Synnestvedt,
Atty.

TITLE: CHAIR-FRAME
INVENTOR: GUSTAVE STICKLEY
ASSIGNEE: NONE

PATENT NUMBER: USD 37,508
PATENT FILED: JUNE 26, 1905
PATENT GRANTED: AUGUST 8, 1905

DESIGN.

No. 37,508.

G. STICKLEY.
CHAIR FRAME.
APPLICATION FILED JUNE 26, 1905.

PATENTED AUG. 8, 1905.

WITNESSES:
B. E. Robinson.
M. M. Nott.

INVENTOR:
Gustave Stickley
BY:
Howard P. Denison
ATTORNEY.

TITLE: REFRIGERATOR
INVENTOR: CHARLES H. BOECK
ASSIGNEE: METAL STAMPING COMPANY

PATENT NUMBER: USD 38,237
PATENT FILED: APRIL 18, 1906
PATENT GRANTED: SEPTEMBER 11, 1906

DESIGN.

No. 38,237.

PATENTED SEPT. 11, 1906.

C. H. BOECK.
REFRIGERATOR.
APPLICATION FILED APR. 18, 1906.

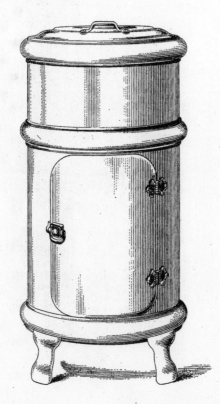

Inventor

Witnesses

Charles H. Boeck
By *Julian C. Dowell Ston*
his Attorneys

TITLE: CABINET FOR TALKING-MACHINES
INVENTOR: JOHN C. ENGLISH
ASSIGNEE: VICTOR TALKING MACHINE COMPANY

PATENT NUMBER: USD 38,537
PATENT FILED: MARCH 22, 1907
PATENT GRANTED: APRIL 23, 1907

DESIGN.

No. 38,537.

PATENTED APR. 23, 1907.

J. C. ENGLISH.
CABINET FOR TALKING MACHINES.
APPLICATION FILED MAR. 22, 1907.

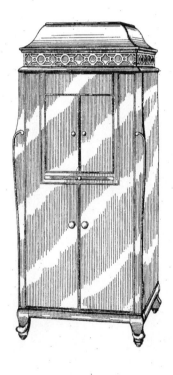

INVENTOR
John C. English.

WITNESSES
F. G. Hartman.
A. G. Gardner.

.BY Horace Pettit

ATTORNEY.

TITLE: CABINET
INVENTOR: ANTON TAMULAITIS
ASSIGNEE: NONE

PATENT NUMBER: USD 38,586
PATENT FILED: APRIL 19, 1907
PATENT GRANTED: MAY 28, 1907

DESIGN.

No. 38,586.

PATENTED MAY 28, 1907.

A. TAMULAITIS.
CABINET.
APPLICATION FILED APR. 19, 1907.

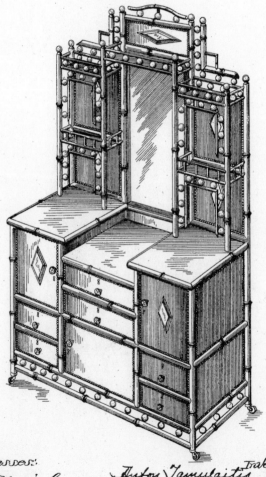

Witnesses:
Am. Hamial
E. M. Lundy

Inventor
Anton Tamulaitis
by Frank L. Thomason
Att

TITLE: WEIGHING AND VENDING MACHINE
INVENTORS: ALBERT HEIMANN & LEO FLATOW
ASSIGNEE: NONE

PATENT NUMBER: USD 38,670
PATENT FILED: JUNE 1, 1907
PATENT GRANTED: JULY 9, 1907

DESIGN.

No. 38,670.

PATENTED JULY 9, 1907.

A. HEIMANN & L. FLATOW.
WEIGHING AND VENDING MACHINE CASE.
APPLICATION FILED JUNE 1, 1907.

WITNESSES
Leon Hauerstein
Harry Goss

INVENTORS
Albert Heimann
Leo Flatow
BY
Chapin Raymond
their ATTORNEYS

TITLE: REFRIGERATOR
INVENTOR: MORRIS ROSE
ASSIGNEE: BELDING-HALL COMPANY

PATENT NUMBER: USD 40,042
PATENT FILED: MARCH 6, 1909
PATENT GRANTED: JUNE 8, 1909

DESIGN.

M. ROSE.
REFRIGERATOR.
APPLICATION FILED MAR. 6, 1909.

40,042.

Patented June 8, 1909.

WITNESSES:
H. Crochen
W. H. Heagerty

INVENTOR.
Morris Rose
BY
Stewart & Stewart
ATTORNEYS

TITLE: COVERED DISH OR SIMILAR ARTICLE
INVENTOR: CHARLES EDWARD HAVILAND
ASSIGNEE: NONE

PATENT NUMBER: USD 40,520
PATENT FILED: DECEMBER 16, 1909
PATENT GRANTED: FEBRUARY 22, 1910

DESIGN.

C. E. HAVILAND.
COVERED DISH OR SIMILAR ARTICLE.
APPLICATION FILED DEC. 16, 1909.

40,520.

Patented Feb. 22, 1910.

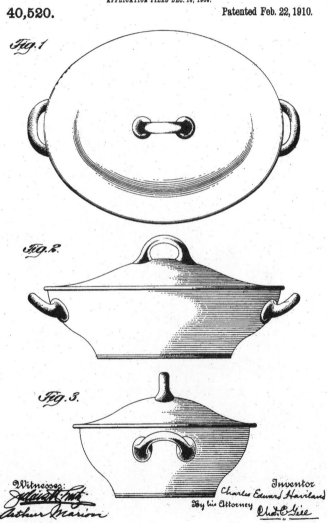

Fig.1

Fig.2.

Fig.3.

Witnesses:

Inventor
Charles Edward Haviland
By his Attorney

TITLE: COMPUTING-SCALE HOUSING
INVENTOR: ALLEN DE VILBISS, JR.
ASSIGNEE: TOLEDO COMPUTING SCALE COMPANY

PATENT NUMBER: USD 40,593
PATENT FILED: DECEMBER 16, 1909
PATENT GRANTED: MARCH 29, 1910

DESIGN.

A. DE VILBISS, JR.
COMPUTING SCALE HOUSING.
APPLICATION FILED DEC. 16, 1909.

40,593.

Patented Mar. 29, 1910.

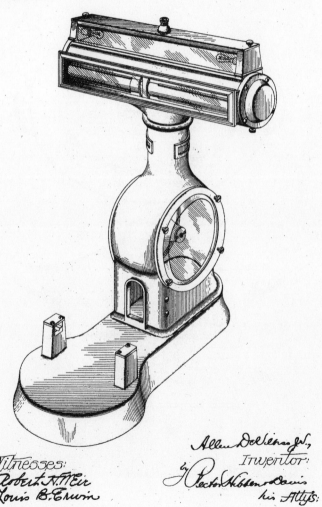

Witnesses:
Robert N. Weir
Louis B. Erwin

Allen De Vilbiss Jr.,
Inventor:
by Rector Hibben Davis
his Attys.

TITLE: CASING FOR PORTABLE SUCTION
CLEANING APPARATUS
INVENTORS: IRVING K. BAXTER & CHARLES F. BARRETT
ASSIGNEE: STANDARD VACUUM CLEANER COMPANY

PATENT NUMBER: USD 41,007
PATENT FILED: JULY 19, 1910
PATENT GRANTED: NOVEMBER 29, 1910

DESIGN.

I. K. BAXTER & C. F. BARRETT.
CASING FOR PORTABLE SUCTION CLEANING APPARATUS.
APPLICATION FILED JULY 19, 1910.

41,007.

Patented Nov. 29, 1910.

2 SHEETS—SHEET 1.

Fig. 1

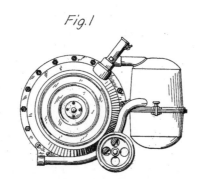

Fig. 2

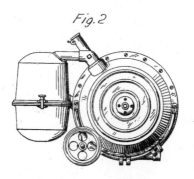

WITNESSES:
H. W. Meade
M. I. Lougden

INVENTORS
Irving K. Baxter
Charles F. Barrett
BY
[signature]
ATTORNEY

TITLE: STREET LAMP
INVENTOR: GEORGE JOSEPH MURRAY
ASSIGNEE: NONE

PATENT NUMBER: USD 41,303
PATENT FILED: JANUARY 27, 1910
PATENT GRANTED: APRIL 11, 1911

DESIGN.

G. J. MURRAY,
STREET LAMP.
APPLICATION FILED JAN. 27, 1910.

41,303.

Patented Apr. 11, 1911.

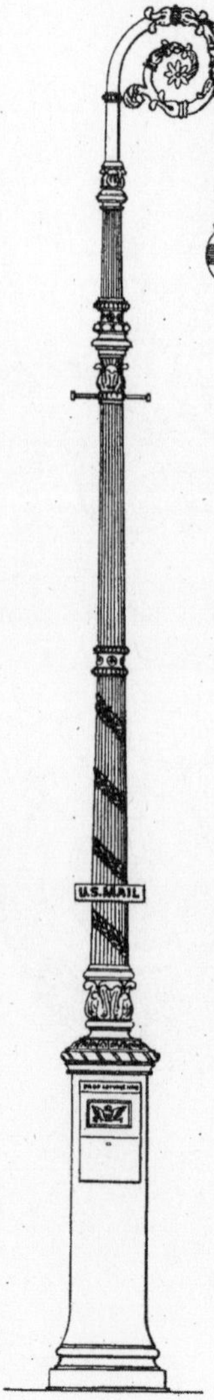

Witnesses:
Geo. A Hoffman
Cuthbert H. Jewell

George J. Murray
Inventor
By his Attorney
Walter W. Pumphrey

TITLE: URINAL
INVENTORS: OLIVER C. G. BRETTELL & JOHN F. BAILEY
ASSIGNEE: NONE

PATENT NUMBER: USD 41,401
PATENT FILED: SEPTEMBER 16, 1909
PATENT GRANTED: MAY 23, 1911

DESIGN.

O. C. G. BRETTELL & J. F. BAILEY.
URINAL.
APPLICATION FILED SEPT. 16, 1909.

41,401.

Patented May 23, 1911.

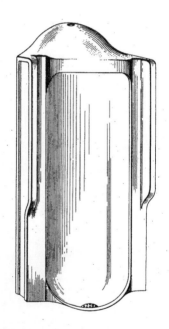

WITNESSES.
Robert C Totten
John F. Will.

INVENTORS
Oliver C G Brettell
& John F Bailey
By Kay & Totten
attorneys.

TITLE: CASING FOR ALARM CLOCKS
INVENTOR: GEORGE KERN
ASSIGNEE: WESTERN CLOCK MANUFACTURING COMPANY

PATENT NUMBER: USD 41,725
PATENT FILED: NOVEMBER 7, 1910
PATENT GRANTED: AUGUST 29, 1911

DESIGN.

G. KERN.
CASING FOR ALARM CLOCKS.
APPLICATION FILED NOV. 7, 1910.

41,725.

Patented Aug. 29, 1911.

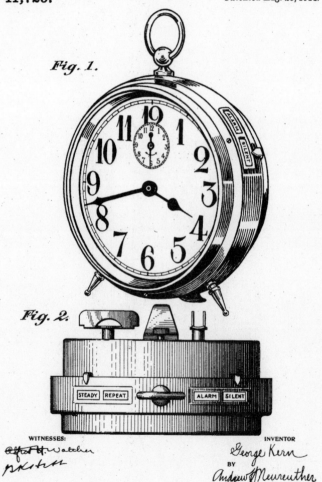

Fig. 1.

Fig. 2.

WITNESSES:

INVENTOR
George Kern
BY
Andrew Neureuther
ATTORNEY

TITLE: CASING FOR DISPENSING APPARATUS
INVENTOR: WALTER O. AMSLER
ASSIGNEE: AUTO-MERCHANDISING COMPANY
OF PITTSBURGH

PATENT NUMBER: USD 41,790
PATENT FILED: JUNE 13, 1911
PATENT GRANTED: SEPTEMBER 19, 1911

DESIGN.

W. O. AMSLER.
CASING FOR DISPENSING APPARATUS.
APPLICATION FILED JUNE 13, 1911.

41,790.   Patented Sept. 19, 1911.

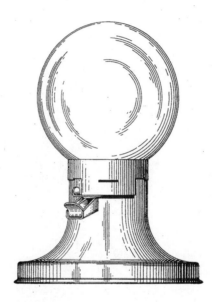

WITNESSES   INVENTOR
F. E. Gaither.   Walter O. Amsler
Lois Wineman.   by W. G. Doolittle
                                          attorneys.

TITLE: STOVE
INVENTOR: GUNNAR CARTENG
ASSIGNEE: ATLANTA STOVE WORKS

PATENT NUMBER: USD 42,728
PATENT FILED: MARCH 4, 1912
PATENT GRANTED: JULY 9, 1912

DESIGN.

G. CARTENG.
STOVE.
APPLICATION FILED MAR. 4, 1912.

42,728.

Patented July 9, 1912.

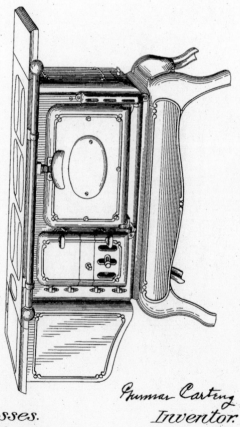

Witnesses.
Wm. J. Stafford
William H. Govert.

Gunnar Carteng
Inventor.

TITLE: SIDEBOARD
INVENTORS: PHILIP MINDUM & LEON HEYNE
ASSIGNEE: NONE

PATENT NUMBER: USD 42,842
PATENT FILED: MARCH 27, 1912
PATENT GRANTED: JULY 30, 1912

DESIGN.

P. MINDUM & L. HEYNE.
SIDEBOARD.
APPLICATION FILED MAR. 27, 1912.

42,842.

Patented July 30, 1912.

Witnesses:

E. B Knudsen,
A. S. Peterson.

Inventors:

P. MINDUM,
L. HEYNE,
By Michael J Stark & Sons, Attys.

TITLE: BOTTLE
INVENTOR: GEORGE R. WEST
ASSIGNEE: NONE

PATENT NUMBER: USD 43,173
PATENT FILED: MAY 11, 1912
PATENT GRANTED: OCTOBER 15, 1912

DESIGN.

G. R. WEST.
BOTTLE.
APPLICATION FILED MAY 11, 1912.

43,173.

Patented Oct. 15, 1912.

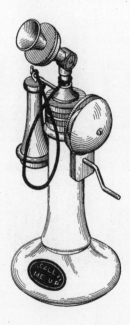

WITNESSES:
Wa. Heckman
Fred. J. Staub.

George R. West INVENTOR
by *C. M. Clarke* Atty

TITLE: CASING AND STAND FOR LIQUID AGITATORS
INVENTOR: CHARLES N. ECKLYN
ASSIGNEE: NONE

PATENT NUMBER: USD 43,991
PATENT FILED: OCTOBER 12, 1912
PATENT GRANTED: MAY 13, 1913

DESIGN.

C. N. ECKLYN.
CASING AND STAND FOR LIQUID AGITATORS.
APPLICATION FILED OCT. 12, 1912.

43,991.

Patented May 13, 1913.

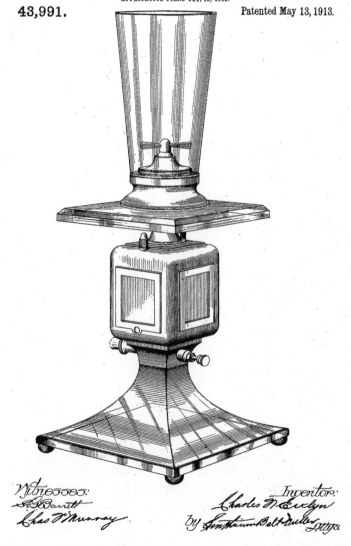

Witnesses:

Inventor:
Charles N. Ecklyn
By Lintham Belt & Miller Attys.

TITLE: CHAIR
INVENTOR: WALTER F. KOKEN
ASSIGNEE: KOKEN BARBERS SUPPLY COMPANY

PATENT NUMBER: USD 44,006
PATENT FILED: FEBRUARY 17, 1913
PATENT GRANTED: MAY 13, 1913

DESIGN.

W. F. KOKEN.
CHAIR.
APPLICATION FILED FEB. 17, 1913.

D 44,006.

Patented May 13, 1913.
2 SHEETS—SHEET 1.

Fig. 1.

Witnesses:
Harry H. Reiss.
George G. Anderson.

Inventor:
Walter F. Koken,
By
Hugh K. Wagner
His Attorney.

TITLE: TUBULAR LANTERN
INVENTOR: JAMES H. HILL
ASSIGNEE: EMBURY MANUFACTURING COMPANY

PATENT NUMBER: USD 44,340
PATENT FILED: APRIL 24, 1913
PATENT GRANTED: JULY 15, 1913

DESIGN.

J. H. HILL.
TUBULAR LANTERN.
APPLICATION FILED APR. 24, 1913.

44,340.

Patented July 15, 1913.

Fig. 1.

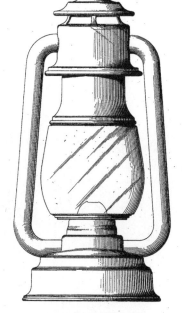

Fig. 2.

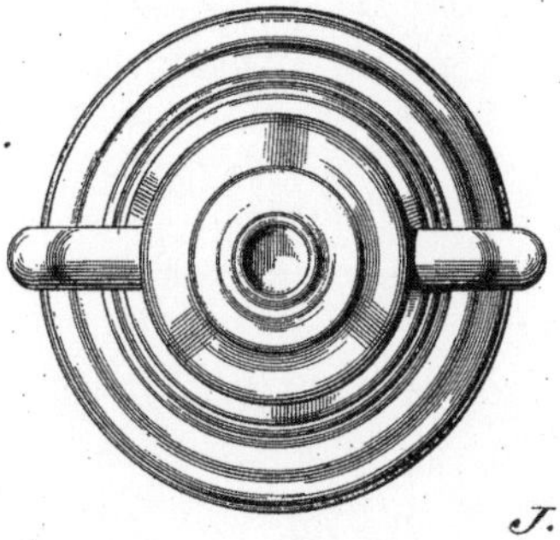

Witnesses
W. A. Williams
F. H. Bivel.

Inventor
J. H. Hill.
By Chas. M. Catlin,
Attorney

65

TITLE: DESK
INVENTOR: HENRY J. MERLE
ASSIGNEE: NONE

PATENT NUMBER: USD 44,770
PATENT FILED: JULY 2, 1913
PATENT GRANTED: OCTOBER 21, 1913

DESIGN.

H. J. MERLE.
DESK.
APPLICATION FILED JULY 2, 1913.

44,770.

Patented Oct. 21, 1913.

Witnesses:

Inventor.

Henry J. Merle

TITLE: SODA-DISPENSING APPARATUS
INVENTOR: JOHN M. TRAVIS
ASSIGNEE: NONE

PATENT NUMBER: USD 45,096
PATENT FILED: SEPTEMBER 26, 1913
PATENT GRANTED: DECEMBER 30, 1913

DESIGN.

J. M. TRAVIS.
SODA DISPENSING APPARATUS.
APPLICATION FILED SEPT. 26, 1913.

45,096.

Patented Dec. 30, 1913.

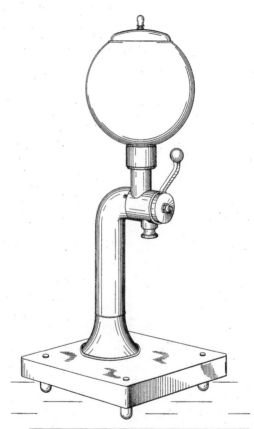

WITNESSES:

Harry A. Beimes

Fannie E. Weber

INVENTOR.
John M. Travis.

BY

Ernst Starek

ATTORNEY.

TITLE: INK BOTTLE
INVENTOR: CHARLES H. HENKELS
ASSIGNEE: THE CARTER'S INK COMPANY

PATENT NUMBER: USD 45,113
PATENT FILED: AUGUST 16, 1913
PATENT GRANTED: JANUARY 6, 1914

DESIGN.

C. H. HENKELS.
INK BOTTLE.
APPLICATION FILED AUG. 16, 1913.

45,113.

Patented Jan. 6, 1914.

WITNESSES:
M. E. Flaherty.
A. E. O'Brien.

INVENTOR:
Charles H. Henkels.
By
Coale & Hayes
his attorneys.

TITLE: SALT OR PEPPER SHAKER
INVENTOR: LOGAN A. BROADDUS
ASSIGNEE: NONE

PATENT NUMBER: USD 45,584
PATENT FILED: FEBRUARY 16, 1914
PATENT GRANTED: APRIL 14, 1914

DESIGN.

L. A. BROADDUS.
SALT OR PEPPER SHAKER.
APPLICATION FILED FEB. 16, 1914.

45,584.

Patented Apr. 14, 1914.

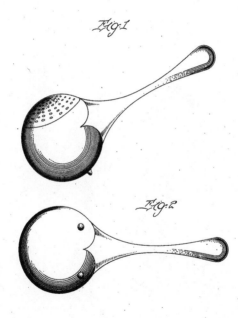

Fig.1

Fig.2

Inventor
L. A. BROADDUS

Witnesses
Robut M. Lutphui.
a. I. Sting

By *Watson E. Coleman*
Attorney

TITLE: SELF HEATING SAD IRON
INVENTOR: GEORGE FINN
ASSIGNEE: NONE

PATENT NUMBER: USD 46,277
PATENT FILED: MAY 29, 1914
PATENT GRANTED: AUGUST 18, 1914

DESIGN.

G. FINN.
SELF HEATING SAD IRON.
APPLICATION FILED MAY 29, 1914.

46,277.

Patented Aug. 18, 1914.

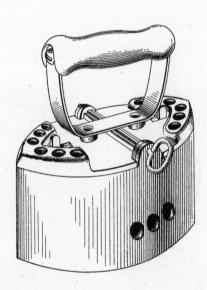

Witnesses:

Arthur Marion.

Inventor:
George Finn,
By his Attorney,
Charles C. Gill

TITLE: VEHICLE BODY
INVENTOR: JAMES S. STEPHENS
ASSIGNEE: NONE

PATENT NUMBER: USD 46,327
PATENT FILED: MAY 20, 1914
PATENT GRANTED: AUGUST 25, 1914

DESIGN.

J. S. STEPHENS,
VEHICLE BODY.
APPLICATION FILED MAY 20, 1914.

46,327.

Patented Aug. 25, 1914.
2 SHEETS—SHEET 1.

Fig.1.

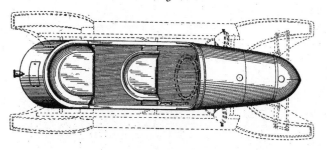

Fig.2.

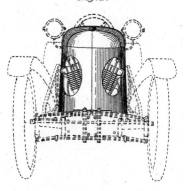

Witnesses
Martin H. Olsen.
Robert S. Martin

Inventor
James S. Stephens.
By Kummler & Kummler, Attys.

71

TITLE: GLASS BLANK FOR PORTABLE ELECTRIC LAMPS
INVENTOR: RICHARD S. GIESE
ASSIGNEE: NONE

PATENT NUMBER: USD 46,928
PATENT FILED: OCTOBER 26, 1914
PATENT GRANTED: FEBRUARY 9, 1915

DESIGN.

R. S. GIESE.

GLASS BLANK FOR PORTABLE ELECTRIC LAMPS.

APPLICATION FILED OCT. 26, 1914.

46,928.

Patented Feb. 9, 1915.

Fig. 1.

Fig. 2

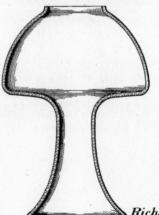

WITNESSES

Jas. F. McCathran

H. F. Riley

Richard S. Giese,
INVENTOR

BY *E. G. Siggers*

ATTORNEY

TITLE: COFFEE MILL CASING
INVENTORS: FRANK F. WEAR & BERNARD M. ELY
ASSIGNEE: ALVEY-FERGUSON COMPANY

PATENT NUMBER: USD 47,660
PATENT FILED: NOVEMBER 14, 1914
PATENT GRANTED: JULY 27, 1915

DESIGN.

F. F. WEAR & B. M. ELY.
COFFEE MILL CASING.
APPLICATION FILED NOV. 14, 1914.

47,660.

Patented July 27, 1915.

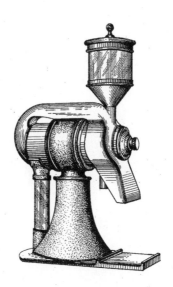

Witnesses:
J. M. Fowler Jr.
L. N. Gillis

Inventors.
F. F. Wear & B. M. Ely
By C. J. Stockman
Atty.

TITLE: PITCHER
INVENTOR: WILLIAM MISCHLER
ASSIGNEE: E.G. WEBSTER & SON

PATENT NUMBER: USD 48,354
PATENT FILED: OCTOBER 14, 1915
PATENT GRANTED: DECEMBER 28, 115

DESIGN.

W. MISCHLER.
PITCHER.
APPLICATION FILED OCT. 14, 1915.

48,354.

Patented Dec. 28, 1915.

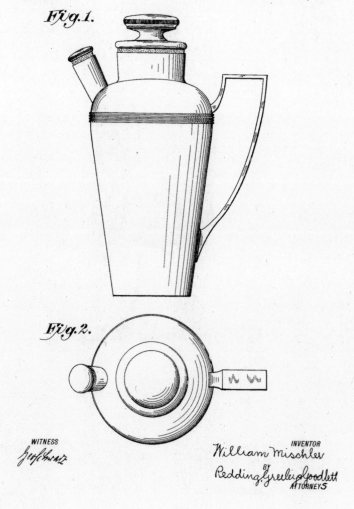

Fig.1.

Fig.2.

WITNESS

INVENTOR
William Mischler
BY
Redding Greeley Goodlett
ATTORNEYS

TITLE: PORTABLE LAMP
INVENTOR: HARRISON D. MCFADDIN
ASSIGNEE: NONE

PATENT NUMBER: USD 48,565
PATENT FILED: DECEMBER 11, 1915
PATENT GRANTED: FEBRUARY 15, 1916

DESIGN.

H. D. McFADDIN.
PORTABLE LAMP.
APPLICATION FILED DEC. 11, 1915.

48,565.

Patented Feb. 15, 1916.

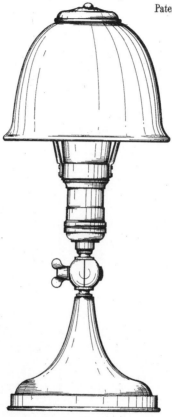

WITNESS

C. Zabriskie.

INVENTOR

Harrison D. McFaddin.

BY

Jas. H. Griffin

Attorneys

TITLE: CASING AND STAND FOR ELECTRIC FANS
INVENTOR: WARREN NOBLE
ASSIGNEE: FRANTZ PREMIER COMPANY

PATENT NUMBER: USD 48,570
PATENT FILED: OCTOBER 18, 1915
PATENT GRANTED: FEBRUARY 15, 1916

DESIGN.

W. NOBLE.
CASING AND STAND FOR ELECTRIC FANS.
APPLICATION FILED OCT. 18, 1915.

48,570.

Patented Feb. 15, 1916.

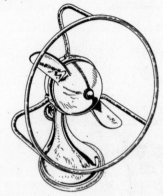

Fig. 1

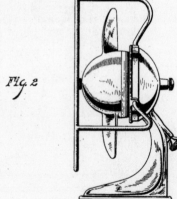

Fig. 2

Inventor

Warren Noble

By Hull, Smith, Brock & West
Attys.

TITLE: FOLDING CAMERA
INVENTOR: JOSEPH GODDARD
ASSIGNEE: SENECA CAMERA MANUFACTURING COMPANY

PATENT NUMBER: USD 48,622
PATENT FILED: SEPTEMBER 16, 1915
PATENT GRANTED: FEBRUARY 22, 1916

DESIGN.

J. GODDARD.
FOLDING CAMERA.
APPLICATION FILED SEPT. 16, 1915.

48,622.

Patented Feb. 22, 1916.

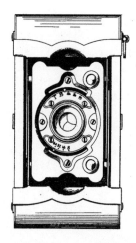

Inventor:
Joseph Goddard
by his attorneys
Davis & Dorsey

TITLE: SAFETY MATCH BOX
INVENTOR: JAMES OSA HAYES
ASSIGNEE: NONE

PATENT NUMBER: USD 49,118
PATENT FILED: FEBRUARY 7, 1916
PATENT GRANTED: MAY 30, 1916

DESIGN.

J. O. HAYES.
SAFETY MATCH BOX.
APPLICATION FILED FEB. 7, 1916.

49,118.

Patented May 30, 1916.

Fig. 1.

Fig. 2.

Inventor
James O. Hayes

By Victor J. Evans

Attorney

Witnesses

TITLE: SCALE CASING
INVENTOR: HALVOR O. HEM
ASSIGNEE: TOLEDO SCALE COMPANY

PATENT NUMBER: USD 49,306
PATENT FILED: JANUARY 7, 1916
PATENT GRANTED: JULY 4, 1916

DESIGN.

H. O. HEM.
SCALE CASING.
APPLICATION FILED JAN. 7, 1916.

49,306.

Patented July 4, 1916.

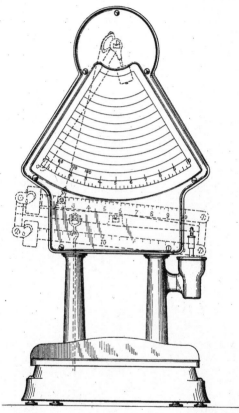

WITNESSES
D. C. Walter
C. J. Jinks

INVENTOR
Halvor O. Hem
By George R. Frye
ATTORNEY

TITLE: CASING FOR WEIGHING SCALES
INVENTOR: HERBERT S. MILLS
ASSIGNEE: NONE

PATENT NUMBER: USD 50,246
PATENT FILED: NOVEMBER 7, 1916
PATENT GRANTED: JANUARY 30, 1917

DESIGN.

H. S. MILLS.
CASING FOR WEIGHING SCALES.
APPLICATION FILED NOV. 7, 1916.

50,246.

Patented Jan. 30, 1917.

Witnesses.

Inventor:
Herbert S. Mills,

TITLE: INKSTAND
INVENTOR: FRANK A. WEEKS
ASSIGNEE: NONE

PATENT NUMBER: USD 51,191
PATENT FILED: JUNE 13, 1917
PATENT GRANTED: AUGUST 21, 1917

DESIGN.

F. A. WEEKS.
INKSTAND.
APPLICATION FILED JUNE 13, 1917.

51,191.

Patented Aug. 21, 1917.

Fig. 1.

Fig. 2.

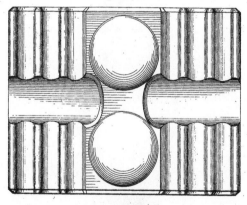

Fig. 3.

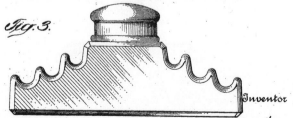

Inventor

By his Attorney Frank A. Weeks

Chas. C. Gill

81

TITLE: PORTABLE LAMP
INVENTORS: JAMES T. ROBB & LORIN W. YOUNG
ASSIGNEE: LIGHTING CORPORATION OF NEW YORK

PATENT NUMBER: USD 51,269
PATENT FILED: JULY 26, 1917
PATENT GRANTED: SEPTEMBER 11, 1917

DESIGN.

J. T. ROBB & L. W. YOUNG.
PORTABLE LAMP.
APPLICATION FILED JULY 26, 1917.

51,269.

Patented Sept. 11, 1917.

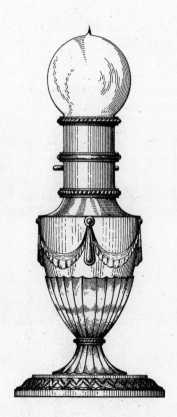

Inventors
James F. Robb
By their Attorney Lorin W. Young
Serrell & Son

TITLE: CLOCK
INVENTOR: NATHAN DREYFUS
ASSIGNEE: NONE

PATENT NUMBER: USD 51,278
PATENT FILED: JULY 18, 1917
PATENT GRANTED: SEPTEMBER 18, 1917

DESIGN.

N. DREYFUS.
CLOCK,
APPLICATION FILED JULY 18, 1917,

51,278.

Patented Sept. 18, 1917.

Fig. 1.

Fig. 2.

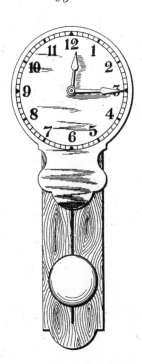

INVENTOR:
Nathan Dreyfus.
BY
Cha. M. Chapman,
ATTORNEY.

TITLE: STREET CLOCK
INVENTOR: FRANK FONTANA
ASSIGNEE: NONE

PATENT NUMBER: USD 51,280
PATENT FILED: AUGUST 1, 1917
PATENT GRANTED: SEPTEMBER 18, 1917

DESIGN.

F. FONTANA.
STREET CLOCK.
APPLICATION FILED AUG. 1, 1917.

51,280

Patented Sept. 18, 1917.

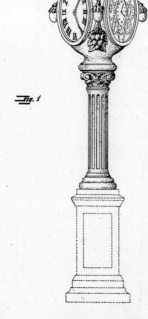

Fig. 1

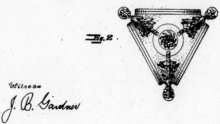

Fig. 2

Witness

J. B. Gardner

INVENTOR
F. FONTANA

By White & Frost

ATTORNEYS

84

TITLE: COMBINATION LAMP AND STREET SIGN
INVENTOR: MARK COPPINGER
ASSIGNEE: NONE

PATENT NUMBER: USD 51,774
PATENT FILED: SEPTEMBER 20, 1917
PATENT GRANTED: FEBRUARY 12, 1918

DESIGN.

M. COPPINGER.
COMBINATION LAMP AND STREET SIGN.
APPLICATION FILED SEPT. 20, 1917.

51,774.

Patented Feb. 12, 1918.

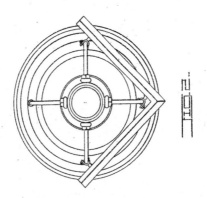

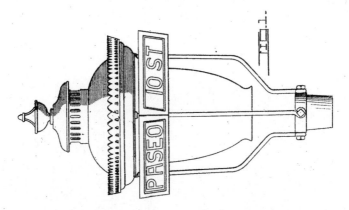

Witness:
L. J. Fischer

Inventor,
Mark Coppinger.
By F. G. Fischer,
atty.

TITLE: LAMP
INVENTOR: LOUIS COMFORT TIFFANY
ASSIGNEE: NONE

PATENT NUMBER: USD 51,800
PATENT FILED: DECEMBER 26, 1917
PATENT GRANTED: FEBRUARY 19, 1918

DESIGN.

L. C. TIFFANY.
LAMP.
APPLICATION FILED DEC. 26, 1917.

51,800.

Patented Feb. 19, 1918.

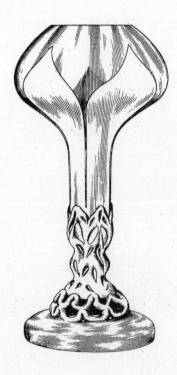

WITNESSES

INVENTOR

Louis C. Tiffany

BY

ATTORNEYS

TITLE: CALLING DEVICE
INVENTOR: OSCAR F. FORSBERG
ASSIGNEE: WESTERN ELECTRIC COMPANY

PATENT NUMBER: USD 52,009
PATENT FILED: JANUARY 25, 1915
PATENT GRANTED: MAY 7, 1918

DESIGN.

O. F. FORSBERG.
CALLING DEVICE.
APPLICATION FILED JAN. 25, 1915.

52,009.

Patented May 7, 1918.

Fig. 1.

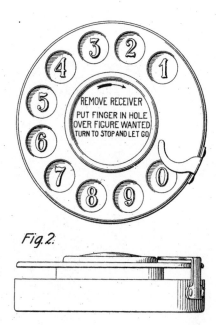

REMOVE RECEIVER
PUT FINGER IN HOLE
OVER FIGURE WANTED
TURN TO STOP AND LET GO

Fig. 2.

Witnesses:
O. D. M. Guthe.
John Waldheim.

Inventor:
Oscar F. Forsberg.
by A. C. Bannel, Att'y

TITLE: CHIP RECEPTACLE FOR PENCIL POINTERS
INVENTOR: ALLEN P. WILSON
ASSIGNEE: BOSTON PENCIL POINTER COMPANY

PATENT NUMBER: USD 52,549
PATENT FILED: JANUARY 29, 1914
PATENT GRANTED: OCTOBER 8, 1918

DESIGN.

A. P. WILSON.
CHIP RECEPTACLE FOR PENCIL POINTERS.
APPLICATION FILED JAN. 29, 1914.

52,549.

Patented Oct. 8, 1918.

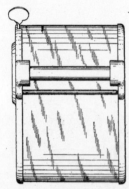

Fig. 1.

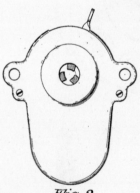

Fig. 2.

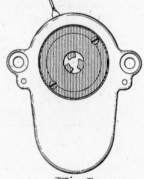

Fig. 3.

Witnesses
J. H. Thurston
E. C. Alford

Inventor
Allen P. Wilson,
By Wilmarth H. Thurston
Attorney.

88

TITLE: TYPE WRITING MACHINE
INVENTOR: LEE S. BURRIDGE
ASSIGNEE: UNDERWOOD TYPEWRITER COMPANY

PATENT NUMBER: USD 52,907
PATENT FILED: JULY 27, 1918
PATENT GRANTED: JANUARY 28, 1919

DESIGN.

L. S. BURRIDGE, DEC'D.
F. O. BURRIDGE, EXECUTOR.
TYPE WRITING MACHINE.
APPLICATION FILED JULY 27, 1918.

52,907.

Patented Jan. 28, 1919.

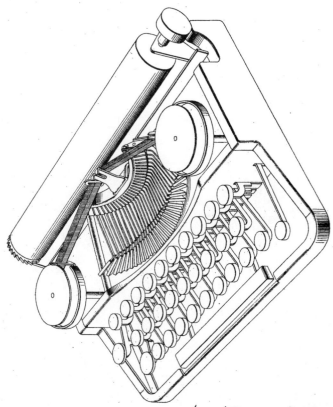

Inventor:
Lee S Burridge deceased
by Francis O Burridge Executor

By B.C. Stickney

Attorney.

89

TITLE: TRACTOR
INVENTOR: HENRY FORD
ASSIGNEE: NONE

PATENT NUMBER: USD 53,898
PATENT FILED: MAY 29, 1919
PATENT GRANTED: OCTOBER 7, 1919

DESIGN.

H. FORD.

TRACTOR.

APPLICATION FILED MAY 29, 1919.

53,898.

Patented Oct. 7, 1919.

Witness
Chas. W. Stauffiger

By

Inventor
Henry Ford,

Attorneys

TITLE: TOY VEHICLE
INVENTOR: ALFRED C. GILBERT
ASSIGNEE: A. C. GILBERT COMPANY

PATENT NUMBER: USD 54,207
PATENT FILED: AUGUST 27, 1919
PATENT GRANTED: NOVEMBER 18, 1919

DESIGN.

A. C. GILBERT.
TOY VEHICLE.
APPLICATION FILED AUG. 27, 1919.

54,207.

Patented Nov. 18, 1919.

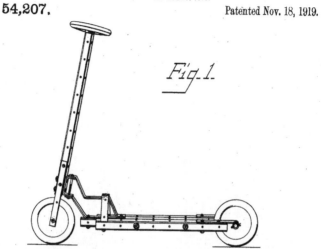

Fig. 1

Fig. 2

Fig. 3

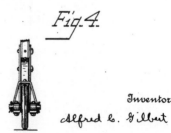

Fig. 4

Inventor
Alfred C. Gilbert
By
Henry E. Rockwell
Attorney

91

TITLE: LIQUID DISPENSING APPARATUS
INVENTOR: VOLNEY E. H. CONE
ASSIGNEE: GILBERT & BARKER MANUFACTURING

PATENT NUMBER: USD 54,243
PATENT FILED: JULY 19, 1919
PATENT GRANTED: DECEMBER 9, 1919

DESIGN.

V. E. H. CONE.
LIQUID DISPENSING APPARATUS.
APPLICATION FILED JULY 19, 1919.

54,243.

Fig. 1

Patented Dec. 9, 1919.

Fig. 2

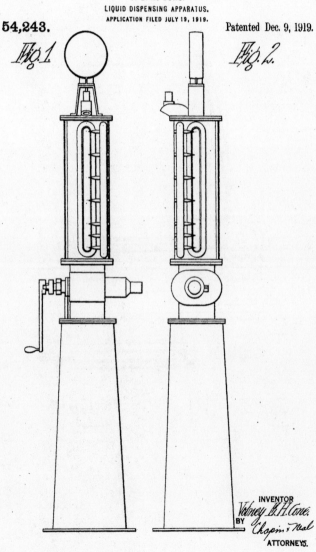

INVENTOR
Volney E. H. Cone.
BY
Chapin & Neal
ATTORNEYS.

TITLE: TOY AIRPLANE
INVENTOR: CHARLES H. GRANT
ASSIGNEE: NONE

PATENT NUMBER: USD 54,256
PATENT FILED: MARCH 21, 1919
PATENT GRANTED: DECEMBER 9, 1919

DESIGN.

C. H. GRANT.

TOY AIRPLANE.

APPLICATION FILED MAR. 21, 1919.

54,256.

Patented Dec. 9, 1919.

2 SHEETS—SHEET 2.

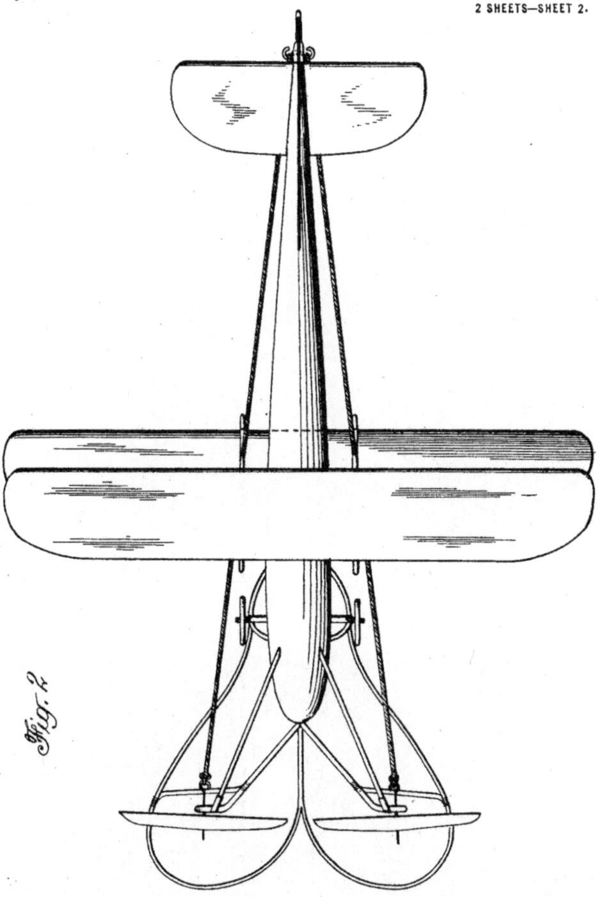

Fig. 2.

INVENTOR.

Charles H. Grant

BY *Lester W. Dittendorfer*

ATTORNEY.

TITLE: MOTORCYCLE
INVENTOR: ADAM ZISKA, JR.
ASSIGNEE: HARLEY-DAVIDSON MOTOR COMPANY

PATENT NUMBER: USD 54,346
PATENT FILED: SEPTEMBER 27, 1919
PATENT GRANTED: DECEMBER 23, 1919

DESIGN.

A. ZISKA, Jr.
MOTORCYCLE.
APPLICATION FILED SEPT. 27, 1919.

54,346.

Patented Dec. 23, 1919.

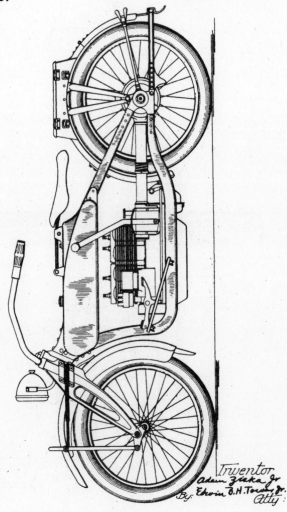

Inventor
Adam Ziska Jr
By: Edwin B.H. Tower Jr.
Atty

TITLE: AUTOMOBILE
INVENTOR: FRED E. BRADFIELD
ASSIGNEE: NONE

PATENT NUMBER: USD 54,589
PATENT FILED: OCTOBER 20, 1919
PATENT GRANTED: MARCH 9, 1920

DESIGN.

F. E. BRADFIELD.

AUTOMOBILE.

APPLICATION FILED OCT. 20, 1919.

54,589.

Patented Mar. 9, 1920.

2 SHEETS—SHEET 2.

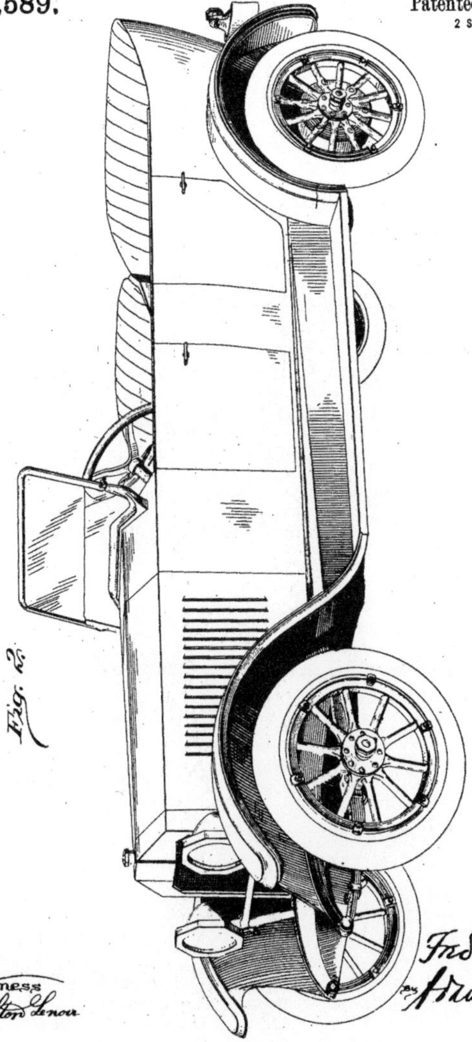

Fig. 2.

Witness
Philton Lenoir

Inventor
Fred E. Bradfield

by Armus Jackton
Attorneys

TITLE: STORE FRONT
INVENTOR: MAURICE GILLETTE
ASSIGNEE: NONE

PATENT NUMBER: USD 54,908
PATENT FILED: OCTOBER 23, 1919
PATENT GRANTED: APRIL 20, 1920

DESIGN.

M. GILLETTE.
STORE FRONT.
APPLICATION FILED OCT. 23, 1919.

54,908.

Patented Apr. 20, 1920.

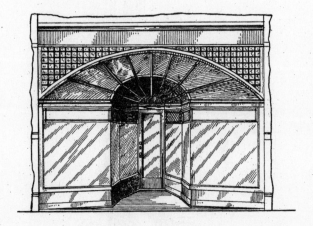

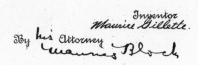

Inventor
Maurice Gillette.

By his Attorney Maurice Block

TITLE: TALKING MACHINE
INVENTOR: ROBERT L. POE
ASSIGNEE: SHELL-O-PHONE TALKING MACHINE COMPANY

PATENT NUMBER: USD 54,989
PATENT FILED: SEPTEMBER 6, 1919
PATENT GRANTED: APRIL 27, 1920

DESIGN.

R. L. POE.
TALKING MACHINE.
APPLICATION FILED SEPT. 6, 1919.

54,989.

Patented Apr. 27, 1920.

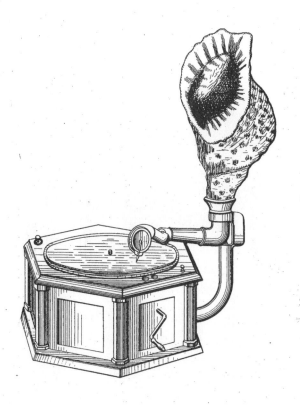

Inventor:
Robert L. Poe
By Sheridan, Jones, Sheridan & Smith.

Attys

TITLE: DISH WASHING MACHINE
INVENTOR: FRANK E. WOLCOTT
ASSIGNEE: NONE

PATENT NUMBER: USD 55,351
PATENT FILED: JANUARY 20, 1920
PATENT GRANTED: MAY 25, 1920

DESIGN.

F. E. WOLCOTT.
DISH WASHING MACHINE.
APPLICATION FILED JAN. 20, 1920.

55,351.

Patented May 25, 1920.

Inventor
Frank E. Wolcott by
Harry R. Williams
Attorney

TITLE: ELECTRIC LAMP
INVENTOR: ALBERT J. D. OHM
ASSIGNEE: LION ELECTRIC APPLIANCE COMPANY

PATENT NUMBER: USD 55,431
PATENT FILED: FEBRUARY 25, 1920
PATENT GRANTED: JUNE 8, 1920

DESIGN.

A. J. D. OHM.
ELECTRIC LAMP.
APPLICATION FILED FEB. 25, 1920.

55,431.

Patented June 8, 1920.

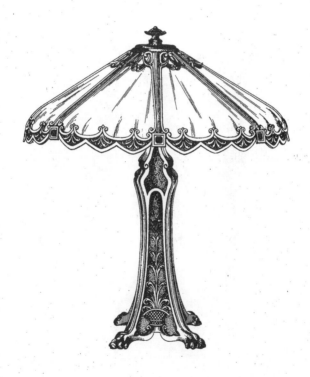

Inventor
Albert J. D. Ohm
By his Attorney
Max F. Ordmann

TITLE: OUIJA BOARD
INVENTOR: CLIFFORD H. MCGLASSON
ASSIGNEE: NONE

PATENT NUMBER: USD 56,449
PATENT FILED: MAY 26, 1920
PATENT GRANTED: OCTOBER 26, 1920

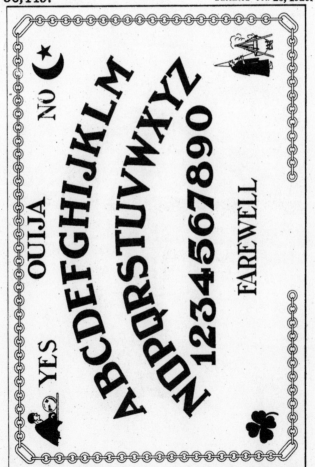

DESIGN.

C. H. McGLASSON.
OUIJA BOARD.
APPLICATION FILED MAY 26, 1920.

56,449.

Patented Oct. 26, 1920.

TITLE: BEVERAGE DISPENSING APPARATUS
INVENTOR: JOHN M. TRAVIS
ASSIGNEE: NONE

PATENT NUMBER: USD 57,950
PATENT FILED: NOVEMBER 19, 1920
PATENT GRANTED: MAY 17, 1921

DESIGN.

J. M. TRAVIS.
BEVERAGE DISPENSING APPARATUS.
APPLICATION FILED NOV. 19, 1920.

57,950.

Patented May 17, **1921.**

Inventor
John M. Travis
by Emil Starek Atty.

TITLE: MOTOR OMNIBUS BODY
INVENTOR: SAMUEL GAGE
ASSIGNEE: LONDON GENERAL OMNIBUS COMPANY

PATENT NUMBER: USD 58,288
PATENT FILED: DECEMBER 28, 1920
PATENT GRANTED: JULY 5, 1921

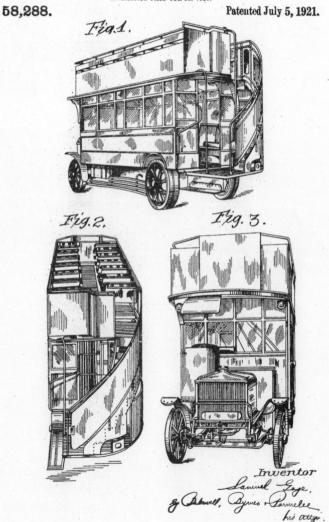

DESIGN.

S. GAGE.

MOTOR OMNIBUS BODY.

APPLICATION FILED DEC. 28, 1920.

58,288.

Patented July 5, 1921.

Fig. 1.

Fig. 2.

Fig. 3.

Inventor
Samuel Gage,
By Bakewell, Byrnes & Parmelee
his attys.

TITLE: SAFETY RAZOR
INVENTOR: CARL ELSENER
ASSIGNEE: NONE

PATENT NUMBER: USD 59,544
PATENT FILED: FEBRUARY 5, 1920
PATENT GRANTED: NOVEMBER 1, 1921

DESIGN.

C. ELSENER.
SAFETY RAZOR.
APPLICATION FILED FEB. 5, 1920.

59,544.

Patented Nov. 1, 1921.

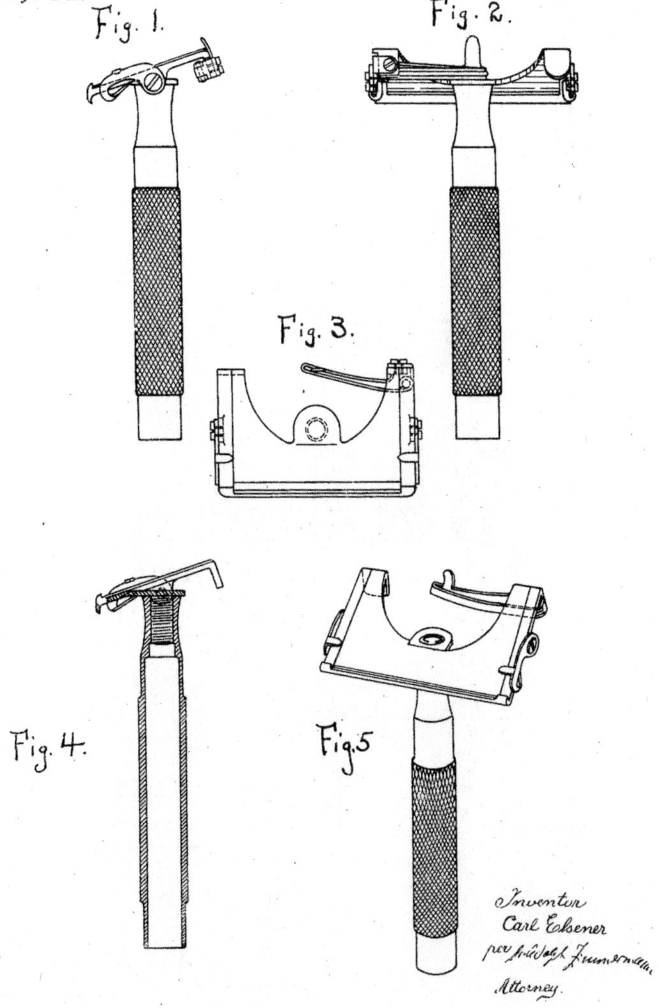

Fig. 1.

Fig. 2.

Fig. 3.

Fig. 4.

Fig. 5.

Inventor
Carl Elsener
per fridolf Zimmermann,
Attorney.

TITLE: COMBINED LAMP AND PHONOGRAPH
INVENTOR: ANTHONY J. BURNS
ASSIGNEE: BURNS-POLLOCK ELECTRIC
MANUFACTURING COMPANY

PATENT NUMBER: USD 61,291
PATENT FILED: NOVEMBER 14, 1921
PATENT GRANTED: AUGUST 1, 1922

DESIGN.

A. J. BURNS.
COMBINED LAMP AND PHONOGRAPH.
APPLICATION FILED NOV. 14, 1921.

61,291.

Patented Aug. 1, 1922.

Inventor
Anthony J. Burns
By *F. V. Cornwall* Atty.

TITLE: GAS HEATER
INVENTOR: EMIL ZETTLER
ASSIGNEE: JAMES B. CLOW & SONS

PATENT NUMBER: USD 61,514
PATENT FILED: JANUARY 30, 1922
PATENT GRANTED: SEPTEMBER 19, 1922

DESIGN.

E. ZETTLER.
GAS HEATER.
APPLICATION FILED JAN. 30, 1922.

61,514.

Patented Sept. 19, 1922.

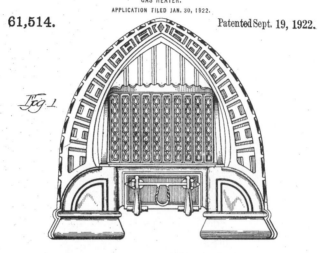

Fig. 1

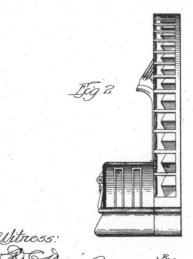

Fig. 2

Witness:

By

Inventor
Emil Zettler

TITLE: WAFFLE IRON
INVENTOR: CHARLES P. RANDOLPH
ASSIGNEE: EDISON ELECTRIC APPLIANCE COMPANY

PATENT NUMBER: USD 61,605
PATENT FILED: MARCH 13, 1922
PATENT GRANTED: OCTOBER 24, 1922

DESIGN.

C. P. RANDOLPH.
WAFFLE IRON.
APPLICATION FILED MAR. 13, 1922.

61,605.

Patented Oct. 24, 1922.

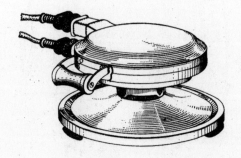

Inventor:
Charles P. Randolph
by *Albert S. Davis*
His Attorney.

TITLE: URN
INVENTOR: GEORGE E. CURTISS
ASSIGNEE: LANDERS, FRARY & CLARK

PATENT NUMBER: USD 62,271
PATENT FILED: AUGUST 31, 1922
PATENT GRANTED: MAY 1, 1923

May 1, 1923.

Des. 62,271

G. E. CURTISS

URN

Filed Aug. 31, 1922

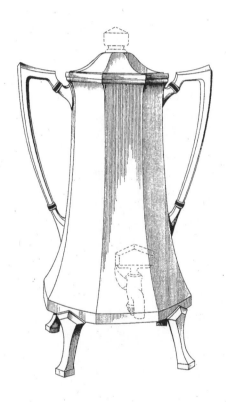

Inventor
George E. Curtiss
By
Attorneys

TITLE: BARBER POLE
INVENTOR: WALTER F. KOKEN
ASSIGNEE: NONE

PATENT NUMBER: USD 62,301
PATENT FILED: MARCH 24, 1922
PATENT GRANTED: MAY 1, 1923

May 1, 1923.　　　　　　　　　　　　　**Des. 62,301**

W. F. KOKEN

BARBER POLE

Filed March 24, 1922

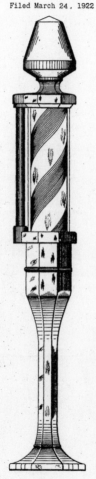

INVENTOR
Walter F. Koken.
By Bakewell & Church
ATTORNEYS

TITLE: BOTTLE
INVENTOR: CHAPMAN J. ROOT
ASSIGNEE: NONE

PATENT NUMBER: USD 63,657
PATENT FILED: FEBRUARY 4, 1922
PATENT GRANTED: DECEMBER 25, 1923

Dec. 25, 1923.

Des. 63,657

C. J. ROOT

BOTTLE

Filed Feb. 4. 1922

Fig. 1.

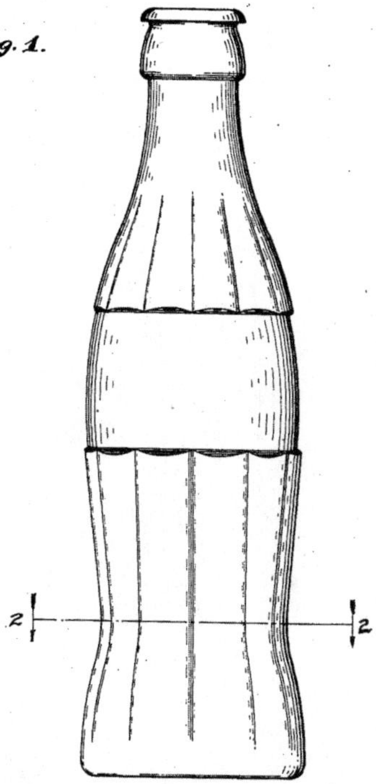

2 | 2

Fig. 2.

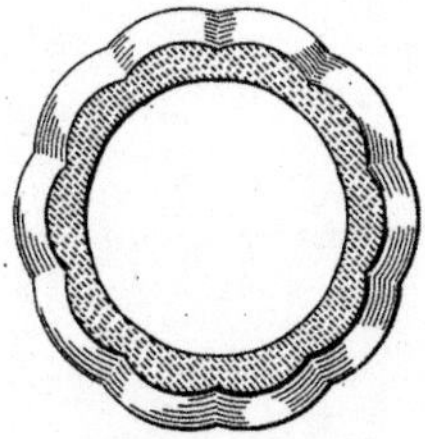

Inventor
Chapman J. Root,

By

Arthur M. Hood
Attorney

TITLE: CABINET FOR RADIOMACHINES
INVENTOR: HARRY C. NAILL
ASSIGNEE: LONG FURNITURE COMPANY

PATENT NUMBER: USD 64,922
PATENT FILED: JULY 28, 1922
PATENT GRANTED: JUNE 17, 1924

June 17, 1924.

Des. 64,922

H. C. NAILL

CABINET FOR RADIOMACHINES

Filed July 28, 1922

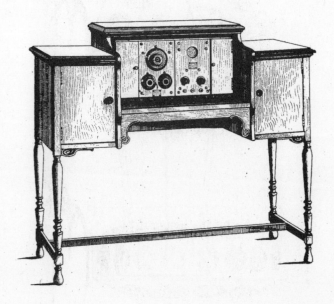

WITNESSES
Charles H. Ourand
Z. P. Smith.

Harry C. Naill
INVENTOR

BY

E. G. Siggers

ATTORNEY

TITLE: CASING FOR A TELEPHONE TRANSMITTER
INVENTOR: GEORGE R. LUM
ASSIGNEE: WESTERN ELECTRIC COMPANY

PATENT NUMBER: USD 65,194
PATENT FILED: OCTOBER 3, 1922
PATENT GRANTED: JULY 15, 1924

July 15, 1924.

G. R. LUM

Des. 65,194

CASING FOR A TELEPHONE TRANSMITTER

Filed Oct. 3, 1922

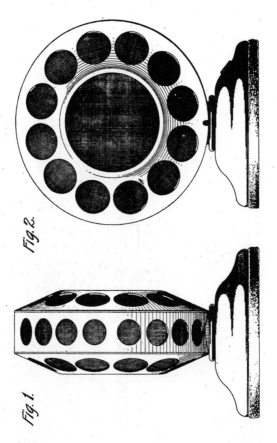

Fig. 2.

Fig. 1.

Inventor:
George R. Lum
by ~~Jne CL. Palmer~~ Atty.

TITLE: DESK STAND FOR HAND TELEPHONES
INVENTOR: GEORGE K. THOMPSON
ASSIGNEE: AMERICAN TELEPHONE AND
TELEGRAPH COMPANY

PATENT NUMBER: USD 65,204
PATENT FILED: DECEMBER 28, 1922
PATENT GRANTED: JULY 15, 1924

July 15, 1924.   Des. 65,204

G. K. THOMPSON

DESK STAND FOR HAND TELEPHONES

Filed Dec. 28, 1922

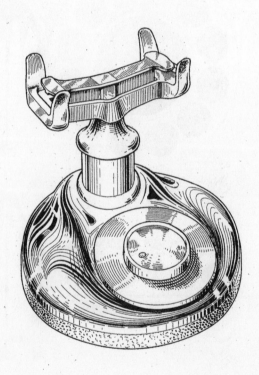

INVENTOR.

G. K. Thompson

BY *gefor*

ATTORNEY

TITLE: TRAFFIC LIGHT
INVENTOR: LOREN W. MCOMBER
ASSIGNEE: NONE

PATENT NUMBER: USD 65,349
PATENT FILED: DECEMBER 12, 1923
PATENT GRANTED: JULY 29, 1924

July 29, 1924.

Des. 65,349

L. W. McOMBER

TRAFFIC LIGHT

Filed Dec. 12, 1923

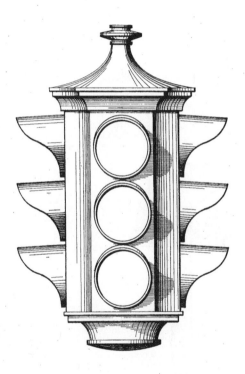

Inventor.
Loren W. McOmber.

Atty.

TITLE: TOY
INVENTOR: LOUIS V. ARONSON
ASSIGNEE: NONE

PATENT NUMBER: USD 65,514
PATENT FILED: MAY 29, 1924
PATENT GRANTED: SEPTEMBER 2, 1924

Sept. 2, 1924.

L. V. ARONSON

Des. 65,514

TOY

Filed May 29, 1924

Fig.1.

Fig.2.

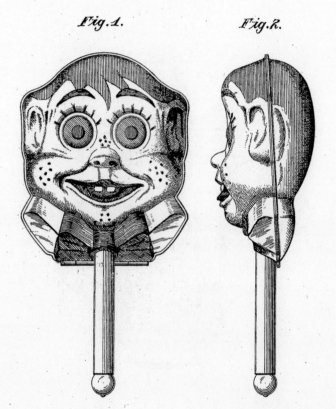

Inventor

Louis V. Aronson

By *Brown & Phelps*

Attorneys

TITLE: SOUND AMPLIFIER OR SIMILAR ARTICLE
INVENTOR: EVERETT WORTHINGTON
ASSIGNEE: RADIO PHONO-KRAFTS

PATENT NUMBER: USD 65,889
PATENT FILED: AUGUST 11, 1924
PATENT GRANTED: OCTOBER 28, 1924

Oct. 28, 1924.   Des. 65,889

E. WORTHINGTON

SOUND AMPLIFIER OR SIMILAR ARTICLE

Filed Aug. 11, 1924

INVENTOR
Everett Worthingtc

by White Prat & Evans.

his ATTORNEYS

TITLE: PORTABLE READING LAMP
INVENTOR: CHARLES ROHLFS
ASSIGNEE: NONE

PATENT NUMBER: USD 66,428
PATENT FILED: JUNE 28, 1923
PATENT GRANTED: JANUARY 13, 1925

Jan. 13, 1925.

Des. 66,428

C. ROHLFS

PORTABLE READING LAMP

Filed June 28, 1923

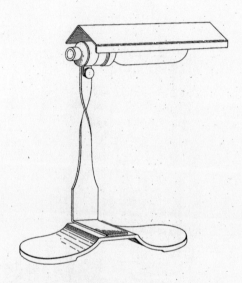

INVENTOR.

Charles Rohlfs.

by Parker Rockwood,

ATTORNEYS.

TITLE: HAND TELEPHONE
INVENTOR: GEORGE K. THOMPSON
ASSIGNEE: AMERICAN TELEPHONE &
TELEGRAPH COMPANY

PATENT NUMBER: USD 66,991
PATENT FILED: DECEMBER 31, 1923
PATENT GRANTED: APRIL 7, 1925

April 7, 1925.

G. K. THOMPSON

HAND TELEPHONE

Filed Dec. 31, 1923

Des. 66,991

INVENTOR

G. K. Thompson

BY

ATTORNEY

TITLE: MOTOR CYCLE
INVENTOR: CARL A. NERACHER
ASSIGNEE: NER-A-CAR CORPORATION

PATENT NUMBER: USD 67,297
PATENT FILED: MARCH 26, 1920
PATENT GRANTED: MAY 12, 1925

May 12, 1925.

Des. 67,297

C. A. NERACHER

MOTOR CYCLE

Filed March 26, 1920

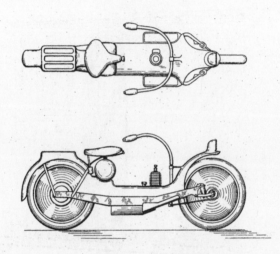

Carl A Neracher
INVENTOR.

BY *Raymond H. Van West*
ATTORNEY

TITLE: CABINET FOR RADIORECEIVERS
INVENTOR: ROBERT C. EDWARDS
ASSIGNEE: RADIO CORPORATION OF AMERICA

PATENT NUMBER: USD 68,850
PATENT FILED: JULY 19, 1924
PATENT GRANTED: NOVEMBER 24, 1925

Nov. 24, 1925.

Des. 68,850

R. C. EDWARDS

CABINET FOR RADIORECEIVERS

Filed July 19, 1924

Inventor
ROBERT C. EDWARDS

By his Attorney *Fra J. Adams*

119

TITLE: LOUD SPEAKER HORN FOR RADIO
RECEIVING SETS
INVENTORS: ALBERT C. FRISCH & JOHN R. FRISCH
ASSIGNEE: NONE

PATENT NUMBER: USD 69,446
PATENT FILED: OCTOBER 19, 1925
PATENT GRANTED: FEBRUARY 16, 1926

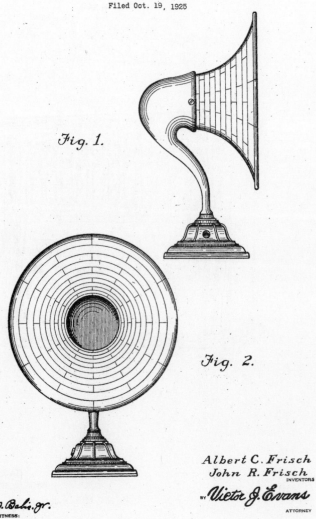

Feb. 16 , 1926.

Des. 69,446

A. C. FRISCH ET AL

LOUD SPEAKER HORN FOR RADIO RECEIVING SETS

Filed Oct. 19, 1925

Fig. 1.

Fig. 2.

Albert C. Frisch
John R. Frisch
INVENTORS

BY Victor J. Evans

ATTORNEY

O. Belis. Jr.
WITNESS:

TITLE: THERMOMETER
INVENTOR: RICHARD E. MANN
ASSIGNEE: NONE

PATENT NUMBER: USD 69,804
PATENT FILED: JANUARY 23, 1926
PATENT GRANTED: MARCH 30, 1926

March 30, 1926.

Des. 69,804

R. E. MANN

THERMOMETER

Filed Jan. 23, 1926

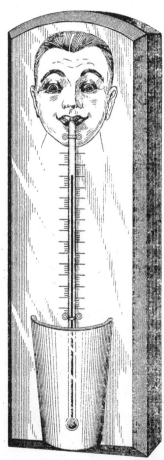

Inventor

RICHARD E. MANN.

By His Attorney

Philip C. Peck

TITLE: COMBINED CASING AND SUPPORT FOR ELECTRIC
HAIR-DRYING MACHINE
INVENTOR: CARL G. GROSS
ASSIGNEE: EASTERN LABORATORIES

PATENT NUMBER: USD 70,667
PATENT FILED: OCTOBER 30, 1924
PATENT GRANTED: JULY 27, 1926

July 27, 1926.　　　　　　　　　　**Des. 70,667**

C. G. GROSS

COMBINED CASING AND SUPPORT FOR ELECTRIC HAIR DRYING MACHINES

Filed Oct. 30, 1924

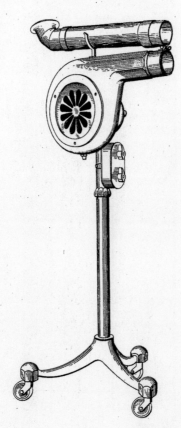

Inventor

Carl G. Gross

By his Attorney

Ramsay Hoguet.

TITLE: ELECTRIC FAN CASING
INVENTOR: SOCRATES A. XIPPAS
ASSIGNEE: NONE

PATENT NUMBER: USD 70,930
PATENT FILED: APRIL 16, 1926
PATENT GRANTED: AUGUST 24, 1926

Aug. 24, 1926.

Des. 70,930

S. A. XIPPAS

ELECTRIC FAN CASING

Filed April 16, 1926

Inventor
S. A. Xippas

By Ralph J. Bassett

Attorney

TITLE: ELECTRIC HEATER
INVENTOR: LINDLEY S. LAWSON
ASSIGNEE: NONE

PATENT NUMBER: USD 71,467
PATENT FILED: SEPTEMBER 3, 1926
PATENT GRANTED: NOVEMBER 9, 1926

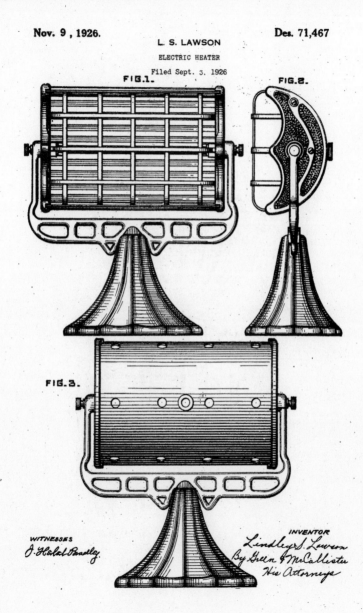

Nov. 9 , 1926.

Des. 71,467

L. S. LAWSON

ELECTRIC HEATER

Filed Sept. 3, 1926

FIG.1.

FIG.2.

FIG.3.

WITNESSES

INVENTOR
Lindley S. Lawson
By Green & McCallister
His Attorneys

TITLE: CASING FOR RADIO SETS
INVENTOR: GEORGE SEIGFRIED BRUSH
ASSIGNEE: NONE

PATENT NUMBER: USD 71,823
PATENT FILED: SEPTEMBER 20, 1926
PATENT GRANTED: JANUARY 11, 1927

Jan. 11, 1927.

Des. 71,823

G. S. BRUSH

CASING FOR RADIO SETS

Filed Sept. 20, 1926

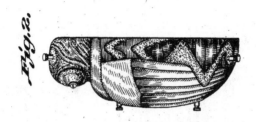

Fig. 2.

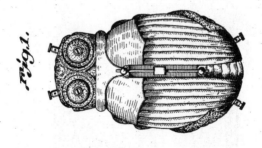

Fig. 1.

Inventor

GEORGE S. BRUSH,

By

Attorney

TITLE: ELECTRIC TOASTER
INVENTOR: CHARLES P. RANDOLPH
ASSIGNEE: EDISON ELECTRIC APPLIANCE COMPANY

PATENT NUMBER: USD 72,495
PATENT FILED: MARCH 22, 1926
PATENT GRANTED: APRIL 19, 1927

April 19, 1927.

C. P. RANDOLPH

ELECTRIC TOASTER

Filed March 22. 1926

Des. 72,495

Inventor:
Charles P. Randolph,

by *Alexander S. Lantz.*

His Attorney.

TITLE: RADIATOR-CAP ORNAMENT
INVENTOR: JOSEPH E. CORKER
ASSIGNEE: PACKARD MOTOR CAR COMPANY

PATENT NUMBER: USD 73,026
PATENT FILED: JUNE 25, 1926
PATENT GRANTED: JULY 12, 1927

July 12, 1927.

J. E. CORKER

RADIATOR CAP ORNAMENT

Filed June 25, 1926

Des. 73,026

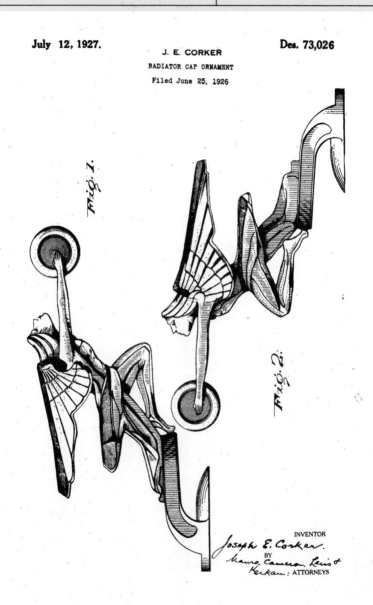

Fig. 1.

Fig. 2.

INVENTOR

Joseph E. Corker.

BY

Mauro, Cameron, Lewis &
Kerkam: ATTORNEYS

TITLE: LOUD SPEAKER
INVENTOR: JOSEPH W. GOSLING
ASSIGNEE: GENERAL ELECTRIC COMPANY

PATENT NUMBER: USD 73,030
PATENT FILED: JANUARY 27, 1927
PATENT GRANTED: JULY 12, 1927

July 12, 1927.

J. W. GOSLING

Des. 73,030

LOUD SPEAKER

Filed Jan. 27, 1927

Inventor:
Joseph W. Gosling,
by *Alexander S. Lent*
His Attorney.

TITLE: DINING CAR BODY
INVENTOR: CHARLES A. WARD
ASSIGNEE: NONE

PATENT NUMBER: USD 73,246
PATENT FILED: JANUARY 17, 1927
PATENT GRANTED: AUGUST 9, 1927

Aug. 9, 1927.

Des. 73,246

C. A. WARD

DINING CAR BODY

Filed Jan. 17, 1927

Fig.1.

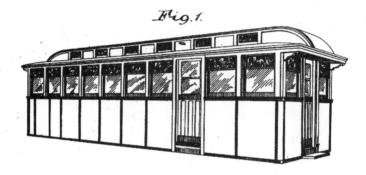

Fig.2.

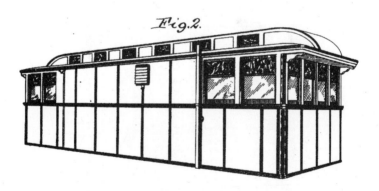

Inventor
Charles A. Ward
by Pofft Powers

TITLE: LANTERN
INVENTOR: FURMAN D. SPEAR
ASSIGNEE: NONE

PATENT NUMBER: USD 73,877
PATENT FILED: OCTOBER 2, 1925
PATENT GRANTED: NOVEMBER 15, 1927

Nov. 15, 1927.   Des. 73,877

F. D. SPEAR

LANTERN

Filed Oct.2, 1925

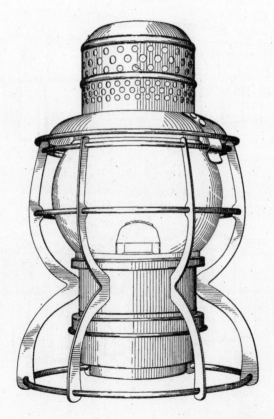

INVENTOR

Furman D. Spear

BY

ATTORNEY

TITLE: CAMERA CASING
INVENTOR: CARL BORNMANN
ASSIGNEE: ANSCO PHOTOPRODUCTS

PATENT NUMBER: USD 74,211
PATENT FILED: JANUARY 22, 1927
PATENT GRANTED: JANUARY 10, 1928

Jan. 10, 1928.

Des. 74,211

C. BORNMANN

CAMERA CASING

Filed Jan. 22, 1927

INVENTOR
CARL BORNMANN.

BY

ATTORNEY

TITLE: BODY CARRIAGE FOR MOTOR CARS
INVENTOR: JACQUES GÉRIN
ASSIGNEE: NONE

PATENT NUMBER: USD 74,498
PATENT FILED: AUGUST 31, 1925
PATENT GRANTED: FEBRUARY 21, 1928

Feb. 21, 1928.   Des. 74,498

J. GERIN

BODY CARRIAGE FOR MOTOR CARS

Filed Aug. 31, 1925

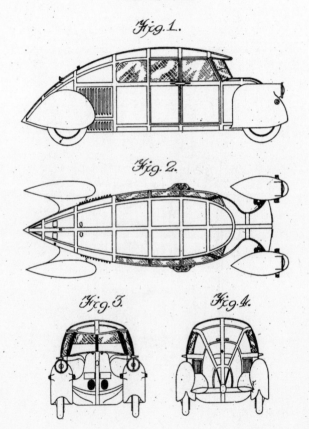

Fig. 1.

Fig. 2.

Fig. 3.   Fig. 4.

INVENTOR
J. Gerin
By marks & clerk
attys

TITLE: PAPER CUP OR SIMILAR ARTICLE
INVENTOR: JOSEPH JOHNSON
ASSIGNEE: INDIVIDUAL DRINKING CUP COMPANY

PATENT NUMBER: USD 74,793
PATENT FILED: DECEMBER 19, 1927
PATENT GRANTED: MARCH 27, 1928

March 27, 1928. **Des. 74,793**

J. JOHNSON

PAPER CUP OR SIMILAR ARTICLE

Filed Dec. 19, 1927

Fig.1.

Fig.2.

Fig.3.

Witnesses:
C. A. Gegowity
M. H. Fenton

Inventor:
Joseph Johnson,
by Milans & Milans
Attys:

TITLE: VASE
INVENTOR: REUBEN HALEY
ASSIGNEE: CONSOLIDATED LAMP & GLASS COMPANY

PATENT NUMBER: USD 74,882
PATENT FILED: FEBRUARY 1, 1928
PATENT GRANTED: APRIL 10, 1928

April 10, 1928.   **Des. 74,882**

R. HALEY

VASE

Filed Feb. 1, 1928

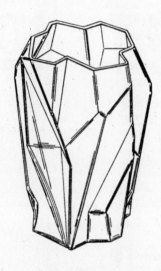

INVENTOR.
Reuben Haley
BY Green & McCallister
His ATTORNEYS.

TITLE: CARTON
INVENTOR: FRED W. TEETZEL
ASSIGNEE: NONE

PATENT NUMBER: USD 74,992
PATENT FILED: DECEMBER 27, 1927
PATENT GRANTED: APRIL 24, 1928

April 24, 1928.   Des. 74,992

F. W. TEETZEL

CARTON

Filed Dec. 27, 1927

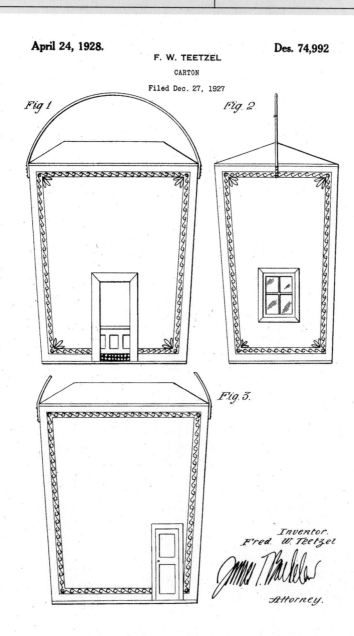

Fig 1

Fig. 2

Fig. 3

Inventor.
Fred. W. Teetzel

Attorney.

135

TITLE: LAMP
INVENTOR: ROBERT BEARDSLEY
ASSIGNEE: NONE

PATENT NUMBER: USD 75,331
PATENT FILED: MARCH 5, 1928
PATENT GRANTED: MAY 29, 1928

May 29, 1928.   Des. 75,331

R. BEARDSLEY

LAMP

Filed March 5, 1928

Fig. 1.

Fig. 2.

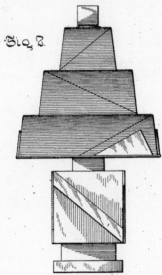

Witness

William P. Kilroy

Inventor,
Robert Beardsley.
By Hill & Hill
Att'ys

136

TITLE: LOUD SPEAKER
INVENTOR: HERMAN L. FAISON
ASSIGNEE: NONE

PATENT NUMBER: USD 75,617
PATENT FILED: JANUARY 28, 1928
PATENT GRANTED: JUNE 26, 1928

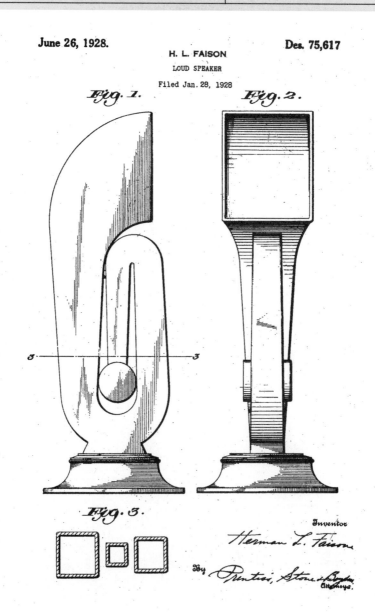

June 26, 1928.

Des. 75,617

H. L. FAISON

LOUD SPEAKER

Filed Jan. 28, 1928

Fig. 1.

Fig. 2.

Fig. 3.

Inventor

Herman L. Faison

By Prentiss, Stone & Boyden
Attorneys.

TITLE: LIGHTING FIXTURE BOWL OR SIMILAR ARTICLE
INVENTOR: NICHOLAS KOPP
ASSIGNEE: KOPP GLASS INCORPORATED

PATENT NUMBER: USD 75,631
PATENT FILED: MARCH 12, 1928
PATENT GRANTED: JUNE 26, 1928

June 26, 1928.   **Des. 75,631**

N. KOPP

LIGHTING FIXTURE BOWL OR SIMILAR ARTICLE

Filed March 12, 1928

Fig. 1.

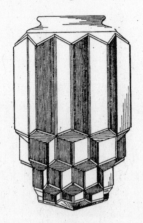

Fig. 2.

INVENTOR

Nicholas Kopp
by W.F. Doolittle
Attorney

TITLE: CAKE PLATE
INVENTOR: ALBERT F. SAUNDERS
ASSIGNEE: T. N. BENEDICT MANUFACTURING COMPANY

PATENT NUMBER: USD 75,655
PATENT FILED: MAY 3, 1928
PATENT GRANTED: JUNE 26, 1928

June 26, 1928.   Des. 75,655

A. F. SAUNDERS

CAKE PLATE

Filed May 3, 1928

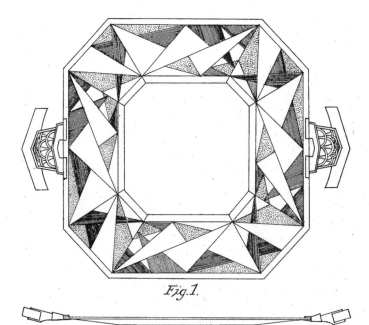

Fig.1.

Fig.2.

Albert F. Saunders

INVENTOR

139

TITLE: ELECTRIC SMOOTHING IRON
INVENTOR: CHARLES T. JOHNSON-VEA
ASSIGNEE: DOVER MANUFACTURING COMPANY

PATENT NUMBER: USD 75,732
PATENT FILED: JUNE 19, 1926
PATENT GRANTED: JULY 10, 1928

July 10, 1928.

C. T. JOHNSON-VEA

ELECTRIC SMOOTHING IRON

Filed June 19, 1926

Des. 75,732

2 Sheets-Sheet 2

Fig. 5.

Inventor

Charles T. Johnson-Vea.

By Erwin Wheeler and Woolard
Attorneys

140

TITLE: SALT AND PEPPER SHAKER
INVENTOR: ALFRED J. FLAUDER
ASSIGNEE: NONE

PATENT NUMBER: USD 75,907
PATENT FILED: MAY 28, 1928
PATENT GRANTED: JULY 31, 1928

July 31, 1928.

A. J. FLAUDER

SALT AND PEPPER SHAKER

Filed May 28, 1928

Des. 75,907

Fig. 1

Fig. 2

Fig. 3

Inventor:
Alfred J. Flauder

By   Chamberlain & Newman
Attorneys.

TITLE: GAME TABLE
INVENTOR: HANS BERG
ASSIGNEE: BRUNSWICK–BALKE–COLLENDER COMPANY

PATENT NUMBER: USD 75,951
PATENT FILED: MAY 25, 1928
PATENT GRANTED: AUGUST 7, 1928

Aug. 7, 1928.

Des. 75,951

H. BERG

GAME TABLE

Filed May 25, 1928

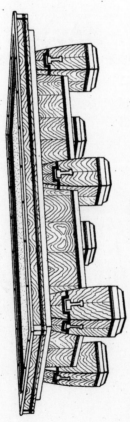

Inventor
Hans Berg.
by James P. Shea
Atty.

TITLE: SHAKER OR SIMILAR ARTICLE
INVENTOR: HOWARD L. BUDD
ASSIGNEE: NONE

PATENT NUMBER: USD 76,285
PATENT FILED: APRIL 9, 1928
PATENT GRANTED: SEPTEMBER 11, 1928

Sept. 11, 1928.

Des. 76,285

H. L. BUDD

'SHAKER OR SIMILAR ARTICLE

Filed April 9, 1928

Fig. 1.

Fig. 2.

INVENTOR
Howard L. Budd
BY

ATTORNEY

TITLE: TABLE LAMP
INVENTOR: JOHN B. SALTERINI
ASSIGNEE: NONE

PATENT NUMBER: USD 76,710
PATENT FILED: AUGUST 22, 1928
PATENT GRANTED: OCTOBER 23, 1928

Oct. 23, 1928.

Des. 76,710

J. B. SALTERINI

TABLE LAMP

Filed Aug. 22, 1928

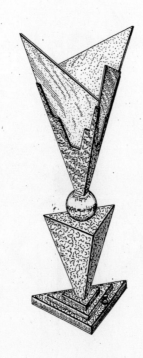

John B. Salterini, Inventor

By Linton, Kellogg & Smith

Attorneys

144

TITLE: AUTOMOBILE FRONT END DECORATION
INVENTORS: ROBERT G. SEALS & EDWARD N. C. KUNTZ
ASSIGNEE: NONE

PATENT NUMBER: USD 76,712
PATENT FILED: JANUARY 23, 1928
PATENT GRANTED: OCTOBER 23, 1928

Oct. 23, 1928.

Des. 76,712

R. G. SEALS ET AL

AUTOMOBILE FRONT END DECORATION

Filed Jan. 23, 1928

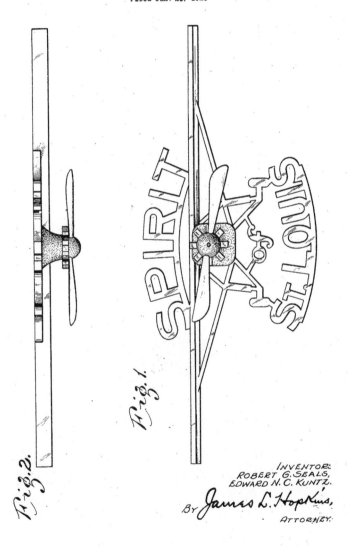

Fig.2.

Fig.1.

INVENTOR:
ROBERT G. SEALS,
EDWARD N. C. KUNTZ.

By James L. Hopkins,

ATTORNEY.

145

TITLE: LAMP
INVENTOR: ARTHUR VON FRANKENBERG
ASSIGNEE: FRANKART

PATENT NUMBER: USD 77,202
PATENT FILED: SEPTEMBER 15, 1928
PATENT GRANTED: DECEMBER 11, 1928

Dec. 11, 1928.

A. VON FRANKENBERG

LAMP

Filed Sept. 15, 1928

Des. 77,202

Arthur von Frankenberg
INVENTOR

BY
Morris Kirschstein
ATTORNEY

TITLE: STORE FRONT
INVENTOR: WARD MELVILLE
ASSIGNEE: MELVILLE SHOE CORPORATION

PATENT NUMBER: USD 77,251
PATENT FILED: JUNE 19, 1928
PATENT GRANTED: DECEMBER 18, 1928

Dec. 18, 1928.

Des. 77,251

W. MELVILLE

STORE FRONT

Filed June 19, 1928

Fig.1.

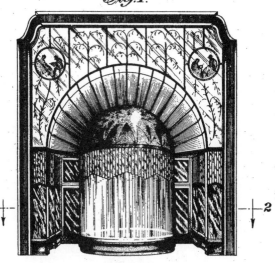

2

2

Fig.2.

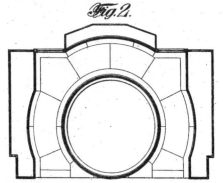

INVENTOR
Ward Melville
BY
Kenyon & Kenyon
ATTORNEYS.

147

TITLE: SERVICE STATION BOOTH
INVENTOR: CARL AUGUST PETERSEN
ASSIGNEE: PURE OIL COMPANY

PATENT NUMBER: USD 77,857
PATENT FILED: OCTOBER 11, 1928
PATENT GRANTED: FEBRUARY 26, 1929

Feb. 26, 1929.

C. A. PETERSEN

SERVICE STATION BOOTH

Filed Oct. 11, 1928

Des. 77,857

3 Sheets—Sheet 1

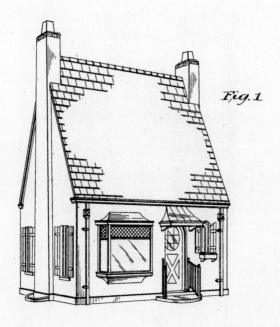

Fig.1

Inventor

Carl A. Petersen

By *W. S. McDowell*

Attorney

TITLE: LAMP
INVENTOR: ARTHUR VON FRANKENBERG
ASSIGNEE: FRANKART

PATENT NUMBER: USD 78,417
PATENT FILED: FEBRUARY 20, 1929
PATENT GRANTED: APRIL 30, 1929

April 30, 1929.   A. VON FRANKENBERG   **Des. 78,417**

LAMP

Filed Feb. 20, 1929

INVENTOR

Arthur von Frankenberg

BY

Morris Hirschstein

ATTORNEY

TITLE: TOASTER
INVENTOR: GEORGE E. CURTISS
ASSIGNEE: LANDERS, FRARY & CLARK

PATENT NUMBER: USD 78,504
PATENT FILED: FEBRUARY 16, 1929
PATENT GRANTED: MAY 14, 1929

May 14, 1929.   G. E. CURTISS   Des. 78,504

TOASTER

Filed Feb. 16, 1929

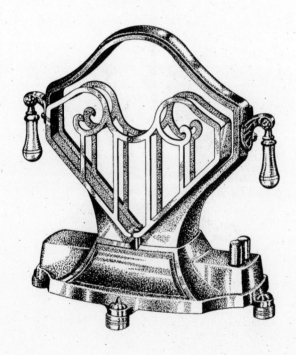

Inventor:
George E. Curtiss

by T. Clay Lindsey
Attorney.

TITLE: WEIGHING SCALE CASING
INVENTOR: JOSEPH SINEL
ASSIGNEE: INTERNATIONAL TICKET
SCALE CORPORATION

PATENT NUMBER: USD 78,592
PATENT FILED: MARCH 26, 1929
PATENT GRANTED: MAY 21, 1929

May 21, 1929.   J. SINEL   Des. 78,592

WEIGHING SCALE CASING

Filed March 26, 1929

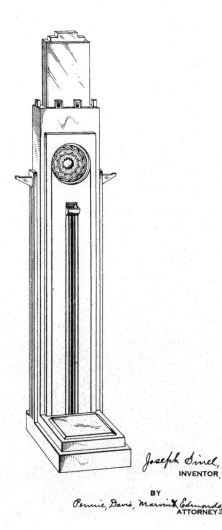

Joseph Sinel,
INVENTOR.

BY

Pennie, Davis, Marvin & Edmonds,
ATTORNEYS.

TITLE: TRAFFIC SIGNAL
INVENTOR: GERALD C. WATERHOUSE
ASSIGNEE: NONE

PATENT NUMBER: USD 78,953
PATENT FILED: DECEMBER 27, 1927
PATENT GRANTED: JULY 9, 1929

July 9, 1929.   G. C. WATERHOUSE   Des. 78,953

TRAFFIC SIGNAL

Filed Dec. 27, 1927

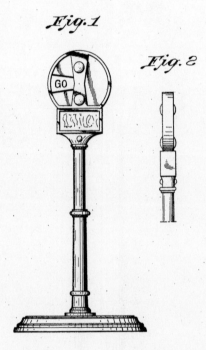

Fig. 1

Fig. 2

INVENTOR.
G.C. Waterhouse

BY Westall and Wallace

ATTORNEYS

TITLE: AUTOMOBILE BODY, HOOD, AND FENDERS
INVENTOR: RAYMOND G. F. LOWEY
ASSIGNEE: NONE

PATENT NUMBER: USD 79,147
PATENT FILED: JULY 9, 1928
PATENT GRANTED: AUGUST 6, 1929

Aug. 6, 1929.   R. G. F. LOEWY   Des. 79,147

COMBINED AUTOMOBILE BODY, HOOD, AND FENDERS

Filed July 9, 1928

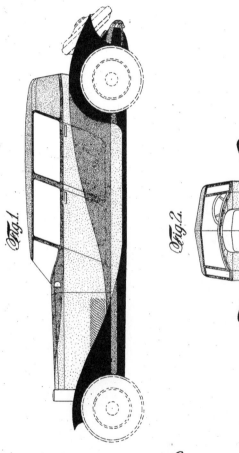

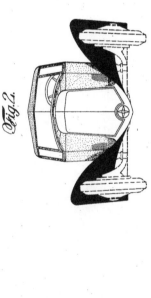

Fig.1.

Fig.2.

Raymond G.F. Lowey
INVENTOR

BY

Wm. S. Pritchard
ATTORNEY

TITLE: CANDLESTICK BASE OR ARTICLE OF
ANALOGOUS NATURE
INVENTOR: LOUIS ZWEIG
ASSIGNEE: SUNRISE LAMP MANUFACTURING COMPANY

PATENT NUMBER: USD 79,347
PATENT FILED: JULY 9, 1929
PATENT GRANTED: SEPTEMBER 3, 1929

Sept. 3, 1929. L. ZWEIG Des. 79,347

CANDLESTICK BASE OR ARTICLE OF ANALOGOUS NATURE

Filed July 9, 1929

INVENTOR
Louis Zweig

BY

ATTORNEY

TITLE: SPOON OR SIMILAR ARTICLE
INVENTOR: ELIEL SAARINEN
ASSIGNEE: REED & BARTON

PATENT NUMBER: USD 79,854
PATENT FILED: JULY 20, 1929
PATENT GRANTED: NOVEMBER 5, 1929

Nov. 5, 1929.   E. SAARINEN   Des. 79,854

SPOON OR SIMILAR ARTICLE

Filed July 20, 1929

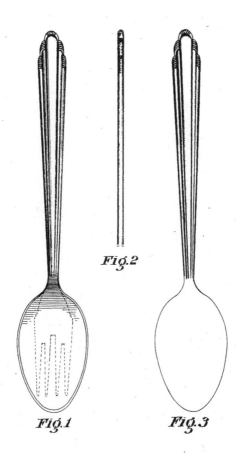

Fig.2

Fig.1

Fig.3

INVENTOR

Eliel Saarinen
by H. Kirchmayer
his Atty.

TITLE: GASOLINE PUMP CASING
INVENTORS: RUDOLPH L. SCHWARTZ
& WILLIAM PAUL MARTIN
ASSIGNEE: NONE

PATENT NUMBER: USD 79,992
PATENT FILED: FEBRUARY 6, 1929
PATENT GRANTED: NOVEMBER 26, 1929

Nov. 26, 1929.   R. L. SCHWARTZ ET AL   Des 79,992

GASOLINE PUMP CASING

Filed Feb. 6, 1929

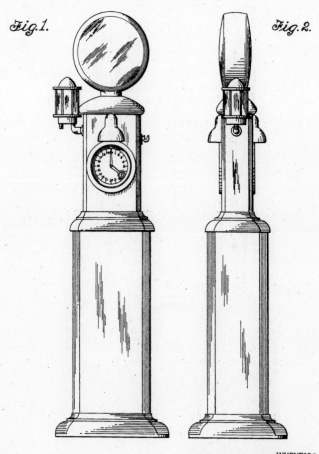

Fig.1.

Fig.2.

INVENTORS
Rudolph L. Schwartz and
William Paul Martin
BY

James F. Splain
ATTORNEY.

TITLE: TEAPOT
INVENTOR: HOWARD H. SCHOTT
ASSIGNEE: ROBESON ROCHESTER CORPORATION

PATENT NUMBER: USD 80,146
PATENT FILED: OCTOBER 3, 1929
PATENT GRANTED: DECEMBER 17, 1929

Dec. 17, 1929.

H. H. SCHOTT

Des. 80,146

TEAPOT

Filed Oct. 3, 1929

Fig.1

Fig.2

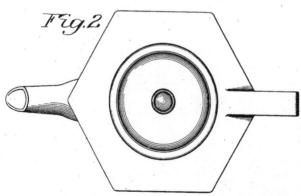

INVENTOR.
Howard H. Schott
BY *Cumpston & Griffith*
his ATTORNEYS

TITLE: CLOSET
INVENTOR: CHARLES R. CRANE, II
ASSIGNEE: NONE

PATENT NUMBER: USD 80,606
PATENT FILED: SEPTEMBER 12, 1929
PATENT GRANTED: MARCH 4, 1930

March 4, 1930.　　　C. R. CRANE, 2D　　　**Des. 80,606**

CLOSET

Filed Sept. 12, 1929

Witness
R.B.Davison.

Inventor:
Charles R.Crane II.
By Ira J.Wilson
Atty

TITLE: LIGHTING DEVICE
INVENTOR: JOSEPH W. GOSLING
ASSIGNEE: GENERAL ELECTRIC COMPANY

PATENT NUMBER: USD 81,233
PATENT FILED: AUGUST 9, 1929
PATENT GRANTED: MAY 27, 1930

May 27, 1930.

J. W. GOSLING

LIGHTING DEVICE

Filed Aug. 9, 1929

Des. 81,233

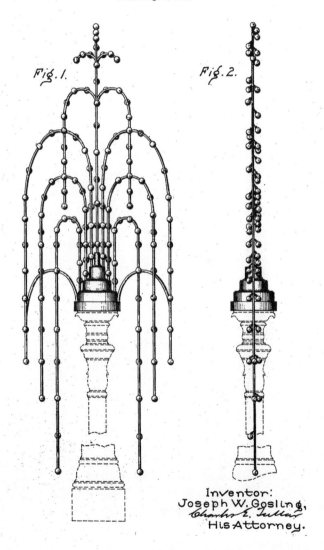

Fig. 1.

Fig. 2.

Inventor:
Joseph W. Gosling,
Charles E. Tuller
His Attorney.

TITLE: FOUNTAIN PEN
INVENTOR: KENNETH S. PARKER
ASSIGNEE: THE PARKER PEN COMPANY

PATENT NUMBER: USD 81,254
PATENT FILED: JULY 8, 1929
PATENT GRANTED: MAY 27, 1930

May 27, 1930.   K. S. PARKER   Des. 81,254

FOUNTAIN PEN

Filed July 8, 1929

Fig.1.

Fig.2.

Inventor:
Kenneth S. Parker.
By Pieton, Hibben, Davis & Macauley attys.

TITLE: CASH REGISTER
INVENTOR: BERNIE M. SHIPLEY
ASSIGNEE: NATIONAL CASH REGISTER COMPANY

PATENT NUMBER: USD 81,411
PATENT FILED: MAY 23, 1929
PATENT GRANTED: JUNE 17, 1930

June 17, 1930.

B. M. SHIPLEY

CASH REGISTER

Filed May 23, 1929

Des. 81,411

3 Sheets–Sheet 1

FIG. 1

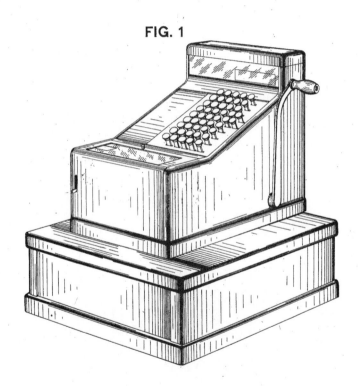

Inventor
Bernis M. Shipley

By *Earl Beust*

Ralph E. Warfield.

His Attorneys

161

TITLE: DESK STAND FOR A HAND TELEPHONE
INVENTOR: JOHN VASSOS
ASSIGNEE: BELL TELEPHONE LABORATORIES

PATENT NUMBER: USD 81,510
PATENT FILED: MAY 10, 1930
PATENT GRANTED: JULY 1, 1930

July 1, 1930.   J. VASSOS   Des. 81,510

DESK STAND FOR A HAND TELEPHONE

Filed May 10, 1930   2 Sheets-Sheet 1

Fig. 1

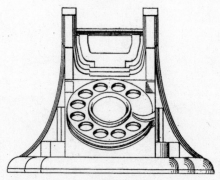

Fig. 2

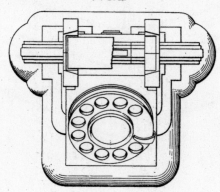

INVENTOR
J. VASSOS
BY   Walter C. Kisel
ATTORNEY

162

TITLE: HAND TELEPHONE
INVENTOR: JOHN VASSOS
ASSIGNEE: THE BELL TELEPHONE LABORATORIES

PATENT NUMBER: USD 81,511
PATENT FILED: MAY 10, 1930
PATENT GRANTED: JULY 1, 1930

July 1, 1930.　　　J. VASSOS　　　Des. 81,511

HAND TELEPHONE

Filed May 10, 1930

Fig. 1

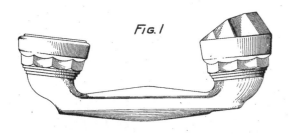

Fig. 2

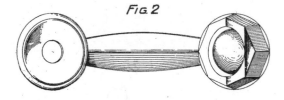

INVENTOR
J. VASSOS

BY
Walter C. Kiesel

ATTORNEY

TITLE: OZONIZING APPARATUS
INVENTOR: WELLINGTON J. SMITH
ASSIGNEE: NONE

PATENT NUMBER: USD 81,815
PATENT FILED: APRIL 24, 1930
PATENT GRANTED: AUGUST 12, 1930

Aug. 12, 1930.　　　　W. J. SMITH　　　　Des. 81,815

OZONIZING APPARATUS

Filed April 24, 1930

Inventor

W. J. Smith.

By

Attorneys

TITLE: GASOLINE-FILLING-STATION BOOTH
INVENTOR: CHARLES D. VARY
ASSIGNEE: NONE

PATENT NUMBER: USD 82,067
PATENT FILED: APRIL 28, 1930
PATENT GRANTED: SEPTEMBER 16, 1930

Sept. 16, 1930.   C. D. VARY   Des. 82,067

PORTABLE GASOLINE FILLING STATION BOOTH

Filed April 28, 1930

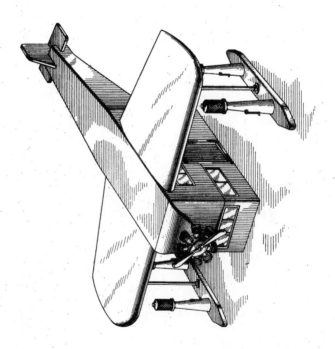

Inventor:
Charles D. Vary.
By Bertha L. MacGregor
Atty.

TITLE: STORE FRONT
INVENTOR: VAHAN HAGOPIAN
ASSIGNEE: A.S. BECK SHOE CORPORATION

PATENT NUMBER: USD 82,150
PATENT FILED: MARCH 13, 1930
PATENT GRANTED: SEPTEMBER 30, 1930

Sept. 30, 1930.

V. HAGOPIAN

Des. 82,150

STORE FRONT

Filed March 13, 1930

2 Sheets—Sheet 1

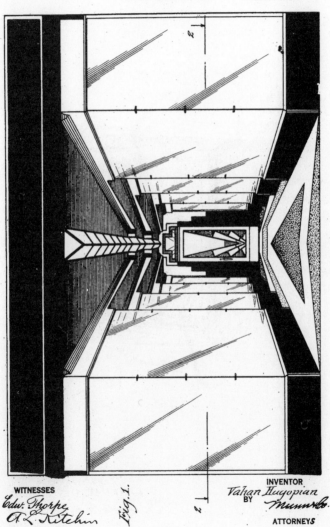

Fig. 1.

WITNESSES

Edw. Thorpe
A. L. Kitchin

INVENTOR
Vahan Hagopian
BY
Munn & Co.
ATTORNEYS

166

TITLE: CLOCK OR THE LIKE
INVENTOR: ERROL W. GOFF
ASSIGNEE: WARREN TELECHRON COMPANY

PATENT NUMBER: USD 82,424
PATENT FILED: JULY 15, 1930
PATENT GRANTED: NOVEMBER 4, 1930

Nov. 4, 1930.　　　E. W. GOFF　　　**Des. 82,424**

CLOCK OR THE LIKE

Filed July 15, 1930

Inventor:
Errol W. Goff,
by *Charles W. Mullen*
His Attorney.

TITLE: AMUSEMENT PARK BUILDING OR
ANALAGOUS STRUCTURE
INVENTOR: EMIL C. HOPPE
ASSIGNEE: NONE

PATENT NUMBER: USD 82,427
PATENT FILED: MAY 31, 1930
PATENT GRANTED: NOVEMBER 4, 1930

Nov. 4, 1930.　　　　E. C. HOPPE　　　　Des. 82,427

AMUSEMENT PARK BUILDING OR ANALOGOUS STRUCTURE

Filed May 31, 1930

INVENTOR
Emil C. Hoppe.
BY
ATTORNEY

TITLE: COMBINED CLOCK CASING AND DIAL THEREFOR
OR SIMILAR ARTICLE
INVENTOR: PAUL T. FRANKL
ASSIGNEE: WARREN TELECHRON COMPANY

PATENT NUMBER: USD 82,548
PATENT FILED: JULY 14, 1930
PATENT GRANTED: NOVEMBER 18, 1930

Nov. 18, 1930.   P. T. FRANKL   Des. 82,548

COMBINED CLOCK CASING AND DIAL THEREFOR OR SIMILAR ARTICLE

Filed July 14, 1930

Fig.1.

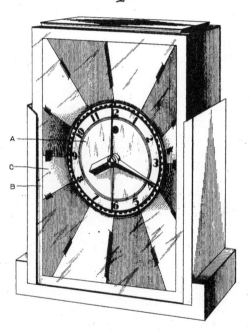

Fig.2.

Inventor:
Paul T. Frankl,
by Charles Mullen
His Attorney.

TITLE: CAMERA CASING OR THE LIKE
INVENTOR: WALTER D. TEAGUE
ASSIGNEE: EASTMAN KODAK COMPANY

PATENT NUMBER: USD 82,918
PATENT FILED: JULY 26, 1930
PATENT GRANTED: DECEMBER 23, 1930

Dec. 23, 1930.

W. D. TEAGUE

Des. 82,918

CAMERA CASING OR THE LIKE

Filed July 26, 1930

Fig. 1

Fig. 2

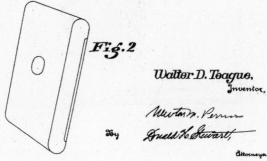

Walter D. Teague,
Inventor,

Newton N. Perrin

By Donald H. Stewart,

Attorneys

TITLE: COMBINED CLOCK FRAME AND FACE
INVENTOR: RAYMOND E. PATTEN
ASSIGNEE: EDISON GENERAL ELECTRIC
APPLIANCE COMPANY

PATENT NUMBER: USD 83,642
PATENT FILED: OCTOBER 23, 1930
PATENT GRANTED: MARCH 10, 1931

March 10, 1931. R. E. PATTEN Des. 83,642

COMBINED CLOCK FRAME AND FACE

Filed Oct. 23, 1930

Inventor:
Raymond E. Patten,
by *Charles V. Tullar*
His Attorney.

TITLE: ELECTRIC FAN
INVENTOR: FREDRIK LJUNGSTRÖM
ASSIGNEE: NONE

PATENT NUMBER: USD 84,642
PATENT FILED: JUNE 1, 1931
PATENT GRANTED: JULY 14, 1931

July 14, 1931.   F. LJUNGSTROM   Des. 84,642

ELECTRIC FAN

Filed June 1, 1931

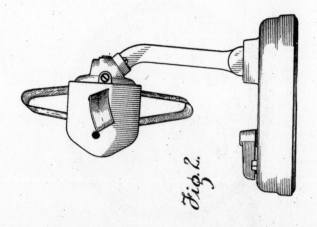

Fig. 2.

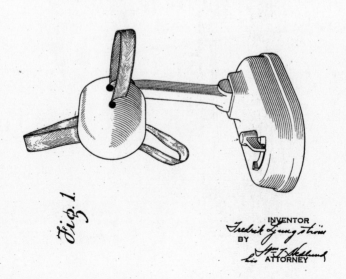

Fig. 1.

INVENTOR
Fredrik Ljungström
BY
his ATTORNEY

TITLE: CLOCK CASE
INVENTOR: HENRY DREYFUSS
ASSIGNEE: WESTERN CLOCK COMPANY

PATENT NUMBER: USD 85,916
PATENT FILED: APRIL 20, 1931
PATENT GRANTED: JANUARY 5, 1932

Jan. 5, 1932.

H. DREYFUSS

Des. 85,916

CLOCK CASE

Filed April 20, 1931

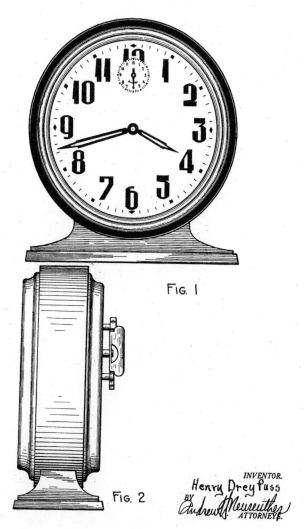

FIG. 1

FIG. 2

INVENTOR.
Henry Dreyfuss
BY Andrew J. Neureuther
ATTORNEYS.

173

TITLE: BOTTLE OR SIMILAR ARTICLE
INVENTOR: RENÉ LALIQUE
ASSIGNEE: LUCIEN LELONG

PATENT NUMBER: USD 86,244
PATENT FILED: NOVEMBER 16, 1931
PATENT GRANTED: FEBRUARY 16, 1932

Feb. 16, 1932.   R. LALIQUE   Des. 86,244

BOTTLE OR SIMILAR ARTICLE

Filed Nov. 16, 1931

FIG. 2

FIG. 1

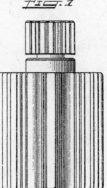

Inventor:
René Lalique.

by: Charles H. Fields Attys.

TITLE: CABINET FOR RADIO RECEIVERS
INVENTOR: JAMES I. BENJAMIN
ASSIGNEE: PILOT RADIO & TUBE CORPORATION

PATENT NUMBER: USD 86,509
PATENT FILED: SEPTEMBER 29, 1931
PATENT GRANTED: MARCH 15, 1932

March 15, 1932.   J. I. BENJAMIN   Des. 86,509

CABINET FOR RADIO RECEIVERS

Filed Sept. 29, 1931

Fig. 1.

Fig. 2.

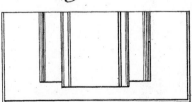

INVENTOR.
James I Benjamin
BY
ATTORNEYS

TITLE: BUILDING OF DIRIGIBLE AIRCRAFT DESIGN
INVENTOR: NICKOLAS G. LAGIOS
ASSIGNEE: NONE

PATENT NUMBER: USD 86,617
PATENT FILED: OCTOBER 19, 1931
PATENT GRANTED: MARCH 29, 1932

March 29, 1932.

N. G. LAGIOS

Des. 86,617

BUILDING OF DIRIGIBLE AIRCRAFT DESIGN

Filed Oct. 19, 1931

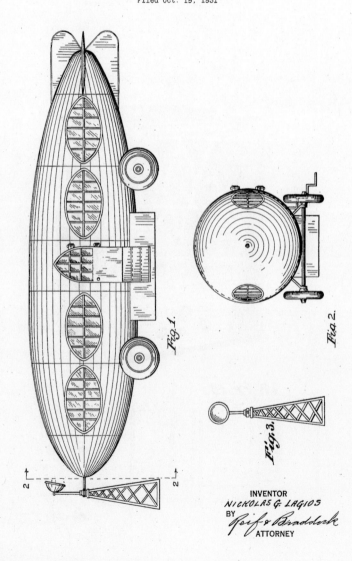

Fig. 1.

Fig. 2.

Fig. 3.

INVENTOR
NICKOLAS G. LAGIOS
BY
Reif & Braddock
ATTORNEY

TITLE: COFFEE POT OR SIMILAR ARTICLE
INVENTOR: LURELLE GUILD
ASSIGNEE: ALUMINUM COOKING UTENSIL COMPANY

PATENT NUMBER: USD 86,671
PATENT FILED: FEBRUARY 1, 1932
PATENT GRANTED: APRIL 5, 1932

April 5, 1932.   L. GUILD   Des. 86,671

COFFEE POT OR SIMILAR ARTICLE

Filed Feb. 1, 1932

Fig. 3.

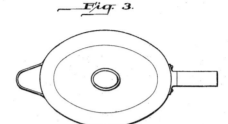

Fig. 1.   _Fig. 2._

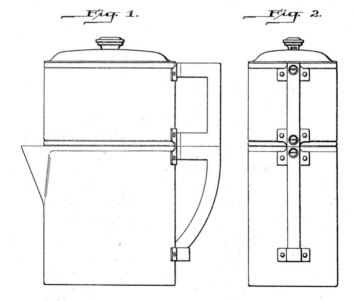

INVENTOR

Lurelle Guild
By
His Attorney

177

TITLE: ELECTRIC TOASTER
INVENTOR: RAYMOND E. PATTEN
ASSIGNEE: EDISON GENERAL ELECTRIC
APPLIANCE COMPANY

PATENT NUMBER: USD 86,804
PATENT FILED: NOVEMBER 27, 1931
PATENT GRANTED: APRIL 19, 1932

April 19, 1932.   R. E. PATTEN   **Des. 86,804**

ELECTRIC TOASTER

Filed Nov. 27, 1931

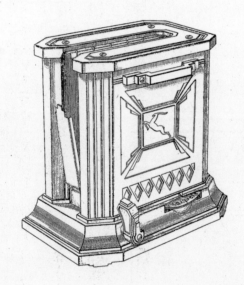

Inventor:
Raymond E. Patten,
by *Charles V. Tuller*
His Attorney.

TITLE: CAMERA
INVENTOR: THOMAS B. LAMB
ASSIGNEE: AGFA-ANSCO CORPORATION

PATENT NUMBER: USD 86,846
PATENT FILED: JANUARY 9, 1932
PATENT GRANTED: APRIL 26, 1932

April 26, 1932.

T. B. LAMB

Des. 86,846

CAMERA

Filed Jan. 9, 1932

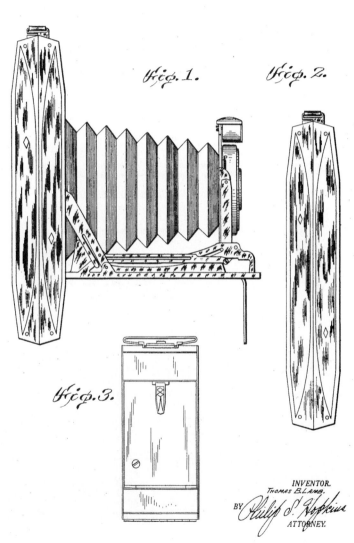

Fig. 1.

Fig. 2.

Fig. 3.

INVENTOR.
Thomas B. Lamb.
BY Philip S. Hopkins
ATTORNEY.

TITLE: BATHTUB
INVENTOR: GEORGE SAKIER
ASSIGNEE: STANDARD SANITARY
MANUFACTURING COMPANY

PATENT NUMBER: USD 86,936
PATENT FILED: JULY 19, 1930
PATENT GRANTED: MAY 10, 1932

May 10, 1932.　　G. SAKIER　　**Des. 86,936**

BATHTUB

Filed July 19, 1930

Fig. 1.

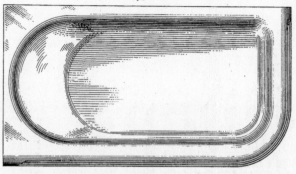

Fig. 2.

Fig. 3.

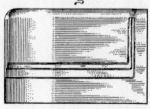

INVENTOR.

George Sakier

BY Conrad A Writeri

his ATTORNEY.

TITLE: TRANSPORT AIRPLANE
INVENTORS: CHARLES N. MONTEITH &
FRANK R. CANNEY
ASSIGNEE: BOEING AIRPLANE COMPANY

PATENT NUMBER: USD 87,440
PATENT FILED: JUNE 7, 1932
PATENT GRANTED: JULY 26, 1932

July 26, 1932.   C. N. MONTEITH ET AL   Des. 87,440

TRANSPORT AIRPLANE

Filed June 7, 1932   2 Sheets—Sheet 2

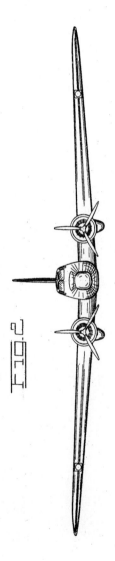

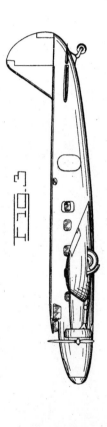

Charles N. Monteith
Frank R. Canney
INVENTORS

BY

Charles L. Reynolds
ATTORNEY

TITLE: AUTOMOBILE RADIATOR CAP
INVENTOR: ALFRED F. MASURY
ASSIGNEE: INTERNATIONAL MOTOR COMPANY

PATENT NUMBER: USD 87,931
PATENT FILED: JULY 2, 1932
PATENT GRANTED: OCTOBER 11, 1932

Oct. 11, 1932.   A. F. MASURY   Des. 87,931

AUTOMOBILE RADIATOR CAP

Filed July 2, 1932

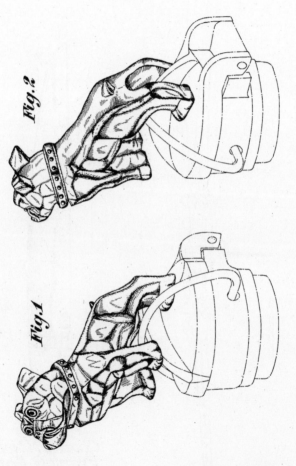

INVENTOR

Alfred F. Masury

BY

Redding, Greeley, O'Shea & Campbell

his ATTORNEYS

182

TITLE: TEAKETTLE
INVENTORS: LURELLE GUILD & JAMES K. MATTER
ASSIGNEE: ALUMINUM COOKING UTENSIL COMPANY

PATENT NUMBER: USD 88,228
PATENT FILED: JUNE 16, 1932
PATENT GRANTED: NOVEMBER 8, 1932

Nov. 8, 1932.

L. GUILD ET AL

Des. 88,228

TEAKETTLE

Filed June 16, 1932

INVENTOR

Lurelle Guild &
James K. Matter
By
attorney

TITLE: BOOK END OR SIMILAR ARTICLE
INVENTOR: WALTER VON NESSEN
ASSIGNEE: THE CHASE COMPANIES

PATENT NUMBER: USD 88,832
PATENT FILED: NOVEMBER 5, 1932
PATENT GRANTED: DECEMBER 27, 1932

Dec. 27, 1932.   W. VON NESSEN   Des. 88,832

BOOK END OR SIMILAR ARTICLE

Filed Nov. 5, 1932

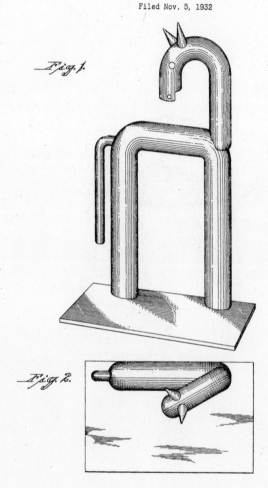

Fig. 1.

Fig. 2.

Inventor
Walter von Nessen
by
Seymour Earle & Nichols
Attys

TITLE: WALL CLOCK
INVENTOR: EARL T. ARNAULT
ASSIGNEE: NONE

PATENT NUMBER: USD 88,849
PATENT FILED: JULY 27, 1932
PATENT GRANTED: JANUARY 3, 1933

Jan. 3, 1933.

E. T. ARNAULT

Des. 88,849

WALL CLOCK

Filed July 27, 1932

Fig. 2

Fig. 1.

Inventor

EARL T. ARNAULT

By

Attorney

TITLE: PLATFORM SCALE CASING
INVENTOR: MATHIAS J. WEBER
ASSIGNEE: HEALTH-O-METER COMPANY

PATENT NUMBER: USD 88,997
PATENT FILED: OCTOBER 17, 1932
PATENT GRANTED: JANUARY 10, 1933

Jan. 10, 1933. M. J. WEBER Des. 88,997

PLATFORM SCALE CASING

Filed Oct. 17, 1932

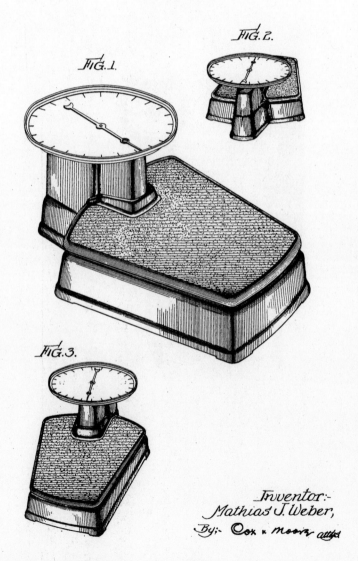

FIG.1.

FIG.2.

FIG.3.

Inventor:-
Mathias J. Weber,
By:- Cox & Moore attys

TITLE: GAS STOVE CASING
INVENTOR: NORMAN BEL GEDDES
ASSIGNEE: STANDARD GAS EQUIPMENT CORPORATION

PATENT NUMBER: USD 90,108
PATENT FILED: APRIL 6, 1933
PATENT GRANTED: JUNE 13, 1933

June 13, 1933.

N. B. GEDDES

Des. 90,108

GAS STOVE CASING

Filed April 6, 1933   2 Sheets—Sheet 1

Fig. 1.

INVENTOR.

Norman Bel Geddes

BY

Morrison, Kennedy & Campbell

ATTORNEYS.

TITLE: MOTOR VEHICLE
INVENTOR: EARL J. W. RAGSDALE
ASSIGNEE: EDWARD G. BUDD MANUFACTURING COMPANY

PATENT NUMBER: USD 90,168
PATENT FILED: MAY 16, 1932
PATENT GRANTED: JUNE 20, 1933

June 20, 1933.   E. J. W. RAGSDALE   Des. 90,168

MOTOR VEHICLE

Filed May 16, 1932   3 Sheets—Sheet 1

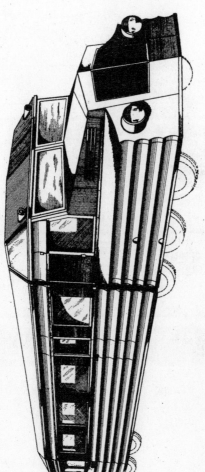

FIG. 1

INVENTOR
EARL J. W. RAGSDALE

BY *John P. Vasbor*

ATTORNEY

TITLE: CHECK WRITING MACHINE
INVENTORS: HENRY DREYFUSS & WALTER B. PAYNE
ASSIGNEE: THE TODD COMPANY

PATENT NUMBER: USD 93,157
PATENT FILED: DECEMBER 29, 1933
PATENT GRANTED: AUGUST 28, 1934

Aug. 28, 1934.   H. DREYFUSS ET AL   Des. 93,157

CHECK WRITING MACHINE

Filed Dec. 29, 1933

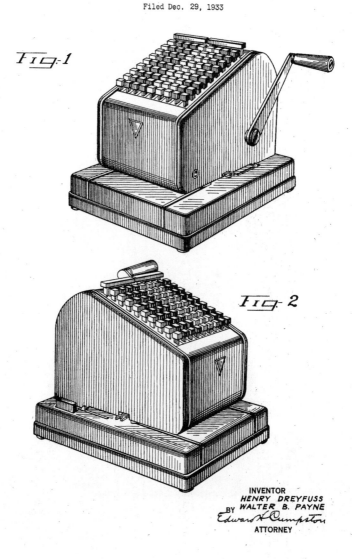

Fig-1

Fig-2

INVENTOR
HENRY DREYFUSS
BY *WALTER B. PAYNE*
Edward H. Cumpston
ATTORNEY

TITLE: CABINET FOR RADIORECEIVER
INVENTOR: RAYMOND G. F. LOEWY
ASSIGNEE: COLONIAL RADIO CORPORATION

PATENT NUMBER: USD 90,586
PATENT FILED: JUNE 24, 1933
PATENT GRANTED: AUGUST 29, 1933

Aug. 29, 1933.   R. G. F. LOEWY   Des. 90,586

CABINET·FOR RADIORECEIVER

Filed June 24, 1933

INVENTOR
RAYMOND G. F. LOEWY
BY
Clyde G. Norton
ATTORNEY

TITLE: SERVICE STATION
INVENTOR: HERBERT O. ALDEN
ASSIGNEE: SHELL OIL COMPANY

PATENT NUMBER: USD 90,642
PATENT FILED: JULY 14, 1933
PATENT GRANTED: SEPTEMBER 12, 1933

Sept. 12, 1933. H. O. ALDEN **Des. 90,642**

SERVICE STATION

Fig. 1 Filed July 14, 1933

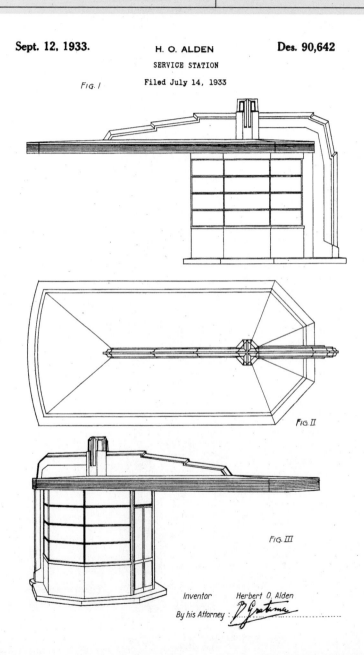

Fig. II

Fig. III

Inventor   Herbert O. Alden

By his Attorney : *[signature]*

TITLE: CLOCK
INVENTOR: ELOF L. CARLSON
ASSIGNEE: THE E. INGRAHAM COMPANY

PATENT NUMBER: USD 91,054
PATENT FILED: SEPTEMBER 28, 1933
PATENT GRANTED: NOVEMBER 21, 1933

Nov. 21, 1933. E. L. CARLSON **Des. 91,054**

CLOCK

Filed Sept. 28, 1933

Fig. 1.

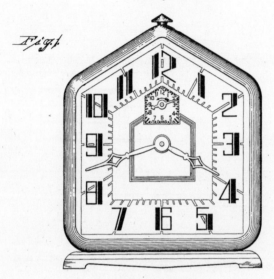

Fig. 2.

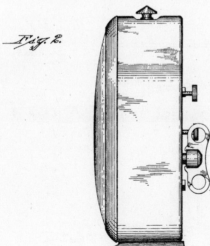

Inventor
Elof L. Carlson
by Seymour Earle & Nichols
Atty.

192

TITLE: RADIOCABINET OR THE LIKE
INVENTOR: EVERETT WORTHINGTON
ASSIGNEE: THE STROMBERG-CARLSON TELEPHONE
MANUFACTURING COMPANY

PATENT NUMBER: USD 91,290
PATENT FILED: NOVEMBER 10, 1933
PATENT GRANTED: JANUARY 2, 1934

Jan. 2, 1934.   E. WORTHINGTON   Des. 91,290

RADIOCABINET OR THE LIKE

Filed Nov. 10, 1933

INVENTOR
Everett Worthington
BY
D. Clyde Jones
ATTORNEY

193

TITLE: COMBINATION SHAKER AND DECANTER
INVENTOR: EDWARD KANTER
ASSIGNEE: NONE

PATENT NUMBER: USD 91,526
PATENT FILED: AUGUST 14, 1933
PATENT GRANTED: FEBRUARY 20, 1934

Feb. 20, 1934.   E. KANTER   Des. 91,526

COMBINATION SHAKER AND DECANTER

Filed Aug. 14, 1933

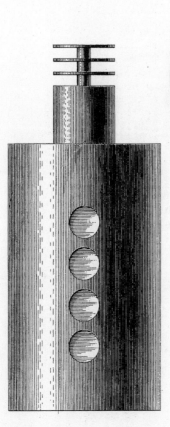

FIG. 2

FIG. 1

INVENTOR
EDWARD KANTER
BY
Hues Brockelbert
ATTORNEY

TITLE: COASTER WAGON
INVENTOR: ANTONIO PASIN
ASSIGNEE: RADIO STEEL & MANUFACTURING COMPANY

PATENT NUMBER: USD 91,540
PATENT FILED: DECEMBER 8, 1933
PATENT GRANTED: FEBRUARY 20, 1934

Feb. 20, 1934. A. PASIN Des. 91,540

COASTER WAGON

Filed Dec. 8, 1933

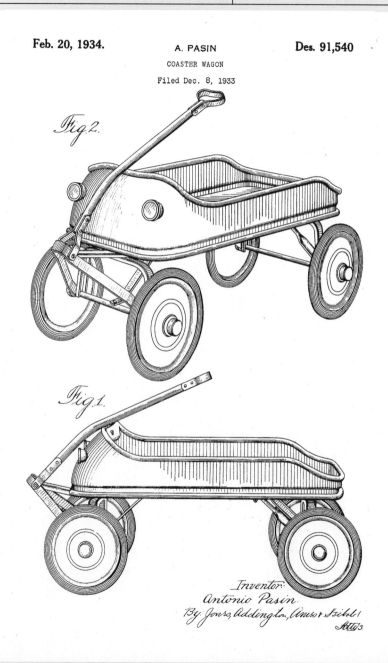

Fig.2.

Fig.1.

Inventor:
Antonio Pasin
By Jones, Addington, Ames & Seibold
Attys

195

TITLE: SALT AND PEPPER SHAKER ASSEMBLY
INVENTOR: HELEN HUGHES DULANY
ASSIGNEE: NONE

PATENT NUMBER: USD 91,555
PATENT FILED: JANUARY 15, 1934
PATENT GRANTED: FEBRUARY 20, 1934

Feb. 20, 1934.   H. H. DULANY   Des. 91,555

SALT AND PEPPER SHAKER ASSEMBLY

Filed Jan. 15, 1934

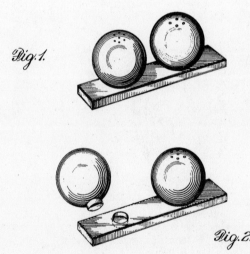

Fig.1.

Fig.2.

Helen Hughes Dulany,
INVENTOR

BY *Albert Grobstein*
ATTORNEY

TITLE: BOAT
INVENTOR: NORMAN BEL GEDDES
ASSIGNEE: NONE

PATENT NUMBER: USD 91,579
PATENT FILED: NOVEMBER 1, 1933
PATENT GRANTED: FEBRUARY 20, 1934

Feb. 20, 1934.　　　N. BEL GEDDES　　　Des. 91,579

BOAT

Filed Nov. 1, 1933

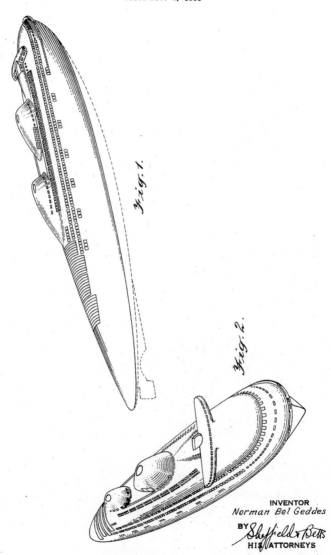

Fig. 1.

Fig. 2.

INVENTOR
Norman Bel Geddes

BY *Sheffield & Betts*
HIS ATTORNEYS

TITLE: PENCIL SHARPENER
INVENTOR: RAYMOND LOEWY
ASSIGNEE: NONE

PATENT NUMBER: USD 91,675
PATENT FILED: MAY 29, 1933
PATENT GRANTED: MARCH 6, 1934

March 6, 1934.　　R. LOEWY　　Des. 91,675

PENCIL SHARPENER

Filed May 29, 1933

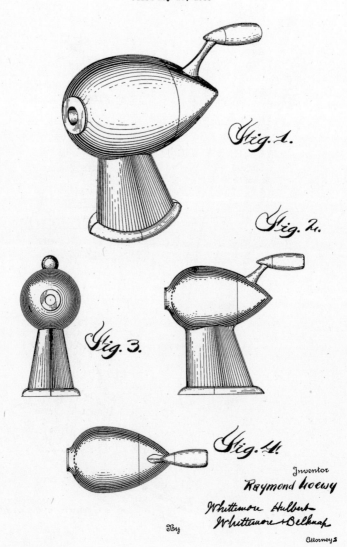

Fig. 1.

Fig. 2.

Fig. 3.

Fig. 4.

Inventor
Raymond Loewy

Whittemore Hulbert
Whittemore + Belknap
Attorneys

By

TITLE: ELECTRIC LAMP
INVENTOR: GLENN E. MCFADDEN
ASSIGNEE: MARKEL ELECTRIC PRODUCTS

PATENT NUMBER: USD 91,679
PATENT FILED: NOVEMBER 29, 1933
PATENT GRANTED: MARCH 6, 1934

March 6, 1934.

G. E. McFADDEN

Des. 91,679

ELECTRIC LAMP

Filed Nov. 29, 1933

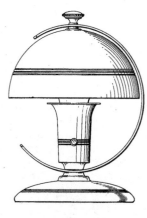

Fig. 1.

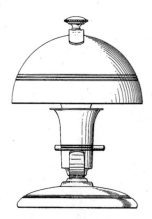

Fig. 2.

Fig. 3.

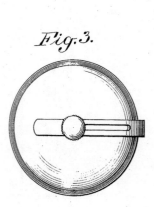

Fig. 4.

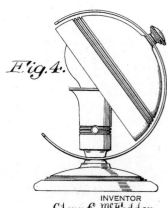

INVENTOR
Glenn E. McFadden
BY
Popp and Powers
ATTORNEYS

TITLE: ELECTRIC SEWING MACHINE
INVENTOR: HERBERT J. GOOSMAN
ASSIGNEE: SINGER MANUFACTURING COMPANY

PATENT NUMBER: USD 91,816
PATENT FILED: JANUARY 25, 1934
PATENT GRANTED: MARCH 27, 1934

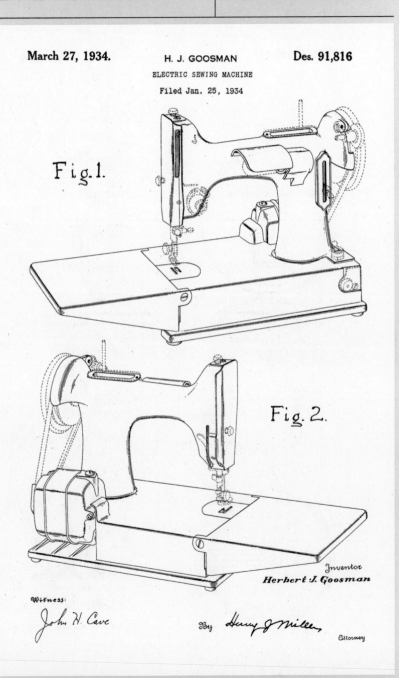

March 27, 1934.

H. J. GOOSMAN

Des. 91,816

ELECTRIC SEWING MACHINE

Filed Jan. 25, 1934

Fig. 1.

Fig. 2.

Inventor
Herbert J. Goosman

Witness:
John H. Cave

By Henry J. Miller
Attorney

TITLE: BUILDING
INVENTOR: SOLIS D. KAPLAN
ASSIGNEE: NONE

PATENT NUMBER: USD 91,828
PATENT FILED: JUNE 17, 1933
PATENT GRANTED: MARCH 27, 1934

March 27, 1934.   S. D. KAPLAN   Des. 91,828

BUILDING

Filed June 17, 1933

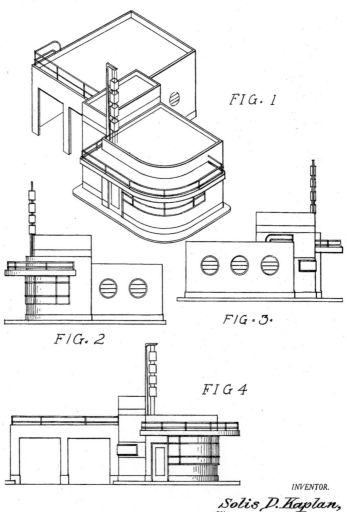

FIG. 1

FIG. 2

FIG. 3.

FIG 4

INVENTOR.

Solis D. Kaplan,

BY

Jas. C. Nobenesmith

ATTORNEY.

TITLE: TELEPHONE INSTRUMENT OR THE LIKE
INVENTOR: EVERETT WORTHINGTON
ASSIGNEE: THE STROMBERG-CARLSON TELEPHONE
MANUFACTURING COMPANY

PATENT NUMBER: USD 92,442
PATENT FILED: APRIL 6, 1934
PATENT GRANTED: JUNE 5, 1934

June 5, 1934. E. WORTHINGTON **Des. 92,442**

TELEPHONE INSTRUMENT OR THE LIKE

Filed April 6, 1934

Fig. 1

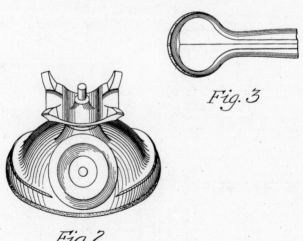

Fig. 3

Fig. 2

INVENTOR
Everett Worthington
BY *D. Clyde Jones*
his ATTORNEY

TITLE: FAUCET
INVENTOR: RAYMOND LOEWY
ASSIGNEE: NONE

PATENT NUMBER: USD 92,480
PATENT FILED: MARCH 15, 1934
PATENT GRANTED: JUNE 12, 1934

June 12, 1934.

R. LOEWY

Des. 92,480

FAUCET

Filed March 15, 1934

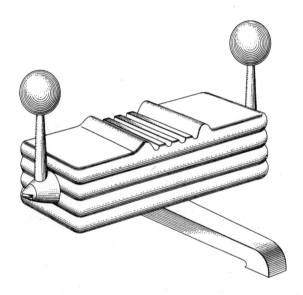

INVENTOR
Raymond Loewy
BY
Blair, Curtis & Dunne
ATTORNEYS

TITLE: BEER BOTTLE
INVENTOR: HARRY ENNEVER
ASSIGNEE: NONE

PATENT NUMBER: USD 92,640
PATENT FILED: DECEMBER 21, 1933
PATENT GRANTED: JUNE 26, 1934

June 26, 1934.   H. ENNEVER   Des. 92,640

BEER BOTTLE

Filed Dec. 21, 1933

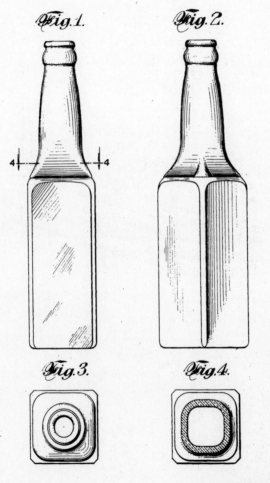

Fig. 1.   Fig. 2.

Fig. 3.   Fig. 4.

4

HARRY ENNEVER
INVENTOR

BY

ATTORNEY

TITLE: PITCHER OR SIMILAR ARTICLE
INVENTOR: MICHAEL W. MCARDLE
ASSIGNEE: CHICAGO FLEXIBLE SHAFT COMPANY

PATENT NUMBER: USD 92,668
PATENT FILED: APRIL 19, 1934
PATENT GRANTED: JULY 3, 1934

July 3, 1934.

M. W. McARDLE

Des. 92,668

PITCHER OR SIMILAR ARTICLE

Filed April 19, 1934

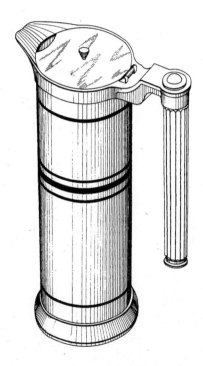

Inventor:
Michael W. McArdle
By
Wilson, Dowell, McComa & Winterain
Attys.

TITLE: ADJUSTABLE LAMP
INVENTOR: EDWARD C. GODFREY
ASSIGNEE: NONE

PATENT NUMBER: USD 92,802
PATENT FILED: MARCH 26, 1934
PATENT GRANTED: JULY 17, 1934

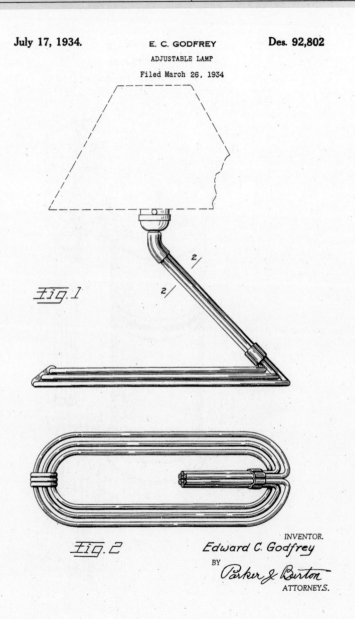

July 17, 1934.

E. C. GODFREY

Des. 92,802

ADJUSTABLE LAMP

Filed March 26, 1934

_Fig._1

_Fig._2

INVENTOR.
Edward C. Godfrey
BY
Parker & Burton
ATTORNEYS.

TITLE: CAMERA CASING
INVENTOR: WALTER D. TEAGUE
ASSIGNEE: EASTMAN KODAK COMPANY

PATENT NUMBER: USD 92,830
PATENT FILED: MARCH 31, 1934
PATENT GRANTED: JULY 17, 1934

July 17, 1934.   W. D. TEAGUE   Des. 92,830

CAMERA CASING

Filed March 31, 1934

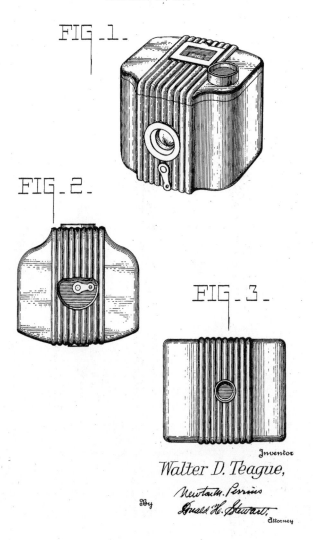

FIG_1_

FIG_2_

FIG_3_

Inventor

Walter D. Teague,

By

Newtown. Perrius

Russell H. Stewart,

Attorney

TITLE: COFFEE MAKING APPARATUS OR THE LIKE
INVENTOR: HOWARD H. SCHOTT
ASSIGNEE: ROBESON-ROCHESTER CORPORATION

PATENT NUMBER: USD 92,980
PATENT FILED: NOVEMBER 14, 1933
PATENT GRANTED: AUGUST 7, 1934

Aug. 7, 1934. H. H. SCHOTT Des. 92,980

COFFEE MAKING APPARATUS OR THE LIKE

Filed Nov. 14, 1933

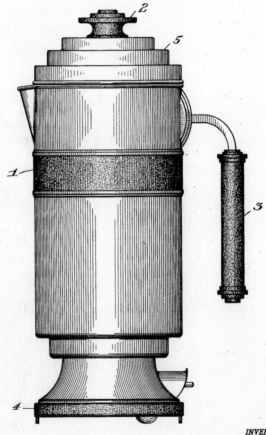

INVENTOR
Howard H. Schott
BY *Edward H. Cumpston*
his ATTORNEY

TITLE: LAMP
INVENTOR: HANNAH PORTER
ASSIGNEE: NONE

PATENT NUMBER: USD 93,047
PATENT FILED: MAY 23, 1934
PATENT GRANTED: AUGUST 14, 1934

Aug. 14, 1934.　　　H. PORTER　　　**Des. 93,047**

LAMP

Filed May 23, 1934

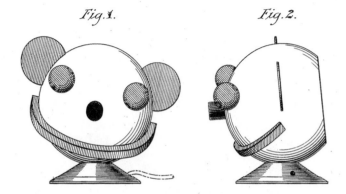

Fig. 1.　　　*Fig. 2.*

Fig. 3.

WITNESSES
Edw. Thorpe.
Chris Feinle.

INVENTOR
Hannah Porter
BY
Munn, Anderson & Liddy.
ATTORNEY

209

TITLE: TOASTER
INVENTOR: WILLIAM A. PENTECOST
ASSIGNEE: ACE MFG. COMPANY

PATENT NUMBER: USD 93,128
PATENT FILED: MAY 24, 1934
PATENT GRANTED: AUGUST 21, 1934

Aug. 21, 1934.   W. A. PENTECOST   Des. 93,128

TOASTER

Filed May 24, 1934

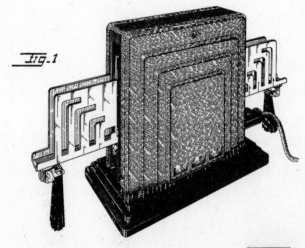

𝐹𝑖𝑔.1

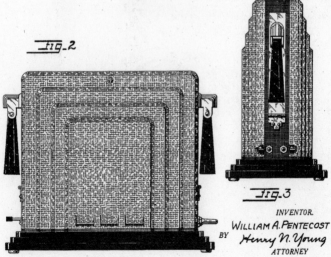

𝐹𝑖𝑔.2

𝐹𝑖𝑔.3

INVENTOR.
WILLIAM A. PENTECOST
BY Henry N. Young
ATTORNEY

210

TITLE: INDICATOR
INVENTOR: ALBERT L. STEMWEDEL
ASSIGNEE: FEE & STEMWEDEL & NEW PROCESS COMPANY

PATENT NUMBER: USD 93,364
PATENT FILED: JULY 9, 1934
PATENT GRANTED: SEPTEMBER 18, 1934

Sept. 18, 1934.   A. L. STEMWEDEL   Des. 93,364

INDICATOR

Filed July 9, 1934

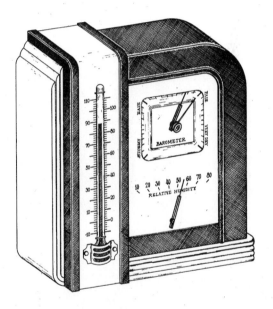

WITNESS

INVENTOR

albert L. Stemwedel

TITLE: AUTOMOBILE
INVENTOR: GORDON MILLER BUEHRIG
ASSIGNEE: CORD CORPORATION

PATENT NUMBER: USD 93,451
PATENT FILED: MAY 17, 1934
PATENT GRANTED: OCTOBER 2, 1934

Oct. 2, 1934.

G. M. BUEHRIG

Des. 93,451

AUTOMOBILE

Filed May 17, 1934

3 Sheets—Sheet 1

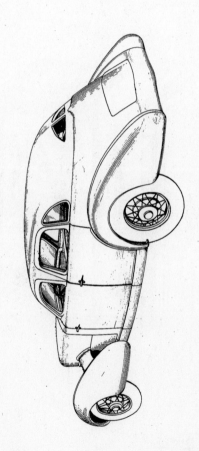

Inventor:
Gordon Miller Buehrig
By Fred L. Gerlach, his Atty.

212

TITLE: EGG BEATER
INVENTOR: JOHN ANDERSON
ASSIGNEE: NONE

PATENT NUMBER: USD 93,596
PATENT FILED: JUNE 8, 1934
PATENT GRANTED: OCTOBER 16, 1934

Oct. 16, 1934.

J. ANDERSON

EGG BEATER

Filed June 8, 1934

Des. 93,596

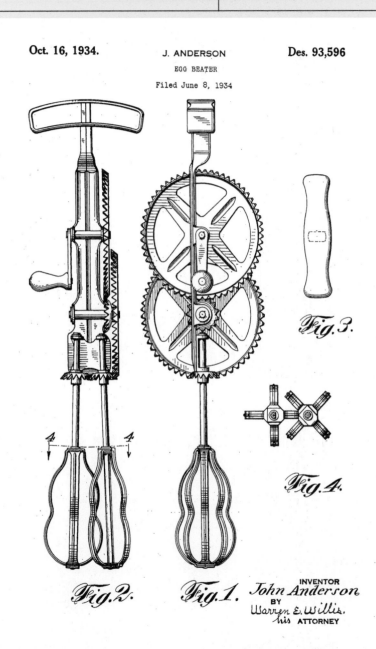

Fig.3.

Fig.4.

Fig.2.

Fig.1.

INVENTOR
John Anderson
BY
Warren E. Willis,
his ATTORNEY

TITLE: CLOCK CASE
INVENTOR: BELLE KOGAN
ASSIGNEE: WARREN TELECHRON COMPANY

PATENT NUMBER: USD 93,662
PATENT FILED: JULY 31, 1934
PATENT GRANTED: OCTOBER 23, 1934

Oct. 23, 1934.

B. KOGAN

Des. 93,662

CLOCK CASE

Filed July 31, 1934

Fig. 2.

Fig. 1.

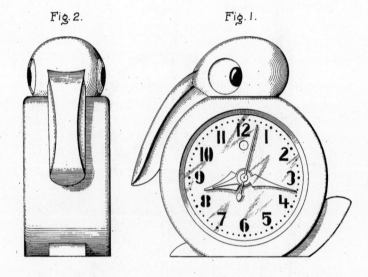

Fig. 3.

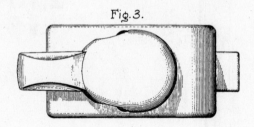

Inventor:
Belle Kogan,
by *Harry E. Dunham*
Her Attorney.

TITLE: AUTOMOBILE OR SIMILAR ARTICLE
INVENTOR: HARLEY J. EARL
ASSIGNEE: GENERAL MOTORS CORPORATION

PATENT NUMBER: USD 93,764
PATENT FILED: MAY 9, 1934
PATENT GRANTED: NOVEMBER 6, 1934

Nov. 6, 1934.   H. J. EARL   Des. 93,764

AUTOMOBILE OR SIMILAR ARTICLE

Filed May 9, 1934   3 Sheets-Sheet 2

Fig. 3

Fig. 2

Harley J. Earl
INVENTOR.

BY
Barnes, Kisselle, Laughlin & Raisch
ATTORNEYS.

TITLE: AUTOMOTIVE VEHICLE
INVENTORS: NORMAN BEL GEDDES, WORTHEN PAXTON
& WILLIAM H. STANGLE
ASSIGNEE: NORMAN BEL GEDDES

PATENT NUMBER: USD 93,863
PATENT FILED: OCTOBER 28, 1933
PATENT GRANTED: NOVEMBER 20, 1934

Nov. 20, 1934.

N. BEL GEDDES ET AL

Des. 93,863

AUTOMOTIVE VEHICLE

Filed Oct. 28, 1933

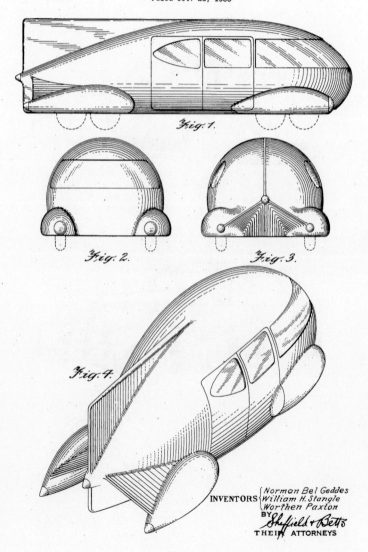

Fig. 1.

Fig. 2.

Fig. 3.

Fig. 4.

INVENTORS { Norman Bel Geddes
William H. Stangle
Worthen Paxton

BY Sheffield & Betts

THEIR ATTORNEYS

216

TITLE: TOASTER
INVENTOR: EVERETT WORTHINGTON
ASSIGNEE: WATERS-GENTER COMPANY

PATENT NUMBER: USD 93,903
PATENT FILED: AUGUST 24, 1934
PATENT GRANTED: NOVEMBER 20, 1934

Nov. 20, 1934.   E. WORTHINGTON   Des. 93,903

TOASTER

Filed Aug. 24, 1934

Inventor
EVERETT WORTHINGTON

By *Paul Carl Moore*

ATTORNEYS

TITLE: STAPLING DEVICE
INVENTOR: EARL C. BUNNELL
ASSIGNEE: NEVA-CLOG PRODUCTS

PATENT NUMBER: USD 94,259
PATENT FILED: OCTOBER 20, 1934
PATENT GRANTED: JANUARY 8, 1935

Jan. 8, 1935.

E. C. BUNNELL

Des. 94,259

STAPLING DEVICE

Filed Oct. 20, 1934

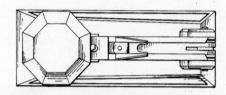

FIG. 3

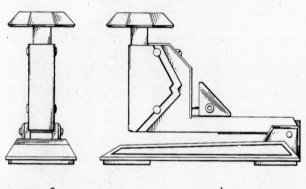

FIG. 2.

FIG. 1

INVENTOR.
EARL C. BUNNELL.
BY
ATTORNEY.

TITLE: LAMP
INVENTOR: FREDRICK DAVID CHAPMAN
ASSIGNEE: MONTGOMERY WARD & COMPANY

PATENT NUMBER: USD 94,409
PATENT FILED: NOVEMBER 8, 1934
PATENT GRANTED: JANUARY 29, 1935

Jan. 29, 1935.

F. D. CHAPMAN

Des. 94,409

LAMP

Filed Nov. 8, 1934

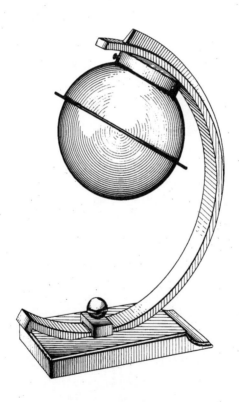

Inventor:
Fredrick David Chapman,
By Cromwell Greist Warden
attys.

TITLE: AIRPLANE
INVENTORS: JAMES H. KINDELBERGER
& ARTHUR E. RAYMOND
ASSIGNEE: DOUGLAS AIRCRAFT COMPANY

PATENT NUMBER: USD 94,427
PATENT FILED: APRIL 9, 1934
PATENT GRANTED: JANUARY 29, 1935

Jan. 29, 1935.   J. H. KINDELBERGER ET AL   Des. 94,427

AIRPLANE

Filed April 9, 1934   2 Sheets—Sheet 2

Fig.4.

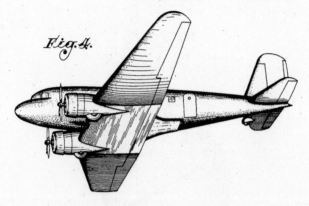

Fig.5.

Fig.6.

INVENTORS
JAMES H. KINDELBERGER
ARTHUR E. RAYMOND

BY *Fad.N.Davis*

ATTORNEY.

TITLE: ROLLER SKATE
INVENTOR: LOUIS MARX
ASSIGNEE: NONE

PATENT NUMBER: USD 95,208
PATENT FILED: SEPTEMBER 13, 1934
PATENT GRANTED: APRIL 16, 1935

April 16, 1935.　　　L. MARX　　　Des. 95,208

ROLLER SKATE

Filed Sept. 13, 1934

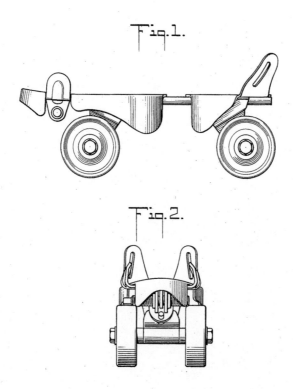

Fig. 1.

Fig. 2.

INVENTOR
Louis Marx
BY

ATTORNEYS

TITLE: AUTOMOBILE OR SIMILAR ARTICLE
INVENTOR: JULES AGRAMONTE
ASSIGNEE: GENERAL MOTORS CORPORATION

PATENT NUMBER: USD 95,302
PATENT FILED: DECEMBER 21, 1933
PATENT GRANTED: APRIL 23, 1935

April 23, 1935.   J. AGRAMONTE   Des. 95,302

AUTOMOBILE OR SIMILAR ARTICLE

Filed Dec. 21, 1933

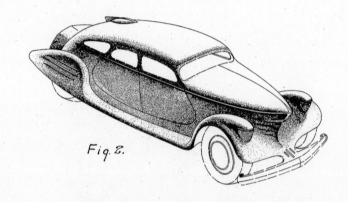

Fig. 2.

Fig. 1.

Jules Agramonte
INVENTOR

BY Barnes, Kisselle
and Laughlin
ATTORNEYS

TITLE: FOOD MIXING APPARATUS
INVENTOR: HERBERT L. JOHNSTON
ASSIGNEE: KITCHENAID MANUFACTURING COMPANY

PATENT NUMBER: USD 95,352
PATENT FILED: JULY 21, 1934
PATENT GRANTED: APRIL 23, 1935

April 23, 1935.   H. L. JOHNSTON   Des. 95,352

FOOD MIXING APPARATUS

Filed July 21, 1934   2 Sheets—Sheet 2

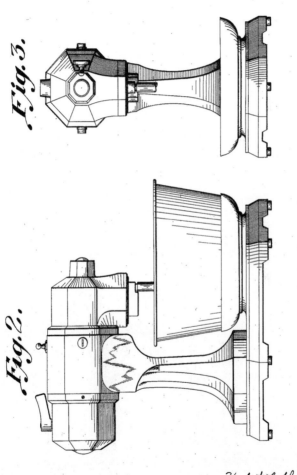

Fig. 3.

Fig. 2.

Inventor
Herbert L. Johnston
By
Marechal & Noe
Attorneys

TITLE: SMOKING STAND
INVENTOR: WILLIAM J. CAMPBELL
ASSIGNEE: CLIMAX MACHINERY COMPANY

PATENT NUMBER: USD 95,401
PATENT FILED: DECEMBER 17, 1934
PATENT GRANTED: APRIL 30, 1935

April 30, 1935.　　　W. J. CAMPBELL　　　Des. 95,401

SMOKING STAND

Filed Dec. 17, 1934

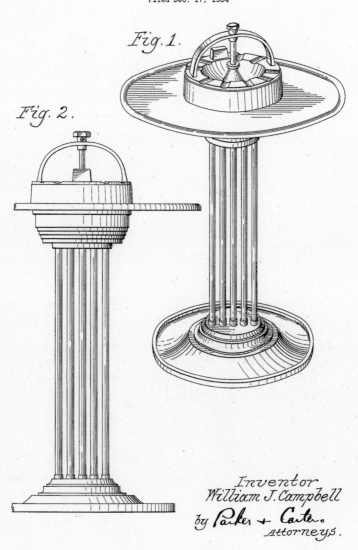

Fig. 1.

Fig. 2.

Inventor
William J. Campbell
by Parker + Carter
Attorneys.

TITLE: LAMP
INVENTOR: BERT A. DICKERSON
ASSIGNEE: FARIES MANUFACTURING COMPANY

PATENT NUMBER: USD 95,668
PATENT FILED: FEBRUARY 20, 1935
PATENT GRANTED: MAY 21, 1935

May 21, 1935.

B. A. DICKERSON

Des. 95,668

LAMP

Filed Feb. 20, 1935

BERT. A. Dickerson

INVENTOR.

BY *Harvey Lea Dodson*

ATTORNEY

TITLE: CHAIR
INVENTOR: WOLFGANG HOFFMANN
ASSIGNEE: W. H. HOWELL COMPANY

PATENT NUMBER: USD 95,745
PATENT FILED: FEBRUARY 5, 1935
PATENT GRANTED: MAY 28, 1935

May 28, 1935.

W. HOFFMANN

Des. 95,745

CHAIR

Filed Feb. 5, 1935

Fig.1

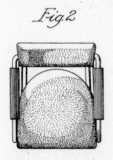

Fig.2

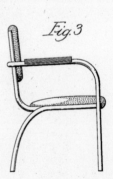

Fig.3

Inventor:
Wolfgang Hoffmann,
By Benning & Benning
Attys.

226

TITLE: DESK STAND FOR A HAND TELEPHONE
INVENTOR: GEORGE R. LUM
ASSIGNEE: BELL TELEPHONE LABORATORIES

PATENT NUMBER: USD 95,765
PATENT FILED: MARCH 27, 1935
PATENT GRANTED: MAY 28, 1935

May 28, 1935.

G. R. LUM

Des. 95,765

DESK STAND FOR A HAND TELEPHONE

Filed March 27, 1935

3 Sheets—Sheet 1

FIG. I

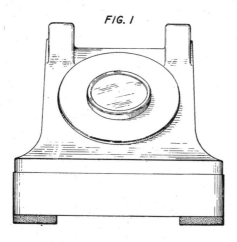

FIG. 2

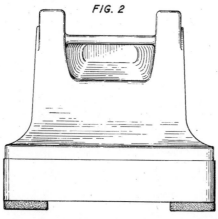

INVENTOR
G. R. LUM

BY

Walter C. Kiesel

ATTORNEY

TITLE: BUILDING
INVENTORS: NORMAN BEL GEDDES & CARL LANDEFELD
ASSIGNEE: SOCONY-VACUUM OIL COMPANY

PATENT NUMBER: USD 95,906
PATENT FILED: APRIL 3, 1935
PATENT GRANTED: JUNE 11, 1935

June 11, 1935.   N. B. GEDDES ET AL   Des. 95,906

BUILDING

Filed April 3, 1935   3 Sheets—Sheet 1

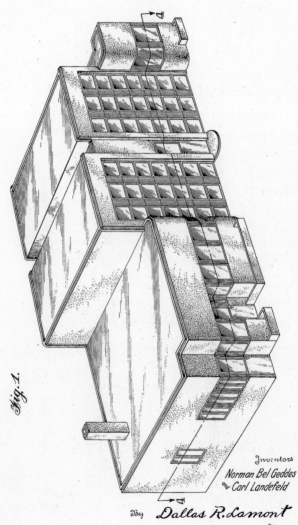

Fig. 1.

Inventors
Norman Bel Geddes
and Carl Landefeld

By Dallas R. Lamont
Attorney

228

TITLE: SCALE
INVENTORS: HAROLD L. VAN DOREN & JOHN G. RIDEOUT
ASSIGNEE: NONE

PATENT NUMBER: USD 96,147
PATENT FILED: MAY 10, 1935
PATENT GRANTED: JULY 2, 1935

July 2, 1935.　　　H. L. VAN DOREN ET AL　　　Des. 96,147

SCALE

Filed May 10, 1935　　　　　2 Sheets—Sheet 1

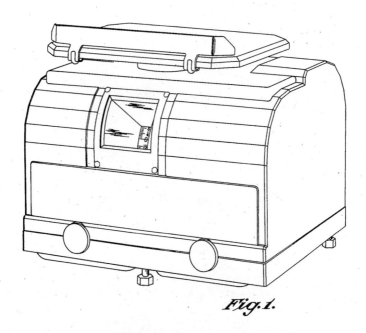

Fig.1.

Harold L. Van Doren
John G. Rideout
INVENTORS

BY *Marshall*
ATTORNEY

TITLE: VELOCIPEDE
INVENTORS: HAROLD L. VAN DOREN & JOHN G. RIDEOUT
ASSIGNEE: AMERICAN-NATIONAL COMPANY

PATENT NUMBER: USD 96,712
PATENT FILED: JUNE 12, 1935
PATENT GRANTED: AUGUST 27, 1935

Aug. 27, 1935.

H. L. VAN DOREN ET AL

Des. 96,712

VELOCIPEDE

Filed June 12, 1935

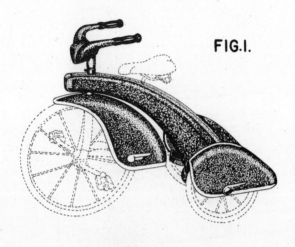

FIG.I.

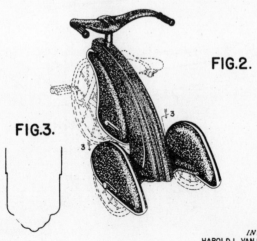

FIG.2.

FIG.3.

INVENTORS
HAROLD L. VAN DOREN
JOHN G. RIDEOUT
BY
Whittemore, Hulbert, Whittemore & Belknap
ATTORNEYS

230

TITLE: CABINET FOR VENDING MACHINES
INVENTOR: GEORGE A. GAST
ASSIGNEE: PLANETELLUS MANUFACTURING
CORPORATION

PATENT NUMBER: USD 96,828
PATENT FILED: JULY 15, 1935
PATENT GRANTED: SEPTEMBER 10, 1935

Sept. 10, 1935.

G. A. GAST

Des. 96,828

CABINET FOR VENDING MACHINES

Filed July 15, 1935

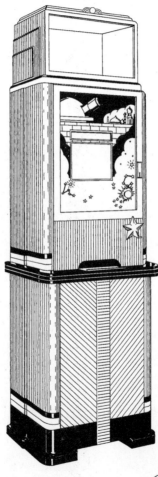

Inventor
George A. Gast
By Paul O. Pippel
Atty.

TITLE: AUTOMOBILE
INVENTOR: CARL BREER
ASSIGNEE: CHRYSLER CORPORATION

PATENT NUMBER: USD 97,574
PATENT FILED: DECEMBER 13, 1933
PATENT GRANTED: NOVEMBER 19, 1935

Nov. 19, 1935.   C. BREER   Des. 97,574

AUTOMOBILE

Original Filed Dec. 13, 1933

Fig.1.

Fig.2.

Fig.3.

INVENTOR
CARL BREER
BY
Harness, Lind, Patie & Harris
ATTORNEYS.

TITLE: WATER CLOSET
INVENTOR: JOHN TJAARDA
ASSIGNEE: BRIGGS MANUFACTURING COMPANY

PATENT NUMBER: USD 97,874
PATENT FILED: APRIL 26, 1935
PATENT GRANTED: DECEMBER 17, 1935

Dec. 17, 1935.

J. TJAARDA

Des. 97,874

WATER CLOSET

Filed April 26, 1935

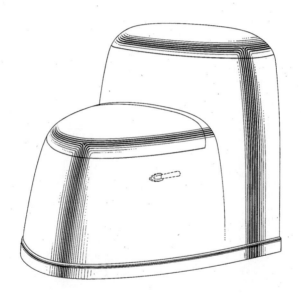

Inventor:
John Tjaarda

By Dike, Calver & Gray
Attorneys.

233

TITLE: LOCOMOTIVE
INVENTOR: EARL J.W. RAGSDALE
ASSIGNEE: EDWARD G. BUDD MANUFACTURING COMPANY

PATENT NUMBER: USD 98,126
PATENT FILED: APRIL 23, 1934
PATENT GRANTED: JANUARY 7, 1936

Jan. 7, 1936.   E. J. W. RAGSDALE   Des. 98,126

LOCOMOTIVE

Original Filed April 23, 1934

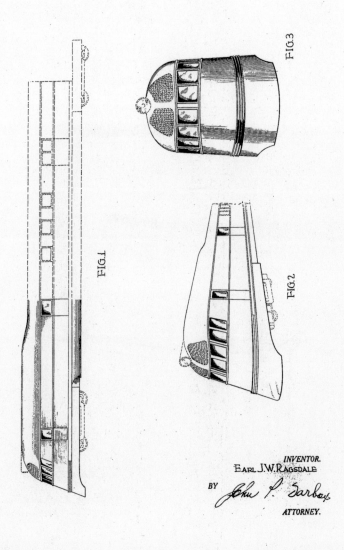

FIG.3

FIG.1

FIG.2

INVENTOR.
EARL J.W. RAGSDALE

BY _John P. Sarbox_

ATTORNEY.

TITLE: SERVICE STATION
INVENTOR: LEONARD D. LONG
ASSIGNEE: SOUTHERN STATES OIL COMPANY

PATENT NUMBER: USD 98,358
PATENT FILED: MAY 28, 1935
PATENT GRANTED: JANUARY 28, 1936

Jan. 28, 1936.   L. D. LONG   Des. 98,358

SERVICE STATION

Filed May 28, 1935

Fig. 1.

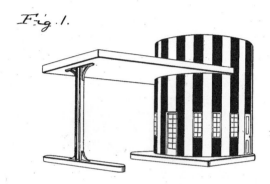

Fig. 2.

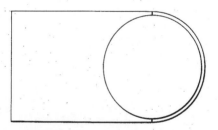

Fig. 3.

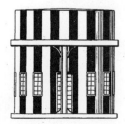

Inventor

L. D. Long

By Clarence A. O'Brien

Attorney

235

TITLE: CAMERA
INVENTOR: GORDON BROWN SCHEIBELL
ASSIGNEE: NONE

PATENT NUMBER: USD 98,369
PATENT FILED: JUNE 21, 1935
PATENT GRANTED: JANUARY 28, 1936

Jan. 28, 1936.   G. B. SCHEIBELL   Des. 98,369

CAMERA

Filed June 21, 1935

Fig_1

Fig_2

INVENTOR
Gordon Brown Scheibell
BY
Wm. J. Herdman
ATTORNEY

236

TITLE: STOVE
INVENTOR: JOHN TJAARDA
ASSIGNEE: BRIGGS MANUFACTURING COMPANY

PATENT NUMBER: USD 98,411
PATENT FILED: DECEMBER 14, 1935
PATENT GRANTED: JANUARY 28, 1936

Jan. 28, 1936.

J. TJAARDA

Des. 98,411

STOVE

Filed Dec. 14, 1935

2 Sheets—Sheet 1

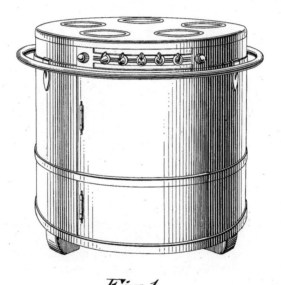

Fig.1

Inventor:
John Tjaarda
By Dike, Calver & Gray
Attorneys.

TITLE: RADIO CABINET
INVENTOR: GUSTAV B. JENSEN
ASSIGNEE: NONE

PATENT NUMBER: USD 98,477
PATENT FILED: DECEMBER 18, 1935
PATENT GRANTED: FEBRUARY 4, 1936

Feb. 4, 1936.　　　　G. B. JENSEN　　　　**Des. 98,477**

RADIO CABINET

Filed Dec. 18, 1935

INVENTOR.

Gustav B. Jensen

BY　　*Darby & Darby*

ATTORNEYS

TITLE: ADJUSTABLE CHAIR
INVENTOR: RUSSEL WRIGHT
ASSIGNEE: NONE

PATENT NUMBER: USD 98,637
PATENT FILED: AUGUST 10, 1935
PATENT GRANTED: FEBRUARY 18, 1936

Feb. 18, 1936.　　　R. WRIGHT　　　**Des. 98,637**

ADJUSTABLE CHAIR

Filed Aug. 10, 1935

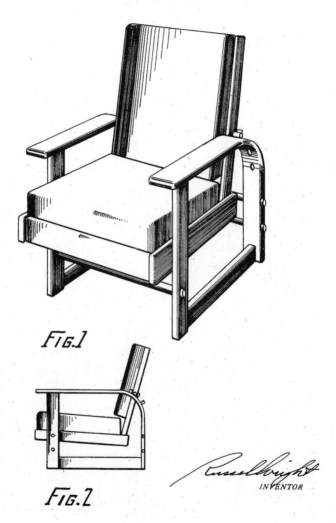

Fig.1

Fig.2

Russel Wright

INVENTOR

TITLE: KETTLE
INVENTOR: EMIL R. ZETTLER
ASSIGNEE: REVERE COPPER & BRASS

PATENT NUMBER: USD 99,425
PATENT FILED: FEBRUARY 12, 1935
PATENT GRANTED: APRIL 21, 1936

April 21, 1936.   E. R. ZETTLER   Des. 99,425

KETTLE

Filed Feb. 12, 1935

Fig. 1.

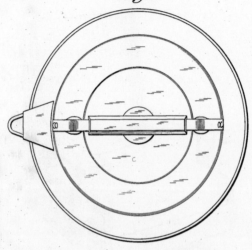

Fig. 2.

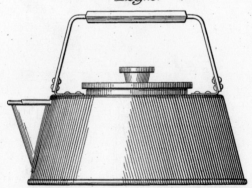

Inventor:
Emil R. Zettler
by Emery Booth Varney & Townsend
Attys

240

TITLE: WEIGHING SCALE
INVENTORS: RUSSEL E. VANDERHOFF
& MATHIAS J. WEBER
ASSIGNEE: CONTINENTAL SCALE WORKS

PATENT NUMBER: USD 99,737
PATENT FILED: MARCH 9, 1936
PATENT GRANTED: MAY 19, 1936

May 19, 1936.   R. E. VANDERHOFF ET AL   Des. 99,737

WEIGHING SCALE

Filed March 9, 1936

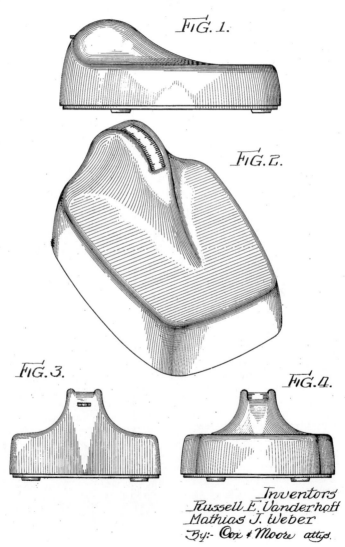

FIG. 1.

FIG. 2.

FIG. 3.

FIG. 4.

Inventors
Russell E. Vanderhoff
Mathias J. Weber
By:- Cox & Moore attys.

241

TITLE: CABINET FOR COIN OPERATED SIMULATED
RACE GAME
INVENTOR: GEORGE A. GAST
ASSIGNEE: RAYMOND T. MOLONEY

PATENT NUMBER: USD 99,746
PATENT FILED: APRIL 8, 1936
PATENT GRANTED: MAY 19, 1936

May 19, 1936.   G. A. GAST   Des. 99,746

CABINET FOR COIN OPERATED SIMULATED RACE GAME

Filed April 8, 1936

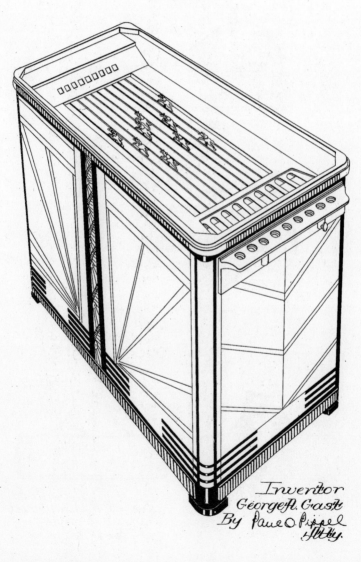

Inventor
George A. Gast
By Paul O. Pippel
Atty.

TITLE: COMBINED WASHING MASHINE CASING
AND WRINGER
INVENTOR: JOHN R. MORGAN
ASSIGNEE: SEARS, ROEBUCK & COMPANY

PATENT NUMBER: USD 99,888
PATENT FILED: APRIL 4, 1936
PATENT GRANTED: JUNE 2, 1936

June 2, 1936.   J. R. MORGAN   **Des. 99,888**

COMBINED WASHING MACHINE CASING AND WRINGER

Filed April 4, 1936

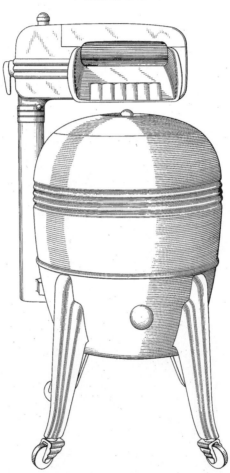

Inventor:
John R. Morgan
By Frank H. Marks, Atty.

243

TITLE: CAMERA
INVENTORS: WALTER D. TEAGUE & CHESTER
W. CRUMRINE
ASSIGNEE: EASTMAN KODAK COMPANY

PATENT NUMBER: USD 99,906
PATENT FILED: APRIL 16, 1936
PATENT GRANTED: JUNE 2, 1936

June 2, 1936.

W. D. TEAGUE ET AL

Des. 99,906

CAMERA

Filed April 16, 1936   2 Sheets—Sheet 1

Fig.1.

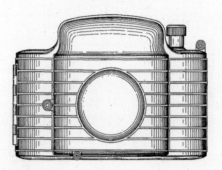

Fig.2.

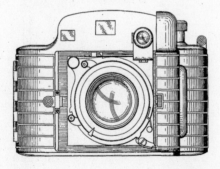

Walter D. Teague & Chester W. Crumrine,
INVENTORS:

BY   *Newton M. Perrior*

Duard H. Stewart
ATTORNEYS.

244

TITLE: ARTICULATED RAIL CAR OR SIMILAR ARTICLE
INVENTORS: EVERETT E. ADAMS, MARTIN P.
BLOMBERG, WILLIAM H. MUSSEY & LIAM B. STOUT
ASSIGNEE: PULLMAN-STANDARD CAR MANUFACTURING

PATENT NUMBER: USD 100,000
PATENT FILED: MAY 9, 1935
PATENT GRANTED: JUNE 16, 1936

June 16, 1936.   E. E. ADAMS ET AL   Des. 100,000

ARTICULATED RAIL CAR OR SIMILAR ARTICLE

Filed May 9, 1935

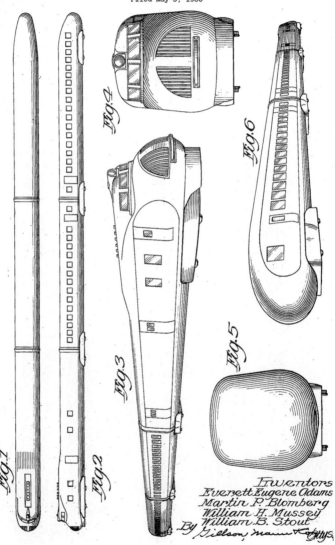

Inventors
Everett Eugene Adams
Martin P. Blomberg
William H. Mussey
William B. Stout
By Gielson, Mann & Cottys

TITLE: RADIO CABINET
INVENTOR: JOHN STEVENS
ASSIGNEE: ZENITH RADIO CORPORATION

PATENT NUMBER: USD 100,131
PATENT FILED: APRIL 16, 1936
PATENT GRANTED: JUNE 23, 1936

June 23, 1936.   J. STEVENS   Des. 100,131

RADIO CABINET

Filed April 16, 1936

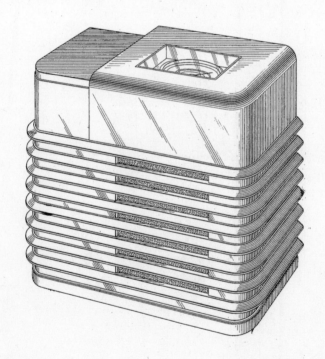

Inventor:
John Stevens
By J. Clarke Hagey Atty.

TITLE: AUTOMOBILE
INVENTOR: DOUGLAS FREDERICK HAROLD FITZMAURICE
ASSIGNEE: NONE

PATENT NUMBER: USD 100,186
PATENT FILED: FEBRUARY 7, 1936
PATENT GRANTED: JUNE 23, 1936

June 23, 1936.   D. F. H. FITZMAURICE   Des. 100,186

AUTOMOBILE

Filed Feb. 7, 1936

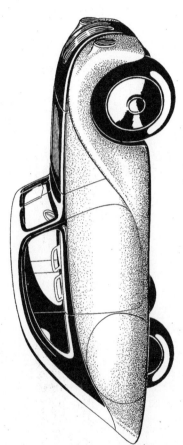

Douglas Frederick Harold Fitzmaurice
INVENTOR

BY *Mock & Blum*
ATTORNEYS

TITLE: COMBINATION TRAVELING & DESK CLOCK
INVENTOR: MAX SCHLENKER
ASSIGNEE: WESTERN CLOCK COMPANY

PATENT NUMBER: USD 100,297
PATENT FILED: MARCH 5, 1936
PATENT GRANTED: JULY 7, 1936

July 7, 1936. M. SCHLENKER **Des. 100,297**

COMBINATION TRAVELING AND DESK CLOCK

Filed March 5, 1936

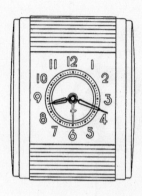

FIG. 1.

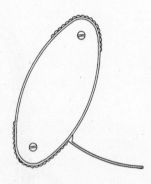

FIG. 2.

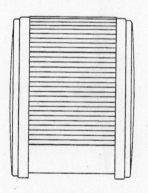

FIG. 3.

FIG. 4.

INVENTOR.
Max Schlenker
BY
Andrew Neureuther
ATTORNEY.

248

TITLE: PORTABLE RADIO CABINET
INVENTOR: JOHN R. MORGAN
ASSIGNEE: SEARS, ROEBUCK & COMPANY

PATENT NUMBER: USD 100,501
PATENT FILED: MAY 25, 1936
PATENT GRANTED: JULY 21, 1936

July 21, 1936.　　　　J. R. MORGAN　　　　Des. 100,501

PORTABLE RADIO CABINET

Filed May 25, 1936

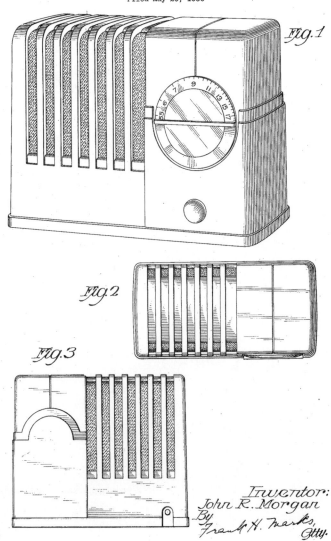

Fig.1

Fig.2

Fig.3

Inventor:
John R. Morgan
By
Frank H. Marks,
Atty.

TITLE: ELECTRIC FAN
INVENTOR: MARSHALL HINDSLEY FRISBIE
ASSIGNEE: THE A.C. GILBERT COMPANY

PATENT NUMBER: USD 100,690
PATENT FILED: DECEMBER 9, 1935
PATENT GRANTED: AUGUST 4, 1936

Aug. 4, 1936.

M. H. FRISBIE

Des. 100,690

ELECTRIC FAN

Filed Dec. 9, 1935

Fig.1.

Fig.2.

Inventor

Marshall Hindsley Frisbie.

By Jerry B. Morehouse

Attorney

250

TITLE: BEVERAGE COOLER CABINET
INVENTOR: RALPH E. KRUCK
ASSIGNEE: WESTINGHOUSE ELECTRIC
& MANUFACTURING COMPANY

PATENT NUMBER: USD 101,370
PATENT FILED: AUGUST 6, 1936
PATENT GRANTED: SEPTEMBER 29, 1936

Sept. 29, 1936.

R. E. KRUCK

Des. 101,370

BEVERAGE COOLER CABINET

Filed Aug. 6, 1936

2 Sheets—Sheet 1

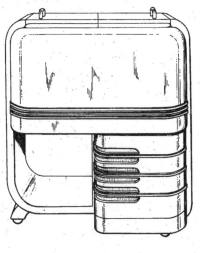

Fig. 1.

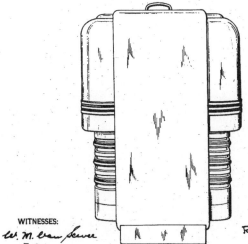

Fig. 2.

WITNESSES:
W. M. van Sewee
E. Lutz

INVENTOR
RALPH E. KRUCK.
BY W.A.Steiger
ATTORNEY

TITLE: TRAY
INVENTOR: NORMAN BEL GEDDES
ASSIGNEE: REVERE COPPER & BRASS

PATENT NUMBER: USD 101,414
PATENT FILED: FEBRUARY 13, 1935
PATENT GRANTED: SEPTEMBER 29, 1936

Sept. 29, 1936.

N. BEL GEDDES

Des. 101,414

TRAY

Filed Feb. 13, 1935

Fig. 1.

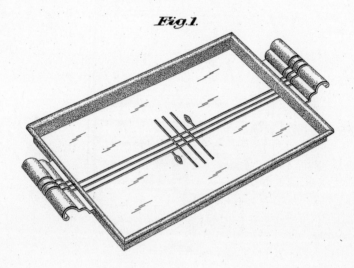

Fig. 2.

Inventor:
Norman Bel Geddes.
By Emery Booth Varney & Townsend
Attys

252

TITLE: ELECTRIC IRON
INVENTOR: DONALD L. HADLEY
ASSIGNEE: WESTINGHOUSE ELECTRIC
& MANUFACTURING COMPANY

PATENT NUMBER: USD 101,495
PATENT FILED: MAY 14, 1936
PATENT GRANTED: OCTOBER 6, 1936

Oct. 6, 1936.

D. L. HADLEY

Des. 101,495

ELECTRIC IRON

Filed May 14, 1936

2 Sheets—Sheet 1

Fig.1.

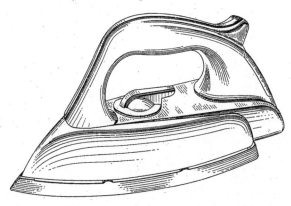

Fig. 2.

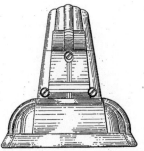

WITNESSES:

C. J. Weller.

R. J. Fitzgerald

INVENTOR

Donald L. Hadley.

BY

W. R. Coley

ATTORNEY

253

TITLE: COMBINED LAVATORY AND PEDESTAL
INVENTORS: HENRY DREYFUSS & ROY H. ZINKIL
ASSIGNEE: CRANE COMPANY

PATENT NUMBER: USD 101,446
PATENT FILED: MAY 15, 1936
PATENT GRANTED: OCTOBER 6, 1936

Oct. 6, 1936.

H. DREYFUSS ET AL

Des. 101,446

COMBINED LAVATORY AND PEDESTAL

Filed May 15, 1936

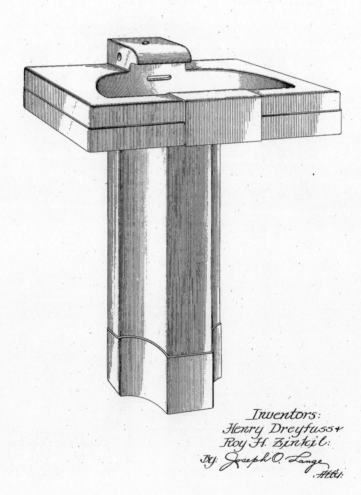

Inventors:
Henry Dreyfuss +
Roy H. Zinkil.
By: Joseph O. Lange
Atty:

TITLE: COCKTAIL SHAKER OR SIMILAR ARTICLE
INVENTOR: EMIL A. SCHUELKE
ASSIGNEE: THE NAPIER COMPANY

PATENT NUMBER: USD 101,559
PATENT FILED: AUGUST 22, 1936
PATENT GRANTED: OCTOBER 13, 1936

Oct. 13, 1936.

E. A. SCHUELKE

Des. 101,559

COCKTAIL SHAKER OR SIMILAR ARTICLE

Filed Aug. 22, 1936

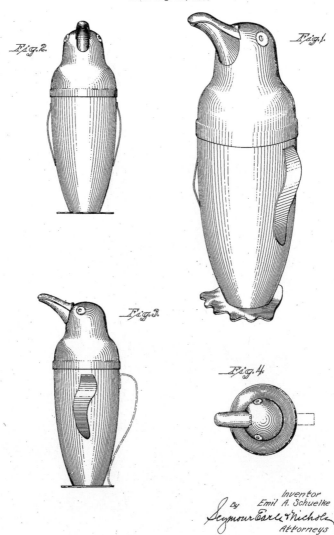

Fig.2.

Fig.1.

Fig.3.

Fig.4

Inventor
Emil A. Schuelke
By
Seymour Earle & Nichols
Attorneys

255

TITLE: ROCKING CHAIR
INVENTOR: WOLFGANG HOFFMANN
ASSIGNEE: THE HOWELL COMPANY

PATENT NUMBER: USD 101,632
PATENT FILED: AUGUST 15, 1936
PATENT GRANTED: OCTOBER 20, 1936

Oct. 20, 1936.

W. HOFFMANN

Des. 101,632

ROCKING CHAIR

Filed Aug. 15, 1936

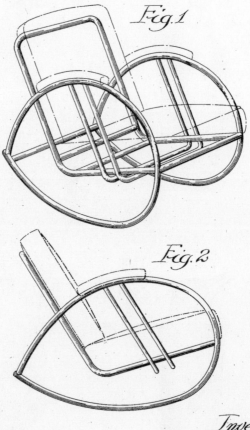

Fig.1

Fig.2

Inventor:
Wolfgang Hoffmann
By Dunning & Dunning
Attys.

TITLE: FLYING BOAT
INVENTORS: ROBERT J. MINSHALL & WELLWOOD
E. BEALL
ASSIGNEE: BOEING AIRCRAFT COMPANY

PATENT NUMBER: USD 101,707
PATENT FILED: JUNE 1, 1936
PATENT GRANTED: OCTOBER 27, 1936

Oct. 27, 1936.   R. J. MINSHALL ET AL   Des. 101,707

FLYING BOAT

Filed June 1, 1936   2 Sheets—Sheet 1

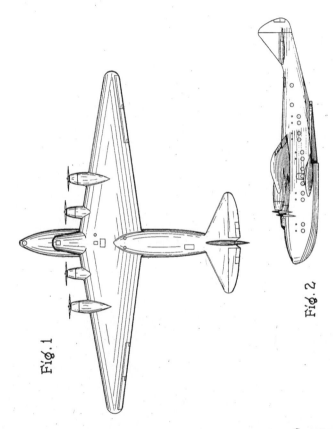

Fig. 1

Fig. 2

Inventor
Robert J. Minshall
Wellwood E. Beall
By Charles L. Reynolds
Attorney

257

TITLE: TEAPOT OR SIMILAR ARTICLE
INVENTOR: BELLE KOGAN
ASSIGNEE: EBELING & REUSS

PATENT NUMBER: USD 101,960
PATENT FILED: SEPTEMBER 24, 1936
PATENT GRANTED: NOVEMBER 17, 1936

Nov. 17, 1936.　　　B. KOGAN　　　**Des. 101,960**

TEAPOT OR SIMILAR ARTICLE

Filed Sept. 24, 1936

Fig.1.

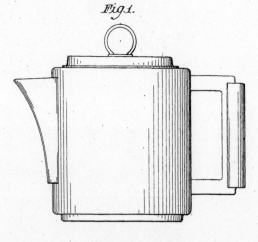

Fig. 2.

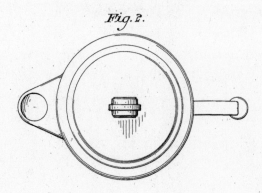

Inventor:
Belle Kogan,
By *Jas. C. Nobenswith*
Attorney.

TITLE: RADIATOR ORNAMENT
INVENTOR: WILFRED R. MILNER
ASSIGNEE: GENERAL MOTORS CORPORATION

PATENT NUMBER: USD 101,998
PATENT FILED: OCTOBER 5, 1936
PATENT GRANTED: NOVEMBER 17, 1936

Nov. 17, 1936.

W. R. MILNER

Des. 101,998

RADIATOR ORNAMENT

Filed Oct. 5, 1936

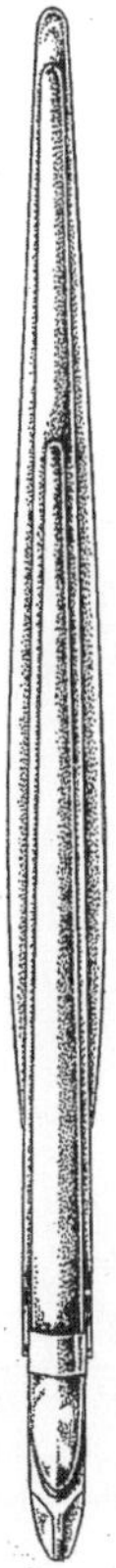

Fig.2

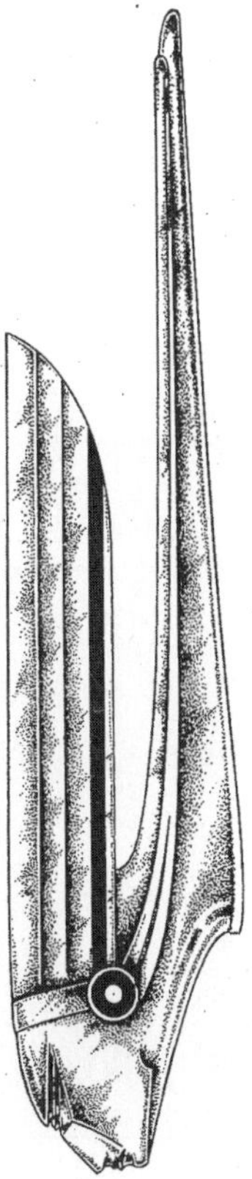

Fig.1

Fig.3

INVENTOR
Wilfred R. Milner
BY
Blackmore, Spencer & Flint
ATTORNEYS

TITLE: REFRIGERATOR
INVENTOR: RAYMOND LOEWY
ASSIGNEE: SEARS, ROEBUCK & COMPANY

PATENT NUMBER: USD 103,023
PATENT FILED: OCTOBER 31, 1934
PATENT GRANTED: FEBRUARY 2, 1937

Feb. 2, 1937.   R. LOEWY   Des. 103,023

REFRIGERATOR

Filed Oct. 31, 1934

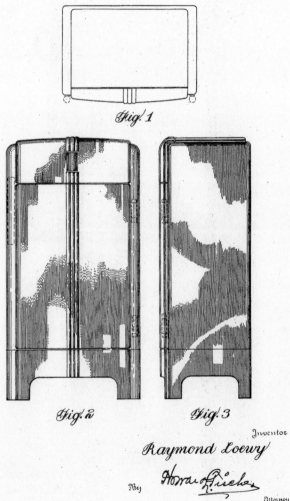

Fig. 1

Fig. 2   Fig. 3

Inventor

Raymond Loewy

By   Howard Richer

Attorney

TITLE: PITCHER
INVENTOR: ANNE SWAINSON
ASSIGNEE: MONTGOMERY WARD & COMPANY

PATENT NUMBER: USD 103,167
PATENT FILED: JUNE 29, 1936
PATENT GRANTED: FEBRUARY 9, 1937

Feb. 9, 1937.　　　　A. SWAINSON　　　　Des. 103,167

PITCHER

Filed June 29, 1936

Fig. 1

Fig. 2

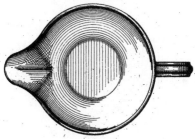

Fig. 3

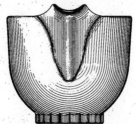

Inventor:
Anne Swainson,
By _____ attys.

TITLE: CLOCK CASE
INVENTOR: WALTER D. TEAGUE
ASSIGNEE: WARREN TELECHRON COMPANY

PATENT NUMBER: USD 103,836
PATENT FILED: FEBRUARY 9, 1937
PATENT GRANTED: MARCH 30, 1937

March 30, 1937.
W. D. TEAGUE
Des. 103,836

CLOCK CASE

Filed Feb. 9, 1937

Inventor:
Walter D. Teague,

by *Harry E. Dunlam*
His Attorney.

TITLE: COMBINED LAMP & DESK SET
INVENTOR: GUSTAV J. SENGBUSCH
ASSIGNEE: NONE

PATENT NUMBER: USD 103,981
PATENT FILED: OCTOBER 5, 1936
PATENT GRANTED: APRIL 6, 1937

April 6, 1937.   G. J. SENGBUSCH   Des. 103,981

COMBINED LAMP AND DESK SET

Filed Oct. 5, 1936

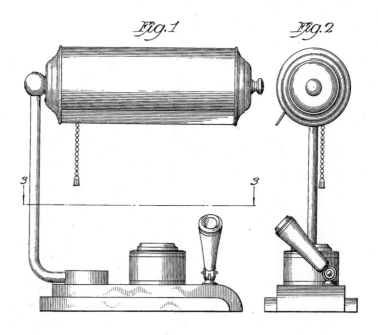

Fig.1   *Fig.2*

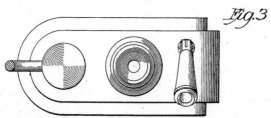

Fig.3

Inventor.
Gustav J. Sengbusch
By
Fisher, Clapp, Soans & Pond Attys.

TITLE: SPACE HEATER
INVENTOR: RALPH E. KRUCK
ASSIGNEE: FLORENCE STOVE COMPANY

PATENT NUMBER: USD 104,193
PATENT FILED: MARCH 4, 1937
PATENT GRANTED: APRIL 20, 1937

April 20, 1937.　　　　R. E. KRUCK　　　　Des. 104,193

SPACE HEATER

Filed March 4, 1937

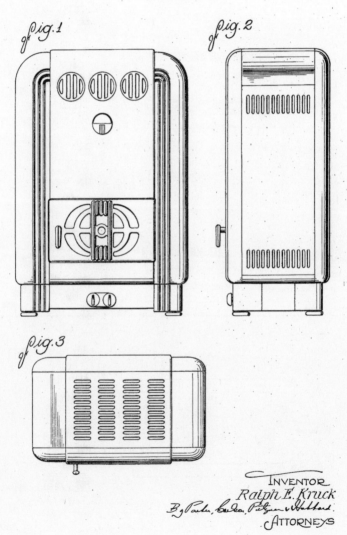

ƒig.1

ƒig.2

ƒig.3

INVENTOR
Ralph E. Kruck
By Parker, Carten, Pitzner & Hubbard
ATTORNEYS

TITLE: COFFEE MAKER OR THE LIKE
INVENTOR: GEORGE T. SCHARFENBERG
ASSIGNEE: CHICAGO FLEXIBLE SHAFT COMPANY

PATENT NUMBER: USD 104,477
PATENT FILED: MARCH 1, 1937
PATENT GRANTED: MAY 11, 1937

May 11, 1937.   G. T. SCHARFENBERG   Des. 104,477

COFFEE MAKER OR THE LIKE

Filed March 1, 1937

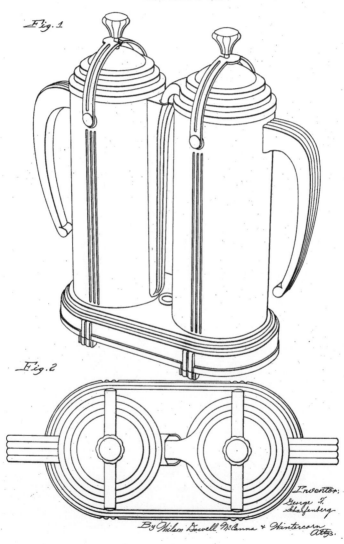

Fig. 1

Fig. 2

Inventor:
George T.
Scharfenberg

By Wilson Dowell McCanna & Wintercorn Attys.

TITLE: PYROPHORIC LIGHTER
INVENTOR: LOUIS V. ARONSON
ASSIGNEE: ART METAL WORKS

PATENT NUMBER: USD 104.955
PATENT FILED: FEBRUARY 9, 1937
PATENT GRANTED: JUNE 15, 1937

June 15, 1937. L. V. ARONSON Des. 104,955

PYROPHORIC LIGHTER

Filed Feb. 9, 1937

Fig. 1.

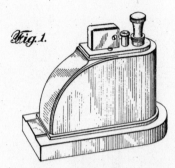

Fig. 2.

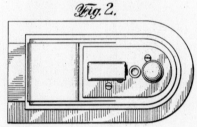

Fig. 3.

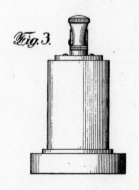

Fig. 4.

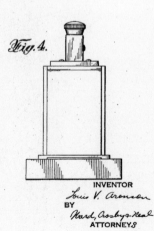

INVENTOR

Louis V. Aronson

BY

Ward, Crosby & Neal

ATTORNEYS

266

TITLE: TRAILER
INVENTOR: JOHN R. MORGAN
ASSIGNEE: SEARS, ROEBUCK & COMPANY

PATENT NUMBER: USD 105,073
PATENT FILED: MAY 10, 1937
PATENT GRANTED: JUNE 22, 1937

June 22, 1937.

J. R. MORGAN

Des. 105,073

TRAILER

Filed May 10, 1937

2 Sheets—Sheet 1

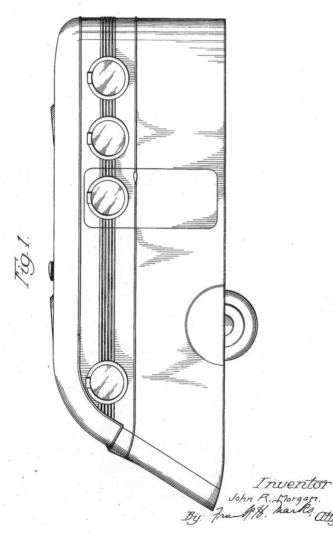

Fig. 1

Inventor
John R. Morgan,
By: Fra___ H. Marks, Atty.

TITLE: WEIGHING SCALE
INVENTOR: JOHN R. MORGAN
ASSIGNEE: SEARS, ROEBUCK & COMPANY

PATENT NUMBER: USD 105,126
PATENT FILED: APRIL 29, 1937
PATENT GRANTED: JUNE 29, 1937

June 29, 1937.

J. R. MORGAN

Des. 105,126

WEIGHING SCALE

Filed April 29, 1937

Fig.1

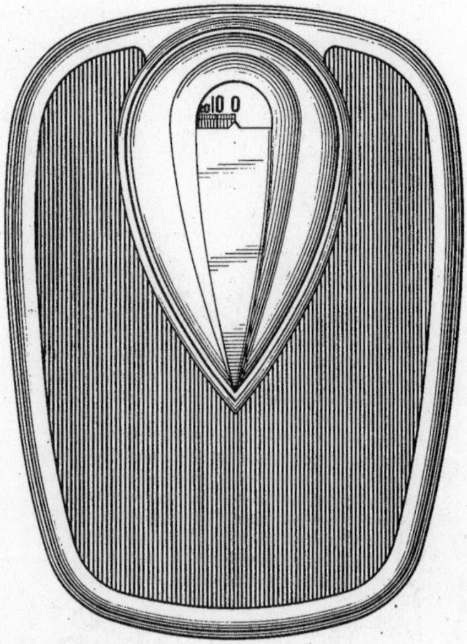

Fig.2

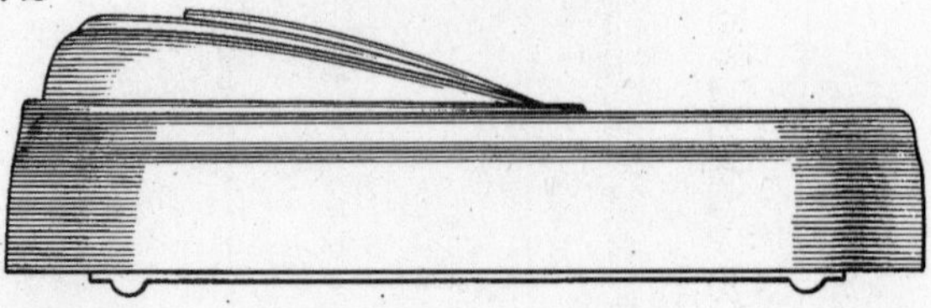

Fig.3

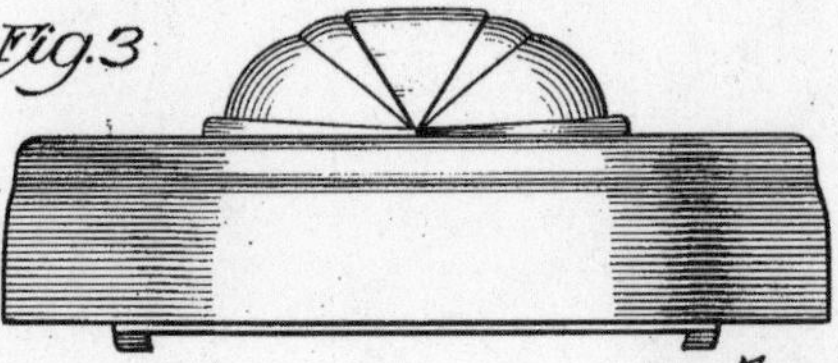

Inventor:
John R. Morgan.
By Frank H. Marks,
Atty.

TITLE: WASHING MACHINE CABINET
INVENTOR: AMOS E. NORTHUP
ASSIGNEE: BENDIX HOME APPLIANCES

PATENT NUMBER: USD 105,228
PATENT FILED: DECEMBER 9, 1936
PATENT GRANTED: JULY 6, 1937

July 6, 1937.   A. E. NORTHUP   Des. 105,228

WASHING MACHINE CABINET

Filed Dec. 9, 1936

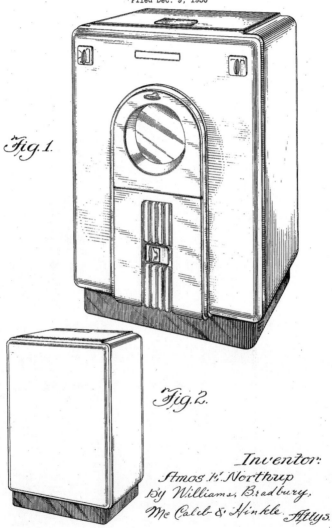

Fig.1.

Fig.2.

Inventor:
Amos E. Northup
By Williams, Bradbury,
Mc Caleb & Hinkle. Attys.

TITLE: FRUIT PRESS
INVENTOR: JOSEPH M. MAJEWSKI, JR.
ASSIGNEE: RIVAL MANUFACTURING COMPANY

PATENT NUMBER: USD 105,335
PATENT FILED: JUNE 5, 1937
PATENT GRANTED: JULY 20, 1937

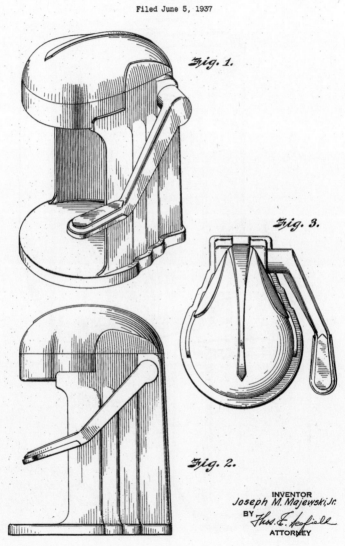

July 20, 1937.

J. M. MAJEWSKI, JR

Des 105,335

FRUIT PRESS

Filed June 5, 1937

Fig. 1.

Fig. 3.

Fig. 2.

INVENTOR
Joseph M. Majewski, Jr.
BY
Thos. E. Scofield
ATTORNEY

TITLE: VACUUM CLEANER
INVENTOR: JOHN R. MORGAN
ASSIGNEE: SEARS, ROEBUCK & COMPANY

PATENT NUMBER: USD 105,495
PATENT FILED: MAY 28, 1937
PATENT GRANTED: AUGUST 3, 1937

Aug. 3, 1937.　　　J. R. MORGAN　　　**Des. 105,495**

VACUUM CLEANER

Filed May 28, 1937

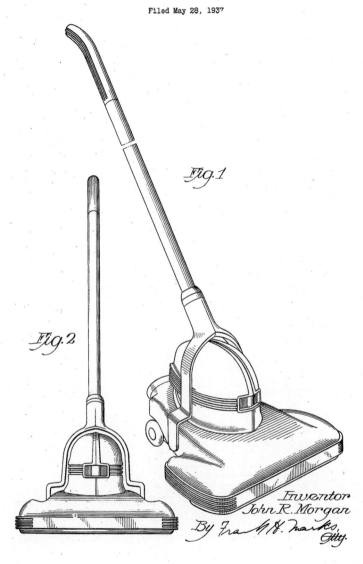

Fig.1

Fig.2

Inventor
John R. Morgan
By Fra... H. Marks,
Atty.

271

TITLE: CAB-OVER-ENGINE FUEL TANK TRUCK
INVENTOR: ALEXIS DE SAKHNOFFSKY
ASSIGNEE: THE WHITE MOTOR COMPANY

PATENT NUMBER: USD 105,899
PATENT FILED: JANUARY 21, 1937
PATENT GRANTED: AUGUST 31, 1937

Aug. 31, 1937.   A. DE SAKHNOFFSKY   Des. 105,899

CAB-OVER-ENGINE FUEL TANK TRUCK

Filed Jan. 21, 1937

Fig.-1

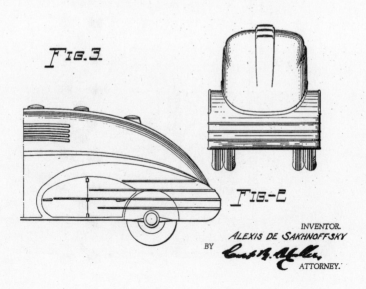

Fig.3

Fig.-2

INVENTOR.
ALEXIS DE SAKHNOFFSKY
BY
ATTORNEY.

TITLE: LOCOMOTIVE
INVENTOR: RAYMOND G.F. LOEWY
ASSIGNEE: PENNSYLVANIA RAILROAD COMPANY

PATENT NUMBER: USD 106,143
PATENT FILED: MARCH 10, 1937
PATENT GRANTED: SEPTEMBER 21, 1937

Sept. 21, 1937.

R. G. F. LOEWY

Des. 106,143

LOCOMOTIVE

Filed March 10, 1937

2 Sheets—Sheet 1

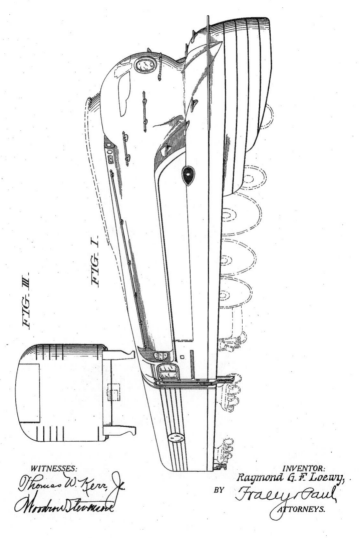

FIG. III.

FIG. I.

WITNESSES:
Thomas W. Kerr, Jr.
Woodrow Stevenson

INVENTOR:
Raymond G. F. Loewy,
BY Fraley Paul
ATTORNEYS.

TITLE: VACUUM CLEANER CASING
INVENTOR: LURELLE GUILD
ASSIGNEE: ELECTROLUX CORPORATION

PATENT NUMBER: USD 106,662
PATENT FILED: MARCH 25, 1937
PATENT GRANTED: OCTOBER 26, 1937

Oct. 26, 1937.

L. GUILD

Des. 106,662

VACUUM CLEANER CASING

Filed March 25, 1937

4 Sheets—Sheet 4

Fig. 5.

INVENTOR,
Lurelle Guild

BY

L. ATTORNEY.

274

TITLE: LOCOMOTIVE BODY
INVENTORS: HAROLD L. HAMILTON, RICHARD M.
DILWORTH, MARTIN P. BLOMBERG, ET AL.
ASSIGNEE: GENERAL MOTORS CORPORATION

PATENT NUMBER: USD 106,918
PATENT FILED: JUNE 24, 1937
PATENT GRANTED: NOVEMBER 9, 1937

Nov. 9, 1937.   H. L. HAMILTON ET AL   Des. 106,918

LOCOMOTIVE BODY

Filed June 24, 1937

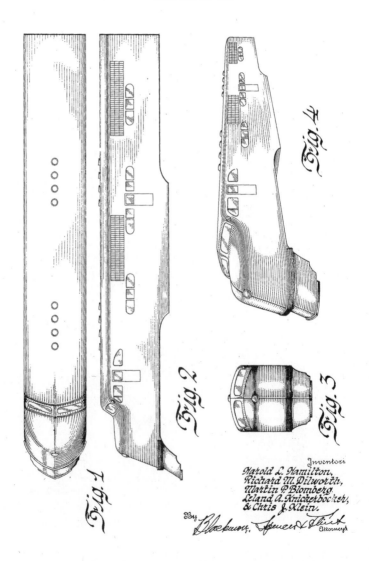

Fig. 4

Fig. 2

Fig. 3

Fig. 1

Inventors
Harold L. Hamilton,
Richard M. Dilworth,
Martin P. Blomberg
Leland A. Knickerbocker,
& Chris J. Klein.

By Blackmore, Spencer & Flint
Attorneys

TITLE: MODEL OF AN ARCHITECTURAL UNIT
INVENTORS: WALLACE K. HARRISON
& JACQUES ANDRE FOUILHOUX
ASSIGNEE: NEW YORK WORLD'S FAIR 1939

PATENT NUMBER: USD 107,425
PATENT FILED: AUGUST 10, 1937
PATENT GRANTED: DECEMBER 14, 1937

Dec. 14, 1937.   W. K. HARRISON ET AL   Des. 107,425

MODEL OF AN ARCHITECTURAL UNIT

Filed Aug. 10, 1937   2 Sheets-Sheet 1

Fig. 1.

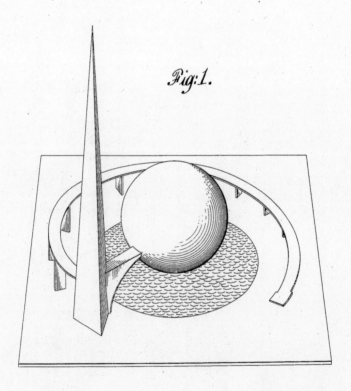

INVENTORS
WALLACE K. HARRISON
BY J. ANDRE FOUILHOUX

William J. Barnes
ATTORNEY

TITLE: TOASTER
INVENTOR: GEORGE T. SCHARFENBERG
ASSIGNEE: CHICAGO FLEXIBLE SHAFT COMPANY

PATENT NUMBER: USD 107,552
PATENT FILED: SEPTEMBER 27, 1937
PATENT GRANTED: DECEMBER 21, 1937

Dec. 21, 1937.   G. T. SCHARFENBERG   Des. 107,552

TOASTER

Filed Sept. 27, 1937

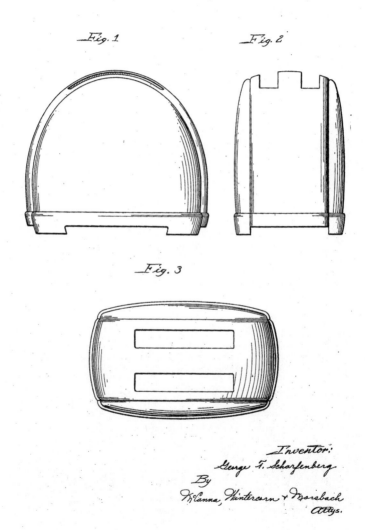

Fig. 1

Fig. 2

Fig. 3

Inventor:
George T. Scharfenberg
By
McCanna, Wintercorn & Morsbach
Attys.

TITLE: ELECTRIC SHAVING DEVICE
INVENTOR: JOHN A. HANLEY
ASSIGNEE: NONE

PATENT NUMBER: USD 108,441
PATENT FILED: NOVEMBER 23, 1937
PATENT GRANTED: FEBRUARY 15, 1938

Feb. 15, 1938.

J. A. HANLEY

ELECTRIC SHAVING DEVICE

Filed Nov. 23, 1937

Des. 108,441

Fig.1.

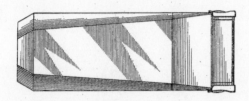

Fig.2.

Fig.3.

Fig.4.

INVENTOR

John A. Hanley

BY

Dean Fairbank & Hirsch

ATTORNEYS

TITLE: CHAIR
INVENTOR: FRANK LLOYD WRIGHT
ASSIGNEE: NONE

PATENT NUMBER: USD 108,473
PATENT FILED: DECEMBER 20, 1937
PATENT GRANTED: FEBRUARY 15, 1938

Feb. 15, 1938.

F. L. WRIGHT

Des. 108,473

CHAIR

Filed Dec. 20, 1937

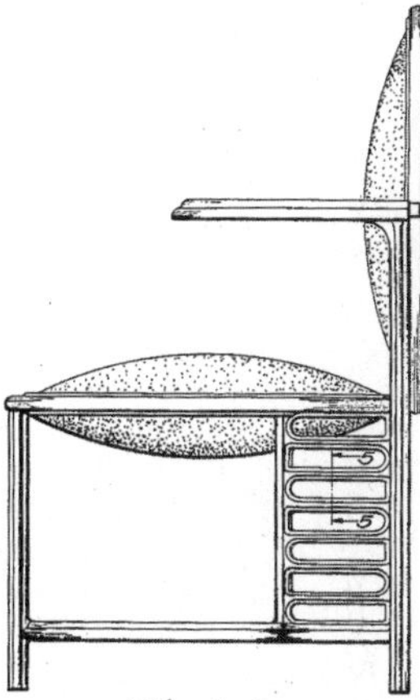

Fig. 1.

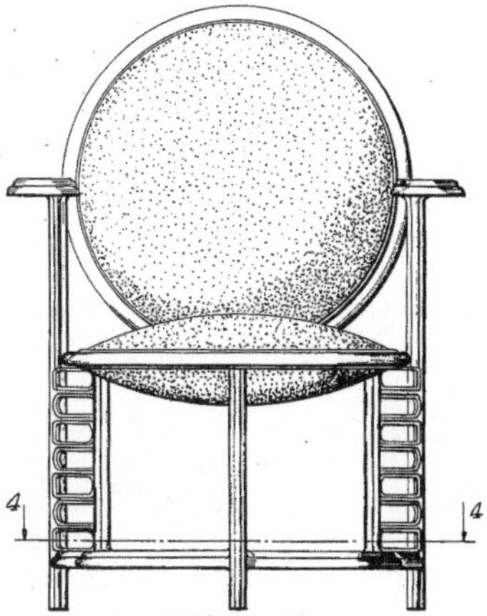

Fig. 2.

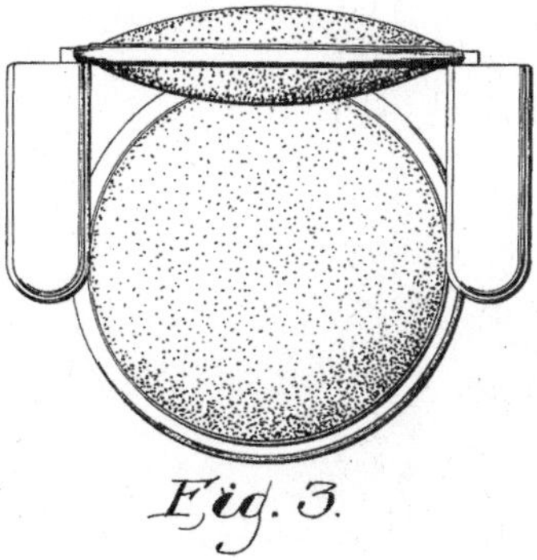

Fig. 3.

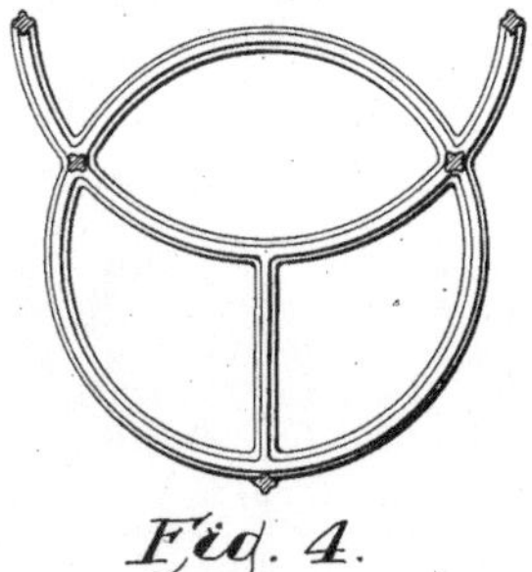

Fig. 4.

Fig. 5.

INVENTOR
Frank Lloyd Wright
BY
Gerald P. Welch
ATTORNEY

279

TITLE: RADIO CASING
INVENTOR: ISAMU NOGUCHI
ASSIGNEE: ZENITH RADIO CORPORATION

PATENT NUMBER: USD 108,837
PATENT FILED: DECEMBER 31, 1937
PATENT GRANTED: MARCH 15, 1938

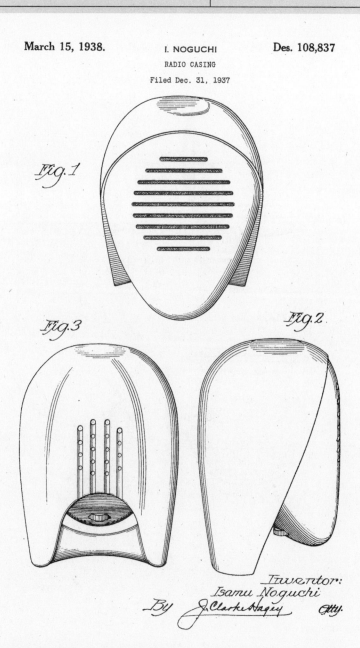

March 15, 1938.

I. NOGUCHI

Des. 108,837

RADIO CASING

Filed Dec. 31, 1937

Fig.1

Fig.3

Fig.2

Inventor:
Isamu Noguchi
By J. Clarke Hagey   Atty.

TITLE: ELECTRIC MIXER BODY
INVENTOR: ROBERT HELLER
ASSIGNEE: A.C. GILBERT COMPANY

PATENT NUMBER: USD 108,946
PATENT FILED: JANUARY 12, 1938
PATENT GRANTED: MARCH 22, 1938

March 22, 1938.　　R. HELLER　　Des. 108,946

ELECTRIC MIXER BODY

Filed Jan. 12, 1939　　2 Sheets—Sheet 1

Fig.1.

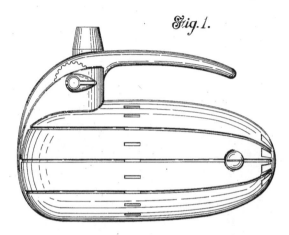

Fig.2.

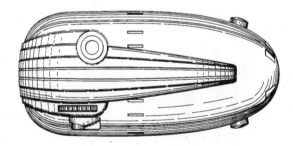

Inventor

Robert Heller

By Rockwell & Barthalaw

Attorneys

TITLE: HIGHWAY AUTOMOTIVE PASSENGER VEHICLE
INVENTOR: CLIFFORD BROOKS STEVENS
ASSIGNEE: NONE

PATENT NUMBER: USD 109,739
PATENT FILED: DECEMBER 18, 1937
PATENT GRANTED: MAY 17, 1938

May 17, 1938.   C. B. STEVENS   Des. 109,739

HIGHWAY AUTOMOTIVE PASSENGER VEHICLE

Filed Dec. 18, 1937

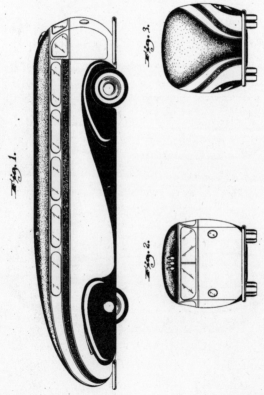

Fig. 1.

Fig. 2.

Fig. 3.

Inventor

Clifford Brooks Stevens

Attorney

TITLE: BILLIARD TABLE
INVENTOR: DONALD DESKEY
ASSIGNEE: BRUNSWICK-BALKE-COLLENDER COMPANY

PATENT NUMBER: USD 110,083
PATENT FILED: FEBRUARY 23, 1938
PATENT GRANTED: JUNE 14, 1938

June 14, 1938.   D. DESKEY   Des. 110,083

BILLIARD TABLE

Filed Feb. 23, 1938

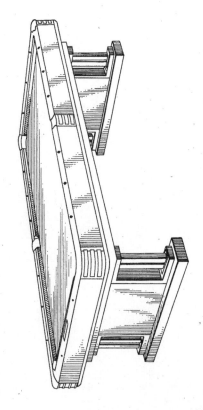

DONALD DESKEY
INVENTOR
PER

Albert G. Fihe

ATTORNEY

TITLE: LAMP
INVENTOR: RAY A. SCHOBER
ASSIGNEE: PREMIUM PRODUCTS
MANUFACTURING COMPANY

PATENT NUMBER: USD 110,196
PATENT FILED: FEBRUARY 18, 1938
PATENT GRANTED: JUNE 21, 1938

June 21, 1938.

R. A. SCHOBER

Des. 110,196

LAMP

Filed Feb. 18, 1938

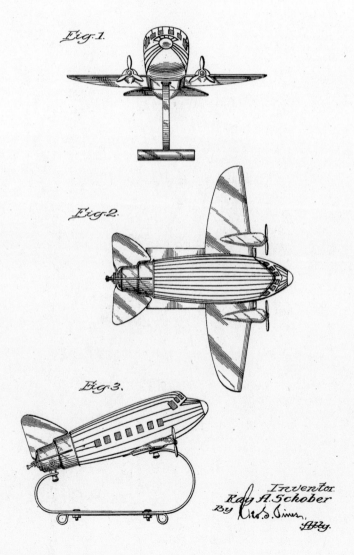

Fig. 1.

Fig. 2.

Fig. 3.

Inventor.
Ray A. Schober
By
Atty.

284

TITLE: FLATIRON
INVENTOR: LEO IVAN BRUCE, JR.
ASSIGNEE: FITZGERALD MANUFACTURING COMPANY

PATENT NUMBER: USD 110,266
PATENT FILED: MARCH 14, 1938
PATENT GRANTED: JUNE 28, 1938

June 28, 1938.   L. I. BRUCE, JR   **Des. 110,266**

FLATIRON

Filed March 14, 1938   2 Sheets—Sheet 1

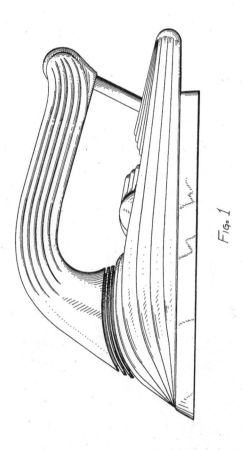

Fig. 1

INVENTOR.
LEO IVAN BRUCE JR.
BY Joshua R. H. Potts
ATTORNEY.

285

TITLE: COMBINATION CLOCK & CALENDAR
INVENTOR: HERBERT W. LAMPORT
ASSIGNEE: JOSEPH C. MORRIS & JIM I. SILVERS

PATENT NUMBER: USD 110,489
PATENT FILED: JULY 3, 1937
PATENT GRANTED: JULY 12, 1938

July 12, 1938.   H. W. LAMPORT   Des. 110,489

COMBINATION CLOCK AND CALENDAR

Filed July 3, 1937   2 Sheets—Sheet 1

Fig.1.

Inventor:
Herbert W. Lamport.

By: Bertha L. MacGregor
Attorney.

TITLE: STAPLING MACHINE
INVENTOR: STEPHEN A. CROSBY
ASSIGNEE: PARROT SPEED FASTENER CORPORATION

PATENT NUMBER: USD 110,796
PATENT FILED: APRIL 26, 1937
PATENT GRANTED: AUGUST 9, 1938

Aug. 9, 1938.   S. A. CROSBY   Des. 110,796

STAPLING MACHINE

Filed April 26, 1937

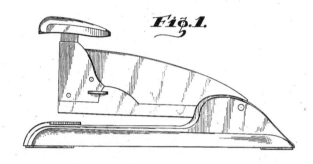

Fig.1.

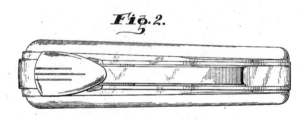

Fig.2.

Fig.3.

S. A. Crosby

INVENTOR

BY

ATTORNEY

TITLE: COMBINATION DESK UNIT
INVENTORS: ALBERT S. BRAND
& LAURENCE W. KENDRICK
ASSIGNEE: THE CARTER'S INK COMPANY

PATENT NUMBER: USD 110,889
PATENT FILED: JUNE 11, 1938
PATENT GRANTED: AUGUST 16, 1938

Aug. 16, 1938.

A. S. BRAND ET AL

Des. 110,889

COMBINATION DESK UNIT

Filed June 11, 1938

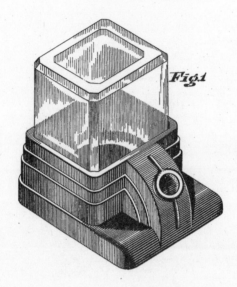

Fig.1

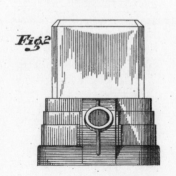

Fig.2

INVENTORS
Albert S. Brand
Laurence W. Kendrick
BY
John E. R. Haines
ATTORNEY

TITLE: ELECTRIC TOOTHBRUSH
INVENTOR: TOMLINSON I. MOSELEY
ASSIGNEE: MOTODENT

PATENT NUMBER: USD 110,928
PATENT FILED: DECEMBER 13, 1937
PATENT GRANTED: AUGUST 16, 1938

Aug. 16, 1938.

T. I. MOSELEY

Des. 110,928

ELECTRIC TOOTH BRUSH

Filed Dec. 13, 1937

Fig.1.

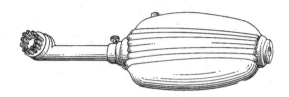

Fig.2.

Fig.4.

Fig.3.

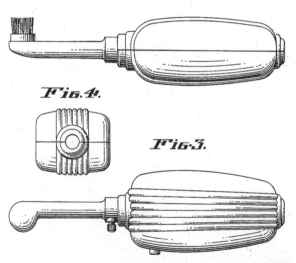

INVENTOR.
TOMLINSON I. MOSELEY
BY
Oscar A. Mellin
ATTORNEY

TITLE: CAKE OF SOAP
INVENTOR: FLORENCE N. LEWIS
ASSIGNEE: ELIZABETH ARDEN

PATENT NUMBER: USD 110,971
PATENT FILED: JUNE 11, 1938
PATENT GRANTED: AUGUST 23, 1938

Aug. 23, 1938.

F. N. LEWIS

Des. 110,971

CAKE OF SOAP

Filed June 11, 1938

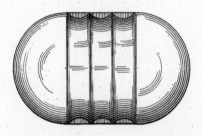

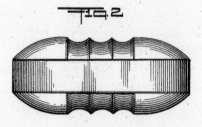

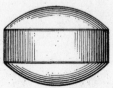

INVENTOR.
Florence N. Lewis

BY

Mock & Blum

ATTORNEYS

TITLE: ACCORDION
INVENTOR: JOHN VASSOS
ASSIGNEE: M. HOHNER

PATENT NUMBER: USD 111,555
PATENT FILED: JUNE 30, 1938
PATENT GRANTED: SEPTEMBER 27, 1938

Sept. 27, 1938.   J. VASSOS   Des. 111,555

ACCORDION

Filed June 30, 1938   3 Sheets—Sheet 1

Fig.1

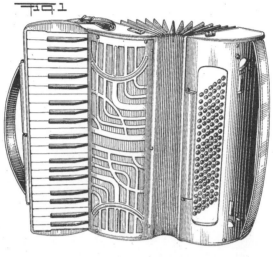

Fig. 2

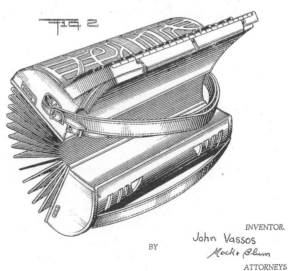

INVENTOR.

John Vassos

BY   *Mock + Blum*

ATTORNEYS

TITLE: ELECTRIC SHAVER
INVENTOR: GEORGE T. SCHARFENBERG
ASSIGNEE: CHICAGO FLEXIBLE SHAFT COMPANY

PATENT NUMBER: USD 111,574
PATENT FILED: MARCH 24, 1938
PATENT GRANTED: OCTOBER 4, 1938

Oct. 4, 1938.

G. T. SCHARFENBERG

Des. 111,574

ELECTRIC SHAVER

Filed March 24, 1938

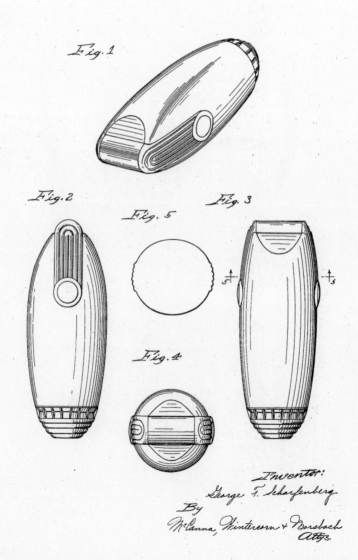

Fig. 1

Fig. 2

Fig. 5

Fig. 3

Fig. 4

Inventor:
George T. Scharfenberg
By
McCanna, Wintercorn & Borsbach
Attys.

292

TITLE: ICE CREAM DISHER
INVENTOR: PATRICK F. DONAHUE
ASSIGNEE: SCOVILL MANUFACTURING COMPANY

PATENT NUMBER: USD 112,040
PATENT FILED: JULY 21, 1938
PATENT GRANTED: NOVEMBER 8, 1938

Nov. 8, 1938.　　　　P. F. DONAHUE　　　**Des. 112,040**

. ICE CREAM DISHER

Filed July 21, 1938

FIG.1.

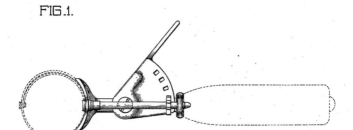

FIG.2.

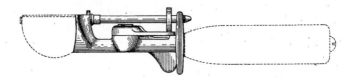

FIG.3.

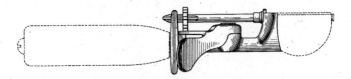

Inventor:
Patrick F. Donahue.
By: Bertha L. MacGregor
Attorney

TITLE: TELEPHONE TRANSMITTER
INVENTOR: ROBERT N. MARSHALL
ASSIGNEE: BELL TELEPHONE LABORATORIES

PATENT NUMBER: USD 112,756
PATENT FILED: JULY 1, 1938
PATENT GRANTED: DECEMBER 27, 1938

Dec. 27, 1938.

R. N. MARSHALL

Des. 112,756

TELEPHONE TRANSMITTER

Filed July 1, 1938

FIG. 1

FIG. 2

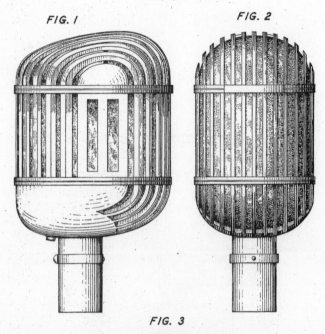

FIG. 3

INVENTOR
R. N. MARSHALL

BY

Walter C. Kiesel

ATTORNEY

TITLE: RADIO RECEIVER CABINET
INVENTOR: CLARENCE KARSTADT
ASSIGNEE: SEARS, ROEBUCK & COMPANY

PATENT NUMBER: USD 113,004
PATENT FILED: NOVEMBER 18, 1938
PATENT GRANTED: JANUARY 24, 1939

Jan. 24, 1939.   C. **KARSTADT**   Des. 113,004

RADIO RECEIVER CABINET

Filed Nov. 18, 1938

Fig.1

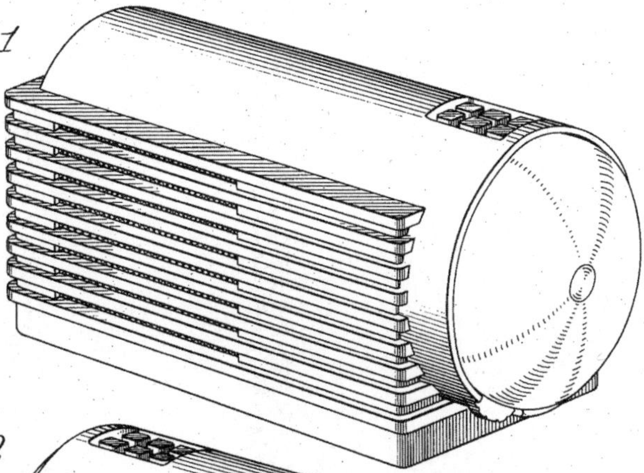

Fig.2

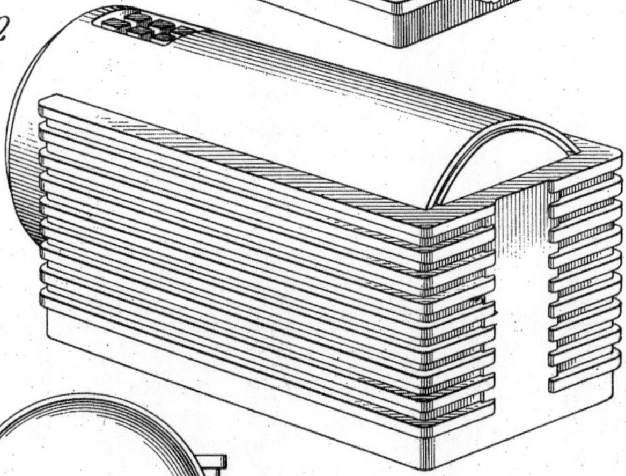

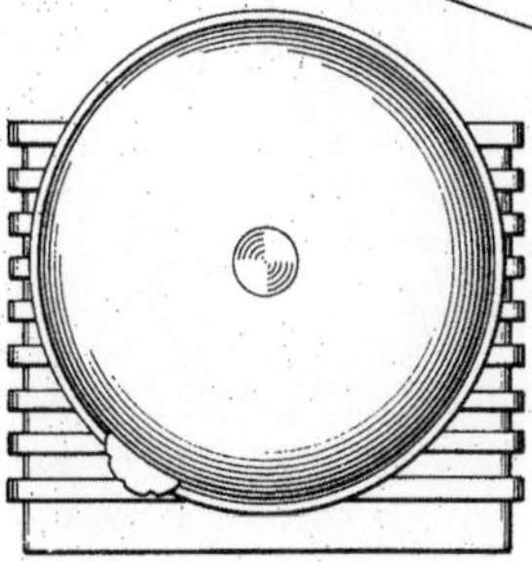

Fig.3

Inventor:
Clarence Karstadt
By Frank H. Marks,
Atty.

TITLE: PHONOGRAPH CABINET
INVENTOR: DAVID C. ROCKOLA
ASSIGNEE: ROCK-OLA MANUFACTURING CORPORATION

PATENT NUMBER: USD 113,287
PATENT FILED: OCTOBER 17, 1938
PATENT GRANTED: FEBRUARY 7, 1939

Feb. 7, 1939.

D. C. ROCKOLA

Des. 113,287

PHONOGRAPH CABINET

Filed Oct. 17, 1938

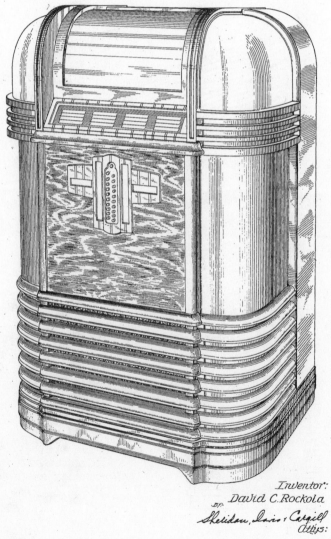

Inventor:
David C. Rockola
BY:
Sheridan, Davis & Cargill
Attys:

TITLE: BEVERAGE SERVICE COUNTER
INVENTOR: LE RAY FOWLER
ASSIGNEES: LE RAY FOWLER, EUGENE T. CONNELLY
& JOHN J. DALY

PATENT NUMBER: USD 113,507
PATENT FILED: AUGUST 9, 1938
PATENT GRANTED: FEBRUARY 28, 1939

Feb. 28, 1939.   LE RAY FOWLER   Des. 113,507

BEVERAGE SERVICE COUNTER

Filed Aug. 9, 1938

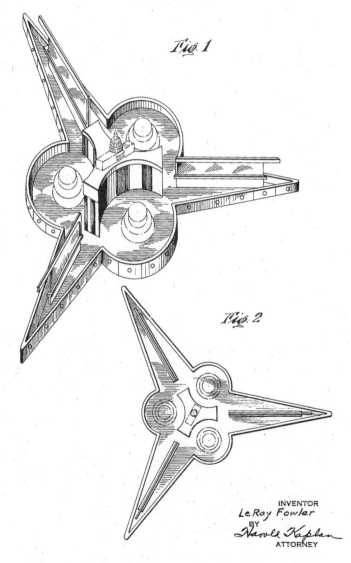

Fig. 1

Fig. 2

INVENTOR
Le Ray Fowler
BY
Harold Kaplan
ATTORNEY

TITLE: TRACTOR
INVENTOR: NELS E. ERICKSON
ASSIGNEE: MINNEAPOLIS—MOLINE POWER
IMPLEMENT COMPANY

PATENT NUMBER: USD 113,554
PATENT FILED: OCTOBER 10, 1938
PATENT GRANTED: FEBRUARY 28, 1939

Feb. 28, 1939.

N. E. ERICKSON

Des. 113,554

TRACTOR

Filed Oct. 10, 1938

3 Sheets—Sheet 1

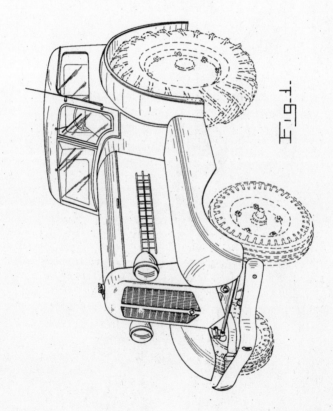

Fig. 1.

Inventor

NELS E. ERKKSON

By *Andrew E. Herlm*

Attorney

TITLE: BICYCLE
INVENTOR: JOHN VASSOS
ASSIGNEE: NONE

PATENT NUMBER: USD 113,584
PATENT FILED: DECEMBER 13, 1938
PATENT GRANTED: FEBRUARY 28, 1939

Feb. 28, 1939.   J. VASSOS   Des. 113,584

BICYCLE

Filed Dec. 13, 1938

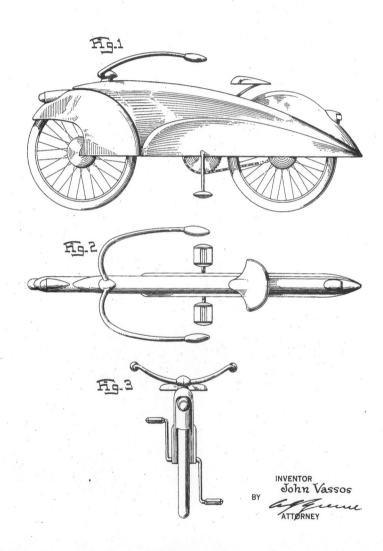

Fig.1

Fig.2

Fig.3

INVENTOR
John Vassos
BY
ATTORNEY

TITLE: CASH REGISTER
INVENTORS: WALTER DORWIN TEAGUE.
WALTER DORWIN TEAGUE JR. & EDWARD W. HERMAN
ASSIGNEE: NATIONAL CASH REGISTER COMPANY

PATENT NUMBER: USD 113,900
PATENT FILED: DECEMBER 16, 1938
PATENT GRANTED: MARCH 21, 1939

March 21, 1939.　　W. D. TEAGUE ET AL　　Des. 113,900

CASH REGISTER

Filed Dec. 16, 1938　　　3 Sheets—Sheet 1

FIG. 1

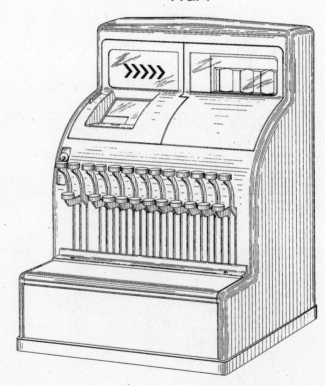

Walter Dorwin Teague
Walter Dorwin Teague, Jr.
and Edward W. Herman
Inventors

By *Karl Beust*

Their Attorney

TITLE: LUNCH BOX OR SIMILAR ARTICLE
INVENTOR: EVERETT WORTHINGTON
ASSIGNEE: AMERICAN CAN COMPANY

PATENT NUMBER: USD 114,202
PATENT FILED: JULY 14, 1938
PATENT GRANTED: APRIL 11, 1939

April 11, 1939.   E. WORTHINGTON   Des. 114,202

LUNCH BOX OR SIMILAR ARTICLE

Filed July 14, 1938

Fig. 1.

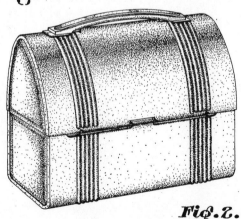

Fig. 2.

INVENTOR.

BY

ATTORNEYS

TITLE: DWELLING
INVENTOR: FRANK LLOYD WRIGHT
ASSIGNEE: NONE

PATENT NUMBER: USD 114,204
PATENT FILED: OCTOBER 12, 1938
PATENT GRANTED: APRIL 11, 1939

April 11, 1939.

F. L. WRIGHT

Des. 114,204

DWELLING

Filed Oct. 12, 1938

2 Sheets—Sheet 1

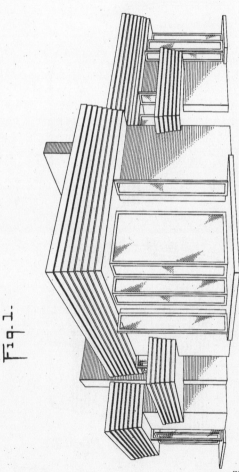

Fig.1.

INVENTOR
Frank Lloyd Wright
BY
Blair, Curtis, Dunne & Hayward
ATTORNEYS

TITLE: CLOCK CASING
INVENTOR: HENRY DREYFUSS
ASSIGNEE: GENERAL TIME INSTRUMENTS CORPORATION

PATENT NUMBER: USD 114,262
PATENT FILED: NOVEMBER 19, 1938
PATENT GRANTED: APRIL 11, 1939

April 11, 1939.   H. DREYFUSS   Des. 114,262

CLOCK CASING

Filed Nov. 19, 1938

FIG. 1

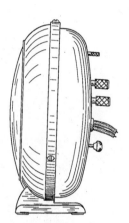

FIG. 2

INVENTOR.
Henry Dreyfuss
BY
ATTORNEY.

303

TITLE: CASING FOR SUCTION CLEANER
INVENTOR: HENRY DREYFUSS
ASSIGNEE: THE HOOVER COMPANY

PATENT NUMBER: USD 115,286
PATENT FILED: FEBRUARY 11, 1939
PATENT GRANTED: JUNE 20, 1939

June 20, 1939. H. DREYFUSS Des. 115,286

CASING FOR SUCTION CLEANERS OR SIMILAR ARTICLES

Filed Feb. 11, 1939

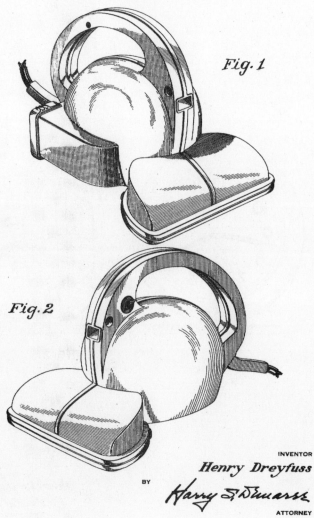

Fig. 1

Fig. 2

INVENTOR

Henry Dreyfuss

BY

Harry S. Dumarse

ATTORNEY

TITLE: STORE FRONT
INVENTOR: HARRY L. WYMAN
ASSIGNEE: NONE

PATENT NUMBER: USD 115,304
PATENT FILED: JULY 29, 1938
PATENT GRANTED: JUNE 20, 1939

June 20, 1939.

H. L. WYMAN

Des. 115,304

STORE FRONT

Filed July 29, 1938

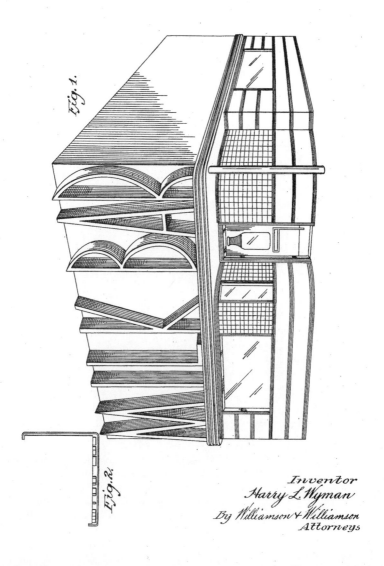

Fig. 1.

Fig. 2.

Inventor
Harry L. Wyman
By Williamson & Williamson
Attorneys

TITLE: BICYCLE
INVENTOR: FRANK W. SCHWINN
ASSIGNEE: NONE

PATENT NUMBER: USD 115,942
PATENT FILED: APRIL 17, 1939
PATENT GRANTED: AUGUST 1, 1939

Aug. 1, 1939   F. W. SCHWINN   Des. 115,942

BICYCLE

Filed April 17, 1939

Inventor:
Frank W. Schwinn
By
Williams, Bradbury, McCaleb & Hinkle.
Attys.

TITLE: LOCOMOTIVE
INVENTOR: HENRY DREYFUSS
ASSIGNEE: NEW YORK CENTRAL RAILROAD COMPANY

PATENT NUMBER: USD 116,180
PATENT FILED: SEPTEMBER 28, 1938
PATENT GRANTED: AUGUST 15, 1939

Aug. 15, 1939.

H. DREYFUSS

Des. 116,180

LOCOMOTIVE

Filed Sept. 28, 1938

2 Sheets—Sheet 1

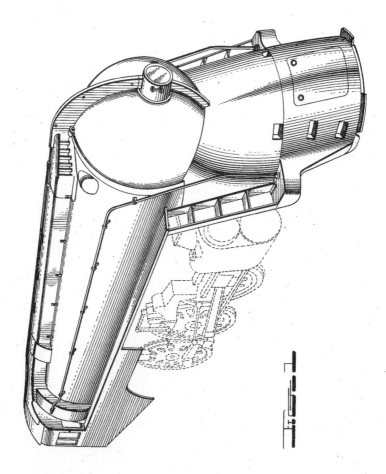

INVENTOR.

Henry Dreyfuss

BY

Edwin S. Clarkson

ATTORNEY.

TITLE: RADIO CABINET
INVENTOR: NORMAN BEL GEDDES
ASSIGNEE: MAJESTIC RADIO & TELEVISION CORPORATION

PATENT NUMBER: USD 117,116
PATENT FILED: JULY 26, 1939
PATENT GRANTED: OCTOBER 10, 1939

Oct. 10, 1939.

N. BEL GEDDES

Des. 117,116

RADIO CABINET

Filed July 26, 1939

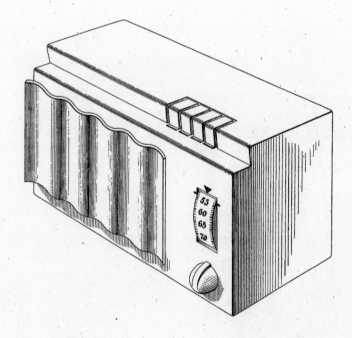

INVENTOR
Norman Bel Geddes
BY
Morgan, Finnegan & Durla
ATTORNEYS

TITLE: STAPLER
INVENTOR: ROBERT HELLER
ASSIGNEE: THE E.H. HOTCHKISS COMPANY

PATENT NUMBER: USD 117,144
PATENT FILED: AUGUST 19, 1938
PATENT GRANTED: OCTOBER 17, 1939

Oct. 17, 1939.   R. HELLER   Des. 117,144

STAPLER

Filed Aug. 19, 1938

Fig. 1

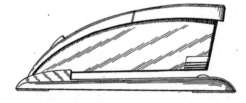

Fig. 2

Fig. 3

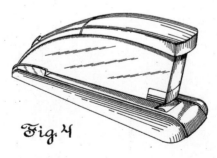

Fig. 4

INVENTOR
Robert Heller,
BY
ATTORNEY

TITLE: RANGE
INVENTOR: DONALD L. HADLEY
ASSIGNEE: WESTINGHOUSE ELECTRIC
& MANUFACTURING COMPANY

PATENT NUMBER: USD 117,561
PATENT FILED: SEPTEMBER 15, 1939
PATENT GRANTED: NOVEMBER 14, 1939

Nov. 14, 1939.

D. L. HADLEY

Des. 117,561

RANGE

Filed Sept. 15, 1939

Fig. 1.

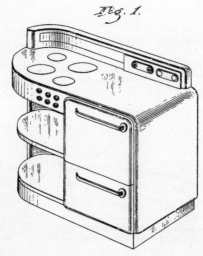

Fig. 2.

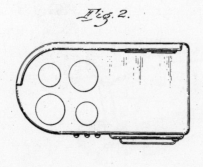

Fig. 3.

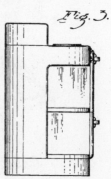

WITNESSES:
E. C. Fridung.
Nw. C. Groome

INVENTOR
Donald L. Hadley.
BY
W. R. Coley
ATTORNEY

310

TITLE: HAIR DRIER OR SIMILAR ARTICLE
INVENTOR: EGMONT ARENS
ASSIGNEE: THE NESTLE-LEMUR COMPANY

PATENT NUMBER: USD 117,942
PATENT FILED: JULY 25, 1939
PATENT GRANTED: DECEMBER 5, 1939

Dec. 5, 1939.　　　　E. ARENS　　　　Des. 117,942

HAIR DRIER OR SIMILAR ARTICLE

Filed July 25, 1939

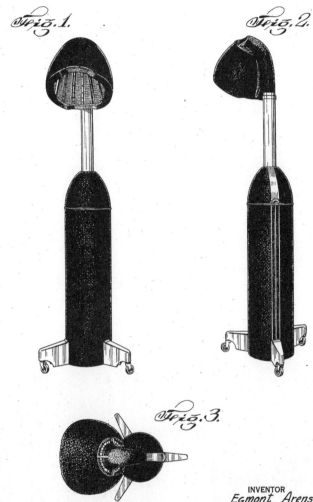

Fig. 1.

Fig. 2.

Fig. 3.

INVENTOR
Egmont Arens
BY
Eforin Sprichstein
ATTORNEY

TITLE: DRINK MIXER
INVENTORS: JAMES F. BARNES & JEAN OTIS REINECKE
ASSIGNEE: SCOVILL MANUFACTURING COMPANY

PATENT NUMBER: USD 118,225
PATENT FILED: OCTOBER 30, 1939
PATENT GRANTED: DECEMBER 26, 1939

Dec. 26, 1939.

J. F. BARNES ET AL

DRINK MIXER

Filed Oct. 30, 1939

Des. 118,225

2 Sheets—Sheet 1

FIG.1.

FIG.2.

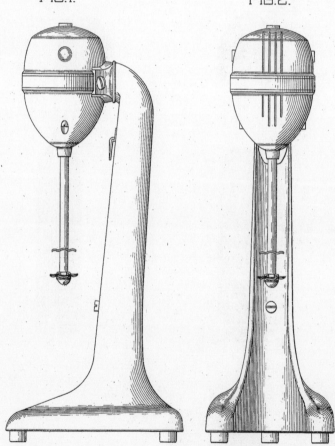

Inventors:
James F. Barnes
Jean Otis Reinecke
By Bertha L. Mac Gregor
Attorney.

TITLE: TAPE DISPENSER
INVENTOR: JEAN OTIS REINECKE
ASSIGNEE: MINNESOTA MINING
& MANUFACTURING COMPANY

PATENT NUMBER: USD 118,629
PATENT FILED: NOVEMBER 24, 1939
PATENT GRANTED: JANUARY 23, 1940

Jan. 23, 1940.

J. O. REINECKE

Des. 118,629

TAPE DISPENSER

Filed Nov. 24, 1939

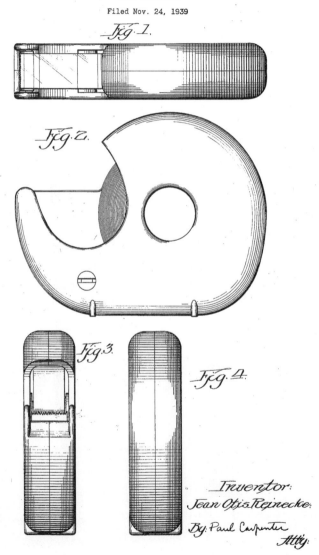

Fig. 1.

Fig. 2.

Fig. 3.

Fig. 4.

Inventor:
Jean Otis Reinecke.

By: Paul Carpenter
Atty.

313

TITLE: FOUNTAIN PEN
INVENTOR: JOHN VASSOS
ASSIGNEE: L.E. WATERMAN COMPANY

PATENT NUMBER: USD 118,872
PATENT FILED: DECEMBER 16, 1939
PATENT GRANTED: FEBRUARY 6, 1940

Feb. 6, 1940.　　　J. VASSOS　　　Des. 118,872

FOUNTAIN PEN

Filed Dec. 16, 1939

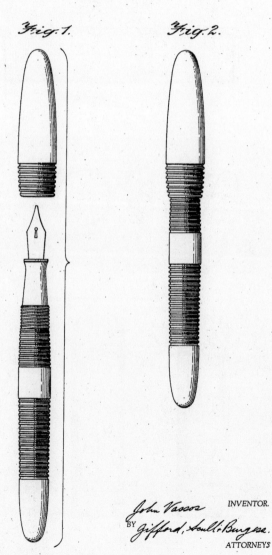

Fig.1.　　　　*Fig.2.*

John Vassos

INVENTOR.

BY *Gifford, Scull & Burgess.*

ATTORNEYS

TITLE: SHEARS
INVENTOR: LURELLE GUILD
ASSIGNEE: THE ACME SHEAR COMPANY

PATENT NUMBER: USD 119,038
PATENT FILED: OCTOBER 23, 1939
PATENT GRANTED: FEBRUARY 20, 1940

Feb. 20, 1940.

L. GUILD

Des. 119,038

SHEARS

Filed Oct. 23, 1939

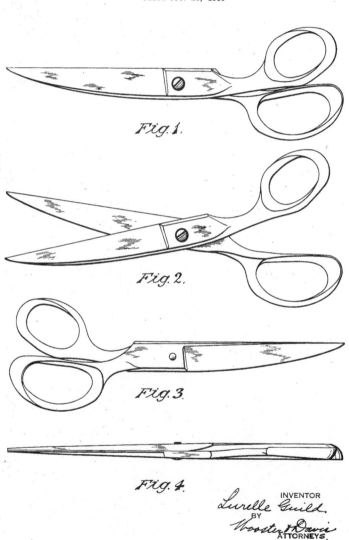

Fig. 1.

Fig. 2.

Fig. 3.

Fig. 4.

INVENTOR

Lurelle Guild.

BY

Wooster & Davis
ATTORNEYS.

TITLE: STENOTYPE MACHINE
INVENTOR: WILLIAM B. PETZOLD
ASSIGNEE: GENERAL ELECTRIC COMPANY

PATENT NUMBER: USD 119,204
PATENT FILED: OCTOBER 24, 1939
PATENT GRANTED: FEBRUARY 27, 1940

Feb. 27, 1940.

W. B. PETZOLD

STENOTYPE MACHINE

Filed Oct. 24, 1939

Des. 119,204

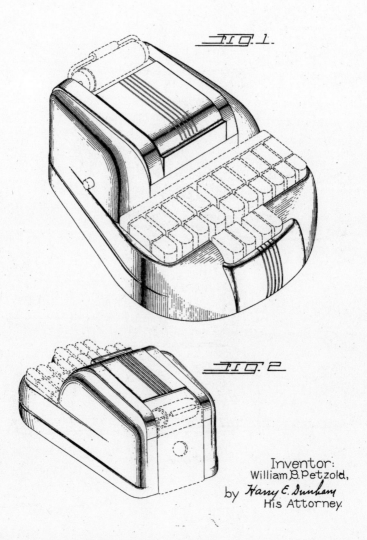

FIG. 1

FIG. 2

Inventor:
William B. Petzold,
by *Harry E. Dunham*
His Attorney.

TITLE: BOTTLE OR SIMILAR ARTICLE
INVENTOR: JAMES S. STEELMAN
ASSIGNEE: PEPSI-COLA COMPANY

PATENT NUMBER: USD 120,277
PATENT FILED: FEBRUARY 6, 1940
PATENT GRANTED: APRIL 30, 1940

April 30, 1940.

J. S. STEELMAN

Des. 120,277

BOTTLE OR SIMILAR ARTICLE

Filed Feb. 6, 1940

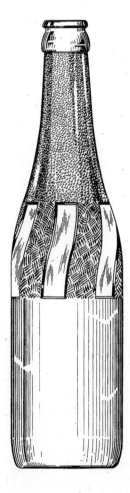

Inventor
James S. Steelman
by
Walter F. Kaufman
Attorney

TITLE: CLOCK
INVENTOR: PETER MULLER-MUNK
ASSIGNEE: PENNWOOD COMPANY

PATENT NUMBER: USD 120,740
PATENT FILED: JANUARY 4, 1940
PATENT GRANTED: MAY 28, 1940

May 28, 1940.   P. MULLER-MUNK   Des. 120,740

CLOCK

Filed Jan. 4, 1940

INVENTOR
Peter Muller-Munk

BY
Ezra D. Savage
ATTORNEY

TITLE: COMFORT STATION
INVENTORS: ARTHUR C. STEWART & KEM WEBER
ASSIGNEE: UNION OIL COMPANY

PATENT NUMBER: USD 121,104
PATENT FILED: MARCH 6, 1939
PATENT GRANTED: JUNE 18, 1940

June 18, 1940.   A. C. STEWART ET AL   Des. 121,104

COMFORT STATION

Filed March 6, 1939

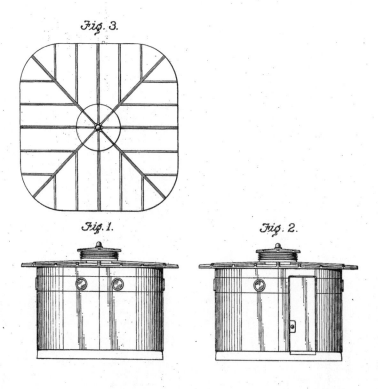

Fig. 3.

Fig. 1.   *Fig. 2.*

INVENTORS
Arthur C. Stewart
& Kem Weber
BY   Philip Subkow
ATTORNEY.

319

TITLE: PHONOGRAPH RECORD PLAYER
INVENTOR: JOHN B. SUOMALA
ASSIGNEE: RADIO CORPORATION OF AMERICA

PATENT NUMBER: USD 121,427
PATENT FILED: APRIL 29, 1939
PATENT GRANTED: JULY 9, 1940

July 9, 1940.   J. B. SUOMALA   Des. 121,427

PHONOGRAPH RECORD PLAYER

Filed April 29, 1939

F1G.1.

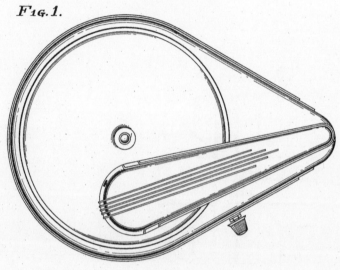

F1G.2.

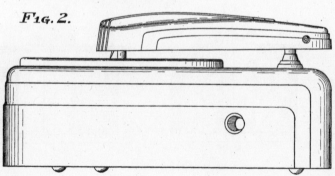

JOHN B. SUOMALA   Inventor

By

Attorney

320

TITLE: RADIO RECEIVER CABINET
INVENTOR: JOHN R. MORGAN
ASSIGNEE: SEARS, ROEBUCK & COMPANY

PATENT NUMBER: USD 123,839
PATENT FILED: SEPTEMBER 19, 1940
PATENT GRANTED: DECEMBER 3, 1940

Dec. 3, 1940.   J. R. MORGAN   Des. 123,839

RADIO RECEIVER CABINET

Filed Sept. 19, 1940

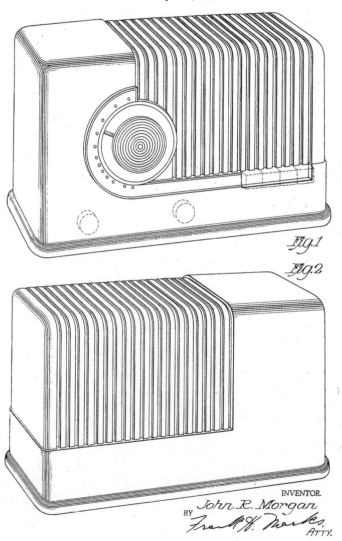

Fig.1

Fig.2

INVENTOR.

John R. Morgan

BY

Frank H. Marks,

ATTY.

TITLE: STOVE
INVENTOR: CLEMENT EHRET
ASSIGNEE: NONE

PATENT NUMBER: USD 124,063
PATENT FILED: AUGUST 10, 1939
PATENT GRANTED: DECEMBER 17, 1940

Dec. 17, 1940.   C. EHRET   Des. 124,063

STOVE

Filed Aug. 10, 1939

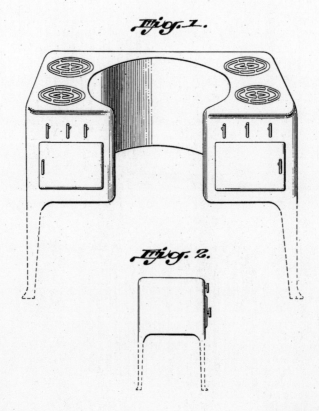

Fig. 1.

Fig. 2.

INVENTOR.
Clement Ehret

BY

Cornelius Zabriskie

ATTORNEY.

TITLE: COMBINED CALENDAR, THERMOMETER
& HUMIDITY INDICATOR
INVENTOR: WILLIAM B. PETZOLD
ASSIGNEE: GENERAL ELECTRIC COMPANY

PATENT NUMBER: USD 125,093
PATENT FILED: NOVEMBER 27, 1940
PATENT GRANTED: FEBRUARY 11, 1941

Feb. 11, 1941.   W. B. FETZOLD   Des. 125,093

COMBINED CALENDAR, THERMOMETER, AND HUMIDITY INDICATOR

Filed Nov. 27, 1940

Fig. 1.

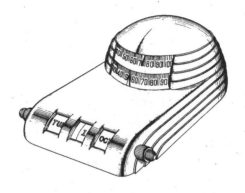

Fig. 2.

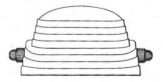

Inventor:
William B. Petzold,
by *Harry E. Dunham*
His Attorney.

323

TITLE: SERVICE STATION
INVENTORS: RALPH N. ALDRICH & ALFRED H. JAEHNE
ASSIGNEE: STANDARD OIL COMPANY OF CALIFORNIA

PATENT NUMBER: USD 125,252
PATENT FILED: DECEMBER 23, 1940
PATENT GRANTED: FEBRUARY 18, 1941

Feb. 18, 1941.   R. N. ALDRICH ET AL   Des. 125,252

SERVICE STATION

Filed Dec. 23, 1940

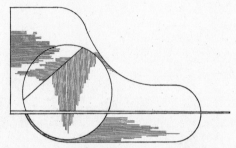

Fig. 1

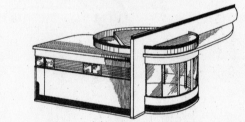

Fig. 2

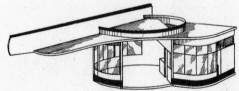

Fig. 3

Inventors

RALPH N. ALDRICH
ALFRED H. JAEHNE

by *J. L. Adams*
Attorney

TITLE: SIPHON OR THE LIKE
INVENTOR: DAVID CHAPMAN
ASSIGNEE: KNAPP-MONARCH COMPANY

PATENT NUMBER: USD 125,632
PATENT FILED: DECEMBER 11, 1940
PATENT GRANTED: MARCH 4, 1941

March 4, 1941.

D. CHAPMAN

Des. 125,632

SIPHON OR THE LIKE

Filed Dec. 11, 1940

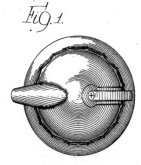

Fig. 1.

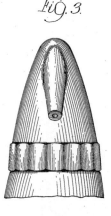

Fig. 3.

Fig. 2.

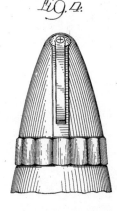

Fig. 4.

INVENTOR.

David Chapman,

BY _Bair & Freeman_

Attys.

TITLE: COLLAPSIBLE TUBE
INVENTOR: DONALD DESKEY
ASSIGNEE: BRISTOL-MYERS COMPANY

PATENT NUMBER: USD 126,431
PATENT FILED: DECEMBER 5, 1940
PATENT GRANTED: APRIL 8, 1941

April 8, 1941.

D. DESKEY

COLLAPSIBLE TUBE

Filed Dec. 5, 1940

Des. 126,431

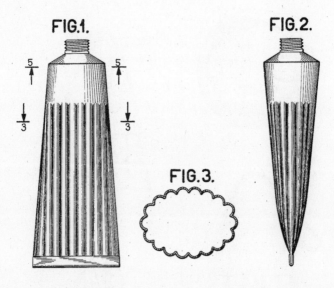

FIG.1.

FIG.2.

FIG.3.

FIG.4.

FIG.5.

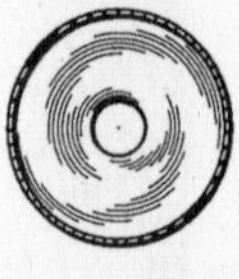

INVENTOR
DONALD DESKEY

BY

H. C. Glieseing

ATTORNEY

TITLE: CHAIR
INVENTOR: GILBERT ROHDE
ASSIGNEE: NONE

PATENT NUMBER: USD 126,593
PATENT FILED: FEBRUARY 9, 1940
PATENT GRANTED: APRIL 15, 1941

April 15, 1941.

G. ROHDE

CHAIR

Filed Feb. 9, 1940

Des. 126,593

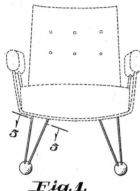

Fig. 1.

Fig. 2.

Fig. 3.

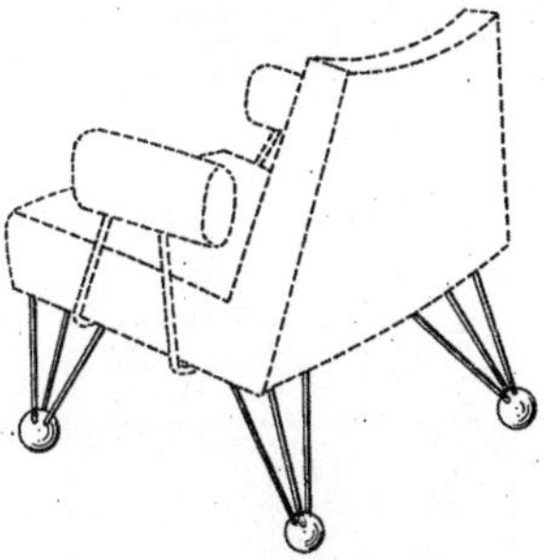

Fig. 5.

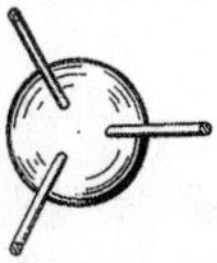

Fig. 4.

GILBERT ROHDE
INVENTOR

BY Richard S. Temke
ATTORNEY

TITLE: MOTOR COACH
INVENTOR: RAYMOND LOEWY
ASSIGNEE: THE GREYHOUND CORPORATION

PATENT NUMBER: USD 127,174
PATENT FILED: SEPTEMBER 11, 1940
PATENT GRANTED: MAY 13, 1941

May 13, 1941.   R. LOEWY   Des. 127,174

MOTOR COACH

Filed Sept. 11, 1940

Fig.1

Fig.2

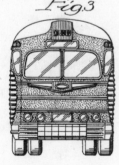

Fig.3

Fig.4

Inventor:
Raymond Loewy.
By Harold Olsen
Attorney.

TITLE: AIR FINNED SMOKING PIPE
INVENTOR: WAYNE LESER
ASSIGNEE: NONE

PATENT NUMBER: USD 127,324
PATENT FILED: JANUARY 30, 1941
PATENT GRANTED: MAY 20, 1941

May 20, 1941.   W. LESER   Des. 127,324

AIR FINNED SMOKING PIPE

Filed Jan. 30, 1941

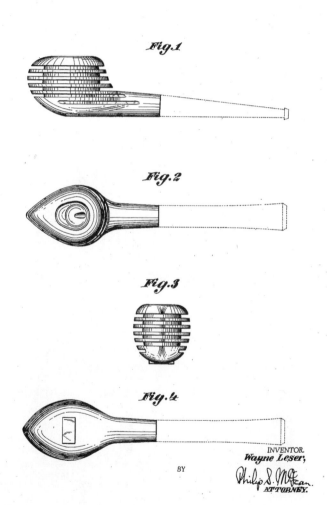

Fig.1

Fig.2

Fig.3

Fig.4

INVENTOR.
Wayne Leser,

BY

Philip S. McLean.
ATTORNEY.

TITLE: TAPE DISPENSER
INVENTOR: JEAN OTIS REINECKE
ASSIGNEE: MINNESOTA MINING
& MANUFACTURING COMPANY

PATENT NUMBER: USD 127,388
PATENT FILED: MARCH 13, 1941
PATENT GRANTED: MAY 20, 1941

May 20, 1941.　　　J. O. REINECKE　　　**Des. 127,388**

TAPE DISPENSER

Filed March 13, 1941

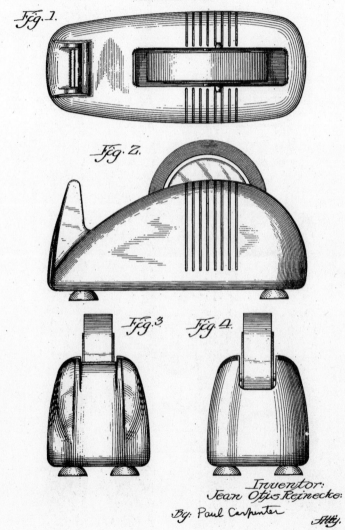

Fig. 1.

Fig. 2.

Fig. 3.　Fig. 4.

Inventor:
Jean Otis Reinecke:
By: Paul Carpenter
Atty.

TITLE: AUTOMOBILE
INVENTOR: RALPH S. ROBERTS
ASSIGNEE: BRIGGS MANUFACTURING COMPANY

PATENT NUMBER: USD 129,619
PATENT FILED: JUNE 28, 1941
PATENT GRANTED: SEPTEMBER 23, 1941

Sept. 23, 1941.   R. S. ROBERTS   Des. 129,619

AUTOMOBILE

Filed June 28, 1941   2 Sheets—Sheet 1

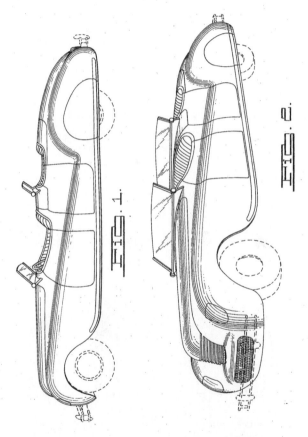

FIG. 1.

FIG. 2.

INVENTOR
Ralph S. Roberts
BY *Gray and Smith*
ATTORNEYS.

TITLE: CAMERA
INVENTORS: JOSEPH MIHALYI & WALTER D. TEAGUE
ASSIGNEE: NONE

PATENT NUMBER: USD 130,202
PATENT FILED: SEPTEMBER 23, 1941
PATENT GRANTED: OCTOBER 28, 1941

Oct. 28, 1941.   J. MIHALYI ET AL   Des. 130,202

CAMERA

Filed Sept. 23, 1941   2 Sheets—Sheet 1

FIG. I.

FIG. 2.

JOSEPH MIHALYI
WALTER D. TEAGUE
INVENTORS

BY

ATTORNEYS

332

TITLE: VEHICLE BODY
INVENTORS: WILLIAM T. ROSSELL,
FRANCIS H. SHEPARD & HARRY J. BADER
ASSIGNEE: NONE

PATENT NUMBER: USD 131,166
PATENT FILED: MARCH 4, 1941
PATENT GRANTED: JANUARY 20, 1942

Jan. 20, 1942.   W. T. ROSSELL ET AL   Des. 131,166

VEHICLE BODY

Filed March 4, 1941

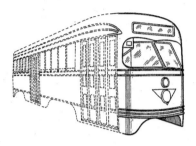

Fig. 4

Fig. 2

Fig. 1

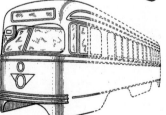

Fig. 3

Inventor
William T. Rossell
Francis H. Shepard
Harry J. Bader
By Marechal + Noz
Attorneys

333

TITLE: ELECTRIC SHAVER
INVENTOR: RAYMOND F. LOEWY
ASSIGNEE: SCHICK

PATENT NUMBER: USD 131,928
PATENT FILED: JANUARY 29, 1942
PATENT GRANTED: APRIL 7, 1942

April 7, 1942.   R. F. LOEWY   Des. 131,928

ELECTRIC SHAVER

Filed Jan. 29, 1942

Fig.1.

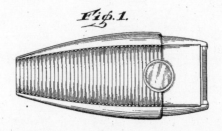

Fig.2.

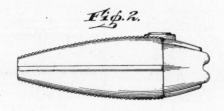

Fig.3.

Raymond F. Loewy
INVENTOR

BY
Reginald Hicks
ATTORNEY

TITLE: CIGARETTE LIGHTER
INVENTOR: A. JAY ACKERMAN
ASSIGNEE: NEW MARTINSVILLE GLASS
MANUFACTURING COMPANY

PATENT NUMBER: USD 132,121
PATENT FILED: AUGUST 2, 1941
PATENT GRANTED: APRIL 21, 1942

April 21, 1942.   A. J. ACKERMAN   Des. 132,121

CIGARETTE LIGHTER

Filed Aug. 2, 1941

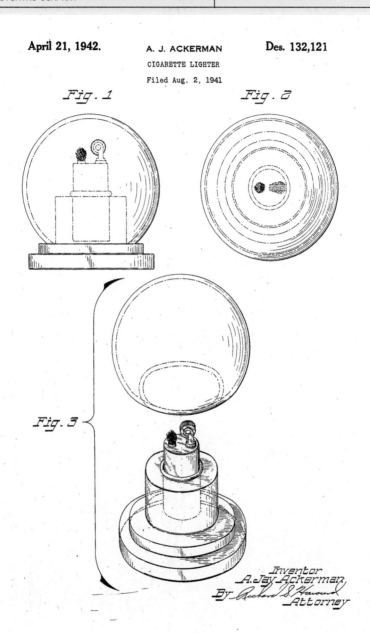

Fig. 1

Fig. 2

Fig. 3

Inventor
A. Jay Ackerman
By Richard S. Howard
Attorney

TITLE: COMBINATION DESK UNIT
INVENTOR: JACQUES MARTIAL
ASSIGNEE: ESTERBROOK STEEL PEN
MANUFACTURING COMPANY

PATENT NUMBER: USD 132,638
PATENT FILED: JUNE 21, 1941
PATENT GRANTED: JUNE 2, 1942

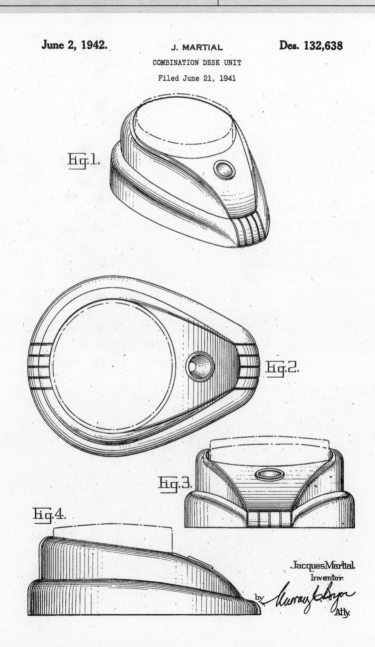

June 2, 1942.

J. MARTIAL

Des. 132,638

COMBINATION DESK UNIT

Filed June 21, 1941

Fig.1.

Fig.2.

Fig.3.

Fig.4.

Jacques Martial.
Inventor.
by
Atty.

TITLE: FRUIT JUICE EXTRACTOR
INVENTOR: HENRY J. TALGE
ASSIGNEE: RIVAL MANUFACTURING COMPANY

PATENT NUMBER: USD 132,678
PATENT FILED: MARCH 23, 1942
PATENT GRANTED: JUNE 9, 1942

June 9, 1942.   H. J. TALGE   Des. 132,678

FRUIT JUICE EXTRACTOR

Filed March 23, 1942

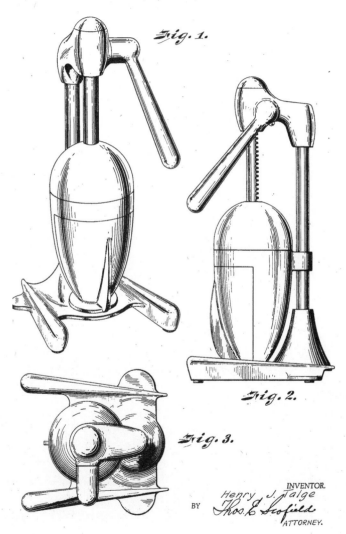

Fig. 1.

Fig. 2.

Fig. 3.

INVENTOR.
Henry J. Talge
BY Thos. E. Scofield
ATTORNEY.

TITLE: JUICE EXTRACTOR
INVENTORS: DON E. GROVE & JACKSON D. COMSTOCK
ASSIGNEE: HOLLYWOOD LIQUEFIER CORPORATION

PATENT NUMBER: USD 132,762
PATENT FILED: APRIL 1, 1941
PATENT GRANTED: JUNE 16, 1942

June 16, 1942.

D. E. GROVE ET AL

Des. 132,762

JUICE EXTRACTOR

Filed April 1, 1941

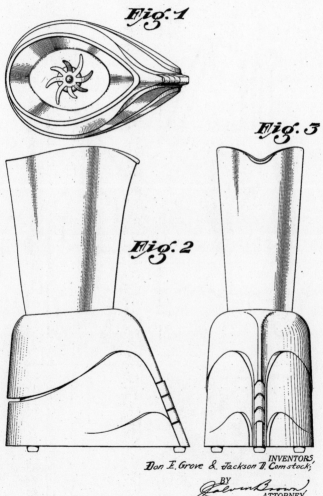

Fig. 1

Fig. 3

Fig. 2

INVENTORS,
Don E. Grove & Jackson D. Comstock;
BY
Calvin Brown
ATTORNEY

338

TITLE: STRIP SERVER
INVENTOR: EGMONT ARENS
ASSIGNEE: NASHUA GUMMED & COATED PAPER COMPANY

PATENT NUMBER: USD 132,802
PATENT FILED: JANUARY 20, 1942
PATENT GRANTED: JUNE 16, 1942

June 16, 1942.

E. ARENS

Des. 132,802

STRIP SERVER

Filed Jan. 20, 1942

Fig. 1.

Fig. 2.

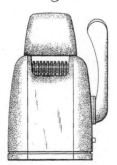

Fig. 3.

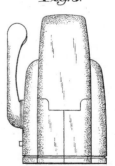

Inventor:
Egmont Arens,
by Emery, Booth, Townsend, Miller & Widner Attys.

339

TITLE: AUTOMOBILE OR SIMILAR ARTICLE
INVENTOR: GEORGE W. WALKER
ASSIGNEE: PACKARD MOTOR CAR COMPANY

PATENT NUMBER: USD 133,122
PATENT FILED: OCTOBER 24, 1941
PATENT GRANTED: JULY 21, 1942

July 21, 1942.   G. W. WALKER   Des. 133,122

AUTOMOBILE OR SIMILAR ARTICLE

Filed Oct. 24, 1941

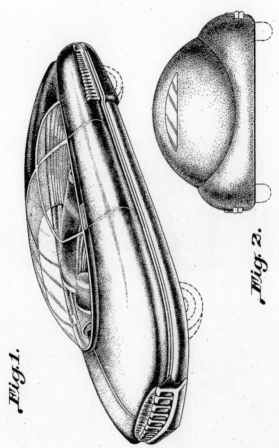

Fig. 1.

Fig. 2.

Inventor.

George W. Walker,

by Tibbetts & Hart,

Attorneys.

TITLE: PREFABRICATED HOUSE
INVENTOR: RICHARD BUCKMINSTER FULLER
ASSIGNEE: THE DYMAXION COMPANY

PATENT NUMBER: USD 133,411
PATENT FILED: MAY 31, 1941
PATENT GRANTED: AUGUST 11, 1942

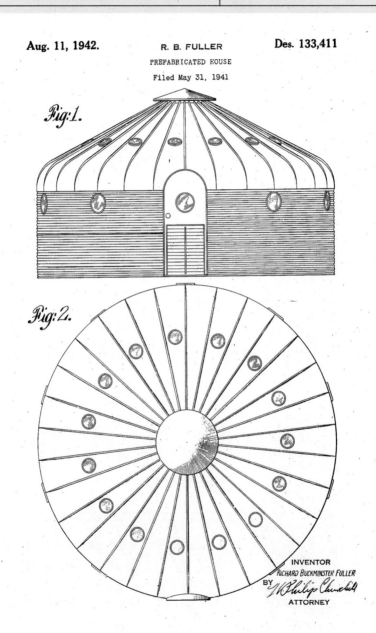

Aug. 11, 1942. R. B. FULLER Des. 133,411

PREFABRICATED HOUSE

Filed May 31, 1941

Fig:1.

Fig:2.

INVENTOR
RICHARD BUCKMINSTER FULLER
BY
J. Philip Churchill
ATTORNEY

TITLE: LAMP
INVENTOR: HORACE EVERETT HOPKINS
ASSIGNEE: NONE

PATENT NUMBER: USD 135,479
PATENT FILED: AUGUST 10, 1942
PATENT GRANTED: APRIL 13, 1943

April 13, 1943.   H. E. HOPKINS   Des. 135,479

LAMP

Filed Aug. 10, 1942

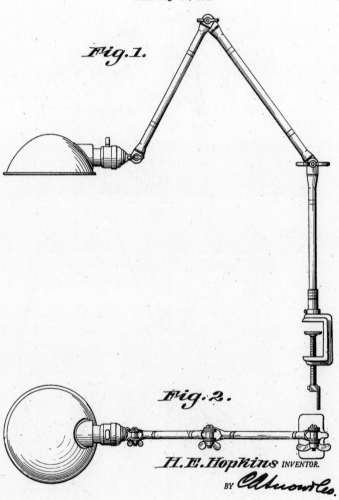

Fig.1.

Fig.2.

H. E. Hopkins INVENTOR.

BY Cdknowles.

342

TITLE: PITCHER OR SIMILAR ARTICLE
INVENTOR: WALTER OEHRLE
ASSIGNEE: BORDEN COMPANY

PATENT NUMBER: USD 136,262
PATENT FILED: JANUARY 7, 1943
PATENT GRANTED: AUGUST 31, 1943

Aug. 31, 1943.   W. OEHRLE   Des. 136,262

PITCHER OR SIMILAR ARTICLE

Filed Jan. 7, 1943

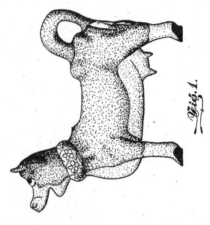

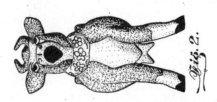

INVENTOR.
WALTER OEHRLE.

BY Arthur C. Mac Mahon

ATTORNEY.

TITLE: AIRPLANE
INVENTORS: HALL L. HIBBARD & CLARENCE L. JOHNSON
ASSIGNEE: LOCKHEED AIRCRAFT CORPORATION

PATENT NUMBER: USD 136,352
PATENT FILED: OCTOBER 5, 1942
PATENT GRANTED: SEPTEMBER 14, 1943

Sept. 14, 1943.   H. L. HIBBARD ET AL   Des. 136,352

AIRPLANE

Filed Oct. 5, 1942   2 Sheets—Sheet 2

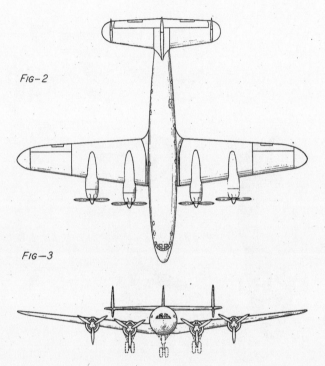

FIG—2

FIG—3

FIG—4

INVENTORS
HALL L. HIBBARD
CLARENCE L. JOHNSON

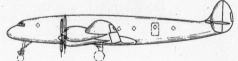

BY *George C. Sullivan*

TITLE: STATION WAGON TYPE AUTOMOBILE
INVENTOR: CLIFFORD BROOKS STEVENS
ASSIGNEE: MONART MOTORS

PATENT NUMBER: USD 136,355
PATENT FILED: JUNE 21, 1943
PATENT GRANTED: SEPTEMBER 14, 1943

Sept. 14, 1943.   C. B. STEVENS   Des. 136,355

STATION WAGON TYPE AUTOMOBILE

Filed June 21, 1943

Fig. 1.

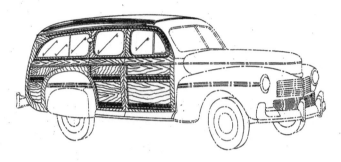

Fig. 2.

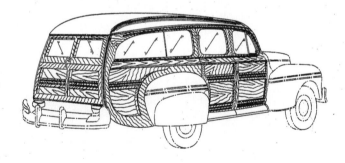

Inventor
Clifford Brooks Stevens
By Ira Milton Jones
Attorney

TITLE: MOTION PICTURE PROJECTOR
INVENTOR: CLARENCE KARSTADT
ASSIGNEE: SEARS, ROEBUCK & COMPANY

PATENT NUMBER: USD 136,623
PATENT FILED: SEPTEMBER 5, 1942
PATENT GRANTED: NOVEMBER 9, 1943

Nov. 9, 1943.   C. KARSTADT   Des. 136,623

MOTION PICTURE PROJECTOR

Filed Sept. 5, 1942   2 Sheets—Sheet 2

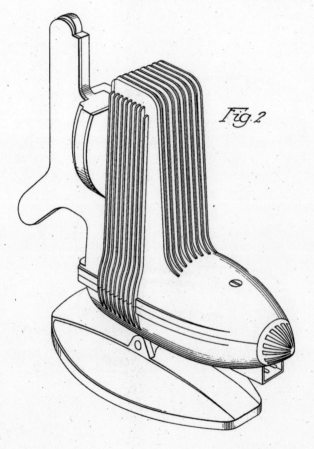

Fig. 2

Inventor
Clarence Karstadt
By: Louis Sheldon Atty.

TITLE: COMBINED RADIO RECEIVER AND CLOCK CASING
INVENTOR: ROBERT D. BUDLONG
ASSIGNEE: ZENITH RADIO CORPORATION

PATENT NUMBER: USD 136,827
PATENT FILED: SEPTEMBER 3, 1943
PATENT GRANTED: DECEMBER 14, 1943

Dec. 14, 1943.   R. D. BUDLONG   Des. 136,827

COMBINED RADIO RECEIVER AND CLOCK CASING

Filed Sept. 3, 1943

Fig. 1

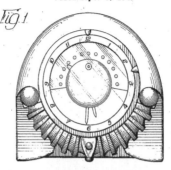

Fig. 2

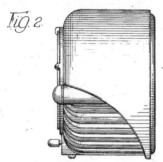

Fig. 3

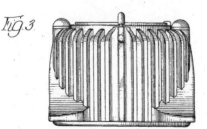

INVENTOR.
Robert D. Budlong,
BY
J. Clarke Hagey
Atty.

347

TITLE: ICE CUBE TRAY
INVENTOR: JOSEPH A. GITS
ASSIGNEE: JOSEPH A. GITS AND JULES P. GITS

PATENT NUMBER: USD 137,122
PATENT FILED: NOVEMBER 12, 1941
PATENT GRANTED: JANUARY 25, 1944

Jan. 25, 1944.　　　　J. A. GITS　　　　Des. 137,122

ICE CUBE TRAY

Filed Nov. 12, 1941

Fig. 1.

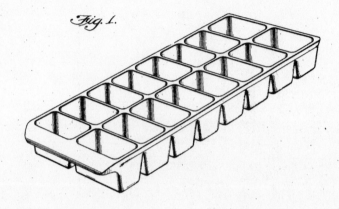

Fig. 2.

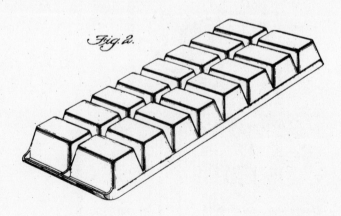

INVENTOR.

Joseph A. Gits

BY *Thiess, Olsen & Mecklenburger.*

Attys.

TITLE: TOY GIRAFFE
INVENTOR: JEAN O. REINECKE
ASSIGNEE: THE FIRESTONE TIRE & RUBBER COMPANY

PATENT NUMBER: USD 137,695
PATENT FILED: DECEMBER 31, 1943
PATENT GRANTED: APRIL 18, 1944

April 18, 1944.   J. O. REINECKE   Des. 137,695

TOY GIRAFFE

Filed Dec. 31, 1943

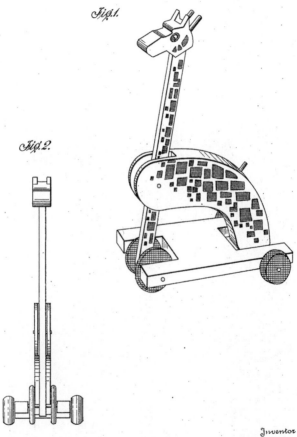

Fig. 1.

Fig. 2.

Inventor

JEAN O. REINECKE

By

Ely & Fiye

Attorneys

TITLE: COMBINED FLASK & HANDLE FOR A COFFEEMAKER
INVENTOR: PETER SCHLUMBOHM
ASSIGNEE: CHEMEX CORPORATION

PATENT NUMBER: USD 137,943
PATENT FILED: JANUARY 12, 1943
PATENT GRANTED: MAY 23, 1944

May 23, 1944.   P. SCHLUMBOHM   Des. 137,943

COMBINED FLASK AND HANDLE, FOR A COFFEEMAKER OR THE LIKE

Filed Jan. 12, 1943   2 Sheets–Sheet 2

Fig. 5.

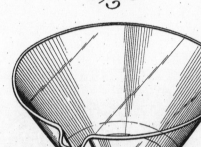

INVENTOR.
PETER SCHLUMBOHM
BY
KARL W. FLOCKS
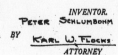
ATTORNEY

TITLE: BATHROOM SCALE
INVENTOR: CARL W. SUNDBERG
ASSIGNEE: NONE

PATENT NUMBER: USD 137,990
PATENT FILED: MARCH 24, 1944
PATENT GRANTED: MAY 30, 1944

May 30, 1944.   C. W. SUNDBERG   Des. 137,990

BATHROOM SCALE

Filed March 24, 1944

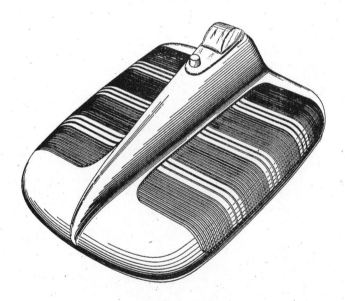

Inventor
Carl W. Sundberg
by Sundbey & Robilland
Attorneys

TITLE: HAIR DRIER OR THE LIKE
INVENTOR: HARRY S. PREBLE JR.
ASSIGNEE: A.C. GILBERT COMPANY

PATENT NUMBER: USD 138,044
PATENT FILED: MARCH 29, 1944
PATENT GRANTED: JUNE 6, 1944

June 6, 1944.   H. S. PREBLE, JR   Des.138,044

HAIR DRIER OR THE LIKE

Filed March 29, 1944

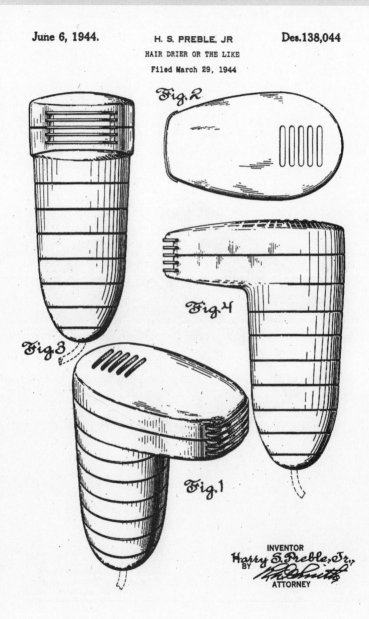

Fig. 2

Fig. 3

Fig. 4

Fig. 1

INVENTOR
Harry S. Preble, Jr.,
BY
ATTORNEY

TITLE: FLASHLIGHT OR LIKE ARTICLE
INVENTOR: JOSHUA GORDON LIPPINCOTT
ASSIGNEE: GUTH, STERN & COMPANY

PATENT NUMBER: USD 139,442
PATENT FILED: JUNE 2, 1944
PATENT GRANTED: NOVEMBER 14, 1944

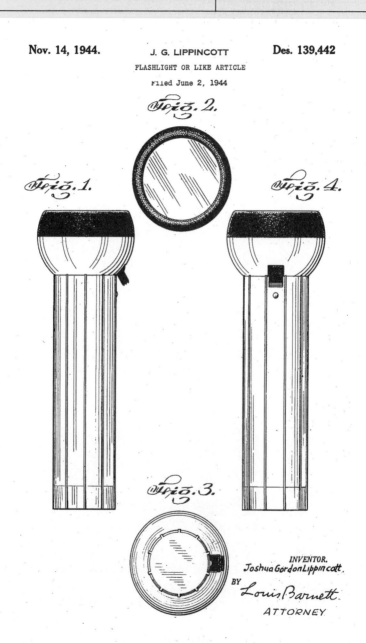

Nov. 14, 1944.   J. G. LIPPINCOTT   Des. 139,442

FLASHLIGHT OR LIKE ARTICLE

Filed June 2, 1944

Fig. 2.

Fig. 1.

Fig. 4.

Fig. 3.

INVENTOR.
Joshua Gordon Lippincott.
BY
Louis Barnett.
ATTORNEY

TITLE: REFRIGERATOR
INVENTOR: GEORGE W. WALKER
ASSIGNEE: BOHN ALUMINUM & BRASS CORPORATION

PATENT NUMBER: USD 139,533
PATENT FILED: SEPTEMBER 1, 1943
PATENT GRANTED: NOVEMBER 28, 1944

Nov. 28, 1944.   G. W. WALKER   Des. 139,533

REFRIGERATOR

Filed Sept. 1, 1943

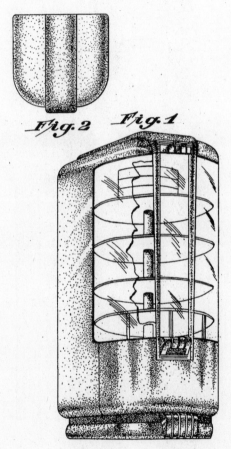

Fig.2   Fig.1

INVENTOR.
George W. Walker
BY

Edwin J. Balluff
ATTORNEY.

TITLE: HAND DRILL
INVENTOR: FRANCESCO COLLURA
ASSIGNEE: MILLERS FALLS COMPANY

PATENT NUMBER: USD 140,811
PATENT FILED: JANUARY 6, 1945
PATENT GRANTED: APRIL 10, 1945

April 10, 1945.   F. COLLURA   Des. 140,811

HAND DRILL

Filed Jan. 6, 1945

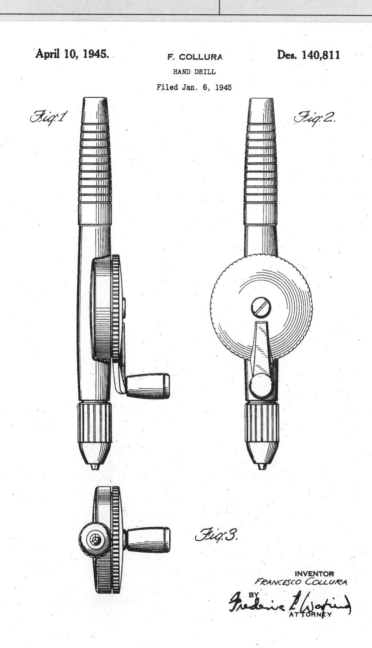

Fig.1

Fig.2

Fig.3

INVENTOR
FRANCESCO COLLURA
BY
Frederick L. Watkins
ATTORNEY

355

TITLE: CHAIR
INVENTOR: JENS RISOM
ASSIGNEE: KNOLL ASSOCIATES

PATENT NUMBER: USD 141,839
PATENT FILED: SEPTEMBER 8, 1943
PATENT GRANTED: JULY 10, 1945

July 10, 1945.   J. RISOM   Des. 141,839

CHAIR

Filed Sept. 8, 1943

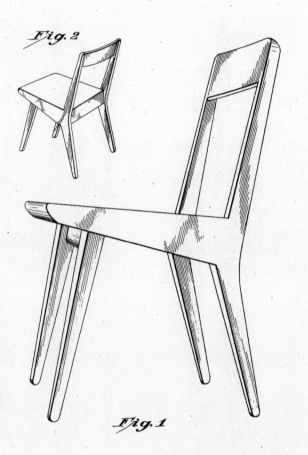

Fig. 2

Fig. 1

JENS RISOM.
INVENTOR.

BY

ATT'Y

TITLE: RADIO RECEIVER CABINET
INVENTOR: CLIFFORD E. GRUBE
ASSIGNEE: BELMONT RADIO CORPORATION

PATENT NUMBER: USD 142,140
PATENT FILED: JUNE 14, 1945
PATENT GRANTED: AUGUST 14, 1945

Aug. 14, 1945.   C. E. GRUBE   Des. 142,140

RADIO RECEIVER CABINET

Filed June 14, 1945

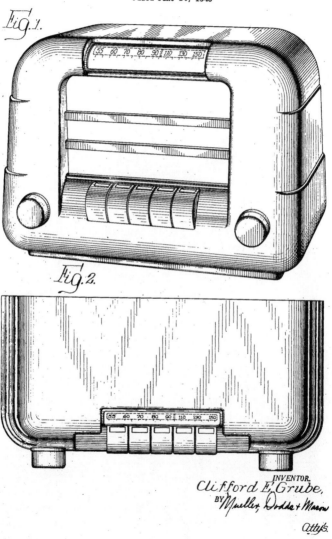

Fig. 1.

Fig. 2.

INVENTOR.
Clifford E. Grube,
BY Mueller, Dodda + Mason

Attys.

357

TITLE: ROTARY POWER HANDSAW
INVENTOR: LOUIS VAVRIK
ASSIGNEE: AMERICAN FLOOR SURFACING
MACHINE COMPANY

PATENT NUMBER: USD 142,235
PATENT FILED: MARCH 26, 1945
PATENT GRANTED: AUGUST 21, 1945

Aug. 21, 1945.   L VAVRIK   Des. 142,235

ROTARY POWER HAND SAW

Filed March 26, 1945   2 Sheets—Sheet 1

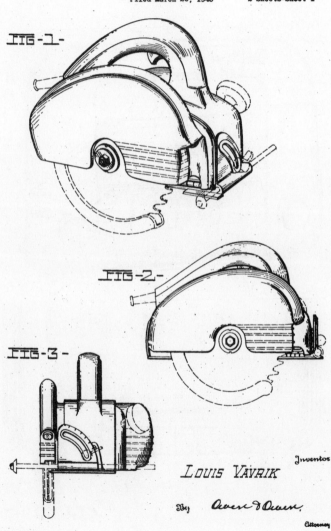

FIG-1-

FIG-2-

FIG-3-

Louis Vavrik   Inventor

By   *Owen & Owen.*

        Attorney

358

TITLE: COMBINATION DESK UNIT
INVENTOR: SCOTT P. AKERS
ASSIGNEE: NONE

PATENT NUMBER: USD 143,109
PATENT FILED: AUGUST 31, 1945
PATENT GRANTED: DECEMBER 11, 1945

Dec. 11, 1945.

S. P. AKERS

Des. 143,109

COMBINATION DESK UNIT

Filed Aug. 31, 1945

Fig. 1.

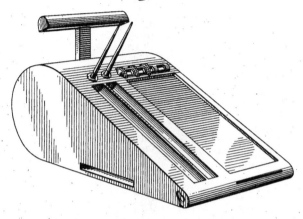

Fig. 2.

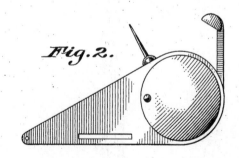

Scott P. Akers

INVENTOR.

BY

Cd Knowles

ATTORNEYS.

TITLE: FAUCET HANDLE OR THE LIKE
INVENTOR: HENRY DREYFUSS
ASSIGNEE: CRANE COMPANY

PATENT NUMBER: USD 143,287
PATENT FILED: APRIL 26, 1945
PATENT GRANTED: DECEMBER 25, 1945

Dec. 25, 1945.

H. DREYFUSS

Des. 143,287

FAUCET HANDLE OR THE LIKE

Filed April 26, 1945

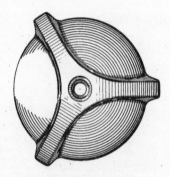

Fig. 1

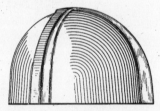

Fig. 2.

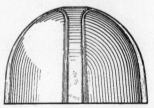

Fig. 3.

Inventor:
Henry Dreyfuss:

By: Joseph O. Lange
Atty.

TITLE: VEGETABLE PEELER
INVENTOR: RALPH P. DE VAULT
ASSIGNEE: NONE

PATENT NUMBER: USD 143,714
PATENT FILED: MARCH 1, 1945
PATENT GRANTED: FEBRUARY 5, 1946

Feb. 5, 1946.   R. P. DE VAULT   Des. 143,714

VEGETABLE PEELER

Filed March 1, 1945

Fig.1

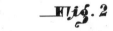

Fig. 2

Fig. 3

Inventor

RALPH P. DE VAULT

By *Jesse P. Whann*

Attorney

TITLE: ELECTRIC FAN
INVENTOR: ROBERT DAVOL BUDLONG
ASSIGNEE: CLIFFORD STROM

PATENT NUMBER: USD 144,034
PATENT FILED: JUNE 9, 1945
PATENT GRANTED: MARCH 5, 1946

March 5, 1946.   R. D. BUDLONG   Des. 144,034

ELECTRIC FAN

Filed June 9, 1945   2 Sheets—Sheet 1

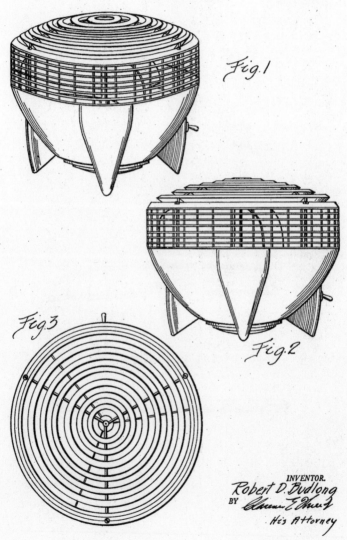

Fig. 1

Fig. 2

Fig. 3

INVENTOR.
Robert D. Budlong
BY
His Attorney

TITLE: MOTH PREVENTIVE TABLET
INVENTOR: DONALD DESKEY
ASSIGNEE: KOPPERS COMPANY

PATENT NUMBER: USD 144,159
PATENT FILED: JUNE 5, 1945
PATENT GRANTED: MARCH 19, 1946

March 19, 1946. D. DESKEY Des. 144,159

MOTH PREVENTIVE TABLET

Filed June 5, 1945

Fig. 3.

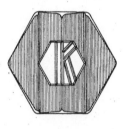

Fig. 1.

Fig. 2.

INVENTOR.
DONALD DESKEY.

BY Edmund M Borders

his ATTORNEY.

363

TITLE: TYPEWRITING MACHINE
INVENTOR: HENRY DREYFUSS
ASSIGNEE: ROYAL TYPEWRITER COMPANY

PATENT NUMBER: USD 144,165
PATENT FILED: AUGUST 2, 1945
PATENT GRANTED: MARCH 19, 1946

March 19, 1946.

H. DREYFUSS

Des. 144,165

TYPEWRITING MACHINE

Filed Aug. 2, 1945

4 Sheets—Sheet 1

Fig.1.

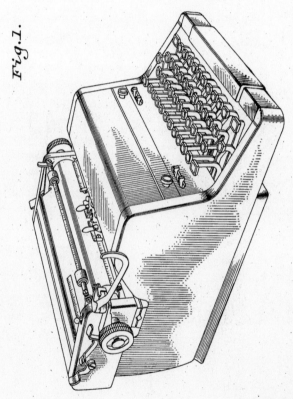

INVENTOR.

Henry Dreyfuss

BY

Baldwin & Wight

his ATTORNEYS

TITLE: AIRPLANE
INVENTORS: EDWARD H. HEINEMANN & LEO J. DEVLIN
ASSIGNEE: DOUGLAS AIRCRAFT COMPANY

PATENT NUMBER: USD 144,714
PATENT FILED: MAY 2, 1945
PATENT GRANTED: MAY 14, 1946

May 14, 1946.   E. H. HEINEMANN ET AL   Des. 144,714

AIRPLANE

Filed May 2, 1945   2 Sheets—Sheet 1

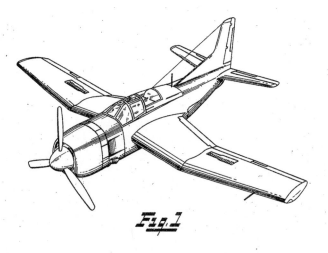

Fig. 1

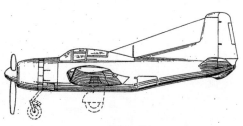

Fig. 2

INVENTOR.
EDWARD H. HEINEMANN
LEO. J. DEVLIN

BY Edwin Coates

ATTORNEY

365

TITLE: PENCIL SHARPENER
INVENTOR: ROBERT B. FLEMING
ASSIGNEE: BERT M. MORRIS COMPANY

PATENT NUMBER: USD 144,777
PATENT FILED: MARCH 12, 1946
PATENT GRANTED: MAY 21, 1946

May 21, 1946.

R. B. FLEMING

Des. 144,777

PENCIL SHARPENER

Filed March 12, 1946

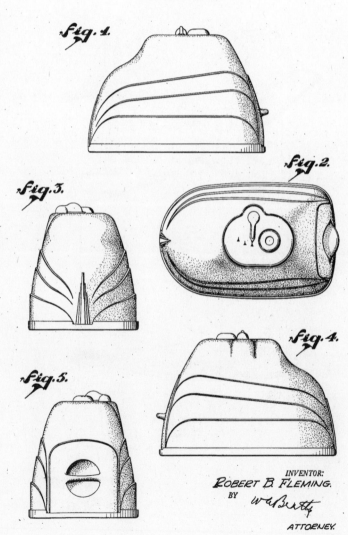

Fig. 1.

Fig. 2.

Fig. 3.

Fig. 4.

Fig. 5.

INVENTOR:
ROBERT B. FLEMING.
BY
W. H. Beatty
ATTORNEY.

TITLE: COMBINATION TOASTER & COOKER
INVENTOR: OTTO E. STELZER
ASSIGNEE: CALKINS APPLIANCE CORPORATION

PATENT NUMBER: USD 145,108
PATENT FILED: AUGUST 1, 1945
PATENT GRANTED: JUNE 25, 1946

June 25, 1946.　　　　O. E. STELZER　　　　**Des. 145,108**

COMBINATION TOASTER AND COOKER

Filed Aug. 1, 1945

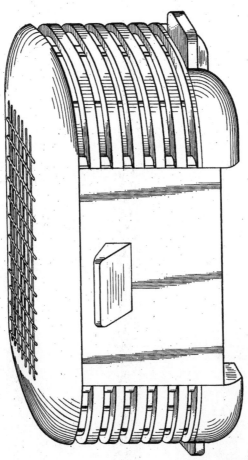

INVENTOR.

OTTO E. STELZER.

BY

Oltach & Knoblock

ATTORNEYS.

TITLE: VACUUM CLEANER CASING
INVENTOR: CLIFFORD BROOKS STEVENS
ASSIGNEE: MODERN HYGIENE CORPORATION

PATENT NUMBER: USD 145,276
PATENT FILED: DECEMBER 22, 1945
PATENT GRANTED: JULY 23, 1946

July 23, 1946.   C. B. STEVENS   Des. 145,276

VACUUM CLEANER CASING

Filed Dec. 22, 1945

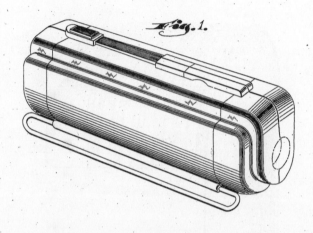

Fig. 1.

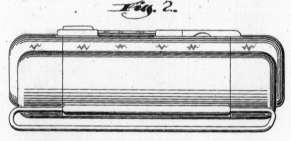

Fig. 2.

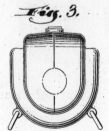

Fig. 3.

Inventor
Clifford Brooks Stevens
By Dewitt Jones
Attorney

368

TITLE: COMBINED WASHING MACHINE AND WRINGER
INVENTOR: CARL W. SUNDBERG
ASSIGNEE: NINETEEN HUNDRED CORPORATION

PATENT NUMBER: USD 145,543
PATENT FILED: SEPTEMBER 19, 1945
PATENT GRANTED: SEPTEMBER 3, 1946

Sept. 3, 1946. C. W. SUNDBERG Des. 145,543

COMBINED WASHING MACHINE AND WRINGER OR SIMILAR ARTICLE

Filed Sept. 19, 1945

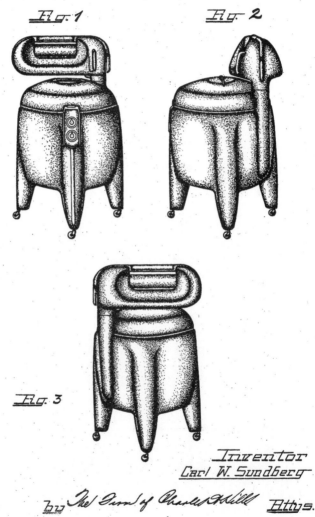

Fig. 1

Fig. 2

Fig. 3

Inventor
Carl W. Sundberg

by The Firm of Charles R. Hill Attys.

TITLE: TAPE DISPENSER
INVENTOR: HARRY PREBLE, JR.
ASSIGNEE: INTERNATIONAL PLASTIC CORPORATION

PATENT NUMBER: USD 145,699
PATENT FILED: JANUARY 26, 1946
PATENT GRANTED: OCTOBER 8, 1946

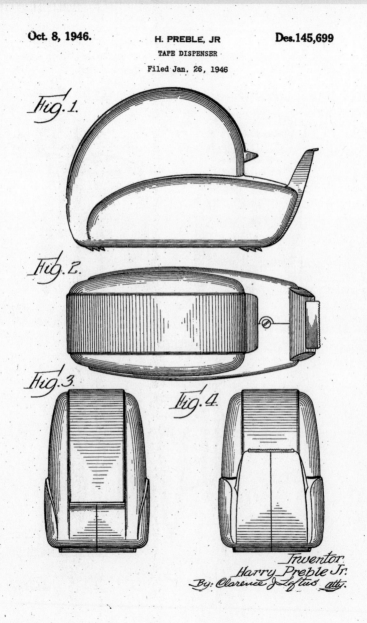

Oct. 8, 1946.

H. PREBLE, JR

Des. 145,699

TAPE DISPENSER

Filed Jan. 26, 1946

Fig. 1.

Fig. 2.

Fig. 3.

Fig. 4.

Inventor
Harry Preble Jr.
By: Clarence J. Loftus atty.

TITLE: PHONOGRAPH CABINET
INVENTOR: PAUL M. FULLER
ASSIGNEE: RUDOLPH WURLITZER COMPANY

PATENT NUMBER: USD 146,175
PATENT FILED: FEBRUARY 21,1946
PATENT GRANTED: JANUARY 7,1947

Jan. 7, 1947.

P. M. FULLER

Des.146,175

PHONOGRAPH CABINET

Filed Feb. 21, 1946

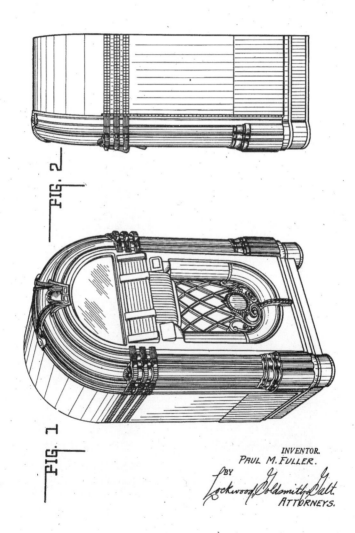

FIG. 2

FIG. 1

INVENTOR.
PAUL M. FULLER.

BY
Lockwood, Goldsmith & Galt.
ATTORNEYS.

TITLE: ELECTRIC IRON
INVENTOR: FRANCESCO COLLURA
ASSIGNEE: NONE

PATENT NUMBER: USD 146,256
PATENT FILED: DECEMBER 7, 1945
PATENT GRANTED: JANUARY 21, 1947

Jan. 21, 1947.

F. COLLURA

Des. 146,256

ELECTRIC IRON

Filed Dec. 7, 1945

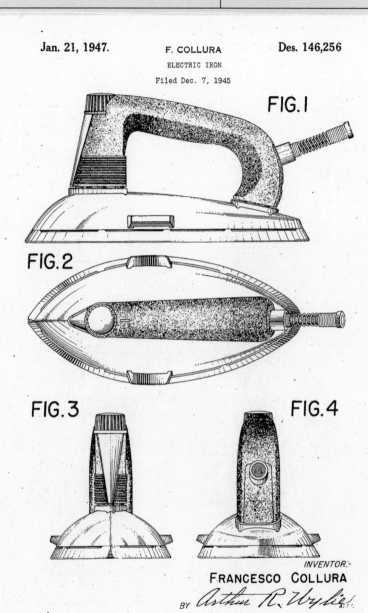

FIG.1

FIG.2

FIG.3

FIG.4

INVENTOR:-

FRANCESCO COLLURA

BY *Arthur R. Wylie*

TITLE: CAMERA
INVENTOR: RAYMOND T. LARSON
ASSIGNEE: NONE

PATENT NUMBER: USD 146,800
PATENT FILED: JUNE 15, 1946
PATENT GRANTED: MAY 20, 1947

May 20, 1947.

R. T. LARSON

Des. 146,800

CAMERA

Filed June 15, 1946

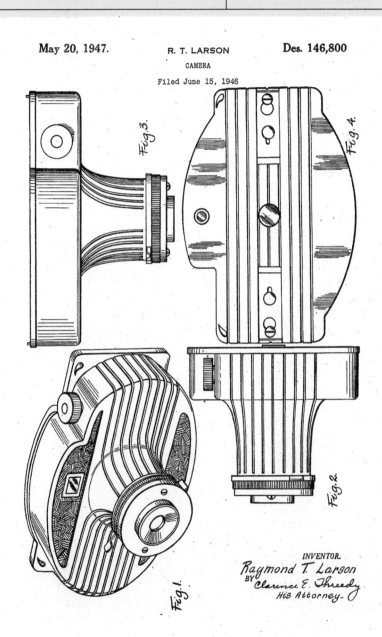

Fig.3.

Fig.4.

Fig.2.

Fig.1.

INVENTOR.
Raymond T. Larson
BY Clarence E. Threedy
His Attorney.

TITLE: FOUNTAIN PEN
INVENTOR: LÁSZLÓ MOHOLY–NAGY
ASSIGNEE: PARKER PEN COMPANY

PATENT NUMBER: USD 146,806
PATENT FILED: FEBRUARY 11, 1946
PATENT GRANTED: MAY 20, 1947

May 20, 1947.

L. MOHOLY-NAGY

Des. 146,806

FOUNTAIN PEN

Filed Feb. 11, 1946

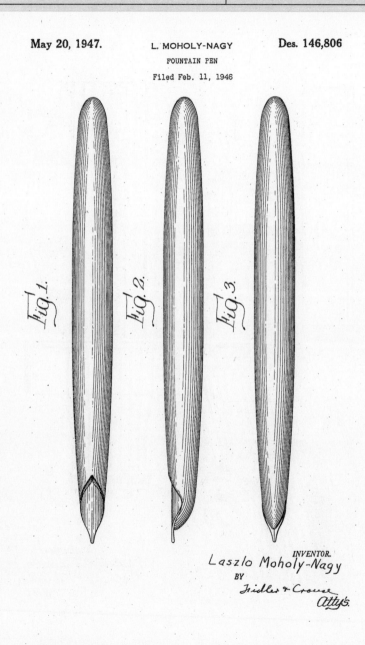

INVENTOR.

Laszlo Moholy-Nagy

BY

Fidler & Crouse

Atty's.

TITLE: PHOTOGRAPHIC SPOTLIGHT
INVENTOR: MARSHALL M. ROBINSON
ASSIGNEE: NATIONAL INSTRUMENT CORPORATION

PATENT NUMBER: USD 146,809
PATENT FILED: AUGUST 17, 1946
PATENT GRANTED: MAY 20, 1947

May 20, 1947.

M. M. ROBINSON

Des. 146,809

PHOTOGRAPHIC SPOT LIGHT

Filed Aug. 17, 1946

2 Sheets—Sheet 1

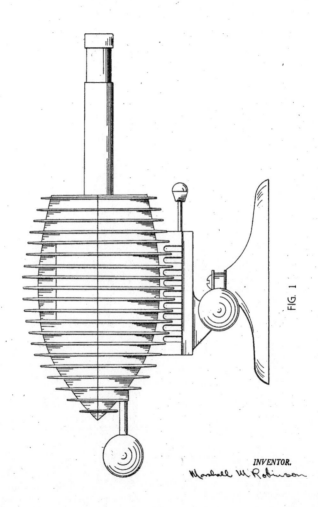

FIG. 1

INVENTOR.

Marshall M. Robinson

TITLE: LAMP
INVENTOR: JEAN O. REINECKE
ASSIGNEE: W.A. SHEAFFER PEN COMPANY

PATENT NUMBER: USD 146,987
PATENT FILED: JANUARY 7, 1946
PATENT GRANTED: JUNE 24, 1947

June 24, 1947.

J. O. REINECKE

Des. 146,987.

LAMP

Filed Jan. 7, 1946

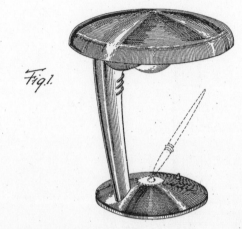

Fig.1.

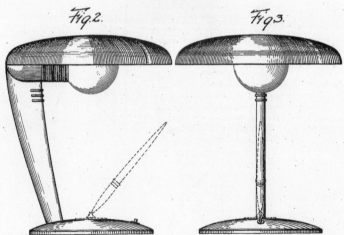

Fig.2.

Fig.3.

Inventor
JEAN O. REINECKE
By Wilbur L. Olson
Atty.

376

TITLE: COCKTAIL SHAKER
INVENTOR: ANDREW CRAVARITIS
ASSIGNEE: NONE

PATENT NUMBER: USD 147,113
PATENT FILED: MAY 8, 1946
PATENT GRANTED: JULY 15, 1947

July 15, 1947.　　　A. CRAVARITIS　　　Des. 147,113

COCKTAIL SHAKER

Filed May 8, 1946

Fig.1.　　　　　*Fig.2.*

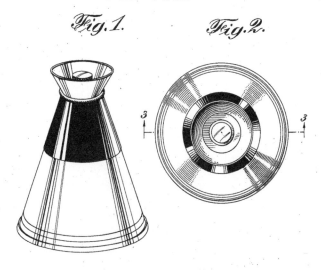

Fig.3.

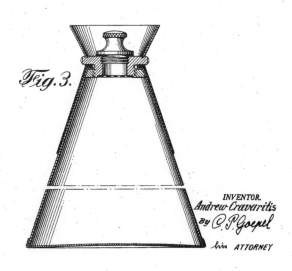

INVENTOR.
Andrew Cravaritis
By *C. P. Goepel*
his ATTORNEY

TITLE: WAGON
INVENTOR: GORDON W. FLORIAN
ASSIGNEE: NONE

PATENT NUMBER: USD 147,645
PATENT FILED: JULY 11, 1946
PATENT GRANTED: OCTOBER 14, 1947

Oct. 14, 1947. G. W. FLORIAN Des. 147,645

WAGON

Filed July 11, 1946

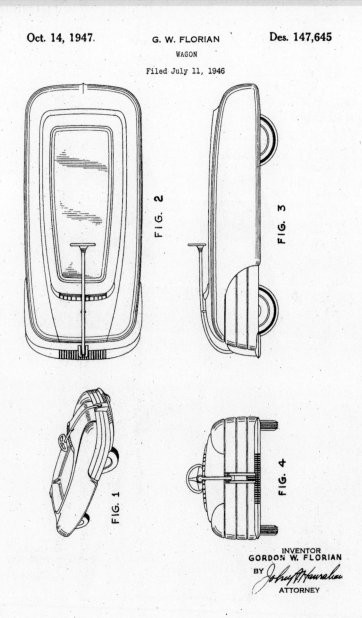

FIG. 2

FIG. 3

FIG. 1

FIG. 4

INVENTOR
GORDON W. FLORIAN

BY

ATTORNEY

TITLE: CONDIMENT RECEPTACLE
INVENTOR: JOHN P. KAMINSKI
ASSIGNEE: NONE

PATENT NUMBER: USD 147,731
PATENT FILED: JANUARY 23, 1946
PATENT GRANTED: OCTOBER 21, 1947

Oct. 21, 1947.   J. P. KAMINSKI   Des. 147,731

CONDIMENT RECEPTACLE

Filed Jan. 23, 1946

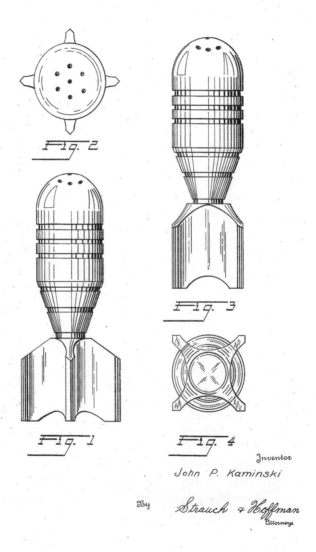

Fig. 2

Fig. 3

Fig. 1

Fig. 4

Inventor

John P. Kaminski

By   Strauch & Hoffman

Attorneys

379

TITLE: TOASTER HOUSING
INVENTOR: CHARLES W. MUSSER
ASSIGNEE: ETC.

PATENT NUMBER: USD 147,734
PATENT FILED: JUNE 22, 1946
PATENT GRANTED: OCTOBER 21, 1947

Oct. 21, 1947.

C. W. MUSSER

TOASTER HOUSING

Filed June 22, 1946

Des. 147,734

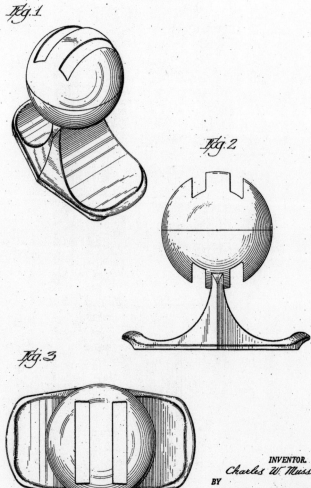

Fig.1

Fig.2

Fig.3

INVENTOR.
Charles W. Musser
BY
Albert G. McCaleb
Atty.

380

TITLE: MILK PITCHER
INVENTOR: ROLF JOHN FALK
ASSIGNEE: SHAWNEE POTTERY COMPANY

PATENT NUMBER: USD 148,056
PATENT FILED: APRIL 20, 1946
PATENT GRANTED: DECEMBER 9, 1947

Dec. 9, 1947.

R. J. FALK

MILK PITCHER

Filed April 20, 1946

Des. 148,056

2 Sheets—Sheet 2

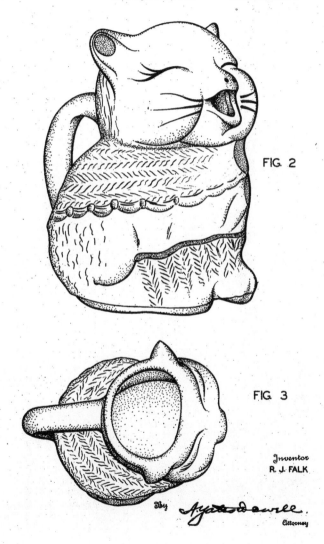

FIG. 2

FIG. 3

Inventor
R. J. FALK

By _Ayato Dowell_.

Attorney

TITLE: SERVICE STATION BUILDING OR THE LIKE
INVENTOR: GEORGE W. TERP
ASSIGNEE: STANDARD OIL COMPANY

PATENT NUMBER: USD 148,196
PATENT FILED: JUNE 26, 1946
PATENT GRANTED: DECEMBER 23, 1947

Dec. 23, 1947.   G. W. TERP   **Des. 148,196**

SERVICE STATION BUILDING OR THE LIKE

Filed June 26, 1946

Fig. 1

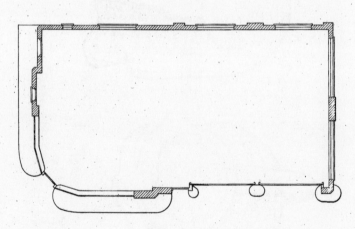

Fig. 2

Inventor
George W. Terp
By *Arthur H. Bransky*
Attorney

382

TITLE: COMBINATION CORKSCREW AND BOTTLE OPENER
INVENTOR: PAUL WYLER
ASSIGNEE: NONE

PATENT NUMBER: USD 148,345
PATENT FILED: JUNE 4, 1946
PATENT GRANTED: JANUARY 6, 1948

Jan. 6, 1948.   P. WYLER   Des. 148,345

COMBINATION CORKSCREW AND BOTTLE OPENER

Filed June 4, 1946

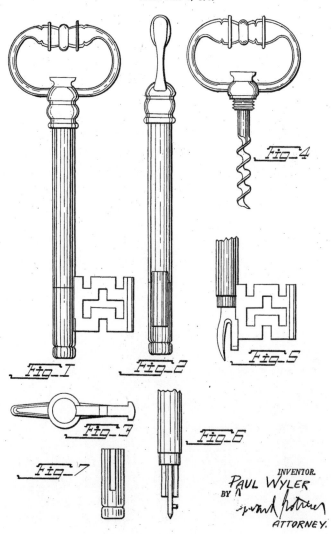

INVENTOR.
PAUL WYLER
BY
ATTORNEY.

TITLE: AUTOMOBILE STATION WAGON
INVENTOR: DELMAR G. ROOS
ASSIGNEE: WILLYS-OVERLAND MOTORS

PATENT NUMBER: USD 148,579
PATENT FILED: APRIL 26, 1946
PATENT GRANTED: FEBRUARY 3, 1948

Feb. 3, 1948.

D. G. ROOS

Des. 148,579

AUTOMOBILE STATION WAGON

Filed April 26, 1946

3 Sheets—Sheet 3

FIG-3-

FIG-4-

INVENTOR.
Delmar G. Roos
BY
Harry O. Ernsberger
ATTORNEY.

384

TITLE: BUILDING
INVENTOR: RAYMOND LOEWY
ASSIGNEE: NONE

PATENT NUMBER: USD 149,076
PATENT FILED: AUGUST 30, 1946
PATENT GRANTED: MARCH 23, 1948

March 23, 1948.

R. LOEWY

Des. 149,076

BUILDING

Filed Aug. 30, 1946

2 Sheets—Sheet 2

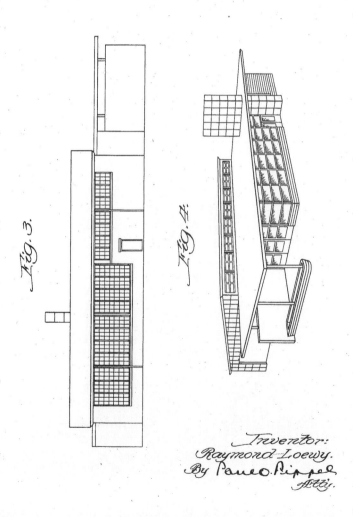

Fig. 3.

Fig. 4.

Inventor:
Raymond Loewy.
By Paulo Rippel
Atty.

TITLE: SINK FIXTURE
INVENTOR: JOHN M. LITTLE
ASSIGNEE: NONE

PATENT NUMBER: USD 149,195
PATENT FILED: OCTOBER 9, 1946
PATENT GRANTED: APRIL 6, 1948

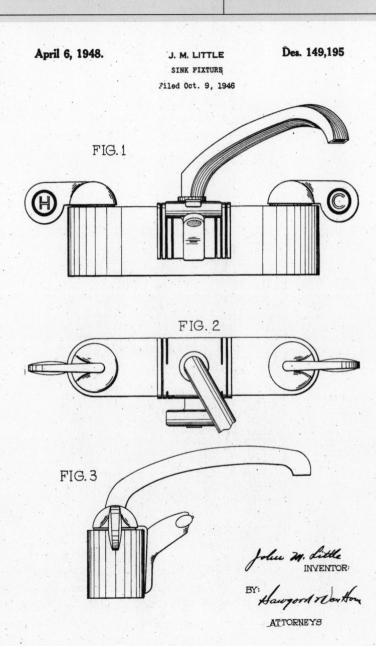

April 6, 1948.

J. M. LITTLE

SINK FIXTURE

Filed Oct. 9, 1946

Des. 149,195

FIG. 1

FIG. 2

FIG. 3

John M. Little

INVENTOR:

BY: *Haugood Norton*

ATTORNEYS

TITLE: PORTABLE ELECTRIC SPACE HEATER
INVENTOR: WAYNE A. GUSTAFSON
ASSIGNEE: M.S. AVIATION COMPANY

PATENT NUMBER: USD 149,266
PATENT FILED: JULY 5, 1946
PATENT GRANTED: APRIL 13, 1948

April 13, 1948.   W. A. GUSTAFSON   Des. 149,266

PORTABLE ELECTRIC SPACE HEATER

Filed July 5, 1946

FIG. 1

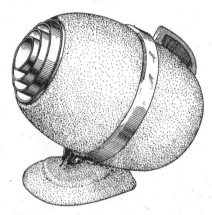

FIG. 2

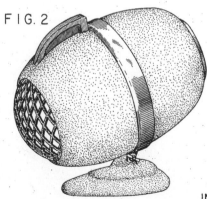

INVENTOR
WAYNE A. GUSTAFSON

BY *Caswell & Laquard*

ATTORNEYS

387

TITLE: WATER KETTLE
INVENTOR: PETER SCHLUMBOHM
ASSIGNEE: NONE

PATENT NUMBER: USD 149,310
PATENT FILED: OCTOBER 7, 1946
PATENT GRANTED: APRIL 13, 1948

April 13, 1948.   P. SCHLUMBOHM   Des. 149,310

WATER KETTLE

Filed Oct. 7, 1946

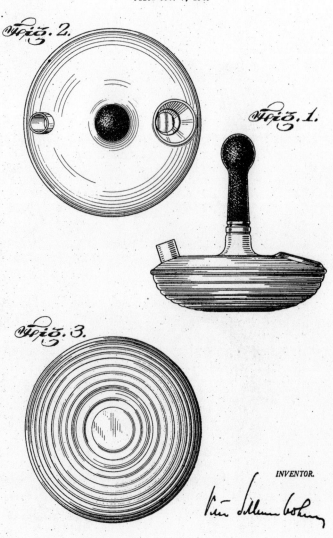

Fig. 2.

Fig. 1.

Fig. 3.

INVENTOR.

TITLE: THEATRE
INVENTOR: ALBERT R. WALKER
ASSIGNEE: FOX WEST COAST THEATRES CORPORATION

PATENT NUMBER: USD 149,324
PATENT FILED: SEPTEMBER 9, 1946
PATENT GRANTED: APRIL 13, 1948

April 13, 1948.　　　A. R. WALKER　　　Des. 149,324

THEATRE

Filed Sept. 9, 1946　　　2 Sheets—Sheet 1

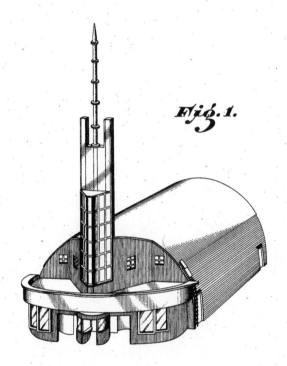

Fig. 1.

Albert R. Walker,
INVENTOR

BY Lyon & Lyon
ATTORNEYS

TITLE: TABLE
INVENTOR: CARL W. SUNDBERG
ASSIGNEE: REYNOLDS METALS COMPANY

PATENT NUMBER: USD 149,524
PATENT FILED: JULY 2, 1946
PATENT GRANTED: MAY 4, 1948

May 4, 1948.   C. W. SUNDBERG   Des. 149,524

TABLE

Filed July 2, 1946

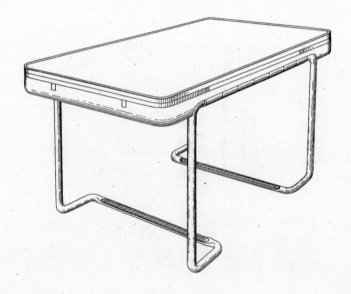

INVENTOR.

Carl W. Sundberg

BY H. Lee Helms

ATTORNEY

TITLE: BEVERAGE DISPENSER
INVENTOR: RAYMOND LOEWY
ASSIGNEE: COCA-COLA COMPANY

PATENT NUMBER: USD 149,656
PATENT FILED: JUNE 17, 1946
PATENT GRANTED: MAY 18, 1948

May 18, 1948.   R. LOEWY   **Des. 149,656**

BEVERAGE DISPENSER

Filed June 17, 1946   3 Sheets—Sheet 1

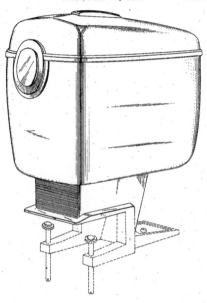

𝕱𝖎𝖌. 1 .

INVENTOR

RAYMOND LOEWY

BY

ATTORNEY

TITLE: TOASTER
INVENTOR: DONALD E. DAILEY
ASSIGNEE: PROCTOR ELECTRIC COMPANY

PATENT NUMBER: USD 149,937
PATENT FILED: APRIL 14, 1947
PATENT GRANTED: JUNE 15, 1948

June 15, 1948.

D. E. DAILEY

Des. 149,937

TOASTER

Filed April 14, 1947

FIG. 1.

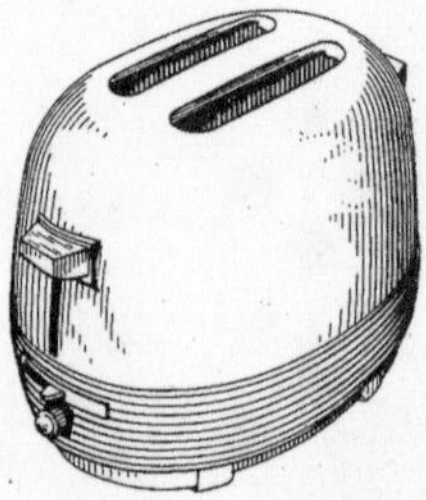

FIG. 2.

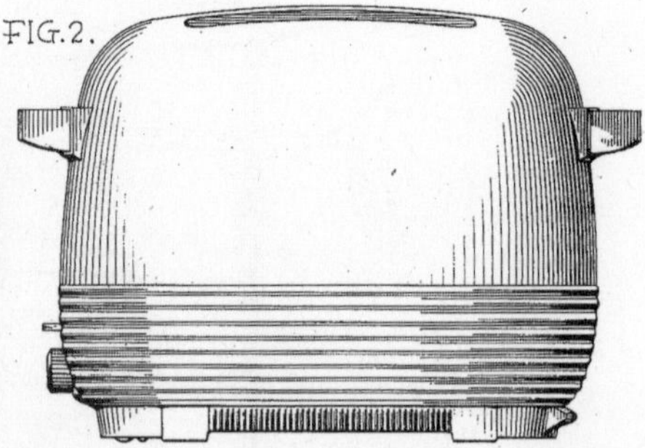

FIG. 3.

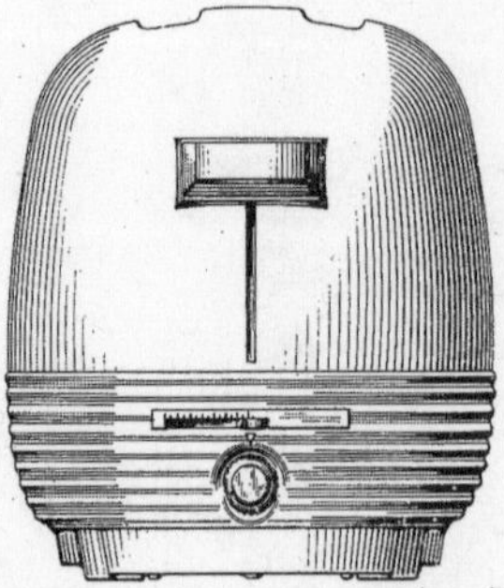

FIG. 4.

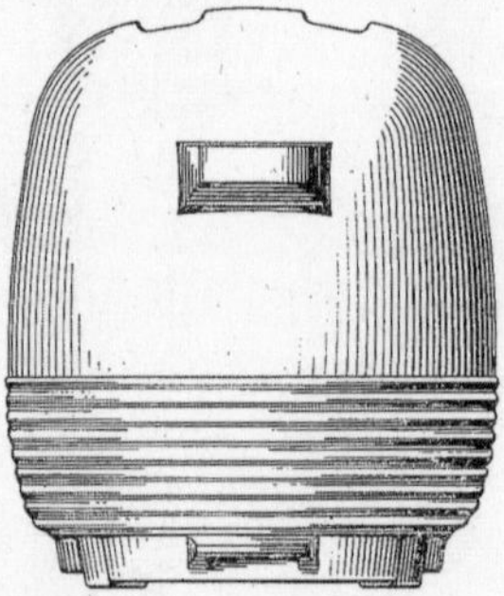

FIG. 5.

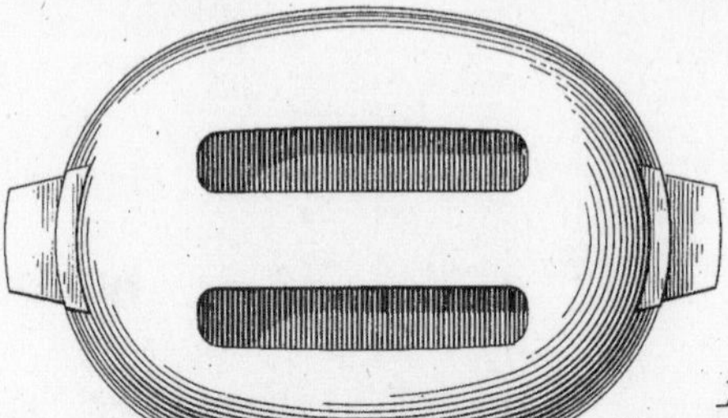

Inventor:
Donald E. Dailey
by his Attorneys
Howson & Howson

TITLE: MOTOR CAR
INVENTOR: ROGER LAURENT JEAN-BAPTISTE SANMORI
ASSIGNEE: NONE

PATENT NUMBER: USD 150,161
PATENT FILED: JUNE 1, 1946
PATENT GRANTED: JULY 6, 1948

July 6, 1948. R. L. JEAN-BAPTISTE SANMORI Des. 150,161

MOTOR CAR

Filed June 1, 1946

3 Sheets—Sheet 1

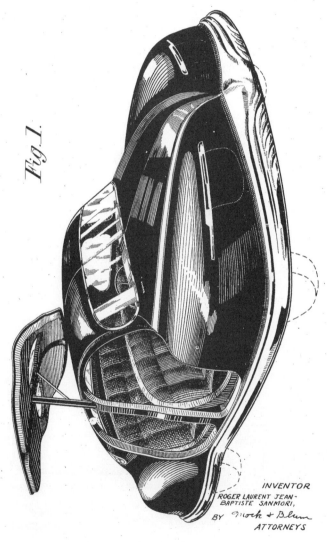

Fig. 1.

INVENTOR
ROGER LAURENT JEAN-
BAPTISTE SANMORI,
BY *Mock & Blum*
ATTORNEYS

TITLE: BOX CAMERA
INVENTOR: ARTHUR H. CRAPSEY, JR.
ASSIGNEE: EASTMAN KODAK COMPANY

PATENT NUMBER: USD 150,289
PATENT FILED: JANUARY 17, 1948
PATENT GRANTED: JULY 20, 1948

July 20, 1948.   A. H. CRAPSEY, JR   Des. 150,289

BOX CAMERA

Filed Jan. 17, 1948

FIG. 1.

FIG. 2.

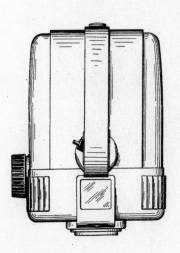

FIG. 3.

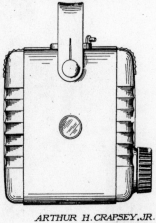

ARTHUR H. CRAPSEY, JR.
INVENTOR

BY
ATTORNEYS

394

TITLE: COASTER CAR
INVENTOR: THOMAS B. BRICKSON
ASSIGNEE: NONE

PATENT NUMBER: USD 150,401
PATENT FILED: AUGUST 31, 1946
PATENT GRANTED: AUGUST 3, 1948

Aug. 3, 1948.

T. B. BRICKSON

Des. 150,401

COASTER CAR

Filed Aug. 31, 1946

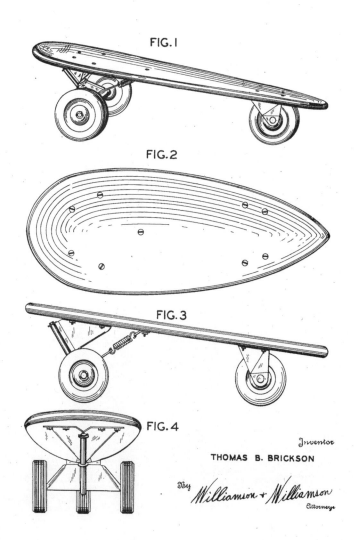

FIG.1

FIG.2

FIG.3

FIG.4

Inventor

THOMAS B. BRICKSON

By Williamson + Williamson
Attorneys

TITLE: CHAISE LONGUE
INVENTOR: ALICE ROTH
ASSIGNEE: TROY SUNSHADE COMPANY

PATENT NUMBER: USD 150,461
PATENT FILED: DECEMBER 26, 1946
PATENT GRANTED: AUGUST 3, 1948

Aug. 3, 1948.

A. ROTH

CHAISE LONGUE

Des. 150,461

Filed Dec. 26, 1946

3 Sheets—Sheet 1

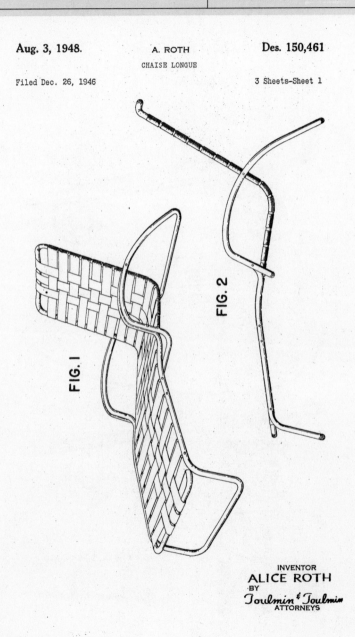

FIG. 1

FIG. 2

INVENTOR
ALICE ROTH
BY
Toulmin & Toulmin
ATTORNEYS

TITLE: RADIO CABINET
INVENTOR: BARTON T. SETCHELL
ASSIGNEE: NONE

PATENT NUMBER: USD 150,660
PATENT FILED: APRIL 24, 1946
PATENT GRANTED: AUGUST 17, 1948

Aug. 17, 1948. B. T. SETCHELL Des. 150,660

RADIO CABINET

Filed April 24, 1946 2 Sheets—Sheet 1

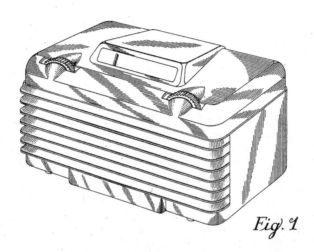

Fig. 1

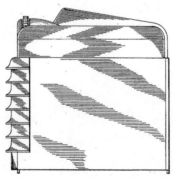

Fig. 2

Inventor

Barton T. Setchell

By Robert M. Dunning

Attorney

TITLE: CHAIR
INVENTOR: CHARLES EAMES
ASSIGNEE: EVANS PRODUCTS COMPANY

PATENT NUMBER: USD 150,683
PATENT FILED: MARCH 27, 1947
PATENT GRANTED: AUGUST 24, 1948

Aug. 24, 1948.

C. EAMES

Des. 150,683

CHAIR

Filed March 27, 1947

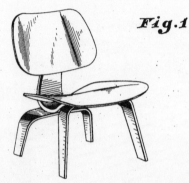

Fig. 1

Fig. 2

Fig. 3

Fig. 4

Inventor

Charles Eames

By

Lyon + Lyon

Attorneys

398

TITLE: FRUIT JAR AND BOTTLE OPENER
INVENTOR: HENRY L. NICHOLS
ASSIGNEE: NONE

PATENT NUMBER: USD 151,065
PATENT FILED: MAY 3, 1946
PATENT GRANTED: SEPTEMBER 21, 1948

Sept. 21, 1948.

H. L. NICHOLS

Des. 151,065

FRUIT JAR AND BOTTLE OPENER

Filed May 3, 1946

Fig. 1

Fig. 2

Inventor
Henry L. Nichols
By
Francis D. Ammen
his Atty.

TITLE: DESK LAMP OR THE LIKE
INVENTOR: HERMAN L. GOEBEL
ASSIGNEE: MITCHELL MANUFACTURING COMPANY

PATENT NUMBER: USD 150,940
PATENT FILED: SEPTEMBER 4, 1946
PATENT GRANTED: SEPTEMBER 14, 1948

Sept. 14, 1948.

H. L. GOEBEL

Des. 150,940

DESK LAMP OR THE LIKE

Filed Sept. 4, 1946

2 Sheets—Sheet 1

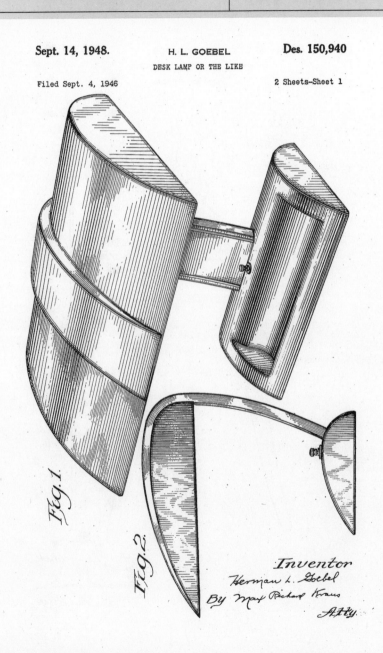

Fig.1

Fig.2

Inventor
Herman L. Goebel
By Max Richard Kraus
Atty.

400

TITLE: RADIO RECEIVER CABINET
INVENTOR: ALBERT L. JENKS
ASSIGNEE: MOTOROLA

PATENT NUMBER: USD 152,156
PATENT FILED: AUGUST 23, 1947
PATENT GRANTED: DECEMBER 21, 1948

Dec. 21, 1948.

A. L. JENKS

Des. 152,156

RADIO RECEIVER CABINET

Filed Aug. 23, 1947

Fig. 1.

Fig. 2.

INVENTOR.
Albert L. Jenks,
BY
Foorman L. Mueller
Atty.

TITLE: PHOTOGRAPHIC CAMERA OR SIMILAR ARTICLE
INVENTORS: WALTER D. TEAGUE, ROBERT H. ENSIGN,
HAROLD R. BEAL & MURRY N. FAIRBANK
ASSIGNEE: POLAROID CORPORATION

PATENT NUMBER: USD 152,229
PATENT FILED: APRIL 30, 1948
PATENT GRANTED: DECEMBER 28, 1948

Dec. 28, 1948.   W. D. TEAGUE ET AL   Des. 152,229

PHOTOGRAPHIC CAMERA OR SIMILAR ARTICLE

Filed April 30, 1948   5 Sheets—Sheet 5

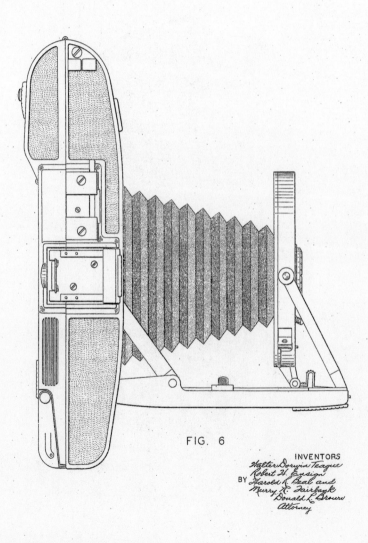

FIG. 6

INVENTORS
Walter Dorwin Teague
Robert H. Ensign
BY Harold R. Beal and
Murry N. Fairbank
Donald L. Brown
Attorney

402

TITLE: TELEVISION RECEIVER CABINET
INVENTOR: ALBERT L. JENKS
ASSIGNEE: MOTOROLA

PATENT NUMBER: USD 152,266
PATENT FILED: FEBRUARY 25, 1948
PATENT GRANTED: JANUARY 4, 1949

Jan. 4, 1949.　　　　A. L. JENKS　　　　Des. 152,266

TELEVISION RECEIVER CABINET

Filed Feb. 25, 1948

Fig. 1.

Fig. 2.

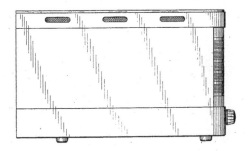

INVENTOR.

Albert L. Jenks,

BY

Foorman L. Mueller

Atty.

TITLE: FACSIMILE RECORDER
INVENTOR: WALTER DORWIN TEAGUE
ASSIGNEE: FINCH TELECOMMUNICATIONS

PATENT NUMBER: USD 152,303
PATENT FILED: APRIL 3, 1946
PATENT GRANTED: JANUARY 4, 1949

Jan. 4, 1949.

W. D. TEAGUE

Des. 152,303

FACSIMILE RECORDER

Filed April 3, 1946

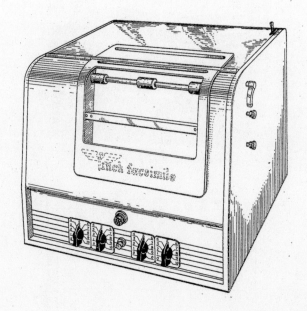

INVENTOR.
WALTER DORWIN TEAGUE
BY *Ostrolenk and Faber*

ATTORNEYS

TITLE: AUTOMOBILE
INVENTOR: VIRGIL M. EXNER
ASSIGNEE: STUDEBAKER CORPORATION

PATENT NUMBER: USD 152,400
PATENT FILED: OCTOBER 10, 1946
PATENT GRANTED: JANUARY 18, 1949

Jan. 18, 1949.

V. M. EXNER

Des. 152,400

AUTOMOBILE

Filed Oct. 10, 1946

2 Sheets—Sheet 1

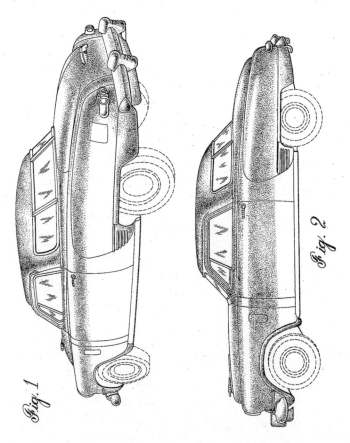

Fig. 1

Fig. 2

INVENTOR.

Virgil M. Exner

BY

Brown, Jackson, Boettcher & Dienner.

ATTORNEYS

405

TITLE: COMBINATION LAMP & ASH TRAY
INVENTOR: ROBERT LEE AULICH
ASSIGNEE: NONE

PATENT NUMBER: USD 152,849
PATENT FILED: JANUARY 26, 1948
PATENT GRANTED: MARCH 1, 1949

March 1, 1949.   R. L. AULICH   Des. 152,849

COMBINATION LAMP AND ASH TRAY

Filed Jan. 26, 1948

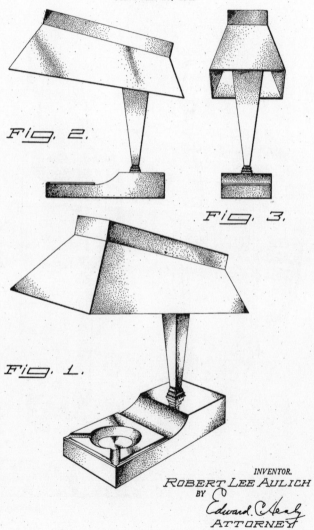

Fig. 2.

Fig. 3.

Fig. 1.

INVENTOR.
ROBERT LEE AULICH
BY
Edward C Healy
ATTORNEY

TITLE: COFFEE TABLE
INVENTOR: CHARLES EAMES
ASSIGNEE: EVANS PRODUCTS COMPANY

PATENT NUMBER: USD 152,949
PATENT FILED: MARCH 27, 1947
PATENT GRANTED: MARCH 8, 1949

March 8, 1949. C. EAMES Des. 152,949

COFFEE TABLE

Filed March 27, 1947

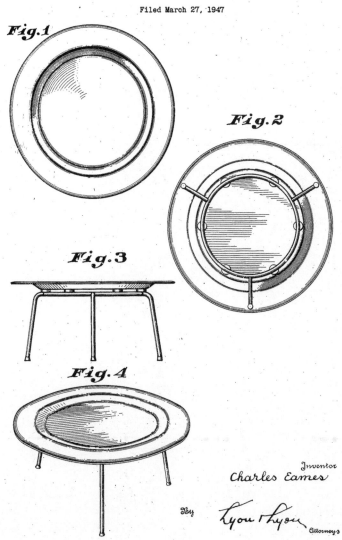

Fig.1

Fig.2

Fig.3

Fig.4

Inventor
Charles Eames

By
Lyon & Lyon
Attorneys

TITLE: ANIMAL TRAP
INVENTOR: GEORGE SAKIER
ASSIGNEE: ANIMAL TRAP COMPANY OF AMERICA

PATENT NUMBER: USD 153,176
PATENT FILED: AUGUST 4, 1947
PATENT GRANTED: MARCH 22, 1949

March 22, 1949. G. SAKIER **Des. 153,176**

ANIMAL TRAP

Filed Aug. 4, 1947

Fig.1.

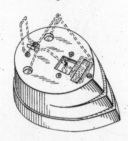

Fig.2.

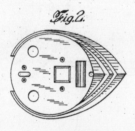

Fig.3.

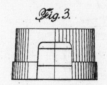

INVENTOR.
GEORGE SAKIER

BY

Robert E. Burns

ATTORNEY

408

TITLE: REMOTE CONTROL SELECTOR CABINET
FOR PHONOGRAPHS
INVENTOR: PAUL M. FULLER
ASSIGNEE: THE RUDOLPH WURLITZER COMPANY

PATENT NUMBER: USD 153,425
PATENT FILED: SEPTEMBER 8, 1947
PATENT GRANTED: APRIL 19, 1949

April 19, 1949.

P. M. FULLER
REMOTE CONTROL SELECTOR
CABINET FOR PHONOGRAPHS
Filed Sept. 8, 1947

Des. 153,425

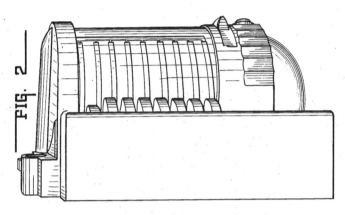

FIG. 2

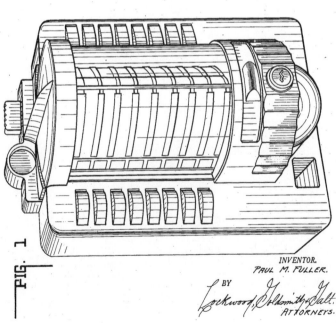

FIG. 1

INVENTOR.
PAUL M. FULLER.

BY

Lockwood, Goldsmith & Galt.
ATTORNEYS.

TITLE: TOY DUCK
INVENTOR: PETER GANINE
ASSIGNEE: NONE

PATENT NUMBER: USD 153,514
PATENT FILED: DECEMBER 29, 1947
PATENT GRANTED: APRIL 26, 1949

April 26, 1949.

P. GANINE

Des. 153,514

TOY DUCK

Filed Dec. 29, 1947

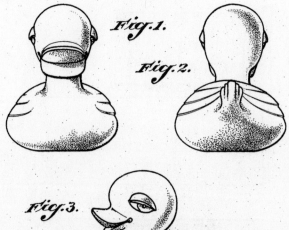

Fig.1.

Fig.2.

Fig.3.

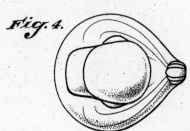

Fig.4.

INVENTOR:
PETER GANINE
BY HIS ATTORNEYS
HARRIS, KIECH, FOSTER & HARRIS,
BY

410

TITLE: CHILD'S SCOOTER
INVENTOR: RICHARD H. ARBIB
ASSIGNEE: UNITED STATES RUBBER COMPANY

PATENT NUMBER: USD 153,575
PATENT FILED: AUGUST 16, 1947
PATENT GRANTED: MAY 3, 1949

May 3, 1949.

R. H. ARBIB

Des. 153,575

CHILD'S SCOOTER

Filed Aug. 16, 1947

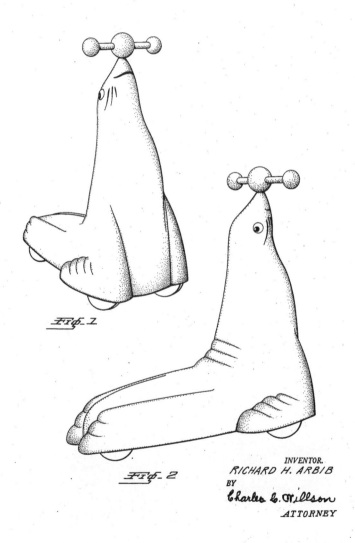

Fig. 1

Fig. 2

INVENTOR.
RICHARD H. ARBIB
BY
Charles C. Willson
ATTORNEY

411

TITLE: LOCOMOTIVE BODY
INVENTOR: RAY PATTEN
ASSIGNEE: GENERAL ELECTRIC COMPANY

PATENT NUMBER: USD 153,896
PATENT FILED: AUGUST 16, 1946
PATENT GRANTED: MAY 24, 1949

May 24, 1949.   R. PATTEN   Des. 153,896

LOCOMOTIVE BODY

Filed Aug. 16, 1946

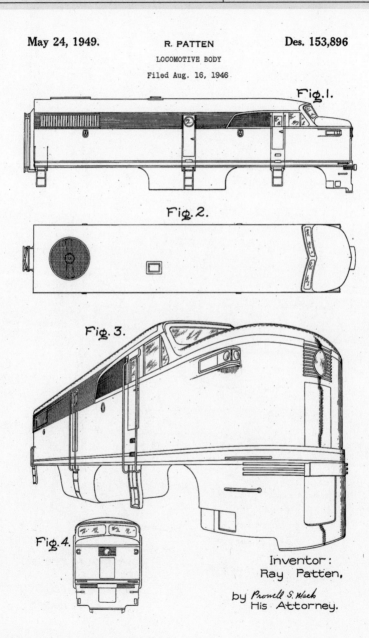

Fig.1.

Fig.2.

Fig.3.

Fig.4.

Inventor:
Ray Patten,

by *Prowell S. Wack*
His Attorney.

TITLE: TOASTER
INVENTOR: JEAN O. REINECKE
ASSIGNEE: MCGRAW ELECTRIC COMPANY

PATENT NUMBER: USD 153,901
PATENT FILED: JULY 9, 1946
PATENT GRANTED: MAY 24, 1949

May 24, 1949.   J. O. REINECKE   Des. 153,901

TOASTER

Filed July 9, 1946   3 Sheets—Sheet 1

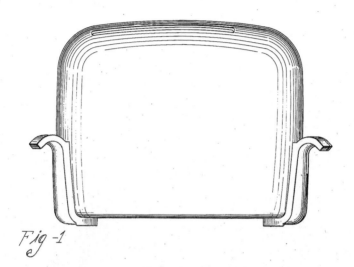

Fig-1

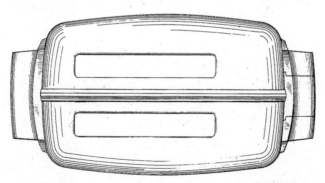

Fig-2

INVENTOR.
JEAN O. REINECKI
BY
ATTY

413

TITLE: WASHING MACHINE
INVENTOR: MELVIN H. BOLDT
ASSIGNEE: BENDIX HOME APPLIANCES

PATENT NUMBER: USD 153,920
PATENT FILED: JULY 31, 1948
PATENT GRANTED: MAY 31, 1949

May 31, 1949.

M. H. BOLDT

Des. 153,920

WASHING MACHINE

Filed July 31, 1948

INVENTOR.
MELVIN H. BOLDT.

BY

W. W. Green
ATTORNEY.

TITLE: DESK STAND FOR A HAND TELEPHONE
INVENTORS: HENRY DREYFUSS & ROBERT H. HOSE
ASSIGNEE: BELL TELEPHONE LABORATORIES

PATENT NUMBER: USD 153,927
PATENT FILED: FEBRUARY 11, 1948
PATENT GRANTED: MAY 31, 1949

May 31, 1949.   H. DREYFUSS ET AL   Des. 153,927

DESK STAND FOR A HAND TELEPHONE

Filed Feb. 11, 1948

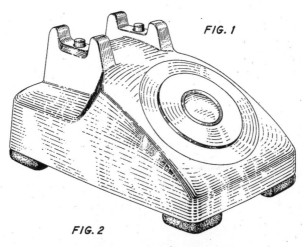

FIG. 1

FIG. 2

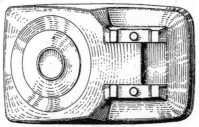

FIG. 3

INVENTORS H. DREYFUSS
            R. H. HOSE
        BY

        ATTORNEY

TITLE: AUTOMOBILE
INVENTOR: PRESTON T. TUCKER
ASSIGNEE: TUCKER CORPORATION

PATENT NUMBER: USD 154,192
PATENT FILED: MARCH 15, 1947
PATENT GRANTED: JUNE 14, 1949

June 14, 1949.

P. T. TUCKER

Des. 154,192

AUTOMOBILE

Filed March 15, 1947

3 Sheets—Sheet 1

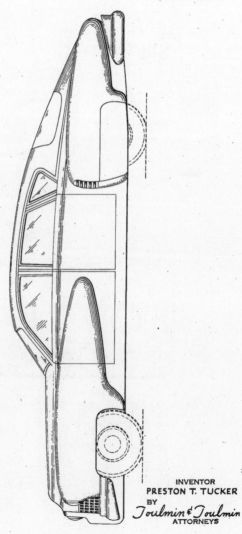

FIG. 1

INVENTOR
PRESTON T. TUCKER
BY
Toulmin & Toulmin
ATTORNEYS

416

TITLE: AIRPLANE
INVENTORS: EDWARD H. HEINEMANN & LEO J. DEVLIN
ASSIGNEE: DOUGLAS AIRCRAFT COMPANY

PATENT NUMBER: USD 154,273
PATENT FILED: DECEMBER 6, 1947
PATENT GRANTED: JUNE 28, 1949

June 28, 1949.   E. H. HEINEMANN ET AL   Des. 154,273

AIRPLANE

Filed Dec. 6, 1947   2 Sheets—Sheet 1

Fig. 1

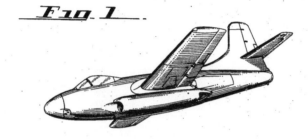

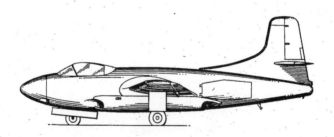

Fig. 2

INVENTORS
EDWARD H. HEINEMANN
AND LEO J. DEVLIN

BY J. Edwin Coates

ATTORNEY

417

TITLE: ELECTRIC IRON
INVENTOR: CLARENCE KARSTADT
ASSIGNEE: BIRTMAN ELECTRIC COMPANY

PATENT NUMBER: USD 154,278
PATENT FILED: FEBRUARY 28, 1947
PATENT GRANTED: JUNE 28, 1949

June 28, 1949.   C. KARSTADT   Des. 154,278

ELECTRIC IRON

Filed Feb. 28, 1947   2 Sheets—Sheet 1

Fig. 1.

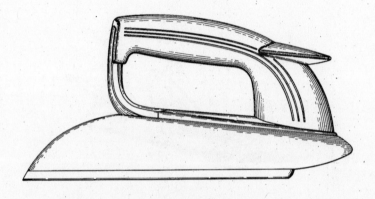

Fig. 2.

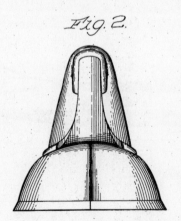

Inventor:
Clarence Karstadt,
By Christler, Schraeder, Merriam & Hofgren,
Attys.

TITLE: PITCHER
INVENTOR: EARL S. TUPPER
ASSIGNEE: NONE

PATENT NUMBER: USD 154,348
PATENT FILED: OCTOBER 5, 1946
PATENT GRANTED: JUNE 28, 1949

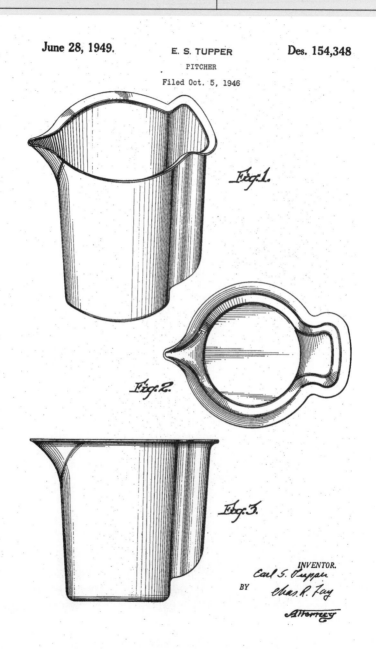

June 28, 1949.

E. S. TUPPER

PITCHER

Filed Oct. 5, 1946

Des. 154,348

Fig.1.

Fig.2.

Fig.3.

INVENTOR.
Earl S. Tupper

BY Chas. R. Fay

Attorney

TITLE: HOUSEHOLD WEIGHING SCALE
INVENTOR: CHARLES T. WALTER
ASSIGNEE: NONE

PATENT NUMBER: USD 154,446
PATENT FILED: JULY 9, 1947
PATENT GRANTED: JULY 5, 1949

July 5, 1949.

C. T. WALTER

Des. 154,446

HOUSEHOLD WEIGHING SCALE

Filed July 9, 1947

Fig. 1

Fig. 2

Fig. 3

INVENTOR.
Charles T. Walter,
BY Brown, Jackson,
Boettcher & Dienner
attys.

420

TITLE: ROOM COOLER OF THE WINDOW TYPE
INVENTORS: LURELLE GUILD & HARPER LANDELL
ASSIGNEE: CARRIER CORPORATION

PATENT NUMBER: USD 154,605
PATENT FILED: OCTOBER 10, 1947
PATENT GRANTED: JULY 26, 1949

July 26, 1949.   L. GUILD ET AL   Des. 154,605

ROOM COOLER OF THE WINDOW TYPE

Filed Oct. 10, 1947

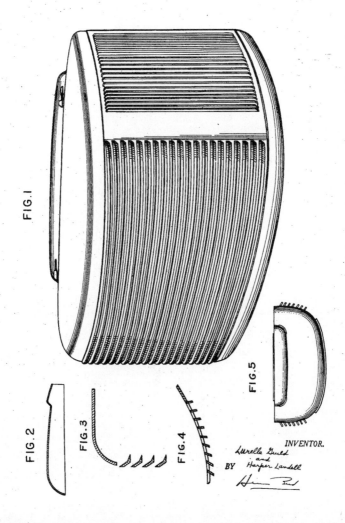

FIG. 1

FIG. 2

FIG. 3

FIG. 4

FIG. 5

INVENTOR.

Lurelle Guild
and
BY Harper Landell

421

TITLE: INTEROFFICE COMMUNICATION CABINET
INVENTOR: JOSEPH PALMA, JR.
ASSIGNEE: THE RAULAND CORPORATION

PATENT NUMBER: USD 154,626
PATENT FILED: OCTOBER 20, 1947
PATENT GRANTED: JULY 26, 1949

July 26, 1949.

J. PALMA, JR
INTEROFFICE COMMUNICATION CABINET
OR SIMILAR ARTICLE
Filed Oct. 20, 1947

Des. 154,626

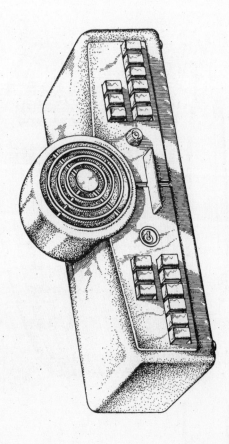

Inventor

JOSEPH PALMA, JR.

By

Attorney

422

TITLE: BUS
INVENTOR: ERIC P. RAMSTRUM
ASSIGNEE: NONE

PATENT NUMBER: USD 154,806
PATENT FILED: OCTOBER 15, 1947
PATENT GRANTED: AUGUST 9, 1949

Aug. 9, 1949.　　　　E. P. RAMSTRUM　　　**Des. 154,806**

BUS

Filed Oct. 15, 1947

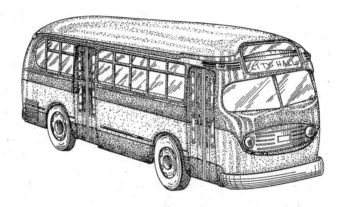

FIG. 1.

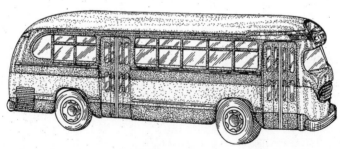

FIG. 2.

E. P. RAMSTRUM
INVENTOR.

BY E. C. McRae
J. R. Faulkner
T. H. Oster

ATTORNEYS

TITLE: CHAIR
INVENTOR: CHARLES EAMES
ASSIGNEE: EVANS PRODUCTS COMPANY

PATENT NUMBER: USD 155,272
PATENT FILED: MARCH 27, 1947
PATENT GRANTED: SEPTEMBER 20, 1949

Sept. 20, 1949.   C. EAMES   Des. 155,272

CHAIR

Filed March 27, 1947.

Fig.1

Fig.2

Fig.4

Fig.3

Inventor

Charles Eames

By

Lyon+Lyon Attorneys

424

TITLE: COFFEE MAKER
INVENTOR: PETER MULLER-MUNK
ASSIGNEE: THE HARTFORD PRODUCTS CORPORATION

PATENT NUMBER: USD 156,147
PATENT FILED: SEPTEMBER 5, 1947
PATENT GRANTED: NOVEMBER 22, 1949

Nov. 22, 1949   P. MULLER-MUNK   Des. 156,147

COFFEE MAKER

Filed Sept. 5, 1947

Fig.1.

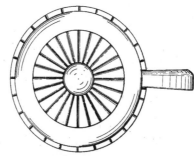

Fig.2.

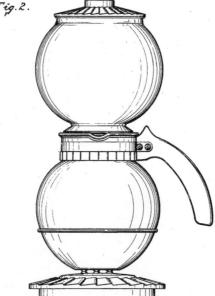

INVENTOR.
Peter Muller-Munk
BY

Louis V. Lucia
ATTORNEY

425

TITLE: MOTOR BICYCLE
INVENTOR: CORRADINO D'ASCANIO
ASSIGNEE: PIAGGIO

PATENT NUMBER: USD 156,609
PATENT FILED: JUNE 19, 1947
PATENT GRANTED: DECEMBER 27, 1949

Dec. 27, 1949

C. D'ASCANIO

MOTOR BICYCLE

Des. 156,609

Filed June 19, 1947

2 Sheets—Sheet 1

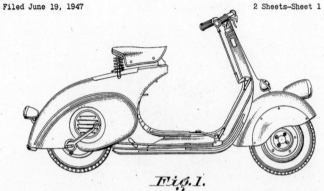

Fig.1.

Fig.2.

Inventor:
Corradino D'ascanio

By Richardson, David and Nordon
Attorneys

426

TITLE: VENDING MACHINE
INVENTOR: CHARLES L. METZLER
ASSIGNEE: ROWE MANUFACTURING COMPANY

PATENT NUMBER: USD 156,647
PATENT FILED: DECEMBER 30, 1947
PATENT GRANTED: DECEMBER 27, 1949

Dec. 27, 1949

C. L. METZLER

Des. 156,647

VENDING MACHINE

Filed Dec. 30, 1947

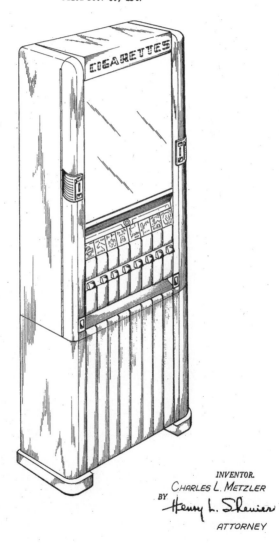

INVENTOR.
CHARLES L. METZLER
BY Henry L. Shevier
ATTORNEY

TITLE: SHOPPING CART
INVENTOR: GEORGE W. CONCKLIN
ASSIGNEE: JOHN CHATILLON & SONS

PATENT NUMBER: USD 156,702
PATENT FILED: JUNE 10, 1948
PATENT GRANTED: JANUARY 3, 1950

Jan. 3, 1950   G. W. CONCKLIN   Des. 156,702

SHOPPING CART OR SIMILAR ARTICLE

Filed June 10, 1948   2 Sheets—Sheet 1

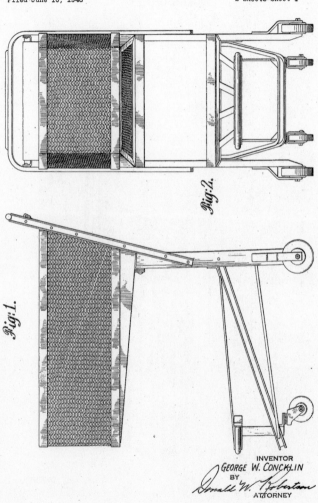

Fig: 2.

Fig: 1.

INVENTOR
GEORGE W. CONCKLIN
BY
Donald W. Robertson
ATTORNEY

TITLE: DISHWASHER CABINET OR THE LIKE
INVENTOR: ELMER H. DANIELS
ASSIGNEE: KAISER FLEETWINGS

PATENT NUMBER: USD 157,240
PATENT FILED: SEPTEMBER 19, 1947
PATENT GRANTED: FEBRUARY 14, 1950

Feb. 14, 1950　　　　E. H. DANIELS　　　　**Des. 157,240**

DISHWASHER CABINET OR THE LIKE

Filed Sept. 19, 1947

INVENTOR.
ELMER H. DANIELS.

BY

James E. Tooney

ATTORNEY

TITLE: AIR CIRCULATOR
INVENTOR: JOSEPH PALMA, JR.
ASSIGNEE: CORY CORPORATION

PATENT NUMBER: USD 157,406
PATENT FILED: NOVEMBER 23, 1948
PATENT GRANTED: FEBRUARY 21, 1950

Feb. 21, 1950

J. PALMA, JR

AIR CIRCULATOR

Des. 157,406

Filed Nov. 23, 1948

2 Sheets—Sheet 1

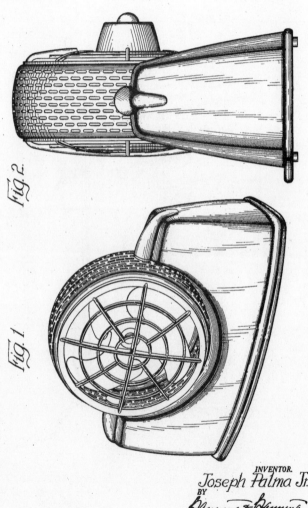

Fig. 2

Fig. 1

INVENTOR.
Joseph Palma Jr.
BY
Blaming & Blaming
Attys:

430

TITLE: ELECTRIC HAND & HAIR DRYER
INVENTORS: GEORGE S. CLEMENS & JAMES TEAGUE
ASSIGNEE: NONE

PATENT NUMBER: USD 157,739
PATENT FILED: MARCH 1, 1949
PATENT GRANTED: MARCH 21, 1950

March 21, 1950   G. S. CLEMENS ET AL   Des. 157,739

ELECTRIC HAND AND HAIR DRIER

Filed March 1, 1949

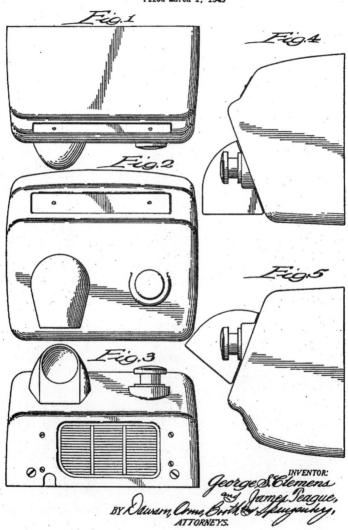

Fig.1

Fig.2

Fig.3

Fig.4

Fig.5

INVENTOR:
George S. Clemens
and James Teague,
BY Dawson, Orme, Broth & Shingauley,
ATTORNEYS.

TITLE: HAND SLED
INVENTOR: LOUIS VAVRIK
ASSIGNEE: KALAMAZOO SLED COMPANY

PATENT NUMBER: USD 158,158
PATENT FILED: DECEMBER 9, 1948
PATENT GRANTED: APRIL 11, 1950

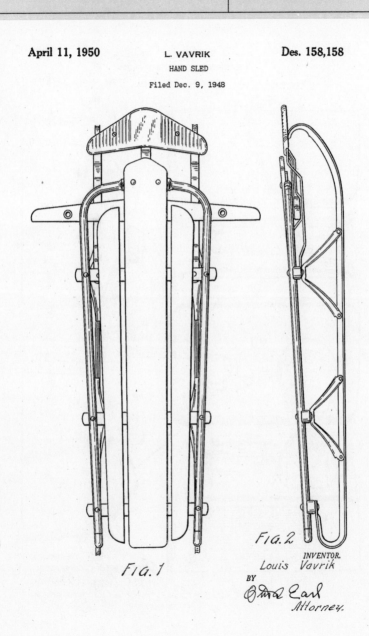

April 11, 1950

L. VAVRIK

HAND SLED

Filed Dec. 9, 1948

Des. 158,158

FIG. 1

FIG. 2

INVENTOR.
Louis Vavrik

BY

Attorney.

432

TITLE: CHAIR OR THE LIKE
INVENTOR: EERO SAARINEN
ASSIGNEE: KNOLL ASSOCIATES

PATENT NUMBER: USD 158,509
PATENT FILED: DECEMBER 22, 1948
PATENT GRANTED: MAY 9, 1950

May 9, 1950

E. SAARINEN

CHAIR OR THE LIKE

Des. 158,509

Filed Dec. 22, 1948

2 Sheets—Sheet 2

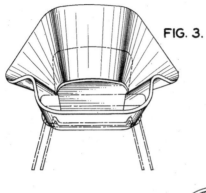

FIG. 3.

FIG. 4.

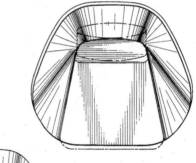

FIG. 5.

INVENTOR.
EERO SAARINEN

BY

ATTORNEY

TITLE: CABINET FOR A TELEVISION RECEIVER
INVENTORS: PETER SCHLADERMUNDT
& CHARLES L. METZLER
ASSIGNEE: AVCO MANUFACTURING CORPORATION

PATENT NUMBER: USD 158,618
PATENT FILED: APRIL 26, 1949
PATENT GRANTED: MAY 16, 1950

May 16, 1950   P. SCHLADERMUNDT ET AL   **Des. 158,618**

CABINET FOR A TELEVISION RECEIVER

Filed April 26, 1949   3 Sheets—Sheet 1

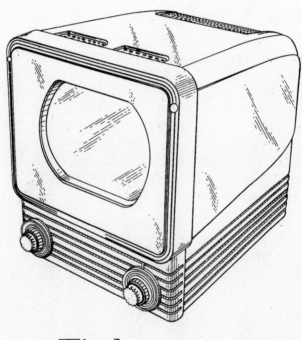

Fig. 1

INVENTORS.
PETER SCHLADERMUNDT.
CHARLES L. METZLER.
BY
Alden D. Redfield,
Charles Marshall Hogan,
ATTYS.

434

TITLE: FOOD MIXER
INVENTOR: WILLIAM F. BISLEY
ASSIGNEE: DORMEYER CORPORATION

PATENT NUMBER: USD 158,835
PATENT FILED: JULY 5, 1947
PATENT GRANTED: JUNE 6, 1950

June 6, 1950   W. F. BISLEY   Des. 158,835

FOOD MIXER

Filed July 5, 1947   2 Sheets—Sheet 1

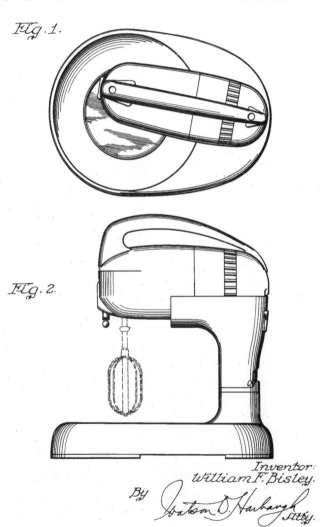

Fig. 1.

Fig. 2.

Inventor:
William F. Bisley.

By

Watson D. Harbaugh
Atty.

435

TITLE: RAILWAY OBSERVATION CAR
INVENTOR: CLIFFORD BROOKS STEVENS
ASSIGNEE: NONE

PATENT NUMBER: USD 159,107
PATENT FILED: FEBRUARY 4, 1949
PATENT GRANTED: JUNE 20, 1950

June 20, 1950   C. B. STEVENS   Des. 159,107

RAILWAY OBSERVATION CAR

Filed Feb. 4, 1949   2 Sheets—Sheet 1

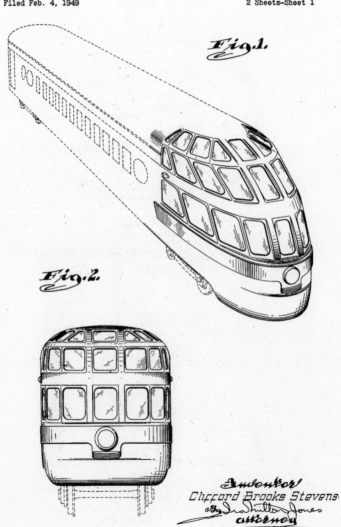

Fig.1.

Fig.2.

Inventor
Clifford Brooks Stevens
attorney

TITLE: SPECTACLE FRAME OR THE LIKE
INVENTOR: SEVERIN JONASSEN
ASSIGNEE: AMERICAN OPTICAL COMPANY

PATENT NUMBER: USD 159,346
PATENT FILED: DECEMBER 16, 1948
PATENT GRANTED: JULY 18, 1950

July 18, 1950   S. JONASSEN   Des. 159,346

SPECTACLE FRAME OR THE LIKE

Filed Dec. 16, 1948

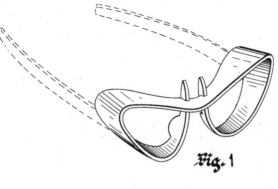

Fig. 1

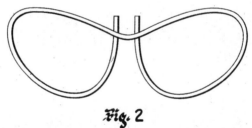

Fig. 2

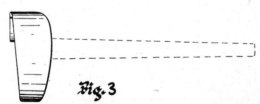

Fig. 3

INVENTOR.
SEVERIN JONASSEN

BY

Louis L. Gagnon

ATTORNEY

437

TITLE: FAN
INVENTOR: FORD SEBASTIAN
ASSIGNEE: CHICAGO ELECTRIC
MANUFACTURING COMPANY

PATENT NUMBER: USD 160,023
PATENT FILED: DECEMBER 20, 1949
PATENT GRANTED: SEPTEMBER 5, 1950

Sept. 5, 1950   F. SE BASTIAN   Des. 160,023

FAN

Filed Dec. 20, 1949

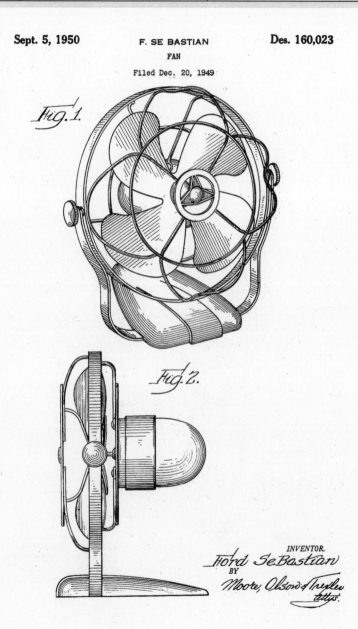

Fig. 1.

Fig. 2.

INVENTOR.
Ford SeBastian
BY
Moore, Olson & Trexler
attys.

438

TITLE: SLIDE PROJECTOR
INVENTOR: KENNETH A. VAN DYCK
ASSIGNEE: EASTMAN KODAK COMPANY

PATENT NUMBER: USD 160,040
PATENT FILED: JUNE 17, 1950
PATENT GRANTED: SEPTEMBER 5, 1950

Sept. 5, 1950   K. A. VAN DYCK   Des. 160,040

SLIDE PROJECTOR

Filed June 17, 1950

FIG. 1

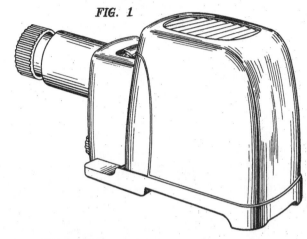

FIG. 2

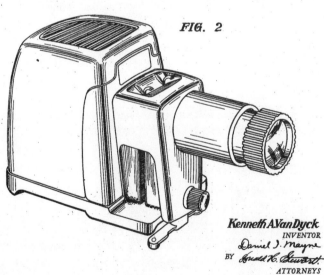

Kenneth A.Van Dyck
INVENTOR
Daniel J. Mayne
BY *Gerald H. Stewart*
ATTORNEYS

TITLE: COACH
INVENTOR: ALBERT A. BOCA
ASSIGNEE: GENERAL MOTORS CORPORATION

PATENT NUMBER: USD 160,059
PATENT FILED: MARCH 4, 1950
PATENT GRANTED: SEPTEMBER 12, 1950

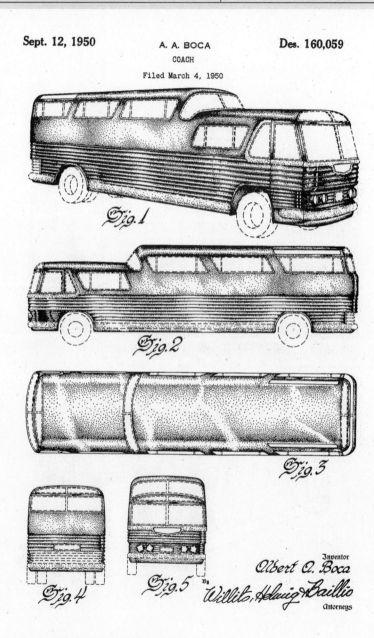

Sept. 12, 1950　　　A. A. BOCA　　　Des. 160,059

COACH

Filed March 4, 1950

Fig.1

Fig.2

Fig.3

Fig.4　Fig.5

Inventor
Albert A. Boca
Willits, Helwig & Baillio
Attorneys

440

TITLE: FLOOR LAMP
INVENTOR: GRETA MAGNUSSON GROSSMAN
ASSIGNEE: NONE

PATENT NUMBER: USD 160,084
PATENT FILED: DECEMBER 24, 1949
PATENT GRANTED: SEPTEMBER 12, 1950

Sept. 12, 1950

G. M. GROSSMAN

Des. 160,084

FLOOR LAMP

Filed Dec. 24, 1949

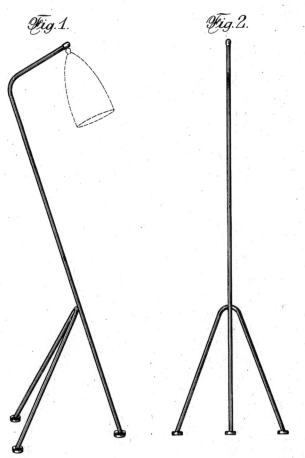

Fig.1.

Fig.2.

Inventor
GRETA MAGNUSSON GROSSMAN
By
C. G. Stratton
Attorney

441

TITLE: TYPEWRITER
INVENTORS: NORMAN BEL GEDDES & ELIOT F. NOYES
ASSIGNEE: INTERNATIONAL BUSINESS
MACHINES CORPORATION

PATENT NUMBER: USD 160,139
PATENT FILED: JANUARY 8, 1949
PATENT GRANTED: SEPTEMBER 19, 1950

Sept. 19, 1950   N. BEL GEDDES ET AL   Des. 160,139

TYPEWRITER

Filed Jan. 8, 1949

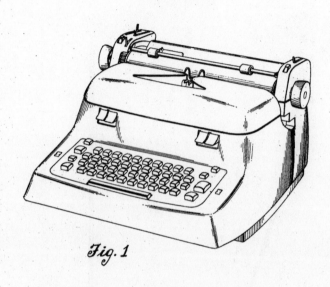

Fig. 1

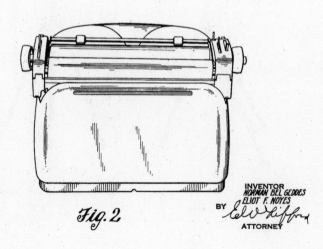

Fig. 2

INVENTOR
NORMAN BEL GEDDES
ELIOT F. NOYES
BY
ATTORNEY

TITLE: TELEVISION RECEIVER CABINET
INVENTOR: WILLIAM H. CLINGMAN
ASSIGNEE: AVCO MANUFACTURING CORPORATION

PATENT NUMBER: USD 160,474
PATENT FILED: APRIL 27, 1950
PATENT GRANTED: OCTOBER 17, 1950

Oct. 17, 1950   W. H. CLINGMAN   Des. 160,474

TELEVISION RECEIVER CABINET

Filed April 27, 1950

INVENTOR.
WILLIAM H. CLINGMAN
BY
Alden E. Redfield
Charles M. Rosen
ATTORNEYS.

TITLE: CABINET FOR A RADIO RECEIVER
INVENTOR: CARL REYNOLDS, JR.
ASSIGNEE: AVCO MANUFACTURING CORPORATION

PATENT NUMBER: USD 160,538
PATENT FILED: APRIL 20, 1950
PATENT GRANTED: OCTOBER 17, 1950

Oct. 17, 1950   C. REYNOLDS, JR   Des. 160,538

CABINET FOR A RADIO RECEIVER

Filed April 20, 1950

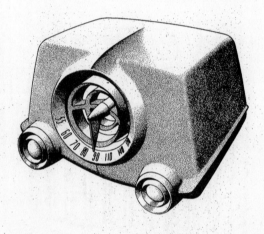

INVENTOR.

CARL REYNOLDS JR.

BY

Algin D. Redfield
Charles M. Logan

ATTORNEYS.

444

TITLE: ELECTRIC HAND MIXER
INVENTOR: JOSEPH PALMA, JR.
ASSIGNEE: NONE

PATENT NUMBER: USD 160,655
PATENT FILED: OCTOBER 7, 1949
PATENT GRANTED: OCTOBER 24, 1950

Oct. 24, 1950

J. PALMA, JR

Des. 160,655

ELECTRIC HAND MIXER

Filed Oct. 7, 1949

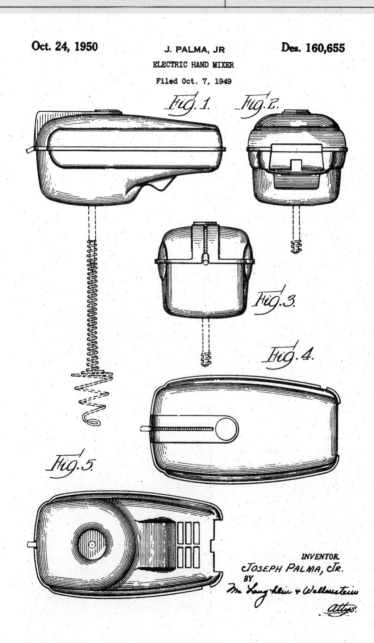

Fig. 1.

Fig. 2.

Fig. 3.

Fig. 4.

Fig. 5.

INVENTOR.
JOSEPH PALMA, JR.
BY
Mc Laughlin & Wallenstein
Attys.

TITLE: COMBINED ASH TRAY & SNUFFER
INVENTOR: ERIC WEDEMEYER
ASSIGNEE: HAMILTON ART METAL CORPORATION

PATENT NUMBER: USD 160,676
PATENT FILED: OCTOBER 29, 1949
PATENT GRANTED: OCTOBER 24, 1950

Oct. 24, 1950   E. WEDEMEYER   Des. 160,676

COMBINED ASH TRAY AND SNUFFER

Filed Oct. 29, 1949

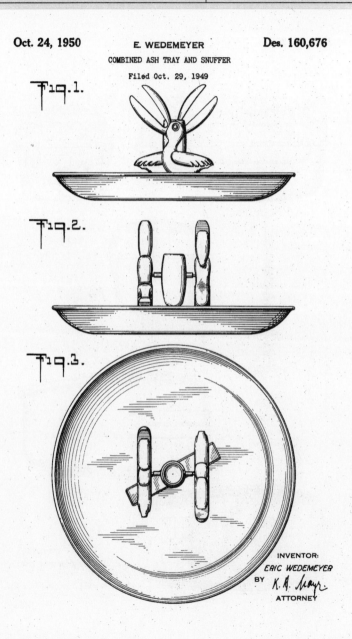

Fig.1.

Fig.2.

Fig.3.

INVENTOR:
ERIC WEDEMEYER
BY K. A. Mayr
ATTORNEY

TITLE: ELECTRIC SHAVER
INVENTOR: CARL L. OTTO
ASSIGNEE: SCHICK INCORPORATED

PATENT NUMBER: USD 160,805
PATENT FILED: JUNE 16, 1950
PATENT GRANTED: NOVEMBER 7, 1950

Nov. 7, 1950

C. L. OTTO

Des. 160,805

ELECTRIC SHAVER

Filed June 16, 1950

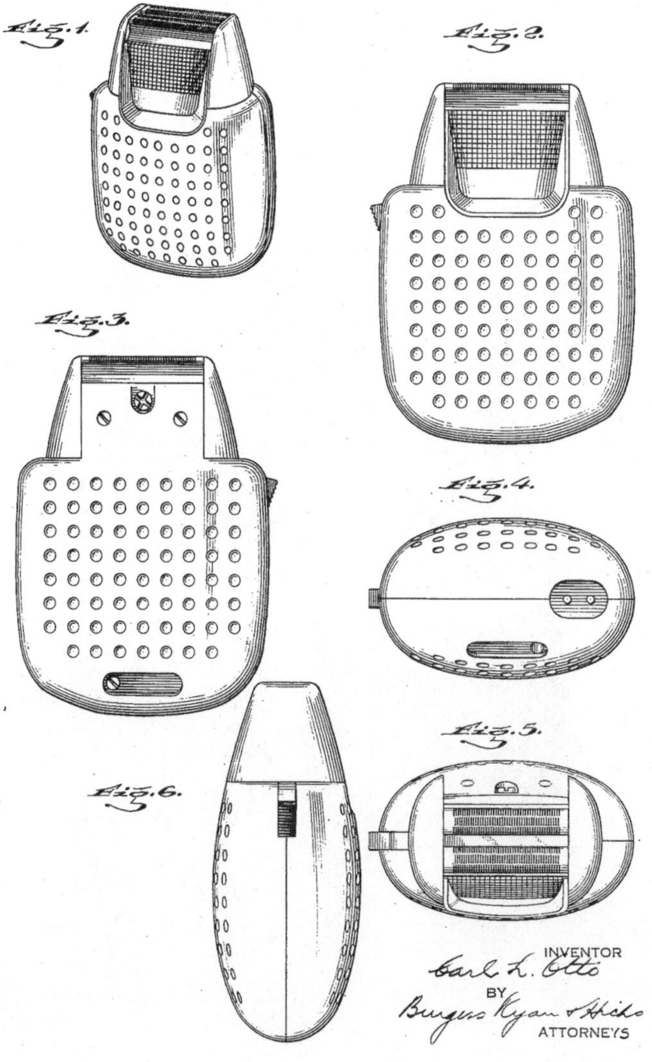

Fig. 1.

Fig. 2.

Fig. 3.

Fig. 4.

Fig. 5.

Fig. 6.

INVENTOR
Carl L. Otto
BY
Burgess Ryan & Hicks
ATTORNEYS

TITLE: CAMERA
INVENTOR: ARTHUR H. CRAPSEY, JR.
ASSIGNEE: EASTMAN KODAK COMPANY

PATENT NUMBER: USD 160,926
PATENT FILED: OCTOBER 27, 1949
PATENT GRANTED: NOVEMBER 21, 1950

Nov. 21, 1950

A. H. CRAPSEY, JR

CAMERA

Des. 160,926

Filed Oct. 27, 1949

2 Sheets—Sheet 1

FIG. 1.

FIG. 2.

ARTHUR H. CRAPSEY, JR.
INVENTOR

Daniel I. Mayne
BY Donald H. Stewart
ATTORNEYS

448

TITLE: BARBECUE GRILL
INVENTOR: A. BAKER BARNHART
ASSIGNEE: MODERN CARPET SWEEPER COMPANY

PATENT NUMBER: USD 161,080
PATENT FILED: JANUARY 21, 1950
PATENT GRANTED: DECEMBER 5, 1950

Dec. 5, 1950

A. B. BARNHART

Des. 161,080

BARBECUE GRILL

Filed Jan. 21, 1950

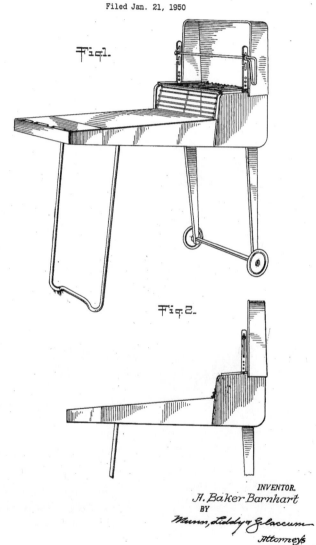

Fig.1.

Fig.2.

INVENTOR.
A. Baker Barnhart
BY
Munn, Liddy & Glaccum
Attorneys

TITLE: TOASTER
INVENTORS: IVAR JEPSON & ROBERT DAVOL BUDLONG
ASSIGNEE: SUNBEAM CORPORATION

PATENT NUMBER: USD 161,266
PATENT FILED: MARCH 24, 1950
PATENT GRANTED: DECEMBER 19, 1950

Dec. 19, 1950   I. JEPSON ET AL   Des. 161,266

TOASTER

Filed March 24, 1950   2 Sheets—Sheet 1

Fig. 1

INVENTORS
Ivar Jepson
Robert Davol Budlong
By *McCenna & Morsbach*
ATTYS.

450

TITLE: RAZOR
INVENTORS: PETER MULLER-MUNK &
CHARLES DELAFONTAINE
ASSIGNEE: REELSHAV CORPORATION

PATENT NUMBER: USD 161,779
PATENT FILED: SEPTEMBER 6, 1950
PATENT GRANTED: JANUARY 30, 1951

Jan. 30, 1951   P. MULLER-MUNK ET AL   Des. 161,779

RAZOR

Filed Sept. 6, 1950

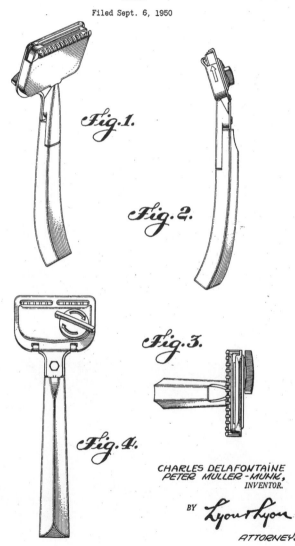

Fig.1.

Fig.2.

Fig.3.

Fig.4.

CHARLES DELAFONTAINE
PETER MULLER-MUNK,
INVENTOR.

BY *Lyon Lyon*

ATTORNEYS

TITLE: BOTTLE
INVENTOR: DONALD DESKEY
ASSIGNEE: PROCTER & GAMBLE

PATENT NUMBER: USD 161,825
PATENT FILED: MARCH 17, 1950
PATENT GRANTED: FEBRUARY 6, 1951

Feb. 6, 1951   D. DESKEY   Des. 161,825

BOTTLE

Filed March 17, 1950

FIG.1.

FIG.2.

FIG.3.

FIG.4.

INVENTOR.
DONALD DESKEY,
BY Allen & Allen

ATTORNEYS.

452

TITLE: MOTION-PICTURE CAMERA
INVENTOR: FREDERICK G. KNOWLES
ASSIGNEE: EASTMAN KODAK COMPANY

PATENT NUMBER: USD 161,940
PATENT FILED: AUGUST 5, 1950
PATENT GRANTED: FEBRUARY 13, 1951

Feb. 13, 1951

F. G. KNOWLES
MOTION-PICTURE CAMERA

Des. 161,940

Filed Aug. 5, 1950

2 Sheets—Sheet 1

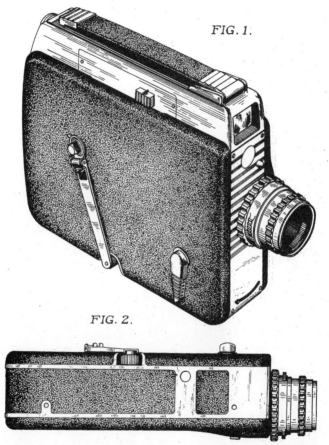

FIG. 1.

FIG. 2.

FREDERICK G. KNOWLES
INVENTOR

BY *Daniel J. Mayne*
Budd C. Stewart.
ATTORNEYS

TITLE: RADIO CABINET
INVENTORS: CARL W. SUNDBERG & MONTGOMERY FERAR
ASSIGNEE: SYLVANIA ELECTRIC PRODUCTS

PATENT NUMBER: USD 162,899
PATENT FILED: JANUARY 3, 1951
PATENT GRANTED: APRIL 10, 1951

April 10, 1951   C. W. SUNDBERG ET AL   Des. 162,899

RADIO CABINET

Filed Jan. 3, 1951

Fig.1

Fig. 2

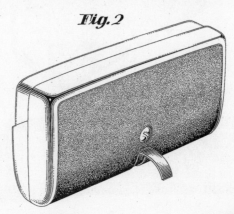

INVENTORS
CARL W. SUNDBERG
MONTGOMERY FERAR
BY *John A. Harvey*
ATTORNEY

TITLE: CLOCK
INVENTOR: GEORGE W. NELSON
ASSIGNEE: HOWARD MILLER CLOCK COMPANY

PATENT NUMBER: USD 162,976
PATENT FILED: MARCH 20, 1950
PATENT GRANTED: APRIL 17, 1951

April 17, 1951   G. W. NELSON   Des. 162,976

CLOCK

Filed March 20, 1950

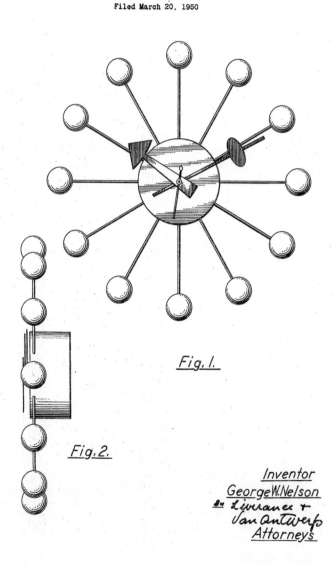

Fig. 1.

Fig. 2.

Inventor
George W. Nelson
By Livrance &
Van Antwerp
Attorneys

TITLE: CONTAINER FOR DAIRY PRODUCTS
AND SOFT DRINKS
INVENTOR: PETER MULLER-MUNK
ASSIGNEE: OTTO MILK COMPANY

PATENT NUMBER: USD 163,132
PATENT FILED: MARCH 24, 1948
PATENT GRANTED: MAY 1, 1951

May 1, 1951   P. MULLER-MUNK   Des. 163,132

CONTAINER FOR DAIRY PRODUCTS AND SOFT DRINKS

Filed March 24, 1948

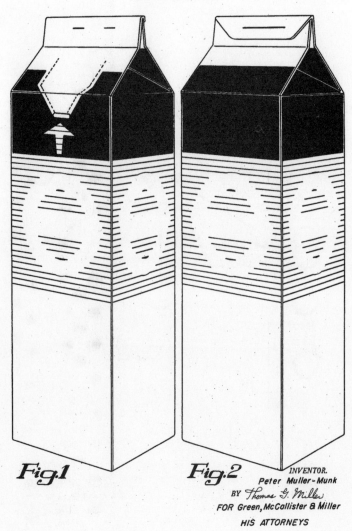

Fig.1   Fig.2

INVENTOR.
Peter Muller-Munk
BY *Thomas G. Miller*
FOR Green, McCallister & Miller
HIS ATTORNEYS

TITLE: CLOCKCASE OR SIMILAR ARTICLE
INVENTOR: JOSEPH F. PUNZAK
ASSIGNEE: UNITED METAL GOODS

PATENT NUMBER: USD 163,138
PATENT FILED: AUGUST 21, 1950
PATENT GRANTED: MAY 1, 1951

May 1, 1951

J. F. PUNZAK

Des. 163,138

CLOCKCASE OR SIMILAR ARTICLE

Filed Aug. 21, 1950

INVENTOR

JOSEPH F. PUNZAK

BY *Fisher & Christen,*

ATTORNEYS

TITLE: AUTOMOTIVE VEHICLE HOOD ORNAMENT
INVENTOR: NED F. NICKLES
ASSIGNEE: GENERAL MOTORS CORPORATION

PATENT NUMBER: USD 163,473
PATENT FILED: FEBRUARY 3, 1950
PATENT GRANTED: MAY 29, 1951

May 29, 1951   N. F. NICKLES   Des. 163,473

AUTOMOTIVE VEHICLE HOOD ORNAMENT

Filed Feb. 3, 1950

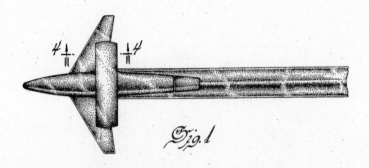

Fig. 1

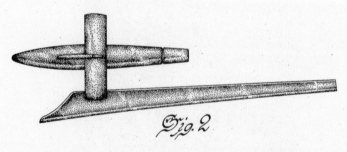

Fig. 2

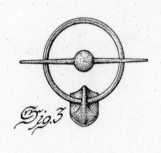

Fig. 3

Fig. 4

Inventor
Ned F. Nickles

By
Willits, Helmig & Baillie
Attorneys

458

TITLE: HOUSING FOR FLUID DISPENSING APPARATUS
INVENTOR: PETER MULLER-MUNK
ASSIGNEE: THE WAYNE PUMP COMPANY

PATENT NUMBER: USD 163,764
PATENT FILED: NOVEMBER 30, 1950
PATENT GRANTED: JUNE 26, 1951

June 26, 1951   P. MULLER-MUNK   Des. 163,764

HOUSING FOR FLUID DISPENSING APPARATUS

Filed Nov. 30, 1950

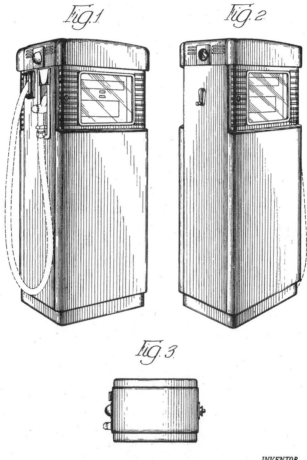

Fig.1   Fig. 2

Fig. 3

INVENTOR.
Peter Muller-Munk,
BY
Wilkinson, Husley, Byron Hume
attys.

TITLE: TABLE LAMP
INVENTOR: KURT VERSEN
ASSIGNEE: NONE

PATENT NUMBER: USD 164,886
PATENT FILED: DECEMBER 11, 1950
PATENT GRANTED: OCTOBER 16, 1951

Oct. 16, 1951   K. VERSEN   Des. 164,886

TABLE LAMP

Filed Dec. 11, 1950

Fig.1.

Fig.2.

INVENTOR.
Kurt Versen

BY *[signature]*

ATTORNEY.

TITLE: RAILWAY OBSERVATION CAR BODY
INVENTORS: ALFRED B. GIRARDY, DONALD W. DOMAN
& RALPH E. MEYERS
ASSIGNEE: PULLMAN-STANDARD CAR MANUFACTURING

PATENT NUMBER: USD 164,917
PATENT FILED: JANUARY 20, 1951
PATENT GRANTED: OCTOBER 23, 1951

Oct. 23, 1951   A. B. GIRARDY ET AL   Des. 164,917

RAILWAY OBSERVATION CAR BODY

Filed Jan. 20, 1951   3 Sheets—Sheet 1

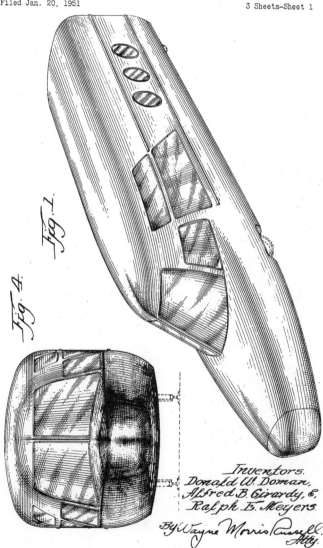

Fig. 1.

Fig. 4.

Inventors.
Donald W. Doman,
Alfred B. Girardy, &
Ralph E. Meyers.

By Wayne Morris Russell,
Atty.

461

TITLE: CLOCK
INVENTOR: ALAN E. KOPLAR
ASSIGNEE: NONE

PATENT NUMBER: USD 165,010
PATENT FILED: JULY 12, 1951
PATENT GRANTED: OCTOBER 30, 1951

Oct. 30, 1951   A. E. KOPLAR   Des. 165,010

CLOCK

Filed July 12, 1951

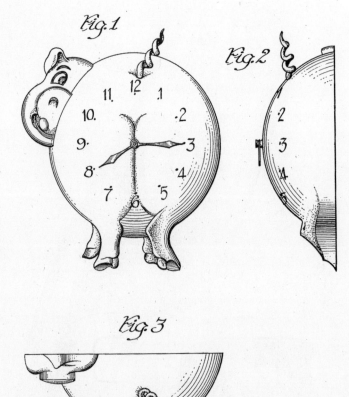

Fig. 1

Fig. 2

Fig. 3

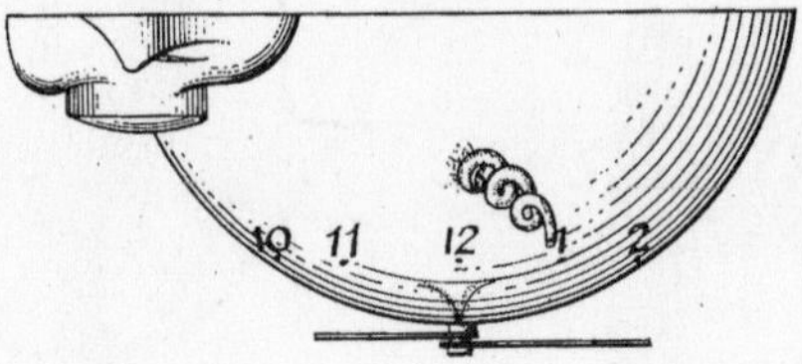

Inventor:
Alan E. Koplar,
by Wm F. Trendenreich, Atty.

TITLE: COMBINED CREAM & SUGAR VESSELS
& TRAY THEREFOR
INVENTOR: JOSEPH A. HILL
ASSIGNEE: NONE

PATENT NUMBER: USD 165,075
PATENT FILED: MAY 19, 1951
PATENT GRANTED: NOVEMBER 6, 1951

Nov. 6, 1951   J. A. HILL   Des. 165,075

COMBINED CREAM AND SUGAR VESSELS AND TRAY THEREFOR

Filed May 19, 1951   2 SHEETS—SHEET 1

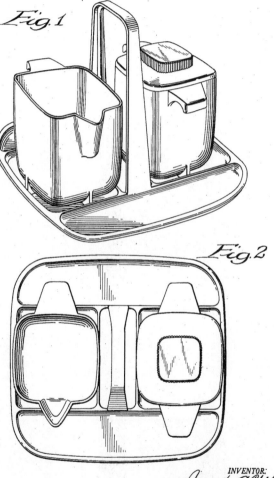

Fig. 1

Fig. 2

INVENTOR:
Joseph A. Hill.
BY
Dawson & Ooms,
ATTORNEYS.

463

TITLE: FLOOR LAMP
INVENTORS: JOHN M. GRAY & ELLIS G. REVNESS
ASSIGNEE: NONE

PATENT NUMBER: USD 165,226
PATENT FILED: AUGUST 4, 1951
PATENT GRANTED: NOVEMBER 20, 1951

Nov. 20, 1951   J. M. GRAY ET AL   Des. 165,226

FLOOR LAMP

Filed Aug. 4, 1951

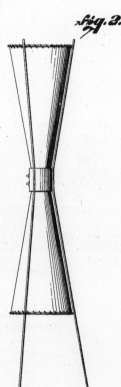

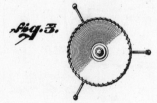

JOHN M. GRAY &
ELLIS G. REVNESS,
INVENTORS.

BY George J. Smyth.

ATTORNEY.

464

TITLE: TABLE LAMP
INVENTOR: KURT VERSEN
ASSIGNEE: NONE

PATENT NUMBER: USD 165,312
PATENT FILED: DECEMBER 11, 1950
PATENT GRANTED: NOVEMBER 27, 1951

Nov. 27, 1951

K. VERSEN

Des. 165,312

TABLE LAMP

Filed Dec. 11, 1950

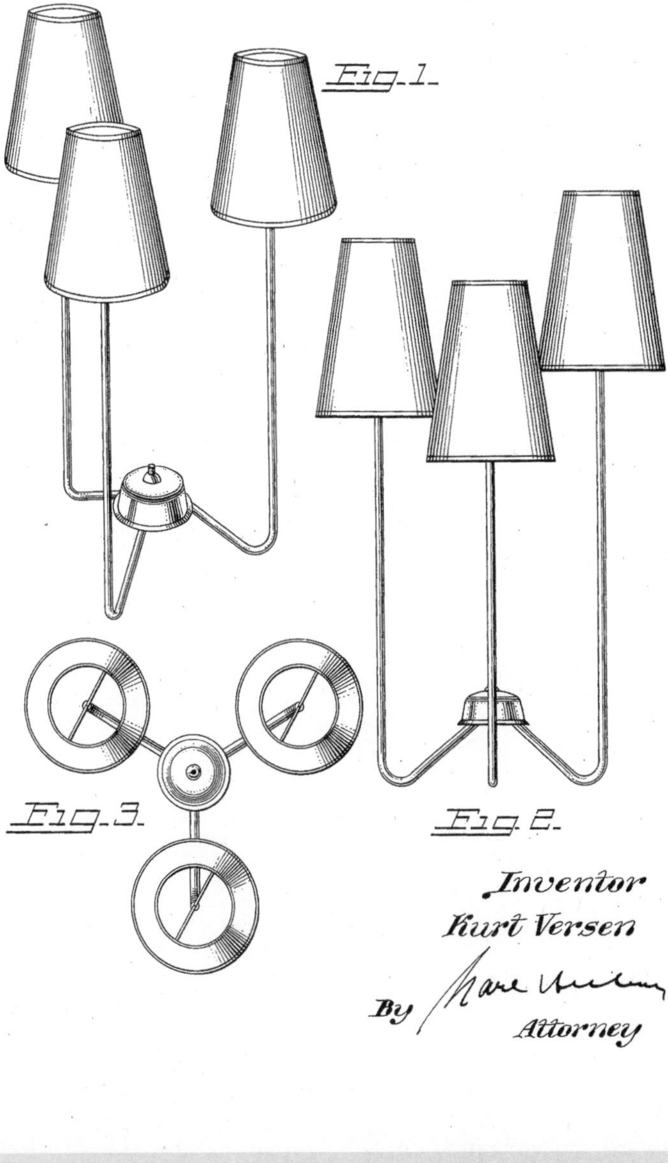

Fig. 1.

Fig. 3.

Fig. 2.

Inventor
Kurt Versen

By

Attorney

TITLE: COMBINED TELEVISION, RADIO,
& PHONOGRAPH CABINET OR SIMILAR ARTICLE
INVENTOR: JACK BAROFSKY
ASSIGNEE: NONE

PATENT NUMBER: USD 165,319
PATENT FILED: APRIL 20, 1951
PATENT GRANTED: DECEMBER 4, 1951

Dec. 4, 1951   J. BAROFSKY   Des. 165,319
COMBINED TELEVISION, RADIO, AND PHONOGRAPH
CABINET OR SIMILAR ARTICLE
Filed April 20, 1951   3 Sheets-Sheet 1

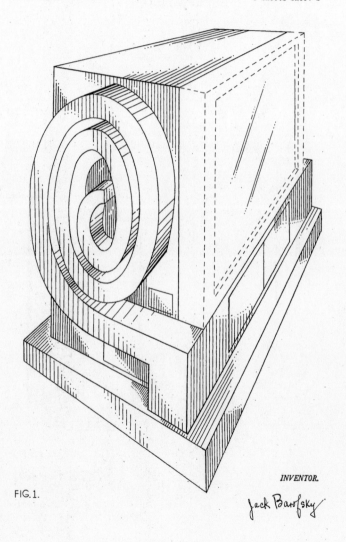

FIG. 1.

INVENTOR.

Jack Barofsky

TITLE: LAMP
INVENTOR: ANTHONY J. INGOLIA, JR.
ASSIGNEE: NONE

PATENT NUMBER: USD 165,652
PATENT FILED: MARCH 31, 1951
PATENT GRANTED: JANUARY 8, 1952

Jan. 8, 1952

A. J. INGOLIA, JR

Des. 165,652

LAMP

Filed March 31, 1951

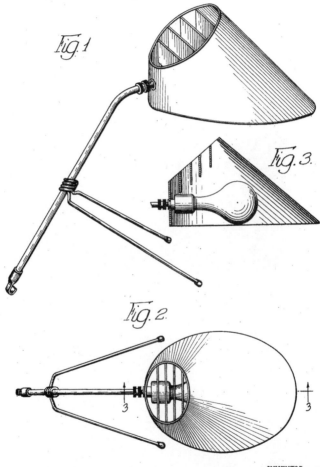

Fig. 1

Fig. 3.

Fig. 2

INVENTOR.
Anthony J. Ingolia, Jr.,
BY
Wilkinson, Huxley, Byron & Irons
attys.

467

TITLE: CLOCK-RADIO HOUSING
INVENTORS: CARL W. SUNDBERG & MONTGOMERY FERAR
ASSIGNEE: SYLVANIA ELECTRIC PRODUCTS

PATENT NUMBER: USD 165,704
PATENT FILED: DECEMBER 23, 1950
PATENT GRANTED: JANUARY 15, 1952

Jan. 15, 1952   C. W. SUNDBERG ET AL   Des. 165,704

CLOCK-RADIO HOUSING

Filed Dec. 23, 1950

INVENTORS
CARL W. SUNDBERG
MONTGOMERY FERAR
BY
ATTORNEY

468

TITLE: LAMP
INVENTOR: GILBERT A. WATROUS
ASSIGNEE: NONE

PATENT NUMBER: USD 165,806
PATENT FILED: MARCH 31, 1951
PATENT GRANTED: JANUARY 29, 1952

Jan. 29, 1952

G. A. WATROUS

Des. 165,806

LAMP

Filed March 31, 1951

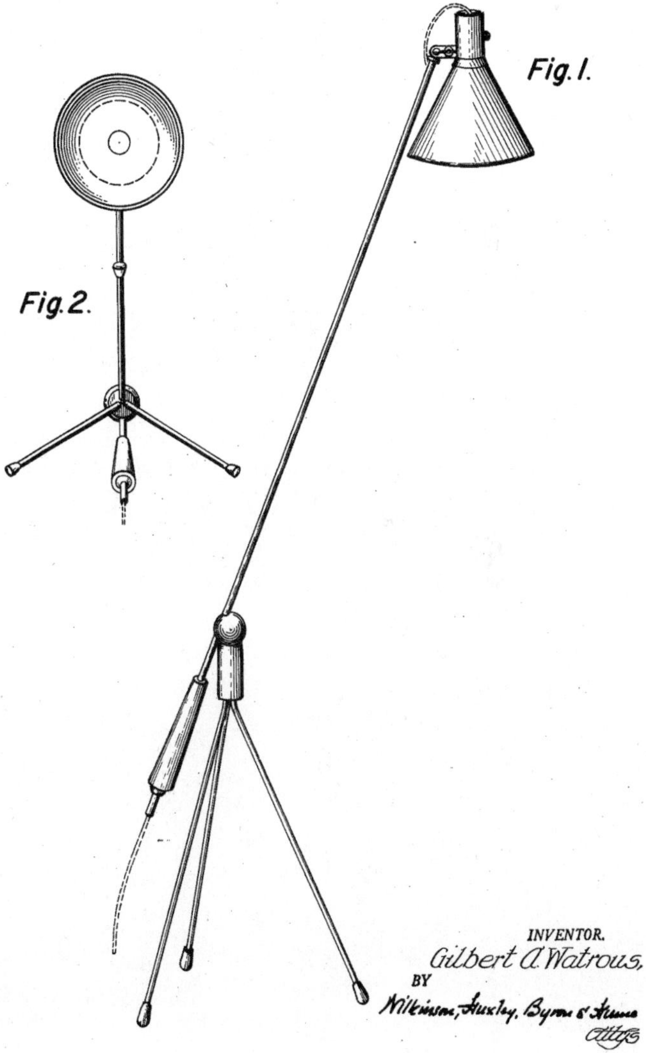

Fig. 1.

Fig. 2.

INVENTOR.
Gilbert A. Watrous,
BY
Wilkinson, Huxley, Byron & Hume
ATTYS.

TITLE: KNIFE
INVENTOR: RUSSEL WRIGHT
ASSIGNEE: NONE

PATENT NUMBER: USD 165,811
PATENT FILED: OCTOBER 25, 1950
PATENT GRANTED: JANUARY 29, 1952

Jan. 29, 1952   R. WRIGHT   Des. 165,811

KNIFE

Filed Oct. 25, 1950

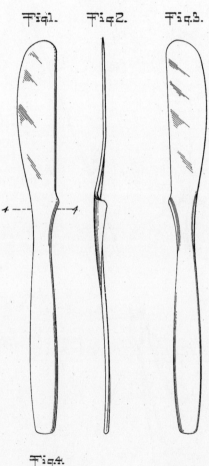

Fig1.   Fig2.   Fig3.

Fig4.

INVENTOR.

Russel Wright

BY

Munn, Liddy & Glaccum
Attorneys

TITLE: ELECTRIC IRON
INVENTOR: FRANCESCO COLLURA
ASSIGNEE: STEAM ELECTRIC PRODUCTS

PATENT NUMBER: USD 165,909
PATENT FILED: DECEMBER 12, 1950
PATENT GRANTED: FEBRUARY 12, 1952

Feb. 12, 1952

F. COLLURA

Des. 165,909

ELECTRIC IRON

Filed Dec. 12, 1950

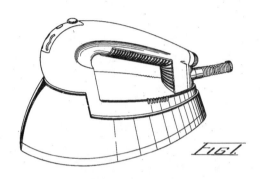

FIG.1

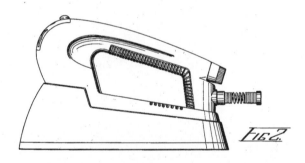

FIG.2

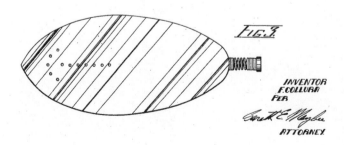

FIG.3

INVENTOR
F.COLLURA
PER

ATTORNEY

471

TITLE: COMBINED FOOD AND BEVERAGE
VENDING STATION
INVENTOR: CHARLES M. KEMPER
ASSIGNEE: NONE

PATENT NUMBER: USD 166,320
PATENT FILED: OCTOBER 26, 1950
PATENT GRANTED: APRIL 1, 1952

April 1, 1952   C. M. KEMPER   Des. 166,320

COMBINED FOOD AND BEVERAGE VENDING STATION

Filed Oct. 26, 1950   2 SHEETS—SHEET 1

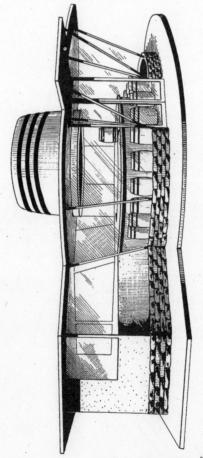

Fig. 1

INVENTOR

Charles M. Kemper

BY

Emery, Varney, Whittemore & Dix

ATTORNEYS

TITLE: CHAIR
INVENTOR: RAY KOMAI
ASSIGNEE: J. G. FURNITURE COMPANY

PATENT NUMBER: USD 166,397
PATENT FILED: FEBRUARY 23, 1950
PATENT GRANTED: APRIL 8, 1952

April 8, 1952   R. KOMAI   **Des. 166,397**

CHAIR

Filed Feb. 23, 1950

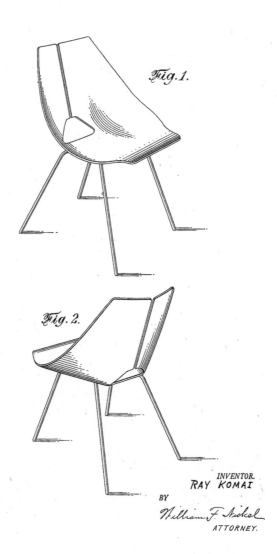

Fig.1.

Fig.2.

INVENTOR.
RAY KOMAI

BY

William F. Nickel

ATTORNEY.

473

TITLE: INTERVAL TIMER
INVENTORS: FREDERICK LUX & HELMUT D. BEERBAUM
ASSIGNEE: LUX CLOCK MANUFACTURING COMPANY

PATENT NUMBER: USD 166,764
PATENT FILED: JUNE 9, 1951
PATENT GRANTED: MAY 13, 1952

May 13, 1952

F. LUX ET AL

INTERVAL TIMER

Filed June 9, 1951

Des. 166,764

Fig.1

Fig.2

Fig.3

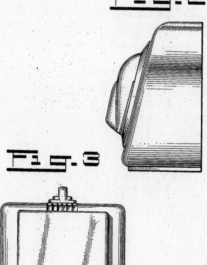

INVENTOR.
FREDERICK LUX
HELMUT D. BEERBAUM
BY

H. G. Manning

ATTORNEY

474

TITLE: POCKET KNIFE
INVENTOR: THOMAS R. ARDEN
ASSIGNEE: BARD-PARKER COMPANY

PATENT NUMBER: USD 166,900
PATENT FILED: MARCH 7, 1951
PATENT GRANTED: JUNE 3, 1952

June 3, 1952

T. R. ARDEN

Des. 166,900

POCKET KNIFE

Filed March 7, 1951

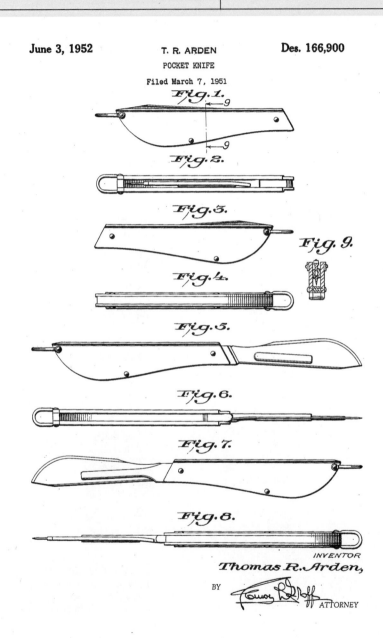

Fig. 1.

Fig. 2.

Fig. 3.

Fig. 9.

Fig. 4.

Fig. 5.

Fig. 6.

Fig. 7.

Fig. 8.

INVENTOR
Thomas R. Arden,
BY
ATTORNEY

TITLE: BOTTLE OR SIMILAR ARTICLE
INVENTOR: EDWARD RACHINS
ASSIGNEE: NONE

PATENT NUMBER: USD 166,995
PATENT FILED: FEBRUARY 14, 1950
PATENT GRANTED: JUNE 10, 1952

June 10, 1952   E. RACHINS   Des. 166,995

BOTTLE OR SIMILAR ARTICLE

Filed Feb. 14, 1950

Fig.1.

Fig.2

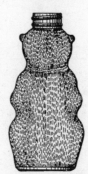

Fig.3.   Fig.4.

Inventor:
Edward Rachins,
by   Thomson & Thomson
Attorney

476

TITLE: COMBINATION CLOCK & RADIO
RECEIVER CABINET
INVENTOR: ROBERT D. BUDLONG
ASSIGNEE: ZENITH RADIO CORPORATION

PATENT NUMBER: USD 167,194
PATENT FILED: FEBRUARY 29, 1952
PATENT GRANTED: JULY 8, 1952

July 8, 1952   R. D. BUDLONG   Des. 167,194

COMBINATION CLOCK AND RADIO RECEIVER CABINET

Filed Feb. 29, 1952

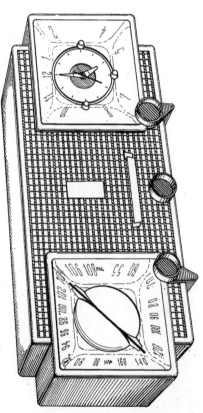

INVENTOR:
ROBERT D. BUDLONG
BY

HIS ATTORNEY.

TITLE: REFRIGERATOR CABINET
INVENTOR: MONTGOMERY FERAR
ASSIGNEE: SEEGER REFRIGERATOR COMPANY

PATENT NUMBER: USD 168,257
PATENT FILED: JULY 18, 1952
PATENT GRANTED: NOVEMBER 25, 1952

Nov. 25, 1952

M. FERAR

Des. 168,257

REFRIGERATOR CABINET

Filed July 18, 1952

2 SHEETS—SHEET 1

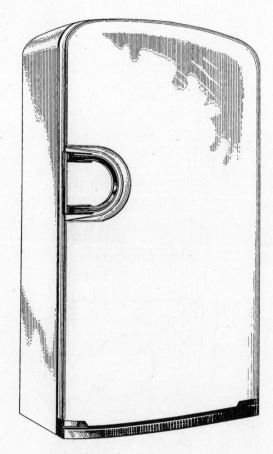

Fig.1.

INVENTOR.
Montgomery Ferar
BY Frank H. Marks
Nathan N. Kraus
ATTORNEYS

TITLE: MEASURING TAPE
INVENTOR: SIDNEY BLUM
ASSIGNEE: OXWALL TOOL COMPANY

PATENT NUMBER: USD 168,329
PATENT FILED: AUGUST 21, 1952
PATENT GRANTED: DECEMBER 9, 1952

Dec. 9, 1952

S. BLUM

Des. 168,329

MEASURING TAPE

Filed Aug. 21, 1952

Fig. 1.

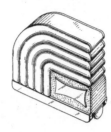

Fig. 2.

Fig. 3.

INVENTOR
SIDNEY BLUM.
BY
ATTORNEY

TITLE: ELECTRIC RANGE
INVENTOR: FOLKE M. GUSTAFSON
ASSIGNEE: AVCO MANUFACTURING CORPORATION

PATENT NUMBER: USD 168,893
PATENT FILED: DECEMBER 23, 1952
PATENT GRANTED: FEBRUARY 24, 1953

Feb. 24, 1953

F. M. GUSTAFSON

ELECTRIC RANGE

Filed Dec. 23, 1952

Des. 168,893

INVENTOR.

FOLKE M. GUSTAFSON.

BY *Alden D. Redfield*

Warren Kunz.

ATTORNEYS.

TITLE: RADIO CABINET
INVENTOR: ROBERT D. BUDLONG
ASSIGNEE: ZENITH RADIO CORPORATION

PATENT NUMBER: USD 169,054
PATENT FILED: FEBRUARY 29, 1952
PATENT GRANTED: MARCH 24, 1953

March 24, 1953

R. D. BUDLONG
RADIO CABINET

Des. 169,054

Filed Feb. 29, 1952

2 SHEETS—SHEET 1

Fig. 1

INVENTOR:
ROBERT D. BUDLONG
BY

HIS ATTORNEY.

TITLE: GUITAR
INVENTOR: CLARENCE L. FENDER
ASSIGNEE: NONE

PATENT NUMBER: USD 169,062
PATENT FILED: NOVEMBER 21, 1952
PATENT GRANTED: MARCH 24, 1953

March 24, 1953

C. L. FENDER

GUITAR

Filed Nov. 21, 1952

Des. 169,062

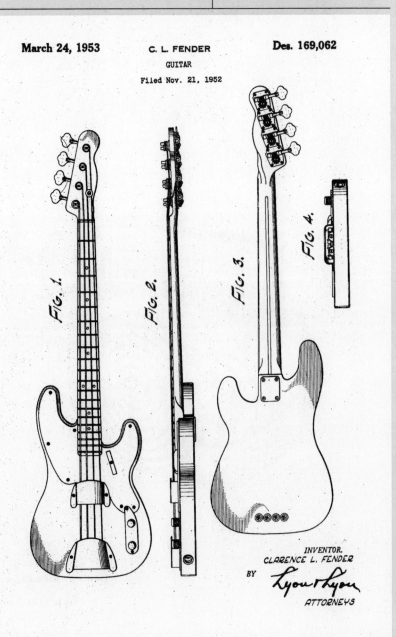

FIG. 1.

FIG. 2.

FIG. 3.

FIG. 4.

INVENTOR.
CLARENCE L. FENDER

BY

Lyon & Lyon

ATTORNEYS

TITLE: POGO STICK
INVENTOR: HARRY H. HOHBERGER
ASSIGNEE: NONE

PATENT NUMBER: USD 169,141
PATENT FILED: AUGUST 1, 1952
PATENT GRANTED: MARCH 31, 1953

March 31, 1953

H. H. HOHBERGER

Des. 169,141

POGO STICK

Filed Aug. 1, 1952

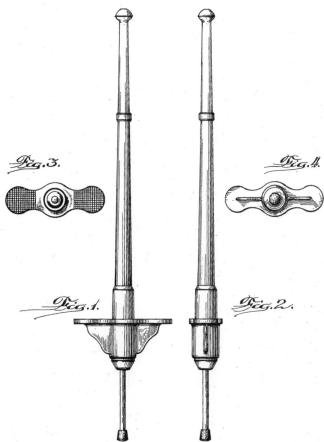

Fig.3. Fig.4. Fig.1. Fig.2.

Inventor:
Harry H. Hohberger
By Ahlberg, Hupper, & Gradolph
Attorneys.

TITLE: DESK
INVENTOR: FLORENCE S. KNOLL
ASSIGNEE: NONE

PATENT NUMBER: USD 169,320
PATENT FILED: JULY 30, 1952
PATENT GRANTED: APRIL 14, 1953

April 14, 1953　　　F. S. KNOLL　　　**Des. 169,320**

DESK

Filed July 30, 1952

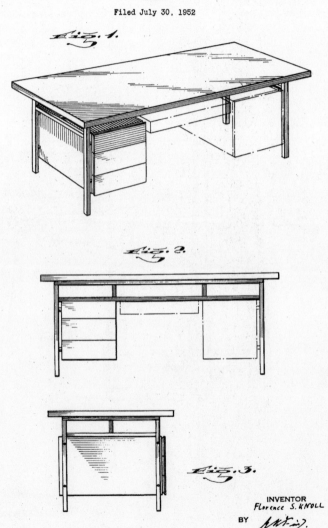

Fig. 1.

Fig. 2.

Fig. 3.

INVENTOR
Florence S. Knoll

BY

ATTORNEY

TITLE: BUILDING
INVENTOR: BENJAMIN F. BRITT
ASSIGNEE: NONE

PATENT NUMBER: USD 169,354
PATENT FILED: NOVEMBER 7, 1952
PATENT GRANTED: APRIL 21, 1953

April 21, 1953

B. F. BRITT

BUILDING

Des. 169,354

Filed Nov. 7, 1952

3 Sheets—Sheet 1

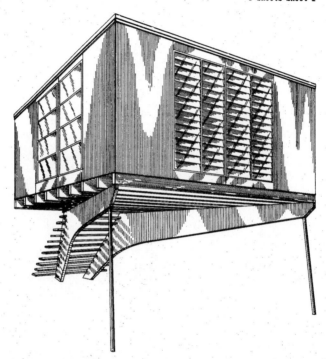

FIG. 1.

INVENTOR.
BENJAMIN F. BRITT,
BY

McMorrow, Berman & Davidson
ATTORNEYS

TITLE: TAPE DISPENSER
INVENTOR: JEAN OTIS REINECKE
ASSIGNEE: MINNESOTA MINING
& MANUFACTURING COMPANY

PATENT NUMBER: USD 169,989
PATENT FILED: JANUARY 24, 1952
PATENT GRANTED: JULY 7, 1953

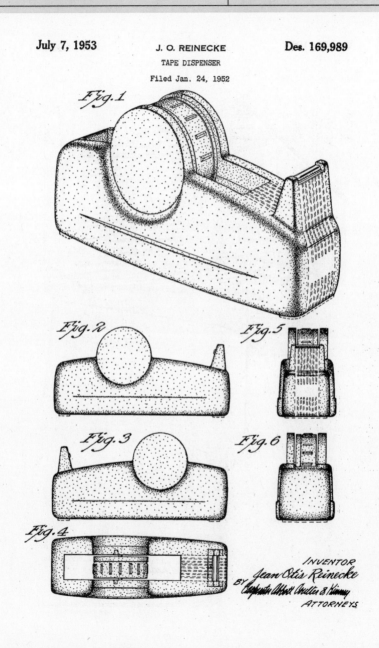

July 7, 1953

J. O. REINECKE

TAPE DISPENSER

Filed Jan. 24, 1952

Des. 169,989

Fig.1

Fig.2

Fig.5

Fig.3

Fig.6

Fig.4

INVENTOR
Jean Otis Reinecke
BY
ATTORNEYS

TITLE: TOY CAP PISTOL OR SIMILAR ARTICLE
INVENTOR: FREDERICK J. MAYWALD
ASSIGNEE: THE J. & E. STEVENS SALES COMPANY

PATENT NUMBER: USD 170,091
PATENT FILED: MARCH 9, 1953
PATENT GRANTED: JULY 28, 1953

July 28, 1953   F. J. MAYWALD   Des. 170,091

TOY CAP PISTOL OR SIMILAR ARTICLE

Filed March 9, 1953

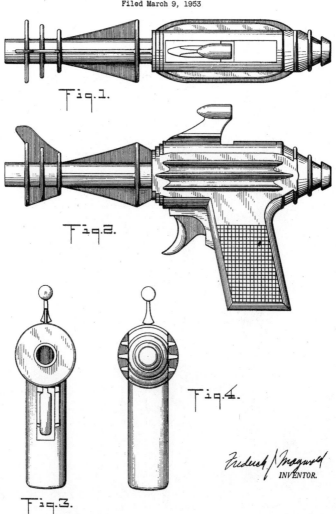

Fig.1.

Fig.2.

Fig.3.

Fig.4.

Frederick J. Maywald
INVENTOR.

TITLE: AUTOMOBILE
INVENTOR: GIOACCHINO COLOMBO
ASSIGNEE: ALFA ROMEO SOCIETÀ

PATENT NUMBER: USD 170,448
PATENT FILED: APRIL 7, 1953
PATENT GRANTED: SEPTEMBER 22, 1953

Sept. 22, 1953   G. COLOMBO   Des. 170,448

AUTOMOBILE

Filed April 7, 1953

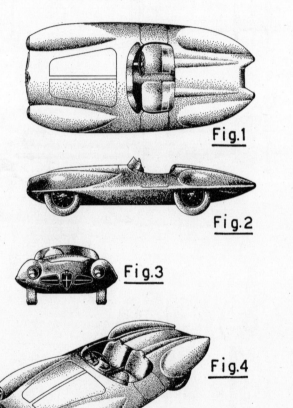

Fig.1

Fig.2

Fig.3

Fig.4

Inventor
G. Colombo
By Howard Downing Rubbel
Attys.

TITLE: DISH OR THE LIKE
INVENTOR: EVA ZEISEL
ASSIGNEE: MIDHURST CHINA COMPANY

PATENT NUMBER: USD 170,788
PATENT FILED: AUGUST 29, 1952
PATENT GRANTED: NOVEMBER 3, 1953

Nov. 3, 1953

E. ZEISEL

Des. 170,788

DISH OR THE LIKE

Filed Aug. 29, 1952

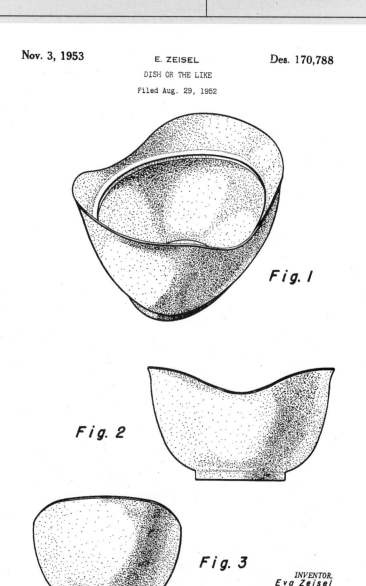

Fig. 1

Fig. 2

Fig. 3

INVENTOR.
Eva Zeisel

BY *Weill, Mackey & Burden*

HER ATTORNEYS

TITLE: CHAIR
INVENTOR: HARRY BERTOIA
ASSIGNEE: KNOLL ASSOCIATES

PATENT NUMBER: USD 170,790
PATENT FILED: JULY 23, 1952
PATENT GRANTED: NOVEMBER 10, 1953

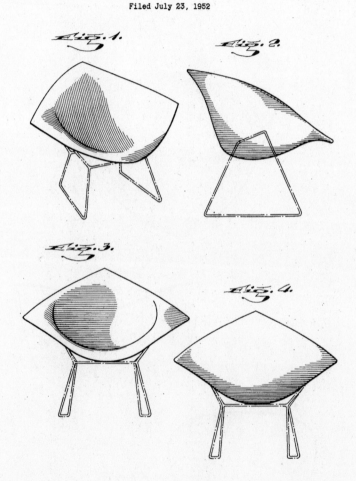

Nov. 10, 1953

H. BERTOIA

CHAIR

Filed July 23, 1952

Des. 170,790

Fig. 1.

Fig. 2.

Fig. 3.

Fig. 4.

INVENTOR
HARRY BERTOIA
BY
ATTORNEY

TITLE: BARBECUE BRAZIER
INVENTOR: JEAN O. REINECKE
ASSIGNEE: MELL-HOFFMANN MANUFACTURING COMPANY

PATENT NUMBER: USD 170,943
PATENT FILED: MARCH 20, 1953
PATENT GRANTED: NOVEMBER 24, 1953

Nov. 24, 1953

J. O. REINECKE

Des. 170,943

BARBECUE BRAZIER

Filed March 20, 1953

INVENTOR.
Jean O. Reinecke
BY
Moore, Olson & Trexler
Attys.

TITLE: AUTOMOTIVE VEHICLE
INVENTOR: CARL G. MAYER
ASSIGNEE: OSCAR MAYER & COMPANY

PATENT NUMBER: USD 171,550
PATENT FILED: SEPTEMBER 27, 1952
PATENT GRANTED: FEBRUARY 23, 1954

Feb. 23, 1954

C. G. MAYER

Des. 171,550

AUTOMOTIVE VEHICLE

Filed Sept. 27, 1952

Fig.1

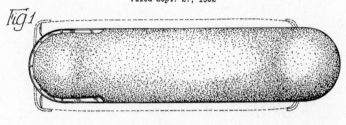

Fig.2

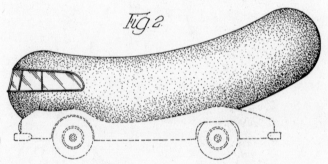

Fig.3

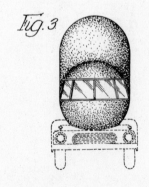

Fig.4

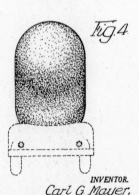

INVENTOR.
Carl G. Mayer,
BY
Cromwell, Greist & Warden
Attys.

492

TITLE: COMBINATION CIGARETTE LIGHTER
AND POCKET KNIFE
INVENTOR: EMIL S. POLK
ASSIGNEE: NONE

PATENT NUMBER: USD 172,725
PATENT FILED: JANUARY 11, 1954
PATENT GRANTED: JULY 27, 1954

July 27, 1954   E. S. POLK   **Des. 172,725**

COMBINATION CIGARETTE LIGHTER AND POCKET KNIFE

Filed Jan. 11, 1954

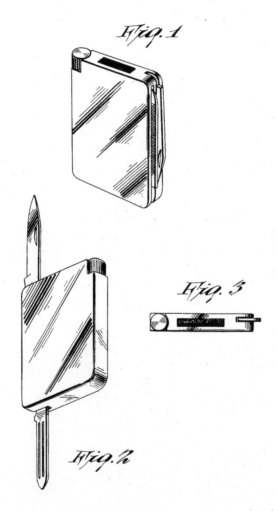

Fig. 1

Fig. 3

Fig. 2

493

TITLE: PAIR OF SPECTACLES
INVENTOR: WALTER DORWIN TEAGUE
ASSIGNEE: POLAROID CORPORATION

PATENT NUMBER: USD 172,730
PATENT FILED: JULY 30, 1953
PATENT GRANTED: JULY 27, 1954

July 27, 1954

W. D. TEAGUE

Des. 172,730

PAIR OF SPECTACLES

Filed July 30, 1953

FIG. I

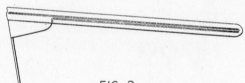

FIG. 2

FIG. 3

INVENTOR

Walter Dorwin Teague

BY *Brown and Mikulka*

ATTORNEYS

494

TITLE: HEIGHT-ADJUSTABLE FLOOR LAMP
INVENTOR: ARTHUR F. JACOBS
ASSIGNEE: BERNARD ROBERTS

PATENT NUMBER: USD 172,792
PATENT FILED: MARCH 8, 1954
PATENT GRANTED: AUGUST 10, 1954

Aug. 10, 1954   A. F. JACOBS   Des. 172,792

HEIGHT-ADJUSTABLE FLOOR LAMP

Filed March 8, 1954

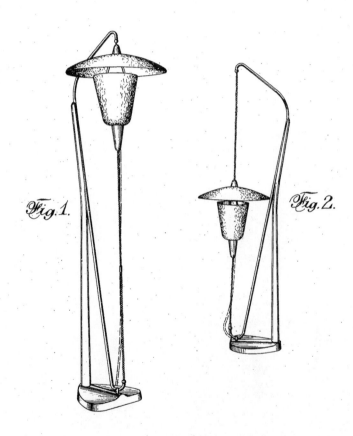

Fig.1.   *Fig.2.*

Inventor

ARTHUR F. JACOBS

By   C. F. Stratton

Attorney

495

TITLE: FORK
INVENTOR: JEAN O. REINECKE
ASSIGNEE: GEORGE W. EMMERT

PATENT NUMBER: USD 172,805
PATENT FILED: FEBRUARY 17, 1954
PATENT GRANTED: AUGUST 10, 1954

Aug. 10, 1954

J. O. REINECKE

Des. 172,805

FORK

Filed Feb. 17, 1954

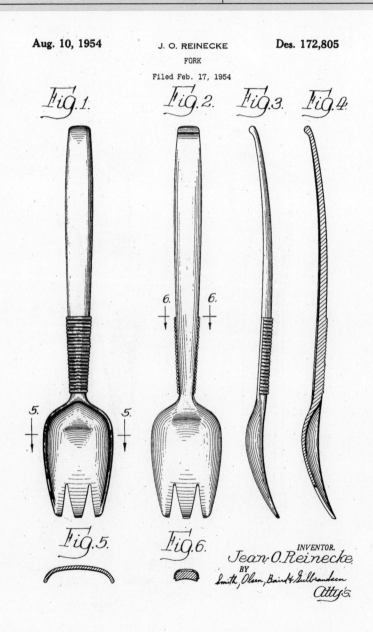

Fig.1. *Fig.2.* *Fig.3.* *Fig.4.*

6. 6.

5. 5.

Fig.5. *Fig.6.*

INVENTOR.
Jean O. Reinecke
BY
Smith, Olson, Baird & Gullbrandsen
Attys.

TITLE: AUTOMATIC TIMER
INVENTOR: CHAUNCEY E. WALTMAN
ASSIGNEE: INTERNATIONAL REGISTER COMPANY

PATENT NUMBER: USD 172,911
PATENT FILED: DECEMBER 1, 1953
PATENT GRANTED: AUGUST 24, 1954

Aug. 24, 1954

C. E. WALTMAN

Des. 172,911

AUTOMATIC TIMER

Filed Dec. 1, 1953

Fig. 1

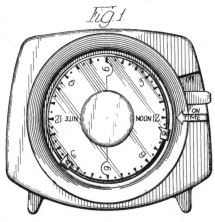

Fig. 2

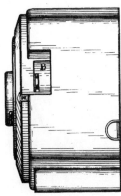

Fig. 3

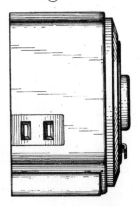

INVENTOR.
Chauncey E. Waltman,
BY Brown, Jackson,
Boettcher & Drenner
Attys.

497

TITLE: TELEVISION LAMP
INVENTOR: FRANK PETTY
ASSIGNEE: PHIL-MAR CORPORATION

PATENT NUMBER: USD 172,984
PATENT FILED: DECEMBER 29, 1953
PATENT GRANTED: SEPTEMBER 7, 1954

Sept. 7, 1954

F. PETTY

TELEVISION LAMP

Des. 172,984

Filed Dec. 29, 1953

2 Sheets—Sheet 1

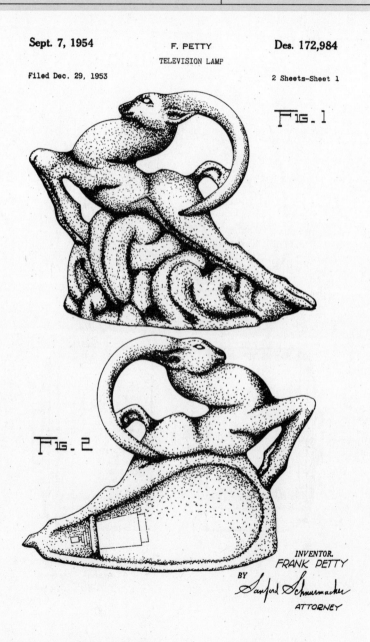

Fig. 1

Fig. 2

INVENTOR.
FRANK PETTY
BY
Sanford Schumacher
ATTORNEY

498

TITLE: HANDLE FOR CUTLERY OR THE LIKE
INVENTOR: THOMAS LAMB
ASSIGNEE: NONE

PATENT NUMBER: USD 173,115
PATENT FILED: DECEMBER 4, 1953
PATENT GRANTED: SEPTEMBER 28, 1954

Sept. 28, 1954   T. LAMB   Des. 173,115

HANDLE FOR CUTLERY OR THE LIKE

Filed Dec. 4, 1953

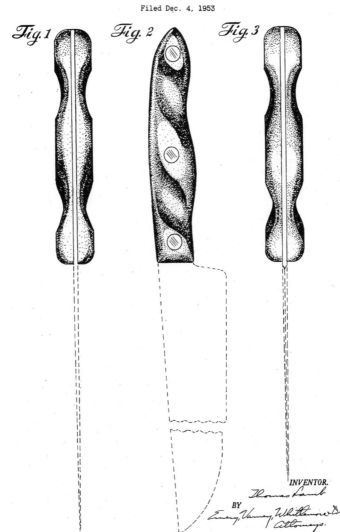

Fig. 1 *Fig. 2* *Fig. 3*

INVENTOR.
Thomas Lamb
BY
Emery, Varney, Whittemore & Dix
Attorneys.

TITLE: COFFEE MAKER OR SIMILAR ARTICLE
INVENTOR: ROBERT D. BUDLONG
ASSIGNEE: CORY CORPORATION

PATENT NUMBER: USD 173,143
PATENT FILED: MARCH 5, 1953
PATENT GRANTED: OCTOBER 5, 1954

Oct. 5, 1954   R. D. BUDLONG   Des 173,143

COFFEE MAKER OR SIMILAR ARTICLE

Filed March 5, 1953

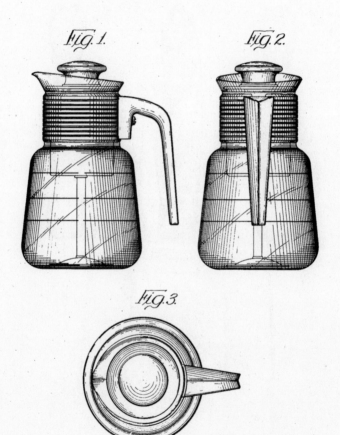

Fig. 1.   *Fig. 2.*

Fig. 3.

INVENTOR.
Robert D. Budlong
BY
Schneider, Mariani,
Hofgren & Beroby   Attys.

TITLE: CLOCK
INVENTOR: LEO I. BRUCE
ASSIGNEE: GENERAL ELECTRIC COMPANY

PATENT NUMBER: USD 173,142
PATENT FILED: MAY 13, 1954
PATENT GRANTED: OCTOBER 5, 1954

Oct. 5, 1954   L. I. BRUCE   **Des 173,142**

CLOCK

Filed May 13, 1954

Inventor:

Leo I. Bruce

by, *Richard E. Hosley*

His Attorney

501

TITLE: DECORATIVE ANIMATED LAMP
INVENTOR: AUBREY B. LEECH
ASSIGNEE: ECONOLITE CORPORATION

PATENT NUMBER: USD 173,621
PATENT FILED: MAY 18, 1954
PATENT GRANTED: DECEMBER 7, 1954

United States Patent Office

Des. 173,621
Patented Dec. 7, 1954

173,621

DECORATIVE ANIMATED LAMP

Aubrey B. Leech, Los Angeles, Calif., assignor to Econolite Corporation, Los Angeles, Calif., a corporation of
California

Application May 18, 1954, Serial No. 30,544

Term of patent 14 years

(Cl. D48—20)

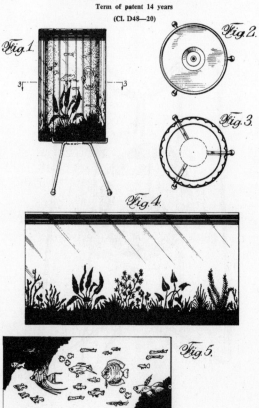

    Be it known that I, Aubrey B. Leech, a citizen of the
United States of America, residing in Los Angeles, county of Los Angeles, and State of California, have invented
a new, original, and ornamental Design for a Decorative Animated Lamp, of which the following is a specification, reference being had to the accompanying drawing, forming part thereof.

    Fig. 1 is a side elevational view of a decorative ani-
mated lamp, showing my new design.

    Fig. 2 is a top plan view thereof.

    Fig. 3 is a cross-sectional view as taken on the plane
of line 3—3 of Fig. 1.

    Fig. 4 is a panoramic view of the outer cylinder.

    Fig. 5 is a panoramic view of the inner cylinder.

I claim:

    The ornamental design for a decorative animated lamp,
substantially as shown.

References Cited in the file of this patent

UNITED STATES PATENTS

Number	Name	Date
D. 156,441	Leech	Dec. 13, 1949
1,333,454	Sato	Mar. 9, 1920

OTHER REFERENCES

Washington (D. C.) Sunday "Star," Nov. 23, 1952,
Woodward and Lothrup advertisement section, page 22,
item 22Q.

TITLE: HOUSEHOLD MIXER
INVENTORS: ALFRED W. MADL & JOSEPH A. HILL
ASSIGNEE: JOHN OSTER MANUFACTURING COMPANY

PATENT NUMBER: USD 173,624
PATENT FILED: MAY 10, 1954
PATENT GRANTED: DECEMBER 7, 1954

United States Patent Office

Des. 173,624
Patented Dec. 7, 1954

173,624

HOUSEHOLD MIXER

Alfred W. Madl, Milwaukee, Wis., and Joseph A. Hill,
Glen Ellyn, Ill., assignors to John Oster Manufacturing
Co., Milwaukee, Wis., a corporation of Wisconsin

Application May 10, 1954, Serial No. 30,390

Term of patent 14 years

(Cl. D44—1)

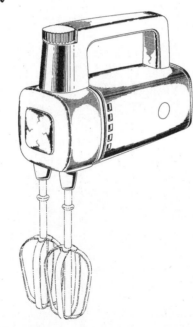

TITLE: TELEVISION RECEIVER CABINET
INVENTOR: ROBERT D. BUDLONG
ASSIGNEE: ZENITH RADIO CORPORATION

PATENT NUMBER: USD 174,109
PATENT FILED: OCTOBER 19, 1954
PATENT GRANTED: MARCH 1, 1955

United States Patent Office

Des. 174,109
Patented Mar. 1, 1955

174,109

TELEVISION RECEIVER CABINET

Robert D. Budlong, Skokie, Ill., assignor to Zenith Radio
Corporation, a corporation of Illinois

Application October 19, 1954, Serial No. 32,713

Term of patent 7 years

(Cl. D56—4)

FIG. 1

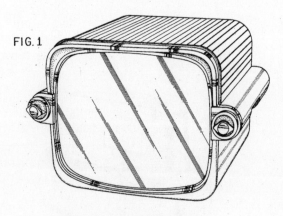

FIG. 2

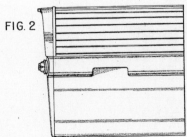

To all whom it may concern:

Be it known that I, Robert D. Budlong, a citizen of the United States, residing at Skokie, in the county of Cook, State of Illinois, have invented a new, original, and ornamental Design for a Television Receiver Cabinet, of which the following is a specification, reference being made to the accompanying drawings, forming a part hereof.

Figure 1 is a perspective view of a television receiver cabinet showing my new design;

Figure 2 is a side elevational view of the television receiver cabinet.

The side of the receiver cabinet not shown is similar to the side shown in Figure 1, and the rear of the cabinet is unornamented.

I claim:

The ornamental design for a television receiver cabinet, substantially as shown and described.

References Cited in the file of this patent

UNITED STATES PATENTS

D. 156,919	Schubert et al.	Jan. 17, 1950
D. 166,047	Portanova	Feb. 26, 1952

TITLE: BILLIARD TABLE
INVENTOR: WILLIAM H. GUNKLACH
ASSIGNEE: NATIONAL BILLIARD
MANUFACTURING COMPANY

PATENT NUMBER: USD 174,550
PATENT FILED: MAY 21, 1953
PATENT GRANTED: APRIL 26, 1955

United States Patent Office

Des. 174,550
Patented Apr. 26, 1955

174,550

BILLIARD TABLE

William H. Gunklach, Cincinnati, Ohio, assignor to The
National Billiard Mfg. Co., Cincinnati, Ohio, a corporation of Ohio

Application May 21, 1953, Serial No. 25,145

Term of patent 14 years

(Cl. D34—3)

To all whom it may concern:

Be it known that I, William H. Gunklach, a citizen of
the United States of America, residing in Cincinnati, in
the county of Hamilton and State of Ohio, have invented
a new, original, and ornamental Design for a Billiard
Table, of which the following is a specification, reference
being had to the accompanying drawing, forming a part
hereof.

The single figure is a perspective view of a billiard
table, showing my new design.

The opposite end of the table, not shown, has substantially the same appearance as the end shown in the single
figure, except that the recess is omitted.

I claim:

The ornamental design for a billiard table, as shown
and described.

References Cited in the file of this patent

UNITED STATES PATENTS

D. 148,119   Anderson et al. _____ Dec. 23, 1947

OTHER REFERENCES

Sporting Goods Dealer, July 1935, page 6, New Brunswick Home Billiard Table.

TITLE: STEREO SLIDE VIEWER
INVENTOR: ARTHUR H. CRAPSEY, JR.
ASSIGNEE: EASTMAN KODAK COMPANY

PATENT NUMBER: USD 174,800
PATENT FILED: OCTOBER 14, 1954
PATENT GRANTED: MAY 24, 1955

United States Patent Office

Des. 174,800
Patented May 24, 1955

174,800

STEREO SLIDE VIEWER

Arthur H. Crapsey, Jr., Rochester, N. Y., assignor to
Eastman Kodak Company, Rochester, N. Y., a corporation of New Jersey

Application October 14, 1954, Serial No. 32,672

Term of patent 14 years

(Cl. D61—1)

Fig. 1

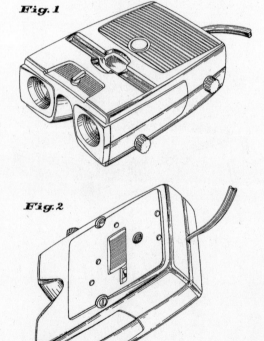

Fig. 2

To all whom it may concern:

Be it known that I, Arthur H. Craspsey, Jr., a citizen
of the United States, residing at Rochester, in the county
of Monroe and State of New York, have invented a new,
original, and ornamental Design for Stereo Slide Viewer,
of which the following is a specification, reference being
had to the drawings, forming a part thereof, in which:

Fig. 1 is a perspective view of the stereo slide viewer
illustrating my new design, this view being taken from
the front and showing parts of the top and side of the
viewer; and

Fig. 2 is a perspective view of the stereo slide viewer
shown in Fig. 1, this view being taken from the bottom
and showing the back and opposite side of the viewer.

I claim:

The ornamental design for a stereo slide viewer, as
shown.

References Cited in the file of this patent
UNITED STATES PATENTS

D. 166,906   Collins _____ June 3, 1952

OTHER REFERENCES

Montgomery Ward Photographic Catalog, 1953,
Item J.

Modern Plastics, February 1954, page 55.

TITLE: CHAISE LONGUE
INVENTOR: ERNEST DAWSON RACE
ASSIGNEE: ERNEST RACE LIMITED

PATENT NUMBER: USD 175,040
PATENT FILED: FEBRUARY 16, 1954
PATENT GRANTED: JUNE 28, 1955

United States Patent Office

Des. 175,040
Patented June 28, 1955

175,040

CHAISE LOUNGE

Ernest Dawson Race, Barnes, London, England, assignor to Ernest Race Limited, London, England, a company of Great Britain and Northern Ireland

Application February 16, 1954, Serial No. 29,052

Claims priority, application Great Britain January 6, 1954

Term of patent 7 years

(Cl. D15—11)

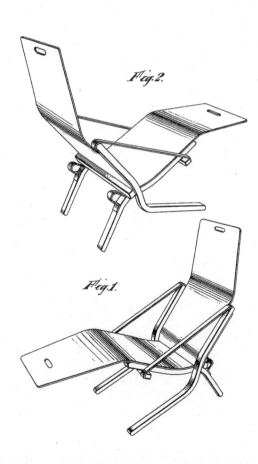

Fig. 2.

Fig. 1.

TITLE: FOOD STORAGE CONTAINER
INVENTOR: EARL S. TUPPER
ASSIGNEE: NONE

PATENT NUMBER: USD 175,202
PATENT FILED: MARCH 23, 1954
PATENT GRANTED: JULY 19, 1955

United States Patent Office

Des. 175,202
Patented July 19, 1955

175,202

FOOD STORAGE CONTAINER

Earl S. Tupper, Upton, Mass.

Application March 23, 1954, Serial No. 29,653

Term of patent 14 years

(Cl. D44—1)

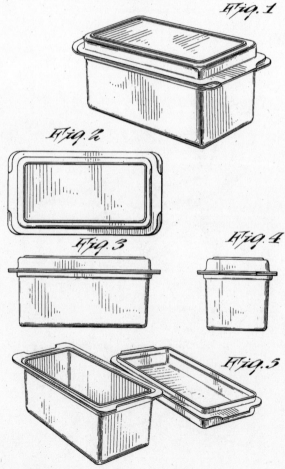

Fig. 1

Fig. 2

Fig. 3

Fig. 4

Fig. 5

Fig. 1 is a perspective view of a food storage container showing my new design;

Fig. 2 is a top plan view thereof;

Fig. 3 is a side elevational view thereof;

Fig. 4 is an end elevational view thereof; and

Fig. 5 is another perspective view thereof with the cover portion removed and lying in an inverted position.

I claim:

The ornamental design for a food storage container, as shown.

References Cited in the file of this patent

Montgomery Ward & Co. (Baltimore), Spring & Summer. 1952, page 646, item #32(86A3775), "Plastic Refrigerator Set."

TITLE: SUCTION CLEANER
INVENTOR: HENRY DREYFUSS
ASSIGNEE: THE HOOVER COMPANY

PATENT NUMBER: USD 175,210
PATENT FILED: JANUARY 18, 1955
PATENT GRANTED: JULY 26, 1955

United States Patent Office

Des. 175,210
Patented July 26, 1955

175,210

SUCTION CLEANER

Henry Dreyfuss, South Pasadena, Calif., assignor to The Hoover Company, North Canton, Ohio, a corporation of Ohio

Application January 18, 1955, Serial No. 34,054

Term of patent 14 years

(Cl. D9—2)

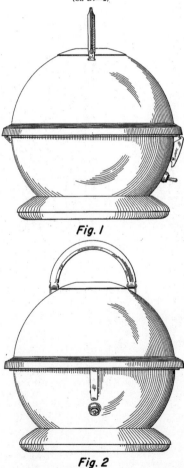

Fig. 1

Fig. 2

Figure 1 is a side elevational view of a suction cleaner showing my new design; and

Figure 2 is a front elevational view of the same.

I claim:

The ornamental design for a suction cleaner, substantially as shown.

References Cited in the file of this patent

UNITED STATES PATENTS

D. 147,874   Senne _____ Nov. 11, 1947

OTHER REFERENCES

House Furnishing Review, October 1949, page 39.

TITLE: MOTOR COACH
INVENTOR: ROLAND E. GEGOUX
ASSIGNEE: GENERAL MOTORS CORPORATION

PATENT NUMBER: USD 175,464
PATENT FILED: NOVEMBER 3, 1954
PATENT GRANTED: AUGUST 30, 1955

United States Patent Office

Des. 175,464
Patented Aug. 30, 1955

175,464

MOTOR COACH

Roland E. Gegoux, Pontiac, Mich., assignor to General Motors Corporation, Detroit, Mich., a corporation of Delaware

Application November 3, 1954, Serial No. 32,936

Term of patent 14 years

(Cl. D14—3)

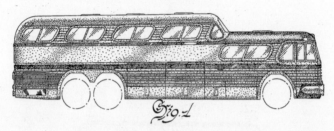

Fig. 1

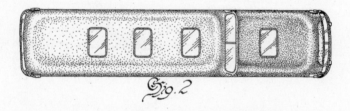

Fig. 2

Fig. 3

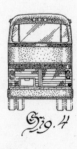

Fig. 4

Figure 1 is a side elevation of a motor coach embodying my new design;

Figure 2 is a top plan view of the coach;

Figure 3 is a front-end view thereof; and

Figure 4 is a rear-end view of the coach.

The dominant features of my design are shown in solid lines in each of the above figures.

I claim:

The ornamental design for a motor coach, substantially as shown and described.

References Cited in the file of this patent

UNITED STATES PATENTS

D. 150,567	Greig	Aug. 17, 1948
D. 160,059	Boca	Sept. 12, 1950
D. 169,856	Kay	June 16, 1953

OTHER REFERENCES

Bus Transportation, September 1952, page 83, pages 85 and 86 which fold out from page 84.

TITLE: DOUGHNUT COOKER OR SIMILAR ARTICLE
INVENTOR: RUTH G. JOSEPHSON
ASSIGNEE: NONE

PATENT NUMBER: USD 175,547
PATENT FILED: MAY 27, 1954
PATENT GRANTED: SEPTEMBER 13, 1955

United States Patent Office

Des. 175,547
Patented Sept. 13, 1955

175,547

DOUGHNUT COOKER OR SIMILAR ARTICLE

Ruth G. Josephson, Middletown, R. I.

Application May 27, 1954, Serial No. 30,698

Term of patent 14 years

(Cl. D81—10)

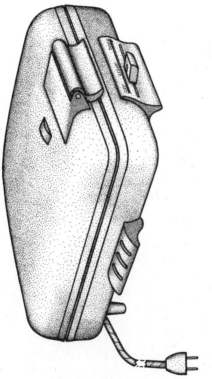

Fig. 1

TITLE: CIGAR LIGHTER OR SIMILAR ARTICLE
INVENTOR: SEYMOUR RAPPOPORT
ASSIGNEE: RONSON CORPORATION

PATENT NUMBER: USD 175,564
PATENT FILED: MAY 11, 1955
PATENT GRANTED: SEPTEMBER 13, 1955

United States Patent Office

Des. 175,564
Patented Sept. 13, 1955

175,564

CIGAR LIGHTER OR SIMILAR ARTICLE

Seymour Rappoport, New York, N. Y., assignor to Ronson Corporation, Newark, N. J., a corporation of New Jersey

Application May 11, 1955, Serial No. 35,929

Term of patent 14 years

(Cl. D48—27)

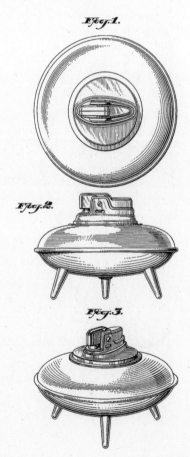

Fig. 1.

Fig. 2.

Fig. 3.

Fig. 1 is a top plan view of a cigar lighter embodying my new design, and

Figs. 2 and 3 are, respectively, a side elevation and perspective view of such lighter.

I claim:

The ornamental design for a cigar lighter or similar article, substantially as shown.

References Cited in the file of this patent

Gift and Art Buyer, April 1952, page 54, lighter at top left.

House Beautiful, July 1953, page 26, lighter at top right.

House Beautiful, April 1954, page 69, lighter in set No. 84F–6–2.

TITLE: CONVERTIBLE PASSENGER AUTOMOBILE
INVENTOR: EDWARD R. MACAULEY
ASSIGNEE: STUDEBAKER-PACKARD CORPORATION

PATENT NUMBER: USD 175,845
PATENT FILED: MAY 11, 1953
PATENT GRANTED: OCTOBER 18, 1955

United States Patent Office

Des. 175,845
Patented Oct. 18, 1955

175,845

**CONVERTIBLE PASSENGER AUTOMOBILE OR
SIMILAR ARTICLE**

Edward R. Macauley, Grosse Pointe Farms, Mich., assignor to Studebaker-Packard Corporation, a corporation of Michigan

Application May 11, 1953, Serial No. 24,937

Term of patent 14 years

(Cl. D14—3)

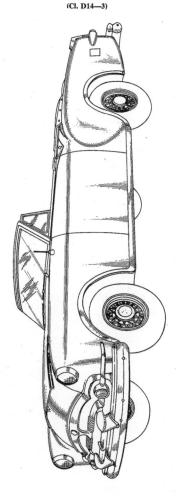

Fig. 1.

TITLE: COMBINED ASH TRAY AND PLANTER
INVENTOR: JACK LANE
ASSIGNEE: NONE

PATENT NUMBER: USD 175,968
PATENT FILED: FEBRUARY 23, 1955
PATENT GRANTED: NOVEMBER 1, 1955

United States Patent Office

Des. 175,968
Patented Nov. 1, 1955

175,968

COMBINED ASH TRAY AND PLANTER OR SIMILAR ARTICLE

Jack Lane, Los Angeles County, Calif.

Application February 23, 1955, Serial No. 34,644

Term of patent 3½ years

(Cl. D85—2)

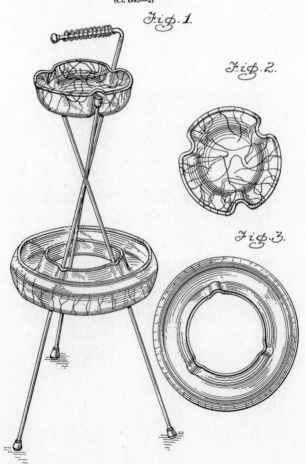

Fig. 1.

Fig. 2.

Fig. 3.

Fig. 1 is a perspective view of a combined ash tray and planter or similar article, showing my new design;

Fig. 2 is a top view of the ash tray portion thereof; and

Fig. 3 is a top view of the planter portion thereof.

I claim:

The ornamental design for a combined ash tray and planter or similar article as shown.

References Cited in the file of this patent

UNITED STATES PATENTS

D. 72,286	Schultz	Mar. 22, 1927
D. 172,865	Clemens	Aug. 24, 1954
902,511	Voska et al.	Oct. 27, 1908

TITLE: PORTABLE RADIO RECEIVER
FOR BROADCAST RECEPTION
INVENTOR: EDWARD KLEIN
ASSIGNEE: MOTOROLA

PATENT NUMBER: USD 176,023
PATENT FILED: JUNE 15, 1955
PATENT GRANTED: NOVEMBER 8, 1955

United States Patent Office

Des. 176,023
Patented Nov. 8, 1955

176,023

PORTABLE RADIO RECEIVER FOR BROADCAST RECEPTION

Edward Klein, Chicago, Ill., assignor to Motorola, Inc., Chicago, Ill., a corporation of Illinois

Application June 15, 1955, Serial No. 36,515

Term of patent 7 years

(Cl. D56—4)

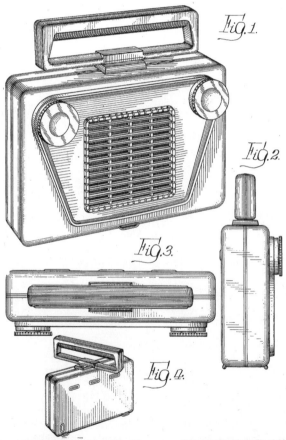

Fig. 1.

Fig. 2.

Fig. 3.

Fig. 4.

Fig. 1 is a front perspective view of a portable radio receiver for broadcast reception showing my new design;

Fig. 2 is a side elevation view thereof;

Fig. 3 is a top plan view thereof; and

Fig. 4 is a rear perspective view with the handle in another position.

I claim:

The ornamental design for a portable radio receiver for broadcast reception, as shown.

References Cited in the file of this patent

UNITED STATES PATENTS

D. 159,460	Adler	Aug. 1, 1950
D. 161,379	Schladermundt et al.	Dec. 26, 1950
D. 161,903	Carlson	Feb. 13, 1951
D. 164,891	Adler	Oct. 23, 1951

TITLE: AUTOMOBILE
INVENTORS: FRIEDRICH K. H. NALLINGER &
RUDOLF E. UHLENHAUT
ASSIGNEE: DAIMLER-BENZ

PATENT NUMBER: USD 176,278
PATENT FILED: FEBRUARY 5, 1954
PATENT GRANTED: DECEMBER 6, 1955

United States Patent Office

Des. 176,278
Patented Dec. 6, 1955

176,278

AUTOMOBILE

Friedrich K. H. Nallinger and Rudolf E. Uhlenhaut,
Stuttgart-N, Germany, assignors to Daimler-Benz
Aktiengesellschaft, Stuttgart-Unterturkheim, Germany

Application February 5, 1954, Serial No. 28,870

Claims priority, application Germany November 14, 1953

Term of patent 14 years

(Cl. D14—3)

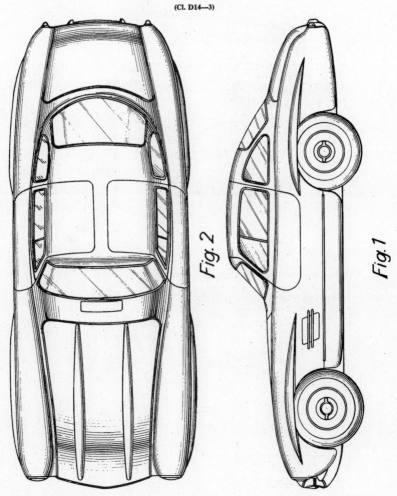

Fig. 2

Fig. 1

TITLE: CLOCK
INVENTOR: ROBERT O. FLETCHER
ASSIGNEE: GENERAL ELECTRIC COMPANY

PATENT NUMBER: USD 176,407
PATENT FILED: AUGUST 2, 1954
PATENT GRANTED: DECEMBER 20, 1955

United States Patent Office

Des. 176,407
Patented Dec. 20, 1955

176,407

CLOCK

Robert O. Fletcher, Ashland, Mass., assignor to General
Electric Company, a corporation of New York
Application August 2, 1954, Serial No. 31,697

Term of patent 3½ years

(Cl. D42—7)

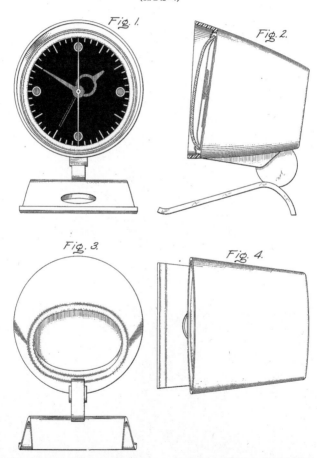

Fig. 1.
Fig. 2.
Fig. 3.
Fig. 4.

Figure 1 is a front elevational view of a clock embodying my new design; Fig. 2 is a side elevational view of the clock shown in Fig. 1 with the front part thereof being shown in cross section; Fig. 3 is a rear elevational view of the clock shown in Fig. 1; and, Fig. 4 is a top plan view of the clock shown in Fig. 1.

I claim:

The ornamental design for a clock, as shown.

References Cited in the file of this patent

Watchmaker & Jeweller, October 1936, page 1342, #3624, Garrard Clocks.

Premium Practice, July 1939, page 40, New Haven Clock Company adv., bicycle clock.

Hagn Merchandiser, No. 522, 1953, page 515, #534C3.

Jewelers' Circular-Keystone, September 1953, page 159, lower left hand item.

Gentry, Spring 1952, page 10, Item C.

TITLE: MINIATURE RADIO RECEIVER
INVENTOR: VICTOR A. PETERTIL
ASSIGNEE: I. D. E. A.

PATENT NUMBER: USD 176,481
PATENT FILED: FEBRUARY 10, 1955
PATENT GRANTED: DECEMBER 27, 1955

United States Patent Office

Des. 176,481
Patented Dec. 27, 1955

176,481

MINIATURE RADIO RECEIVER

Victor A. Petertil, Oak Park, Ill., assignor to I. D. E. A., Inc., Indianapolis, Ind., a corporation of Indiana

Application February 10, 1955, Serial No. 34,445

Term of patent 3½ years

(Cl. D56—4)

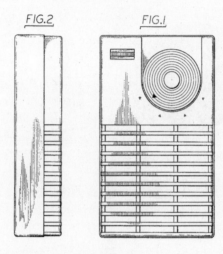

FIG.2   FIG.1

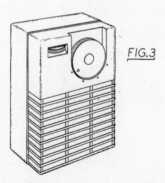

FIG.3

Fig. 1 is a front elevational view of a miniature radio receiver showing my new design;

Fig. 2 is a side elevation thereof; and

Fig. 3 is a perspective view.

I claim:

The ornamental design for a miniature radio receiver, as shown.

References Cited in the file of this patent

UNITED STATES PATENTS

D. 153,881	Kress	May 24, 1949
D. 170,923	Israel et al.	Nov. 24, 1953

OTHER REFERENCES

Radio and Television Retailing, January 1951 (Directory Issue), page 50, RCA Portable Radio, top center of page.

TITLE: LAUNDRY MACHINE CABINET
INVENTOR: MELVIN H. BOLDT
ASSIGNEE: AVCO MANUFACTURING CORPORATION

PATENT NUMBER: USD 177,010
PATENT FILED: JANUARY 18, 1955
PATENT GRANTED: MARCH 6, 1956

United States Patent Office

Des. 177,010
Patented Mar. 6, 1956

177,010

LAUNDRY MACHINE CABINET

Melvin H. Boldt, Glenview, Ill., assignor to Avco Manufacturing Corporation, Cincinnati, Ohio, a corporation
of Delaware

Application January 18, 1955, Serial No. 34,034

Term of patent 14 years

(Cl. D49—1)

The single figure is a perspective view of a laundry
machine cabinet showing my new design. The side and
back, not shown, are substantially plain.

The characteristic features of the design for the cabinet
disclosed reside in the portions on the upper front and
top having the configurations and appearance shown.

I claim:

The ornamental design for a laundry machine cabinet,
substantially as shown and described.

References Cited in the file of this patent

UNITED STATES PATENTS

D. 169,351   Boldt _____ Apr. 21, 1953

TITLE: RECORD PLAYER
INVENTOR: MARCEL JULES HELENE STAAR
ASSIGNEE: USINES GUSTAVE STAAR

PATENT NUMBER: USD 177,075
PATENT FILED: AUGUST 31, 1955
PATENT GRANTED: MARCH 6, 1956

United States Patent Office

Des. 177,075
Patented Mar. 6, 1956

177,075

RECORD PLAYER

Marcel Jules Helene Staar, Brussels, Belgium, assignor to
Usines Gustave Staar, S. A., a corporation of Belgium

Application August 31, 1955, Serial No. 37,732

Term of patent 7 years

(Cl. D56—4)

FIG. 1

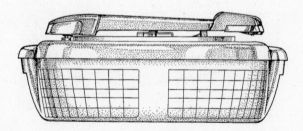

FIG. 3

TITLE: BOTTLE
INVENTOR: JAMES NASH
ASSIGNEE: ORANGE-CRUSH COMPANY

PATENT NUMBER: USD 177,271
PATENT FILED: JULY 11, 1955
PATENT GRANTED: MARCH 27, 1956

United States Patent Office

Des. 177,271
Patented Mar. 27, 1956

177,271

BOTTLE

James Nash, New York, N. Y., assignor to Orange-Crush
Company, a corporation of Illinois

Application July 11, 1955, Serial No. 36,918

Term of patent 14 years

(Cl. D58—8)

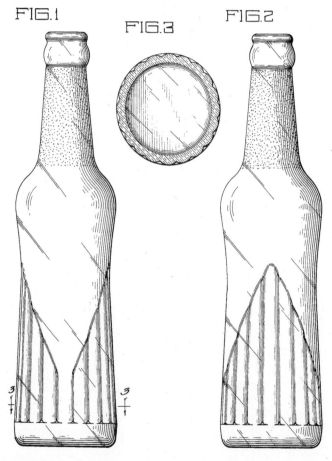

FIG.1   FIG.3   FIG.2

Fig. 1 is a front elevational view of a bottle showing my new design;

Fig. 2 is a side elevational view thereof; and

Fig. 3 is a cross-sectional view taken substantially on the section line 3—3 of Fig. 1.

I claim:

The ornamental design for a bottle, as shown.

References Cited in the file of this patent

UNITED STATES PATENTS

D. 75,789   Ginter _____ July 17, 1928

OTHER REFERENCES

Owens-Illinois Glass Company, Beverage and Brewery Catalog, page 27, Item G-217.

TITLE: TABLET ARM CHAIR
INVENTOR: RUSSEL WRIGHT
ASSIGNEE: SHWAYDER BROTHERS

PATENT NUMBER: USD 177,296
PATENT FILED: FEBRUARY 24, 1955
PATENT GRANTED: MARCH 27, 1956

United States Patent Office

Des. 177,296
Patented Mar. 27, 1956

177,296

TABLET ARM CHAIR

Russel Wright, New York, N. Y., assignor to Shwayder
Brothers, Ecorse, Mich., a corporation of Colorado

Application February 24, 1955, Serial No. 34,656

Term of patent 14 years

(Cl. D15—1)

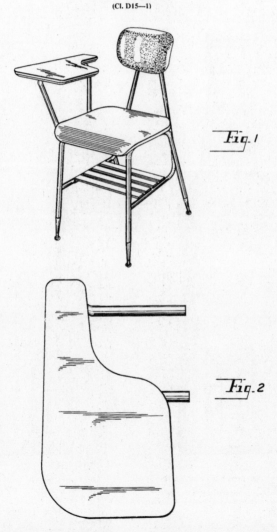

Fig. 1

Fig. 2

TITLE: LAVATORY
INVENTOR: GIOVANNI PONTI
ASSIGNEE: AMERICAN RADIATOR & STANDARD
SANITARY CORPORATION

PATENT NUMBER: USD 177,587
PATENT FILED: JULY 22, 1954
PATENT GRANTED: MAY 1, 1956

United States Patent Office

Des. 177,587
Patented May 1, 1956

177,587

LAVATORY

Giovanni Ponti, Milan, Italy, assignor to American Radiator & Standard Sanitary Corporation, Pittsburgh, Pa., a corporation of Delaware

Application July 22, 1954, Serial No. 31,541

Term of patent 14 years

(Cl. D4—2)

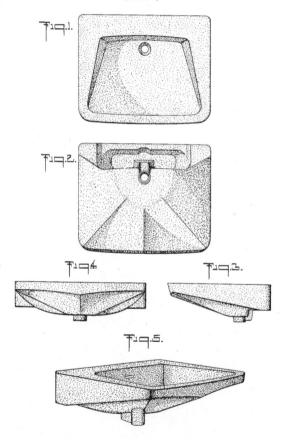

Fig. 1 is a top plan view of the lavatory,
Fig. 2 is a bottom plan view thereof,
Fig. 3 is a view of the lavatory in side elevation,
Fig. 4 is a front view thereof, and
Fig. 5 is a top perspective view taken from the left front corner of the lavatory.

I claim:

The ornamental design for a lavatory, substantially as shown.

References Cited in the file of this patent

UNITED STATES PATENTS

D. 157,278	Muller-Munk	Feb. 14, 1950
D. 160,767	Brown	Nov. 7, 1950
D. 169,348	Young	Apr. 14, 1953
D. 170,530	Hendrickson	Oct. 6, 1953

OTHER REFERENCES

Stile Industria, October 1954, page 13.

TITLE: AUTOMOBILE
INVENTOR: CLIFFORD BROOKS STEVENS
ASSIGNEE: NONE

PATENT NUMBER: USD 177,650
PATENT FILED: OCTOBER 10, 1955
PATENT GRANTED: MAY 8, 1956

United States Patent Office

Des. 177,650
Patented May 8, 1956

177,650

AUTOMOBILE

Clifford Brooks Stevens, Milwaukee, Wis.

Application October 10, 1955, Serial No. 38,317

Term of patent 3½ years

(Cl. D14—3)

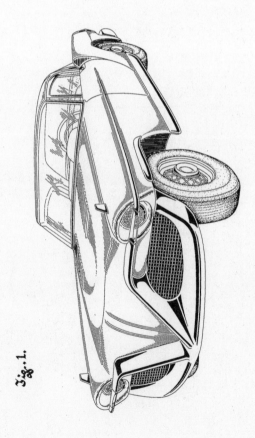

Fig. 1.

TITLE: RADIO CABINET OR SIMILAR ARTICLE
INVENTOR: JON W. HAUSER
ASSIGNEE: HAWLEY PRODUCTS COMPANY

PATENT NUMBER: USD 177,728
PATENT FILED: NOVEMBER 10, 1955
PATENT GRANTED: MAY 22, 1956

United States Patent Office

Des. 177,728
Patented May 22, 1956

177,728

RADIO CABINET OR SIMILAR ARTICLE

Jon W. Hauser, St. Charles, Ill., assignor to Hawley Products Company, St. Charles, Ill., a corporation of Delaware

Application November 10, 1955, Serial No. 38,829

Term of patent 14 years

(Cl. D56—4)

FIG. 1

FIG. 2

FIG. 3

FIG. 4

Fig. 1 is a front elevational view of a radio cabinet or similar article, embodying my new design;

Fig. 2 is a side view thereof;

Fig. 3 is back elevational view thereof; and

Fig. 4 is a top plan view thereof.

I claim:

The ornamental design for a radio cabinet or similar article, as shown.

References Cited in the file of this patent

Mart, June 1954, page 56, Raytheon "Challenger" TV Set, middle item in left column of page.

Industrial Design, Aug. 1954, page 125, Zenith cabinet and table model.

TITLE: LOCOMOTIVE BODY
INVENTORS: CHARLES M. JORDAN & MASAJI B. SUGANO
ASSIGNEE: GENERAL MOTORS CORPORATION

PATENT NUMBER: USD 177,814
PATENT FILED: AUGUST 16, 1955
PATENT GRANTED: MAY 29, 1956

United States Patent Office

Des. 177,814
Patented May 29, 1956

177,814

LOCOMOTIVE BODY

Charles M. Jordan, Birmingham, and Masaji B. Sugano, Detroit, Mich., assignors to General Motors Corporation, Detroit, Mich., a corporation of Delaware

Application August 16, 1955, Serial No. 37,506

Term of patent 7 years

(Cl. D66—1)

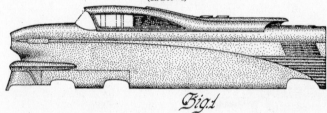

Fig.1

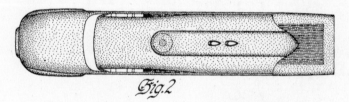

Fig.2

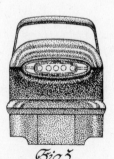

Fig.3

Fig.4

Fig. 1 is a side elevational view of a locomotive body embodying our new design;

Fig. 2 is a top view thereof;

Fig. 3 is a front end view thereof;

Fig. 4 is a rear end view thereof.

The dominant features of our design are shown in solid lines in each of the above figures.

We claim:

The ornamental design for a locomotive body, substantially as shown and described.

References Cited in the file of this patent

UNITED STATES PATENTS

D. 136,261	Loewy	Aug. 31, 1943
D. 154,120	Hadley et al.	June 14, 1949
D. 164,915	Girardy et al.	Oct. 23, 1951
49,227	Calthrop	Aug. 8, 1865

TITLE: RADIO RECEIVER CABINET
INVENTOR: JACK DE YOUNG
ASSIGNEE: ZENITH RADIO CORPORATION

PATENT NUMBER: USD 178,115
PATENT FILED: JANUARY 19,1956
PATENT GRANTED: JUNE 26,1956

United States Patent Office

Des. 178,115
Patented June 26, 1956

178,115

RADIO RECEIVER CABINET

Jack De Young, Spring Lake, Mich., assignor to Zenith
Radio Corporation, a corporation of Illinois

Application January 19, 1956, Serial No. 39,852

Term of patent 14 years

(Cl. D56—4)

The drawing is a perspective view of a radio receiver cabinet showing my new design.

That side of the radio receiver cabinet not shown in the drawing is identical to the corresponding side shown.

The bottom of the radio receiver cabinet is identical to the top, and the back of the radio receiver cabinet is unornamented.

I claim:

The ornamental design for a radio receiver cabinet, substantially as shown and described.

References Cited in the file of this patent

Electrical Merchandising, March 1954, page 112, Zenith's "The Voyager," Model L406R.

Mart, April 1954, RCA Victor portable radio, Model 2B400, page 29.

TITLE: COMBINATION FREEZER AND REFRIGERATOR
CABINET OR SIMILAR ARTICLE
INVENTOR: JEAN O. REINECKE
ASSIGNEE: AMANA REFRIGERATION

PATENT NUMBER: USD 178,149
PATENT FILED: SEPTEMBER 6, 1955
PATENT GRANTED: JUNE 26, 1956

United States Patent Office

Des. 178,149
Patented June 26, 1956

178,149

COMBINATION FREEZER AND REFRIGERATOR CABINET OR SIMILAR ARTICLE

Jean O. Reinecke, Oak Park, Ill., assignor to Amana Refrigeration, Inc., Amana, Iowa, a corporation of Iowa

Application September 6, 1955, Serial No. 37,801

Term of patent 14 years

(Cl. D67—3)

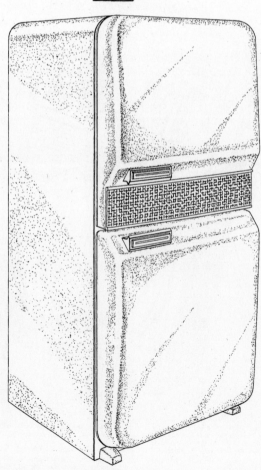

TITLE: PORTABLE ELECTRIC DRILL UNIT
INVENTOR: ROBERT O. ERNEST
ASSIGNEE: SUNBEAM CORPORATION

PATENT NUMBER: USD 178,227
PATENT FILED: JUNE 24, 1955
PATENT GRANTED: JULY 10, 1956

United States Patent Office

Des. 178,227
Patented July 10, 1956

178,227

PORTABLE ELECTRIC DRILL UNIT

Robert O. Ernest, Oak Park, Ill., assignor to Sunbeam
Corporation, Chicago, Ill., a corporation of Illinois

Application June 24, 1955, Serial No. 36,665

Term of patent 14 years

(Cl. D54—14)

Fig. 1.

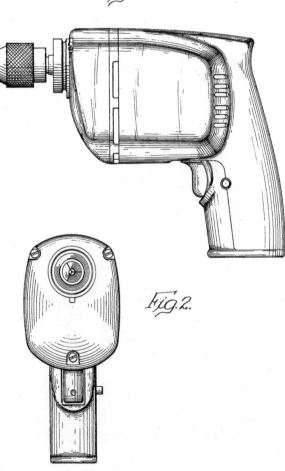

Fig. 2.

TITLE: CASE FOR MOTION PICTURE CAMERAS
INVENTOR: PETER MULLER-MUNK
ASSIGNEE: BELL & HOWELL COMPANY

PATENT NUMBER: USD 178,533
PATENT FILED: NOVEMBER 6, 1953
PATENT GRANTED: AUGUST 14, 1956

United States Patent Office

Des. 178,533
Patented Aug. 14, 1956

178,533

CASE FOR MOTION PICTURE CAMERAS
OR THE LIKE

Peter Muller-Munk, Pittsburgh, Pa., assignor to Bell &
Howell Company, Chicago, Ill., a corporation of
Illinois

Application November 6, 1953, Serial No. 27,485

Term of patent 14 years

(Cl. D61—2)

FIG.1.

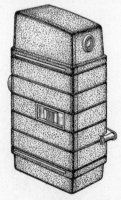

FIG.2.

Figure 1 is a perspective view of a case for motion
picture cameras or the like embodying my new design;
and

Figure 2 is a perspective view of the same showing
the sides thereof opposite those shown in Figure 1.

I claim:

The ornamental design for a case for motion picture
cameras or the like, as shown.

References Cited in the file of this patent

UNITED STATES PATENTS

D. 161,824   Davis ------------------ Feb. 6, 1951

OTHER REFERENCES

Sears, Roebuck & Company, Catalog #204, Spring
and Summer, 1952, page 850, Revere "50" and Revere
"55", top of page in left corner.

Lafayette Camera, Catalog #81R, Lafayette Radio
Corporation, New York, received June 1941, page 19,
items PH2007x and PH2009x.

TITLE: STATION WAGON
INVENTOR: DAVID E. SCOTT
ASSIGNEE: CHRYSLER CORPORATION

PATENT NUMBER: USD 178,542
PATENT FILED: DECEMBER 19, 1955
PATENT GRANTED: AUGUST 14, 1956

United States Patent Office

Des. 178,542
Patented Aug. 14, 1956

178,542

STATION WAGON

David E. Scott, Royal Oak, Mich., assignor to Chrysler
Corporation, Highland Park, Mich., a corporation of
Delaware

Application December 19, 1955, Serial No. 39,368

Term of patent 7 years

(Cl. D14—3)

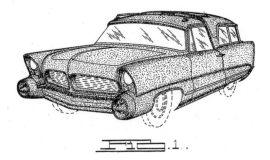

FIG. 1.

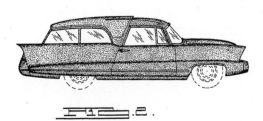

FIG. 2.

TITLE: BOAT
INVENTOR: CLIFFORD BROOKS STEVENS
ASSIGNEE: OUTBOARD MARINE
& MANUFACTURING COMPANY

PATENT NUMBER: USD 178,552
PATENT FILED: JANUARY 12, 1956
PATENT GRANTED: AUGUST 14, 1956

Des. 178,552

PAGE 3

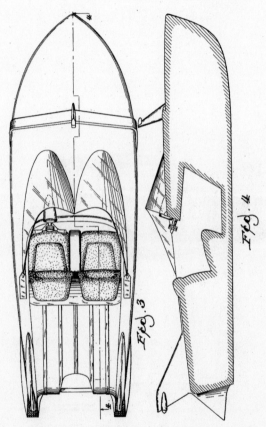

Fig. 1 is a front perspective view of a boat showing my new design.

Fig. 2 is a rear perspective view thereof.

Fig. 3 is a top plan view thereof.

Fig. 4 is an outline sectional view thereof on line 4—4 of Fig. 3.

The side not shown is like the side shown.

I claim:

The ornamental design for a boat, as shown described.

No references cited.

TITLE: VACUUM CLEANER
INVENTOR: EARL R. HEAVNER
ASSIGNEE: NONE

PATENT NUMBER: USD 178,774
PATENT FILED: JULY 13, 1955
PATENT GRANTED: SEPTEMBER 18, 1956

United States Patent Office

Des. 178,774
Patented Sept. 18, 1956

178,774

VACUUM CLEANER

Earl R. Heavner, Dayton, Ohio

Application July 13, 1955, Serial No. 36,957

Term of patent 14 years

(Cl. D9—2)

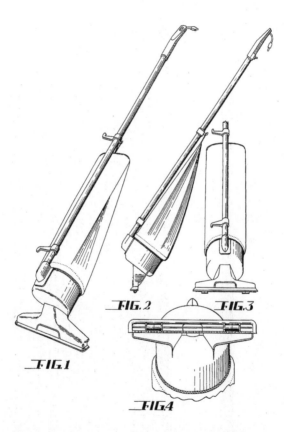

FIG. 1
FIG. 2
FIG. 3
FIG. 4

Figure 1 is a perspective view of a vacuum cleaner embodying my new design.

Figure 2 is a side elevational view thereof.

Figure 3 is a front elevational view with a portion of the handle broken away for the convenience of illustration only.

Figure 4 is a fragmentary, enlarged bottom perspective view thereof.

I claim:

The ornamental design for a vacuum cleaner, as shown and described.

References Cited in the file of this patent

UNITED STATES PATENTS

D. 82,003   Smellie ----------------- Sept. 9, 1930
D. 103,255   Stone et al. ------------ Feb. 16, 1937

TITLE: AUTOMOBILE BODY
INVENTOR: ANTOINE BRUEDER
ASSIGNEE: SOCIETE ANONYME ANDRE CITROEN

PATENT NUMBER: USD 179,115
PATENT FILED: MARCH 19, 1956
PATENT GRANTED: NOVEMBER 6, 1956

Des. 179,115

PAGE 2

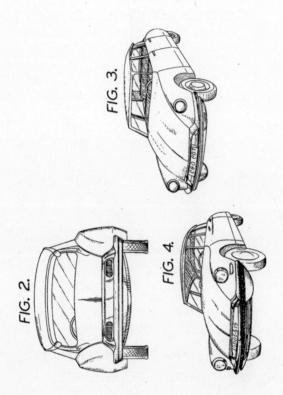

FIG. 3.

FIG. 2.

FIG. 4.

Fig. 1 is a side elevational view of an automobile body showing my new design;

Fig. 2 is a rear elevational view;

Fig. 3 is a front perspective view;

Fig. 4 is another front perspective view taken at a different angle from that shown in Fig. 3.

I claim:

The ornamental design for an automobile body, substantially as shown.

References Cited in the file of this patent

Car Life, May 1954, page 63, middle of pag
La Vie Automobile, October 1954, page 285, of page, La Dyne.

Motor Life, December 1955, page 9, lower ri

TITLE: COMBINED CONDIMENT DISPENSER SET
& HOLDER THEREFOR
INVENTOR: SEVERNS HILTON
ASSIGNEE: MENSCHIK-GOLDMAN COMPANY

PATENT NUMBER: USD 179,293
PATENT FILED: JULY 17, 1956
PATENT GRANTED: NOVEMBER 27, 1956

United States Patent Office

Des. 179,293
Patented Nov. 27, 1956

179,293

COMBINED CONDIMENT DISPENSER SET AND HOLDER THEREFOR

Severns Hilton, Wilton, Maine, assignor to Menschik-
Goldman Company, New York, N. Y., a partnership

Application July 17, 1956, Serial No. 42,278

Term of patent 3½ years

(Cl. D44—22)

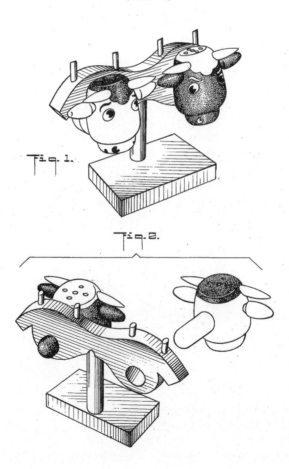

Fig. 1.

Fig. 2.

TITLE: COMBINED FRONT CONTROL PANEL
& GRILL FOR AN AIR CONDITIONER
INVENTOR: HENRY DREYFUSS
ASSIGNEE: WHIRLPOOL-SEEGER CORPORATION

PATENT NUMBER: USD 179,887
PATENT FILED: MARCH 22, 1956
PATENT GRANTED: MARCH 19, 1957

United States Patent Office

Des. 179,887
Patented Mar. 19, 1957

179,887

COMBINED FRONT CONTROL PANEL AND GRILL
FOR AN AIR CONDITIONER

Henry Dreyfuss, South Pasadena, Calif., assignor to
Whirlpool-Seeger Corporation, St. Joseph, Mich., a corporation of Delaware

Application March 22, 1956, Serial No. 40,722

Term of patent 14 years

(Cl. D62—4)

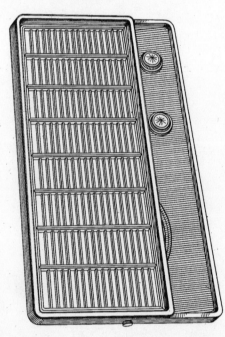

Figure 1 is a perspective view of a combined front control panel and grill for an air conditioner showing my new design; and

Figure 2 is a side view thereof.

I claim:

The ornamental design for a combined front control panel and grill for an air conditioner, substantially as shown.

References Cited in the file of this patent

UNITED STATES PATENTS

D. 173,790   Chuboff _____ Jan. 4, 195
D. 178,664   Howe _____ Sept. 4, 195

536

TITLE: LAWN CHAIR OR THE LIKE
INVENTORS: SIEGMUND WERNER & RAYMOND BOTHUN
ASSIGNEE: NONE

PATENT NUMBER: USD 179,926
PATENT FILED: MARCH 29, 1956
PATENT GRANTED: MARCH 19, 1957

United States Patent Office

Des. 179,926
Patented Mar. 19, 1957

179,926

LAWN CHAIR OR THE LIKE

Siegmund Werner, South Orange, N. J., and Raymond Bothun, Huntington Park, Calif.

Application March 29, 1956, Serial No. 40,829

Term of patent 3½ years

(Cl. D15—1)

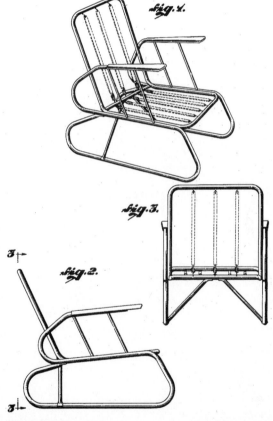

Figure 1 is a front perspective view of a lawn chair embodying our design.

Figure 2 is a side view thereof.

Figure 3 is a rear view taken in the direction of the arrows 3—3 of Figure 2.

The dominant features of the design reside in the portions shown in full lines.

We claim:

The ornamental design for a lawn chair or the like, substantially as shown and described.

References Cited in the file of this patent

UNITED STATES PATENTS

D. 101,632	Hoffmann	Oct. 20, 1936
2,079,767	Larsen	May 11, 1937
2,437,303	Molla	Mar. 9, 1948

FOREIGN PATENTS

134,596	Austria	Aug. 25, 1933

TITLE: DOILY
INVENTOR: EARL S. TUPPER
ASSIGNEE: NONE

PATENT NUMBER: USD 180,165
PATENT FILED: OCTOBER 25, 1956
PATENT GRANTED: APRIL 23, 1957

United States Patent Office

Des. 180,165
Patented Apr. 23, 1957

180,165

DOILY

Earl S. Tupper, Smithfield, R. I.

Application October 25, 1956, Serial No. 43,531

Term of patent 14 years

(Cl. D3—9)

Fig. 1

Fig. 2

Figure 1 is a top plan view of a doily embodying my new design; and

Figure 2 is a side view in elevation thereof.

I claim:

The ornamental design for a doily, substantially as shown.

References Cited in the file of this patent

UNITED STATES PATENTS

D. 159,418	Karfiol	---------------	July 25, 1950
D. 179,188	Cole	---------------	Nov. 13, 1956
529,719	Eils	---------------	Nov. 27, 1894

OTHER REFERENCES

British Plastics, July 1953, page 254, plastic place mats.

TITLE: SPOON
INVENTOR: ISAMU NOGUCHI
ASSIGNEE: NONE

PATENT NUMBER: USD 180,411
PATENT FILED: AUGUST 30, 1956
PATENT GRANTED: JUNE 4, 1957

United States Patent Office

Des. 180,411
Patented June 4, 1957

180,411

SPOON

Isamu Noguchi, Carmel, N. Y.

Application August 30, 1956, Serial No. 42,794

Claims priority, application Japan April 28, 1956

Term of patent 14 years

(Cl. D54—12)

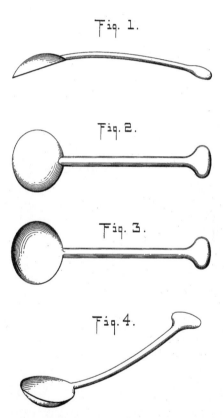

Fig. 1.

Fig. 2.

Fig. 3.

Fig. 4.

Fig. 1 is an elevational view of a spoon embodying my new design;

Fig. 2 is a top plan view of the spoon of Fig. 1;

Fig. 3 is a bottom plan view of the spoon of Fig. 1; and

Fig. 4 is a perspective view of the spoon of Fig. 1.

I claim:

The ornamental design for a spoon, substantially as shown.

References Cited in the file of this patent

UNITED STATES PATENTS

D. 29,695	Swalm	Nov. 22, 1898
D. 102,748	Erikson	Jan. 19, 1937
D. 138,750	Swenson	Sept. 5, 1944
D. 144,599	Tupper	Apr. 30, 1946

TITLE: AUTOMOBILE
INVENTOR: HARLEY J. EARL
ASSIGNEE: GENERAL MOTORS CORPORATION

PATENT NUMBER: USD 180,509
PATENT FILED: AUGUST 31, 1956
PATENT GRANTED: JUNE 25, 1957

United States Patent Office

Des. 180,509
Patented June 25, 1957

180,509

AUTOMOBILE

Harley J. Earl, Grosse Pointe Farms, Mich., assignor to
General Motors Corporation, Detroit, Mich., a corporation of Delaware

Application August 31, 1956, Serial No. 42,798

Term of patent 7 years

(Cl. D14—3)

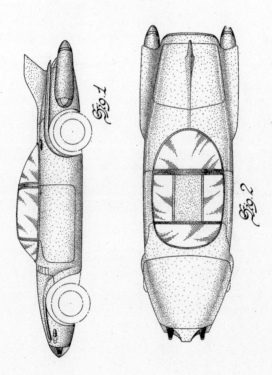

TITLE: COMBINATION THERMOMETER & BAROMETER
INVENTOR: GORDON W. FLORIAN
ASSIGNEE: TAYLOR INSTRUMENT COMPANIES

PATENT NUMBER: USD 180,826
PATENT FILED: SEPTEMBER 4, 1956
PATENT GRANTED: AUGUST 20, 1957

United States Patent Office

Des. 180,826
Patented Aug. 20, 1957

180,826

COMBINATION THERMOMETER AND BAROMETER

Gordon W. Florian, Bridgeport, Conn., assignor to Taylor Instrument Companies, Rochester, N. Y., a corporation of New York

Application September 4, 1956, Serial No. 42,830

Term of patent 14 years

(Cl. D52—7)

FIG. I   FIG. 2

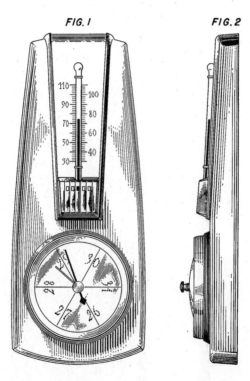

Fig. 1 is a front view and Fig. 2 is a side view of a combination thermometer and barometer, showing my new design.

I claim:

The ornamental design for a combination thermometer and barometer, as shown.

References Cited in the file of this patent

UNITED STATES PATENTS

D. 157,103   Teague et al. _____ Jan. 31, 1950

OTHER REFERENCES

Taylor Instruments Catalog No. 5000, July 1951, Edition (in bound copies), rec'd March 23, 1953, upper left corner of page 8.

TITLE: DESK SET
INVENTOR: DOROTHY HARCOURT TURNER
ASSIGNEE: SCRIPTO

PATENT NUMBER: USD 181,114
PATENT FILED: OCTOBER 30, 1956
PATENT GRANTED: OCTOBER 1, 1957

United States Patent Office

Des. 181,114
Patented Oct. 1, 1957

181,114

DESK SET

Dorothy Harcourt Turner, Atlanta, Ga., assignor to
Scripto, Inc., a corporation of Georgia

Application October 30, 1956, Serial No. 43,596

Term of patent 14 years

(Cl. D74—1)

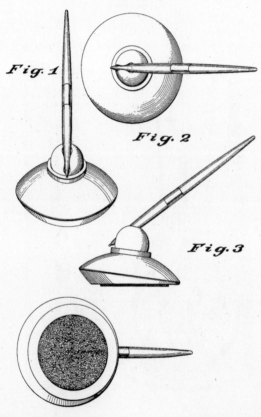

Fig. 1

Fig. 2

Fig. 3

Fig. 1 is a front perspective view of a desk set, showing my new design;
Fig. 2 is a top plan view thereof;
Fig. 3 is a side elevational view thereof; and
Fig. 4 is a bottom plan view thereof.
I claim:
The ornamental design for a desk set, as shown.

References Cited in the file of this patent
UNITED STATES PATENTS

D. 153,763	Campbell	May 17, 1949
D. 172,847	Spatz	Aug. 17, 1954
D. 173,918	Vogel	Jan. 25, 1955
D. 179,560	Doman	Jan. 22, 1957
1,620,529	Ferris	Mar. 8, 1927

OTHER REFERENCES

"Newsweek" clipping, May 3, 1954, Esterbrook advertisement, page 75.

TITLE: LAMP
INVENTOR: ALBERT N. BROOKS
ASSIGNEE: NONE

PATENT NUMBER: USD 181,182
PATENT FILED: MAY 24, 1956
PATENT GRANTED: OCTOBER 15, 1957

United States Patent Office

Des. 181,182
Patented Oct. 15, 1957

181,182

LAMP

Albert N. Brooks, Chicago, Ill.

Application May 24, 1956, Serial No. 41,628

Term of patent 14 years

(Cl. D48—19)

Fig. 1.

Fig. 2.

TITLE: SURFACE TREATING MACHINE
INVENTORS: BENGT ERIK NILSSON & CARL SIXTEN
ANDERSSON-SASON
ASSIGNEE: AKTIEBOLAGET ELEKTROLUX

PATENT NUMBER: USD 181,225
PATENT FILED: AUGUST 28, 1956
PATENT GRANTED: OCTOBER 15, 1957

United States Patent Office

Des. 181,225
Patented Oct. 15, 1957

181,225

SURFACE TREATING MACHINE

Bengt Erik Nilsson, Hagersten, and Carl Sixten Andersson-Sason, Solna, Sweden, assignors to Aktiebolaget Elektrolux, Stockholm Sweden, a corporation of Sweden

Application August 28, 1956, Serial No. 42,758

Claims priority, application Sweden March 29, 1956

Term of patent 14 years

(Cl. D9—2)

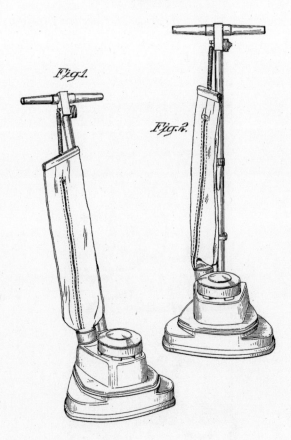

Fig.1.

Fig.2.

TITLE: WIRE STAPLE REMOVING TOOL
INVENTOR: WILLIAM G. PANKONIN
ASSIGNEE: TRIANGLE TOOL & MANUFACTURING COMPANY

PATENT NUMBER: USD 181,226
PATENT FILED: JANUARY 7, 1957
PATENT GRANTED: OCTOBER 15, 1957

United States Patent Office

Des. 181,226
Patented Oct. 15, 1957

181,226

WIRE STAPLE REMOVING TOOL

William G. Pankonin, Chicago, Ill., assignor to Triangle
Tool & Manufacturing Company, Chicago, Ill., a corporation of Illinois

Application January 7, 1957, Serial No. 44,428

Term of patent 14 years

(Cl. D74—1)

FIG. 1

FIG. 2

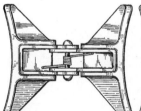

FIG. 3

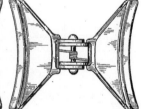

FIG. 4

Fig. 1 is a side view;
Fig. 2 is a front view;
Fig. 3 is a bottom view; and
Fig. 4 is a top view of a wire staple removing tool,
showing my new design.
I claim:
The ornamental design for a wire staple removing tool,
as shown.

References Cited in the file of this patent
UNITED STATES PATENTS

D. 158,608   Pankonin _____ May 16, 1950
D. 160,420   Pankonin _____ Oct. 10, 1950

TITLE: VENDING MACHINE FOR CIGARETTES,
CANDY AND THE LIKE
INVENTOR: WALTER E. MOORE
ASSIGNEE: NATIONAL VENDORS

PATENT NUMBER: USD 181,804
PATENT FILED: FEBRUARY 4, 1957
PATENT GRANTED: DECEMBER 31, 1957

United States Patent Office

Des. 181,804
Patented Dec. 31, 1957

181,804

VENDING MACHINE FOR CIGARETTES, CANDY AND THE LIKE

Walter E. Moore, Bel-Nor, Mo., assignor to National
Vendors, Inc., St. Louis, Mo., a corporation of Missouri

Application February 4, 1957, Serial No. 44,727

Term of patent 14 years

(Cl. D52—3)

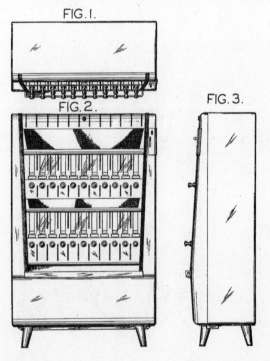

FIG. 1.

FIG. 2.

FIG. 3.

Fig. 1 is a top plan view of a vending machine for
cigarettes, candy and the like showing my new design;
Fig. 2 is a front elevation of Fig. 1; and,
Fig. 3 is a right side elevation of Fig. 2.
The undisclosed side of the vending machine is substantially the same in appearance as the side shown, and
the rear is plain and unadorned.

I claim:
The ornamental design for a vending machine for
cigarettes, candy and the like, substantially as shown
and described.

References Cited in the file of this patent
UNITED STATES PATENTS

D. 174,587	Moore	_____	Apr. 26, 1955
D. 175,002	Abeles et al.	_____	June 28, 1955
D. 177,424	Moore	_____	Apr. 10, 1956

TITLE: STRINGED MUSICAL INSTRUMENT
INVENTOR: THEODORE M. MCCARTY
ASSIGNEE: GIBSON

PATENT NUMBER: USD 181,867
PATENT FILED: JUNE 27, 1957
PATENT GRANTED: JANUARY 7, 1958

United States Patent Office

Des. 181,867
Patented Jan. 7, 1958

181,867

STRINGED MUSICAL INSTRUMENT

Theodore M. McCarty, Kalamazoo, Mich., assignor to
Gibson, Inc., Kalamazoo, Mich., a corporation of
Michigan

Application June 27, 1957, Serial No. 46,764

Term of patent 14 years

(Cl. D56—9)

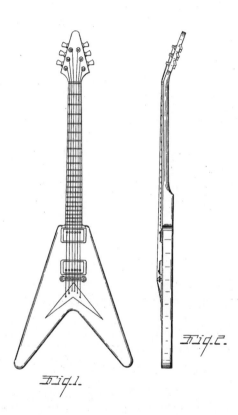

Fig. 1.

Fig. 2.

Fig. 1 is a top plan view of a stringed musical instrument, showing my new design, and

Fig. 2 is a side elevational view thereof.

The back of the article is substantially plain.

I claim:

The ornamental design for a stringed musical instrument, as shown and described.

References Cited in the file of this patent

UNITED STATES PATENTS

D. 17,888	Darbyshire	Nov. 22, 1887
D. 155,881	Evers	Nov. 8, 1949
D. 162,521	Crowle et al.	Mar. 20, 1951
D. 175,328	Van Pelt	Aug. 9, 1955
1,208,077	Ashley	Dec. 12, 1916

TITLE: CHAIR OR THE LIKE
INVENTOR: EERO SAARINEN
ASSIGNEE: NONE

PATENT NUMBER: USD 181,945
PATENT FILED: MARCH 1, 1957
PATENT GRANTED: JANUARY 21, 1958

United States Patent Office

Des. 181,945
Patented Jan. 21, 1958

181,945

CHAIR OR THE LIKE

Eero Saarinen, Bloomfield Hills, Mich.

Application March 1, 1957, Serial No. 45,040

Term of patent 14 years

(Cl. D15—1)

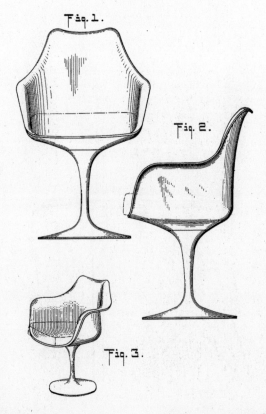

Fig. 1.

Fig. 2.

Fig. 3.

Fig. 1 is a front elevational view of a chair embodying the invention;

Fig. 2 is a side elevational view of the chair of Fig. 1; and

Fig. 3 is a perspective view of the chair of Figs. 1 and 2.

The characteristic features of my design reside in the portion shown by means of full lines in the drawing.

I claim:

The ornamental design for a chair or the like, substantially as shown and described.

References Cited in the file of this patent

"Cramer" Posture Chair Company Incorporated G. S. A., Federal Supply Schedule, January 1–December 31, 1952, received May 27, 1927 see item on back cover of folder—Model 8–150 special purpose chair (note pedestal).

"Interiors," vol. 114, August 1954, January 1955, see issue of August 1954, page 79, Item No. 7.

TITLE: FAN HOUSING
INVENTOR: HAROLD L. KIRK
ASSIGNEE: MEIER ELECTRIC & MACHINE COMPANY

PATENT NUMBER: USD 182,029
PATENT FILED: DECEMBER 3, 1956
PATENT GRANTED: FEBRUARY 4, 1958

United States Patent Office

Des. 182,029
Patented Feb. 4, 1958

182,029

FAN HOUSING

Harold L. Kirk, Indianapolis, Ind., assignor to Meier Electric and Machine Company, Inc., Indianapolis, Ind., a corporation

Application December 3, 1956, Serial No. 44,050

Term of patent 7 years

(Cl. D26—7)

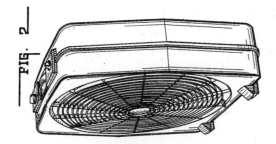

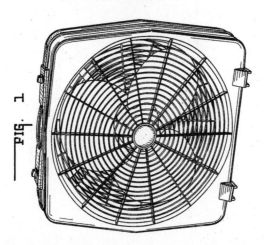

Fig. 1 is a front perspective view of a fan housing, showing my new design.

Fig. 2 is a side perspective view thereof.

I claim:

The ornamental design for a fan housing, as shown.

References Cited in the file of this patent

UNITED STATES PATENTS

D. 159,008   Seil et al. _____ June 13, 1950

OTHER REFERENCES

Television Retailing, January 1953, pages 56 and 57, items: Fresh'nd-Aire Window Fan, fourth from left at bottom of page 56; Fresh'nd-Aire Window Air-Conditioner, top page 56.

Electrical Merchandising, April 1957, page 45, Diehl fan, second down left side.

TITLE: TABLE OR THE LIKE
INVENTOR: ISAMU NOGUCHI
ASSIGNEE: NONE

PATENT NUMBER: USD 182,037
PATENT FILED: JANUARY 3, 1956
PATENT GRANTED: FEBRUARY 4, 1958

United States Patent Office

Des. 182,037
Patented Feb. 4, 1958

182,037

TABLE OR THE LIKE

Isamu Noguchi, Carmel, N. Y.

Application January 3, 1956, Serial No. 39,549

Term of patent 14 years

(Cl. D33—14)

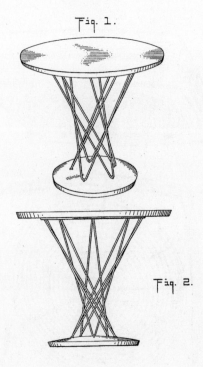

Fig. 1.

Fig. 2.

Fig. 1 is a perspective view of a table embodying my new design; and

Fig. 2 is an elevational view of the table of Fig. 1.

I claim:

The ornamental design for a table or the like, substantially as shown.

References Cited in the file of this patent

UNITED STATES PATENTS

D. 159,561   Tanier ------------------ Aug. 1, 1950

OTHER REFERENCES

Howell Modern Chromsteel Furniture, Catalog No. 20, © 1939, page 26, No. 350 at top right of page (description on page 27).

Lloyd Chromium Furniture, Catalog No. 41–A, 1949, page 44, item T–59–C.

House Beautiful, March 1955, page 83, Brancusi adv., at top right of page.

TITLE: ELECTRIC OVEN AND STOVE COMBINATION
INVENTOR: RAY C. SANDIN
ASSIGNEE: GENERAL ELECTRIC COMPANY

PATENT NUMBER: USD 182,084
PATENT FILED: OCTOBER 19, 1956
PATENT GRANTED: FEBRUARY 11, 1958

United States Patent Office

Des. 182,084
Patented Feb. 11, 1958

182,084

ELECTRIC OVEN AND STOVE COMBINATION

Ray C. Sandin, Northbrook, Ill., assignor to General
Electric Company, a corporation of New York

Application October 19, 1956, Serial No. 43,416

Term of patent 14 years

(Cl. D81—4)

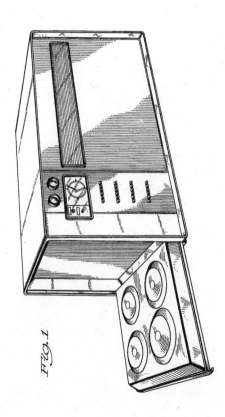

FIG. 1

TITLE: PHONOGRAPH CABINET
INVENTOR: MELVIN H. BOLDT
ASSIGNEE: AMI

PATENT NUMBER: USD 182,103
PATENT FILED: MAY 1, 1957
PATENT GRANTED: FEBRUARY 18, 1958

United States Patent Office

Des. 182,103
Patented Feb. 18, 1958

182,103

PHONOGRAPH CABINET

Melvin H. Boldt, Glenview, Ill., assignor to AMI Incorporated, Grand Rapids, Mich., a corporation of Delaware

Application May 1, 1957, Serial No. 45,960

Term of patent 14 years

(Cl. D56—4)

Fig. 1.

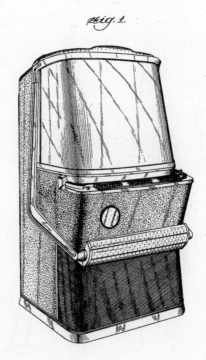

TITLE: DESK TELEPHONE
INVENTOR: PETER ALEKSA
ASSIGNEE: GENERAL TELEPHONE LABORATORIES

PATENT NUMBER: USD 182,450
PATENT FILED: JUNE 10, 1957
PATENT GRANTED: APRIL 8, 1958

United States Patent Office

Des. 182,450
Patented Apr. 8, 1958

182,450

DESK TELEPHONE

Peter Aleksa, Chicago, Ill., assignor to General Telephone
Laboratories, Incorporated, Chicago, Ill., a corporation of Delaware

Application June 10, 1957, Serial No. 46,536

Term of patent 14 years

(Cl. D26—14)

FIG. 1

FIG. 2

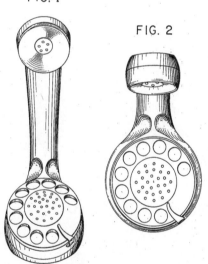

TITLE: CLOCK OR SIMILAR ARTICLE
INVENTOR: WILLIAM V. JUDSON
ASSIGNEE: GENERAL ELECTRIC COMPANY

PATENT NUMBER: USD 182,723
PATENT FILED: MAY 2, 1957
PATENT GRANTED: MAY 6, 1958

United States Patent Office

Des. 182,723
Patented May 6, 1958

182,723

CLOCK OR SIMILAR ARTICLE

William V. Judson, Dover, Mass., assignor to General Electric Company, a corporation of New York

Application May 2, 1957, Serial No. 45,979

Term of patent 14 years

(Cl. D42—7)

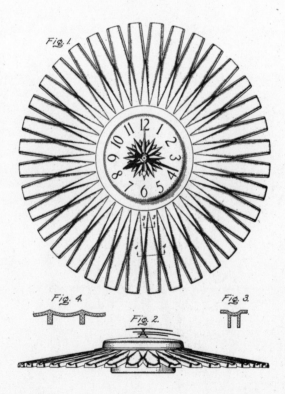

Fig. 1

Fig. 4

Fig. 2

Fig. 3

Fig. 1 is a front elevational view of a clock embodying my new design;

Fig. 2 is a top plan view of the clock shown in Fig. 1;

Fig. 3 is a fragmentary cross-sectional view of a portion of the clock shown in Fig. 1 taken along the line 3—3 of Fig. 1; and,

Fig. 4 is a fragmentary cross-sectional view of a portion of the clock shown in Fig. 1 taken along the line 4—4 of Fig. 1.

I claim:

The ornamental design for a clock or similar article, substantially as shown.

References Cited in the file of this patent

UNITED STATES PATENTS

D. 108,488   Carpenter _____ Feb. 15, 1938

OTHER REFERENCES

Sears, Roebuck and Company 1955 Christmas Book, page 19, item L.

Interiors, August 1954, page 109, asterisk clock, Howard Miller Clock Company adv.

TITLE: DISHWASHER
INVENTORS: HARRISON K. LINGER & ROBERT W. BLEE
ASSIGNEE: THE GENERAL ELECTRIC COMPANY

PATENT NUMBER: USD 182,968
PATENT FILED: MARCH 21, 1957
PATENT GRANTED: JUNE 3, 1958

United States Patent Office

Des. 182,968
Patented June 3, 1958

182,968

DISHWASHER

Harrison K. Linger and Robert W. Blee, Jefferson County,
Ky., assignors to General Electric Company, a corporation of New York

Application March 21, 1957, Serial No. 45,377

Term of patent 14 years

(Cl. D49—1)

The single figure is a perspective view of a dishwasher
embodying our design.

The dominant features of our design reside in the portions shown in full lines.

We claim:

The ornamental design for a dishwasher, as shown and
described.

References Cited in the file of this patent

UNITED STATES PATENTS

D. 161,876   Sandin et al. _____ Feb. 6, 1951
D. 176,493   Becker et al. _____ Jan. 3, 1956

OTHER REFERENCES

Electrical Merchandising, vol. 88, January–March 1956,
January 1956, pages 214 and 215, American Kitchens
adv., "Roll-o-matic" mobile dishwasher.

TITLE: MOTOR COACH
INVENTORS: ROLAND E. GEGOUX & WILLIAM P. STRONG
ASSIGNEE: GENERAL MOTORS CORPORATION

PATENT NUMBER: USD 182,998
PATENT FILED: DECEMBER 4, 1957
PATENT GRANTED: JUNE 10, 1958

United States Patent Office

Des. 182,998
Patented June 10, 1958

182,998

MOTOR COACH

Roland E. Gegoux and William P. Strong, Pontiac, Mich.,
assignors to General Motors Corporation, Detroit,
Mich., a corporation of Delaware

Application December 4, 1957, Serial No. 48,769

Term of patent 7 years

(Cl. D14—3)

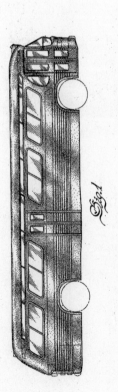

TITLE: LAMP
INVENTOR: GERALD MOSS
ASSIGNEE: NONE

PATENT NUMBER: USD 183,137
PATENT FILED: JUNE 19, 1957
PATENT GRANTED: JULY 1, 1958

United States Patent Office

Des. 183,137
Patented July 1, 1958

183,137

LAMP

Gerald Moss, San Francisco, Calif.

Application June 19, 1957, Serial No. 46,650

Term of patent 14 years

(Cl. D48—20)

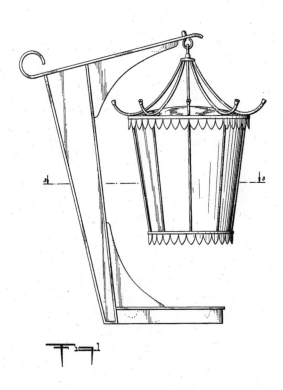

TITLE: LAWN SPRINKLER
INVENTOR: FREDERICK DAVID CHAPMAN
ASSIGNEE: SCOVILL MANUFACTURING COMPANY

PATENT NUMBER: USD 183,510
PATENT FILED: OCTOBER 15, 1957
PATENT GRANTED: SEPTEMBER 16, 1958

United States Patent Office

Des. 183,510
Patented Sept. 16, 1958

183,510

LAWN SPRINKLER

Frederick David Chapman, Chicago, Ill., assignor to Scovill Manufacturing Company, Waterbury, Conn., a corporation of Connecticut

Application October 15, 1957, Serial No. 48,099

Term of patent 14 years

(Cl. D91—1)

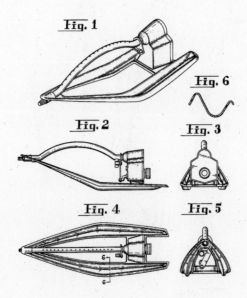

Fig. 1
Fig. 6
Fig. 2
Fig. 3
Fig. 4
Fig. 5

Fig. 1 is a perspective view of a lawn sprinkler showing my new design;

Fig. 2 is a front elevational view of the sprinkler shown on a slightly reduced scale;

Fig. 3 is an end elevational view taken from the right of Fig. 2;

Fig. 4 is a top plan view thereof;

Fig. 5 is an end elevational view taken from the left of Fig. 2;

Fig. 6 is a sectional view taken along the line 6—6 of Fig. 4.

I claim:

The ornamental design of a lawn sprinkler, as shown.

References Cited in the file of this patent

UNITED STATES PATENTS

D. 178,782   Jepson   _____ Sept. 18, 1956

TITLE: TELEVISION RECEIVER
INVENTORS: RICHARD J. WHIPPLE & SEVERIN JONASSEN
ASSIGNEE: PHILCO CORPORATION

PATENT NUMBER: USD 183,780
PATENT FILED: NOVEMBER 19, 1957
PATENT GRANTED: OCTOBER 21, 1958

United States Patent Office

Des. 183,780
Patented Oct. 21, 1958

183,780

TELEVISION RECEIVER

Richard J. Whipple, Abington, and Severin Jonassen,
Lafayette Hill, Pa., assignors to Philco Corporation,
Philadelphia, Pa., a corporation of Pennsylvania

Application November 19, 1957, Serial No. 48,550

Term of patent 14 years

(Cl. D56—4)

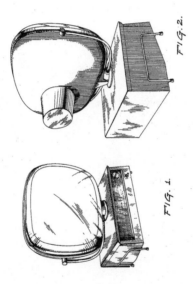

Figure 1 is a front perspective view of a television receiver, showing our new design; and

Figure 2 is a rear perspective view thereof.

The side of the television receiver not shown is substantially the same in appearance as the side shown.

We claim:

The ornamental design for a television receiver, substantially as shown and described.

References Cited in the file of this patent

UNITED STATES PATENTS

D. 152,341	Kromhout	Jan. 11, 1949
D. 156,919	Schubert et al.	Jan. 17, 1950
D. 161,245	Carrier	Dec. 19, 1950
D. 170,882	McGunnigle	Nov. 17, 1953

OTHER REFERENCES

Allied Radio Catalog No. 144, © 1955, page 61, item 610, bottom right hand corner.

Stile Industria, April 1957, page 17, television sets, right hand column.

Industrial Design, February, 1955, page 91, second row, first and second cabinets from left.

TITLE: WEATHER VANE DESK ORNAMENT
INVENTOR: RICHARD A. DONGES
ASSIGNEE: PETER PEPPER PRODUCTS

PATENT NUMBER: USD 183,791
PATENT FILED: FEBRUARY 24, 1958
PATENT GRANTED: OCTOBER 28, 1958

United States Patent Office

Des. 183,791
Patented Oct. 28, 1958

183,791

WEATHER VANE DESK ORNAMENT

Richard A. Donges, Inglewood, Calif., assignor to Peter Pepper Products, Inc., Lomita, Calif., a corporation of California

Application February 24, 1958, Serial No. 49,771

Term of patent 7 years

(Cl. D52—9)

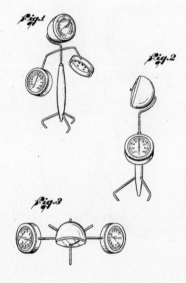

Figure 1 is a perspective view of a weather vane desk ornament showing my new design;

Figure 2 is a side elevational view thereof; and

Figure 3 is a top plan view thereof.

I claim:

The ornamental design for a weather vane desk ornament, substantially as shown.

References Cited in the file of this patent

UNITED STATES PATENTS

D. 138,647	Dubke	Aug. 29,	1944
D. 159,937	Stoddard	Aug. 29,	1950
1,141,459	Gregg	June 1	1915

TITLE: ARM CHAIR
INVENTORS: GEORGE NELSON & JOHN F. PILE
ASSIGNEE: HERMAN MILLER FURNITURE COMPANY

PATENT NUMBER: USD 184,111
PATENT FILED: OCTOBER 3, 1957
PATENT GRANTED: DECEMBER 16, 1958

United States Patent Office

Des. 184,111
Patented Dec. 16, 1958

184,111

ARM CHAIR

George Nelson, Quogue, and John F. Pile, Brooklyn, N. Y., assignors to Herman Miller Furniture Company, Zeeland, Mich., a corporation of Michigan

Application October 3, 1957, Serial No. 47,954

Term of patent 14 years

(Cl. D15—1)

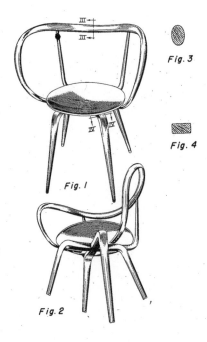

Fig. 3

Fig. 4

Fig. 1

Fig. 2

Fig. 1 is an oblique front elevation view of the arm chair.

Fig. 2 is an oblique bottom view of the chair.

Fig. 3 is a sectional view taken along the plane III—III of Fig. 1.

Fig. 4 is a sectional view taken along the plane IV—IV of Fig. 1.

The essential features of our design reside in the portions shown in solid lines on the drawings.

We claim:

The ornamental design for an arm chair, as shown and described.

References Cited in the file of this patent

"Interiors" Bd., vol. 115, February-July 1956, see issue of February 1956, page 31, note chair legs on chairs illustrated at bottom of page in "Micarta" advertisement.

"Domus" Bd., vol. 314–319, January-June 1956, see issue of June 1956, page 24, note figure-stool base.

"Domus" Bd., vol. 326–331, January-June 1957, see issue of April 1957, page 6, note bases on chairs at bottom of page.

"Office Appliances," December 1936, page 92, note item "A."

TITLE: DICTATION TRANSCRIBING MACHINE
INVENTOR: GORDON W. FLORIAN
ASSIGNEE: DICTAPHONE CORPORATION

PATENT NUMBER: USD 184,254
PATENT FILED: OCTOBER 7, 1957
PATENT GRANTED: JANUARY 13, 1959

United States Patent Office

Des. 184,254
Patented Jan. 13, 1959

184,254

DICTATION TRANSCRIBING MACHINE OR SIMILAR ARTICLE

Gordon W. Florian, Fairfield, Conn., assignor to Dictaphone Corporation, Bridgeport, Conn., a corporation of New York

Application October 7, 1957, Serial No. 47,989

Term of patent 14 years

(Cl. D26—14)

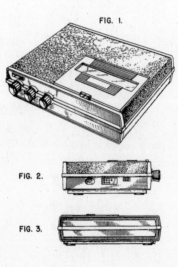

FIG. 1.

FIG. 2.

FIG. 3.

Fig. 1 is a perspective view of a dictation transcribing machine or similar article, showing my new design;

Fig. 2 is a side elevational view; and

Fig. 3 is a rear elevational view thereof.

I claim:

The ornamental design for a dictation transcribing machine or similar article, substantially as shown.

References Cited in the file of this patent

UNITED STATES PATENTS

D. 153,414	Berlant		Apr. 19, 1949
D. 169,559	Otto		May 12, 1953
D. 169,566	Somers		May 12, 1953
D. 173,024	Florian		Sept. 14, 1954
D. 175,490	Aucoin		Sept. 6, 1955

OTHER REFERENCES

Popular Science magazine, January 1953, page 160, Briefcase dictating machine, VP. Voicewriter, by Edison of West Orange, N. J.

Technician magazine, December 1954, page 28, Mohawk Tape recorder by Mohawk Business Machines Corp., 944 Halsey St., Brooklyn 33, N. Y.

TITLE: TIMER
INVENTOR: MELVIN H. BOLDT
ASSIGNEE: NATIONAL PRESTO INDUSTRIES

PATENT NUMBER: USD 184,300
PATENT FILED: DECEMBER 13, 1957
PATENT GRANTED: JANUARY 27, 1959

United States Patent Office

Des. 184,300
Patented Jan. 27, 1959

184,300

TIMER

Melvin H. Boldt, Glenview, Ill., assignor to National
Presto Industries, Inc., Eau Claire, Wis., a corporation
of Wisconsin

Application December 13, 1957, Serial No. 48,895

Term of patent 14 years

(Cl. D42—7)

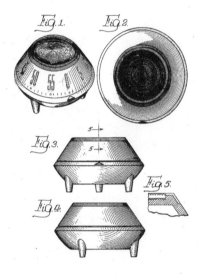

Figure 1 is a perspective view of a timing device showing my new design;

Figure 2 is a top plan view thereof;

Figure 3 is a front elevational view of the timer;

Figure 4 is a side elevation thereof; and

Figure 5 is an enlarged fragmented sectional view taken along **5—5** in Figure 3 to show the concentric grooves in the top surface of the timer and to show the radially extending grooves which are at the periphery of the top of the timer.

The dominant features of the design reside in the por~~ns~~ shown in full lines.

I claim:

The ornamental design for a timer, substantially as shown and described.

References Cited in the file of this patent

Electrical Merchandising, September 1955, page 111, Robertshaw-Fulton Controls Co. adv., thermostat and timer controls.

Mart, February 1957, page 21, Electronics Inc. adv., "Magic Genie."

TITLE: WALL MOUNTING FOR TELEPHONE HANDSET
INVENTOR: E. BURTON BENJAMIN
ASSIGNEE: GENERAL TELEPHONE LABORATORIES

PATENT NUMBER: USD 185,259
PATENT FILED: APRIL 28, 1958
PATENT GRANTED: MAY 26, 1959

United States Patent Office

Des. 185,259
Patented May 26, 1959

185,259

WALL MOUNTING FOR TELEPHONE HANDSET

E Burton Benjamin, Chicago, Ill., assignor to General
Telephone Laboratories, Incorporated, Northlake, Ill.,
a corporation of Delaware

Application April 28, 1958, Serial No. 50,640

Term of patent 14 years

(Cl. D26—14)

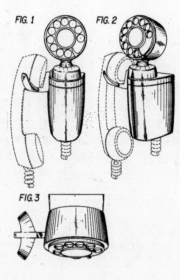

Fig. 1 is a front perspective view of a wall mounting
for telephone handset showing my new design;

Fig. 2 is a side perspective view thereof; and

Fig. 3 is a top plan view thereof.

The broken line showing of the handset and fragmentary portions of connecting cord in Figs. 1 and 2
are for illustrative purposes only.

I claim:

The ornamental design for a wall mounting for telephone handset, substantially as shown and described.

References Cited in the file of this patent
UNITED STATES PATENTS

1,790,930   Lawton _____ Feb. 3, 1931

OTHER REFERENCES

Bell Telephone Brochure received November 12, 1956,
page 3, central portion, top panel.

TITLE: FOOD & DRINK MIXER
INVENTOR: ALFRED W. MADL
ASSIGNEE: THE JOHN OSTER MANUFACTURING COMPANY

PATENT NUMBER: USD 185,765
PATENT FILED: FEBRUARY 13, 1959
PATENT GRANTED: JULY 28, 1959

United States Patent Office

Des. 185,765
Patented July 28, 1959

185,765

FOOD AND DRINK MIXER

Alfred W. Madl, Milwaukee, Wis., assignor to The John
Oster Manufacturing Co., Milwaukee, Wis., a corporation of Wisconsin

Application February 13, 1959, Serial No. 54,598

Term of patent 14 years

(Cl. D44—1)

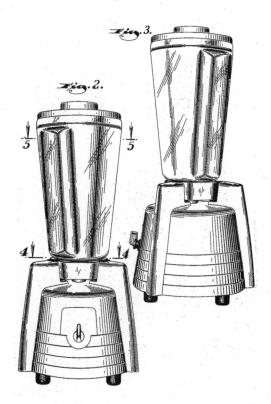

TITLE: ARCHITECTURAL SCREEN OR SIMILAR ARTICLE
INVENTOR: ERWIN FRANZ HAUER
ASSIGNEE: NONE

PATENT NUMBER: USD 186,216
PATENT FILED: APRIL 26, 1957
PATENT GRANTED: SEPTEMBER 29, 1959

United States Patent Office

Des. 186,216
Patented Sept. 29, 1959

186,216

ARCHITECTURAL SCREEN OR SIMILAR ARTICLE

Erwin Franz Hauer, New Haven, Conn.

Application April 26, 1957, Serial No. 45,909

Term of patent 14 years

(Cl. D18—2)

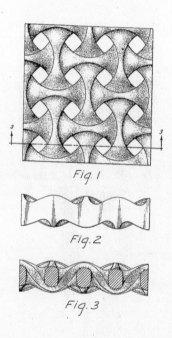

Fig. 1

Fig. 2

Fig. 3

Figure 1 is a front elevation of an architectural screen or similar article showing my new design;

Figure 2 is an edge view taken from the bottom of Fig. 1; and

Figure 3 is a section taken along the line 3—3 of Figure 1.

I claim:

The ornamental design for an architectural screen or similar article, as shown.

References Cited in the file of this patent

UNITED STATES PATENTS

D. 74,115   Mandalian _____ Dec. 20, 1927
1,907,056   Galloway _____ May 2, 1933

TITLE: CLOCK
INVENTORS: FREDERIC MARTI & GEORGES BRAUNSCHWEIG
ASSIGNEE: NONE

PATENT NUMBER: USD 186,530
PATENT FILED: SEPTEMBER 13, 1957
PATENT GRANTED: NOVEMBER 3, 1959

United States Patent Office

Des. 186,530
Patented Nov. 3, 1959

186,530

CLOCK

**Frederic Marti and Georges Braunschweig,
La Chaux de Fonds, Switzerland**

Application September 13, 1957, Serial No. 47,728

Term of patent 14 years

(Cl. D42—7)

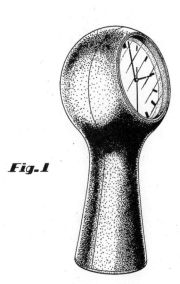

Fig. 1

TITLE: CLOCK OR SIMILAR ARTICLE
INVENTOR: CARL N. JOHNSON
ASSIGNEE: GENERAL ELECTRIC COMPANY

PATENT NUMBER: USD 186,780
PATENT FILED: JULY 28, 1959
PATENT GRANTED: DECEMBER 1, 1959

United States Patent Office

Des. 186,780
Patented Dec. 1, 1959

186,780

CLOCK OR SIMILAR ARTICLE

Carl N. Johnson, Stratford, Conn., assignor to General
Electric Company, a corporation of New York

Application July 28, 1959, Serial No. 56,969

Term of patent 7 years

(Cl. D42—7)

Fig. 1.

TITLE: DWELLING
INVENTOR: AUGUST H. STARK
ASSIGNEE: NONE

PATENT NUMBER: USD 186,976
PATENT FILED: SEPTEMBER 25, 1957
PATENT GRANTED: JANUARY 5, 1960

United States Patent Office

Des. 186,976
Patented Jan. 5, 1960

186,976

DWELLING

August H. Stark, Denver, Colo.

Application September 25, 1957, Serial No. 47,863

Term of patent 7 years

(Cl. D13—1)

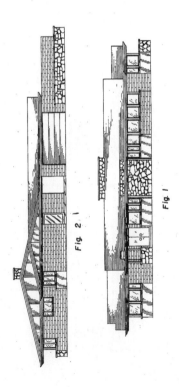

Fig. 2

Fig. 1

TITLE: PHOTOGRAPHIC CAMERA OR SIMILAR ARTICLE
INVENTOR: KEIICHI SOMEHA
ASSIGNEE: KABUSHIKI KAISHA YASHICA

PATENT NUMBER: USD 187,563
PATENT FILED: AUGUST 21, 1959
PATENT GRANTED: MARCH 29, 1960

United States Patent Office

Des. 187,563
Patented Mar. 29, 1960

187,563

PHOTOGRAPHIC CAMERA OR SIMILAR ARTICLE

Keiichi Someha, Shinjuku-ku, Tokyo, Japan, assignor to
Kabushiki Kaisha Yashica, Tokyo, Japan, a corporation of Japan

Application August 21, 1959, Serial No. 57,251

Claims priority, application Japan March 6, 1959

Term of patent 14 years

(Cl. D61—1)

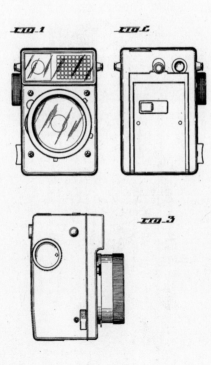

TITLE: COMBINED AUTOMOBILE & HELICOPTER
INVENTOR: STEVEN POSTELSON APOSTOLESCU
ASSIGNEE: NONE

PATENT NUMBER: USD 187,625
PATENT FILED: FEBRUARY 12, 1959
PATENT GRANTED: APRIL 5, 1960

United States Patent Office

Des. 187,625
Patented Apr. 5, 1960

187,625

COMBINED AUTOMOBILE AND HELICOPTER

Steven Postelson Apostolescu, New York, N.Y.

Application February 12, 1959, Serial No. 54,590

Term of patent 14 years

(Cl. D71—1)

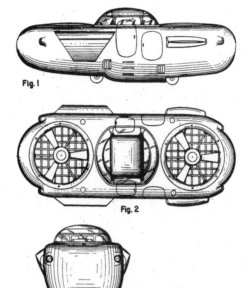

Fig. 1

Fig. 2

Fig. 3

Fig. 1 is a side elevational view of a combined automobile and helicopter showing my new design, and the appearance from the rear is substantially the same as the front appearance shown in Fig. 3, as indicated in Fig. 2.

Fig. 2 is a top plan view thereof.

Fig. 3 is a front view thereof.

The side of the combined automobile and helicopter not shown is a mirror image of the side shown in Fig. 1.

I claim:

The ornamental design for a combined automobile and helicopter, as shown and described.

References Cited in the file of this patent

UNITED STATES PATENTS

D. 169,720   Apostolescu _____ June 2, 1953
D. 183,816   Simmons _____ Oct. 28, 1958

OTHER REFERENCES

Popular Mechanics, vol. 108, No. 1, July 1957, page 74, aerial vehicle at top of page by Hiller Helicopters.

TITLE: TABLE OR THE LIKE
INVENTOR: EERO SAARINEN
ASSIGNEE: NONE

PATENT NUMBER: USD 187,797
PATENT FILED: MAY 3, 1957
PATENT GRANTED: MAY 3, 1960

United States Patent Office

Des. 187,797
Patented May 3, 1960

187,797

TABLE OR THE LIKE

Eero Saarinen, Bloomfield Hills, Mich.

Application May 3, 1957, Serial No. 46,001

Term of patent 14 years

(Cl. D33—14)

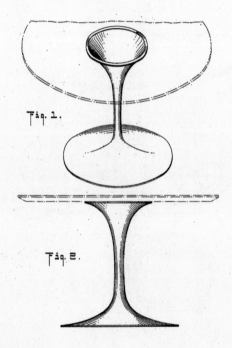

Fig. 1.

Fig. 2.

Fig. 1 is a perspective view of a table embodying the new design; and

Fig. 2 is an elevational view of the table of Fig. 1.

The dominant features of my design reside in those portions shown in full lines in the drawing.

I claim:

The ornamental design for a table or the like, as shown and described.

References Cited in the file of this patent

Lloyd Chromium Furniture Cat., No. 41–A, © 1941, page 46, item T–70–C–AR, ash receiver; page 44, item T–72–C, table.

Interiors, August 1954, page 14, left center of page, "Stalagmite Cave."

TITLE: LAMP
INVENTOR: GERALD E. THURSTON
ASSIGNEE: LIGHTOLIER

PATENT NUMBER: USD 187,814
PATENT FILED: MARCH 26, 1959
PATENT GRANTED: MAY 3, 1960

United States Patent Office

Des. 187,814
Patented May 3, 1960

187,814

LAMP

Gerald E. Thurston, Cranford, N.J., assignor to Lightolier
Incorporated, a corporation of New York

Application March 26, 1959, Serial No. 55,194

Term of patent 7 years

(Cl. D48—20)

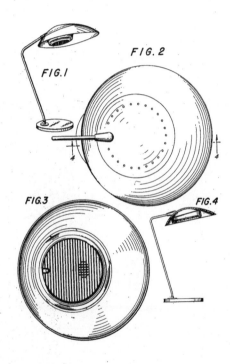

FIG.1
FIG.2
FIG.3
FIG.4

Fig. 1 is a reduced perspective view of the lamp, showing my new design.

Fig. 2 is a top plan view thereof,

Fig. 3 is a bottom plan view of the shade portion of the lamp, and

Fig. 4 is a reduced partial sectional view taken along line 4—4 of Fig. 2.

I claim:

The ornamental design for a lamp, substantially as shown.

References Cited in the file of this patent

Lighting and Lamps, March 1952, page 56, Raytomic Lamp, bottom center of page.

Sweet's Architectural File, 1956, Sec. 31a/Pr, page 11, Lamp BT–33, bottom right of page.

TITLE: ELECTRIC TOASTER
INVENTOR: WALTER E. MOORE
ASSIGNEE: KNAPP-MONARCH COMPANY

PATENT NUMBER: USD 187,836
PATENT FILED: DECEMBER 14, 1959
PATENT GRANTED: MAY 3, 1960

United States Patent Office

Des. 187,836
Patented May 3, 1960

187,836

ELECTRIC TOASTER

Walter E. Moore, St. Louis, Mo., assignor to Knapp-Monarch Company, St. Louis, Mo., a corporation of Delaware

Application December 14, 1959, Serial No. 58,664

Term of patent 14 years

(Cl. D81—10)

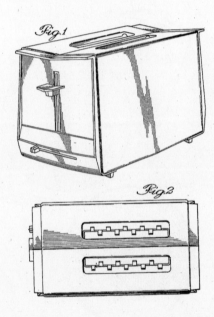

Fig.1

Fig.2

TITLE: SAUCEPAN
INVENTOR: RAYMOND LOEWY
ASSIGNEE: LE CREUSET

PATENT NUMBER: USD 187,995
PATENT FILED: JULY 23, 1959
PATENT GRANTED: MAY 24, 1960

United States Patent Office

Des. 187,995
Patented May 24, 1960

187,995

SAUCEPAN

Raymond Loewy, New York, N.Y., assignor to Le Creuset, Aisne, France, a corporation of France

Filed July 23, 1959, Ser. No. 56,907

Claims priority, application France Jan. 28, 1959

Term of patent 14 years

(Cl. D44—1)

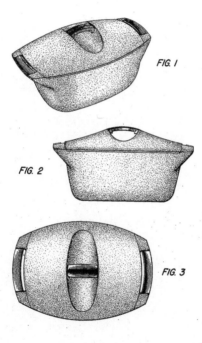

FIG. 1

FIG. 2

FIG. 3

Fig. 1 is a perspective view of the saucepan;
Fig. 2 is a side view;
Fig. 3 is a plan view.
I claim:
The ornamental design for a saucepan, as shown.

References Cited in the file of this patent

UNITED STATES PATENTS

D. 100,992   Fay _____ Aug. 25, 1936
D. 173,094   Schreckengost _____ Sept. 21, 1954

TITLE: EGG CARTON
INVENTOR: HARRY E. LAMBERT
ASSIGNEE: PACKAGING CORPORATION OF AMERICA

PATENT NUMBER: USD 188,472
PATENT FILED: FEBRUARY 9, 1959
PATENT GRANTED: JULY 26, 1960

United States Patent Office

Des. 188,472
Patented July 26, 1960

188,472

EGG CARTON

Harry E. Lambert, Gary, Ind., assignor to Packaging
Corporation of America, a corporation of Delaware

Filed Feb. 9, 1959, Ser. No. 54,516

Term of patent 14 years

(Cl. D58—13)

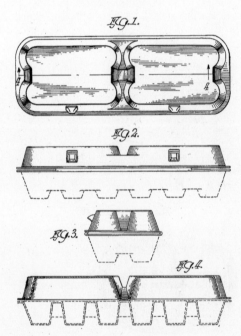

Fig. 1.

Fig. 2.

Fig. 3.

Fig. 4.

Figure 1 is a top plan view of an egg carton, showing my new design;

Fig. 2 is a front elevation thereof;

Fig. 3 is an end elevation; and

Fig. 4 is a vertical longitudinal sectional view on the line 4—4 of Figure 1.

The dominant features of my design reside in the portions shown in full lines.

I claim:

The ornamental design for an egg carton, substantially as shown and described.

References Cited in the file of this patent

UNITED STATES PATENTS

D. 95,291   Sherman _____ Apr. 16, 1935
D. 159,869   Shepard _____ Aug. 22, 1950

TITLE: TABLEWARE DRYING PAN OR SIMILAR ARTICLE
INVENTORS: BENJAMIN H. STANSBURY, JR. & WALTER
DORWIN TEAGUE JR.
ASSIGNEE: COLUMBUS PLASTIC PRODUCTS

PATENT NUMBER: USD 188,864
PATENT FILED: MAY 13, 1960
PATENT GRANTED: SEPTEMBER 20, 1960

United States Patent Office

Des. 188,864
Patented Sept. 20, 1960

188,864

TABLEWARE DRYING PAN OR SIMILAR ARTICLE

Benjamin H. Stansbury, Jr., and Walter Dorwin Teague,
Jr., Alpine, N.J., assignors to Columbus Plastic Products, Inc., Columbus, Ohio, a corporation of Ohio

Filed May 13, 1960, Ser. No. 60,564

Term of patent 14 years

(Cl. D44—29)

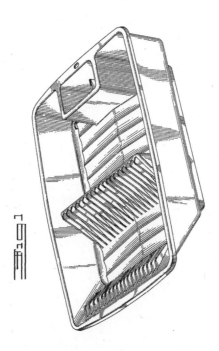

TITLE: PORTABLE BARBECUE GRILL
INVENTORS: ALLEN W. GAUSS & WILLIAM J. CAIN
ASSIGNEE: UNION STEEL PRODUCTS COMPANY

PATENT NUMBER: USD 188,879
PATENT FILED: FEBRUARY 25, 1959
PATENT GRANTED: SEPTEMBER 20, 1960

United States Patent Office

Des. 188,879
Patented Sept. 20, 1960

188,879

PORTABLE BARBECUE GRILL

Allen W. Gauss, Albion, and William J. Cain, Spring
Arbor, Mich., assignors to Union Steel Products Company, Albion, Mich., a corporation of Michigan

Filed Feb. 25, 1959, Ser. No. 54,730

Term of patent 14 years

(Cl. D81—10)

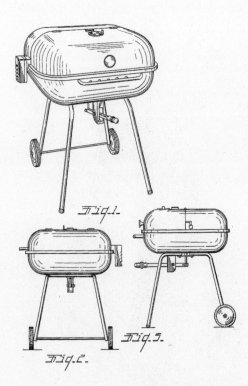

Fig. 1

Fig. 2

Fig. 3

Fig. 1 is a front perspective view of a portable barbecue grill showing our new design;

Fig. 2 is a rear elevational view on a reduced scale;
and

Fig. 3 is a side elevational view from the left of Fig. 2.

We claim:

The ornamental design for a portable barbecue grill,
as shown.

References Cited in the file of this patent

Simmons Hardware Co. Cat., 1939, page 5, oblong
and oval roasters at top right of page.

Better Homes and Gardens, June 1956, page 79, item
8 and item 15; page 93, Hemp and Company Inc. adv.
charcoal grills.

Better Homes and Gardens, June 1957, page 108, control box of top grill and rotisserie at top right of page.

Washington Evening Star, Sunday, March 16, 1958,
page 3, Hecht Co. adv.

TITLE: FORK OR SIMILAR ARTICLE
INVENTOR: JENS H. QUISTGAARD
ASSIGNEE: DANSK DESIGNS

PATENT NUMBER: USD 189,370
PATENT FILED: MARCH 25, 1959
PATENT GRANTED: NOVEMBER 29, 1960

United States Patent Office

Des. 189,370
Patented Nov. 29, 1960

189,370

FORK OR SIMILAR ARTICLE

Jens H. Quistgaard, Copenhagen, Denmark, assignor to
Dansk Designs Inc., Great Neck, N.Y.

Filed Mar. 25, 1959, Ser. No. 55,175

Term of patent 14 years

(Cl. D54—12)

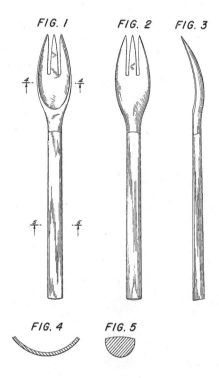

FIG. 1   FIG. 2   FIG. 3

FIG. 4   FIG. 5

Fig. 1 is a front plan view of a fork, showing my new design;

Fig. 2 is a reverse plan view thereof;

Fig. 3 is a side view thereof;

Fig. 4 is an enlarged section taken approximately along lines 4—4 of Fig. 1; and

Fig. 5 is an enlarged section taken approximately along lines 5—5 of Fig. 1.

I claim:

The ornamental design for a fork or similar article, substantially as shown.

References Cited in the file of this patent

UNITED STATES PATENTS

D. 141,695   Nock _____ June 26, 1945
D. 173,048   Wallance _____ Sept. 14, 1954

OTHER REFERENCES

Modern Plastics, June 1936, page 28, item 1—Plastic handled chrome spoon and fork.

Home Furnishings Daily, Aug. 5, 1957, page 1, "Strength in Style" panel, fork at left.

TITLE: AUTOMOBILE
INVENTOR: WILHELM HOFMEISTER
ASSIGNEE: BAYERISCHE MOTOREN WERKE

PATENT NUMBER: USD 189,474
PATENT FILED: JANUARY 13, 1960
PATENT GRANTED: DECEMBER 27, 1960

United States Patent Office

Des. 189,474
Patented Dec. 27, 1960

189,474

AUTOMOBILE

Wilhelm Hofmeister, Munich, Germany, assignor to Bayerische Motoren Werke Aktiengesellschaft, Munich, Germany

Filed Jan. 13, 1960, Ser. No. 59,029

Claims priority, application Germany July 13, 1959

Term of patent 7 years

(Cl. D14—3)

FIG.1

FIG.2

TITLE: TELEVISION CONTROL KNOB
INVENTOR: MELVIN H. BOLDT
ASSIGNEE: ZENITH RADIO CORPORATION

PATENT NUMBER: USD 189,534
PATENT FILED: JULY 28, 1960
PATENT GRANTED: JANUARY 3, 1961

United States Patent Office

Des. 189,534
Patented Jan. 3, 1961

189,534

TELEVISION CONTROL KNOB

Melvin H. Boldt, Glenview, Ill., assignor to Zenith Radio
Corporation, a corporation of Delaware

Filed July 28, 1960, Ser. No. 61,561

Term of patent 14 years

(Cl. D26—13)

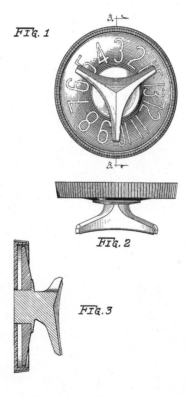

FIG. 1

FIG. 2

FIG. 3

Figure 1 is a front elevational view of a television control knob showing my new design;

Figure 2 is a top plan view thereof; and

Figure 3 is a vertical sectional view thereof as seen from line 3—3 of Figure 1.

The indicia, shown by means of dashed lines in Figure 1, are illustrative only.

I claim:

The ornamental design for a television control knob, substantially as shown and described.

References Cited in the file of this patent

UNITED STATES PATENTS

D. 114,315   Brodbeck _____ Apr. 18, 1939

OTHER REFERENCES

Lafayette Radio Catalog 305, copyrighted 1957, page 39, Fig. P Multi-speaker selector switch.

Lafayette Radio Catolog 600, copyrighted 1959, page 96, 3 speaker selector switch MS–567, at bottom left corner of page.

Radio's Master, 18th edition, 1953–A, page U–123, Knob 920SS and plate 1070 combination.

TITLE: COMBINATION BOWLING BALL RACK
& SCORE TABLE
INVENTOR: HENRY DREYFUSS
ASSIGNEE: AMERICAN MACHINE & FOUNDRY COMPANY

PATENT NUMBER: USD 189,536
PATENT FILED: JUNE 25, 1959
PATENT GRANTED: JANUARY 3, 1961

United States Patent Office

Des. 189,536
Patented Jan. 3, 1961

189,536

COMBINATION BOWLING BALL RACK AND SCORE TABLE

Henry Dreyfuss, New York, N.Y., assignor to American
Machine & Foundry Company, a corporation of New
Jersey

Filed June 25, 1959, Ser. No. 56,538

Term of patent 14 years

(Cl. D34—5)

FIG. 1

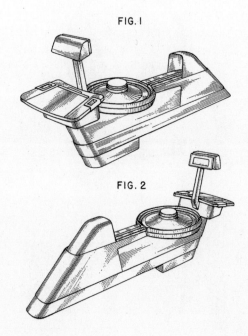

FIG. 2

Fig. 1 is a rear perspective of a combination bowling
ball rack and score table, showing my new design; and
Fig. 2 is a front perspective thereof.

I claim:

The ornamental design for a combination bowling ball
rack and score table, as shown.

References Cited in the file of this patent

UNITED STATES PATENTS

D. 128,988	Cloutier	Aug. 19, 1941
D. 148,838	Anderson et al.	Mar. 2, 1948
D. 178,136	Martin	June 26, 1956

TITLE: HANDLE FOR FAUCETS OR THE LIKE
INVENTOR: FREDERICK DAVID CHAPMAN
ASSIGNEE: MURRAY CORPORATION

PATENT NUMBER: USD 189,712
PATENT FILED: JANUARY 15, 1960
PATENT GRANTED: JANUARY 31, 1961

United States Patent Office

Des. 189,712
Patented Jan. 31, 1961

189,712

HANDLE FOR FAUCETS OR THE LIKE

Frederick David Chapman, Chicago, Ill., assignor to The
Murray Corporation of America, Pittsburgh, Pa., a
corporation of Delaware

Filed Jan. 15, 1960, Ser. No. 59,060

Term of patent 14 years

(Cl. D91—3)

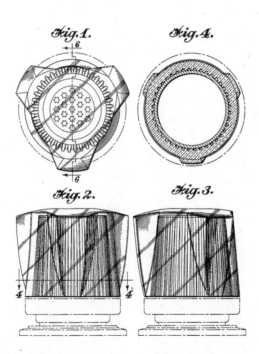

Fig. 1.   Fig. 4.

Fig. 2.   Fig. 3.

TITLE: CASE FOR A CONTACT EXPOSURE MACHINE
INVENTOR: JOSEPH PALMA, JR.
ASSIGNEE: DITTO

PATENT NUMBER: USD 189,703
PATENT FILED: MARCH 30, 1960
PATENT GRANTED: JANUARY 31, 1961

United States Patent Office

Des. 189,703
Patented Jan. 31, 1961

189,703

CASE FOR A CONTACT EXPOSURE MACHINE OR SIMILAR ARTICLE

Joseph Palma, Jr., River Forest, Ill., assignor to Ditto
Incorporated, Chicago, Ill., a corporation of Illinois

Filed Mar. 30, 1960, Ser. No. 59,937

Term of patent 14 years

(Cl. D61—1)

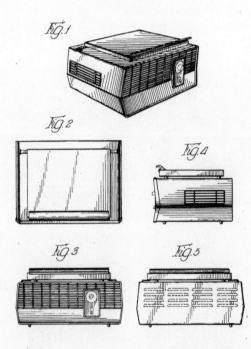

Figure 1 is a perspective view of a case for a contact exposure machine or similar article, showing my new design;

Figure 2 is a top plan view thereof;

Figure 3 is a front elevation thereof;

Figure 4 is a side elevation thereof, showing the side not shown in Figure 1; and

Figure 5 is a rear elevation thereof.

The essential features of my new design are shown in solid lines in the drawing.

I claim:

The ornamental design for a case for a contact exposure machine or similar article, substantially as shown and described.

References Cited in the file of this patent

UNITED STATES PATENTS

D. 115,776	Wolters et al.	July 18, 1939
D. 119,883	Greenblau	Apr. 9, 1940
D. 123,245	Moore	Oct. 22, 1940
D. 170,496	Egan	Sept. 29, 1953
D. 183,766	Petrie	Oct. 21, 1958
2,034,231	Fox	Mar. 17, 1936

OTHER REFERENCES

Masters 1958 Catalog, page 29, Air Conditioners.

TITLE: DESK TELEVISION APPARATUS
FOR INTERCOMMUNICATION SYSTEMS
INVENTOR: RUNE GOTTHARD MONÖ
ASSIGNEE: AKTIEBOLAGET GYLLING & COMPANY

PATENT NUMBER: USD 190,234
PATENT FILED: DECEMBER 31, 1959
PATENT GRANTED: MAY 2, 1961

United States Patent Office

Des. 190,234
Patented May 2, 1961

190,234

DESK TELEPHONE APPARATUS FOR INTER-COMMUNICATION SYSTEMS

Rune Gotthard Monö, Roslags-Nasby, Sweden, assignor to Aktiebolaget Gylling & Co., Stockholm-Grondal, Sweden

Filed Dec. 31, 1959, Ser. No. 58,866

Claims priority, application Norway Sept. 10, 1959

Term of patent 14 years

(Cl. D26—14)

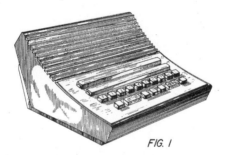

FIG. 1

FIG. 2

TITLE: COMBINED CLOCK & RECEIVER CABINET
INVENTOR: ALFRED R. GILBERT
ASSIGNEE: PHILCO CORPORATION

PATENT NUMBER: USD 190,244
PATENT FILED: MAY 27, 1960
PATENT GRANTED: MAY 2, 1961

United States Patent Office

Des. 190,244
Patented May 2, 1961

190,244

COMBINED CLOCK AND RECEIVER CABINET

Alfred R. Gilbert, Paoli, Pa., assignor to Philco Corporation, Philadelphia, Pa., a corporation of Pennsylvania

Filed May 27, 1960, Ser. No. 60,764

Term of patent 14 years

(Cl. D42—7)

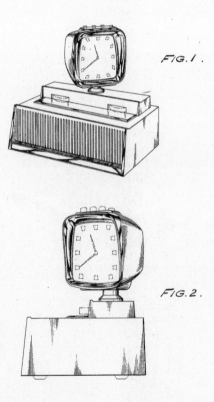

FIG. 1.

FIG. 2.

Figure 1 is a front perspective view of a combined clock and receiver cabinet showing my new design; and

Figure 2 is a side elevational view thereof.

The appearance of the side of the lower cabinet portion of the combined clock and receiver cabinet, not shown in Figures 1 and 2, is generally similar to that shown in said figures. The essential features of the design reside in the portions shown in full lines.

I claim:

The ornamental design for a combined clock and receiver cabinet, as shown and described.

References Cited in the file of this patent

UNITED STATES PATENTS

D. 116,130   Ambrose --------------- Aug. 15, 1939
D. 183,780   Whipple et al. ----------- Oct. 21, 1958
2,872,677   Whipple et al. ----------- Feb. 3, 1953

TITLE: ELEVATED STORAGE TANK
INVENTORS: CLARENCE D. MILLER & JOHN N. PIROK
ASSIGNEE: CHICAGO BRIDGE & IRON COMPANY

PATENT NUMBER: USD 190,464
PATENT FILED: FEBRUARY 8, 1960
PATENT GRANTED: MAY 30, 1961

United States Patent Office

Des. 190,464
Patented May 30, 1961

190,464

ELEVATED STORAGE TANK

Clarence D. Miller, Chicago, and John N. Pirok, Evergreen Park, Ill., assignors to Chicago Bridge & Iron Company, Chicago, Ill., a corporation of Illinois

Continuation of design applications Ser. Nos. 52,856, 52,587, 52,858, and 52,859, Oct. 2, 1958. This application Feb. 8, 1960, Ser. No. 59,300

Term of patent 14 years

(Cl. D91—1)

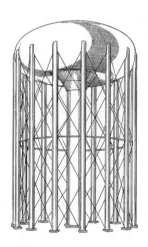

FIGURE 1

TITLE: AUTOMOBILE
INVENTOR: VIRGIL M. EXNER
ASSIGNEE: CHRYSLER CORPORATION

PATENT NUMBER: USD 190,563
PATENT FILED: JULY 5, 1960
PATENT GRANTED: JUNE 13, 1961

United States Patent Office

Des. 190,563
Patented June 13, 1961

190,563

AUTOMOBILE

Virgil M. Exner, Birmingham, Mich., assignor to Chrysler
Corporation, Highland Park, Mich., a corporation of
Delaware

Filed July 5, 1960, Ser. No. 61,228

Term of patent 7 years

(Cl. D14—3)

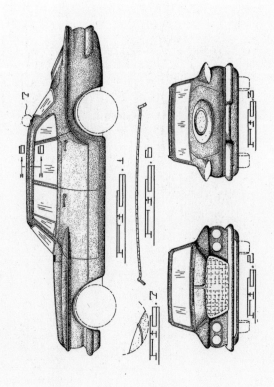

TITLE: ELECTRIC SHAVER
INVENTOR: CARL L. OTTO
ASSIGNEE: SCHICK

PATENT NUMBER: USD 188,244
PATENT FILED: JULY 30, 1959
PATENT GRANTED: JUNE 21, 1961

United States Patent Office

Des. 188,244
Patented June 21, 1960

188,244

ELECTRIC SHAVER

Carl L. Otto, New York, N.Y., assignor to Schick Incorporated, Lancaster, Pa., a corporation of Delaware

Filed July 30, 1959, Ser. No. 57,010

Term of patent 14 years

(Cl. D22—3)

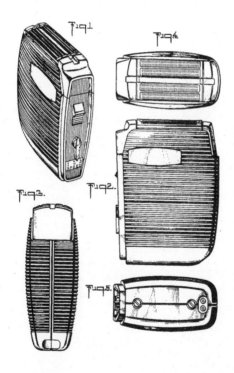

Fig. 1 is a front perspective view of an electric shaver showing my new design;

Fig. 2 is a rear elevational view thereof;

Fig. 3 is a side elevational view thereof;

Fig. 4 is a top plan view; and

Fig. 5 is a bottom plan view thereof.

The essential features of my design reside in the portions shown in solid lines on the drawing.

I claim:

The ornamental design for an electric shaver, substantially as shown and described.

References Cited in the file of this patent

UNITED STATES PATENTS

D. 178,929   Otto _____ Oct. 9, 1956
2,725,625   Muntz _____ Dec. 6, 1955

OTHER REFERENCES

Spors 1956 Wholesale Catalog #84, page 454, center of page, Ronson razor item.

TITLE: TAPE DISPENSER
INVENTOR: JEAN OTIS REINECKE
ASSIGNEE: MINNESOTA MINING
AND MANUFACTURING COMPANY

PATENT NUMBER: USD 190,781
PATENT FILED: NOVEMBER 9, 1959
PATENT GRANTED: JUNE 27, 1961

United States Patent Office

Des. 190,781
Patented June 27, 1961

190,781

TAPE DISPENSER

Jean Otis Reinecke, Chicago, Ill., assignor to Minnesota
Mining and Manufacturing Company, St. Paul, Minn.,
a corporation of Delaware

Filed Nov. 9, 1959, Ser. No. 58,261

Term of patent 14 years

(Cl. D74—1)

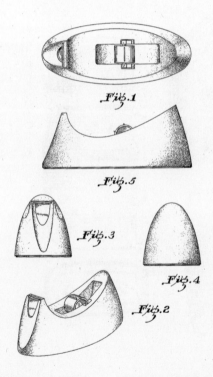

Fig.1

Fig.5

Fig.3

Fig.4

Fig.2

FIGURE 1 is a top plan view of a tape dispenser,
showing my new design;
FIGURE 2 is a side perspective view thereof;
FIGURE 3 is an end elevational view looking from
the left of FIGURE 2;
FIGURE 4 is an end elevational view looking from
the right of FIGURE 2; and
FIGURE 5 is a side elevational view thereof.
I claim:
The ornamental design for a tape dispenser, as shown.

References Cited in the file of this patent

UNITED STATES PATENTS

D. 109,930	Reinecke	May 31, 1938
D. 145,773	Bronfman	Oct. 22, 1946
D. 169,989	Reinecke	July 7, 1953
D. 179,196	Gershen	Nov. 13, 1956
2,540,697	Staples	Feb. 6, 1951

TITLE: CHAIR
INVENTOR: DONALD DESKEY
ASSIGNEE: CHARAK FURNITURE COMPANY

PATENT NUMBER: USD 190,805
PATENT FILED: JANUARY 29, 1959
PATENT GRANTED: JULY 4, 1961

United States Patent Office

Des. 190,805
Patented July 4, 1961

190,805

CHAIR

Donald Deskey, New York, N.Y., assignor to Charak
Furniture Company, Boston, Mass.

Filed Jan. 29, 1959, Ser. No. 54,377

Term of patent 14 years

(Cl. D15—1)

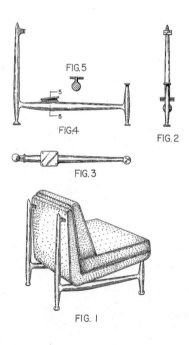

FIG.5

FIG.4

FIG. 2

FIG. 3

FIG. 1

FIGURE 1 is a rear perspective view of a chair showing my design;
FIGURE 2 is a front elevational view of one of the leg supports;
FIGURE 3 is a top plan view thereof;
FIGURE 4 is a side elevational view of one of the identical leg supports; and
FIGURE 5 is a sectional view taken along line 5—5 of FIGURE 4.
The design is characterized by a pair of spaced frame members each being somewhat L-shaped in form, the legs and braces thereof being tapered from the center to the respective end portions as shown.

I claim:
The ornamental design for a chair, as shown and described.

References Cited in the file of this patent

Interiors, August 1956, page 152, bottom right, chair by Cannell and Lincoln.
Interiors, August 1953, page 90, top right, item A–29 chair.
Interiors, March 1954, page 77, bottom right, chair.
Interiors, November 1957, page 65, left, chair.

TITLE: TELEPHONE HANDSET
INVENTORS: HENRY DREYFUSS & ROBERT H. HOSE
ASSIGNEE: BELL TELEPHONE LABORATORIES

PATENT NUMBER: USD 190,810
PATENT FILED: JULY 18, 1960
PATENT GRANTED: JULY 4, 1961

United States Patent Office

Des. 190,810

Patented July 4, 1961

190,810

TELEPHONE HANDSET

Henry Dreyfuss, South Pasadena, Calif., and Robert H. Hose, Mountainside, N.J., assignors to Bell Telephone Laboratories, Incorporated, New York, N.Y., a corporation of New York

Filed July 18, 1960, Ser. No. 61,437

Term of patent 14 years

(Cl. D26—14)

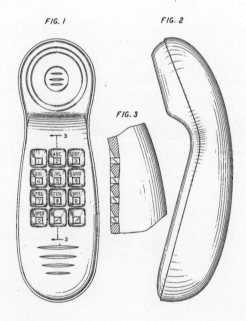

FIG. 1

FIG. 2

FIG. 3

FIG. 1 is a front elevational view of a telephone handset showing our new design;

FIG. 2 is a side elevational view, the opposite side being substantially a mirror image thereof; and

FIG. 3 is a partially sectioned side elevational view taken along section line 3—3 of FIG. 1.

The broken line showing of legible matter is for illustrative purposes only.

We claim:

The ornamental design for a telephone handset, substantially as shown and described.

References Cited in the file of this patent

UNITED STATES PATENTS

D. 184,307   Dreyfuss et al. ---------- Jan. 27, 1959

OTHER REFERENCES

Industrial Design, August 1957, p. 43, telephone set at bottom left corner of page.

Industrial design, December 1959, p. 97, illustrations 190 Dial-in-hand phone, 192 Push-button phone, Bell Telephone Laboratories, New York, Henry Dreyfuss, designers.

TITLE: CASSEROLE
INVENTOR: JENS H. QUISTGAARD
ASSIGNEE: DANSK IMPORTING COMPANY

PATENT NUMBER: USD 190,962
PATENT FILED: NOVEMBER 22, 1960
PATENT GRANTED: JULY 25, 1961

United States Patent Office

Des. 190,962
Patented July 25, 1961

190,962

CASSEROLE

Jens H. Quistgaard, Copenhagen, Denmark, assignor to Dansk Importing Company, Inc., a corporation of New York

Filed Nov. 22, 1960, Ser. No. 62,924

Term of patent 14 years

(Cl. D44—15)

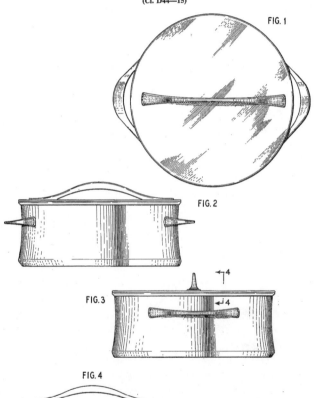

FIG. 1

FIG. 2

FIG. 3

FIG. 4

FIG. 1 is a top plan view of a casserole, showing my new design;

FIGS. 2 and 3 are side elevational views taken at right angles to each other; and

FIG. 4 is a sectional view through the cover, taken on line 4—4 of FIG. 3.

I claim:

The ornamental design for a casserole, as shown.

References Cited in the file of this patent

UNITED STATES PATENTS

D. 96,504   Rantsch _____ Aug. 6, 1935
D. 171,372   Barnhart _____ Feb. 2, 1954

OTHER REFERENCES

Stile Industria, #10, February 1957, p. 14, covered casserole in center panel.

Crockery and Glass Journal, Mar. 3, 1958, p. 26, covered casserole in center of page, note side handles.

TITLE: TEA KETTLE
INVENTOR: IVAR JEPSON
ASSIGNEE: SUNBEAM CORPORATION

PATENT NUMBER: USD 191,005
PATENT FILED: MARCH 16, 1961
PATENT GRANTED: AUGUST 1, 1961

United States Patent Office

Des. 191,005
Patented Aug. 1, 1961

191,005

TEA KETTLE

Ivar Jepson, Oak Park, Ill., assignor to Sunbeam Corporation, Chicago, Ill., a corporation of Illinois

Filed Mar. 16, 1961, Ser. No. 64,339

Term of patent 14 years

(Cl. D44—25)

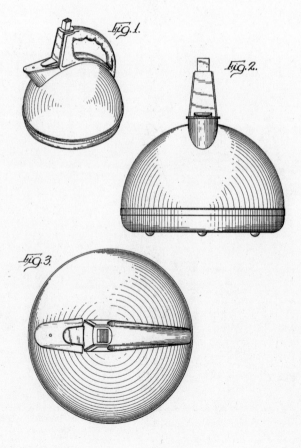

Fig. 1.

Fig. 2.

Fig. 3.

TITLE: WATER CLOSET
INVENTOR: FREDERICK DAVID CHAPMAN
ASSIGNEE: THE MURRAY CORPORATION OF AMERICA

PATENT NUMBER: USD 191,160
PATENT FILED: JANUARY 15, 1960
PATENT GRANTED: AUGUST 22, 1961

United States Patent Office

Des. 191,160
Patented Aug. 22, 1961

191,160

WATER CLOSET

Frederick David Chapman, Chicago, Ill., assignor to The
Murray Corporation of America, Pittsburgh, Pa., a
corporation of Delaware

Filed Jan. 15, 1960, Ser. No. 59,053

Term of patent 14 years

(Cl. D4—5)

FIG. I

TITLE: RESTAURANT
INVENTOR: JOSEPH A. CICCO
ASSIGNEE: NONE

PATENT NUMBER: USD 191,198
PATENT FILED: MAY 8, 1961
PATENT GRANTED: AUGUST 29, 1961

United States Patent Office

Des. 191,198
Patented Aug. 29, 1961

191,198

RESTAURANT

Joseph A. Cicco, 12 Squanto Road, Quincy, Mass.

Filed May 8, 1961, Ser. No. 65,062

Term of patent 14 years

(Cl. D13—1)

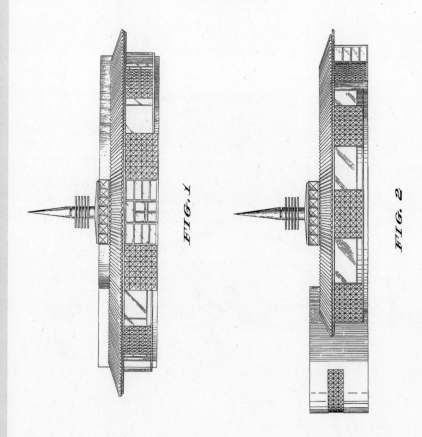

FIG. 1

FIG. 2

596

TITLE: RADIANT HEATER
INVENTOR: JON W. HAUSER
ASSIGNEE: MCGRAW-EDISON COMPANY

PATENT NUMBER: USD 191,384
PATENT FILED: FEBRUARY 6, 1959
PATENT GRANTED: SEPTEMBER 19, 1961

United States Patent Office

Des. 191,384
Patented Sept. 19, 1961

191,384

RADIANT HEATER

Jon W. Hauser, St. Charles Township, Kane County, Ill., assignor to McGraw-Edison Company, Elgin, Ill., a corporation of Delaware

Filed Feb. 6, 1959, Ser. No. 54,481

Term of patent 14 years

(Cl. D81—10)

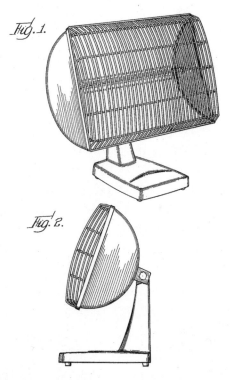

Fig. 1.

Fig. 2.

FIG. 1 is a perspective view showing the front and right side of a radiant heater embodying my new design, the rear thereof being plain; and

FIG. 2 is an elevation showing the left side thereof.

The dominant features of the design reside in the portions shown in full lines.

I claim:

The ornamental design for a radiant heater, substantially as shown and described.

References Cited in the file of this patent

UNITED STATES PATENTS

D. 155,243   Sundberg _____ Sept. 13, 1949
2,512,061   Huck _____ June 20, 1950

FOREIGN PATENTS

191,523   Austria _____ Aug. 26, 1957

OTHER REFERENCES

Industrial Design, June 1954, page 108, British Ferranti cast-iron heater.

Electrical Merchandising, July 1945, page 124, ultra violet lamp adv. by SunKraft Inc.

Electrical Merchandising, August 1945, page 146, germicidal lamp adv. by Federal Engineering Company.

Electrical Merchandising, December 1957, page 68, Dominion Fan No. 2030.

Electrical Merchandising, January 1958, page 44, Hobart Manufacturing Company adv., food preparer.

TITLE: WALL CLOCK
INVENTOR: DAVID A. PATIENCE
ASSIGNEE: RUBBER PRODUCTS

PATENT NUMBER: USD 191,525
PATENT FILED: FEBRUARY 8, 1961
PATENT GRANTED: OCTOBER 10, 1961

United States Patent Office

Des. 191,525

Patented Oct. 10, 1961

191,525

WALL CLOCK

David A. Patience, Melrose Park, Ill., assignor to Rubber
Products, Inc., Chicago, Ill., a corporation of Illinois

Filed Feb. 8, 1961, Ser. No. 63,864

Term of patent 3½ years

(Cl. D42—7)

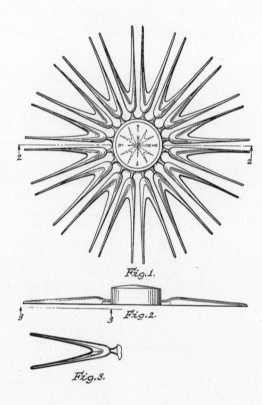

Fig.1.

Fig.2.

Fig.3.

FIG. 1 is a front elevational view of a wall clock, showing my new design;

FIG. 2 is a fragmentary sectional detail view taken on
line 2—2 of FIG. 1;

FIG. 3 is a fragmentary sectional detail view taken on
line 3—3 of FIG. 2.

The essential features of my design reside in the portions
shown in full lines in the drawings.

I claim:

The ornamental design for a wall clock, as shown and
described.

References Cited in the file of this patent

Office Appliances, September 1958, page 120: wall
clocks.

Jewelers' Circular-Keystone, September 1960, page 152;
clock.

TITLE: ADDING MACHINE
INVENTORS: CARL W. SUNDBERG & MONTGOMERY FERAR
ASSIGNEE: SPERRY RAND CORPORATION

PATENT NUMBER: USD 191,644
PATENT FILED: JUNE 7, 1961
PATENT GRANTED: OCTOBER 24, 1961

United States Patent Office

Des. 191,644
Patented Oct. 24, 1961

191,644

ADDING MACHINE

Carl W. Sundberg, Bloomfield Hills, and Montgomery
Ferar, Huntington Woods, Mich., assignors to Sperry
Rand Corporation, New York, N.Y., a corporation of
Delaware

Filed June 7, 1961, Ser. No. 65,509

Term of patent 14 years

(Cl. D64—11)

FIG. I

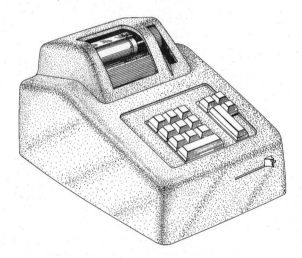

TITLE: POWER LAWN MOWER
INVENTOR: ROBERT O. ERNEST
ASSIGNEE: SUNBEAM CORPORATION

PATENT NUMBER: USD 191,675
PATENT FILED: MAY 8, 1961
PATENT GRANTED: OCTOBER 31, 1961

United States Patent Office

Des. 191,675
Patented Oct. 31, 1961

191,675

POWER LAWN MOWER

Robert O. Ernest, Oak Park, Ill., assignor to Sunbeam
Corporation, Chicago, Ill., a corporation of Illinois

Filed May 8, 1961, Ser. No. 65,049

Term of patent 14 years

(Cl. D40—1)

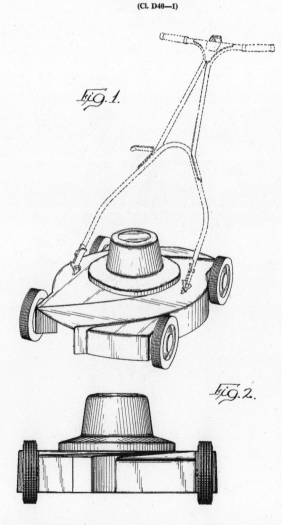

Fig. 1.

Fig. 2.

TITLE: TELEVISION RECEIVER
INVENTORS: RUDOLPH W. KROLLOP
& EDWIN O. STASTNY
ASSIGNEE: MOTOROLA

PATENT NUMBER: USD 191,768
PATENT FILED: OCTOBER 14, 1960
PATENT GRANTED: NOVEMBER 14, 1961

United States Patent Office

Des. 191,768
Patented Nov. 14, 1961

191,768

TELEVISION RECEIVER

Rudolph W. Krolopp, Villa Park, and Edwin O. Stastny,
Lombard, Ill., assignors to Motorola, Inc., Chicago,
Ill., a corporation of Illinois

Filed Oct. 14, 1960, Ser. No. 62,497

Term of patent 14 years

(Cl. D56—4)

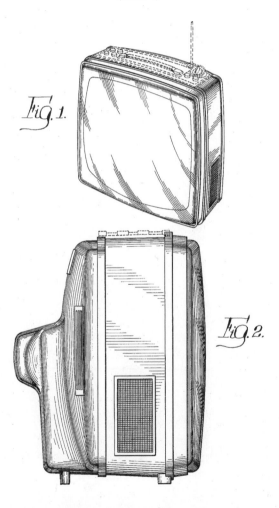

Fig. 1.

Fig. 2.

TITLE: TYPEWRITER
INVENTOR: ELIOT NOYES
ASSIGNEE: INTERNATIONAL BUSINESS
MACHINES CORPORATION

PATENT NUMBER: USD 192,829
PATENT FILED: APRIL 21, 1960
PATENT GRANTED: MAY 15, 1962

United States Patent Office

Des. 192,829
Patented May 15, 1962

192,829

TYPEWRITER

Eliot Noyes, New Canaan, Conn., assignor to International Business Machines Corporation, New York, N.Y., a corporation of New York

Filed Apr. 21, 1961, Ser. No. 64,841

Term of patent 14 years

(Cl. D64—11)

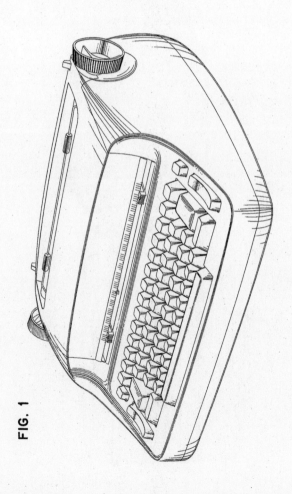

FIG. 1

TITLE: GASOLINE PUMP
INVENTOR: GEORGE B. KAMP
ASSIGNEE: BOWSER

PATENT NUMBER: USD 193,209
PATENT FILED: AUGUST 31, 1961
PATENT GRANTED: JULY 10, 1962

United States Patent Office

Des. 193,209
Patented July 10, 1962

193,209

GASOLINE PUMP

George B. Kamp, Springfield, Pa., assignor to Bowser, Inc., Fort Wayne, Ind., a corporation of Indiana

Filed Aug. 31, 1961, Ser. No. 66,564

Term of patent 14 years

(Cl. D52—2)

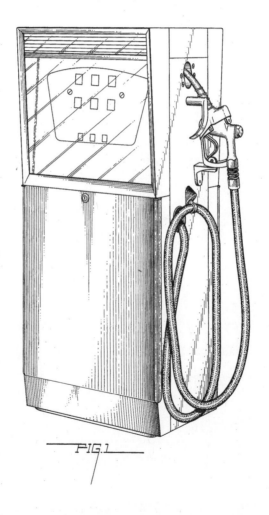

FIG. 1

TITLE: STOVE
INVENTORS: ROBERT A. CLARK & PETER L. HELGESON
ASSIGNEE: CALORIC APPLIANCE CORPORATION

PATENT NUMBER: USD 193,822
PATENT FILED: JULY 26, 1961
PATENT GRANTED: OCTOBER 9, 1962

United States Patent Office

Des. 193,822
Patented Oct. 9, 1962

193,822

STOVE

Robert A. Clark, Allentown, and Peter L. Helgeson, Wes-
cosville, Pa., assignors to Caloric Appliance Corporation, Topton, Pa., a corporation of Pennsylvania

Filed July 26, 1961, Ser. No. 66,070

Term of patent 14 years

(Cl. D81—4)

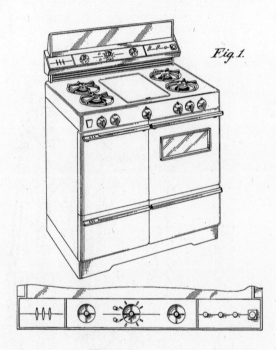

Fig. 1.

Fig. 2.

FIG. 1 is a perspective view of a stove showing our
new design; and

FIG. 2 is an enlarged fragmentary view showing the
control panel element of the stove.

The undisclosed side of the stove is a mirror image of
the side shown and the rear of the stove is substantially
plain.

We claim:

The ornamental design for a stove, as shown and described.

References Cited in the file of this patent

Sears Roebuck and Co. Cat., Fall and Winter, 1960,
No. 221, Philadelphia, page 1243, Kenmore ranges.

Mart, July 1960, page 28, Waste King Corp. adv.

TITLE: INK MARKER
INVENTOR: SAMUEL AYERS, JR.
ASSIGNEE: THE CARTER'S INK COMPANY

PATENT NUMBER: USD 193,918
PATENT FILED: NOVEMBER 14, 1961
PATENT GRANTED: OCTOBER 23, 1962

United States Patent Office

Des. 193,918
Patented Oct. 23, 1962

193,918

INK MARKER

Samuel Ayres, Jr., Marblehead, Mass., assignor to The Carter's Ink Company, Cambridge, Mass., a corporation of Massachusetts

Filed Nov. 14, 1961, Ser. No. 67,518

Term of patent 14 years

(Cl. D74—1)

FIG. 4

FIG. 3

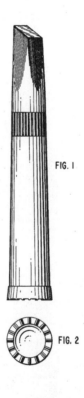

FIG. I

FIG. 2

FIG. 1 is a side elevational view of an ink marker showing my new design;

FIG. 2 is a bottom plan view;

FIG. 3 is an exploded elevational view thereof; and

FIG. 4 is a top plan view of the cap portion.

The essential features of my design reside in the portions shown in solid lines of the drawings. The conventional felt nib portion has been omitted for convenience of illustration.

I claim:

The ornamental design for an ink marker, substantially as shown and described.

References Cited in the file of this patent

UNITED STATES PATENTS

D.	82,821	Furedy _____	Dec. 16, 1930
D.	188,267	Bunn et al. _____	June 21, 1960
D.	189,896	Vuillemenot _____	Mar. 14, 1961
	2,713,176	Rosenthal _____	July 19, 1955

OTHER REFERENCES

Office Appliances, November 1960, page 86.
Office Appliances, November 1960, page 85.

TITLE: AUTOMOBILE
INVENTOR: WILHELM HOFMEISTER
ASSIGNEE: BAYERISCHE MOTOREN WERKE

PATENT NUMBER: USD 194,179
PATENT FILED: JANUARY 25, 1962
PATENT GRANTED: DECEMBER 4, 1962

United States Patent Office

Des. 194,179
Patented Dec. 4, 1962

194,179

AUTOMOBILE

Wilhelm Hofmeister, Munich, Germany, assignor to Bayerische Motoren Werke Aktiengesellschaft, Munich,
Germany

Filed Jan. 25, 1962, Ser. No. 68,514

Term of patent 14 years

Claims priority, application Germany Aug. 1, 1961

(Cl. D14—3)

FIG.1

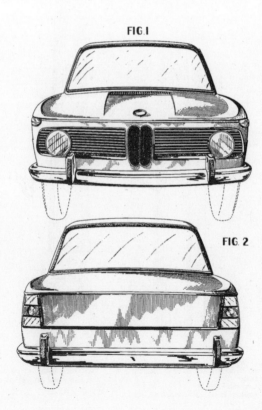

FIG. 2

TITLE: ELECTRIC APPLIANCE FOR COOKING SANDWICHES,
COOKIES, PASTRIES AND OTHER FOOD ARTICLES
INVENTOR: ROSS E. CORNWELL
ASSIGNEE: SUNBEAM CORPORATION

PATENT NUMBER: USD 194,336
PATENT FILED: APRIL 6, 1961
PATENT GRANTED: JANUARY 1, 1963

United States Patent Office

Des. 194,336
Patented Jan. 1, 1963

194,336

**ELECTRIC APPLIANCE FOR COOKING SAND-
WICHES, COOKIES, PASTRIES AND OTHER
FOOD ARTICLES**

Ross E. Cornwell, Chicago, Ill., assignor to Sunbeam Corporation, Chicago, Ill., a corporation of Illinois

Filed Apr. 6, 1961, Ser. No. 64,636

Term of patent 14 years

(Cl. D81—10)

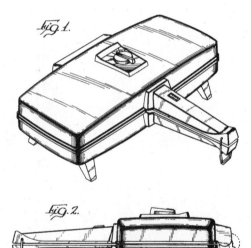

Fig. 1.

Fig. 2.

TITLE: CHAISE LONGUE OR THE LIKE
INVENTOR: MOSES RICHARD SCHULTZ
ASSIGNEE: KNOLL ASSOSIATES

PATENT NUMBER: USD 194,461
PATENT FILED: MAY 12,1961
PATENT GRANTED: JANUARY 29,1963

United States Patent Office

Des. 194,461
Patented Jan. 29, 1963

194,461

CHAISE LONGUE OR THE LIKE

Moses Richard Schultz, Barto, Pa., assignor to Knoll Associates, Inc., New York, N.Y., a corporation of New York

Filed May 12, 1961, Ser. No. 65,146

Term of patent 14 years

(Cl. D15—11)

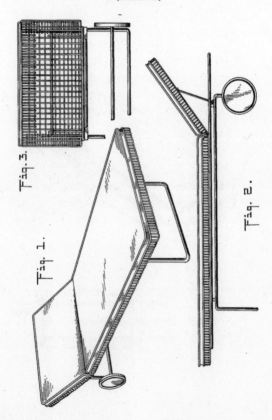

FIG. 1 is a perspective view of the chaise longue embodying my new design;

FIG. 2 is a side elevation of the chaise longue taken at the far side thereof in FIG. 1;

FIG. 3 is an end elevational view taken from the right in FIG. 2, one of the wheeled corner portions being omitted for convenience of illustration.

I claim:

The ornamental design for a chaise longue or the like, as shown.

References Cited in the file of this patent

Sears, Roebuck & Co. cat. No. 214, S. & S. 1957, page 805, item FF, steel chaise.

House and Garden, April 1960, page 195, lower left, swivel canopy by John Salterini.

Design Catalog, No. 68, issue for August 1954, page 39, left center, lounge chair by George Boake.

TITLE: TELEPHONE HANDSET
INVENTOR: RONALD ERNEST CHARLES BROWN
ASSIGNEE: ASSOCIATED ELECTRICAL INDUSTRIES

PATENT NUMBER: USD 194,538
PATENT FILED: MAY 8, 1961
PATENT GRANTED: FEBRUARY 12, 1963

United States Patent Office

Des. 194,538
Patented Feb. 12, 1963

194,538

TELEPHONE HANDSET

Ronald Ernest Charles Brown, Orpington, Kent, England, assignor to Associated Electrical Industries Limited, London, England, a British company

Filed May 8, 1961, Ser. No. 65,048

Claims priority, application Great Britain Dec. 28, 1960

Term of patent 14 years

(Cl. D26—14)

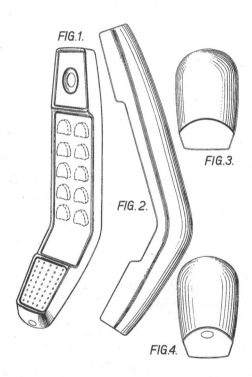

FIG.1.

FIG.2.

FIG.3.

FIG.4.

FIGURE 1 is a perspective view of the telephone handset embodying my new design;

FIGURE 2 is a side view looking from the right of FIGURE 1;

FIGURE 3 is an end view looking down from above FIGURE 1, and

FIGURE 4 is an end view looking up from below FIGURE 1.

The dominant features of my design reside in the portions shown in solid lines.

I claim:

The ornamental design for a telephone handset, as shown and described.

References Cited in the file of this patent

UNITED STATES PATENTS

D. 190,810   Dreyfuss et al. _____ July 4, 1961

OTHER REFERENCES

Plastics Magazine, January 1948, page 45, Televisaphone design by Product Technicians, Inc.

Industrial Design Magazine, June 1955, page 40, handset by Pierre Debs, Pratt Institute.

Industrial Design, October 1957, page 61, headset in center illustration.

TITLE: TELEVISION RECEIVER, OR SIMILAR ARTICLE
INVENTORS: KOZO YAMAMOTO, KAZUNORI JODAI,
SHUHEI TANIGUCHI, NOBUO KITAMURA, ET AL.
ASSIGNEE: SONY CORPORATION

PATENT NUMBER: USD 194,628
PATENT FILED: JUNE 26, 1962
PATENT GRANTED: FEBRUARY 19, 1963

United States Patent Office

Des. 194,628
Patented Feb. 19, 1963

194,628

TELEVISION RECEIVER, OR SIMILAR ARTICLE

Kozo Yamamoto, Kazunori Jodai, and Shuhei Taniguchi,
Tokyo, Nobuo Kitamura, Kawasaki-shi, Kanagawa-ken,
and Tadashi Saito and Akira Shibazaki, Tokyo, Japan,
assignors to Sony Corporation, Kitashinagawa, Shina-
gawa-ku, Tokyo, Japan, a corporation of Japan

Filed June 26, 1962, Ser. No. 70,690

Claims priority, application Japan Dec. 28, 1961

Term of patent 14 years

(Cl. D56—4)

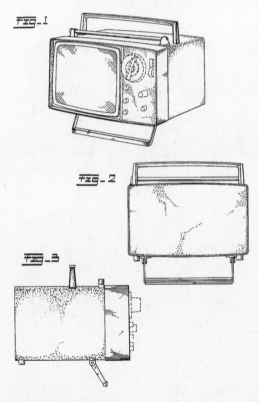

Fig. 1

Fig. 2

Fig. 3

FIGURE 1 is a front perspective view of the television
receiver, or similar article, showing our new design;
FIGURE 2 is a rear elevational view thereof; and
FIGURE 3 is a side elevational view thereof.
The dominant features of our design reside in the por-
tion shown in full lines.
We claim:
The ornamental design for a television receiver, or
similar article, substantially as shown and described.

References Cited in the file of this patent

UNITED STATES PATENTS

D. 175,290	Aeschliman	Aug. 9, 1955
D. 186,697	Beggy	Nov. 17, 1959
D. 188,108	Sundberg	June 7, 1960
D. 191,228	Shimada	Aug. 29, 1961
D. 191,788	Beggy	Nov. 21, 1961

TITLE: BICYCLE
INVENTOR: VIKTOR SCHRECKENGOST
ASSIGNEE: THE MURRAY OHIO MANUFACTURING COMPANY

PATENT NUMBER: USD 195,019
PATENT FILED: JANUARY 30, 1963
PATENT GRANTED: APRIL 9, 1963

United States Patent Office

Des. 195,019
Patented Apr. 9, 1963

195,019

BICYCLE

Viktor Schreckengost, Cleveland Heights, Ohio, assignor
to The Murray Ohio Manufacturing Company, Nashville, Tenn., a corporation of Ohio

Continuation of design applications Ser. No. 66,073, July
26, 1961, and Ser. No. 66,268, Aug. 9, 1961. This application Jan. 30, 1963, Ser. No. 73,408

Term of patent 14 years

(Cl. D90—8)

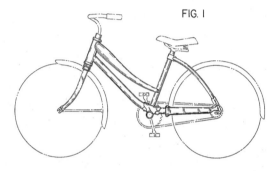

FIG. I

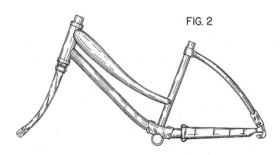

FIG. 2

TITLE: HEADPHONE
INVENTORS: JOHN MCLEOD LITTLE & JAMES L. NELSON
ASSIGNEE: CLEVITE CORPORATION

PATENT NUMBER: USD 195,304
PATENT FILED: MAY 19, 1961
PATENT GRANTED: MAY 28, 1963

United States Patent Office

Des. 195,304
Patented May 28, 1963

195,304

HEADPHONE

John McLeod Little and James J. Nelson, both of Toledo, Ohio, assignors to Clevite Corporation, a corporation of Ohio

Filed May 19, 1961, Ser. No. 65,239

Term of patent 14 years

(Cl. D26—14)

The FIGURE is an isometric view of a headphone; showing our new design.

The inside of the earpiece on the left is the same as that seen on the right, and the outside of the earpiece on the right is the same as that seen on the left.

We claim:

The ornamental design for a headphone, substantially as shown and described.

References Cited in the file of this patent

Industrial Equipment News, February 1960, page 34, earphones with antenna, top center.

Radio Shack, mail order catalogue No. 85, © 1959, page 97, item G, headphones.

TITLE: VACUUM JUG OR SIMILAR ARTICLE
INVENTORS: SIGVARD BERNADOTTE & ACTON BJØRN
ASSIGNEE: NONE

PATENT NUMBER: USD 195,598
PATENT FILED: APRIL 24, 1962
PATENT GRANTED: JULY 2, 1963

United States Patent Office

Des. 195,598
Patented July 2, 1963

195,598

VACUUM JUG OR SIMILAR ARTICLE

Sigvard Bernadotte, Styrmansgatan 57, Stockholm, Sweden, and Acton Bjørn, Toldbodgade 71, Copenhagen, Denmark

Filed Apr. 24, 1962, Ser. No. 69,827

Claims priority, application Sweden Oct. 25, 1961

Term of patent 14 years

(Cl. D58—5)

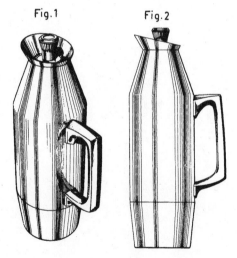

Fig.1   Fig.2

FIGURE 1 is a top perspective view of a vacuum jug, showing our new design; and FIGURE 2 is a side elevational view thereof.

We claim:

The ornamental design for a vacuum jug or similar article as shown.

References Cited in the file of this patent

UNITED STATES PATENTS

D. 91,265   Christman _____ Jan 2, 1934
D.184,265   Cornelius et al. _____ Mar. 31, 1959

OTHER REFERENCES

Modern Plastics, December 1961, page 42, container marked 9″ by 24″, lower left.

TITLE: COMBINED SLIDE PROJECTOR AND SLIDE TRAY
INVENTORS: RICHARD J. OLSON & FRANK A. ZAGARA
ASSIGNEE: EASTMAN KODAK COMPANY

PATENT NUMBER: USD 195,910
PATENT FILED: DECEMBER 22, 1961
PATENT GRANTED: AUGUST 6, 1963

United States Patent Office

Des. 195,910
Patented Aug. 6, 1963

195,910

COMBINED SLIDE PROJECTOR AND SLIDE TRAY

Richard J. Olson, Lima, and Frank A. Zagara, Rochester,
N.Y., assignors to Eastman Kodak Company, Rochester,
N.Y., a corporation of New Jersey

Filed Dec. 22, 1961, Ser. No. 68,028

Term of patent 14 years

(Cl. D61—1)

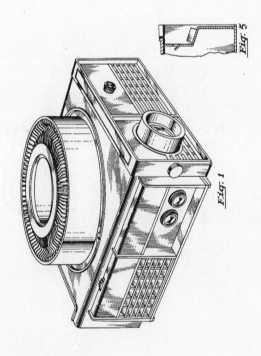

Fig. 5

Fig. 1

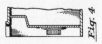

Fig. 4

TITLE: HAND OPERATED TAPE EMBOSSING TOOL
INVENTOR: DANE H. PEDERSEN
ASSIGNEE: DYMO INDUSTRIES

PATENT NUMBER: USD 196,398
PATENT FILED: MARCH 4, 1963
PATENT GRANTED: SEPTEMBER 24, 1963

United States Patent Office

Des. 196,398
Patented Sept. 24, 1963

196,398

HAND OPERATED TAPE EMBOSSING TOOL

Dane H. Pedersen, Moraga, Calif., assignor to Dymo Industries, Inc., Emeryville, Calif., a corporation of California

Filed Mar. 4, 1963, Ser. No. 73,802

Term of patent 14 years

(Cl. D64—10)

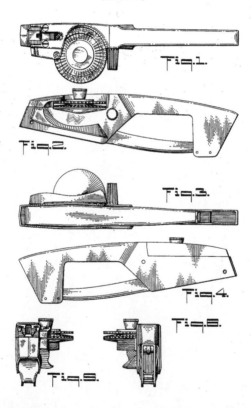

FIGURE 1 is a top plan view of a hand operated tape embossing tool, showing my new design;

FIGURE 2 is a left hand side elevational view thereof;

FIGURE 3 is a bottom plan view thereof;

FIGURE 4 is a right hand side elevational view thereof;

FIGURE 5 is a front end elevational view thereof; and

FIGURE 6 is a rear end elevational view thereof.

The dominant features of my design reside in the solid line portion of the drawing.

I claim:

The ornamental design for a hand operated tape embossing tool, substantially as shown and described.

References Cited in the file of this patent

UNITED STATES PATENTS

D. 191,382	Travaglio	Sept. 19, 1961
D. 194,891	Albrecht et al.	Mar. 26, 1963
2,275,670	Zipf	Mar. 10, 1942

OTHER REFERENCES

Dymo Co. flyer, Dymo M–55 tapewriter, rec'd 4/19/63.
Dymo Co. flyer, Dymo M–5 label maker, rec'd 2/25/63.

TITLE: CANDLEHOLDER
INVENTOR: JENS H. QUISTGAARD
ASSIGNEE: DANSK DESIGNS-WITH-LIGHT

PATENT NUMBER: USD 196,449
PATENT FILED: MARCH 1, 1963
PATENT GRANTED: OCTOBER 1, 1963

United States Patent Office

Des. 196,449
Patented Oct. 1, 1963

196,449

CANDLEHOLDER

Jens H. Quistgaard, Lucerne, Switzerland, assignor to Dansk Designs-With-Light, Inc., Great Neck, N.Y., a corporation of New York

Filed Mar. 1, 1963, Ser. No. 73,774

Term of patent 14 years

(Cl. D48—2)

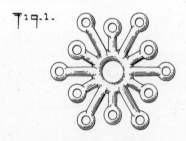

Fig. 1.

Fig. 2.

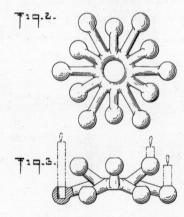

Fig. 3.

FIG. 1 is a top plan view of a candleholder embodying my new design;

FIG. 2 is a bottom plan view thereof; and

FIG. 3 is a side elevational view, partly cut away, thereof with candles shown in dotted lines for illustrative purposes only.

I claim:

The ornamental design for a candleholder, as shown and described.

References Cited in the file of this patent

UNITED STATES PATENTS

D. 142,555	Furst	Oct. 16, 1945
2,219,112	O'Day	Oct. 22, 1940

TITLE: TELEVISION REMOTE CONTROL
INVENTOR: MELVIN H. BOLDT
ASSIGNEE: ZENITH RADIO CORPORATION

PATENT NUMBER: USD 196,647
PATENT FILED: JANUARY 8, 1962
PATENT GRANTED: OCTOBER 22, 1963

United States Patent Office

Des. 196,647
Patented Oct. 22, 1963

196,647

TELEVISION REMOTE CONTROL OR SIMILAR ARTICLE

Melvin H. Boldt, Glenview, Ill., assignor to Zenith Radio
Corporation, Chicago, Ill., a corporation of Delaware

Filed Jan. 8, 1962, Ser. No. 68,217

Term of patent 14 years

(Cl. D26—5)

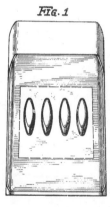

Fig. 1

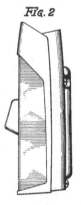

Fig. 2

Fig. 3

TITLE: SEWING MACHINE OR SIMILAR ARTICLE
INVENTOR: HENRY DREYFUSS
ASSIGNEE: THE SINGER COMPANY

PATENT NUMBER: USD 196,822
PATENT FILED: NOVEMBER 15, 1961
PATENT GRANTED: NOVEMBER 5, 1963

United States Patent Office

Des. 196,822
Patented Nov. 5, 1963

196,822

SEWING MACHINE OR SIMILAR ARTICLE

Henry Dreyfuss, South Pasadena, Calif., assignor to The
Singer Company, a corporation of New Jersey

Filed Nov. 15, 1961, Ser. No. 67,532

Term of patent 14 years

(Cl. D70—1)

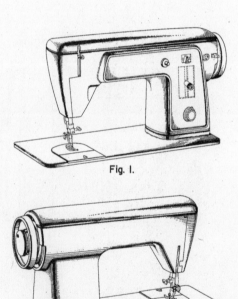

Fig. 1.

Fig. 2.

TITLE: CABINET FOR TELEVISION RECEIVER SETS
INVENTORS: WILLIAM M. EVANS & BEVERLEY H.
MOSELEY, JR.
ASSIGNEE: RADIOHIO

PATENT NUMBER: USD 197,144
PATENT FILED: JUNE 25, 1963
PATENT GRANTED: DECEMBER 17, 1963

United States Patent Office

Des. 197,144
Patented Dec. 17, 1963

197,144

CABINET FOR TELEVISION RECEIVER SETS

William M. Evans, Columbus, and Beverley H. Moseley, Jr., Grove City, Ohio, assignors to RadiOhio Incorporated, Columbus, Ohio, a corporation of Ohio

Filed June 25, 1963, Ser. No. 75,509

Term of patent 14 years

(Cl. D56—4)

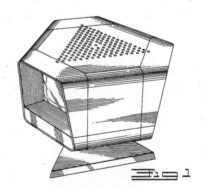

Fig 1

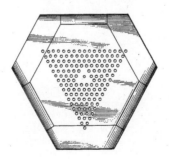

Fig 2

TITLE: PENCIL SHARPENER
INVENTOR: HARRY PREBLE
ASSIGNEE: GENERAL SLICING MACHINE COMPANY

PATENT NUMBER: USD 197,319
PATENT FILED: FEBRUARY 25, 1963
PATENT GRANTED: JANUARY 7, 1964

United States Patent Office

Des. 197,319
Patented Jan. 7, 1964

197,319

PENCIL SHARPENER

Harry Preble, Cross River, N.Y., assignor to General Slicing Machine Co., Inc., Walden, N.Y., a corporation of New York

Filed Feb. 25, 1963, Ser. No. 73,700

Term of patent 14 years

(Cl. D74—21)

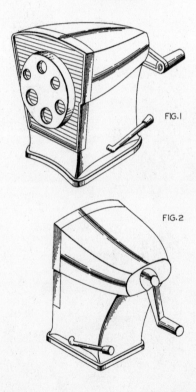

FIG.1

FIG.2

FIG. 1 is a perspective front view; and

FIG. 2 is a perspective rear view of a pencil sharpener embodying my new design.

Both sides of the pencil sharpener are identical, except that there is no operating lever at the side opposite to that shown.

I claim:

The ornamental design for a pencil sharpener, substantially as shown and described.

References Cited in the file of this patent

UNITED STATES PATENTS

D. 151,456   Kihlberg _____ Oct. 19, 1948
D. 152,554   May _____ Feb. 1, 1949
D. 186,344   Fleming _____ Oct. 13, 1959

OTHER REFERENCES

Office Appliances, May 1950, page 74, upper left Apsco Deluxe pencil sharpeners.

Beckley-Cardy Co., Cat. #94, March 19, 1953, page 85, Deluxe Premier self-feed sharpener.

Office Appliances, November 1956, page 70, pencil sharpener item.

TITLE: PHONOGRAPH CABINET
INVENTOR: MELVIN H. BOLDT
ASSIGNEE: AUTOMATIC CANTEEN COMPANY OF AMERICA

PATENT NUMBER: USD 198,231
PATENT FILED: NOVEMBER 12, 1963
PATENT GRANTED: MAY 19, 1964

United States Patent Office

Des. 198,231
Patented May 19, 1964

198,231

PHONOGRAPH CABINET

Melvin H. Boldt, Glenview, Ill., assignor to Automatic
Canteen Company of America, Chicago, Ill., a corporation of Delaware

Filed Nov. 12, 1963, Ser. No. 77,373

Term of patent 14 years

(Cl. D56—4)

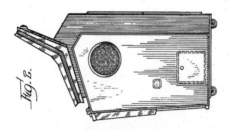

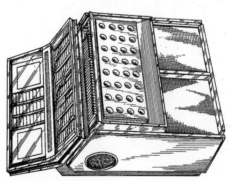

TITLE: DISPENSER FOR TAPE
INVENTOR: BJORN A. LARSEN
ASSIGNEE: STERLING COATED MATERIALS

PATENT NUMBER: USD 198,958
PATENT FILED: JUNE 21, 1963
PATENT GRANTED: AUGUST 18, 1964

United States Patent Office

Des. 198,958
Patented Aug. 18, 1964

198,958

DISPENSER FOR TAPE

Bjorn A. Larsen, Oslo, Norway, assignor to Sterling
Coated Materials Ltd., Stalybridge, England, a British
corporation

Filed June 21, 1963, Ser. No. 77,018

Claims priority, application Great Britain Jan. 16, 1963

Term of patent 7 years

(Cl. D74—1)

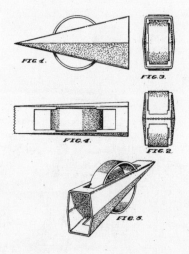

FIG. 1 is a side elevational view of a dispenser for tape showing my new design;

FIG. 2 is a front elevational view;

FIG. 3 is a rear elevational view;

FIG. 4 is a bottom plan view thereof; and

FIG. 5 is a perspective view of the side opposite to that shown in FIG. 1.

I claim:

The ornamental design for a dispenser for tape, substantially as shown.

References Cited in the file of this patent

UNITED STATES PATENTS

D. 164,733	Pretzfelder		Oct. 2, 1951
1,408,499	Casterline et al.		Mar. 7, 1922
2,663,510	Rodgers		Dec. 22, 1953
3,007,619	Burcz		Nov. 7, 1961

TITLE: LAMP
INVENTOR: WILLIAM E. CURRY
ASSIGNEE: NONE

PATENT NUMBER: USD 199,141
PATENT FILED: MARCH 19, 1963
PATENT GRANTED: SEPTEMBER 15, 1964

United States Patent Office

Des. 199,141
Patented Sept. 15, 1964

199,141
LAMP

William E. Curry, 9314 Trask Ave.,
Playa Del Rey, Calif.

Filed Mar. 19, 1963, Ser. No. 74,046

Term of patent 14 years

(Cl. D48—20)

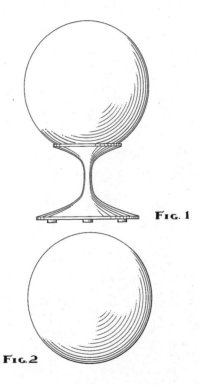

FIG. 1

FIG. 2

FIGURE 1 is a front elevational view of a lamp showing my new design, the undisclosed sides and rear elevations being substantially identical with the front elevation; and

FIGURE 2 is a plan view of the lamp illustrated in elevation in FIGURE 1.

The bottom of the lamp contains three elevating feet which are uniformly spaced near the peripheral edge thereof as best shown in FIG. 1.

This application is a continuation-in-part of my earlier filed, copending application, Serial No. D. 67,712, filed November 27, 1961, and now abandoned.

I claim:

The ornamental design for a lamp, substantially as shown and described.

References Cited by the Examiner
UNITED STATES PATENTS

D– 74,848	4/28	Whelan	D–48/20
D–158,821	5/50	Walter	D–48/20
D–177,744	5/56	Minea	D–48/20
D–187,797	5/60	Saarinen	D–33/14
D–187,941	5/60	Latham	D–33/14
730,619	6/03	Drain.	

WALLACE R. BURKE, *Acting Primary Examiner.*

ADELINE B. HANNAH, *Examiner.*

TITLE: ELECTRIC FAN HEATER
INVENTOR: LYN TREVOR EVANS
ASSIGNEE: THE GENERAL ELECTRIC COMPANY

PATENT NUMBER: USD 199,219
PATENT FILED: JUNE 11, 1963
PATENT GRANTED: SEPTEMBER 22, 1964

United States Patent Office

Des. 199,219
Patented Sept. 22, 1964

199,219

ELECTRIC FAN HEATER

Lyn Trevor Evans, Welwyn Garden City, England, assignor to The General Electric Company Limited, London, England

Filed June 11, 1963, Ser. No. 75,315

Claims priority, application Great Britain Dec. 12, 1962

Term of patent 7 years

(Cl. D81—10)

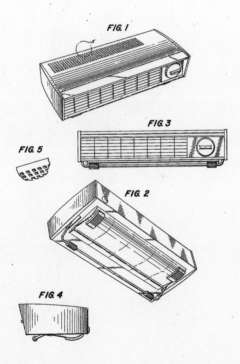

FIG. 1

FIG. 3

FIG. 5

FIG. 2

FIG. 4

FIGURE 1 is a top front perspective view of an electric fan heater showing my new design.

FIGURE 2 is a rear perspective view from below.

FIGURE 3 is a front view.

FIGURE 4 is a side view.

FIGURE 5 is an enlarged fragmentary perspective view taken in the area 5 of FIGURE 1.

I claim:

The ornamental design for an electric fan heater, as shown.

References Cited by the Examiner

Hardware Age, July 16, 1959, page 311, upper right-hand corner, item No. 6, heater.

Home Furnishings Daily, July 19, 1962, page 20, upper right corner, "Hanovia" heater.

WALLACE R. BURKE, *Acting Primary Examiner.*

ADELINE B. HANNAH, *Examiner.*

TITLE: CAN OPENER OR SIMILAR ARTICLE
INVENTORS: ARTHUR M. FELSKE & MAX HAUENSTEIN
ASSIGNEE: GENERAL ELECTRIC COMPANY

PATENT NUMBER: USD 199,311
PATENT FILED: JANUARY 22, 1964
PATENT GRANTED: OCTOBER 6, 1964

United States Patent Office

Des. 199,311
Patented Oct. 6, 1964

199,311

CAN OPENER OR SIMILAR ARTICLE

Arthur M. Felske, Westport, and Max C. Hauenstein,
Monroe, Conn., assignors to General Electric Company,
a corporation of New York

Filed Jan. 22, 1964, Ser. No. 78,306

Term of patent 14 years

(Cl. D22—2)

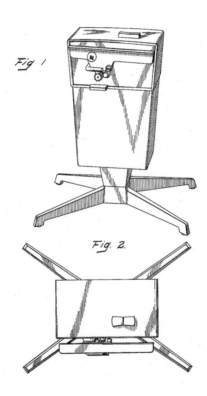

Fig. 1

Fig. 2.

TITLE: ILLUMINATED SIGN
INVENTOR: ROBERT M. CHENAULT
ASSIGNEE: ROBERT M. CHENAULT & ROBERT
BRUCE WILSON

PATENT NUMBER: USD 199,349
PATENT FILED: FEBRUARY 11, 1963
PATENT GRANTED: OCTOBER 13, 1964

United States Patent Office

Des. 199,349
Patented Oct. 13, 1964

199,349

ILLUMINATED SIGN

Robert M. Chenault, P.O. Box 6340, Fort Worth, Tex.,
assignor of one-half to Robert Bruce Wilson, Fort
Worth, Tex.

Filed Feb. 11, 1963, Ser. No. 73,496

Term of patent 14 years

(Cl. D1—12)

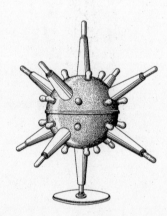

The figure is a perspective view taken from one side of an illuminated sign embodying my new design.

The undisclosed side is the same as the side shown. The conventional light bulbs are arranged symmetrically in relationship to the conical-shaped arms.

I claim:

The ornamental design for an illuminated sign, as shown and described.

References Cited by the Examiner

UNITED STATES PATENTS

790,900   5/05   Junghans.

1,429,408	9/22	Cole	240—10
2,603,738	7/52	Schubert et al.	
3,018,362	1/62	Joyce.	

OTHER REFERENCES

Sears, Roebuck and Co., Cat., Chicago, Spring and Summer 1958, page 1181, lower right items "D" and "E."

WALLACE R. BURKE, *Acting Primary Examiner.*

ADELINE B. HANNAH, *Examiner.*

TITLE: AUTOMOBILE
INVENTOR: FERDINAND ALEXANDER PORSCHE, JR.
ASSIGNEE: FIRMA PORSCHE

PATENT NUMBER: USD 199,433
PATENT FILED: NOVEMBER 14, 1963
PATENT GRANTED: OCTOBER 27, 1964

United States Patent Office

Des. 199,433
Patented Oct. 27, 1964

199,433

AUTOMOBILE

Ferdinand Alexander Porsche, Jr., Doffingen, Kreis Boblingen, Germany, assignor to Firma Dr.-Ing. h.c.F. Porsche K.G., Stuttgart-Zuffenhausen, Germany

Filed Nov. 14, 1963, Ser. No. 77,436

Claims priority, application Germany Sept. 5, 1963

Term of patent 14 years

(Cl. D14—3)

FIG. 1

FIG. 2

FIG. 3

TITLE: HAIR DRIER
INVENTOR: LEE S. WATLINGTON
ASSIGNEE: NONE

PATENT NUMBER: USD 199,949
PATENT FILED: JANUARY 23, 1963
PATENT GRANTED: DECEMBER 29, 1964

United States Patent Office

Des. 199,949
Patented Dec. 29, 1964

199,949

HAIR DRIER

Lee S. Watlington, 1204 N. Linden, Bloomington, Ill.

Filed Jan. 23, 1963, Ser. No. 73,288

Term of patent 7 years

(Cl. D86—10)

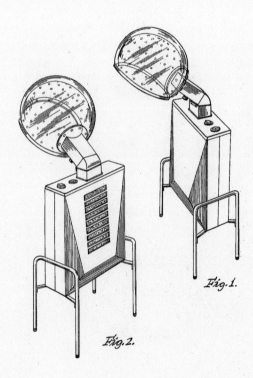

Fig. 1.

Fig. 2.

TITLE: MAILBOX
INVENTORS: ALAN W. DUNCAN & JOSEPH A. BURLINI
ASSIGNEE: SEARS, ROEBUCK AND COMPANY

PATENT NUMBER: USD 200,452
PATENT FILED: APRIL 22, 1963
PATENT GRANTED: FEBRUARY 23, 1965

United States Patent Office

Des. 200,452
Patented Feb. 23, 1965

200,452

MAILBOX

Alan W. Duncan, Itasca, and Joseph A. Burlini, Morton
Grove, Ill., assignors to Sears, Roebuck and Co., Chicago, Ill., a corporation of New York

Filed Apr. 22, 1963, Ser. No. 74,568

Term of patent 14 years

(Cl. D74—9)

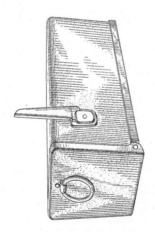

The figure on the drawing is a front, side and top perspective view of a mailbox embodying our new design.

The bottom and back are plain and the side not shown
is similar to the side shown in the drawing except that it
lacks the signal member and support for same.

We claim:

The ornamental design for a mailbox, as shown and
described.

References Cited by the Examiner

UNITED STATES PATENTS

D. 122,006	8/40	Smith	D74—9
D. 183,942	11/58	Masso	D74—9
3,095,140	6/63	Buedingen.	

OTHER REFERENCES

Housewares Review, September 1962, p. 89, upper right
suburban mailbox item.

TITLE: AUTOMOBILE
INVENTORS: KARL WILFERT & BÉLA BARÉNYI
ASSIGNEE: DAIMLER—BENZ

PATENT NUMBER: USD 200,899
PATENT FILED: SEPTEMBER 13, 1963
PATENT GRANTED: APRIL 20, 1965

United States Patent Office

Des. 200,899
Patented Apr. 20, 1965

200,899

AUTOMOBILE

Karl Wilfert, Gerlingen-Waldstadt, and Béla Barényi,
Stuttgart-Vaihingen, Germany, assignors to Daimler-
Benz Aktiengesellschaft, Stuttgart, Unterturkheim,
Germany

Filed Sept. 13, 1963, Ser. No. 76,591

Claims priority, application Germany Mar. 13, 1963

Term of patent 14 years

(Cl. D14—3)

FIG.1

FIG.2

TITLE: BOWL BRUSH
INVENTOR: JON W. HAUSER
ASSIGNEE: NATIONAL BRUSH COMPANY

PATENT NUMBER: USD 201,007
PATENT FILED: JULY 14, 1964
PATENT GRANTED: MAY 4, 1965

United States Patent Office

Des. 201,007
Patented May 4, 1965

201,007

BOWL BRUSH

Jon W. Hauser, St. Charles, Ill., assignor to National
Brush Company, Aurora, Ill., a corporation of Illinois

Filed July 14, 1964, Ser. No. 80,868

Term of patent 14 years

(Cl. D9—2)

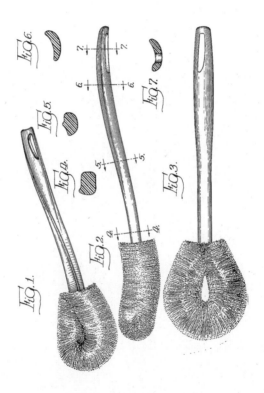

FIGURE 1 is a top perspective view of a bowl brush
showing my new design;
FIGURE 2 is a side elevational view thereof;
FIGURE 3 is a bottom plan view thereof; and
FIGURES 4, 5, 6 and 7 are sectional views taken along
the lines 4—4, 5—5, 6—6 and 7—7, respectively, of
FIG. 2.
My design for the bowl brush disclosed is characterized
by the handle portion having the configuration as shown.

I claim:
The ornamental design for a bowl brush, as shown and
described.

References Cited by the Examiner
UNITED STATES PATENTS

D. 20,486   1/91   Thompson _____ D9—2
D. 176,156   11/55   Racicot _____ D9—2

WALLACE R. BURKE, *Primary Examiner.*

TITLE: VENDING MACHINE FOR CANDY OR THE LIKE
INVENTOR: WALTER E. MOORE
ASSIGNEE: UNIVERSAL MATCH CORPORATION

PATENT NUMBER: USD 201,299
PATENT FILED: MAY 4, 1964
PATENT GRANTED: JUNE 8, 1965

United States Patent Office

Des. 201,299
Patented June 8, 1965

201,299

VENDING MACHINE FOR CANDY OR THE LIKE

Walter E. Moore, Bel-Nor, Mo., assignor to Universal Match Corporation, St. Louis, Mo., a corporation of Delaware

Filed May 4, 1964, Ser. No. 79,796

Term of patent 14 years

(Cl. D52—3)

FIG. 1.

FIG. 3.   FIG. 2.

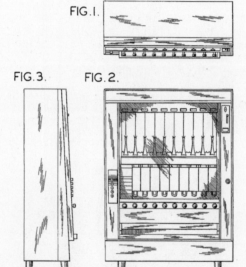

TITLE: LAMP
INVENTOR: LEO H. KLAUSEN
ASSIGNEE: NONE

PATENT NUMBER: USD 201,824
PATENT FILED: JULY 20, 1964
PATENT GRANTED: AUGUST 3, 1965

United States Patent Office

Des. 201,824
Patented Aug. 3, 1965

201,824

LAMP

Leo H. Klausen, 338 Hillcrest Ave., Willowdale,
Ontario, Canada

Filed July 20, 1964, Ser. No. 80,922

Term of patent 14 years

(Cl. D48—20)

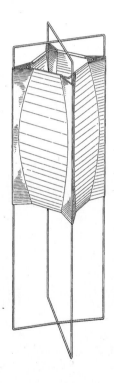

The figure is a perspective view of a lamp showing my new design, the undisclosed sides being similar in appearance.

I claim:

The ornamental design for a lamp, as shown and described.

References Cited by the Examiner

Better Design, June 1952, p. 20, bottom picture, center lamp in rectangular wire frame.

Home Furnishings, June 1952, p. 35, center picture, left hand item, lamp by Archie Kaplan.

WALLACE R. BURKE, *Acting Primary Examiner.*

TITLE: ROTARY SLIDE TRAY
INVENTOR: WALTER J. HALL
ASSIGNEE: NONE

PATENT NUMBER: USD 202.141
PATENT FILED: FEBRUARY 25, 1963
PATENT GRANTED: AUGUST 31, 1965

United States Patent Office

Des. 202,141
Patented Aug. 31, 1965

202,141

ROTARY SLIDE TRAY

Walter J. Hall, 1408 Jonquil Terrace, Chicago, Ill.

Filed Feb. 25, 1963, Ser. No. 73,711

Term of patent 14 years

(Cl. D61—1)

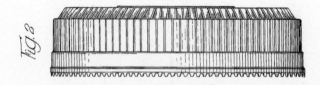

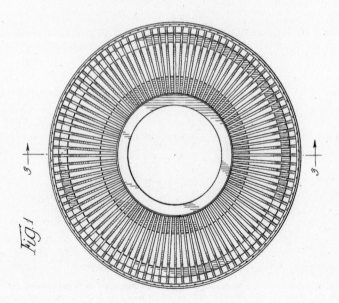

TITLE: RESTAURANT BUILDING
INVENTOR: ELDON C. DAVIS
ASSIGNEE: BY THE NUMBERS

PATENT NUMBER: USD 202,333
PATENT FILED: SEPTEMBER 28, 1964
PATENT GRANTED: SEPTEMBER 21, 1965

United States Patent Office

Des. 202,333
Patented Sept. 21, 1965

202,333

RESTAURANT BUILDING

Eldon C. Davis, Los Angeles, Calif., assignor to By The Numbers, Inc., Fort Wayne, Ind., a corporation of Indiana

Filed Sept. 28, 1964, Ser. No. 81,902

Term of patent 14 years

(Cl. D13—1)

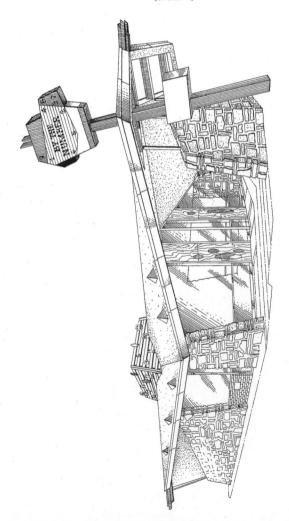

FIG. 1

TITLE: COMBINED OUTDOOR LIGHTING STANDARD
& LUMINAIRES THEREFOR
INVENTORS: DONALD DESKEY & ALEXANDER LURKIS
ASSIGNEE: CITY OF NEW YORK

PATENT NUMBER: USD 202,372
PATENT FILED: FEBRUARY 17, 1964
PATENT GRANTED: SEPTEMBER 21, 1965

United States Patent Office

Des. 202,372
Patented Sept. 21, 1965

202,372

COMBINED OUTDOOR LIGHTING STANDARD AND LUMINAIRES THEREFOR

**Donald Deskey, New York, and Alexander Lurkis, Hollis-
wood, N.Y.; said Deskey assignor to the City of New
York**

Filed Feb. 17, 1964, Ser. No. 78,702

Term of patent 14 years

(Cl. D48—31)

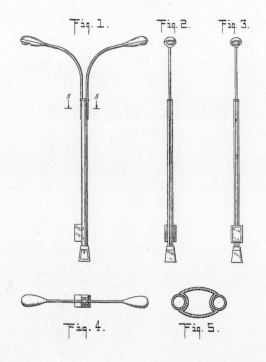

Fig. 1.　　Fig. 2.　　Fig. 3.

Fig. 4.　　Fig. 5.

FIGURE 1 is a side view.
FIGURE 2 is a front view.
FIGURE 3 is a rear view.
FIGURE 4 is a top view.
FIGURE 5 is a cross-sectional view along the line
5—5 of FIGURE 1.

We claim:

The ornamental design for a combined outdoor lighting standard and luminaires therefor, as shown and described.

References Cited by the Examiner

UNITED STATES PATENTS

D. 195,310　5/63　Zagel ---------------- D48—31
2,597,783　5/52　Ferm.

OTHER REFERENCES

Light and Lighting (England) November 1962, page
345, lighting fixture at bottom of page.
Lighting, November 1960, p. 55, luminaire at center
right of page.
Machine Design, December 1949, page 125, item No.
4 in bottom left illustration.
Van Huffel Catalog L.–56, published 1–53, page 93,
item 2245/.062.

WALLACE R. BURKE, *Acting Primary Examiner.*

TITLE: THERMOPLASTIC CEMENT DISPENSER
INVENTOR: RUDOLPH M. BABEL
ASSIGNEE: UNITED SHOE MACHINERY CORPORATION

PATENT NUMBER: USD 202,737
PATENT FILED: FEBRUARY 15, 1965
PATENT GRANTED: NOVEMBER 2, 1965

United States Patent Office

Des. 202,737
Patented Nov. 2, 1965

202,737

THERMOPLASTIC CEMENT DISPENSER

Rudolph M. Babel, Pawtucket, R.I., assignor to United
Shoe Machinery Corporation, Flemington, N.J., a corporation of New Jersey

Filed Feb. 15, 1965, Ser. No. 83,816

Term of patent 14 years

(Cl. D54—13)

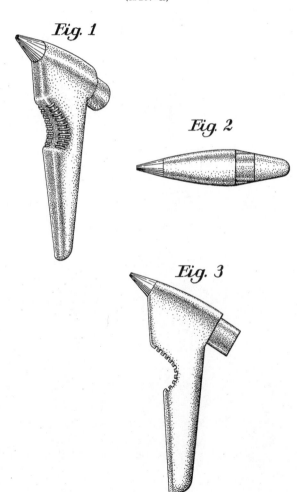

Fig. 1

Fig. 2

Fig. 3

TITLE: TELEPHONE HANDSET
INVENTORS: HENRY DREYFUSS & LIONEL W. MOSING
& ROBERT E. PRESCOTT
ASSIGNEE: BELL TELEPHONE LABORATORIES

PATENT NUMBER: USD 202,788
PATENT FILED: SEPTEMBER 21, 1964
PATENT GRANTED: NOVEMBER 9, 1965

United States Patent Office

Des. 202,788

Patented Nov. 9, 1965

202,788

TELEPHONE HANDSET

Henry Dreyfuss, South Pasadena, Calif., and Lionel W.
Mosing, Springfield, and Robert E. Prescott, Rumson,
N.J., assignors to Bell Telephone Laboratories, Incor-
porated, New York, N.Y., a corporation of New York

Filed Sept. 21, 1964, Ser. No. 81,798

Term of patent 14 years

(Cl. D26—14)

FIG. 1

FIG. 5

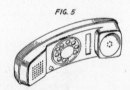

TITLE: BUILDING
INVENTORS: RICHARD D. BURKE & BEN J. KINGDON
ASSIGNEE: PIZZA HUT

PATENT NUMBER: USD 202,878
PATENT FILED: JANUARY 18, 1965
PATENT GRANTED: NOVEMBER 16, 1965

United States Patent Office

Des. 202,878
Patented Nov. 16, 1965

202,878

BUILDING

Richard D. Burke and Ben J. Kingdon, Wichita, Kans.,
assignors to Pizza Hut, Inc., Wichita, Kans., a corporation of Kansas

Filed Jan. 18, 1965, Ser. No. 83,477

Term of patent 14 years

(Cl. D13—1)

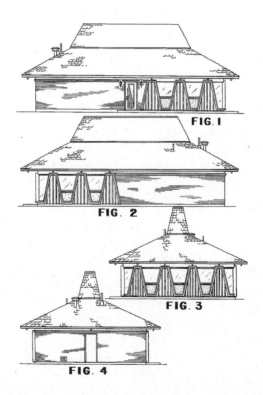

FIG. 1

FIG. 2

FIG. 3

FIG. 4

FIG. 1 is an entry side elevation view of a building
showing our new design; and
FIG. 2 is the opposite side view as same; and
FIG. 3 is a front end elevation view of same; and
FIG. 4 is a rear end elevation view of same.
We claim:
The ornamental design for a building, substantially as
shown.

References Cited by the Examiner
UNITED STATES PATENTS
D. 109,026   3/1938   Petersen _____ D13—1

OTHER REFERENCES
Architectural Record, November 1954, page 332, Japanese house at top of page.

WALLACE R. BURKE, *Primary Examiner.*

A. HUGO WORD, *Assistant Examiner.*

TITLE: PHOTOGRAPHIC CAMERA OR SIMILAR ARTICLE
INVENTORS: JAMES M. CONNER & HENRY DREYFUSS
ASSIGNEE: POLAROID CORPORATION

PATENT NUMBER: USD 204,834
PATENT FILED: MAY 12, 1965
PATENT GRANTED: MAY 17, 1966

United States Patent Office

Des. 204,834
Patented May 17, 1966

204,834

PHOTOGRAPHIC CAMERA OR SIMILAR ARTICLE

James M. Conner, Glendale, and Henry Dreyfuss, South Pasadena, Calif., assignors to Polaroid Corporation, Cambridge, Mass., a corporation of Delaware

Filed May 12, 1965, Ser. No. 85,232

Term of patent 14 years

(Cl. D61—1)

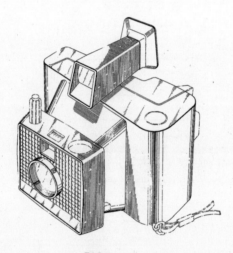

FIG. I

TITLE: PORTABLE TABLE LAMP, OR SIMILAR ARTICLE
INVENTOR: HARRY ZELENKO
ASSIGNEE: NONE

PATENT NUMBER: USD 205,463
PATENT FILED: MAY 25, 1965
PATENT GRANTED: AUGUST 9, 1966

United States Patent Office

Des. 205,463
Patented August 9, 1966

205,463

PORTABLE TABLE LAMP, OR SIMILAR ARTICLE

Harry Zelenko, 10 E. 54th St., New York, N.Y.

Filed May 25, 1965, Ser. No. 85,451

Term of patent 14 years

(Cl. D48—20)

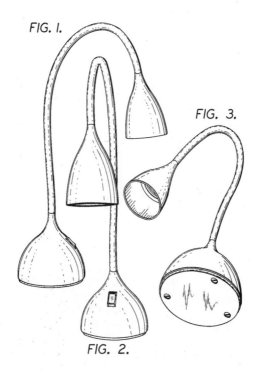

FIG. I.

FIG. 3.

FIG. 2.

FIG. 1 is a side elevational view of a portable table lamp, showing my new design;

FIG. 2 is a front elevational view thereof; and

FIG. 3 is a perspective view thereof as seen from the bottom of the lamp.

I claim:

The ornamental design for a portable table lamp, or similar article, as shown.

References Cited by the Examiner

Eagle Skandia Lights Catalog, received in Patent Office April 27, 1953, page 5, #204 1 light ceiling mount with 5 inch flexarm shown at right center of page.

Interiors, May 1957, page 144, hanging fixture numbered 5 at right of page.

Lamp Journal, August 1964, page 23, floor lamp by Sheridan at lower left of page.

WALLACE R. BURKE, *Primary Examiner.*

WILLIAM C. WATSON, *Assistant Examiner.*

TITLE: CHILD'S CHAIR
INVENTOR: MARCO ZANUSO
ASSIGNEE: NONE

PATENT NUMBER: USD 205,657
PATENT FILED: FEBRUARY 24, 1965
PATENT GRANTED: SEPTEMBER 6, 1966

United States Patent Office

Des. 205,657
Patented Sept. 6, 1966

205,657
CHILD'S CHAIR
Marco Zanuso, Via Laveno 6, Milan, Italy
Filed Feb. 24, 1965, Ser. No. 83,964
Term of patent 7 years
(Cl. D15—1)

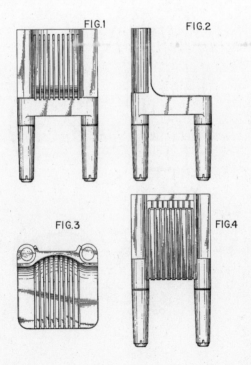

FIG.1   FIG.2

FIG.3   FIG.4

TITLE: PORTABLE RADIO CABINET
INVENTOR: MELVIN H. BOLDT
ASSIGNEE: ZENITH RADIO CORPORATION

PATENT NUMBER: USD 205,727
PATENT FILED: FEBRUARY 4, 1966
PATENT GRANTED: SEPTEMBER 13, 1966

United States Patent Office

Des. 205,727
Patented Sept. 13, 1966

205,727

PORTABLE RADIO CABINET

Melvin H. Boldt, Glenview, Ill., assignor to Zenith Radio
Corporation, Chicago, Ill., a corporation of Delaware

Filed Feb. 4, 1966, Ser. No. 921

Term of patent 14 years

(Cl. D56—4)

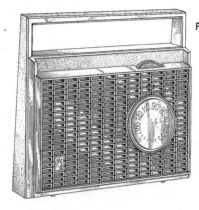

FIG. 1

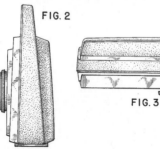

FIG. 2

FIG. 3

FIGURE 1 is a perspective view of my design for a portable radio cabinet;

FIGURE 2 is a side elevational view thereof; and

FIGURE 3 is a top plan view thereof.

The back and bottom of my design are plain and unornamented and the dominant features of my design reside in those portions of the drawing shown by means of full lines.

I claim:

The ornamental design for a portable radio cabinet, substantially as shown and described.

References Cited by the Examiner

UNITED STATES PATENTS

D. 180,742   8/1957   Mason _____ D56—4
D. 198,051   4/1964   Frankel _____ D56—4

OTHER REFERENCES

Home Furnishings Daily, Thursday, May 31, 1962, p. 41, radio by Sony in top right corner.

Jewelers' Circular-Keystone, August 1961, p. 100, model DT-495 radio by Matsushita.

Mart, February 1958, p. 88, model 6RT-1 radio by Packard-Bell Electronics Corp., Los Angeles.

EDWIN H. HUNTER, *Primary Examiner.*

WILLIAM M. HENRY, *Assistant Examiner.*

TITLE: MOTION PICTURE CAMERA
INVENTOR: MONTE L. LEVIN
ASSIGNEE: DEJUR-AMSCO CORPORATION

PATENT NUMBER: USD 205,914
PATENT FILED: JULY 14, 1965
PATENT GRANTED: OCTOBER 4, 1966

United States Patent Office

Des. 205,914
Patented Oct. 4, 1966

205,914

MOTION PICTURE CAMERA

Monte L. Levin, Roslyn Heights, N.Y., assignor to Dejur-
Amsco Corporation, Long Island City, N.Y., a corporation of New York

Filed July 14, 1965, Ser. No. 86,145

Term of patent 14 years

(Cl. D61—1)

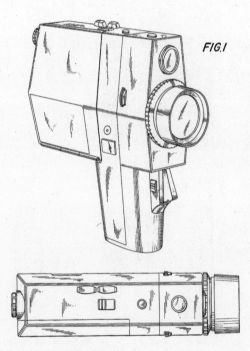

FIG.1

FIG.3

TITLE: STOVE
INVENTORS: WALTER F. ROGERS & JOHN C. ROGERS
ASSIGNEE: CROWN STOVE WORKS

PATENT NUMBER: USD 205,979
PATENT FILED: DECEMBER 30, 1965
PATENT GRANTED: OCTOBER 11, 1966

United States Patent Office

Des. 205,979
Patented Oct. 11, 1966

205,979

STOVE

Walter F. Rogers, Oak Park, and John C. Rogers, River
Forest, Ill., assignors to Crown Stove Works, Chicago,
Ill., a corporation of Illinois

Filed Dec. 30, 1965, Ser. No. 378

Term of patent 14 years

(Cl. D81—4)

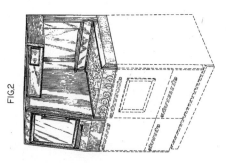

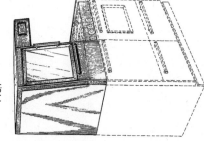

FIGURE 1 is a perspective view of a stove embodying
our new design taken from one side of the stove; and
FIGURE 2 is a perspective view thereof taken from
the opposite side of the stove.
The dominant features of our design are shown in solid
lines.
We claim:
The ornamental design for a stove, as shown and described.

References Cited by the Examiner

Better Homes and Gardens, April 1950, page 28, Universal range.
House and Home, January 1957, page 196a, Hotpoint
oven control panel at upper right.

WALLACE R. BURKE, *Primary Examiner.*

J. PAUL GUERTIN, *Assistant Examiner.*

TITLE: DISPENSING ISLAND
INVENTORS: ELIOT F. NOYES, ERNEST M. BEVILACQUA
& ROBERT E. GRAF
ASSIGNEE: MOBIL OIL CORPORATION

PATENT NUMBER: USD 206,319
PATENT FILED: MARCH 21, 1966
PATENT GRANTED: NOVEMBER 29, 1966

United States Patent Office

Des. 206,319
Patented Nov. 29, 1966

206,319

DISPENSING ISLAND

Eliot F. Noyes, New Canaan, Ernest M. Bevilacqua, Wilton, and Robert E. Graf, New Canaan, Conn., assignors to Mobil Oil Corporation, a corporation of New York

Filed Mar. 21, 1966, Ser. No. 1,574

Term of patent 14 years

(Cl. D13—1)

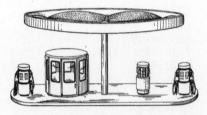

FIG. 1

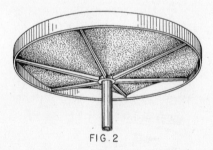

FIG. 2

FIGURE 1 is a top perspective view of a dispensing island showing our new design.

FIGURE 2 is a bottom perspective view of the circular shelter shown in FIGURE 1 with the base shown fragmentarily for convenience of illustration.

We claim:

The ornamental design for a dispensing island, as shown and described.

References Cited by the Examiner
UNITED STATES PATENTS

D. 50,281	2/1917	Norcross	D13—1
D. 144,669	5/1946	Adams	D13—1
D. 199,353	10/1964	Harper	D13—1
2,800,574	7/1957	Belbes et al.	
2,959,826	11/1960	Larsen et al.	

OTHER REFERENCES

National Petroleum News, February 1964, page 20, Island in Fina's Dallas Station illustration.

A. HUGO WORD, *Acting Primary Examiner.*

TITLE: COMBINED WRITING INSTRUMENT
AND POCKET KNIFE
INVENTOR: ALFRED MOSCH
ASSIGNEE: NONE

PATENT NUMBER: USD 206,875
PATENT FILED: JUNE 10, 1966
PATENT GRANTED: FEBRUARY 7, 1967

United States Patent Office

Des. 206,875
Patented Feb. 7, 1967

206,875

COMBINED WRITING INSTRUMENT AND POCKET KNIFE

Alfred Mosch, 31—24 86th St.,
Jackson Heights, N.Y. 11369

Filed June 10, 1966, Ser. No. 2,642

Term of patent 14 years

(Cl. D22—3)

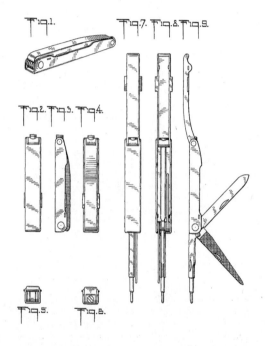

FIG. 1 is a side perspective view of a combined writing instrument and pocket knife, showing my new design;

FIG. 2 is a bottom plan view thereof;

FIG. 3 is a side elevational view thereof, the side opposite presenting a similar appearance;

FIG. 4 is a top plan view thereof;

FIG. 5 is an end elevational view thereof, looking from the left side of FIG. 1;

FIG. 6 is an end elevational view thereof; looking from the right side of FIG. 1;

FIG. 7 is a bottom plan view thereof as it appears in open position;

FIG. 8 is a top plan view thereof as it appears in open position;

FIG. 9 is a side elevational view thereof as its appears in open position, the side opposite presenting a similar appearance.

This is a continuation-in-part of design application Serial No. 86, 253, filed July 22, 1965, and now abandoned.

I claim:

The ornamental design for a combined writing instrument and pocket knife, as shown and described.

References Cited by the Examiner

UNITED STATES PATENTS

D. 114,390	4/1939	Bocchino	D86—10
D. 137,339	2/1944	Liukko	D22—3
209,359	10/1878	Rahner.	
2,798,290	7/1957	Bassett.	
3,119,377	1/1964	Johmann.	

EDWIN H. HUNTER, *Primary Examiner.*

WINIFRED E. HERRMANN, *Assistant Examiner.*

TITLE: CYLINDRICAL LIQUID DISPENSING PUMP
INVENTORS: ELIOT F. NOYES, ERNEST M. BEVILACQUA
& ROBERT E. GRAF
ASSIGNEE: MOBIL OIL CORPORATION

PATENT NUMBER: USD 206,904
PATENT FILED: MARCH 21, 1966
PATENT GRANTED: FEBRUARY 7, 1967

United States Patent Office

Des. 206,904
Patented Feb. 7, 1967

206,904

CYLINDRICAL LIQUID DISPENSING PUMP

Eliot F. Noyes, New Canaan, Ernest M. Bevilacqua, Wilton, and Robert E. Graf, New Canaan, Conn., assignors to Mobil Oil Corporation, a corporation of New York

Filed Mar. 21, 1966, Ser. No. 1,575

Term of patent 14 years

(Cl. D52—2)

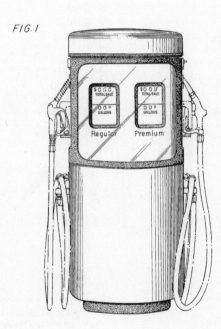

FIG. 1

TITLE: MOTORCYCLE
INVENTORS: NORIMOTO OTSUKA & MAKOTO HORI
ASSIGNEE: KABUSHIKI KAISHA HONDA
GIJUTSU KENKYUSHO

PATENT NUMBER: USD 207,042
PATENT FILED: APRIL 21, 1966
PATENT GRANTED: FEBRUARY 21, 1967

United States Patent Office

Des. 207,042
Patented Feb. 21, 1967

207,042

MOTORCYCLE

Norimoto Otsuka, Tokyo, and Makoto Hori, Yamato-machi, Kitaadachi-gun, Japan, assignors to Kabushiki Kaisha Honda Gijutsu Kenkyusho, Saitama-ken, Japan

Filed Apr. 21, 1966, Ser. No. 1,969

Claims priority, application Japan Oct. 26, 1965

Term of patent 14 years

(Cl. D90—8)

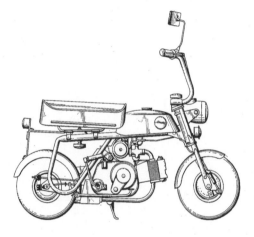

Fig.1

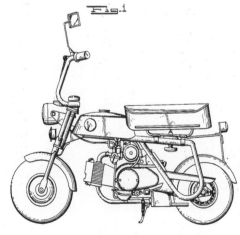

Fig.2

TITLE: MICROWAVE OVEN
INVENTOR: ROBERT I. BRUDER
ASSIGNEE: LITTON PRECISION PRODUCTS

PATENT NUMBER: USD 207,286
PATENT FILED: AUGUST 25, 1966
PATENT GRANTED: MARCH 28, 1967

United States Patent Office

Des. 207,286
Patented Mar. 28, 1967

207,286

MICROWAVE OVEN

Robert I. Bruder, Shaker Heights, Ohio, assignor to Litton Precision Products, Inc., Palo Alto, Calif., a corporation of Delaware

Filed Aug. 25, 1966, Ser. No. 3,582

Term of patent 14 years

(Cl. D81—26)

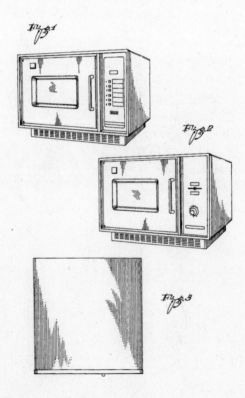

TITLE: TELEPHONE SET
INVENTORS: MARCO ZANUSO & RICHARD SAPPER
ASSIGNEE: SOCIETÀ ITALIANA
TELECOMUNICAZIONI SIEMENS

PATENT NUMBER: USD 207,491
PATENT FILED: JUNE 10, 1966
PATENT GRANTED: APRIL 25, 1967

United States Patent Office

Des. 207,491
Patented Apr. 25, 1967

207,491

TELEPHONE SET

Marco Zanuso, Milan, Italy, and Richard Sapper, Stuttgart-Degerloch, Germany, assignors to Società Italiana
Telecomunicazioni Siemens S.p.A., Milan, Italy

Filed June 10, 1966, Ser. No. 2,639

Term of patent 14 years

(Cl. D26—14)

FIG. 1

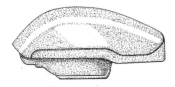

FIG. 4

TITLE: FOOD MIXER AND THE LIKE
INVENTOR: REINHOLD WEISS
ASSIGNEE: BRAUN

PATENT NUMBER: USD 207,859
PATENT FILED: FEBRUARY 1, 1966
PATENT GRANTED: JUNE 6, 1967

United States Patent Office

Des. 207,859
Patented June 6, 1967

207,859

FOOD MIXER AND THE LIKE

Reinhold Weiss, Frankfurt am Main, Germany, assignor
to Braun Aktiengesellschaft

Filed Feb. 1, 1966, Ser. No. 829

Claims priority, application Germany Aug. 13, 1965

Term of patent 7 years

(Cl. D44—1)

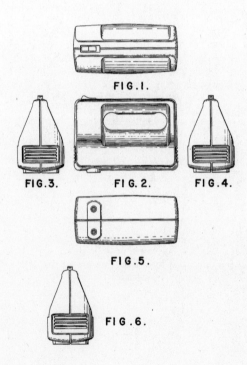

FIG. 1.

FIG. 3. FIG. 2. FIG. 4.

FIG. 5.

FIG. 6.

FIG. 1 is a top plan view of a food mixer and the like showing my new design;
FIG. 2 is a side elevational view;
FIG. 3 is a front elevational view;
FIG. 4 is a rear elevational view;
FIG. 5 is a bottom plan view;
FIG. 6 is a front elevational view of a food mixer and the like showing another form of my new design wherein the front vent panel is raised upwardly in relation to the bottom edge of the mixer and the slots therein are eccentric with respect to the lower line of the panel.

I claim:
The ornamental design for a food mixer and the like, as shown and described.

References Cited

UNITED STATES PATENTS

D. 203,761   2/1966   Frost _____ D44—1

JOEL STEARMAN, *Primary Examiner.*

TITLE: ELECTRIC KNIFE HANDLE
INVENTOR: JEROLD R. PETERSON
ASSIGNEE: SUNBEAM CORPORATION

PATENT NUMBER: USD 208,083
PATENT FILED: DECEMBER 27, 1966
PATENT GRANTED: JULY 11, 1967

United States Patent Office

Des. 208,083

Patented July 11, 1967

208,083

ELECTRIC KNIFE HANDLE

Jerold R. Peterson, Roselle, Ill., assignor to Sunbeam
Corporation, Chicago, Ill., a corporation of Illinois

Filed Dec. 27, 1966, Ser. No. 5,181

Term of patent 14 years

(Cl. D95—3)

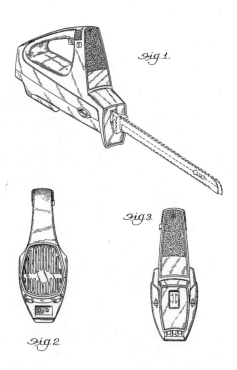

Fig. 1.

Fig. 3.

Fig. 2.

TITLE: TELEVISION RECEIVER OR SIMILAR ARTICLE
INVENTOR: GEORGE P. ROEGNER
ASSIGNEE: WESTINGHOUSE ELECTRIC CORPORATION

PATENT NUMBER: USD 208,330
PATENT FILED: MAY 17, 1965
PATENT GRANTED: AUGUST 15, 1967

United States Patent Office

Des. 208,330
Patented Aug. 15, 1967

208,330

TELEVISION RECEIVER OR SIMILAR ARTICLE

George P. Roegner, Brick Township, Normandy Beach,
N.J., assignor to Westinghouse Electric Corporation, a
corporation of Pennsylvania

Filed May 17, 1965, Ser. No. 85,326

Term of patent 14 years

(Cl. D56—4)

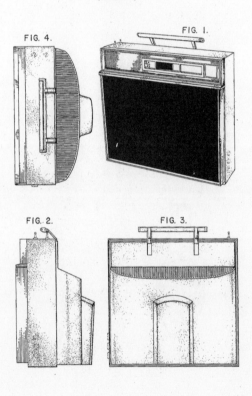

FIG. 4.

FIG. 1.

FIG. 2.

FIG. 3.

TITLE: CALCULATING MACHINE
INVENTOR: ETTORE SOTTSASS, JR.
ASSIGNEE: OLIVETTI

PATENT NUMBER: USD 209,638
PATENT FILED: OCTOBER 3, 1966
PATENT GRANTED: DECEMBER 19, 1967

United States Patent Office

Des. 209,638
Patented Dec. 19, 1967

209,638

CALCULATING MACHINE

Ettore Sottsass, Milan, Italy, assignor to Ing. C. Olivetti
& C., S.p.A., Ivrea, Turin, Italy, a corporation of Italy

Filed Oct. 3, 1966, Ser. No. 4,133

Claims priority, application Italy Apr. 13, 1966

Term of patent 14 Years

(Cl. D64—11)

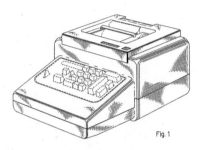

Fig. 1

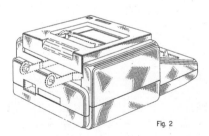

Fig. 2

FIG. 1 is a front perspective view of a calculating machine showing my new design;

FIG. 2 is a rear perspective view thereof,

The essential features of the design reside in the portions shown in full lines on the drawing.

I claim:

The ornamental design for a calculating machine, substantially as shown and described.

References Cited

UNITED STATES PATENTS

D. 192,057   1/1962   Sieber _____ D64—11.3
D. 192,273   2/1962   Nizzoli _____ D64—11.3
D. 205,971   10/1966   Sottsass _____ D64—11.1

EDWIN H. HUNTER, *Primary Examiner.*

LOUIS J. PERLSTEIN, *Examiner.*

TITLE: COUNTERTOP DISHWASHER
INVENTOR: CARL A. PETERSON
ASSIGNEE: WESTINGHOUSE ELECTRIC CORPORATION

PATENT NUMBER: USD 210,799
PATENT FILED: SEPTEMBER 8, 1967
PATENT GRANTED: APRIL 16, 1968

United States Patent Office

Des. 210,799
Patented Apr. 16, 1968

210,799

COUNTERTOP DISHWASHER

Carl A. Peterson, Columbus, Ohio, assignor to Westinghouse Electric Corporation, a corporation of Pennsylvania

Filed Sept. 8, 1967, Ser. No. 8,529

Term of patent 14 years

(Cl. D49—1)

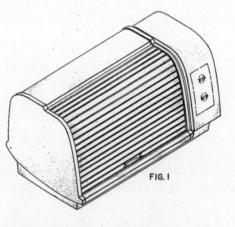

FIG. I

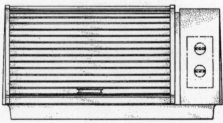

FIG. 2

TITLE: TELEPHONE BOOTH UNIT
INVENTOR: HENRY DREYFUSS
ASSIGNEE: BELL TELEPHONE LABORATORIES

PATENT NUMBER: USD 211,012
PATENT FILED: JULY 3, 1967
PATENT GRANTED: MAY 14, 1968

United States Patent Office

Des. 211,012
Patented May 14, 1968

211,012

TELEPHONE BOOTH UNIT

Henry Dreyfuss, South Pasadena, Calif., assignor to Bell
Telephone Laboratories, Incorporated, Murray Hill,
N.J., a corporation of New York

Filed July 3, 1967, Ser. No. 7,678

Term of patent 14 years

(Cl. D13—1)

FIG. 1

TITLE: TYPEWRITER
INVENTOR: REGINALD R. GALLANT
& RICHARD H. RUSSELL
ASSIGNEE: OLIVETTI UNDERWOOD CORPORATION

PATENT NUMBER: USD 211,063
PATENT FILED: DECEMBER 21, 1966
PATENT GRANTED: MAY 14, 1968

United States Patent Office

Des. 211,063
Patented May 14, 1968

211,063

TYPEWRITER

Reginald R. Gallant, Bristol, and Richard H. Russell, Farmington, Conn., assignors to Olivetti Underwood Corporation, New York, N.Y., a corporation of Delaware

Filed Dec. 21, 1966, Ser. No. 5,138

Term of patent 14 years

(Cl. D64—11)

FIG. 1

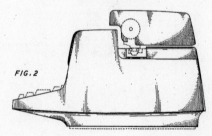

FIG. 2

TITLE: SPORT VEHICLE
INVENTOR: FERDINAND ALEXANDER PORSCHE
ASSIGNEE: NONE

PATENT NUMBER: USD 211,136
PATENT FILED: NOVEMBER 17, 1966
PATENT GRANTED: MAY 21, 1968

United States Patent Office

Des. 211,136
Patented May 21, 1968

211,136

SPORT VEHICLE

Ferdinand Alexander Porsche, Doffingen,
Boblingen, Germany

Filed Nov. 17, 1966, Ser. No. 4,712

Term of patent 14 years

(Cl. D71—1)

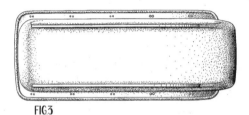

FIG3

FIG.1

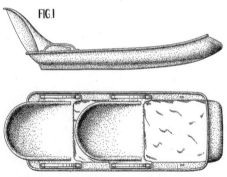

FIG. 2

TITLE: ARMCHAIR
INVENTOR: MOSES RICHARD SCHULTZ
ASSIGNEE: KNOLL ASSOCIATES

PATENT NUMBER: USD 211,334
PATENT FILED: NOVEMBER 8, 1965
PATENT GRANTED: JUNE 11, 1968

United States Patent Office

Des. 211,334
Patented June 11, 1968

211,334

ARMCHAIR

Moses Richard Schultz, Barto, Pa., assignor to Knoll Associates, Inc., New York, N.Y., a corporation of New York

Filed Nov. 8, 1965, Ser. No. 88,044

Term of patent 14 years

(Cl. D15—1)

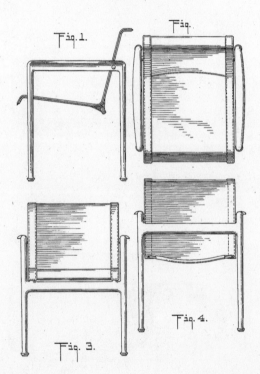

FIG. 1 is a side view of an armchair embodying the new design.
FIG. 2 is a top view of the chair of FIG. 1.
FIG. 3 is a front view of the chair of FIG. 1.
FIG. 4 is a rear view of the chair of FIG. 1.
I claim:
The ornamental design for an armchair, as shown.

References Cited

UNITED STATES PATENTS

D. 137,587   4/1944   Harasty _____ D15—1
D. 188,046   5/1960   Galloway _____ D15—1
D. 190,645   6/1961   Sundberg et al. _____ D15—1

OTHER REFERENCES

Interiors, July 1959, p. 95, chair in view 3.
Interiors, February 1965, p. 149, chair in views 22 and 23.

BRUCE W. DUNKINS, *Primary Examiner.*

EDWIN H. HUNTER, *Examiner.*

TITLE: TABLE LIGHTER
INVENTOR: DIETER RAMS
ASSIGNEE: BRAUN

PATENT NUMBER: USD 211,823
PATENT FILED: AUGUST 21, 1967
PATENT GRANTED: JULY 30, 1968

United States Patent Office

Des. 211,823
Patented July 30, 1968

211,823

TABLE LIGHTER

Dieter Rams, Koenigstein, Taunus, Germany, assignor to Braun Aktiengesellschaft, Frankfurt am Main, Germany

Filed Aug. 21, 1967, Ser. No. 8,323

Term of patent 7 years

(Cl. D48—27)

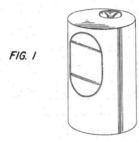

FIG. 1

FIG. 2

FIG. 1 is a perspective front view; and

FIG. 2 is a perspective side view of a table lighter of our design.

The bottom face of the lighter has a flat surface and the side and rear face of the lighter not appearing in the drawing having a cylindrical surface.

I claim:

The ornamental design for a table lighter, as shown and described.

References Cited

UNITED STATES PATENTS

D. 144,876   5/1946   Specht _____ D48—27
1,140,142   5/1915   Faile.

OTHER REFERENCES

National Jeweler, March 1962, p. 46, lighter at lower right of page.

A. HUGO WORD, *Primary Examiner.*

TITLE: AUTOMOBILE
INVENTOR: HENRY G. HAGA
ASSIGNEE: GENERAL MOTORS CORPORATION

PATENT NUMBER: USD 212,152
PATENT FILED: JANUARY 16, 1968
PATENT GRANTED: SEPTEMBER 3, 1968

United States Patent Office

Des. 212,152
Patented Sept. 3, 1968

212,152

AUTOMOBILE

Henry G. Haga, Bloomfield Hills, Mich., assignor to General Motors Corporation, Detroit, Mich., a corporation of Delaware

Filed Jan. 16, 1968, Ser. No. 10,183

Term of patent 14 years

(Cl. D14—3)

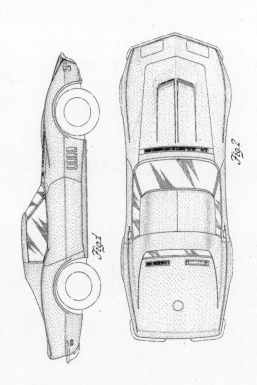

TITLE: AIRPLANE
INVENTORS: JOSEPH F. SUTTER, ROWLAND E. BROWN,
DONALD W. FINLAY, MILTON HEINEMANN, ET AL.
ASSIGNEE: BOEING COMPANY

PATENT NUMBER: USD 212,564
PATENT FILED: DECEMBER 20, 1966
PATENT GRANTED: OCTOBER 29, 1968

United States Patent Office

Des. 212,564
Patented Oct. 29, 1968

212,564

AIRPLANE

Joseph F. Sutter, Rowland E. Brown, Donald W. Finlay,
Milton Heinemann, Kenneth C. Plewes, and Everette
L. Webb, King County, Wash., assignors to The Boeing
Company, Seattle, Wash., a corporation of Delaware

Filed Dec. 20, 1966, Ser. No. 5,128

Term of patent 14 years

(Cl. D71—1)

Fig. 1.

Fig. 2.

663

TITLE: VIDEOTELEPHONE TRANSCEIVER
INVENTORS: HENRY DREYFUSS & REMBERT R. STOKES
ASSIGNEE: BELL TELEPHONE LABORATORIES

PATENT NUMBER: USD 213,108
PATENT FILED: NOVEMBER 24, 1967
PATENT GRANTED: JANUARY 7, 1969

United States Patent Office

Des. 213,108
Patented Jan. 7, 1969

213,108

VIDEOTELEPHONE TRANSCEIVER

Henry Dreyfuss, South Pasadena, Calif., and Rembert R. Stokes, Middletown, N.J., assignors to Bell Telephone Laboratories, Incorporated, Murray Hill, N.J., a corporation of New York

Filed Nov. 24, 1967, Ser. No. 9,548

Term of patent 14 years

U.S. Cl. D26—14
Int. Cl. D14—03

FIG. 1

FIG. 2

TITLE: CLOCK RADIO
INVENTOR: MAXIME DUCHARME
ASSIGNEE: NORTH AMERICAN PHILIPS COMPANY

PATENT NUMBER: USD 213,648
PATENT FILED: JULY 27, 1967
PATENT GRANTED: MARCH 25, 1969

United States Patent Office

Des. 213,648
Patented Mar. 25, 1969

213,648

CLOCK RADIO

Maxime Ducharme, Toronto, Ontario, Canada, assignor to
North American Philips Co., Inc.

Filed July 27, 1967, Ser. No. 8,038

Claims priority, application Switzerland Jan. 30, 1967

Term of patent 14 years

Int. Cl. D10—*03;* D14—*03*

U.S. Cl. D56—4

Fig. 1

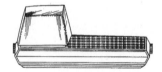

Fig. 2

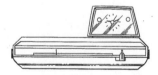

Fig. 3

TITLE: HAND DRILL
INVENTOR: MELVIN H. BOLDT
ASSIGNEE: G. W. MURPHY INDUSTRIES

PATENT NUMBER: USD 213,850
PATENT FILED: APRIL 23, 1968
PATENT GRANTED: APRIL 15, 1969

United States Patent Office

Des. 213,850
Patented Apr. 15, 1969

213,850

HAND DRILL

Melvin H. Boldt, Glenview, Ill., assignor to G. W. Murphy Industries, Inc., Houston, Tex., a corporation of Texas

Filed Apr. 23, 1968, Ser. No. 11,587

Term of patent 14 years

Int. Cl. D8—02

U.S. Cl. D54—14

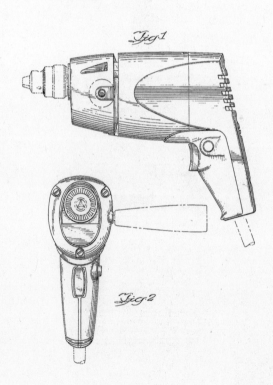

Fig. 1

Fig. 2

TITLE: PEDESTAL OR THE LIKE
INVENTOR: WARREN PLATNER
ASSIGNEE: ART METAL-KNOLL CORPORATION

PATENT NUMBER: USD 213,976
PATENT FILED: AUGUST 31, 1965
PATENT GRANTED: APRIL 29, 1969

United States Patent Office

Des. 213,976
Patented Apr. 29, 1969

213,976

PEDESTAL OR THE LIKE

Warren Platner, North Haven, Conn., assignor to Art Metal-Knoll Corporation, a corporation of Delaware

Continuation-in-part of design application Ser. No. 86,788, Aug. 31, 1965. This application Aug. 1, 1967, Ser. No. 8,082

Term of patent 14 years

Int. Cl. D6—*01*

U.S. Cl. D33—14

Fig. 1.

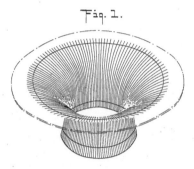

Fig. 2.

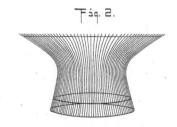

TITLE: BOTTLE
INVENTOR: MASSIMO VIGNELLI
ASSIGNEE: THE GILLETTE COMPANY

PATENT NUMBER: USD 214,307
PATENT FILED: APRIL 25, 1967
PATENT GRANTED: JUNE 3, 1969

United States Patent Office

Des. 214,307
Patented June 3, 1969

214,307

BOTTLE

Massimo Vignelli, New York, N.Y., assignor to The Gillette Company, Boston, Mass., a corporation of Delaware

Filed Apr. 25, 1967, Ser. No. 6,828

Term of patent 14 years

Int. Cl. D9—*01*

U.S. Cl. D9—139

The figure is a view in elevation of a bottle, showing my new design.

The bottle is round in all cross-sections.

I claim:

The ornamental design for a bottle, substantially as shown and described.

References Cited

UNITED STATES PATENTS

D. 91,372   1/1934   Stein ---------------- D58—8

OTHER REFERENCES

Beauty Fashion, February 1966, p. 55, closure cap on Golden Cologne bottle.

House Beautiful, May 1950, p. 38, Pyrex Flagon.

ROBERT C. SPANGLER, *Primary Examiner.*

TITLE: BICYCLE
INVENTORS: JOHN MACGREGOR GORDON, HARRY
LETHERLAND & THOMAS JOSEF DERRIK PAUL KAREN
ASSIGNEE: NONE

PATENT NUMBER: USD 214,820
PATENT FILED: JUNE 11, 1968
PATENT GRANTED: JULY 29, 1969

United States Patent Office

Des. 214,820
Patented July 29, 1969

214,820

BICYCLE

John MacGregor Gordon, 42 Horsendale Ave., Nottingham, Nuthall, England; Harry Letherland, 47 Sandy Lane, Nottingham, Brancote Hill, England; and Thomas Josef Derrick Paul Karen, The Cottage, Hertfordshire, Ashwell, England

Filed June 11, 1968, Ser. No. 12,303

Term of patent 3½ years

Claims priority, application Great Britain Dec. 12 1967

Int. Cl. D12—11

U.S. Cl. D90—8

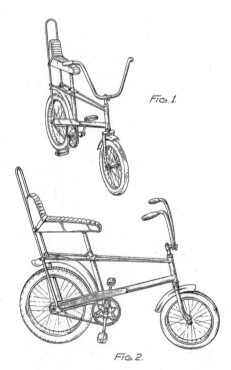

FIG. 1.

FIG. 2.

TITLE: SEWING MACHINE
INVENTORS: MARCO ZANUSO & RICHARD F. SAPPER
ASSIGNEE: NECCHI

PATENT NUMBER: USD 215,368
PATENT FILED: MAY 10, 1968
PATENT GRANTED: SEPTEMBER 23, 1969

United States Patent Office

Des. 215,368
Patented Sept. 23, 1969

215,368

DESIGN FOR A SEWING MACHINE

Marco Zanuso, Milan, Italy, and Richard F. Sapper,
Stuttgart-Degerloch, Germany, assignors to Necchi
Società per Azioni, Pavia, Italy

Filed May 10, 1968, Ser. No. 11,886

Term of patent 14 years

Claims priority, application Italy Nov. 14, 1967

Int. Cl. D15—09

U.S. Cl. D70—1

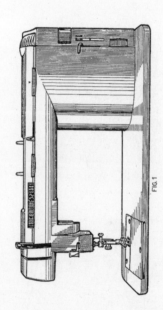

FIG. 1

TITLE: ELECTRIC PENCIL SHARPENER
INVENTORS: KOHJI MIZUNO & DAISUKE KAJIWARA
ASSIGNEE: MATSUSHITA ELECTRIC
INDUSTRIAL COMPANY

PATENT NUMBER: USD 215,379
PATENT FILED: SEPTEMBER 4, 1968
PATENT GRANTED: SEPTEMBER 23, 1969

United States Patent Office

Des. 215,379
Patented Sept. 23, 1969

215,379

ELECTRIC PENCIL SHARPENER

Kohji Mizuno, Amagasaki-shi, and Daisuke Kajiwara, Moriguchi-shi, Japan, assignors to Matsushita Electric Industrial Co., Ltd., Kadoma, Osaka, Japan, a corporation of Japan

Filed Sept. 4, 1968, Ser. No. 13,390

Term of patent 14 years

Claims priority, application Japan Mar. 8, 1968

Int. Cl. D19—99

U.S. Cl. D74—21

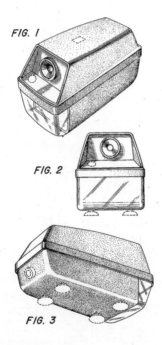

FIG. 1

FIG. 2

FIG. 3

FIG. 1 is a top and front perspective view of an electric pencil sharpener showing our new design;

FIG. 2 is a front view thereof, and

FIG. 3 is a bottom and rear perspective view thereof.

The dominant features of our design reside in the full line portions on the drawing, conventional feet and other elements being shown in broken lines.

We claim:

The ornamental design for an electric pencil sharpener, as shown and described.

References Cited

UNITED STATES PATENTS

D. 199,473	10/1964	Shuler	D74—21
D. 211,297	6/1968	LaZar	D74—21

OTHER REFERENCES

Office Appliances, November 1966, p. 74, "Boston" sharpener.

Premium Practice, March 1966, p. 284, "Jetric" sharpener.

EDWIN H. HUNTER, Primary Examiner

LOUIS J. PERLSTEIN, Assistant Examiner

TITLE: SUCTION CLEANER
INVENTORS: CARROLL M. GANTZ, ROBERT H. HOSE
& JOSEPH T. SESTAK
ASSIGNEE: THE HOOVER COMPANY

PATENT NUMBER: USD 215,489
PATENT FILED: OCTOBER 9, 1968
PATENT GRANTED: SEPTEMBER 30, 1969

United States Patent Office

Des. 215,489
Patented Sept. 30, 1969

215,489

SUCTION CLEANER

Carroll M. Gantz, North Canton, Ohio, Robert H. Hose,
Mountainside, N.J., and Joseph T. Sestak, Pittsburgh,
Pa., assignors to The Hoover Company, North Can-
ton, Ohio, a corporation of Delaware

Filed Oct. 9, 1968, Ser. No. 13,904

Term of patent 14 years

Int. Cl. D15—07

U.S. Cl. D49—14.1

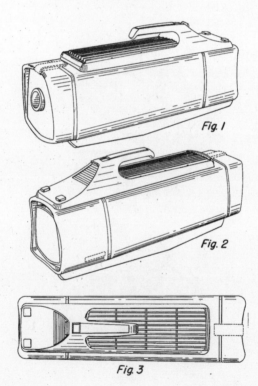

Fig. 1

Fig. 2

Fig. 3

FIGURE 1 is a front perspective view of a suction
cleaner embodying our new design;
FIGURE 2 is a rear perspective view taken diagonally
of that shown in FIGURE 1; and
FIGURE 3 is a top plan view.
The dominant features of our design reside in the por-
tions of the drawing shown in full lines.
We claim:
The ornamental design for a suction cleaner, as shown
and described.

References Cited

UNITED STATES PATENTS

D. 170,256	8/1953	Dreyfuss	D49—13
D. 172,835	8/1954	Kelly	D49—13

OTHER REFERENCES

Modern Plastics, vol. 25, September 1947–February
1948, December 1947, p. 108.

A. HUGO WORD, Primary Examiner

TITLE: HOLDER FOR A COMBINED
SAFETY RAZOR & MOUNT
INVENTOR: IRVING HARPER
ASSIGNEE: WILKINSON SWORD

PATENT NUMBER: USD 215,995
PATENT FILED: OCTOBER 16, 1968
PATENT GRANTED: NOVEMBER 11, 1969

United States Patent Office

Des. 215,995
Patented Nov. 11, 1969

215,995

HOLDER FOR A COMBINED SAFETY RAZOR AND MOUNT

Irving Harper, Rye, N.Y., assignor to Wilkinson Sword
Limited, London, England, a British company

Filed Oct. 16, 1968, Ser. No. 14,022

Claims priority, application Great Britain Apr. 24, 1968

Term of patent 14 years

Int. Cl. D28—03

U.S. Cl. D95—3

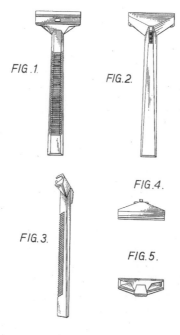

FIG. 1.

FIG. 2.

FIG. 3.

FIG. 4.

FIG. 5.

FIGURE 1 is a front elevational view of a holder for a combined safety razor blade and mount showing my new design;

FIGURE 2 is a rear elevational view thereof;

FIGURE 3 is an elevational view of one side thereof, the opposite side having the same appearance being a mirror image of FIGURE 3;

FIGURE 4 is a top plan view thereof; and

FIGURE 5 is a bottom plan view thereof.

I claim:

The ornamental design for a holder for a combined safety razor blade and mount, as shown and described.

References Cited

UNITED STATES PATENTS

D. 193,299   7/1962   Dreyfuss _____ D95—3

JOEL STEARMAN, Primary Examiner

TITLE: GLOBE CHAIR
INVENTOR: EERO AARNIO
ASSIGNEE: ASKO OSAKEYHTIO

PATENT NUMBER: USD 212,801
PATENT FILED: JULY 22, 1966
PATENT GRANTED: NOVEMBER 26, 1968

United States Patent Office

Des. 212,801
Patented Nov. 26, 1968

212,801

GLOBE CHAIR

Eero Aarnio, Helsinki, Finland, assignor to Asko
Osakeyhtio, Lahti, Finland, a firm of Finland

Filed July 22, 1966, Ser. No. 3,184

Term of patent 14 years

(Cl. D15—11)

Fig. 1

Fig. 2

Fig. 3

Fig. 4

FIGURE 1 is a front elevational view of a globe chair;
FIGURE 2 is a rear elevational view of a globe chair;
FIGURE 3 is a side elevational view of a globe chair;
FIGURE 4 is a top plan view of a globe chair.

The dominant features of my design reside in those
portions shown in full lines on the drawing.

I claim:

The ornamental design for a globe chair, as shown
and described.

References Cited

UNITED STATES PATENTS

D. 191,705   11/1961   Galloway ----------- D15—11

OTHER REFERENCES

Design Cat., March 1962, p. 53, chair top left of Grier-son.

Interiors, April 1962, p. 133, chair at center background
by Pierre Paulin.

Interiors, July 1962, p. 95, chair by Panton at right
center background.

Interiors, November 1965, p. 111, chair by Stendig.

BRUCE W. DUNKINS, *Primary Examiner.*

TITLE: STREET LAMP
INVENTOR: GEORGE E. KOSTRITSKY
ASSIGNEE: RTKL

PATENT NUMBER: USD 216,274
PATENT FILED: MARCH 10, 1969
PATENT GRANTED: DECEMBER 9, 1969

United States Patent Office

Des. 216,274
Patented Dec. 9, 1969

216,274

STREET LAMP

George E. Kostritsky, Baltimore, Md., assignor to RTKL Inc., Baltimore, Md., a corporation of Maryland

Continuation of design application Ser. No. 10,436, Feb. 5, 1968. This application Mar. 10, 1969, Ser. No. 17,174

Term of patent 14 years

Int. Cl. D26—03

U.S. Cl. D48—31

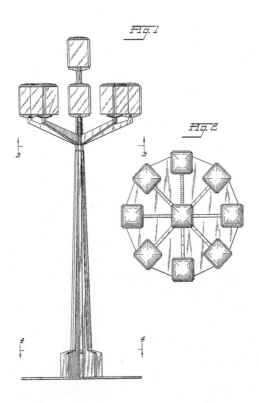

Fig. 1

Fig. 2

TITLE: HOUSE
INVENTOR: MATTI J. SUURONEN
ASSIGNEE: POLYKEM

PATENT NUMBER: USD 216,542
PATENT FILED: NOVEMBER 21, 1968
PATENT GRANTED: FEBRUARY 10, 1970

United States Patent Office

Des. 216,542
Patented Feb. 10, 1970

216,542

HOUSE

Matti J. Suuronen, Westend, Finland, assignor to Oy
Polykem AB, Helsinki, Finland, a firm of Finland

Filed Nov. 21, 1968, Ser. No. 14,587

Term of patent 14 years

Int. Cl. D25—04

U.S. Cl. D13—1

FIG.1

FIG.2

TITLE: BEVERAGE SERVER OR THE LIKE
INVENTOR: ARNE JACOBSEN
ASSIGNEE: NONE

PATENT NUMBER: USD 216,599
PATENT FILED: SEPTEMBER 30, 1968
PATENT GRANTED: FEBRUARY 17, 1970

United States Patent Office

Des. 216,599
Patented Feb. 17, 1970

216,599

BEVERAGE SERVER OR THE LIKE

Arne Jacobsen, 403 Lyngbyvej, Gentofte, Denmark

Filed Sept. 30, 1968, Ser. No. 13,778

Term of patent 14 years

Int. Cl. D7—*01*

U.S. Cl. D44—21

FIG. 1

FIG. 2

FIGURE 1 is a perspective view of a beverage server or the like showing my new design, in the size and proportions of a coffee pot; and

FIGURE 2 is a side elevational view thereof, the opposite side being a mirror image;

proportions of a tea pot.

I claim:

The ornamental design for beverage server or the like, as shown and described.

References Cited

UNITED STATES PATENTS

D. 78,525	5/1929	Lindley	D44—26
D. 116,379	8/1939	Ramsthal	D44—26
D. 139,489	11/1944	Moore	D44—29
D. 155,438	10/1949	Muller-Munk	D44—29
D. 189,983	3/1961	Krause	D44—29

OTHER REFERENCES

Design, #142, October 1960, p. 93, coffee pot in upper right corner.

Tableware, April 1964, p. 302, coffee pot.

JOEL STEARMAN, Primary Examiner

TITLE: FLASHLIGHT
INVENTORS: HANS GUGELOT & FRANZ PREISINGER
ASSIGNEE: BRAUN

PATENT NUMBER: USD 217,065
PATENT FILED: DECEMBER 5, 1968
PATENT GRANTED: MARCH 31, 1970

United States Patent Office

Des. 217,065
Patented Mar. 31, 1970

217,065

FLASHLIGHT

Hans Gugelot, Ulm am Hochstraess, and Franz Preisinger, Oberelchingen, Germany, assignor to Braun Aktiengesellschaft, Frankfurt am Main, Germany

Filed Dec. 5, 1968, Ser. No. 15,008

Claims priority, application Germany June 6, 1968

Term of patent 14 years

Int. Cl. D26—04

U.S. Cl. D48—24

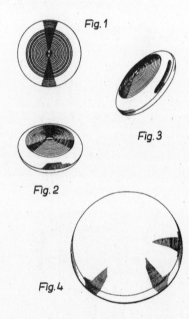

Fig. 1

Fig. 3

Fig. 2

Fig. 4

FIG. 1 is a top view of this flashlight showing our new design;
FIG. 2 is a perspective side view;
FIG. 3 is another perspective side view; and
FIG. 4 is a perspective rear view of this flashlight.
We claim:
The ornamental design for a flashlight, substantially as shown and described.

References Cited

UNITED STATES PATENTS

D. 86,734	4/1932	Mitchell	D48—24
1,074,376	9/1913	Neudorffer	240—10.6
1,757,889	5/1930	Wheat.	

WALLACE R. BURKE, Primary Examiner

S. J. MERCER, Assistant Examiner

TITLE: DESK LAMP
INVENTOR: SHOJI ISHIKAWA
ASSIGNEE: MATSUSHITA ELECTRIC
INDUSTRIAL COMPANY

PATENT NUMBER: USD 217,382
PATENT FILED: MARCH 18, 1969
PATENT GRANTED: APRIL 28, 1970

United States Patent Office

Des. 217,382
Patented Apr. 28, 1970

217,382

DESK LAMP

Shoji Ishikawa, Nara, Japan, assignor to Matsushita Electric Industrial Co., Ltd., Kadoma, Osaka, Japan, a corporation of Japan

Filed Mar. 18, 1969, Ser. No. 16,310

Claims priority, application Japan Sept. 18, 1968

Term of patent 14 years

Int. Cl. D26—02

U.S. Cl. D48—20

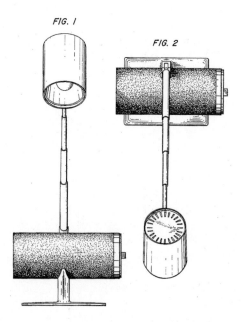

FIG. 1

FIG. 2

TITLE: HEATING FAN
INVENTOR: DIETER RAMS
ASSIGNEE: BRAUN

PATENT NUMBER: USD 217,459
PATENT FILED: JANUARY 6, 1969
PATENT GRANTED: MAY 5, 1970

United States Patent Office

Des. 217,459
Patented May 5, 1970

217,459

HEATING FAN

Dieter Rams, Koenigstein, Taunus, Germany, assignor to Braun Aktiengesellschaft, Frankfurt am Main, Germany, a firm

Filed Jan. 6, 1969, Ser. No. 15,212

Claims priority, application Germany July 4, 1968

Term of patent 14 years

Int. Cl. D23—03

U.S. Cl. D23—73

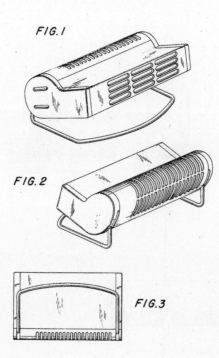

FIG. 1

FIG. 2

FIG. 3

FIG. 1 is a perspective front view of this heating fan, showing my new design;

FIG. 2 is a perspective rear view; and

FIG. 3 is a bottom view.

The characteristic feature of my design reside in the specific configuration of the heater housing.

I claim:

The ornamental design for a heating fan, substantially as shown and described.

References Cited

UNITED STATES PATENTS

D. 152,778   2/1949   Fox -------------- D23—162
3,223,313   12/1965   Kinsworthy.

WALLACE R. BURKE, Primary Examiner

S. J. MERCER, Assistant Examiner

TITLE: SEWING MACHINE
INVENTORS: MARCO ZANUSO & RICHARD SAPPER
ASSIGNEE: NECCHI

PATENT NUMBER: USD 217,511
PATENT FILED: DECEMBER 23, 1968
PATENT GRANTED: MAY 5, 1970

United States Patent Office

Des. 217,511
Patented May 5, 1970

217,511

SEWING MACHINE

Marco Zanuso, Milan, Italy, and Richard Sapper, Stuttgart, Germany, assignors to Necchi Società per Azioni, Via Rismond, Pavia, Italy

Filed Dec. 23, 1968, Ser. No. 15,167

Claims priority, application Italy July 19, 1968

Term of patent 14 years

Int. Cl. D15—09

U.S. Cl. D70—1

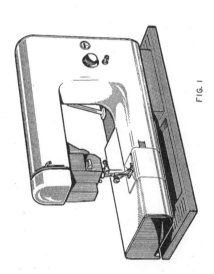

FIG. 1

TITLE: COFFEE GRINDER
INVENTOR: DIETER RAMS
ASSIGNEE: BRAUN

PATENT NUMBER: USD 218,256
PATENT FILED: JUNE 9, 1969
PATENT GRANTED: AUGUST 4, 1970

United States Patent Office

Des. 218,256
Patented Aug. 4, 1970

218,256

COFFEE GRINDER

Dieter Rams, Konigstein, Germany, assignor to Braun
Aktiengesellschaft, Frankfurt am Main, Germany

Filed June 9, 1969, Ser. No. 17,572
Claims priority, application Germany Dec. 9, 1968

Term of patent 14 years

Int. Cl. D7—05

U.S. Cl. D55—1

FIG.1

FIG.2

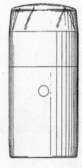 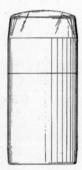

FIG.3

FIG. 1 is a front view of this coffee grinder showing
my new design;
FIG. 2 is a rear view of this coffee grinder; and
FIG. 3 is a top view of this coffee grinder showing my
new design.
I claim:
The ornamental design for a coffee grinder, substan-
tially as shown and described.

References Cited

UNITED STATES PATENTS

D. 212,260	9/1968	Cabell	D55—1
D. 196,323	9/1963	Allen et al.	D55—1
D. 189,393	12/1960	Schlumbohm	D94—3
D. 183,562	9/1958	De Angelis et al.	D55—1
D. 96,679	8/1935	Kopf	D55—1

WALLACE R. BURKE, Primary Examiner

A. P. DOUGLAS, Assistant Examiner

TITLE: LOUD SPEAKER ENCLOSURE
INVENTOR: CARL R. YURDIN
ASSIGNEE: HARMAN-KARDON

PATENT NUMBER: USD 218,614
PATENT FILED: OCTOBER 15, 1969
PATENT GRANTED: SEPTEMBER 8, 1970

United States Patent Office

Des. 218,614
Patented Sept. 8, 1970

218,614

LOUD SPEAKER ENCLOSURE

Carl R. Yurdin, Port Washington, N.Y., assignor to Harman-Kardon, Incorporated, Plainview, Long Island, N.Y., a corporation of Delaware

Filed Oct. 15, 1969, Ser. No. 19,577

Term of patent 14 years

Int. Cl. D14—01

U.S. Cl. D26—14

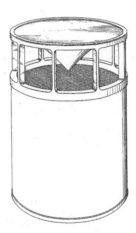

The figure is a perspective view of a loud speaker enclosure showing my new design.

I claim:

The ornamental design for a loud speaker enclosure, as shown and described.

References Cited

UNITED STATES PATENTS

D. 211,180   5/1968   Boldt --------------- D26—14
D. 215,007   8/1969   Levow --------------- D26—14
3,387,531   6/1968   Hesse.

FOREIGN PATENTS

1,158,572   12/1963   Germany.

BERNARD ANSHER, Primary Examiner

TITLE: RADIO CABINET
INVENTORS: MELVIN H. BOLDT & GEORGE A. WILSON
ASSIGNEE: NONE

PATENT NUMBER: USD 218,648
PATENT FILED: MAY 27, 1969
PATENT GRANTED: SEPTEMBER 8, 1970

United States Patent Office

Des. 218,648
Patented Sept. 8, 1970

218,648

RADIO CABINET

Melvin H. Boldt, 933 N. Glenayre Drive, Genview, Ill.
60025, and George A. Wilson, 738½ Hinman Ave.,
Evanston, Ill. 60402

Filed May 27, 1969, Ser. No. 17,374

Term of patent 14 years

Int. Cl. D14—03

U.S. Cl. D56—4

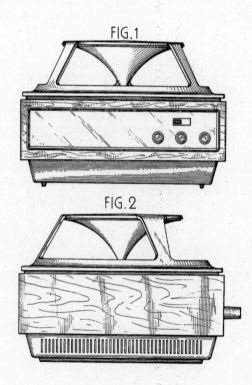

FIG. 1

FIG. 2

TITLE: TELEPHONE INSTRUMENT
INVENTOR: JOHN F. TYSON
ASSIGNEE: NORTHERN ELECTRIC COMPANY

PATENT NUMBER: USD 218,940
PATENT FILED: MARCH 11, 1969
PATENT GRANTED: OCTOBER 13, 1970

United States Patent Office

Des. 218,940
Patented Oct. 13, 1970

218,940

TELEPHONE INSTRUMENT

John F. Tyson, Ottawa, Ontario, Canada, assignor to Northern Electric Company Limited, Montreal, Quebec, Canada

Continuation-in-part of design application Ser. No. 12,072, May 24, 1968, which is a continuation-in-part of design application Ser. No. 4,666, Nov. 15, 1966, now design Patent No. 212,691, dated Nov. 12, 1968. This application Mar. 11, 1969, Ser. No. 16,175

Claims priority, application Canada Mar. 20, 1968

Term of patent 14 years

Int. Cl. D14—*03*

U.S. Cl. D26—14

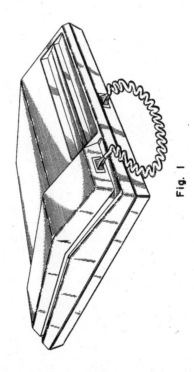

Fig. 1

TITLE: SERVING TRAY OR SIMILAR ARTICLE
INVENTORS: PETER M. BEREND & RICHARD D. DILYARD
ASSIGNEE: RUBBERMAID

PATENT NUMBER: USD 219,049
PATENT FILED: SEPTEMBER 9, 1969
PATENT GRANTED: OCTOBER 27, 1970

United States Patent Office

Des. 219,049
Patented Oct. 27, 1970

219,049

SERVING TRAY OR SIMILAR ARTICLE

Peter M. Berend and Richard D. Dilyard, Wooster, Ohio,
assignors to Rubbermaid Incorporated, Wooster, Ohio,
a corporation of Ohio

Filed Sept. 9, 1969, Ser. No. 19,068

Term of patent 14 years

Int. Cl. D7—99

U.S. Cl. D44—10

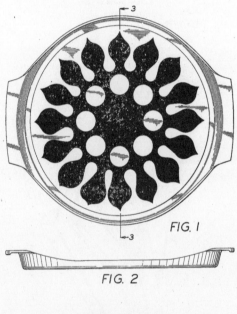

FIG. 1

FIG. 2

FIG. 3

FIG. 1 is a top plan view of a serving tray showing our new design.

FIG. 2 is a side elevational view thereof.

FIG. 3 is a sectional view on line 3—3 of FIG. 1.

We claim:

The ornamental design for a serving tray or similar article, as shown.

References Cited

UNITED STATES PATENTS

D. 211,042	5/1968	Stageberg	D44—7
D. 211,534	6/1968	Gerow	D44—15

OTHER REFERENCES

Gift and Art Buyer, July 1962, p. 22, No. 7096 tray, left center of page.

JOEL STEARMAN, Primary Examiner

TITLE: TEA POT
INVENTOR: WALTER G. GROPIUS
ASSIGNEE: ROSENTHAL

PATENT NUMBER: USD 219,165
PATENT FILED: MAY 23, 1969
PATENT GRANTED: NOVEMBER 10, 1970

United States Patent Office

Des. 219,165
Patented Nov. 10, 1970

219,165

TEA POT

Walter G. Gropius, Lincoln, Mass., assignor to Rosenthal Aktiengesellschaft, Selb, Bavaria, Germany, a corporation of Germany

Filed May 23, 1969, Ser. No. 17,309

Term of patent 14 years

Int. Cl. D7—02

U.S. Cl. D44—26

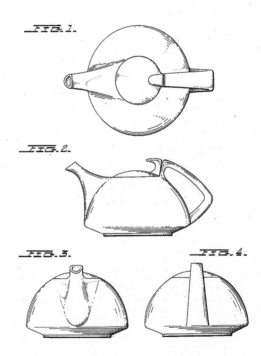

FIG. 1.

FIG. 2.

FIG. 3.

FIG. 4.

FIG. 1 is a top plan view of a tea pot showing my new design;
FIG. 2 is a side elevational view;
FIG. 3 is a front elevational view; and
FIG. 4 is a rear elevational view.
I claim:
The ornamental design for a tea pot, as shown.

References Cited
UNITED STATES PATENTS

D. 175,856   10/1955   Rowan _____ D44—25
D. 178,658   9/1956   Guild et al. _____ D44—25

JOEL STEARMAN, Primary Examiner

TITLE: LOUNGE
INVENTOR: CHARLES EAMES
ASSIGNEE: HERMAN MILLER

PATENT NUMBER: USD 219,212
PATENT FILED: MARCH 3, 1969
PATENT GRANTED: NOVEMBER 17, 1970

United States Patent Office

Des. 219,212
Patented Nov. 17, 1970

219,212

LOUNGE

Charles Eames, Venice, Calif., assignor to Herman Miller,
Inc., Zeeland, Mich., a corporation of Michigan

Filed Mar. 3, 1969, Ser. No. 16,006

Term of patent 14 years

Int. Cl. D6—*01*

U.S. Cl. D15—11

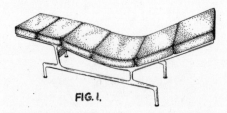

FIG. I.

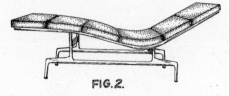

FIG. 2.

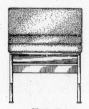

FIG. 3.

TITLE: ELECTRIC SHAVER
INVENTOR: MAARTEN WILLEM VAN LELYVELD
ASSIGNEE: UNITED STATES PHILIPS CORPORATION

PATENT NUMBER: USD 219,901
PATENT FILED: JUNE 24, 1967
PATENT GRANTED: FEBRUARY 9, 1971

United States Patent Office

Des. 219,901
Patented Feb. 9, 1971

219,901

ELECTRIC SHAVER

Maarten Willem van Lelyveld, Drachten, Netherlands,
assignor to United States Philips Corporation

Filed June 24, 1967, Ser. No. 17,846

Claims priority, application Switzerland Dec. 27, 1968

Term of patent 14 years

Int. Cl. D28—03

U.S. Cl. D95—3

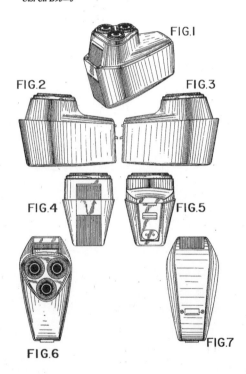

FIG.1

FIG.2

FIG.3

FIG.4

FIG.5

FIG.6

FIG.7

FIG. 1 is a perspective view of the electric shaver showing my new design;
FIG. 2 is a side elevational view thereof;
FIG. 3 is an elevational view of the opposite side thereof;
FIG. 4 is a front elevational view;
FIG. 5 is a rear elevational view;
FIG. 6 is a top plan view thereof;
FIG. 7 is a bottom plan view thereof.

I claim:
The ornamental design for an electric shaver, as shown.

References Cited

Jeweler's Circular-Keystone, August 1966, p. 116,
Norelco "Tripleheader."

JOEL STEARMAN, Primary Examiner

689

TITLE: COMBINED SHAKER & SERVER
INVENTORS: SARA L. BALBACH & RICHARD W. GREGER
& ALLEN J. SAMUELS
ASSIGNEE: CORNING GLASS WORKS

PATENT NUMBER: USD 220,160
PATENT FILED: JANUARY 10, 1969
PATENT GRANTED: MARCH 9, 1971

United States Patent Office

Des. 220,160
Patented Mar. 9, 1971

220,160

COMBINED SHAKER AND SERVER

Sara L. Balbach, Corning, Richard W. Greger, Elmira, and Allen J. Samuels, Corning, N.Y., assignors to Corning Glass Works, Corning, N.Y.

Filed Jan. 10, 1969, Ser. No. 15,302

Term of patent 14 years

Int. Cl. D7—02

U.S. Cl. D94—3

Fig. 1

Fig. 2

Fig. 3

FIG. 1 is an elevational view of a combined shaker and server embodying our new design, with a portion of the cover cut away to show a central recess;

FIG. 2 is a top plan view;

FIG. 3 is a fragmental elevational view showing the top portion of the combined shaker and server with the cover removed.

We claim:

The ornamental design for a combined shaker and server, as shown.

References Cited
UNITED STATES PATENTS

D. 4,752	4/1871	Hoare	D9—119
D. 208,935	10/1967	Marien et al.	D44—21
D. 209,482	12/1967	Noyes	D9—267
1,312,569	8/1919	Paige.	
3,006,510	10/1961	Sagarin	D9—258UX

WALLACE R. BURKE, Primary Examiner

S. J. MERCER, Assistant Examiner

TITLE: PORTABLE TYPEWRITER
INVENTOR: ETTORE SOTTSASS, JR.
ASSIGNEE: NONE

PATENT NUMBER: USD 220,292
PATENT FILED: NOVEMBER 3, 1969
PATENT GRANTED: MARCH 23, 1971

United States Patent Office

Des. 220,292
Patented Mar. 23, 1971

220,292

PORTABLE TYPEWRITER

Ettore Sottsass, Jr., 14 Via Manzoni,
20121 Milan, Italy

Filed Nov. 3, 1969, Ser. No. 19,893

Claims priority, application Italy May 3, 1969

Term of patent 14 years

Int. Cl. D18—*01*

U.S. Cl. D64—11

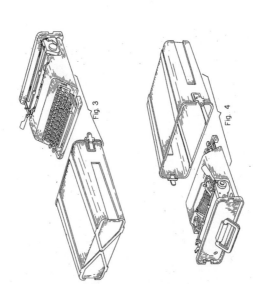

Fig. 3

Fig. 4

TITLE: BOTTLE
INVENTOR: TAPIO WIRKKALA
ASSIGNEE: ALKO

PATENT NUMBER: USD 220,469
PATENT FILED: OCTOBER 2, 1969
PATENT GRANTED: APRIL 20, 1971

United States Patent Office

Des. 220,469
Patented Apr. 20, 1971

220,469

BOTTLE

Tapio Wirkkala, Helsinki, Finland, assignor to
Oy Alko Ab, Helsinki, Finland

Filed Oct. 2, 1969, Ser. No. 19,375

Term of patent 14 years

Int. Cl. D9—01

U.S. Cl. D9—80

FIG.1

FIG.2

FIG.3

FIG. 1 is an elevational view of a bottle showing my new design;

FIG. 2 is a top plan view thereof; and

FIG. 3 is a bottom plan view thereof.

The side opposite that in FIG. 1 is the same as that shown.

I claim:

The ornamental design for a bottle, as shown and described.

References Cited

UNITED STATES PATENTS

D. 79,296	8/1929	Maddaford	D9—78
D. 93,932	11/1934	Levine	D9—78
D. 170,298	9/1953	Barbee	D9—93

ROBERT C. SPANGLER, Primary Examiner

TITLE: BEVERAGE MAKER
INVENTORS: CHESTER H. WICKENBERG
& GEORGE B. JENSEN
ASSIGNEE: NONE

PATENT NUMBER: USD 220,579
PATENT FILED: MARCH 11, 1970
PATENT GRANTED: APRIL 27, 1971

United States Patent Office

Des. 220,579
Patented Apr. 27, 1971

220,579

BEVERAGE MAKER

Chester H. Wickenberg, 1125 Forest Drive, Elgin, Ill.
60120, and George B. Jensen, 1430 Astor St., Chicago,
Ill. 60610

Filed Mar. 11, 1970, Ser. No. 21,851

Term of patent 14 years

Int. Cl. D7—04

U.S. Cl. D44—26

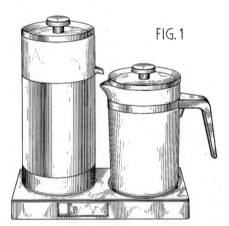

FIG. 1

FIG. 2

693

TITLE: CANDELABRA
INVENTOR: JENS H. QUISTGAARD
ASSIGNEE: DANSK DESIGNS

PATENT NUMBER: USD 220,713
PATENT FILED: MARCH 9, 1970
PATENT GRANTED: MAY 11, 1971

United States Patent Office

Des. 220,713
Patented May 11, 1971

220,713

CANDELABRA

Jens H. Quistgaard, Copenhagen, Denmark, assignor to
Dansk Designs, Ltd., Mount Kisco, N.Y.

Filed Mar. 9, 1970, Ser. No. 21,805

Term of patent 14 years

Int. Cl. D26—05

U.S. Cl. D48—2

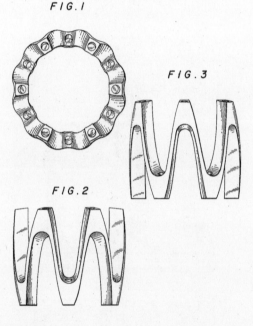

FIG. 1

FIG. 3

FIG. 2

FIG. 1 is a top plan view of a candelabra embodying my new design;

FIG. 2 is a side elevational view thereof; and

FIG. 3 is an end elevational view thereof.

The bottom plan view is a mirror image of the top plan view with the bores for the candles being omitted. The opposite sides of each of the elevational views are mirror images of the view shown.

I claim:

The ornamental design for a candelabra, as shown and described.

References Cited

UNITED STATES PATENTS

D. 206,816   1/1967   Myers et al. _____ D48—2

WALLACE R. BURKE, Primary Examiner

S. J. MERCER, Assistant Examiner

TITLE: TABLE FAN
INVENTOR: PETRUS JOANNES STUT
ASSIGNEE: UNITED STATES PHILIPS CORPORATION

PATENT NUMBER: USD 221,077
PATENT FILED: OCTOBER 30, 1969
PATENT GRANTED: JULY 6, 1971

United States Patent Office

Des. 221,077
Patented July 6, 1971

221,077

TABLE FAN

Petrus Joannes Stut, Drachten, Netherlands, assignor to
United States Philips Corporation

Filed Oct. 30, 1969, Ser. No. 19,844

Claims priority, application Switzerland May 8, 1969

Term of patent 14 years

Int. Cl. D23—*04*

U.S. Cl. D23—155

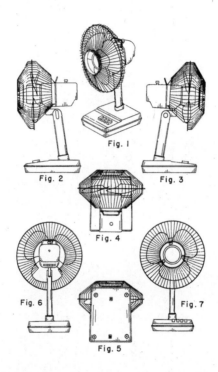

Fig. 1

Fig. 2

Fig. 3

Fig. 4

Fig. 6

Fig. 7

Fig. 5

FIG. 1 is a perspective view of the table fan, showing my new design;

FIG. 2 is a side elevational view thereof;

FIG. 3 is an elevational view of the opposite side thereof;

FIG. 4 is a top plan view thereof;

FIG. 5 is a bottom plan view thereof;

FIG. 6 is a rear elevational view thereof; and

FIG. 7 is a front elevational view thereof.

I claim:

The ornamental design for a table fan, as shown.

References Cited

UNITED STATES PATENTS

3,446,429   5/1969   Suzuki et al. _____ 230—276X

FOREIGN PATENTS

203,580   9/1962   Japan _____ D23—155
213,060   9/1962   Japan _____ D23—155
213,525   5/1962   Japan _____ D23—155

WALLACE R. BURKE, Primary Examiner

S. J. MERCER, Assistant Examiner

TITLE: FOLDABLE LAWN CHAIR
INVENTOR: CHARLES W. MCCOMAS
ASSIGNEE: NONE

PATENT NUMBER: USD 221,146
PATENT FILED: FEBRUARY 2, 1970
PATENT GRANTED: JULY 13, 1971

United States Patent Office

Des. 221,146
Patented July 13, 1971

221,146

FOLDABLE LAWN CHAIR

Charles W. McComas, 116 S. Delaware St.,
Hobart, Ind. 46342

Filed Feb. 2, 1970, Ser. No. 21,180

Term of patent 14 years

Int. Cl. D6—*01*

U.S. Cl. D15—1

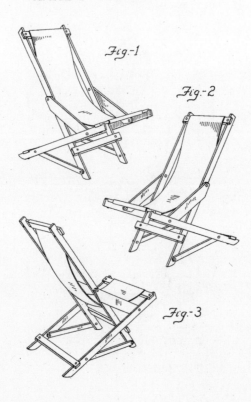

Fig.-1

Fig.-2

Fig.-3

FIG. 1 is a perspective view of the foldable lawn chair embodying the design of my invention as viewed from the front right side thereof;

FIG. 2 is a perspective view of my invention as viewed from the front left side thereof; and

FIG. 3 is a perspective view thereof as viewed from the back right side thereof.

I claim:

The ornamental design for a foldable lawn chair, substantially as shown.

References Cited

UNITED STATES PATENTS

571,823	11/1896	Briggs.
1,979,278	11/1934	McMurtry.
2,080,761	5/1937	Crawford.

BRUCE W. DUNKINS, Primary Examiner

TITLE: CLOCK OR SIMILAR ARTICLE
INVENTOR: WALTER C. ANDERSON
ASSIGNEE: GENERAL ELECTRIC COMPANY

PATENT NUMBER: USD 221,171
PATENT FILED: JUNE 12, 1970
PATENT GRANTED: JULY 13, 1971

United States Patent Office

Des. 221,171
Patented July 13, 1971

221,171

CLOCK OR SIMILAR ARTICLE

Walter C. Anderson, Redding, Conn., assignor to
General Electric Company

Filed June 12, 1970, Ser. No. 23,457

Term of patent 7 years

Int. Cl. D10—*01*

U.S. Cl. D42—7

Fig. 1.

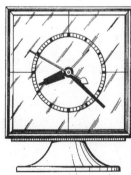

Fig. 2.

TITLE: KITCHEN MIXER
INVENTORS: ARTHUR C. CHRISTENSEN
& MONTE L. LEVIN
ASSIGNEE: SCOVILL MANUFACTURING COMPANY

PATENT NUMBER: USD 221,575
PATENT FILED: JUNE 3, 1970
PATENT GRANTED: AUGUST 24, 1971

United States Patent Office

Des. 221,575
Patented Aug. 24, 1971

221,575

KITCHEN MIXER

Arthur C. Christensen, Thomaston, Conn., and Monte
L. Levin, New York, N.Y., assignors to Scovill Manufacturing Company, Waterbury, Conn.

Filed June 3, 1970, Ser. No. 23,264

Term of patent 14 years

Int. Cl. D7—05

U.S. Cl. D44—1

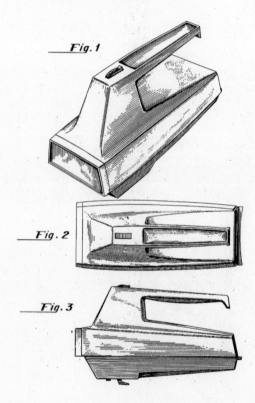

Fig. 1

Fig. 2

Fig. 3

698

TITLE: HAIR DRYER
INVENTOR: MELVIN H. BOLDT
ASSIGNEE: NATIONAL PRESTO INDUSTRIES

PATENT NUMBER: USD 222,198
PATENT FILED: JUNE 15, 1970
PATENT GRANTED: OCTOBER 5, 1971

United States Patent Office

Des. 222,198
Patented Oct. 5, 1971

222,198

HAIR DRYER

Melvin H. Boldt, Glenview, Ill., assignor to National
Presto Industries, Inc., Eau Claire, Wis.

Filed June 15, 1970, Ser. No. 23,471

Term of patent 14 years

Int. Cl. D28—03

U.S. Cl. D86—10

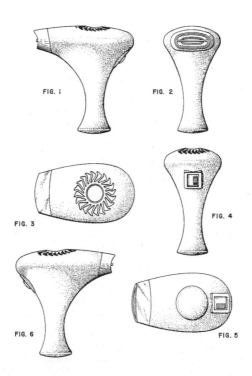

FIG. 1

FIG. 2

FIG. 3

FIG. 4

FIG. 6

FIG. 5

FIG. 1 is a side elevational view of a hair dryer show-
ing my new design;
FIG. 2 is a front end view of the hair dryer;
FIG. 3 is a top plan view thereof;
FIG. 4 is a rear end view thereof;
FIG. 5 is a bottom plan view thereof; and
FIG. 6 is an elevational view of the opposite side of
the hair dryer shown in FIG. 1.
I claim:
The ornamental design for a hair dryer, substantially
as shown.

References Cited

UNITED STATES PATENTS

D. 138,044   6/1944   Preble, Jr. _____ D86—10
D. 155,828   11/1949   Meltzer _____ D86—10

OTHER REFERENCES

Jeweler's Circular Keystone, August 1965, p. 54, Sunbeam hair dryer shown, Model HHD.

EDWIN H. HUNTER, Primary Examiner

L. S. LANIER, Assistant Examiner

TITLE: ELECTRIC CAN OPENER
INVENTOR: MONTE L. LEVIN
ASSIGNEE: SCOVILL MANUFACTURING COMPANY

PATENT NUMBER: USD 222,330
PATENT FILED: JUNE 3, 1970
PATENT GRANTED: OCTOBER 19, 1971

United States Patent Office

Des. 222,330
Patented Oct. 19, 1971

222,330

ELECTRIC CAN OPENER

Monte L. Levin, New York, N.Y., assignor to Scovill
Manufacturing Company, Waterbury, Conn.

Filed June 3, 1970, Ser. No. 23,269

Term of patent 14 years

Int. Cl. D8—05

U.S. Cl. D8—36

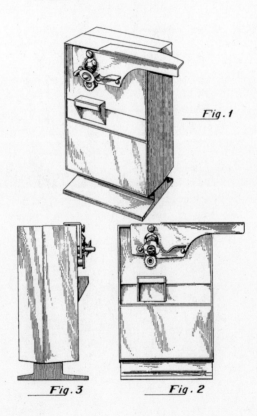

Fig. 1

Fig. 3

Fig. 2

TITLE: HOUSING FOR TABLE LAMP
INVENTOR: LODOVICO MAGISTRETTI
ASSIGNEE: NONE

PATENT NUMBER: USD 222,555
PATENT FILED: AUGUST 12, 1970
PATENT GRANTED: NOVEMBER 2, 1971

United States Patent Office

Des. 222,555
Patented Nov. 2, 1971

222,555

HOUSING FOR TABLE LAMP

Lodovico Magistretti, Via Conservatorio 20,
Milan, Italy

Filed Aug. 12, 1970, Ser. No. 24,447

Term of patent 7 years

Int. Cl. D26—05

U.S. Cl. D48—20

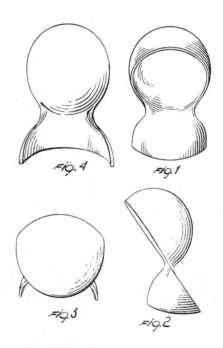

FIG. 4 FIG. 1

FIG. 3 FIG. 2

FIG. 1 is a front elevational view of a housing for table lamp showing my new design;
FIG. 2 is a side view thereof;
FIG. 3 is a top plan view thereof;
FIG. 4 is a rear elevational view thereof.
I claim:
The ornamental design for a housing for table lamp, as shown.

References Cited

Lamp Journal, July 1968, p. 23, top right corner table lamp.

WALLACE R. BURKE, Primary Examiner

S. J. MERCER, Assistant Examiner

TITLE: AUTOMOBILE BODY
INVENTORS: KARL WILFERT & FREDRICH GEIGER
ASSIGNEE: DAIMLER-BENZ

PATENT NUMBER: USD 222,639
PATENT FILED: FEBRUARY 5, 1970
PATENT GRANTED: NOVEMBER 23, 1971

United States Patent Office

Des. 222,639
Patented Nov. 23, 1971

222,639

AUTOMOBILE BODY

Karl Wilfert, Gerlingen-Waldstadt, and Fredrich Geiger,
Boblingen, Germany, assignors to Daimler-Benz Aktiengesellschaft, Stuttgart-Unterturkheim, Germany

Filed Feb. 5, 1970, Ser. No. 21,298

Claims priority, application Germany Aug. 5, 1969

Term of patent 14 years

Int. Cl. D12—08

U.S. Cl. D14—3

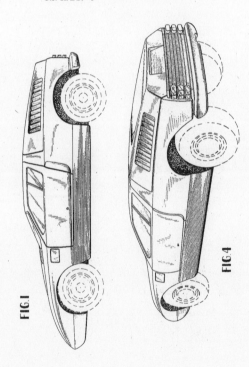

FIG. 1

FIG. 4

TITLE: CAMERA
INVENTORS: MUTSUHIDE MATSUDA & EIICHI YOSHIOKA
ASSIGNEE: CANON KABUSHIKI KAISHA

PATENT NUMBER: USD 222,845
PATENT FILED: AUGUST 24, 1970
PATENT GRANTED: JANUARY 11, 1972

United States Patent Office

Des. 222,845
Patented Jan. 11, 1972

222,845

CAMERA

Mutsuhide Matsuda and Eiichi Yoshioka, Tokyo, Japan,
assignors to Canon Kabushiki Kaisha, Tokyo, Japan

Filed Aug. 24, 1970, Ser. No. 24,675

Claims priority, application Japan Mar. 2, 1970

Term of patent 14 years

Int. Cl. D16—01

U.S. Cl. D61—1

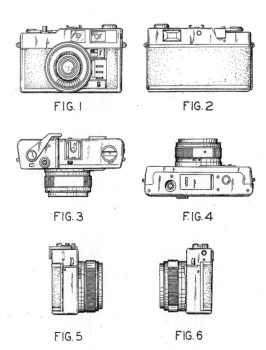

FIG. 1

FIG. 2

FIG. 3

FIG. 4

FIG. 5

FIG. 6

TITLE: MAGNETIC TAPE CASSETTE
INVENTORS: REINHOLD M. WEISS &
T. MICHAEL DENNEHEY
ASSIGNEE: MEMOREX CORPORATION

PATENT NUMBER: USD 222,911
PATENT FILED: SEPTEMBER 14, 1970
PATENT GRANTED: FEBRUARY 1, 1972

United States Patent Office

Des. 222,911
Patented Feb. 1, 1972

222,911

MAGNETIC TAPE CASSETTE

Reinhold M. Weiss, Chicago, and T. Michael Dennehey,
La Grange, Ill., assignors to Memorex Corporation

Filed Sept. 14, 1970, Ser. No. 24,971

Term of patent 14 years

Int. Cl. D14—*01*

U.S. Cl. D26—14

FIG. 1.

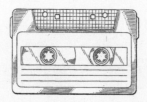

FIG. 2.

FIG. 1 is a perspective view of the novel magnetic tape cassette design of this invention;

FIG. 2 is a side elevational view thereof, the other side being substantially a mirror image thereof.

The undisclosed bottom side of the magnetic tape cassette is substantially plane and unornamented.

We claim:

The ornamental design for a magnetic tape cassette, as shown and described.

References Cited

UNITED STATES PATENTS

D. 206,719	1/1967	Dietrich	D26—14
3,439,127	4/1969	Weigel	179—100.2
3,532,211	10/1970	Gellert	206—52

OTHER REFERENCES

Lafayette Radio Electronics, Cat. 690©, 1969, page 80.

BERNARD ANSHER, Primary Examiner

TITLE: CHAIR
INVENTOR: THOMAS LAMB
ASSIGNEE: NONE

PATENT NUMBER: USD 223,347
PATENT FILED: DECEMBER 1, 1970
PATENT GRANTED: APRIL 11, 1972

United States Patent Office

Des. 223,347

Patented Apr. 11, 1972

223,347

CHAIR

Thomas Lamb, 349 Wellesley St. E.,
Toronto, Ontario, Canada

Filed Dec. 1, 1970, Ser. No. 26,239

Term of patent 14 years

Int. Cl. D6—*02*

U.S. Cl. D15—1

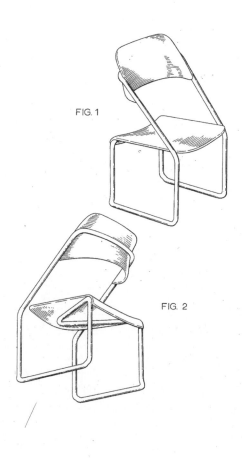

FIG. 1

FIG. 2

TITLE: MOTION PICTURE CAMERA
INVENTOR: ROBERT OBERHEIM
ASSIGNEE: BRAUN

PATENT NUMBER: USD 223,514
PATENT FILED: NOVEMBER 12, 1970
PATENT GRANTED: APRIL 25, 1972

United States Patent Office

Des. 223,514
Patented Apr. 25, 1972

223,514

MOTION PICTURE CAMERA

Robert Oberheim, Neu-Isenburg, Germany, assignor to
Braun A.G., Frankfurt am Main, Germany

Filed Nov. 12, 1970, Ser. No. 25,944

Claims priority, application Germany May 20, 1970

Term of patent 14 years

Int. Cl. D16—01

U.S. Cl. D61—1

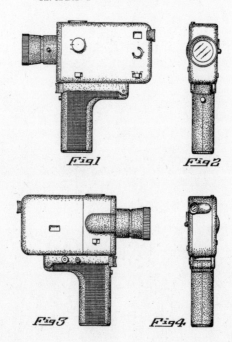

Fig 1

Fig 2

Fig 3

Fig 4

TITLE: TELEVISION RECEIVER
INVENTORS: YASUNOBU NAKAMURA, TADASHI SUMINO,
OSAMU SUGIHARA, KAZUHIRO UEDA & MAKOTO TERAUCHI
ASSIGNEE: MATSUSHITA ELECTRIC INDUSTRIAL COMPANY

PATENT NUMBER: USD 224,346
PATENT FILED: MARCH 15, 1971
PATENT GRANTED: JULY 18, 1972

United States Patent Office

Des. 224,346
Patented July 18, 1972

224,346

TELEVISION RECEIVER

Yasunobu Nakamura, Suita, Tadashi Sumino, Osamu
Sugihara and Kazuhiro Ueda, Takatsuki, and Makoto
Terauchi, Ibaragi, Japan, assignors to Matsushita Elec-
tric Industrial Co., Ltd., Osaka, Japan

Filed Mar. 15, 1971, Ser. No. 124,651

Claims priority, application Japan Sept. 16, 1970

Term of patent 14 years

Int. Cl. D14—03

U.S. Cl. D56—4

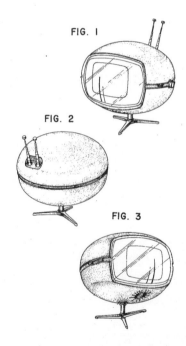

FIG. 1

FIG. 2

FIG. 3

FIG. 1 is a front and right side perspective view of a
television receiver showing our new design,

FIG. 2 is a rear and left side perspective view thereof,
and

FIG. 3 is a front, left side and bottom perspective view
thereof.

We claim:

The ornamental design for a television receiver, as
shown.

References Cited

UNITED STATES PATENTS

D. 179,857	3/1957	Mason	D56—4
D. 183,782	10/1958	Winkler et al.	D56—4

OTHER REFERENCES

Home Furnishings Daily, June 14, 1971, p. 1, Space
Helmet TV by JVC America, Inc.

JOEL STEARMAN, Primary Examiner

W. M. HENRY, Assistant Examiner

TITLE: BATHROOM SCALE
INVENTOR: DIETER RAMS
ASSIGNEE: BRAUN

PATENT NUMBER: USD 224,443
PATENT FILED: JANUARY 27, 1971
PATENT GRANTED: JULY 25, 1972

United States Patent Office

Des. 224,443

Patented July 25, 1972

224,443

BATHROOM SCALE

Dieter Rams, Konigstein, Germany, assignor to Braun
Aktiengesellschaft, Frankfurt am Main, Germany

Filed Jan. 27, 1971, Ser. No. 110,368

Claims priority, application Germany Oct. 17, 1970

Term of patent 14 years

Int. Cl. D10—*04*

U.S. Cl. D52—10

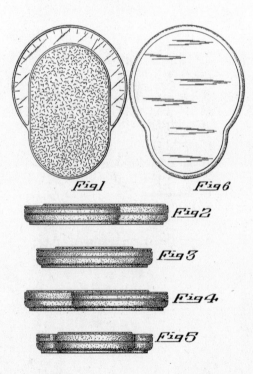

Fig 1
Fig 6
Fig 2
Fig 3
Fig 4
Fig 5

FIG. 1 is a top plan view of a bathroom scale showing my new design;
FIG. 2 is a left side elevational view thereof;
FIG. 3 is a rear elevational view thereof;
FIG. 4 is a right side elevational view thereof;
FIG. 5 is a front elevational view thereof; and
FIG. 6 is a bottom plan view thereof.

I claim:
The ornamental design for a bathroom scale, substantially as shown.

References Cited
UNITED STATES PATENTS

D. 46,750	12/1914	Reeves	D52—10
D. 93,858	11/1934	Weber	D52—10
2,821,376	1/1958	Aston	177—168 XR
2,039,528	5/1936	Garbell	177—168
1,982,938	12/1934	Weber	177—170

JOEL STEARMAN, Primary Examiner

N. C. HOLTJE, Assistant Examiner

TITLE: PORTABLE MICROWAVE OVEN
INVENTORS: THOMAS J. BINZER,
CHARLES H. SCHMITT & PETER H. WOODING
ASSIGNEE: GENERAL ELECTRIC COMPANY

PATENT NUMBER: USD 225,780
PATENT FILED: AUGUST 26, 1970
PATENT GRANTED: JANUARY 2, 1973

United States Patent Office

Des. 225,780
Patented Jan. 2, 1973

225,780

PORTABLE MICROWAVE OVEN OR SIMILAR ARTICLE

Thomas J. Binzer, Charles H. Schmitt, and Peter H. Wooding, Jefferson County, Ky., assignors to General Electric Company

Filed Aug. 26, 1970, Ser. No. 24,693

Term of Patent 14 years

Int. Cl. D7—02

U.S. Cl. D81—4

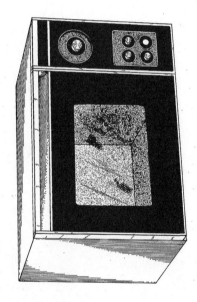

FIG. 1

TITLE: HAIR DRYING & STYLING COMB
INVENTOR: MONTE L. LEVIN
ASSIGNEE: SCOVILL MANUFACTURING COMPANY

PATENT NUMBER: USD 225,786
PATENT FILED: OCTOBER 20, 1971
PATENT GRANTED: JANUARY 2, 1973

United States Patent Office

Des. 225,786
Patented Jan. 2, 1973

225,786

HAIR DRYING AND STYLING COMB

Monte L. Levin, New York, N.Y., assignor to Scovill
Manufacturing Company, Waterbury, Conn.

Filed Oct. 20, 1971, Ser. No. 191,144

Term of patent 14 years

Int. Cl. D28—*03*

U.S. Cl. D86—8

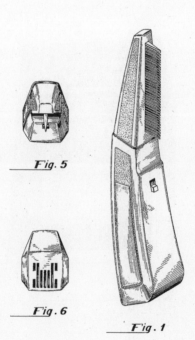

Fig. 5

Fig. 6

Fig. 1

TITLE: OUTDOOR LIGHTING FIXTURE
INVENTOR: ANTHONY C. DONATO
ASSIGNEE: LIGHTOLIER

PATENT NUMBER: USD 226,129
PATENT FILED: JUNE 30, 1971
PATENT GRANTED: JANUARY 23, 1973

United States Patent Office

Des. 226,129
Patented Jan. 23, 1973

226,129

OUTDOOR LIGHTING FIXTURE

Anthony C. Donato, Westfield, N.J., assignor to Lightolier
Incorporated, Jersey City, N.J.

Filed June 30, 1971, Ser. No. 130,050

Term of patent 14 years

Int. Cl. D26—03

U.S. Cl. D48—31

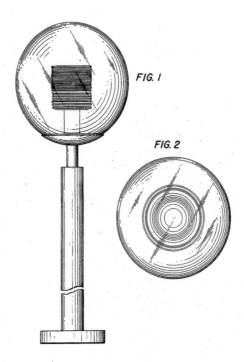

FIG. 1

FIG. 2

FIG. 1 is an elevational view of an outdoor lighting fixture showing my new design with the pole broken away to indicate indeterminate length.

FIG. 2 is a top plan view thereof.

I claim:

The ornamental design for an outdoor lighting fixture, substantially as shown and described.

References Cited

Design, March 1959, p. 47, hanging lamp (bottom right).

Lighting and Electrical Design, March 1968, p. 9, spherical lighting fixture.

WALLACE R. BURKE, Primary Examiner

S. J. MERCER, Assistant Examiner

TITLE: TELEPHONE INSTRUMENT
INVENTOR: CARL-ARNE BREGER
ASSIGNEE: TELEFONAKTIEBOLAGET LM ERICSSON

PATENT NUMBER: USD 226,199
PATENT FILED: MARCH 31, 1971
PATENT GRANTED: JANUARY 30, 1973

United States Patent Office

Des. 226,199
Patented Jan. 30, 1973

226,199

TELEPHONE INSTRUMENT

Carl-Arne Breger, Malmo, Sweden, assignor to Telefonaktiebolaget LM Ericsson, Stockholm, Sweden

Filed Mar. 31, 1971, Ser. No. 130,063

Claims priority, application Sweden Oct. 1, 1970

Term of patent 14 years

Int. Cl. D14—*03*

U.S. Cl. D26—14 A

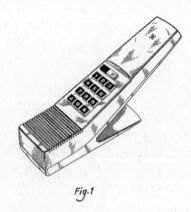

Fig.1

TITLE: TOASTER
INVENTOR: REINHOLD M. WEISS.
ASSIGNEE: THE GILLETTE COMPANY

PATENT NUMBER: USD 226,242
PATENT FILED: JUNE 25, 1971
PATENT GRANTED: JANUARY 30, 1973

United States Patent Office

Des. 226,242
Patented Jan. 30, 1973

226,242

TOASTER

Reinhold M. Weiss, Chicago, Ill., assignor to The
Gillette Company, Boston, Mass.

Filed June 25, 1971, Ser. No. 157,085

Term of patent 14 years

Int. Cl. D7—02

U.S. Cl. D81—10

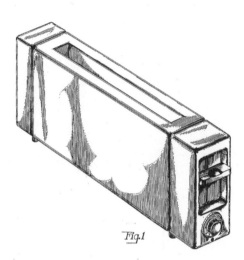

Fig.1

TITLE: AUTOMATIC JUICE MAKER
INVENTOR: JURGEN GREUBEL
ASSIGNEE: BRAUN

PATENT NUMBER: USD 226,345
PATENT FILED: NOVEMBER 25, 1970
PATENT GRANTED: FEBRUARY 13, 1973

United States Patent Office

Des. 226,345
Patented Feb. 13, 1973

226,345

AUTOMATIC JUICE MAKER

Jurgen Greubel, Eschenhahn, Germany, assignor to Braun
A.G., Frankfurt am Main, Germany

Filed Nov. 25, 1970, Ser. No. 26,153

Claims priority, application Germany July 1, 1970

Term of patent 14 years

Int. Cl. D7—04

U.S. Cl. D89—1 A

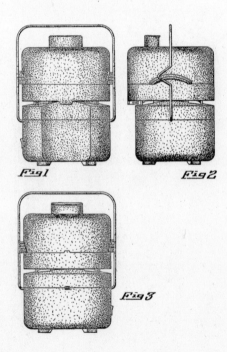

Fig 1   *Fig 2*

Fig 3

TITLE: RIDING MOWER
INVENTOR: VIKTOR SCHRECKENGOST
ASSIGNEE: THE MURRAY OHIO MANUFACTURING COMPANY

PATENT NUMBER: USD 226,391
PATENT FILED: JUNE 19, 1972
PATENT GRANTED: FEBRUARY 27, 1973

United States Patent Office

Des. 226,391
Patented Feb. 27, 1973

226,391

RIDING MOWER

Viktor Schreckengost, Cleveland Heights, Ohio, assignor to The Murray Ohio Manufacturing Co., Nashville, Tenn.

Filed June 19, 1972, Ser. No. 264,009

Term of patent 14 years

Int. Cl. D15—*03*

U.S. Cl. D40—1 D

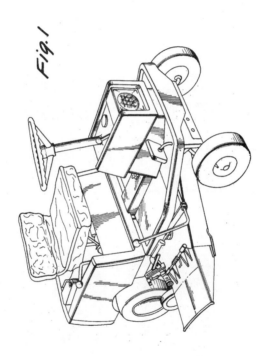

Fig. 1

TITLE: BARBECUE GRILL AND OVEN UNIT
AND STAND THEREFOR
INVENTOR: CHARLES D. DUSHEK
ASSIGNEE: SEARS, ROEBUCK & COMPANY

PATENT NUMBER: USD 226,540
PATENT FILED: MAY 19, 1971
PATENT GRANTED: MARCH 20, 1973

United States Patent Office

Des. 226,540
Patented Mar. 20, 1973

226,540

**BARBECUE GRILL AND OVEN UNIT AND
STAND THEREFOR**

Charles D. Dushek, Lisle, Ill., assignor to Sears,
Roebuck and Co., Chicago, Ill.

Filed May 19, 1971, Ser. No. 145,121

Term of patent 14 years

Int. Cl. D7—02

U.S. Cl. D81—10 E

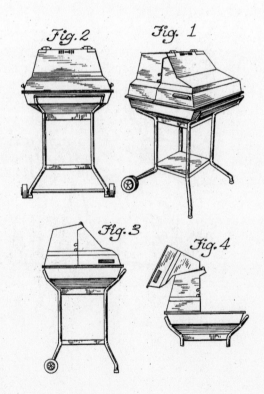

Fig. 2   Fig. 1

Fig. 3   Fig. 4

TITLE: PHOTOGRAPHIC CAMERA OR SIMILAR ARTICLE
INVENTORS: JAMES M. CONNER & MILTON S. DIETZ
ASSIGNEE: POLAROID CORPORATION

PATENT NUMBER: USD 226,731
PATENT FILED: MARCH 15, 1971
PATENT GRANTED: APRIL 17, 1973

United States Patent Office

Des. 226,731
Patented Apr. 17, 1973

226,731

PHOTOGRAPHIC CAMERA OR SIMILAR ARTICLE

James M. Conner, Mamaroneck, N.Y., and Milton S. Dietz, Lexington, Mass., assignors to Polaroid Corporation, Cambridge, Mass.

Filed Mar. 15, 1971, Ser. No. 124,616

Term of patent 14 years

Int. Cl. D16—*01*

U.S. Cl. D61—1 B

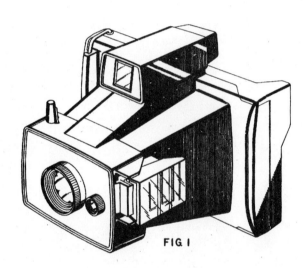

FIG. I

TITLE: ROLLER SKATE
INVENTOR: CHOY CHEUNG TAT
ASSIGNEE: GRACE ARTIFICIAL JEWELLERY
MANUFACTURING COMPANY

PATENT NUMBER: USD 226,812
PATENT FILED: JUNE 7, 1971
PATENT GRANTED: MAY 1, 1973

United States Patent Office

Des. 226,812
Patented May 1, 1973

226,812

ROLLER SKATE

Choy Cheung Tat, Kowloon, Hong Kong, assignor to
Grace Artificial Jewellery Manufacturing Co. Ltd.,
Kowloon, Hong Kong

Filed June 7, 1971, Ser. No. 150,884

Claims priority, application Great Britain Apr. 21, 1971

Term of patent 7 years

Int. Cl. D21—01
U.S. Cl. D34—14 C

FIG. 1.

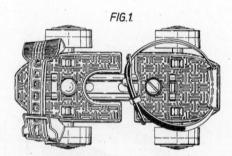

FIG. 2.

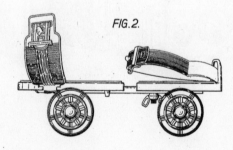

TITLE: CALCULATOR
INVENTORS: GEORGE W. CONE & DONALD C. STEPHAN
ASSIGNEE: GARRETT COMTRONICS CORPORATION

PATENT NUMBER: USD 226,921
PATENT FILED: JUNE 5, 1972
PATENT GRANTED: MAY 15, 1973

United States Patent Office

Des. 226,921
Patented May 15, 1973

226,921

CALCULATOR

George W. Cone, La Jolla, and Donald C. Stephan, San Diego, Calif., assignors to Garrett Comtronics Corporation, San Diego, Calif.

Filed June 5, 1972, Ser. No. 260,060

Term of patent 14 years

Int. Cl. D14—02

U.S. Cl. D26—5 C

Fig: 1.

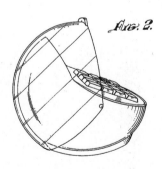

Fig: 2.

TITLE: SCISSORS
INVENTOR: OLOF BACKSTROM
ASSIGNEE: FISKARS

PATENT NUMBER: USD 227,338
PATENT FILED: MAY 24, 1971
PATENT GRANTED: JUNE 19, 1973

United States Patent Office

Des. 227,338
Patented June 19, 1973

227,338

SCISSORS

Olof Backstrom, Fiskars, Finland, assignor to Oy Fiskars AB, Helsinki, Finland

Filed May 24, 1971, Ser. No. 146,611

Claims priority, application Belgium Jan. 22, 1971

Term of patent 14 years

Int. Cl. D8—03

U.S. Cl. D8—57

FIG.5

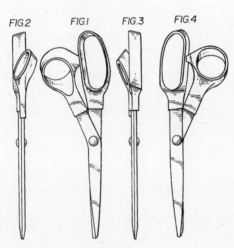

FIG.2　FIG.1　FIG.3　FIG.4

FIG.6

FIG. 1 is schematic front elevational view of scissors showing my new design;
FIG. 2 is a side elevational view thereof;
FIG. 3 is a side elevational view of the other side thereof;
FIG. 4 is a schematic rear elevational view;
FIG. 5 is a top plan view; and
FIG. 6 is a bottom plan view.
I claim:
The ornamental design for scissors, as shown.

References Cited

UNITED STATES PATENTS

893,669	7/1908	Steel	30—229
2,574,066	11/1951	See	30—230
2,701,415	2/1955	Carney	30—230

LOIS S. LANIER, Primary Examiner

TITLE: FLOOR LAMP
INVENTOR: MOTOKO ISHII
ASSIGNEE: YAMAGIWA ELECTRIC COMPANY

PATENT NUMBER: USD 227,592
PATENT FILED: APRIL 13, 1971
PATENT GRANTED: JULY 3, 1973

United States Patent Office

Des. 227,592
Patented July 3, 1973

227,592

FLOOR LAMP

Motoko Ishii, Tokyo, Japan, assignor to Yamagiwa
Electric Company Ltd., Tokyo, Japan

Filed Apr. 13, 1971, Ser. No. 133,771

Term of patent 14 years

Int. Cl. D26—05

U.S. Cl. D48—20 A

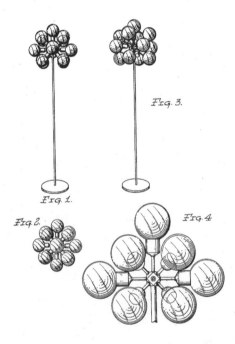

Fig. 1.

Fig. 2.

Fig. 3.

Fig. 4

FIG. 1 is a front view of the floor lamp showing my new design according to the invention;

FIG. 2 is a top plan view thereof;

FIG. 3 is a side view thereof; and

FIG. 4 is an enlarged fragmentary view thereof, the floor lamp being fragmentarily shown for convenience of illustration and purposes of disclosure.

I claim:

The ornamental design for a floor lamp, as shown and described.

References Cited

UNITED STATES PATENTS

D. 210,407   3/1968   Rodriguez .... D48—20
1,192,585   7/1916   Tregoning .... 240—10.1

OTHER REFERENCES

Interiors, September 1968, p. 166, globe tree.
Interiors, August 1959, p. 135, chandelier.
Prescolite Chandeline Catalog (C–1L), Nov. 1, 1963, p. 6, chandelier (3rd from top).

WALLACE R. BURKE, Primary Examiner

S. J. MERCER, Assistant Examiner

TITLE: CLOCK
INVENTOR: ROLAND B. MONROE
ASSIGNEE: NONE

PATENT NUMBER: USD 228,303
PATENT FILED: MAY 8, 1972
PATENT GRANTED: SEPTEMBER 4, 1973

United States Patent Office

Des. 228,303
Patented Sept. 4, 1973

228,303

CLOCK

Ronald B. Monroe, 532 W. 111th St.,
New York, N.Y. 10025

Filed May 8, 1972, Ser. No. 251,562

Term of patent 14 years

Int. Cl. D10—01

U.S. Cl. D42—7 R

FIG. 1

FIG. 2

FIG. 1 is a front elevational view of a clock showing
my new design; and
FIG. 2 is a bottom plan view thereof.
I claim:
The ornamental design for a clock, as shown.

References Cited

Design, November 1966, p. 85, clock @ bottom-center.

JOEL STEARMAN, Primary Examiner
N. C. HOLTJE, Assistant Examiner

TITLE: DIGITAL CLOCK
INVENTOR: RIKI WATANABE
ASSIGNEE: KABUSHIKI KAISHA KOPARU

PATENT NUMBER: USD 228,938
PATENT FILED: AUGUST 1, 1972
PATENT GRANTED: OCTOBER 30, 1973

United States Patent Office

Des. 228,938
Patented Oct. 30, 1973

228,938

DIGITAL CLOCK

Riki Watanabe, Tokyo, Japan, assignor to Kabushiki
Kaisha Koparu, Tokyo-tu, Japan

Filed Aug. 1, 1972, Ser. No. 277,037

Claims priority, application Japan Feb. 2, 1972

Term of patent 14 years

Int. Cl. D10—*01*

U.S. Cl. D42—7 R

FIG. 1

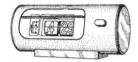

FIG. 2

FIG. 3

FIG. 1 is a front perspective view of a digital clock showing my new design;
FIG. 2 is a rear perspective view thereof;
FIG. 3 is a side elevational view thereof.
I claim:
The ornamental design for a digital clock, substantially as shown.

References Cited

UNITED STATES PATENTS

2,762,190   9/1956   Holzner _____ D42—7 R

OTHER REFERENCES

The Washington Post, Potomac, Oct. 24, 1971, p. 8, digital clock at bottom.
Incentive Marketing, September 1971, p. 4, digital clock at bottom center.
Jeweler's Circular, Keystone, May 1968, p. 65, digital clock at top right.

JOEL STEARMAN, Primary Examiner

N. C. HOLTJE, Assistant Examiner

TITLE: CREDIT CARD IMPRINTER OR THE LIKE
INVENTOR: CHARLES G. SCOTT
ASSIGNEE: NONE

PATENT NUMBER: USD 228,959
PATENT FILED: SEPTEMBER 1, 1971
PATENT GRANTED: OCTOBER 30, 1973

United States Patent Office

Des. 228,959
Patented Oct. 30, 1973

228,959

CREDIT CARD IMPRINTER MACHINE OR THE LIKE

Charles G. Scott, 5083 Kingston Way,
San Jose, Calif. 95130

Continuation-in-part of design application Ser. No. 23,232,
June 1, 1970. This application Sept. 1, 1971, Ser. No.
177,201

Term of patent 14 years

Int. Cl. D18—02

U.S. Cl. D64—11 B

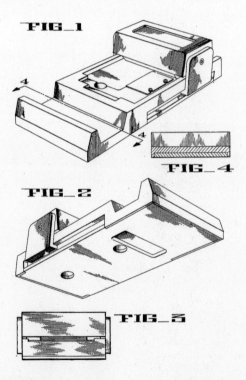

FIG_1

FIG_4

FIG_2

FIG_3

FIG. 1 is a top perspective view of a credit card imprinter machine or the like showing my new design;

FIG. 2 is a bottom perspective view of the credit card imprinter machine or the like;

FIG. 3 is a rear elevational view of the credit card imprinter machine or the like shown in FIGS. 1 and 2; and

FIG. 4 is a partial sectional view taken along the line 4—4 of FIG. 1.

This application is a continuation-in-part of my design application Ser. No. D. 23,232 filed June 1, 1970 and now abandoned.

I claim:

The ornamental design for a credit card imprinter machine or the like, substantially as shown and described.

References Cited

UNITED STATES PATENTS

D. 193,743	10/1962	Maul	D64—11 B
D. 218,991	10/1970	Allport	D64—11 B
D. 217,398	4/1970	Barbour	D64—11 B
D. 225,376	12/1972	Yamamoto	D64—11 B
D. 204,519	4/1966	Barbour	D64—11 B

JOEL STEARMAN, Primary Examiner

L. J. PERLSTEIN, Assistant Examiner

TITLE: COFFEE BREWER
INVENTOR: VINCENT G. MAROTTA
ASSIGNEE: NONE

PATENT NUMBER: USD 229,158
PATENT FILED: JUNE 29, 1971
PATENT GRANTED: NOVEMBER 13, 1973

United States Patent Office

Des. 229,158
Patented Nov. 13, 1973

229,158

COFFEE BREWER

Vincent G. Marotta, 2712 Rocklyn Road,
Shaker Heights, Ohio 44122

Filed June 29, 1971, Ser. No. 158,146

Term of patent 14 years

Int. Cl. D7—02

U.S. Cl. D7—94

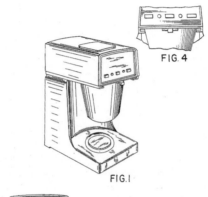

FIG. 4

FIG. I

FIG.3

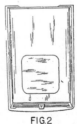

FIG.2

FIG. 1 is a perspective view of a coffee brewer showing my new design;
FIG. 2 is a top plan view thereof;
FIG. 3 is a rear elevational view thereof; and
FIG. 4 is a fragmentary front elevational view thereof.
I claim:
The ornamental design for a coffee brewer, as shown.

References Cited

UNITED STATES PATENTS

D. 177,864	5/1956	Wells et al.	D94—3 B
D. 209,125	10/1967	Martin	D94—3 B
D. 212,317	9/1968	Hausam	D94—3 B
D. 221,202	7/1971	Lorang	D94—3 B
3,387,903	6/1968	Karlen.	

JOEL STEARMAN, Primary Examiner

TITLE: RADIO RECEIVER OR SIMILAR ARTICLE
INVENTOR: DAISUKE KAJIWARA
ASSIGNEE: MATSUSHITA ELECTRIC
INDUSTRIAL COMPANY

PATENT NUMBER: USD 229,347
PATENT FILED: OCTOBER 12, 1971
PATENT GRANTED: NOVEMBER 20, 1973

United States Patent Office

Des. 229,347
Patented Nov. 20, 1973

229,347

RADIO RECEIVER OR SIMILAR ARTICLE

Daisuke Kajiwara, Fukuoka, Japan, assignor to Matsushita
Electric Industrial Co., Ltd., Osaka, Japan

Filed Oct. 12, 1971, Ser. No. 188,653

Claims priority, application Japan Apr. 15, 1971

Term of patent 14 years

Int. Cl. D14—*03*

U.S. Cl. D56—4 B

FIG. 1

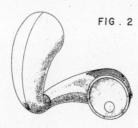

FIG. 2

TITLE: TELEVISION RECEIVER
INVENTORS: KAZUHIRO UEDA, YASUNOBU NAKAMURA,
OSAMU SUGIHARA, TADASHI SUMINO, ET AL.
ASSIGNEE: MATSUSHITA ELECTRIC INDUSTRIAL

PATENT NUMBER: USD 229,348
PATENT FILED: DECEMBER 17, 1971
PATENT GRANTED: NOVEMBER 20, 1973

United States Patent Office

Des. 229,348
Patented Nov. 20, 1973

229,348

TELEVISION RECEIVER

Kazuhiro Ueda, Takatsuki, Yasunobu Nakamura, Suita, Osamu Sugihara and Tadashi Sumino, Takatsuki, and Makoto Terauchi and Kiyoshi Suzuki, Ibaragi, Japan, assignors to Matsushita Electric Industrial Co., Ltd., Kadoma, Osaka, Japan

Filed Dec. 17, 1971, Ser. No. 209,499

Claims priority, application Japan June 18, 1971

Term of patent 14 years

Int. Cl. D14—*03*

U.S. Cl. D56—4 D

FIG. 1

FIG. 2

FIG. 3

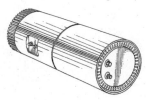

FIG. 1 is a front perspective view of television receiver showing our new design;

FIG. 2 is a bottom plan view; and

FIG. 3 is a top perspective view thereof showing retracted position.

We claim:

The ornamental design for a television receiver, as shown and described.

References Cited

UNITED STATES PATENTS

D. 205,547	8/1966	Celestin	D56—4 D
.D. 214,081	5/1969	Araki	D48—20 G
3,315,073	4/1967	Araki.	

OTHER REFERENCES

National Jeweler, May 1969, p. 43, GBC Autoscan.

Home Furnishings Daily, June 21, 1971, p. 49, sec. 1, prototype foldable 3-inch black-and-white television set with a high intensity lamp by Panasonic.

Lamp Journal, June 1965, p. 55, Lloyd's Hi Lite by Brunswick-Fanta Inc.

JOEL STEARMAN, Primary Examiner

W. M. HENRY, Assistant Examiner

TITLE: AUTOMOBILE
INVENTOR: GIAN PAOLO BOANO
ASSIGNEE: FIAT

PATENT NUMBER: USD 230,577
PATENT FILED: MARCH 29, 1972
PATENT GRANTED: MARCH 5, 1974

United States Patent Office

Des. 230,577
Patented Mar. 5, 1974

230,577

AUTOMOBILE

Gian Paolo Boano, Turin, Italy, assignor to Fiat
Societa per Azioni, Turin, Italy

Filed Mar. 29, 1972, Ser. No. 239,399

Claims priority, application Italy Oct. 8, 1971

Term of patent 14 years

Int. Cl. D12—08

U.S. Cl. D12—91

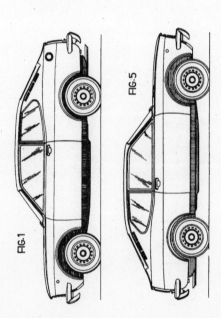

FIG. 1

FIG. 5

TITLE: ELECTRONIC CALCULATOR
INVENTOR: TEISUKE KUROSU
ASSIGNEE: MATSUSHITA ELECTRIC
INDUSTRIAL COMPANY

PATENT NUMBER: USD 230,859
PATENT FILED: NOVEMBER 30, 1972
PATENT GRANTED: MARCH 19, 1974

United States Patent Office

Des. 230,859
Patented Mar. 19, 1974

230,859

ELECTRONIC CALCULATOR

Teisuke Kurosu, Tokyo, Japan, assignor to Matsushit .
Electric Industrial Co., Ltd., Osaka, Japan

Filed Nov. 30, 1972, Ser. No. 310,927

Claims priority, application Japan June 9, 1972

Term of patent 14 years

Int. Cl. D14—02

U.S. Cl. D26—5 C

FIG. 1

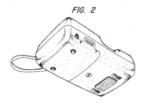

FIG. 2

FIG. 1 is a top and left side perspective view of an electronic calculator showing my new design, and

FIG. 2 is a bottom and left side perspective view thereof.

I claim:

The ornamental design for an electronic calculator, as shown.

References Cited

UNITED STATES PATENTS

D. 222,266	10/1971	Morita	D26—5 C
D. 222,302	10/1971	Yamamoto	D64—11 C
D. 226,004	1/1973	Hazama	D26—5 C
D. 226,922	5/1973	Gore	D26—5 C
D. 227,768	7/1973	Benedetto	D26—5 C
D. 227,769	7/1973	Yamamoto	D26—5 C

OTHER REFERENCES

Office Products, November 1972, p. 54, center left item.

JAMES R. LARGEN, Primary Examiner

TITLE: SCALE FOR LIQUIDS
INVENTOR: MARCO ZANUSO
ASSIGNEE: TERRAILLON

PATENT NUMBER: USD 231,016
PATENT FILED: FEBRUARY 28, 1972
PATENT GRANTED: MARCH 26, 1974

United States Patent Office

Des. 231,016
Patented Mar. 26, 1974

231,016

SCALE FOR LIQUIDS

Marco Zanuso, Milan, Italy, assignor to
Terraillon, Annemasse, France

Filed Feb. 28, 1972, Ser. No. 230,174

Claims priority, application Switzerland Sept. 1, 1971

Term of patent 14 years

Int. Cl. D10—*04*
U.S. Cl. D52—10 R

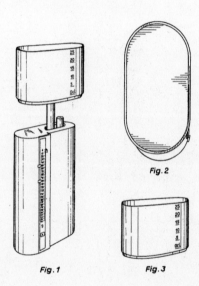

Fig. 2

Fig. 1   Fig. 3

FIG. 1 is a front perspective view of a scale for liquids showing my new design, the rear being flat, plain and unornamented;

FIG. 2 is a top plan view thereof; and

FIG. 3 is a front perspective view of the liquid container/weighing pan, the rear being flat, plain and unornamented.

I claim:

The ornamental design for a scale for liquids, as shown and described.

References Cited

UNITED STATES PATENTS

D. 193,682	9/1962	Bieger	D52—10 R
D. 154,446	7/1949	Walter	D52—10 R
1,787,352	12/1930	Bensinger	177—233
196,245	10/1977	Mery	177—233
57,097	8/1866	Dailey	177—233

JOEL STEARMAN, Primary Examiner

N. C. HOLTJE, Assistant Examiner

TITLE: HAMBURGER COOKER OR SIMILAR ARTICLE
INVENTOR: MELVIN H. BOLDT
ASSIGNEE: NATIONAL PRESTO INDUSTRIES

PATENT NUMBER: USD 231,069
PATENT FILED: APRIL 17, 1972
PATENT GRANTED: APRIL 2, 1974

United States Patent Office

Des. 231,069
Patented Apr. 2, 1974

231,069

HAMBURGER COOKER OR SIMILAR ARTICLE

Melvin H. Boldt, Glenview, Ill., assignor to National
Presto Industries, Inc., Eau Claire, Wis.

Filed Apr. 17, 1972, Ser. No. 245,023

Term of patent 14 years

Int. Cl. D7—02

U.S. Cl. D7—94

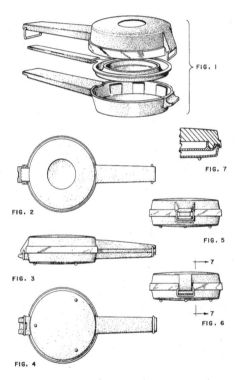

FIG. 1

FIG. 7

FIG. 2

FIG. 5

FIG. 3

FIG. 6

FIG. 4

FIG. 1 is an exploded perspective view of a hamburger
cooker or similar article showing my new design;
FIG. 2 is a top plan view thereof;
FIG. 3 is a side elevational view thereof, the opposite
side being a mirror image thereof;
FIG. 4 is a bottom plan view thereof;
FIG. 5 is an end view thereof;
FIG. 6 is a view taken of its opposite end; and
FIG. 7 is a fragmented sectional view taken along lines
7—7 of FIG. 6 and illustrates the continuous depending
rib about the periphery of the inner flat side of the cover
member which fits within the peripherally disposed recess
of the intermediate or pan member when the cover member, pan member and base member are closed together
as illustrated in FIG. 3.

I claim:
The ornamental design for a hamburger cooker or similar article, substantially as shown and described.

References Cited

UNITED STATES PATENTS

D. 129,963	10/1941	Eck	D7—86
D. 173,987	1/1955	Cunningham et al.	D7—95
3,007,595	11/1961	Remley.	
3,632,962	1/1972	Cherniak	D7—88 UX

WINIFRED E. HERRMANN, Primary Examiner

TITLE: RADIO RECEIVER
INVENTOR: RYUZO FUJITA
ASSIGNEE: RYUJIN COMPANY

PATENT NUMBER: USD 231,401
PATENT FILED: APRIL 17, 1972
PATENT GRANTED: APRIL 16, 1974

United States Patent Office

Des. 231,401
Patented Apr. 16, 1974

231,401

RADIO RECEIVER

Ryuzo Fujita, Tokyo, Japan, assignor to Ryujin Co.,
Ltd., Tokyo, Japan

Filed Apr. 17, 1972, Ser. No. 245,033

Claims priority, application Japan Nov. 9, 1971

Term of patent 14 years

Int. Cl. D14—*03*

U.S. Cl. D56—4 B

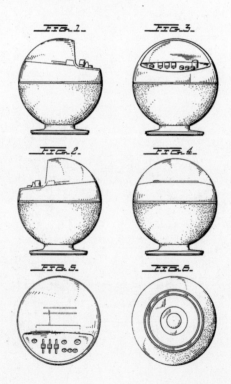

FIG. 1 is a left side elevational view of a radio receiver,
showing my new design;
FIG. 2 is a right side elevational view;
FIG. 3 is a front elevational view;
FIG. 4 is a rear elevational view;
FIG. 5 is a top plan view; and
FIG. 6 is a bottom plan view thereof.
The drawing figures are stippled to indicate contrast
in appearance.
I claim:
The ornamental design for a radio receiver, as shown
and described.

References Cited

UNITED STATES PATENTS

D. 183,779	10/1958	Whipple	D56—4 D
D. 224,159	7/1972	Griffin	D56—4 B
D. 199,811	12/1964	Becerra	D56—4 D

OTHER REFERENCES

Home Furnishings Daily, Feb. 13, 1968, p. 6, spherical
chairs in center of room.

WINIFRED E. HERRMANN, Primary Examiner

W. M. HENRY, Assistant Examiner

TITLE: PORTABLE TELEVISION RECEIVER
INVENTOR: BORIS ROZMAN
ASSIGNEE: NONE

PATENT NUMBER: USD 231,856
PATENT FILED: JUNE 20, 1972
PATENT GRANTED: JUNE 18, 1974

United States Patent Office

Des. 231,856
Patented June 18, 1974

231,856

PORTABLE TELEVISION RECEIVER

Boris Rozman, Knezova 7, Ljubljana, Yugoslavia

Filed June 20, 1972, Ser. No. 264,495

Claims priority, application Yugoslavia Dec. 20, 1971

Term of patent 7 years

Int. Cl. D14—*03*

U.S. Cl. D56—4 D

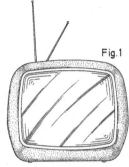

Fig. 1

Fig. 2

TITLE: TABLE LAMP
INVENTOR: GAE AULENTI
ASSIGNEE: NONE

PATENT NUMBER: USD 232.655
PATENT FILED: SEPTEMBER 22.1972
PATENT GRANTED: SEPTEMBER 3.1974

United States Patent Office

Des. 232,655
Patented Sept. 3, 1974

232,655

TABLE LAMP

Gae Aulenti, Via dell'Annunciata 7, Milan, Italy

Filed Sept. 22, 1972, Ser. No. 291,413

Claims priority, application Italy Mar. 23, 1972

Term of patent 7 years

Int. Cl. D26—05

U.S. Cl. D48—20 R

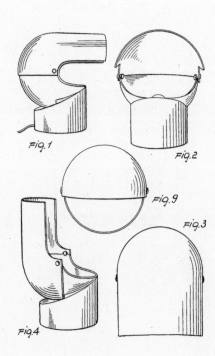

Fig.1
Fig.2
Fig.9
Fig.3
Fig.4

TITLE: ASHTRAY
INVENTOR: ETTORE SOTTSASS, JR.
ASSIGNEE: OLIVETTI

PATENT NUMBER: USD 232,664
PATENT FILED: APRIL 27, 1973
PATENT GRANTED: SEPTEMBER 3, 1974

United States Patent Office

Des. 232,664
Patented Sept. 3, 1974

232,664

ASHTRAY

Ettore Sottsass, Jr., Milan, Italy, assignor to Ing. C.
Olivetti & C., S.p.A., Ivrea, Turin, Italy

Filed Apr. 27, 1973, Ser. No. 355,244

Claims priority, application Italy Nov. 2, 1972

Term of patent 14 years

Int. Cl. D27—03

U.S. Cl. D85—2 H

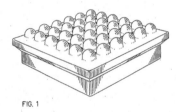

FIG. 1

FIG. 2

TITLE: RADIO RECEIVER
INVENTOR: BENITO MISHIRO
ASSIGNEE: MATSUSHITA ELECTRIC
INDUSTRIAL COMPANY

PATENT NUMBER: USD 232,768
PATENT FILED: MARCH 21, 1973
PATENT GRANTED: SEPTEMBER 10, 1974

United States Patent Office

Des. 232,768
Patented Sept. 10, 1974

232,768

RADIO RECEIVER

Benito Mishiro, Sakai, Japan, assignor to Matsushita
Electric Industrial Co., Ltd., Osaka, Japan

Filed Mar. 21, 1973, Ser. No. 343,409

Claims priority, application Japan Dec. 8, 1972

Term of patent 14 years

Int. Cl. D14—*03*

U.S. Cl. D56—4 B

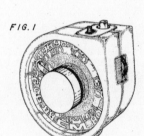

FIG. 1

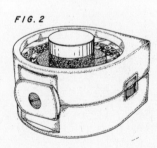

FIG. 2

TITLE: STAPLING MACHINE
INVENTOR: JOHN J. POWER
ASSIGNEE: SWINGLINE

PATENT NUMBER: USD 232,804
PATENT FILED: NOVEMBER 9, 1972
PATENT GRANTED: SEPTEMBER 17, 1974

United States Patent Office

Des. 232,804
Patented Sept. 17, 1974

232,804

STAPLING MACHINE

John J. Power, Westbury, N.Y., assignor to Swingline
Inc., Long Island City, N.Y.

Filed Nov. 9, 1972, Ser. No. 304,989

Term of patent 14 years

Int. Cl. D19—*02*

U.S. Cl. D8—50

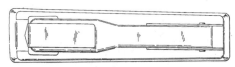

FIG. 1

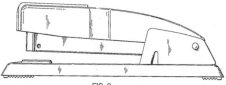

FIG. 2

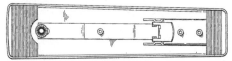

FIG. 3

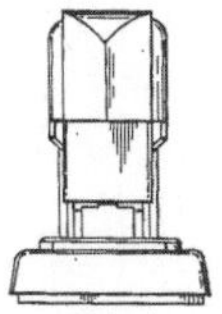

FIG. 4

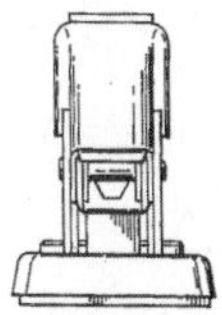

FIG. 5

FIG. 1 is a top plan view of a stapling machine showing my new design;
FIG. 2 is a front elevational view;
FIG. 3 is a bottom plan view;
FIG. 4 is a left end elevational view; and
FIG. 5 is a right end elevational view.
I claim:
The ornamental design for a stapling machine, substantially as shown and described.

References Cited

A.C.C.O. Cat.-#SC–50–469, July 1969, p. 3, Monarch #10.
Office Appliances Cat., February 1962, p. 109.
Office Products Cat., February 1971, pp. 10–11.
Bostitch Flyer #AD589B, Model #B12 Deluxe.

JOEL STEARMAN, Primary Examiner

G. P. WORD, Assistant Examiner

TITLE: PHOTOGRAPHIC CAMERA OR SIMILAR ARTICLE
INVENTORS: EDWIN H. LAND & RICHARD R. WAREHAM
ASSIGNEE: POLAROID CORPORATION

PATENT NUMBER: USD 233,171
PATENT FILED: OCTOBER 12, 1972
PATENT GRANTED: OCTOBER 8, 1974

United States Patent Office

Des. 233,171
Patented Oct. 8, 1974

233,171

PHOTOGRAPHIC CAMERA OR SIMILAR ARTICLE

Edwin H. Land, Cambridge, and Richard R. Wareham,
Marblehead, Mass., assignors to Polaroid Corporation,
Cambridge, Mass.

Filed Oct. 12, 1972, Ser. No. 299,877

Term of patent 14 years

Int. Cl. D16—*01*

U.S. Cl. D61—1 B

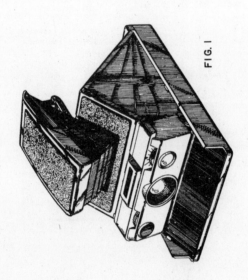

FIG. 1

TITLE: PORTABLE CALCULATOR
INVENTOR: MARIO BELLINI
ASSIGNEE: OLIVETTI

PATENT NUMBER: USD 233,350
PATENT FILED: JUNE 26, 1973
PATENT GRANTED: OCTOBER 22, 1974

United States Patent Office

Des. 233,350
Patented Oct. 22, 1974

233,350

PORTABLE CALCULATOR

Mario Bellini, Milan, Italy, assignor to Ing. C. Olivetti
& C., S.p.A, Torino, Italy

Filed June 26, 1973, Ser. No 373,710

Claims priority, application Italy Dec. 29, 1972

Term of patent 14 years

Int. Cl. D14—02

U.S. Cl. D26—5 C

FIG. 1

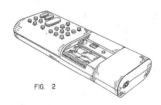

FIG. 2

FIG. 3

TITLE: FOOD SCALE
INVENTOR: MARCO ZANUSO
ASSIGNEE: TERRAILLON

PATENT NUMBER: USD 233,657
PATENT FILED: JUNE 18, 1973
PATENT GRANTED: NOVEMBER 19, 1974

United States Patent Office

Des. 233,657
Patented Nov. 19, 1974

233,657

FOOD SCALE

Marco Zanuso, Milan, Italy, assignor to
Terraillon, Annemasse, France

Original design application Feb. 28, 1972, Ser. No.
230,174, now Patent No. 231,016. Divided and this
application June 18, 1973, Ser. No. 371,144

Claims priority, application Switzerland Sept. 1, 1971

Term of patent 14 years

Int. Cl. D10—*04*

U.S. Cl. D10—89

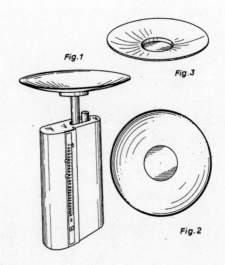

Fig.1

Fig.3

Fig.2

FIG. 1 is a front perspective view of a food scale showing my new design;

FIG. 2 is a top plan view thereof; and

FIG. 3 is a top perspective view of the food pan per se. The rear of the scale is substantially flat, plain and unornamented.

This application is a division of Ser. No. 230,174, filed Feb. 28, 1972, now Pat. No. D. 231,016.

I claim:

The ornamental design for a food scale, as shown and described.

References Cited

UNITED STATES PATENTS

D. 231,016	3/1974	Zanuso	D52—10 R
3,685,603	8/1972	Codina	177—Dig. 005
3,308,899	3/1967	Dinsmore	177—185
2,487,664	11/1949	Morgan	177—243
1,787,352	12/1930	Bensinger	177—233
196,295	10/1877	Mery	177—233
478,699	7/1892	Kovsky	177—233

NELSON C. HOLTJE, Primary Examiner

TITLE: FLOOR AND CARPET SWEEPER
INVENTOR: CARL ARNE BREGER
ASSIGNEE: NONE

PATENT NUMBER: USD 233,724
PATENT FILED: JANUARY 10, 1972
PATENT GRANTED: NOVEMBER 26, 1974

United States Patent Office

Des. 233,724
Patented Nov. 26, 1974

233,724

FLOOR AND CARPET SWEEPER

Carl Arne Breger, Lilla Molleberga, S–230,
Kvarnby 31, Sweden

Filed Jan. 10, 1972, Ser. No. 216,897

Claims priority, application Sweden June 30, 1971

Term of patent 14 years

Int. Cl. D7—*05*

U.S. Cl. D7—176

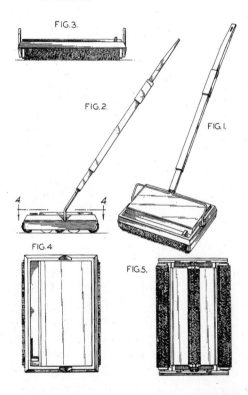

FIG. 3.

FIG. 2.

FIG. 1.

FIG. 4

FIG. 5.

FIG. 1 is a perspective view of my design for a floor and carpet sweeper;
FIG. 2 is a side elevational view thereof;
FIG. 3 is a front view not showing the handle;
FIG. 4 is a view taken on lines 4—4 of FIG. 2; and
FIG. 5 is a bottom plane view thereof.
I claim:
The ornamental design for a floor and carpet sweeper, as shown and described.

References Cited

UNITED STATES PATENTS

D. 37,176	10/1904	Dryden	D7—176
349,684	9/1886	Bissell et al.	15—41 R
879,977	2/1908	Morrison et al.	15—41 A
3,199,138	8/1965	Nordeen	15—410 X

OTHER REFERENCES

Premium Practice: April 1962, p. 189, Shetland Model #63.

WALLACE R. BURKE, Primary Examiner

C. E. O'HARA, Assistant Examiner

TITLE: PORTABLE RADIO TELEPHONE
INVENTOR: KENNETH W. LARSON
ASSIGNEE: MOTOROLA

PATENT NUMBER: USD 234,605
PATENT FILED: MAY 31, 1973
PATENT GRANTED: MARCH 25, 1975

United States Patent

Des. 234,605
Patented Mar. 25, 1975

234,605

PORTABLE RADIO TELEPHONE

Kenneth W. Larson, Elmhurst, Ill., assignor to
Motorola, Inc., Chicago, Ill.

Filed May 31, 1973, Ser. No. 365,772

Term of patent 14 years

Int. Cl. D14—*03*

U.S. Cl. D26—14 K

FIG.1

TITLE: CHAIR
INVENTOR: RODNEY WILLIAM KINSMAN
ASSIGNEE: NONE

PATENT NUMBER: USD 236,395
PATENT FILED: DECEMBER 10, 1973
PATENT GRANTED: AUGUST 26, 1975

United States Patent

Des. 236,395
Patented Aug. 26, 1975

236,395

CHAIR

Rodney William Kinsman, 14 Bruton Place,
London, W. 1, England

Filed Dec. 10, 1973, Ser. No. 423,288

Claims priority, application Great Britain June 11, 1973

Term of patent 14 years

Int. Cl. D6—01

U.S. Cl. D6—75

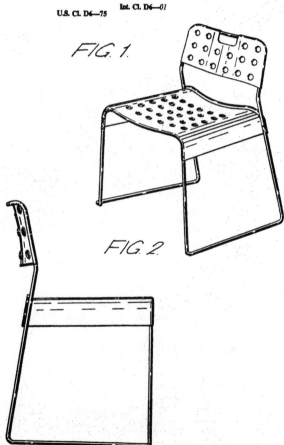

FIG. 1.

FIG. 2.

TITLE: TABLE KNIFE
INVENTORS: MARIA BENKTZON & SVEN-ERIC JUHLIN
ASSIGNEE: AB GUSTAVSBERGS FABRIKER

PATENT NUMBER: USD 236,793
PATENT FILED: APRIL 10, 1974
PATENT GRANTED: SEPTEMBER 16, 1975

United States Patent

Des. 236,793
Patented Sept. 16, 1975

236,793

TABLE KNIFE

Maria Benktzon, Sollentuna, and Sven-Eric Juhlin, Gustavsberg, Sweden, assignors to AB Gustavsbergs Fabriker, Gustavsberg, Sweden

Filed Apr. 10, 1974, Ser. No. 459,773

Claims priority, application Sweden Oct. 10, 1973

Term of patent 14 years

Int. Cl. D7—03

U.S. Cl. D7—137

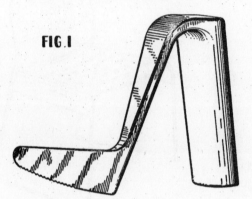

FIG. 1

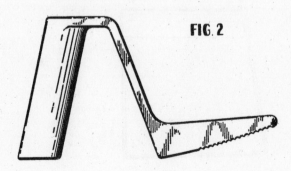

FIG. 2

TITLE: PORTABLE RADIO
INVENTORS: GEORGE M. BUCKLER & KEN-ICHI FUKUNAGA
ASSIGNEE: GENERAL ELECTRIC COMPANY

PATENT NUMBER: USD 238,392
PATENT FILED: MAY 17, 1973
PATENT GRANTED: JANUARY 6, 1976

United States Patent

Des. 238,392
Patented Jan. 6, 1976

238,392

PORTABLE RADIO

George M. Buckler, Dewitt, N.Y., and Ken-ichi Fukunaga, Tokyo, Japan, assignors to General Electric Company, Syracuse, N.Y.

Filed May 17, 1973, Ser. No. 361,221

Term of patent 14 years

Int. Cl. D14—03

U.S. Cl. D56—4 B

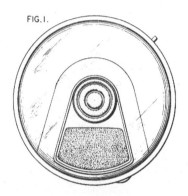

FIG.1.

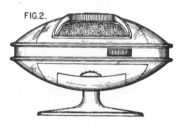

FIG.2.

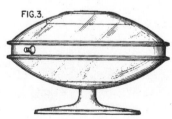

FIG.3.

TITLE: BUILDING STRUCTURE
INVENTOR: WILLIAM A. CURCI
ASSIGNEE: NONE

PATENT NUMBER: USD 238,943
PATENT FILED: OCTOBER 26, 1973
PATENT GRANTED: FEBRUARY 24, 1976

United States Patent

Des. 238,943
Patented Feb. 24, 1976

238,943

BUILDING STRUCTURE

William A. Curci, 4947 Fulton Drive NW.,
Canton, Ohio   44718

Filed Oct. 26, 1973, Ser. No. 410,196

Term of patent 14 years

Int. Cl. D25—*03*

U.S. Cl. D13—1 A

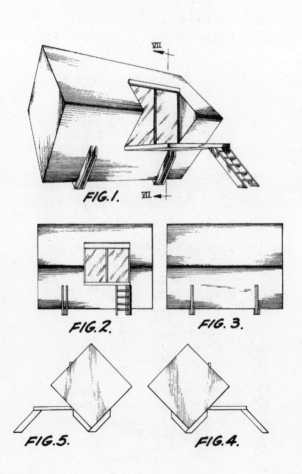

FIG. 1.

FIG. 2.

FIG. 3.

FIG. 5.

FIG. 4.

TITLE: LAMP
INVENTOR: MASAYUKI KUROKAWA
ASSIGNEE: YAMAGIWA ELECTRIC COMPANY

PATENT NUMBER: USD 238,959
PATENT FILED: JUNE 6, 1974
PATENT GRANTED: FEBRUARY 24, 1976

United States Patent

Des. 238,959
Patented Feb. 24, 1976

238,959

LAMP

Masayuki Kurokawa, Tokyo, Japan, assignor to
Yamagiwa Electric Co., Ltd., Tokyo, Japan

Filed June 6, 1974, Ser. No. 476,965

Term of patent 14 years

Int. Cl. D26—05

U.S. Cl. D48—20 F

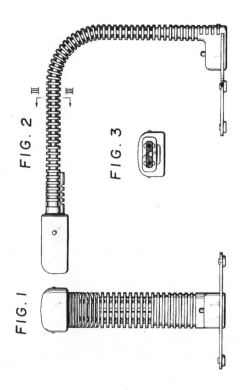

FIG. 2

FIG. 3

FIG. I

TITLE: LIGHTING FIXTURE
INVENTOR: TOBIA SCARPA
ASSIGNEE: NONE

PATENT NUMBER: USD 239,860
PATENT FILED: NOVEMBER 25, 1974
PATENT GRANTED: MAY 11, 1976

United States Patent

Des. 239,860
Patented May 11, 1976

239,860

LIGHTING FIXTURE

Tobia Scarpa, Via Campagna 3, Trevignano,
Treviso, Italy

Filed Nov. 25, 1974, Ser. No. 526,835

Claims priority, application Italy Sept. 30, 1974

Term of patent 14 years

Int. Cl. D26—03

U.S. Cl. D48—31

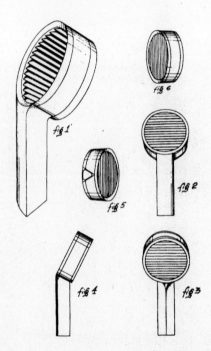

FIG. 1 is a perspective view of a lighting fixture embodying my new design;

FIG. 2 is a rear elevational view thereof on a reduced scale;

FIG. 3 is a front elevational view thereof on a reduced scale;

FIG. 4 is a side elevational view thereof, the opposite side being identical thereto on a reduced scale;

FIG. 5 is a bottom plan view thereof on a reduced scale; and

FIG. 6 is a top plan view thereof on a reduced scale.

I claim:

The ornamental design for a lighting fixture, as shown and described.

References Cited

FOREIGN PATENTS

| 1,444,217 | 5/1966 | France | 240—84 |
| 164,033 | 12/1933 | Switzerland | 240—25 |

OTHER REFERENCES

Chain Store Age, March 1968, p. E44, exterior luminaire.

Sweets Architectural Catalog File, 1972, sec. 16.8/MCP, p. 4, exterior lamp No. 16B–31.

SUSIE J. MERCER, Primary Examiner

TITLE: FAN
INVENTOR: NOEL THOMAS PATTON
ASSIGNEE: NONE

PATENT NUMBER: USD 240,231
PATENT FILED: JANUARY 31, 1975
PATENT GRANTED: JUNE 8, 1976

United States Patent

Des. 240,231
Patented June 8, 1976

240,231

FAN

Noel Thomas Patton, 8227 Westridge Road,
Fort Wayne, Ind. 46825

Filed Jan. 31, 1975, Ser. No. 546,090

Term of patent 14 years

Int. Cl. D23—*04*

U.S. Cl. D23—156

FIG. 1

TITLE: DRINKING GLASS
INVENTOR: TIMO TAPANI SARPANEVA
ASSIGNEE: A. AHLSTROM OSAKEYHTIO

PATENT NUMBER: USD 240,287
PATENT FILED: AUGUST 26, 1974
PATENT GRANTED: JUNE 15, 1976

United States Patent

Des. 240,287
Patented June 15, 1976

240,287

DRINKING GLASS

Timo Tapani Sarpaneva, Helsinki, Finland, assignor to
A. Ahlstrom Osakeyhtio, Iittala, Finland

Filed Aug. 26, 1974, Ser. No. 500,660

Claims priority, application Finland Feb. 25, 1974

Term of patent 14 years

Int. Cl. D7—01

U.S. Cl. D7—11

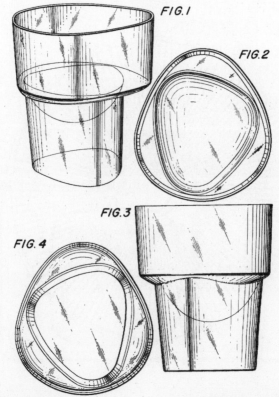

FIG. 1
FIG. 2
FIG. 3
FIG. 4

FIG. 1 is a front perspective view showing my new design for a drinking glass;
FIG. 2 is a top plan view thereof;
FIG. 3 is a side elevation view thereof; and
FIG. 4 is a bottom plan view thereof.
I claim:
The ornamental design for a drinking glass, substantially as shown.

References Cited

UNITED STATES PATENTS

D. 168,218 11/1952 Falk ----------------- D7—9

OTHER REFERENCES

Gift and Tableware Reporter, Sept. 2, 1968, p. 8, plastic stackers, drinkware.
Tableware International, May 1972, p. 11, "Gralglas" cup shown at right, potash-crystal.
Idea 55, © 1955, George Wittenborn, Inc., New York, N.Y., p. 34, Palmqvist stemware, Sweden, right goblets.

WINIFRED E. HERRMANN, Primary Examiner

TITLE: ELECTRIC FOOD COOKER
INVENTOR: MONTE L. LEVIN
ASSIGNEE: SCOVILL MANUFACTURING COMPANY

PATENT NUMBER: USD 240,993
PATENT FILED: SEPTEMBER 15, 1975
PATENT GRANTED: AUGUST 17, 1976

United States Patent

Des. 240,993
Patented Aug. 17, 1976

240,993

ELECTRIC FOOD COOKER

Monte L. Levin, New York, N.Y., assignor to Scovill
Manufacturing Company, Waterbury, Conn.

Filed Sept. 15, 1975, Ser. No. 613,616

Term of patent 14 years

Int. Cl. D7—*02*

U.S. Cl. D7—94

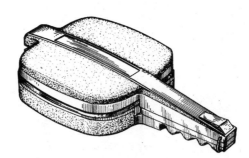

Fig. 1

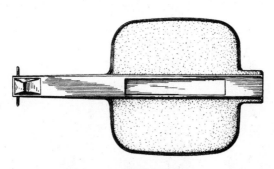

Fig. 2

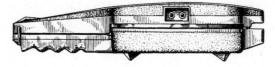

Fig. 3

TITLE: DIGITAL CLOCK RADIO
INVENTOR: MASANORI HAMADA
ASSIGNEE: MATSUSHITA ELECTRIC
INDUSTRIAL COMPANY

PATENT NUMBER: USD 242,385
PATENT FILED: DECEMBER 30, 1974
PATENT GRANTED: NOVEMBER 16, 1976

United States Patent

Des. 242,385
Patented Nov. 16, 1976

242,385

DIGITAL CLOCK RADIO

Masanori Hamada, Osaka, Japan, assignor to Matsushita
Electric Industrial Co., Ltd., Kadoma-shi, Osaka, Japan

Filed Dec. 30, 1974, Ser. No. 537,509

Claims priority, application Japan July 3, 1974

Term of patent 14 years

Int. Cl. D10—*01*; D14—*03*
U.S. Cl. D56—4 B

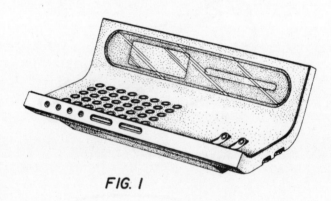

FIG. 1

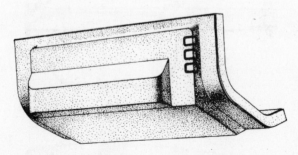

FIG. 2

TITLE: LIGHTER
INVENTOR: FRANZ ALBAN STUETZER
ASSIGNEE: ROWENTA-WERKE

PATENT NUMBER: USD 243,026
PATENT FILED: NOVEMBER 24, 1975
PATENT GRANTED: JANUARY 11, 1977

United States Patent [19]

Stuetzer

[11] **Des. 243,026**

[45] ** **Jan. 11, 1977**

[54] **LIGHTER**

[75] Inventor: **Franz Alban Stuetzer,** Mulheim (Main), Germany

[73] Assignee: **Rowenta-Werke, GmbH,** Offenbach(Main), Germany

[**] Term: **14 Years**

[21] Appl. No.: **634,956**

[22] Filed: **Nov. 24, 1975**

[30] **Foreign Application Priority Data**

May 30, 1975 Germany .... 5 MR 9869

[51] **Int. Cl.** .... D27—05
[52] **U.S. Cl.** D27/42
[58] **Field of Search** D27/36, 39, 42; 431/124, 127–142, 254, 255, 256, 273, 274

[56] **References Cited**

U.S. PATENT DOCUMENTS

2,617,286 11/1952 Prusack .... D27/42 UX

3,240,034 3/1966 Zellweger et al. 431/130
D. 217,067 3/1970 Rams D27/42

OTHER PUBLICATIONS

National Jeweler, Sept. 1956, p. 15, Lighter No. 504.

Primary Examiner—Susie J. Mercer
Attorney, Agent, or Firm—George R. Clark

[57] **CLAIM**

The ornamental design for a lighter, as shown and described.

DESCRIPTION

FIG. 1 is a perspective view thereof including the top, front and one side of a lighter showing my new design;
FIG. 2 is a perspective view thereof including the top, rear and the side opposite that shown in FIG. 1; and
FIG. 3 is a top plan view thereof.
The bottom of the lighter is substantially plain and unornamented.

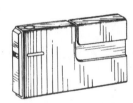

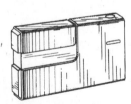

TITLE: PORTABLE TAPE PLAYER
INVENTOR: YOICHI HISANO
ASSIGNEE: MATSUSHITA ELECTRIC
INDUSTRIAL COMPANY

PATENT NUMBER: USD 243,538
PATENT FILED: FEBRUARY 11, 1976
PATENT GRANTED: MARCH 1, 1977

United States Patent [19]

Hisano

[11] **Des. 243,538**

[45] ** **Mar. 1, 1977**

[54] **PORTABLE TAPE PLAYER**

[75] Inventor: **Yoichi Hisano**, Neyagawa, Japan

[73] Assignee: **Matsushita Electric Industrial Co., Ltd.**, Kadoma, Japan

[**] Term: **14 Years**

[21] Appl. No.: **657,328**

[22] Filed: **Feb. 11, 1976**

[30] **Foreign Application Priority Data**

Nov. 20, 1975 Japan 50-46226

[51] **Int. Cl.** .... **D14—01**
[52] **U.S. Cl.** **D14/6**
[58] **Field of Search** .... D26/14 B; D56/4 B; 360/137, 60, 96, 105

[56] **References Cited**

U.S. PATENT DOCUMENTS

3,899,795	8/1975	Watanabe	360/137
D. 171,383	2/1954	Budlong	D56/4 B
D. 218,440	8/1970	Willday	D26/14 B
D. 220,340	3/1971	Sasaki	D26/14 B
D. 224,410	7/1972	Ebata	D26/14 B
D. 230,609	3/1974	Ebata	D26/14 B

Primary Examiner—Bernard Ansher
Attorney, Agent, or Firm—Richard C. Sughrue

[57] **CLAIM**

The ornamental design for a portable tape player, as shown.

DESCRIPTION

FIG. 1 is a front, top and right side perspective view of a portable tape player showing my new design; and FIG. 2 is a rear, bottom and left side perspective view.

754

TITLE: AUTOMOBILE
INVENTORS: KATSUSUKE KOMURO & SHINYA IWAKURA
ASSIGNEE: HONDA GIKEN KOGYO KABUSHIKI KAISHA

PATENT NUMBER: USD 243,668
PATENT FILED: DECEMBER 22, 1975
PATENT GRANTED: MARCH 15, 1977

United States Patent [19]

Komuro et al.

[11] **Des. 243,668**

[45]** **Mar. 15, 1977**

[54] **AUTOMOBILE**

[75] Inventors: **Katsusuke Komuro,** Chofu; **Shinya Iwakura,** Tokyo, both of Japan

[73] Assignee: **Honda Giken Kogyo Kabushiki Kaisha,** Tokyo, Japan

[**] Term: **14 Years**

[21] Appl. No.: **643,841**

[22] Filed: **Dec. 22, 1975**

[30] **Foreign Application Priority Data**

June 30, 1975 Japan 50-27521

[51] **Int. Cl.** .... **D12—08**
[52] **U.S. Cl.** **D12/91**
[58] **Field of Search** .... D12/91, 92; 296/28 R

[56] **References Cited**

U.S. PATENT DOCUMENTS

D. 226,807   5/1973   Tixier D12/91

D. 230,577   3/1974   Boano D12/91

OTHER PUBLICATIONS

Austo Motor, 1/75, p. 39, Mazda 929, top of page, Hot Rod, 10/73, p. 56, Ford Mustang II, bottom of page.

Primary Examiner—Wallace R. Burke
Assistant Examiner—James M. Gandy
Attorney, Agent, or Firm—Eric H. Waters

[57] **CLAIM**

The ornamental design for an automobile, as shown.

DESCRIPTION

FIG. 1 is a top plan view of an automobile showing my new design;
FIG. 2 is a left side elevational view thereof;
FIG. 3 is a right side elevational view thereof;
FIG. 4 is a front elevational view thereof; and
FIG. 5 is a rear elevational view thereof.

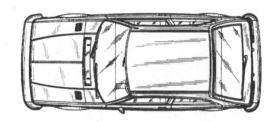

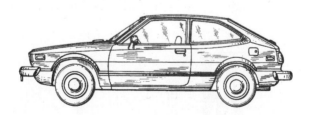

TITLE: CUP & SAUCER COMBINATION
INVENTOR: SVEN-ERIC JUHLIN
ASSIGNEE: AKTIEBOLAGET GUSTAVSBERGS FABRIKER

PATENT NUMBER: USD 244,738
PATENT FILED: MARCH 9, 1976
PATENT GRANTED: JUNE 21, 1977

FIG.I

FIG.2

FIG.4

FIG.3

FIG.5

TITLE: END CLOSURE FOR CONTAINER
INVENTOR: DANIEL F. CUDZIK
ASSIGNEE: REYNOLDS METALS COMPANY

PATENT NUMBER: USD 244,915
PATENT FILED: AUGUST 20, 1975
PATENT GRANTED: JULY 5, 1977

U.S. Patent   July 5, 1977   **Des. 244,915**

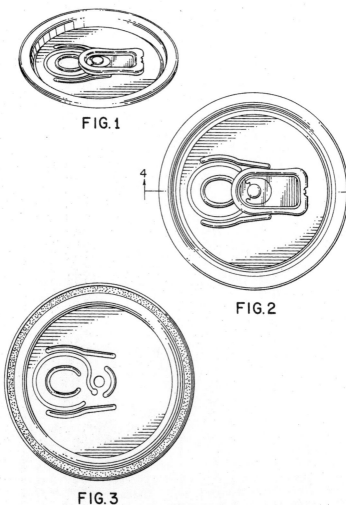

FIG. 1

FIG. 2

FIG. 3

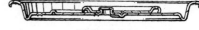

FIG. 4

TITLE: FRONT COVER FOR A BANKING MACHINE
TERMINAL OR SIMILAR ARTICLE
INVENTOR: THOMAS L. HERMANN
ASSIGNEE: NCR CORPORATION

PATENT NUMBER: USD 245,023
PATENT FILED: OCTOBER 17, 1975
PATENT GRANTED: JULY 12, 1977

United States Patent [19]

Hermann

[11] **Des. 245,023**

[45] ** **July 12, 1977**

[54] **FRONT COVER FOR A BANKING MACHINE TERMINAL OR SIMILAR ARTICLE**

[75] Inventor: **Thomas L. Hermann**, Springfield, Ohio

[73] Assignee: **NCR Corporation**, Dayton, Ohio

[**] Term: **14 Years**

[21] Appl. No.: **623,297**

[22] Filed: **Oct. 17, 1975**

Related U.S. Application Data

[62] Division of Ser. No. 420,928, Dec. 3, 1973, Pat. No. Des. 238,429.

[51] Int. Cl. .... **D14—02**
[52] U.S. Cl. **D31/22**
[58] Field of Search .... D26/5 R, 5 C; 235/61.11 F, 61.11 K, 61.7 R, 61.7 A, 61.7 B; 340/146.3 R, 146.3 C, 149 R, 149 A

[56] **References Cited**

U.S. PATENT DOCUMENTS

3,648,020	3/1972	Tateisi et al.	340/149 A X
3,662,343	5/1972	Goldstein et al.	340/149 A
3,778,595	12/1973	Hatanaka et al.	340/149 A X
3,833,885	9/1974	Gentile et al.	340/149 A X
3,862,716	1/1975	Black et al.	340/149 A X
3,941,977	3/1976	Voss et al.	340/149 A X
3,943,335	3/1976	Kinker et al.	340/149 A X
3,970,992	7/1976	Boothroyd et al.	340/149 A X
D. 238,429	1/1976	Hermann	D26/5 C

Primary Examiner—Wallace R. Burke
Assistant Examiner—Catherine Kemper
Attorney, Agent, or Firm—Albert L. Sessler, Jr.

[57] **CLAIM**

The ornamental design for a front cover for a banking machine terminal or similar article, as shown and described.

DESCRIPTION

The FIGURE is a front perspective view of a front cover for a banking machine terminal or similar article, showing my new design.

TITLE: COMBINED RADIO RECEIVER AND CASSETTE
TAPE RECORDER
INVENTORS: TAKEMI EBATA & YOICHI HISANO
ASSIGNEE: MATSUSHITA ELECTRIC INDUSTRIAL COMPANY

PATENT NUMBER: USD 245,038
PATENT FILED: DECEMBER 11, 1975
PATENT GRANTED: JULY 12, 1977

United States Patent [19]

Ebata et al.

[11] **Des. 245,038**

[45] ** **July 12, 1977**

[54] **COMBINED RADIO RECEIVER AND CASSETTE TAPE RECORDER**

[75] Inventors: **Takemi Ebata,** Kyoto; **Yoichi Hisano,** Neyagawa, both of Japan

[73] Assignee: **Matsushita Electric Industrial Co., Ltd.,** Kodama, Japan

[**] Term: **14 Years**

[21] Appl. No.: **639,815**

[22] Filed: **Dec. 11, 1975**

[30] **Foreign Application Priority Data**
June 20, 1975   Japan 50-25225

[51] **Int. Cl.** .... **D14—03; D14—01**
[52] **U.S. Cl.** .... **D56/4 B**
[58] **Field of Search** .... D56/4 R, 4 B; D26/14 B, D26/14 K, 14 L; 312/7 R; 325/300, 311, 352, 361; 179/100.11–100.12 A

[56] **References Cited**

U.S. PATENT DOCUMENTS

D. 237,543	11/1975	Yamamura et al.	.... D56/4 B
D. 240,455	7/1976	Kawano et al.	.... D56/4 B
D. 240,857	8/1976	Murakami et al.	.... D56/4 B

OTHER PUBLICATIONS

The New Yorker, Feb. 24, 1975, p. 25, Panasonic RS–451S (right).

Primary Examiner—Joel Stearman
Assistant Examiner—Louis S. Zarfas
Attorney, Agent, or Firm—Eric H. Waters

[57] **CLAIM**

The ornamental design for a combined radio receiver and cassette tape recorder, as shown.

DESCRIPTION

FIG. 1 is a front, top and right side perspective view of a combined radio receiver and cassette tape recorder showing our new design, and
FIG. 2 is a rear, bottom and left side perspective view thereof.

TITLE: ELECTRONIC CALCULATOR
INVENTOR: BARRY R. MATHIS
ASSIGNEE: HEWLETT-PACKARD COMPANY

PATENT NUMBER: USD 245,107
PATENT FILED: OCTOBER 1, 1975
PATENT GRANTED: JULY 19, 1977

United States Patent [19]

Mathis

[11] **Des. 245,107**

[45] ** **July 19, 1977**

[54] **ELECTRONIC CALCULATOR**

[75] Inventor: **Barry R. Mathis**, Loveland, Colo.

[73] Assignee: **Hewlett-Packard Company**, Palo Alto, Calif.

[**] Term: **14 Years**

[21] Appl. No.: **618,670**

[22] Filed: **Oct. 1, 1975**

[51] Int. Cl. .... **D18—01**
[52] U.S. Cl. .... **D64/11 B**
[58] **Field of Search** .... D26/5 R, 5 C; D64/11 R, D64/11 B, 11 C; 235/145 R; 197/98

[56] **References Cited**

U.S. PATENT DOCUMENTS

D. 213,003	12/1968	Sellers	D26/5 C
D. 218,433	8/1970	Oliver et al.	D64/11 C X
D. 228,189	8/1973	Beitler et al.	D26/5 C
D. 236,350	8/1975	Stoltz et al.	D26/5 C

Primary Examiner—Wallace R. Burke
Assistant Examiner—Catherine Kemper
Attorney, Agent, or Firm—William E. Hein

[57] **CLAIM**

The ornamental design for an electronic calculator, as shown and described.

DESCRIPTION

FIG. 1 is a front perspective view of an electronic calculator showing my new design;

FIG. 2 is a side elevational view thereof, the opposite side being a mirror image thereof.

TITLE: CAMERA
INVENTOR: HIROSHI FUKUDA
ASSIGNEE: FUJI PHOTO FILM COMPANY

PATENT NUMBER: USD 245,986
PATENT FILED: MAY 3, 1976
PATENT GRANTED: OCTOBER 4, 1977

U.S. Patent Oct. 4, 1977 **Des. 245,986**

Fig. 1

Fig. 2

Fig. 3

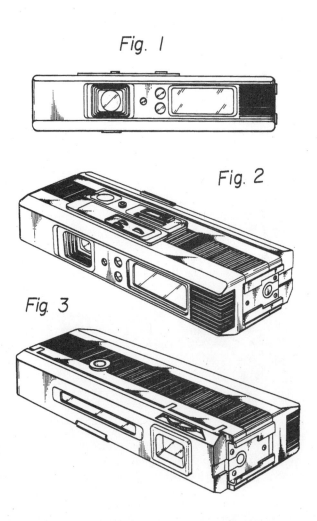

TITLE: HEADPHONE
INVENTOR: MARIO BELLINI
ASSIGNEE: NIPPON GAKKI SEIZO KABUSHIKI KAISHA

PATENT NUMBER: USD 246,242
PATENT FILED: OCTOBER 15, 1975
PATENT GRANTED: NOVEMBER 1, 1977

United States Patent [19]

Bellini

[11] **Des. 246,242**

[45] ** **Nov. 1, 1977**

[54] **HEADPHONE**

[75] Inventor: **Mario Bellini**, Lugano, Switzerland

[73] Assignee: **Nippon Gakki Seizo Kabushiki Kaisha**, Japan

[**] Term: **14 Years**

[21] Appl. No.: **622,467**

[22] Filed: **Oct. 15, 1975**

[51] Int. Cl. .... **D14—03**
[52] U.S. Cl. **D14/36**
[58] Field of Search .... D26/14 H; 179/182 R, 179/156 R; 181/33 R; D14/36

[56] **References Cited**

U.S. PATENT DOCUMENTS

3,488,457	1/1970	Lahti	179/182 R
3,682,268	8/1972	Gorike	D26/14 H X
D. 229,312	11/1973	Itagaki	D26/14 H
D. 235,210	5/1975	Hill	D26/14 H

Primary Examiner—Bernard Ansher
Attorney, Agent, or Firm—Sidney G. Faber

[57] **CLAIM**

The ornamental design for a headphone, as shown.

DESCRIPTION

FIG. 1 is a front elevation of a headphone showing my new design;
FIG. 2 is a side elevation thereof; and
FIG. 3 is a perspective view thereof.

TITLE: HAIR DRYER
INVENTORS: MORISON S. COUSINS & MICHAEL
A. COUSINS
ASSIGNEE: THE GILLETTE COMPANY

PATENT NUMBER: USD 248,048
PATENT FILED: JULY 30, 1976
PATENT GRANTED: MAY 30, 1978

United States Patent [19]

Cousins et al.

[11] **Des. 248,048**

[45] ** **May 30, 1978**

[54] **HAIR DRYER**

[75] Inventors: **Morison S. Cousins,** Plainview; **Michael A. Cousins,** Huntington, both of N.Y.

[73] Assignee: **The Gillette Company,** Boston, Mass.

[**] Term: **14 Years**

[21] Appl. No.: **710,271**

[22] Filed: **Jul. 30, 1976**

[51] Int. Cl. .... **D28—03**
[52] U.S. Cl. **D28/13**
[58] Field of Search .... D28/9, 10, 12–16, D28/18, 24; D4/13, 14, 17; 34/96–101; 219/222; 132/7, 9, 11 R, 11 A, 118; D8/77

[56] **References Cited**

PUBLICATIONS

Sears Supplement to the Washington Post, Wed. 6/12/1974, back cover – professional dryer a.
The Washington Post, Wed. 12/18/1974, p. A25 – Gillette "Promax" at top left.
Stile Industria, Dec. 1961, p. 26 – hair drier.

Primary Examiner—Joel Stearman
Assistant Examiner—Louis S. Zarfas
Attorney, Agent, or Firm—Richard A. Wise

[57] **CLAIM**

The ornamental design for a hair dryer, as shown and described.

DESCRIPTION

FIG. 1 is a perspective view of a hair dryer showing our new design;
FIG. 2 is a rear elevational view thereof;
FIG. 3 is a top plan view thereof;
FIG. 4 is a bottom plan view thereof;
FIG. 5 is a back end elevational view thereof; and
FIG. 6 is a front end elevational view thereof.

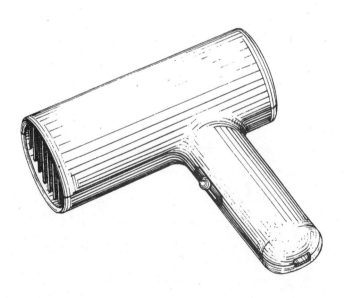

TITLE: TAPE DISPENSER
INVENTORS: HARTLAND W. DEERING, JR.
ASSIGNEE: MINNESOTA MINING AND
MANUFACTURING COMPANY

PATENT NUMBER: USD 248,561
PATENT FILED: JANUARY 10, 1977
PATENT GRANTED: JULY 18, 1978

U.S. Patent   July 18, 1978   Des. 248,561

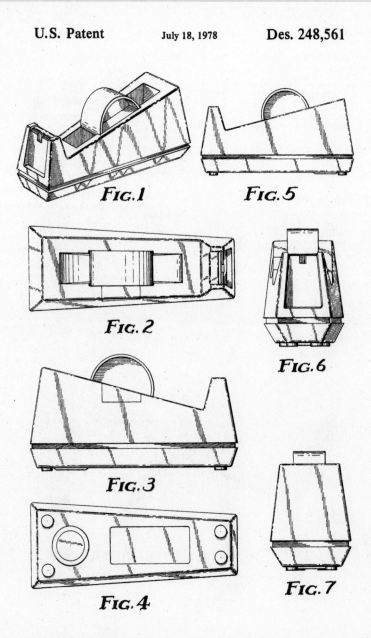

FIG. 1

FIG. 5

FIG. 2

FIG. 6

FIG. 3

FIG. 4

FIG. 7

TITLE: VEHICULAR TELEPHONE APPARATUS
INVENTORS: RUDOLPH WILLIAM KROLOPP & ORVILLE
WALTER LARSON
ASSIGNEE: MOTOROLA

PATENT NUMBER: USD 248,758
PATENT FILED: AUGUST 12, 1976
PATENT GRANTED: AUGUST 1, 1978

U.S. Patent Aug. 1, 1978 Sheet 1 of 2 **Des. 248,758**

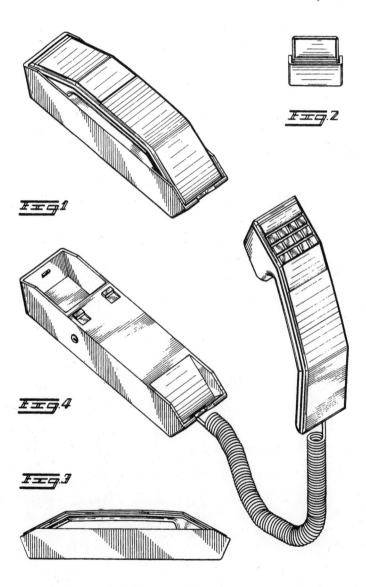

FIG.1

FIG.2

FIG.4

FIG.3

TITLE: VIDEO GAME CABINET
INVENTOR: LONNIE C. POGUE
ASSIGNEE: GREMLIN INDUSTRIES

PATENT NUMBER: USD 248,885
PATENT FILED: DECEMBER 13, 1976
PATENT GRANTED: AUGUST 8, 1978

U.S. Patent   Aug. 8, 1978   Sheet 1 of 2   **Des. 248,885**

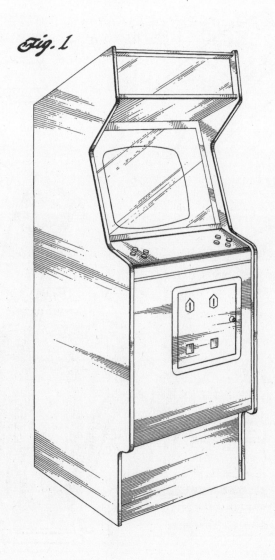

Fig. 1

TITLE: PORTABLE TOILET BUILDING
INVENTORS: FRANK T. SARGENT & SAMUEL C. CROSBY
ASSIGNEE: THETFORD CORPORATION

PATENT NUMBER: USD 250,350
PATENT FILED: SEPTEMBER 19, 1977
PATENT GRANTED: NOVEMBER 21, 1978

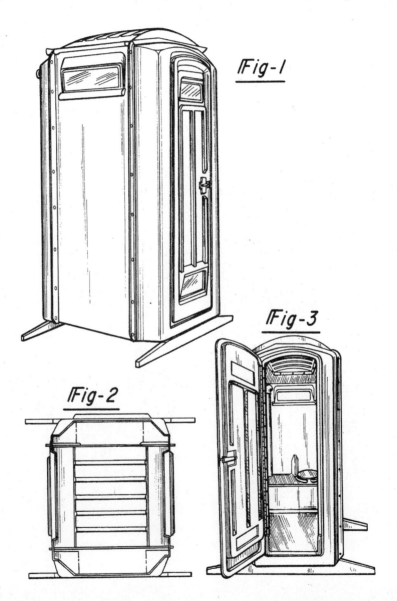

Fig-1

Fig-3

Fig-2

TITLE: TAPE RECORDER
INVENTOR: TOSHIHIKO KADOTA
ASSIGNEE: OLYMPUS OPTICAL COMPANY

PATENT NUMBER: USD 250,473
PATENT FILED: APRIL 11, 1977
PATENT GRANTED: DECEMBER 5, 1978

United States Patent [19]

Kadota

[11] **Des. 250,473**

[45] ** **Dec. 5, 1978**

[54] **TAPE RECORDER**

[75] Inventor: **Toshihiko Kadota**, Hachioji, Japan

[73] Assignee: **Olympus Optical Company Ltd.,** Tokyo, Japan

[**] Term: **14 Years**

[21] Appl. No.: **786,334**

[22] Filed: **Apr. 11, 1977**

[30] **Foreign Application Priority Data**

Oct. 15, 1976 [JP] Japan 51/40843

[51] **Int. Cl.** .... **D14—01**
[52] **U.S. Cl.** **D14/6**
[58] **Field of Search** D14/2, 5–6; 274/17, 2, 21; 360/82, 83, 55; 242/99

[56] **References Cited**

U.S. PATENT DOCUMENTS

D. 236,009	7/1975	Hattori	D14/6
D. 236,504	8/1975	Hattori	D14/6
D. 244,699	6/1977	Okamoto	D14/6
3,218,080	11/1965	Best	274/17

Primary Examiner—Bernard Ansher
Attorney, Agent, or Firm—Louis Weinstein

[57] **CLAIM**

The ornamental design for a tape recorder, as shown.

DESCRIPTION

FIG. 1 is a top front perspective view of a tape recorder, showing my new design; and
FIG. 2 is a bottom rear perspective thereof.

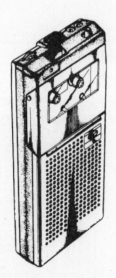
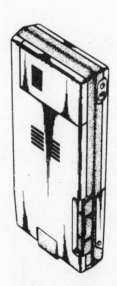

TITLE: VIDEO TAPE CASSETTE
INVENTOR: KOICHI NISHIGAKI
ASSIGNEE: VICTOR COMPANY OF JAPAN

PATENT NUMBER: USD 250,474
PATENT FILED: APRIL 20, 1977
PATENT GRANTED: DECEMBER 5, 1978

U.S. Patent   Dec. 5, 1978   Des. 250,474

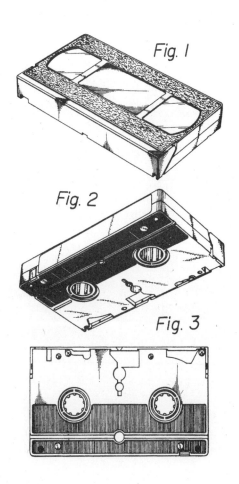

Fig. 1

Fig. 2

Fig. 3

TITLE: FAST SERVICE RESTAURANT BUILDING
INVENTOR: D. PAT. FRALEY
ASSIGNEE: CHURCH'S FRIED CHICKEN

PATENT NUMBER: USD 250,842
PATENT FILED: MAY 9, 1977
PATENT GRANTED: JANUARY 16, 1979

United States Patent [19]

Fraley

[11] **Des. 250,842**

[45] ** **Jan. 16, 1979**

[54] **FAST SERVICE RESTAURANT BUILDING**

[75] Inventor: **D. Pat. Fraley,** Richardson, Tex.

[73] Assignee: **Church's Fried Chicken, Inc.,** San Antonio, Tex.

[**] Term: **14 Years**

[21] Appl. No.: **794,752**

[22] Filed: **May 9, 1977**

[51] **Int. Cl.** .... **D25—03**
[52] **U.S. Cl.** **D25/25; D25/22; D25/33**
[58] **Field of Search** D25/1, 22, 23, 24, 25, D25/26, 56

[56] **References Cited**

U.S. PATENT DOCUMENTS

| D. 227,241 | 6/1973 | Lane | D25/25 |
| D. 243,696 | 3/1977 | Butz | D25/25 |

OTHER PUBLICATIONS

National Petroleum News, Nov., 1971, p. 44, building at lower left.

Primary Examiner—A. Hugo Word
Attorney, Agent, or Firm—Donald R. Comuzzi

[57] **CLAIM**

The ornamental design for a fast service restaurant building, as shown.

DESCRIPTION

FIG. 1 is a perspective view of the restaurant building.
FIG. 2 is a side elevation of the entrance to the restaurant.
FIG. 3 is a right side elevation view of the restaurant.
FIG. 4 is an elevation of the back side of the restaurant.
FIG. 5 is a left side elevation view of the restaurant.

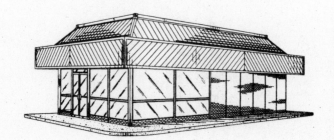

TITLE: PORTABLE TYPEWRITING MACHINE
INVENTOR: MARIO BELLINI
ASSIGNEE: OLIVETTI

PATENT NUMBER: USD 250,914
PATENT FILED: MAY 25, 1976
PATENT GRANTED: JANUARY 23, 1979

United States Patent [19]

Bellini

[11] **Des. 250,914**

[45] ** **Jan. 23, 1979**

[54] **PORTABLE TYPEWRITING MACHINE**

[75] Inventor: **Mario Bellini**, Milan, Italy

[73] Assignee: **Ing. C. Olivetti & C., S.p.A.**, Ivrea (Turin), Italy

[**] Term: **14 Years**

[21] Appl. No.: **689,916**

[22] Filed: **May 25, 1976**

[30] **Foreign Application Priority Data**

Jul. 10, 1975 [IT]   Italy 53215 B/75

[51] **Int. Cl.** .... **D18—01**
[52] **U.S. Cl.** **D18/1**
[58] **Field of Search** .... D64/11 A; 197/186 R

[56] **References Cited**

U.S. PATENT DOCUMENTS

D. 221,357   8/1971   Penney .... D64/11 A
D. 237,216   10/1975   Bellini .... D64/11 A

Primary Examiner—Louis S. Zarfas
Attorney, Agent, or Firm—William E. Schuyler, Jr.

[57] **CLAIM**

The ornamental design for a portable typewriting machine, substantially as shown and described.

DESCRIPTION

FIG. 1 is a front and right perspective view of a portable typewriting machine showing my new design;
FIG. 2 is a rear and left perspective view thereof;
FIG. 3 is a front elevational view thereof; and
FIG. 4 is a left side elevational view thereof.

TITLE: GAME CONTROL CONSOLE
INVENTORS: DOUGLAS A. HARDY
& FREDERICK W. THOMPSON
ASSIGNEE: ATARI

PATENT NUMBER: USD 251,143
PATENT FILED: AUGUST 19, 1977
PATENT GRANTED: FEBRUARY 20, 1979

United States Patent [19]

Hardy et al.

[11] **Des. 251,143**

[45] ** **Feb. 20, 1979**

[54] **GAME CONTROL CONSOLE**

[75] Inventors: **Douglas A. Hardy**, Portola Valley; **Frederick W. Thompson**, Soquel, both of Calif.

[73] Assignee: **Atari, Inc.,** Sunnyvale, Calif.

[**] Term: **14 Years**

[21] Appl. No.: **826,047**

[22] Filed: **Aug. 19, 1977**

[51] Int. Cl. .... **D21—01**
[52] U.S. Cl. .... **D34/5 R**
[58] Field of Search ..... D34/5 R; 273/1 E, DIG. 28; D13/32, 40

[56] **References Cited**

PUBLICATIONS

Popular Science, Nov. 1976, p. 88, TV Game controls.
Playthings, Feb. 1976, p. 195, "Tele-Pong" control.

Primary Examiner—Melvin B. Feifer
Attorney, Agent, or Firm—Stephen S. Townsend

[57] **CLAIM**

The ornamental design for a game control console, as shown and described.

DESCRIPTION

FIG. 1 is a perspective view of the game control console employing our new design.
FIG. 2 is a front elevational view of the game control console shown in FIG. 1.
FIG. 3 is a right side elevational view of the game control console shown in FIG. 1.
FIG. 4 is a top plan view of the game control console shown in FIG. 1.
FIG. 5 is a rear elevational view of the game control console shown in FIG. 1.
FIG. 6 is a bottom plan view of the game control console shown in FIG. 1.
The left side elevation of the game control console is a mirror image of the right side.

TITLE: LIGHT FIXTURE
INVENTOR: ACHILLE CASTIGLIONI
ASSIGNEE: NONE

PATENT NUMBER: USD 251,869
PATENT FILED: MARCH 17, 1977
PATENT GRANTED: MAY 15, 1979

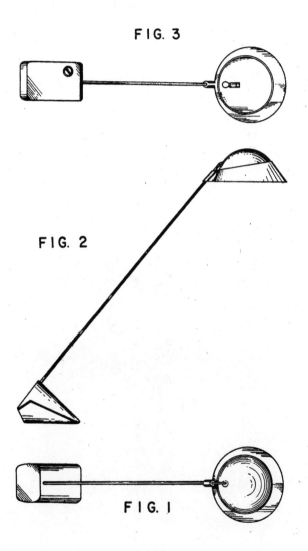

FIG. 3

FIG. 2

FIG. I

773

TITLE: CHAIR
INVENTOR: ENZO MARI
ASSIGNEE: NONE

PATENT NUMBER: USD 251,943
PATENT FILED: MARCH 17, 1977
PATENT GRANTED: MAY 29, 1979

United States Patent [19]

Mari

[11] **Des. 251,943**

[45] ✱✱ **May 29, 1979**

[54] **CHAIR**

[76] Inventor: **Enzo Mari**, P.le Baracca, 10, Milano, Italy, 20100

[✱✱] Term: **14 Years**

[21] Appl. No.: **778,570**

[22] Filed: **Mar. 17, 1977**

[30]   **Foreign Application Priority Data**

Sep. 17, 1976 [IT]   Italy .... 36019/76[U]

[51] Int. Cl. .... **D6—01**
[52] U.S. Cl. **D6/76; D6/78**
[58] Field of Search **D6/47–78,**
D6/186; 297/445

[56]   **References Cited**

U.S. PATENT DOCUMENTS

D. 236,395   8/1975   Kinsman .... D6/76 X

OTHER PUBLICATIONS

Domus Catalog, 9–1975, p. 47, Chair at right center.

Primary Examiner—Bruce W. Dunkins
Attorney, Agent, or Firm—Armand E. Lackenbach

[57]   **CLAIM**

The ornamental design for a chair, substantially as shown and described.

DESCRIPTION

FIG. 1 is a perspective view of the chair of my design taken from above and from the side and back of the chair;
FIG. 2 is a front elevational view thereof;
FIG. 3 is a side elevational view thereof, the side not shown being a mirror image thereof; and
FIG. 4 is a top plan view thereof.

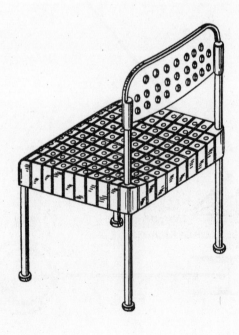

TITLE: AUTOMOBILE
INVENTOR: GIORGETTO GIUGIARO
ASSIGNEE: BAYERISCHE MOTOREN WERKE

PATENT NUMBER: USD 252,020
PATENT FILED: NOVEMBER 7, 1977
PATENT GRANTED: JUNE 5, 1979

United States Patent [19]

Giugiaro

[11] **Des. 252,020**

[45] ✱✱ **Jun. 5, 1979**

[54] **AUTOMOBILE**

[75] Inventor: **Giorgetto Giugiaro**, Moncalieri, Italy

[73] Assignee: **Bayerische Motoren Werke Aktiengesellschaft**, Munich, Fed. Rep. of Germany

[**] Term: **14 Years**

[21] Appl. No.: **849,434**

[22] Filed: **Nov. 7, 1977**

[30] **Foreign Application Priority Data**

May 6, 1977 [DE] Fed. Rep. of Germany 10973

[51] Int. Cl. .... **D12—08**
[52] U.S. Cl. **D12/91**
[58] **Field of Search** .... D12/90–92; D34/15 AJ; 296/15, 28 R, 31 P

[56] **References Cited**

U.S. PATENT DOCUMENTS

D. 222,639 11/1971 Wilfert et al. D12/91

OTHER PUBLICATIONS

Road & Track, 3/73, pp. 49 & 50, Lamborghini, top right side of page.
Bricklin Flyer, Bricklin Automobile.
Motor Trend, 9/73, pp. 90 & 91, BMW Turbo Car.

Primary Examiner—James M. Gandy
Attorney, Agent, or Firm—Craig and Antonelli

[57] **CLAIM**

The ornamental design for an automobile, as shown and described.

DESCRIPTION

FIG. 1 is a left side elevational view of an automobile showing my novel design;
FIG. 2 is a greatly enlarged front elevational view thereof;
FIG. 3 is a greatly enlarged rear elevational view thereof;
FIG. 4 is a perspective view from the left and front thereof;
FIG. 5 is a perspective view from the right and rear thereof; and
The top of the automobile is substantially flat and unornamented.

TITLE: TELEVISION RECEIVER
INVENTOR: TOSHIO OHYA
ASSIGNEE: SONY CORPORATION

PATENT NUMBER: USD 252,395
PATENT FILED: JULY 15, 1977
PATENT GRANTED: JULY 17, 1979

United States Patent [19]

Ohya

[11] **Des. 252,395**

[45] ** **Jul. 17, 1979**

[54] **TELEVISION RECEIVER**

[75] Inventor: **Toshio Ohya,** Omiya, Japan

[73] Assignee: **Sony Corporation,** Tokyo, Japan

[**] Term: **14 Years**

[21] Appl. No.: **816,161**

[22] Filed: **Jul. 15, 1977**

[30]   **Foreign Application Priority Data**

Jan. 18, 1977 [JP]   Japan 52-1103

[51] **Int. Cl.** .... **D14—03**
[52] **U.S. Cl.** **D14/80;** D14/81
[58] **Field of Search** D14/1, 21, 52, 77, 79,
                    D14/82–84, 99; 358/231, 250, 254

[56]   **References Cited**

U.S. PATENT DOCUMENTS

D. 237,826 11/1975 MacDonald et al. D14/81

FOREIGN PATENT DOCUMENTS

889447 2/1962 Fed. Rep. of Germany 358/254

OTHER PUBLICATIONS

Domus, 3–75, p. 49.
Merchandising, 3–76, p. 51, bottom-most item.
Sylvania Cat. #AD75012–0, prior to 4–23–76, p. 17,
item #CA5111SL.
Merchandising, 4–76, p 57.

Primary Examiner—Joel Stearman
Assistant Examiner—Jane E. Corrigan
Attorney, Agent, or Firm—Lewis H. Eslinger

[57]   **CLAIM**

The ornamental design for a television receiver, as shown.

DESCRIPTION

FIG. 1 is a front and partial right side perspective view of a television receiver showing my new design;
FIG. 2 is a top plan view;
FIG. 3 is a left side elevational view;
FIG. 4 is a rear elevational view; and
FIG. 5 is a bottom plan view.

TITLE: CAN RECYCLING PRESS
INVENTORS: ALTON W. HUBBARD & PETE A. JOHNSON
ASSIGNEE: JAHS ENTERPRISES

PATENT NUMBER: USD 253,771
PATENT FILED: APRIL 11, 1977
PATENT GRANTED: DECEMBER 25, 1979

United States Patent [19]

Hubbard et al.

[11] **Des. 253,771**

[45] ⁑ **Dec. 25, 1979**

[54] **CAN RECYCLING PRESS**

[75] Inventors: **Alton W. Hubbard,** Fortuna; **Pete A. Johnson,** Eureka, both of Calif.

[73] Assignee: **Jahs Enterprises, Inc.,** Eureka, Calif.

[**] Term: **14 Years**

[21] Appl. No.: **786,123**

[22] Filed: **Apr. 11, 1977**

[51] Int. Cl. .... D23—02; D15—99
[52] U.S. Cl. **D15/123**
[58] Field of Search D15/123; 100/DIG. 2, 100/45, 49, 53, 229, 220, 48, 289, 218, 232, 290, 295, 216, 233, 278

[56] **References Cited**

U.S. PATENT DOCUMENTS

D. 124,327	12/1940	Muller	D15/123
D. 231,256	4/1974	Longo	D15/123
3,799,051	3/1974	Liberman	D15/123 UX
3,802,336	4/1974	Toppins	100/49
3,862,595	1/1975	Longo	D15/123 X
3,934,498	1/1976	Hochanadel	100/DIG. 2
4,103,609	8/1978	Hiatt	100/218

Primary Examiner—Bernard Ansher
Attorney, Agent, or Firm—Frank A. Neal

[57] **CLAIM**

The ornamental design for a can recycling press, as shown and described.

DESCRIPTION

FIG. 1 is a rear, top and right side perspective view of a can recycling press showing our new design;
FIG. 2 is a top plan view;
FIG. 3 is a rear elevational view;
FIG. 4 is a right side elevational view, the left side being a mirror image thereof;
FIG. 5 is a cross-sectional view taken on the plane designated by line 5—5 of FIG. 4; and,
FIG. 6 is a bottom plan view.

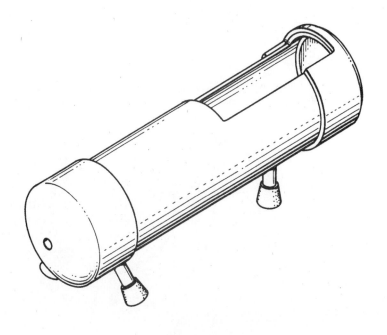

TITLE: ELECTRONIC GAME HOUSING
INVENTOR: DOUGLAS P. MONTAGUE
ASSIGNEE: MARVIN GLASS & ASSOCIATES

PATENT NUMBER: USD 253,786
PATENT FILED: APRIL 13, 1978
PATENT GRANTED: DECEMBER 25, 1979

U.S. Patent Dec. 25, 1979 **Des. 253,786**

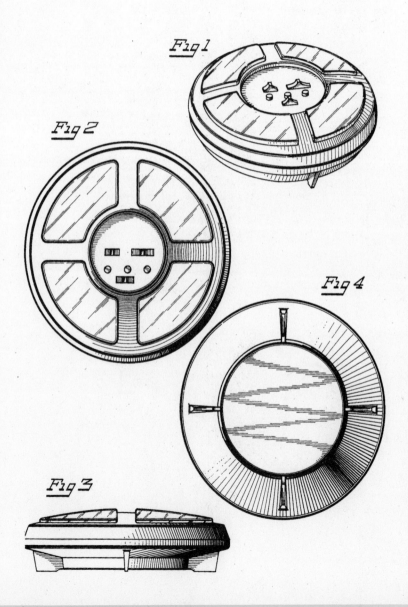

Fig 1

Fig 2

Fig 4

Fig 3

TITLE: COLLAPSIBLE CAMERA
INVENTORS: OTTO STEMME & PETER LERMANN
ASSIGNEE: ROBERT BOSCH

PATENT NUMBER: USD 254,136
PATENT FILED: NOVEMBER 2, 1976
PATENT GRANTED: FEBRUARY 5, 1980

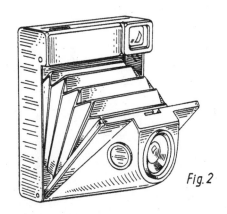

Fig. 2

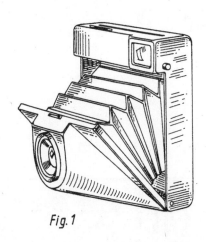

Fig. 1

TITLE: CASSETTE TAPE RECORDER AND PLAYER
OR SIMILAR ARTICLE
INVENTOR: RICHARD CULBERTSON
ASSIGNEE: GENERAL ELECTRIC COMPANY

PATENT NUMBER: USD 254,489
PATENT FILED: SEPTEMBER 26, 1977
PATENT GRANTED: MARCH 18, 1980

Fig. 1.   Fig. 2.

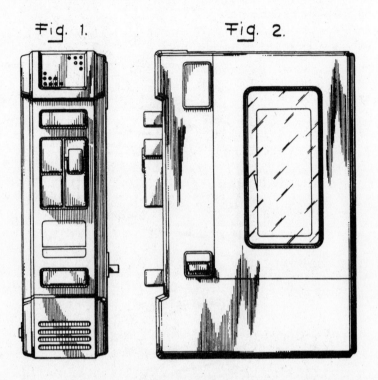

Fig. 3.

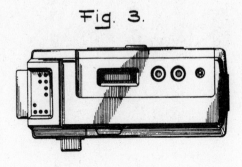

TITLE: PROGRAMMABLE DIGITAL CLOCK
INVENTOR: NICHOLAS F. TALESFORE
ASSIGNEE: FAIRCHILD CAMERA AND
INSTRUMENT CORPORATION

PATENT NUMBER: USD 254,601
PATENT FILED: JANUARY 11, 1978
PATENT GRANTED: APRIL 1, 1980

United States Patent [19]

Talesfore

[11] **Des. 254,601**

[45] ** **Apr. 1, 1980**

[54] **PROGRAMMABLE DIGITAL CLOCK**

[75] Inventor: **Nicholas F. Talesfore,** San Jose, Calif.

[73] Assignee: **Fairchild Camera and Instrument Corp.,** Mountain View, Calif.

[**] Term: **14 Years**

[21] Appl. No.: **868,605**

[22] Filed: **Jan. 11, 1978**

[51] Int. Cl. .... D10—01
[52] U.S. Cl. D10/15
[58] Field of Search D10/1, 2, 15, 18, 21,
D10/24–27, 39, 122–128; 58/23 R, 23 C, 16 D,
53–56, 125 B, 126 R, 126 A, 127 R, 152 R, 152
G

[56] **References Cited**

U.S. PATENT DOCUMENTS

D. 212,493	10/1968	Newman	.... D10/15 X
D. 246,105	10/1977	Coons	.... D10/15 X
D. 246,309	11/1977	Nakamura	.... D14/73

OTHER PUBLICATIONS

Home Furnishings Daily, 7/13/76, p. 9, Digital Clock, Model EC-1100 at left–center–top.

Primary Examiner—Nelson C. Holtje
Attorney, Agent, or Firm—Alan H. MacPherson; Ronald J. Meetin; Robert C. Colwell

[57] **CLAIM**

The ornamental design for a programmable digital clock, substantially as shown and described.

DESCRIPTION

FIG. 1 is a right front perspective view of a programmable digital clock showing my new design;
FIG. 2 is a front elevational view thereof;
FIG. 3 is a top plan view thereof, the bottom being substantially flat, plain and unornamented;
FIG. 4 is right side view elevational thereof, the left side view being a mirror image thereto;
FIG. 5 is a top plan view thereof with the keyboard cover in the opened position; and
FIG. 6 is a rear elevational view thereof.

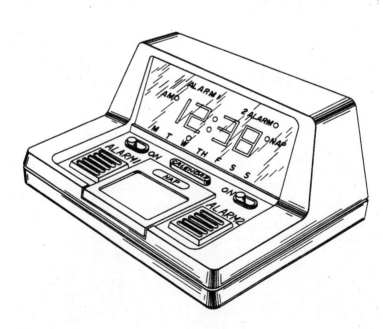

TITLE: CLOCK
INVENTOR: DIETRICH LUBS
ASSIGNEE: BRAUN

PATENT NUMBER: USD 255,876
PATENT FILED: JUNE 13, 1978
PATENT GRANTED: JULY 15, 1980

United States Patent [19]

Lubs

[11] **Des. 255,876**

[45] ** **Jul. 15, 1980**

[54] **CLOCK**

[75] Inventor: **Dietrich Lubs,** Bad Homburg, Fed. Rep. of Germany

[73] Assignee: **Braun Aktiengesellschaft,** Kronberg, Fed. Rep. of Germany

[**] Term: **14 Years**

[21] Appl. No.: **915,101**

[22] Filed: **Jun. 13, 1978**

[30] **Foreign Application Priority Data**

Dec. 13, 1977 [DE] Fed. Rep. of Germany ... 73 MR 8670

[51] **Int. Cl.** .... **D10—01**
[52] **U.S. Cl.** **D10/26**
[58] **Field of Search** .... D10/1, 2, 15, 18, 21–23, D10/24–26, 122–126; 58/53–56, 88 R, 88 G, 88 W, 50 R, 23 R, 126 R, 126 A, 127 R

[56] **References Cited**

U.S. PATENT DOCUMENTS

D. 145,352 8/1946 Collura D10/1
D. 173,302 10/1954 Bruce D10/26

OTHER PUBLICATIONS

Jeweler's Circular-Keystone, Mar. 1972, p. 27, Clock at bottom.
European Jeweler, May 1974, p. 44, Clock at bottom right.
Jeweler's Circular-Keystone, Mar. 1977, p. 23, Clock—.

Primary Examiner—Nelson C. Holtje
Attorney, Agent, or Firm—Richard C. Sughrue

[57] **CLAIM**

The ornamental design for a clock, as shown.

DESCRIPTION

FIG. 1 is a top and right front perspective view of a clock showing my new design;
FIG. 2 is a front elevational view thereof;
FIG. 3 is a front elevational view thereof with the rocker switch on the top depressed forwardly;
FIG. 4 is a left side elevational view thereof;
FIG. 5 is a right side elevational view thereof;
FIG. 6 is a right side elevational view of FIG. 3;
FIG. 7 is a top plan view thereof;
FIG. 8 is a bottom plan view thereof;
FIG. 9 is a rear elevational view thereof.

TITLE: HOT AIR CORN POPPER
INVENTORS: MELVIN H. BOLDT, THURBER H. MORRISON
& WAYNE J. FRANEK
ASSIGNEE: NATIONAL PRESTO INDUSTRIES

PATENT NUMBER: USD 256,019
PATENT FILED: APRIL 10, 1978
PATENT GRANTED: JULY 22, 1980

United States Patent [19]

Boldt et al.

[11] **Des. 256,019**

[45] ** **Jul. 22, 1980**

[54] **HOT AIR CORN POPPER**

[75] Inventors: **Melvin H. Boldt,** Glenview; **Thurber H. Morrison,** Evanston; **Wayne J. Franek,** Palatine, all of Ill.

[73] Assignee: **National Presto Industries, Inc.,** Eau Claire, Wis.

[**] Term: **14 Years**

[21] Appl. No.: **895,003**

[22] Filed: **Apr. 10, 1978**

[51] Int. Cl. .... D15—08
[52] U.S. Cl. D15/105
[58] Field of Search D15/105; D7/59, 60, D7/62, 94; 99/323.5, 323.6, 323.7, 323.8, 323.9, 323.11

[56] **References Cited**

U.S. PATENT DOCUMENTS

3,570,388   3/1971   Gottlieb 99/323.5

3,665,839   5/1972   Gottlieb 99/323.5
4,072,091   2/1978   Richardson 99/323.5
4,120,236   10/1978 Blomberg 99/323.9
4,152,974   5/1979   Tienor 99/323.8

OTHER PUBLICATIONS

Retail Home Furnishings, Dec. 19, 1977, "The Popcorn Pumper".

Primary Examiner—Catherine E. Kemper
Attorney, Agent, or Firm—John D. Gould

[57]   **CLAIM**

The ornamental design for a hot air corn popper, substantially as shown.

DESCRIPTION

FIG. 1 is a top front perspective view of a hot air corn popper, showing our new design;
FIG. 2 is a top plan view thereof;
FIG. 3 is a bottom plan view thereof;
FIG. 4 is a side elevational view thereof;
FIG. 5 is a front elevational view thereof;
FIG. 6 is a rear elevational view thereof.

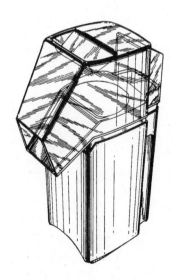

TITLE: VIDEO DISC PLAYER
INVENTORS: MARIAN H. POLHEMUS & ANDREW L. ALGER
ASSIGNEE: RCA CORPORATION

PATENT NUMBER: USD 256,117
PATENT FILED: JANUARY 3, 1978
PATENT GRANTED: JULY 29, 1980

United States Patent [19]

Polhemus et al.

[11] **Des. 256,117**

[45] ** **Jul. 29, 1980**

[54] **VIDEO DISC PLAYER**

[75] Inventors: **Marian H. Polhemus,** Chicago;
Andrew L. Alger, Wilmette, both of
Ill.

[73] Assignee: **RCA Corporation,** New York, N.Y.

[**] Term: **14 Years**

[21] Appl. No.: **866,607**

[22] Filed: **Jan. 3, 1978**

[51] Int. Cl. .... **D14—01**
[52] U.S. Cl. **D14/2; D14/6**
[58] Field of Search D24/1, 2; 360/33–38,
360/79; D14/2, 36

[56] **References Cited**

U.S. PATENT DOCUMENTS

D. 244,053	4/1977	Van De Poel	D14/2
D. 250,470	12/1978	Nishigaki	D14/2
D. 250,471	12/1978	Nishigaki	D14/2
3,493,676	2/1970	Guerin	360/33

OTHER PUBLICATIONS

3,493,676 02001970 Guerin 360 33
Eduology, vol. 4, Issue I, 1973, cover sheet, Philips
Video Disc Player.
Electronics, McGraw–Hill, New York, New York, pp.
106 and 107, Video Cassette Recorder, Nov. 24, 1977.

Primary Examiner—Bernard Ansher
Attorney, Agent, or Firm—Eugene M. Whitacre

[57] **CLAIM**

The ornamental design for a video disc player, as shown
and described.

DESCRIPTION

FIG. **1** is a front perspective view of a video disc player,
showing our new design;
FIG. **2** is a front view thereof;
FIG. **3** is a side perspective thereof;
FIG. **4** is a rear view thereof; and
FIG. **5** is a top rear perspective thereof.

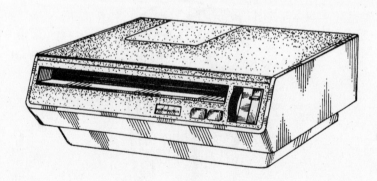

TITLE: TELEPHONE SET
INVENTOR: TAKAO KONTO
ASSIGNEE: NONE

PATENT NUMBER: USD 256,121
PATENT FILED: MARCH 30, 1979
PATENT GRANTED: JULY 29, 1980

United States Patent [19]

Konto

[11] **Des. 256,121**

[45] ** **Jul. 29, 1980**

[54] **TELEPHONE SET**

[76] Inventor: **Takao Konto**, No. 12-6,
Minamiaoyama 7-chome, Minato-ku,
Tokyo, Japan

[**] Term: **7 Years**

[21] Appl. No.: **25,545**

[22] Filed: **Mar. 30, 1979**

[51] **Int. Cl.** .... **D14—03**
[52] **U.S. Cl.** D14/53; D14/63
[58] **Field of Search** D14/53, 63, 66;
170/100 R, 100 D, 100 L, 103, 178, 179

[56] **References Cited**

U.S. PATENT DOCUMENTS

D. 182,450   4/1958   Aleksa D14/53
D. 211,362   6/1968   Janda D14/53
D. 238,079   12/1975   Heribertson et al. D14/53

D. 244,209   5/1977   Bliven D14/53
D. 251,005   2/1979   Breger D14/53

FOREIGN PATENT DOCUMENTS

2247585   4/1974   Fed. Rep. of Germany ...... 179/100 D

Primary Examiner—Bernard Ansher
Attorney, Agent, or Firm—Thomas R. Morrison

[57] **CLAIM**

The ornamental design for a telephone set, substantially as shown.

DESCRIPTION

FIG. 1 is a top plan view of a telephone set showing my new design;
FIG. 2 is a front elevation thereof;
FIG. 3 is a side elevation thereof;
FIG. 4 is an elevation as seen from the side opposite FIG. 3;
FIG. 5 is a rear elevation thereof; and
FIG. 6 is a bottom plan view thereof.

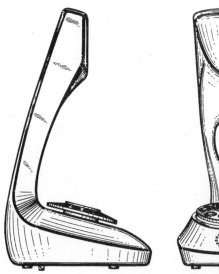

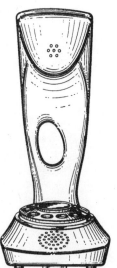

TITLE: STEAM IRON
INVENTORS: ERICH R. BAUMGARTNER,
PETER DOEHLER, DIETER RAMS & JÜRGEN GREUBEL
ASSIGNEE: BRAUN

PATENT NUMBER: USD 257,209
PATENT FILED: FEBRUARY 27, 1978
PATENT GRANTED: OCTOBER 7, 1980

United States Patent [19]

Baumgartner et al.

[11] **Des. 257,209**

[45] **** Oct. 7, 1980**

[54] **STEAM IRON**

[75] Inventors: **Erich R. Baumgartner; Peter Doehler,** both of Munich; **Dieter Rams,** Kronberg; **Jürgen Greubel,** Heidenrod, all of Fed. Rep. of Germany

[73] Assignee: **Braun Aktiengesellschaft,** Kronberg, Fed. Rep. of Germany

[**] Term: **7 Years**

[21] Appl. No.: **881,877**

[22] Filed: **Feb. 27, 1978**

[30] **Foreign Application Priority Data**

Aug. 25, 1977 [DE] Fed. Rep. of Germany 738649

[51] Int. Cl. .... D7—05
[52] U.S. Cl. D7/203
[58] Field of Search D7/202, 203; 38/74, 38/75, 77.1–77.9, 88, 89, 90

[56] **References Cited**

U.S. PATENT DOCUMENTS

D. 221,249	7/1971	Russell	D7/202
2,861,363	11/1958	Finlayson	38/77.83
3,486,256	12/1969	Kapr et al.	38/88
3,718,997	3/1973	Murphy	38/90

Primary Examiner—Catherine E. Kemper
Attorney, Agent, or Firm—William L. Androlia

[57] **CLAIM**

The ornamental design for a steam iron, substantially as shown and described.

DESCRIPTION

FIG. 1 is a right side elevational view of a steam iron showing our new design;
FIG. 2 is a left side elevational view thereof;
FIG. 3 is a front elevational view thereof;
FIG. 4 is a rear elevational view thereof;
FIG. 5 is a top plan view thereof;
FIG. 6 is a bottom view thereof; and
FIG. 7 is a perspective view thereof.
The conventional electric cord has been shown fragmentarily for convenience of illustration.

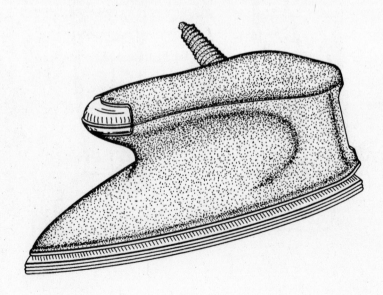

TITLE: PORTABLE VACUUM CLEANER
INVENTOR: CARROLL M. GANTZ
ASSIGNEE: BLACK & DECKER

PATENT NUMBER: USD 257,661
PATENT FILED: DECEMBER 7, 1978
PATENT GRANTED: DECEMBER 23, 1980

FIG. 1

FIG. 2

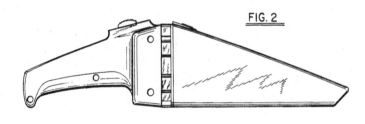

FIG. 3

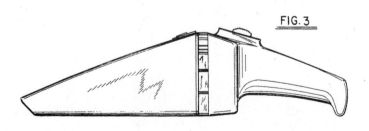

TITLE: BALL POINT PEN OR SIMILAR ARTICLE
INVENTOR: SHIGEO OKA
ASSIGNEE: PENTEL KABUSHIKI KAISHA

PATENT NUMBER: USD 258,218
PATENT FILED: APRIL 5, 1979
PATENT GRANTED: FEBRUARY 10, 1981

U.S. Patent   Feb. 10, 1981   Des. 258,218

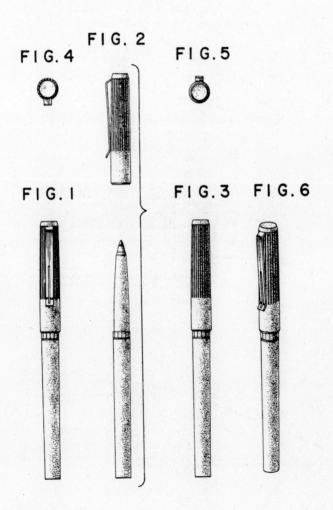

FIG. 4

FIG. 2

FIG. 5

FIG. 1

FIG. 3

FIG. 6

TITLE: CAMERA
INVENTOR: HIDETAKA MINESHIMA
ASSIGNEE: TIZER COMPANY

PATENT NUMBER: USD 258,444
PATENT FILED: MAY 19, 1978
PATENT GRANTED: MARCH 3, 1981

U.S. Patent   Mar. 3, 1981   Sheet 1 of 2   **Des. 258,444**

F I G. 1

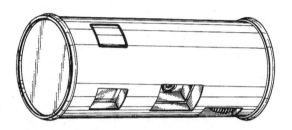

F I G. 2

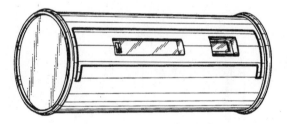

F I G. 3

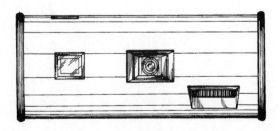

789

TITLE: PORTABLE CALCULATOR
INVENTOR: MARIO BELLINI
ASSIGNEE: OLIVETTI

PATENT NUMBER: USD 258,451
PATENT FILED: OCTOBER 13, 1978
PATENT GRANTED: MARCH 3, 1981

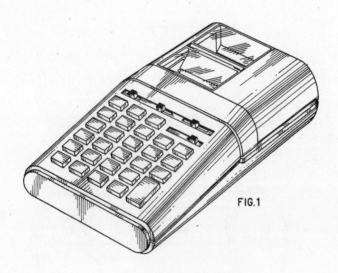

FIG.1

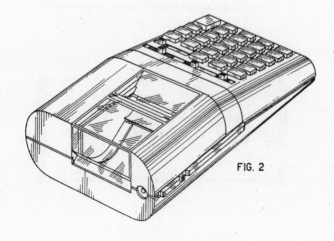

FIG. 2

TITLE: ROTARY CARD FILE
INVENTOR: HILDAUR L. NIELSEN
ASSIGNEE: ROLODEX CORPORATION

PATENT NUMBER: USD 258,669
PATENT FILED: MARCH 31, 1977
PATENT GRANTED: MARCH 24, 1981

FIG. 1

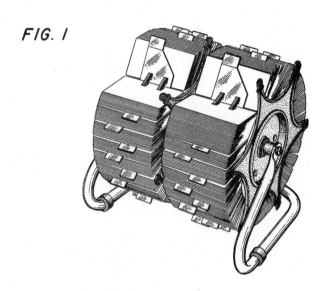

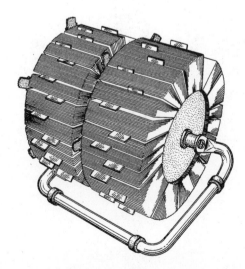

FIG. 2

TITLE: LOUNGE CHAIR
INVENTOR: THOMAS LAMB
ASSIGNEE: NONE

PATENT NUMBER: USD 260,459
PATENT FILED: OCTOBER 30, 1978
PATENT GRANTED: SEPTEMBER 1, 1981

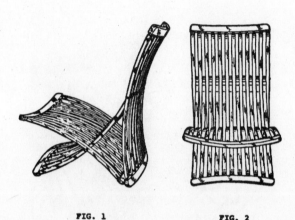

FIG. 1   FIG. 2

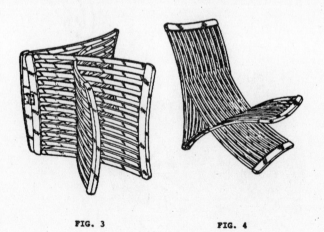

FIG. 3   FIG. 4

TITLE: HOUSING FOR HAND VACUUM AND THE LIKE
INVENTORS: OLIVER W. MASTERSON, CHARLES A.
HARRISON & BUCKLEY A. SINGLETARY
ASSIGNEE: SEARS, ROEBUCK & COMPANY

PATENT NUMBER: USD 261,851
PATENT FILED: MARCH 9, 1979
PATENT GRANTED: NOVEMBER 17, 1981

United States Patent [19]

Masterson et al.

[11] **Des. 261,851**

[45] ** **Nov. 17, 1981**

[54] **HOUSING FOR HAND VACUUM AND THE LIKE**

[75] Inventors: **Oliver W. Masterson,** Chicago;
Charles A. Harrison, Evanston;
Buckley A. Singletary, Plainfield, all
of Ill.

[73] Assignee: **Sears, Roebuck & Co.,** Chicago, Ill.

[**] Term: **14 Years**

[21] Appl. No.: **18,929**

[22] Filed: **Mar. 9, 1979**

[51] **Int. Cl.** .... **D7—05**
[52] **U.S. Cl.** **D32/18**
[58] **Field of Search** D7/164; D15/52–55;
15/344

[56] References Cited

U.S. PATENT DOCUMENTS

2,491,007	12/1949	Koch	69/20
3,872,539	3/1975	Doyel	15/344
3,914,820	10/1975	Hankel	15/344

Primary Examiner—Catherine E. Kemper
Attorney, Agent, or Firm—Arnstein, Gluck & Lehr

[57] **CLAIM**

The ornamental design for a housing for hand vacuum
and the like, as shown and described.

DESCRIPTION

FIG. **1** is a front perspective view of a hand vacuum
housing showing our new design;
FIG. **2** is a side elevational view thereof, shown on an
enlarged scale;
FIG. **3** is a bottom plan view thereof;
FIG. **4** is a top plan view thereof;
FIG. **5** is a front elevational view of our design of FIG.
1 taken along line 5—5 of FIG. **2**; and
FIG. **6** is a rear elevational view thereof.
The side of the housing not shown, is a mirror image of
the side shown.

TITLE: FOUNTAIN PEN
INVENTOR: BERNT SPIEGEL
ASSIGNEE: C. JOSEPH LAMY

PATENT NUMBER: USD 264,854
PATENT FILED: JULY 31, 1980
PATENT GRANTED: JUNE 8, 1982

U.S. Patent   Jun. 8, 1982   Des. 264,854

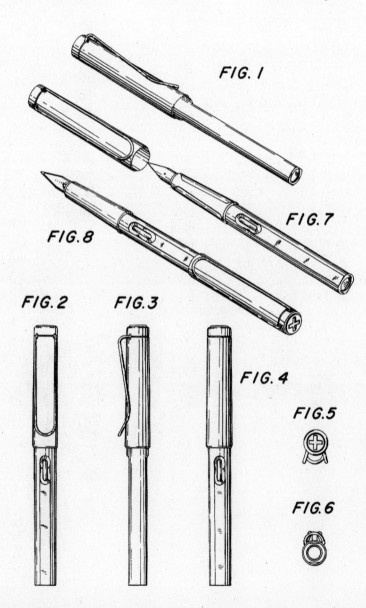

FIG. 1

FIG. 7

FIG. 8

FIG. 2

FIG. 3

FIG. 4

FIG. 5

FIG. 6

TITLE: PORTABLE CASSETTE TAPE RECORDER
INVENTOR: KUNISHIGE MIKI
ASSIGNEE: MATSUSHITA ELECTRIC
INDUSTRIAL COMPANY

PATENT NUMBER: USD 265,901
PATENT FILED: JUNE 10, 1980
PATENT GRANTED: AUGUST 24, 1982

FIG. 1

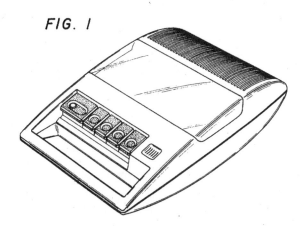

FIG. 2

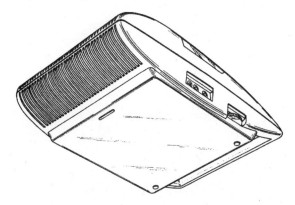

TITLE: COMBINED CASSETTE PLAYER, HEADSET
AND RADIO
INVENTOR: DAMASO PEREZ
ASSIGNEE: NONE

PATENT NUMBER: USD 266,417
PATENT FILED: SEPTEMBER 11, 1980
PATENT GRANTED: OCTOBER 5, 1982

Fig.1

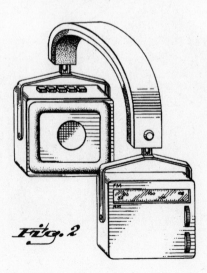

Fig.2

TITLE: PACKAGE OF BEVERAGE BOTTLES
INVENTOR: JEAN-CLAUDE BETON
ASSIGNEE: COMPAGNIE FRANÇAISE DES
PRODUITS ORANGINA

PATENT NUMBER: USD 266,646
PATENT FILED: NOVEMBER 19, 1980
PATENT GRANTED: OCTOBER 26, 1982

Fig. 1

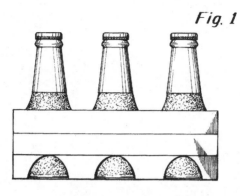

Fig. 2

Fig. 3

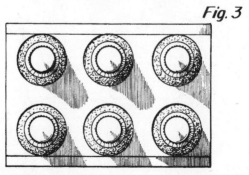

TITLE: MICRO-WAVE OVEN
INVENTORS: MASAMICHI YAMAMURA, TOSHIO HARADA
& MICHIO TANAKA
ASSIGNEE: MATSUSHITA ELECTRIC INDUSTRIAL COMPANY

PATENT NUMBER: USD 267,222
PATENT FILED: DECEMBER 18, 1980
PATENT GRANTED: DECEMBER 14, 1982

U.S. Patent   Dec. 14, 1982   Sheet 1 of 2   Des. 267,222

Fig. 1

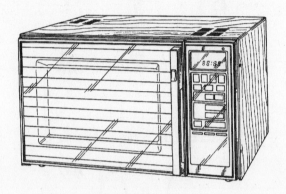

Fig. 2

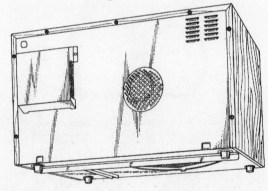

TITLE: MOTORCYCLE
INVENTOR: YUKIHIKO MATSUE
ASSIGNEE: YAMAHA HATSUDOKI KABUSHIKI KAISHA

PATENT NUMBER: USD 267,560
PATENT FILED: OCTOBER 8, 1980
PATENT GRANTED: JANUARY 11, 1983

United States Patent [19]

Matsue

[11] **Des. 267,560**

[45] ✷✷ **Jan. 11, 1983**

[54] **MOTORCYCLE**

[75] Inventor: **Yukihiko Matsue**, Tokyo, Japan

[73] Assignee: **Yamaha Hatsudoki Kabushiki Kaisha**, Japan

[**] Term: **14 Years**

[21] Appl. No.: **194,962**

[22] Filed: **Oct. 8, 1980**

[30] **Foreign Application Priority Data**

Apr. 26, 1980 [JP] Japan 55-16810

[51] Int. Cl. .... **D12—11**

[52] U.S. Cl. **D12/110**

[58] Field of Search D12/110; 180/219, 223

[56] **References Cited**

U.S. PATENT DOCUMENTS

2,436,991 3/1948 Dirksen D6/48.1

OTHER PUBLICATIONS

Cycle World, 2/79, p. 14, Honda XR250.
Cycle World, 6/79, p. 36, Honda CR125R, top of page.
Cycle World, 6/78, p. 73, Honda XL–250S.

Primary Examiner—James M. Gandy
Attorney, Agent, or Firm—Ostrolenk, Faber, Gerb & Soffen

[57] **CLAIM**

The ornamental design for a motorcycle, as shown.

DESCRIPTION

FIG. 1 is a front, left side perspective view of a motorcycle showing my new design;
FIG. 2 is a right side elevational view thereof;
FIG. 3 is a left side elevational view thereof;
FIG. 4 is a front elevational view thereof;
FIG. 5 is a rear elevational view thereof; and
FIG. 6 is a top plan view thereof.

TITLE: TOY SPACE VEHICLE
INVENTORS: GEORGE W. LUCAS, JR. & JOSEPH
E. JOHNSTON
ASSIGNEE: LUCASFILM

PATENT NUMBER: USD 268,200
PATENT FILED: APRIL 18, 1980
PATENT GRANTED: MARCH 8, 1983

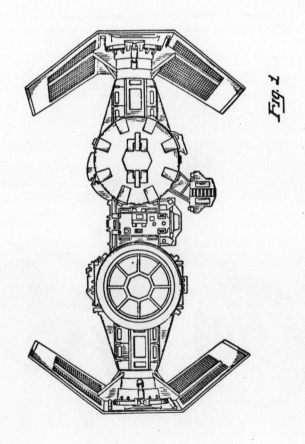

Fig. 1

TITLE: PERSONAL COMPUTER
INVENTORS: STEVEN P. JOBS, JERROLD C. MANOCK
DEAN A. HOVEY & DAVID M. KELLEY
ASSIGNEE: APPLE COMPUTER

PATENT NUMBER: USD 268,584
PATENT FILED: NOVEMBER 3, 1980
PATENT GRANTED: APRIL 12, 1983

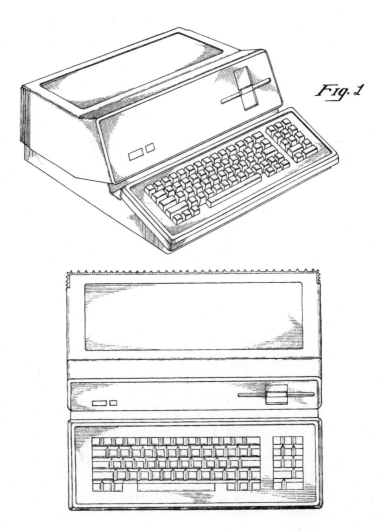

Fig. 1

Fig. 2

TITLE: TAPE PLAYER
INVENTOR: KAORU SUMITA
ASSIGNEE: SONY CORPORATION

PATENT NUMBER: USD 269,266
PATENT FILED: APRIL 30,1981
PATENT GRANTED: JUNE 7 ,1983

FIG. 7

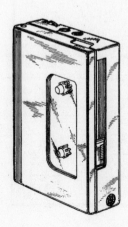

FIG. 8

802

TITLE: PORTABLE RADIO TELEPHONE
INVENTORS: ALBERT L. NAGELE
& KENNETH W. LARSON
ASSIGNEE: MOTOROLA

PATENT NUMBER: USD 269,873
PATENT FILED: FEBRUARY 4, 1981
PATENT GRANTED: JULY 26, 1983

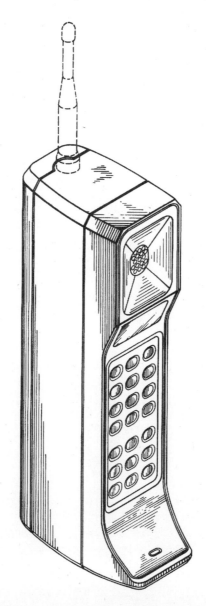

ᴴ==ᴳ.1

803

TITLE: COMPACT FLUORESCENT LAMP
OR SIMILAR ARTICLE FOR A LIGHTING UNIT
INVENTOR: ROBERT G. YOUNG
ASSIGNEE: NORTH AMERICAN PHILIPS ELECTRIC

PATENT NUMBER: USD 270,480
PATENT FILED: NOVEMBER 26, 1979
PATENT GRANTED: SEPTEMBER 6, 1983

United States Patent [19]

Young

[11] **Des. 270,480**

[45] ** **Sep. 6, 1983**

[54] **COMPACT FLUORESCENT LAMP OR SIMILAR ARTICLE FOR A LIGHTING UNIT**

[75] Inventor: **Robert G. Young,** Nutley, N.J.

[73] Assignee: **North American Philips Electric Corp.,** New York, N.Y.

[**] Term: **14 Years**

[21] Appl. No.: **97,280**

[22] Filed: **Nov. 26, 1979**

[51] Int. Cl. .... **D26—04**
[52] U.S. Cl. **D26/3**
[58] Field of Search 313/204, 220, 221, 222, 313/315, 316, 317, 318, 493; D26/2, 3; 362/216, 217, 222, 223, 224, 225

[56] **References Cited**

U.S. PATENT DOCUMENTS

1,898,615 2/1933 Byrnes .... 313/204 X

2,001,511	5/1935	Uyterhoeven et al.	.... 313/204 X
2,170,338	8/1939	Plummer et al.	.... 313/204 X
2,173,234	9/1939	Linder	.... 313/204 X
2,200,940	5/1940	Uyterhoeven et al.	.... 313/204 X

FOREIGN PATENT DOCUMENTS

51-437860	9/1976	Japan	.... 313/220
1514281	6/1978	United Kingdom	.... 313/220

Primary Examiner—Susan J. Lucas

[57] **CLAIM**

The ornamental design for a compact fluorescent lamp or similar article for a lighting unit, as shown and described.

DESCRIPTION

FIG. 1 is a perspective view of a compact fluorescent lamp or similar article for a lighting unit embodying my new design;
FIG. 2 is a back elevational view thereof;
FIG. 3 is a side elevational view thereof; and
FIG. 4 is a top plan view thereof.

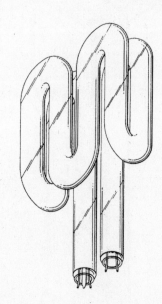

TITLE: HAND HELD ELECTRIC MIXER
INVENTOR: JOSE Z. ZIMNOWICZ
ASSIGNEE: BRAUN ESPANOLA

PATENT NUMBER: USD 271,176
PATENT FILED: OCTOBER 22, 1980
PATENT GRANTED: NOVEMBER 1, 1983

United States Patent [19]

Zimnowicz

[11] **Des. 271,176**

[45] ∗∗ **Nov. 1, 1983**

[54] **HAND HELD ELECTRIC MIXER**

[75] Inventor: **Jose Z. Zimnowicz,** Barcelona, Spain

[73] Assignee: **Braun Espanola, S.A.,** Spain

[∗∗] Term: **14 Years**

[21] Appl. No.: **199,621**

[22] Filed: **Oct. 22, 1980**

[30] **Foreign Application Priority Data**

Apr. 23, 1980 [ES] Spain 96876

[51] Int. Cl. .... **D7—04**
[52] U.S. Cl. **D7/379**
[58] Field of Search D7/41, 157, 158, 159,
D7/139, 160, 379, 380, 376, 377, 412, 415;
366/129

[56] **References Cited**

U.S. PATENT DOCUMENTS

D. 121,299	7/1940	Krebs	D7/158
D. 206,388	12/1966	Clemente	D7/158
1,766,171	6/1930	Hetherington	D7/157 X
2,804,290	8/1957	Kaufman	D7/158 X
2,805,050	9/1957	Choppinet	366/129 X

3,117,769	1/1964	Spingler	366/129
3,333,830	8/1967	Spingler et al.	366/129

FOREIGN PATENT DOCUMENTS

241728	8/1965	Austria	366/129
633260	12/1949	United Kingdom	366/129

OTHER PUBLICATIONS

Design 128, Aug. 1959, p. 54, top left Panel–Hand Mixer for Nova, Belgium, 1959 Signe d'or.

Primary Examiner—Winifred E. Herrmann
Attorney, Agent, or Firm—Scully, Scott, Murphy & Presser

[57] **CLAIM**

The ornamental design for a hand held electric mixer, as shown and described.

DESCRIPTION

FIG. 1 is a rear elevational view of a hand held electric mixer showing my new design;
FIG. 2 is a side elevational view thereof from the left of FIG. 1, the side opposite being a mirror image thereof;
FIG. 3 is a front elevational view thereof;
FIG. 4 is a top plan view thereof; and
FIG. 5 is a bottom plan view thereof.

 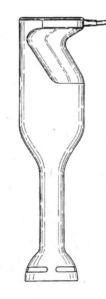 

TITLE: VIDEO GAME CONTROLLER
INVENTOR: ROY M. NISHI
ASSIGNEE: ATARI

PATENT NUMBER: USD 271,313
PATENT FILED: JANUARY 7, 1982
PATENT GRANTED: NOVEMBER 8, 1983

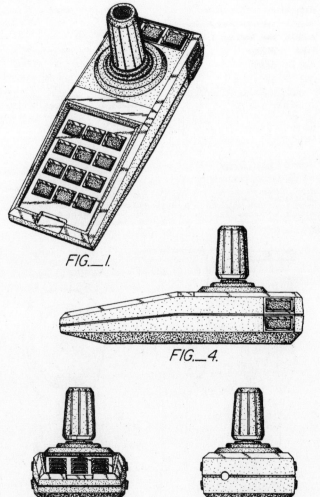

FIG.__1.

FIG.__4.

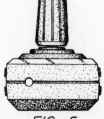

FIG.__3.

FIG.__5.

TITLE: EARPHONE
INVENTOR: TAKEYOSHI KAWANO
ASSIGNEE: SONY CORPORATION

PATENT NUMBER: USD 272,904
PATENT FILED: AUGUST 17, 1981
PATENT GRANTED: MARCH 6, 1984

United States Patent [19]

Kawano

[11] **Des. 272,904**

[45] ** **Mar. 6, 1984**

[54] **EARPHONE**

[75] Inventor: **Takeyoshi Kawano**, Kunitachi, Japan

[73] Assignee: **Sony Corporation**, Tokyo, Japan

[**] Term: **14 Years**

[21] Appl. No.: **293,609**

[22] Filed: **Aug. 17, 1981**

[30] **Foreign Application Priority Data**

Feb. 17, 1981 [JP] Japan 56-6077

[51] Int. Cl. .... **D14—03**
[52] U.S. Cl. **D14/30; D14/36**
[58] Field of Search .... D14/1, 30, 36, 68, 70, D14/76, 99, 67; D24/35; 179/107 H, 182 R

[56] **References Cited**

U.S. PATENT DOCUMENTS

D. 248,158 6/1978 Read .... D14/67 X
2,474,135 6/1949 White .... 179/107 H

3,906,478 9/1975 Smey .... 179/107 H X

FOREIGN PATENT DOCUMENTS

436377 10/1926 Fed. Rep. of Germany ... 179/182 R

Primary Examiner—Jane E. Corrigan
Attorney, Agent, or Firm—Lewis H. Eslinger; Alvin Sinderbrand

[57] **CLAIM**

The ornamental design for an earphone, as shown.

DESCRIPTION

FIG. 1 is a front elevational view of an earphone showing my new design;
FIG. 2 is a right side elevational view;
FIG. 3 is a top plan view;
FIG. 4 is a rear elevational view;
FIG. 5 is a left side elevational view;
FIG. 6 is a bottom plan view;
FIG. 7 is a front perspective view; and
FIG. 8 is a rear perspective view.

TITLE: TELEVISION RECEIVER
INVENTOR: TOSHIYUKI MATSUO
ASSIGNEE: SONY CORPORATION

PATENT NUMBER: USD 272,908
PATENT FILED: OCTOBER 6, 1981
PATENT GRANTED: MARCH 6, 1984

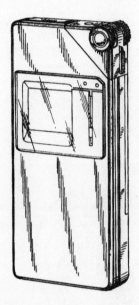

FIG.7

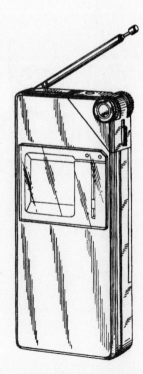

FIG.8

TITLE: COMPUTER
INVENTOR: IRA VELINSKY
ASSIGNEE: COMMODORE ELECTRONICS

PATENT NUMBER: USD 277,857
PATENT FILED: AUGUST 27, 1982
PATENT GRANTED: MARCH 5, 1985

United States Patent [19]

Velinsky

[11] **Patent Number: Des. 277,857**

[45] **Date of Patent:** ₊₊ **Mar. 5, 1985**

[54] **COMPUTER**

[75] Inventor: **Ira Velinsky,** Plainfield, N.J.

[73] Assignee: **Commodore Electronics Limited,** Wayne, Pa.

[**] Term: **14 Years**

[21] Appl. No.: **412,310**

[22] Filed: **Aug. 27, 1982**

[52] **U.S. Cl.** **D14/106**

[58] **Field of Search** .... D14/100, 101, 105–116; 364/900, 708, 709; 340/365 R, 700, 711

[56] **References Cited**

U.S. PATENT DOCUMENTS

D. 227,899 7/1973 Genaro et al. D14/106

OTHER PUBLICATIONS

Datamation, 1–1981, p. 168, Informer Computer Terminal.
Infosystems, 5–1980, p. 63, Vydec Inc. Terminal #2000.
Office Products, 8–1980, p. 33, Cado C.A.T. Computer.
Racal–Milgo ™ Data Communication Products Catalog 5–1978, p. 16, "40+" Display System.

Primary Examiner—Susan J. Lucas
Attorney, Agent, or Firm—Davis, Hoxie, Faithfull & Hapgood

[57] **CLAIM**

The ornamental design for a computer, as shown.

DESCRIPTION

FIG. **1** is a perspective view of a computer showing my new design;
FIG. **2** is a side elevational view thereof;
FIG. **3** is a rear elevational view thereof;
FIG. **4** is an exploded perspective view thereof.

TITLE: ELECTRIC RICE COOKER
INVENTORS: TAKEICHI OBATA & SHINJI OE
ASSIGNEE: HITACHI HEATING APPLIANCES COMPANY

PATENT NUMBER: USD 280,064
PATENT FILED: MARCH 9, 1983
PATENT GRANTED: AUGUST 13, 1985

FIG. 1

FIG. 2

TITLE: PORTABLE COMPUTER
INVENTORS: WILLIAM G. MOGGRIDGE, DAVID C.
PAULSEN, GLENN T. EDENS & STEPHEN R. HOBSON
ASSIGNEE: GRID SYSTEMS CORPORATION

PATENT NUMBER: USD 280,511
PATENT FILED: OCTOBER 18, 1982
PATENT GRANTED: SEPTEMBER 10, 1985

FIG. 1

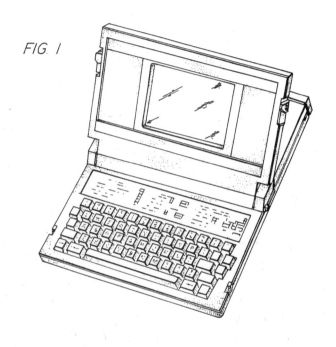

FIG. 2

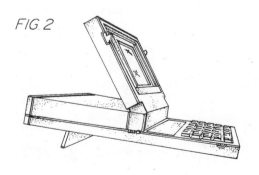

TITLE: LARGE BUTTON TELEPHONE
INVENTOR: KENNETH REICHENSTEIN
ASSIGNEE: NONE

PATENT NUMBER: USD 281,243
PATENT FILED: JULY 25, 1983
PATENT GRANTED: NOVEMBER 5, 1985

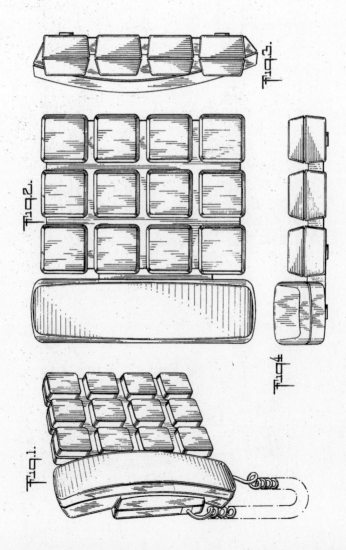

Fig. 3.

Fig. 2.

Fig. 4.

Fig. 1.

TITLE: AUTOMOBILE
INVENTOR: GIORGETTO GIUGIARO
ASSIGNEE: DELOREAN MOTOR COMPANY

PATENT NUMBER: USD 283,882
PATENT FILED: JUNE 12, 1981
PATENT GRANTED: MAY 20, 1986

United States Patent [19]

Giugiaro

[11] **Patent Number:** **Des. 283,882**

[45] **Date of Patent:** ∗∗ **May 20, 1986**

[54] **AUTOMOBILE**

[75] Inventor: **Giorgetto Giugiaro,** Turin, Italy

[73] Assignee: **Delorean Motor Company**

[**] Term: **14 Years**

[21] Appl. No.: **273,091**

[22] Filed: **Jun. 12, 1981**
[52] **U.S. Cl.** **D12/91**
[58] **Field of Search** D12/91, 92; 296/185

[56] **References Cited**

PUBLICATIONS

Road & Track, 3/73, p. 50, Lamborghini P250 Uracco, top right side of page.

Primary Examiner—James M. Gandy
Attorney, Agent, or Firm—David A. Maxon

[57] **CLAIM**

The ornamental design for an automobile, as shown and described.

DESCRIPTION

FIG. **1** is a front perspective view of an automobile showing my new design;
FIG. **2** is a rear perspective view thereof;
FIG. **3** is a front elevational view thereof; and
FIG. **4** is a rear elevational view thereof.
The side opposite to that shown in FIGS. **1** and **2** of the drawing is substantially a mirror image thereof.

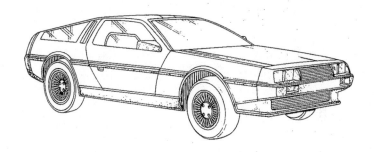

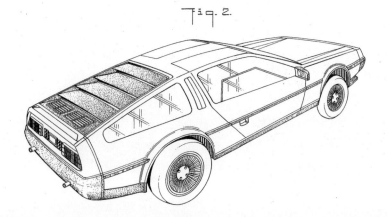

Fig. 2.

TITLE: FLOPPY DISC
INVENTOR: KAZUMI FUJIMOTO
ASSIGNEE: SONY CORPORATION

PATENT NUMBER: USD 283,893
PATENT FILED: MARCH 29, 1983
PATENT GRANTED: MAY 20, 1986

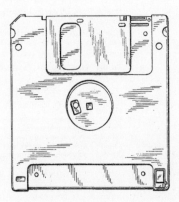

FIG. 5

FIG. 6

FIG. 7

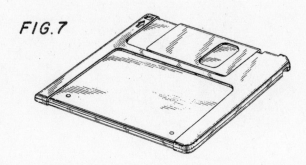

TITLE: ADJUSTABLE TABLE LAMP
INVENTOR: RODOLFO BONETTO
ASSIGNEE: IGUZZINI ILLUMINAZIONE

PATENT NUMBER: USD 284,108
PATENT FILED: JANUARY 4, 1984
PATENT GRANTED: JUNE 3, 1986

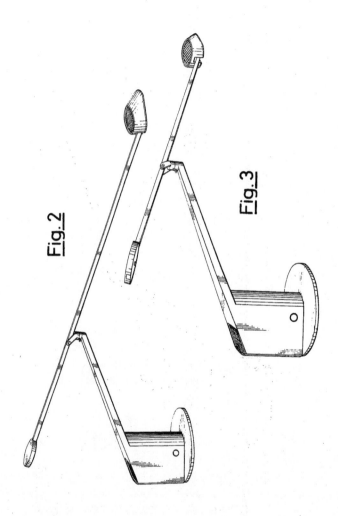

Fig.2

Fig.3

TITLE: HOUSING FOR MOVABLE CURSOR CONTROL
INVENTORS: JERROLD C. MANOCK, TERRELL A. OYAMA
& JAMES R. YURCHENCO
ASSIGNEE: APPLE COMPUTER

PATENT NUMBER: USD 284,284
PATENT FILED: OCTOBER 13, 1983
PATENT GRANTED: JUNE 17, 1986

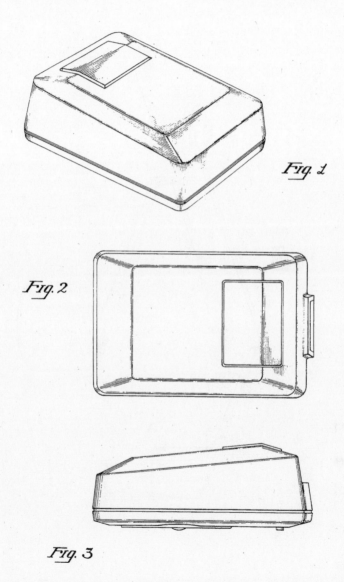

Fig. 1

Fig. 2

Fig. 3

TITLE: FLOATING LANTERN
INVENTORS: JOHN F. SCHOSSER, ROGER F. GLEASON,
CHARLES M. DOLE, RICHARD F. GALYA, ET AL.
ASSIGNEE: DURACELL

PATENT NUMBER: USD 284,309
PATENT FILED: FEBRUARY 22, 1983
PATENT GRANTED: JUNE 17, 1986

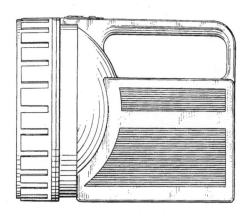

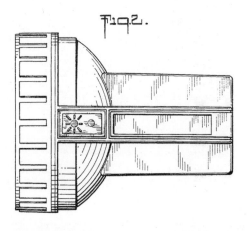

TITLE: ADJUSTABLE LOUNGE CHAIR
INVENTOR: RODRIGO RODRIGUEZ
ASSIGNEE: CASSINA

PATENT NUMBER: USD 285,630
PATENT FILED: MARCH 9, 1984
PATENT GRANTED: SEPTEMBER 16, 1986

United States Patent [19]

Rodriquez

[11] **Patent Number:** **Des. 285,630**

[45] **Date of Patent:** ** Sep. 16, 1986

[54] **ADJUSTABLE LOUNGE CHAIR**

[75] Inventor: **Rodrigo Rodriquez**, Carimate, Italy

[73] Assignee: **Cassina S.p.A.**, Milan, Italy

[**] Term: **14 Years**

[21] Appl. No.: **587,932**

[22] Filed: **Mar. 9, 1984**

[30] **Foreign Application Priority Data**

Sep. 9, 1983 [IT] Italy .... 22896/83[U]
[52] **U.S. Cl.** D6/367; D6/360;
D6/361
[58] **Field of Search** D6/334, 360, 361, 367,
D6/368, 374

[56] **References Cited**

U.S. PATENT DOCUMENTS

D. 230,444	2/1974	Kogoj et al.	D6/375 X
D. 248,344	7/1978	Uchida	D6/375 X
D. 256,407	8/1980	Nakisbendi	D6/334
D. 280,051	8/1985	Offredi	D6/334
D. 280,955	10/1985	Hopfer	D6/381 X
D. 282,126	1/1986	Hopfer	D6/367
D. 282,224	1/1986	Huldt	D6/375

OTHER PUBLICATIONS

Schoner Wohnen, Aug. 1979, p. 70, Settee top right.

Primary Examiner—Bruce W. Dunkins
Attorney, Agent, or Firm—Karl F. Ross; Herbert Dubno

[57] **CLAIM**

The ornamental design for an adjustable lounge chair, as shown and described.

DESCRIPTION

FIG. 1 is a front perspective view of an adjustable lounge chair showing my design;

FIG. 2 is a front elevational view thereof;

FIG. 3 is a perspective view showing one of the two identical sides;

FIG. 4 is a rear elevational view of the adjustable lounge chair as shown in FIG. 1;

FIG. 5 is a front perspective view of the adjustable lounge chair of FIG. 1 showing the backrest in a substantially vertical position;

FIG. 6 is a front perspective view of the adjustable lounge chair of FIG. 5 wherein the leg rest is shown in extended position; and

FIG. 7 is a perspective view of the adjustable lounge chair of FIG. 6 wherein the backrest is shown in an inclined position.

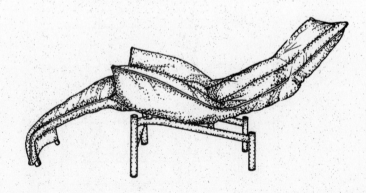

TITLE: COMPUTER HOUSING
INVENTORS: JERROLD C. MANOCK, TERRELL A. OYAMA
& STEVEN R. JOBS
ASSIGNEE: JERROLD C. MANOCK

PATENT NUMBER: USD 285,687
PATENT FILED: OCTOBER 13, 1983
PATENT GRANTED: SEPTEMBER 16, 1986

United States Patent [19]

Manock et al.

[11] **Patent Number:** **Des. 285,687**

[45] **Date of Patent:** ** * Sep. 16, 1986**

[54] **COMPUTER HOUSING**

[75] Inventors: **Jerrold C. Manock**, 2350 Harvard St., Palo Alto, Calif. 94306; **Terrell A. Oyama,** Los Altos; **Steven P. Jobs,** Los Gatos, both of Calif.

[73] Assignee: **Jerrold C. Manock,** Calif.

[*] Notice: The portion of the term of this patent subsequent to Sep. 16, 2000 has been disclaimed.

[**] Term: **14 Years**

[21] Appl. No.: **541,714**

[22] Filed: **Oct. 13, 1983**

[52] **U.S. Cl.** **D14/106**

[58] **Field of Search** 340/700, 711, 710; D14/106, 113, 115

[56] **References Cited**

U.S. PATENT DOCUMENTS

D. 227,256	6/1973	Conway et al.	D14/106
D. 266,426	10/1982	Dresselhaus	D14/115
D. 270,158	8/1983	Fossella et al.	D14/106
D. 272,353	1/1984	Dillon	D14/113
D. 275,955	10/1984	Moraine	D14/106
D. 277,673	2/1985	Dresselhaus et al.	D14/106

OTHER PUBLICATIONS

Computer Design, 8-1982, p. 47, Hewlett Packard Color Graphics Terminal.
Office Products, 8-1980, p. 33, Computer/Word Processor.

Primary Examiner—Susan J. Lucas
Attorney, Agent, or Firm—Blakely, Sokoloff, Taylor & Zafman

[57] **CLAIM**

The ornamental design for a computer housing, substantially as shown.

DESCRIPTION

FIG. 1 is a perspective view of the computer housing showing our new design;
FIG. 2 is a front elevational view thereof;
FIG. 3 is a top plan view thereof;
FIG. 4 is a right side elevational view thereof;
FIG. 5 is a bottom plan view thereof;
FIG. 6 is a rear elevational view thereof.

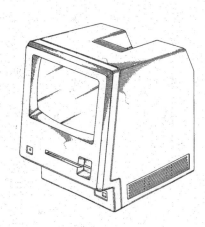

TITLE: STEAM IRON
INVENTORS: FRANZ A. STUTZER & MICHAEL KNOCHNER
ASSIGNEE: ROWENTA-WERKE

PATENT NUMBER: USD 285,737
PATENT FILED: AUGUST 2, 1984
PATENT GRANTED: SEPTEMBER 16, 1986

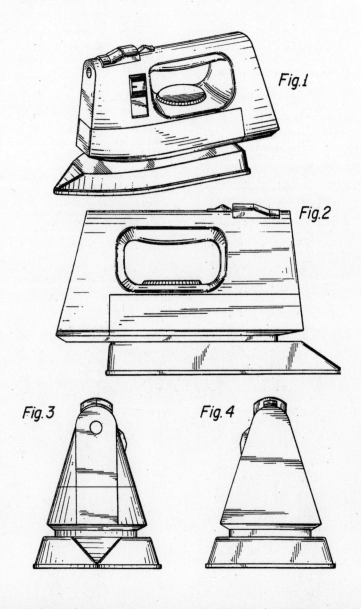

Fig.1

Fig.2

Fig.3

Fig.4

TITLE: MOTORCYCLE
INVENTORS: KATSUSUKE KOMURO, TOSHIYUKI YAMADA
& MATSUO HIROSE
ASSIGNEE: HONDA GIKEN KOGYO KABUSHIKI KAISHA

PATENT NUMBER: USD 286,519
PATENT FILED: NOVEMBER 30, 1983
PATENT GRANTED: NOVEMBER 4, 1986

f IG.4.

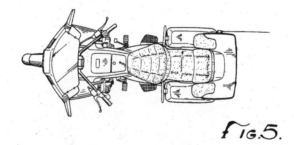

f IG.5.

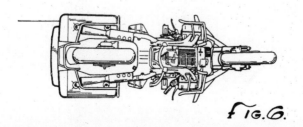

f IG.6.

TITLE: COMBINED HEATER AND FAN
INVENTOR: JORDAN KAHN
ASSIGNEE: HOLMES PRODUCTS CORPORATION

PATENT NUMBER: USD 286,673
PATENT FILED: DECEMBER 9, 1985
PATENT GRANTED: NOVEMBER 11, 1986

United States Patent [19]

Kahn

[11] **Patent Number:** **Des. 286,673**

[45] **Date of Patent:** ✱✱ **Nov. 11, 1986**

[54] **COMBINED HEATER AND FAN**

[75] Inventor: **Jordan Kahn,** Wellesley, Mass.

[73] Assignee: **Holmes Products Corp.,** Holliston, Mass.

[**] Term: **14 Years**

[21] Appl. No.: **806,396**

[22] Filed: **Dec. 9, 1985**
[52] **U.S. Cl.** **D23/122**
[58] **Field of Search** D23/93, 110–116, D23/122–124, 139, 151, 155; 219/366, 369, 370, 371, 367, 368

[56] **References Cited**

U.S. PATENT DOCUMENTS

D. 257,059 9/1980 Schade D23/122

FOREIGN PATENT DOCUMENTS

2535029 4/1984 France 219/370

OTHER PUBLICATIONS

Housewares, Jul. 1–7, 1980–p. 78–Krups Heaters.

Primary Examiner—Catherine E. Kemper
Attorney, Agent, or Firm—Irving M. Kriegsman

[57] **CLAIM**

The ornamental design for a combined heater and fan, as shown and described.

DESCRIPTION

FIG. 1 is a perspective view taken from the front of a combined heater and fan showing my new design;
FIG. 2 is a front view thereof;
FIG. 3 is a side elevational view thereof;
FIG. 4 is a back view thereof; and
FIG. 5 is a bottom view thereof.

TITLE: AUTOMOBILE BODY
INVENTORS: WILLIAM A. DAYTON, JOHN E. CRAIN
& ROBERT N. HUBBACH
ASSIGNEE: CHRYSLER CORPORATION

PATENT NUMBER: USD 286,865
PATENT FILED: DECEMBER 19, 1983
PATENT GRANTED: NOVEMBER 25, 1986

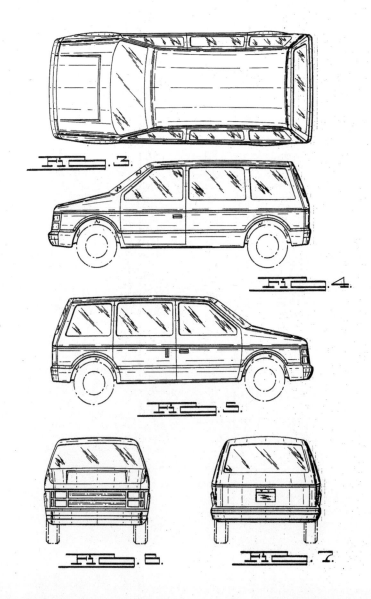

TITLE: CHAIR
INVENTOR: PETER OPSVIK
ASSIGNEE: NONE

PATENT NUMBER: USD 287,669
PATENT FILED: APRIL 2, 1984
PATENT GRANTED: JANUARY 13, 1987

U.S. Patent   Jan. 13, 1987   **Des. 287,669**

Fig. 1.

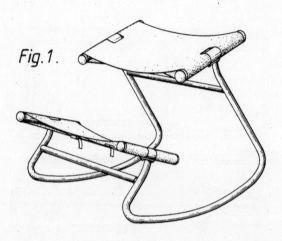

Fig. 2.

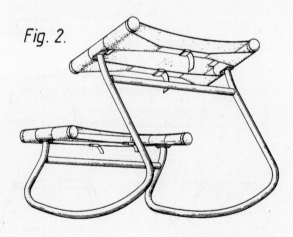

824

TITLE: TABLE BASE
INVENTOR: ROBERT VENTURI
ASSIGNEE: KNOLL INTERNATIONAL

PATENT NUMBER: USD 287,798
PATENT FILED: FEBRUARY 22, 1984
PATENT GRANTED: JANUARY 20, 1987

United States Patent [19]

Venturi

[11] **Patent Number:** **Des. 287,798**

[45] **Date of Patent:** ** Jan. 20, 1987

[54] **TABLE BASE**

[75] Inventor: **Robert Venturi**, Philadelphia, Pa.

[73] Assignee: **Knoll International, Inc.**, New York, N.Y.

[**] Term: **14 Years**

[21] Appl. No.: **582,325**

[22] Filed: **Feb. 22, 1984**

[52] **U.S. Cl.** **D6/498**

[58] **Field of Search** D6/429, 430, 480, 484, D6/486, 487, 488, 495, 496, 498

[56] **References Cited**

U.S. PATENT DOCUMENTS

D. 158,878	6/1950	Marx	D6/429
D. 212,238	9/1968	Belotte	D6/490
D. 225,710	1/1973	McIntosh	D6/488
D. 263,438	3/1982	Watson	D6/484
D. 271,846	12/1983	Hernandez	D6/498 X
D. 280,789	10/1985	Murphy, Jr.	D6/480 X

Primary Examiner—Bruce W. Dunkins
Attorney, Agent, or Firm—Thomas A. O'Rourke

[57] **CLAIM**

The ornamental design for a table base, as shown and described.

DESCRIPTION

FIG. 1 is a side elevational view of a table base showing my design; and
FIG. 2 is a top plan view thereof.
The undisclosed side faces of the leg members are the same in appearance as the disclosed leg faces shown in FIG. 1.

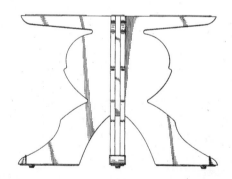

TITLE: TOASTER
INVENTORS: FRANZ A. STUTZER & MICHEAL KNOCHNER
ASSIGNEE: ROWENTA-WERKE

PATENT NUMBER: USD 287,808
PATENT FILED: NOVEMBER 28, 1984
PATENT GRANTED: JANUARY 20, 1987

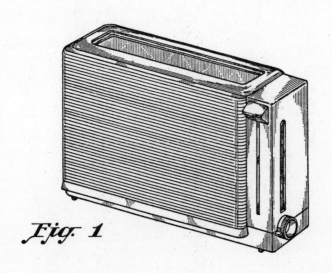

Fig. 1

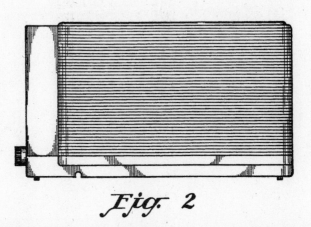

Fig. 2

TITLE: MOTORCYCLE
INVENTORS: KENTARO ITO & CHIHARU SASAKI
ASSIGNEE: HONDA GIKEN KOGYO KABUSHIKI KAISHA

PATENT NUMBER: USD 287,834
PATENT FILED: FEBRUARY 24, 1984
PATENT GRANTED: JANUARY 20, 1987

fIG.7.

fIG.8.

TITLE: BUILDING
INVENTORS: JOSEPH C. LEAGUE, JR. BRIAN H.
TERRELL & HENRI V. JOVA
ASSIGNEE: BANK SOUTH CORPORATION

PATENT NUMBER: USD 288,611
PATENT FILED: MAY 15, 1984
PATENT GRANTED: MARCH 3, 1987

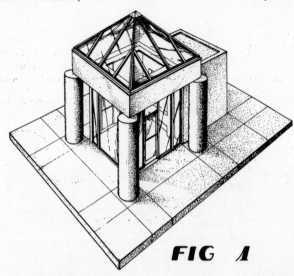

FIG 1

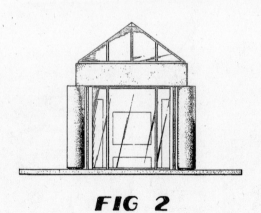

FIG 2

TITLE: WEIGHING SCALE
INVENTOR: RIDO BUSSE
ASSIGNEE: SOEHNLE-WAAGEN

PATENT NUMBER: USD 289,386
PATENT FILED: SEPTEMBER 7, 1984
PATENT GRANTED: APRIL 21, 1987

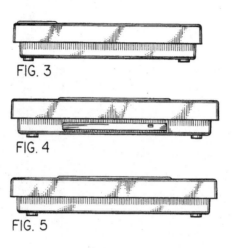

FIG. 3

FIG. 4

FIG. 5

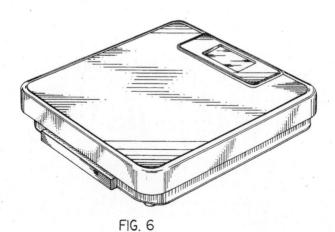

FIG. 6

TITLE: PORTABLE COMPUTER
INVENTOR: RICHARD SAPPER
ASSIGNEE: INTERNATIONAL BUSINESS
MACHINES CORPORATION

PATENT NUMBER: USD 290,256
PATENT FILED: JANUARY 17, 1986
PATENT GRANTED: JUNE 9, 1987

United States Patent [19]

Sapper

[11] **Patent Number: Des. 290,256**

[45] **Date of Patent: ** Jun. 9, 1987**

[54] **PORTABLE COMPUTER**

[75] Inventor: **Richard Sapper**, Baden-Baden, Fed. Rep. of Germany

[73] Assignee: **International Business Machines Corporation**, Armonk, N.Y.

[**] Term: **14 Years**

[21] Appl. No.: **820,461**

[22] Filed: **Jan. 17, 1986**

[52] **U.S. Cl.** **D14/106**

[58] **Field of Search** .... D14/100, 105, 106, 107, D14/113, 114; D18/1, 7, 4; 340/700, 711, 365 R; 364/708, 709

[56] **References Cited**

U.S. PATENT DOCUMENTS

D. 280,511   9/1985   Moggridge et al. D14/106

FOREIGN PATENT DOCUMENTS

2139762   11/1984   United Kingdom .... 340/365 R

OTHER PUBLICATIONS

Datamation, 10–15–1984, pp. 58 & 59, Data General-/One Portable Computer.
Personal Computing, 4–1984, p. 173, Visual Technology Inc. "Commuter" TM Portable Computer.

Primary Examiner—Susan J. Lucas
Attorney, Agent, or Firm—J. F. Villella, Jr.

[57] **CLAIM**

The ornamental design for a portable computer, substantially as shown and described.

DESCRIPTION

FIG. 1 is a perspective view of a portable computer or the like showing my new design, the computer being in a closed condition;
FIG. 2 is a front elevational view thereof;
FIG. 3 is a top plan view thereof;
FIG. 4 is a rear elevational view thereof;
FIG. 5 is a bottom plan view thereof;
FIG. 6 is a side elevational view thereof;
FIG. 7 is an opposite side elevational view thereof;
FIG. 8 is a perspective view thereof in an open condition.

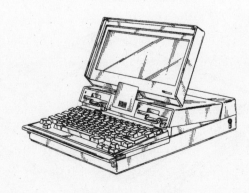

TITLE: SCOOTER
INVENTOR: CLIFFORD F. MUELLER
ASSIGNEE: SCHWINN BICYCLE COMPANY

PATENT NUMBER: USD 292,221
PATENT FILED: DECEMBER 19, 1986
PATENT GRANTED: OCTOBER 6, 1987

FIG. 3

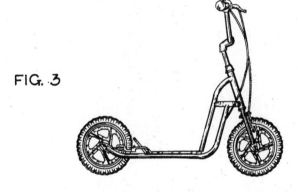

FIG. 4

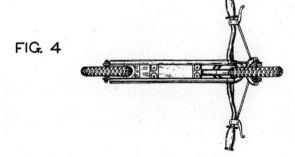

TITLE: COLOR TELEVISION SET
INVENTOR: ENNIO BRION
ASSIGNEE: BRIONVEGA

PATENT NUMBER: USD 293,108
PATENT FILED: OCTOBER 9, 1984
PATENT GRANTED: DECEMBER 8, 1987

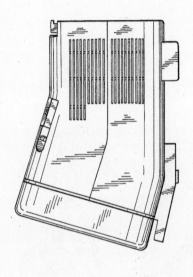

FIG. 6

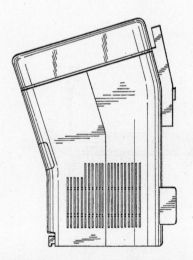

FIG. 5

832

TITLE: COMBINED VIDEO CAMERA AND TAPE RECORDER
INVENTORS: SHIN MIYASHITA & ATSUSHI FUKUTOMI
ASSIGNEE: SONY CORPORATION

PATENT NUMBER: USD 293,784
PATENT FILED: MARCH 22, 1985
PATENT GRANTED: JANUARY 19, 1988

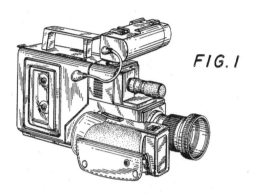

FIG. I

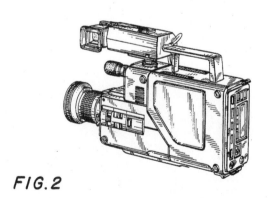

FIG.2

TITLE: FOIL CUTTER FOR WINE BOTTLES
INVENTOR: HERBERT ALLEN
ASSIGNEE: HALLEN COMPANY

PATENT NUMBER: USD 297,201
PATENT FILED: OCTOBER 22, 1985
PATENT GRANTED: AUGUST 16, 1988

U.S. Patent   Aug. 16, 1988   **D297,201**

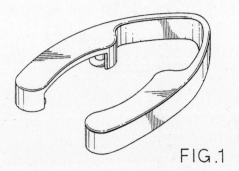

FIG.1

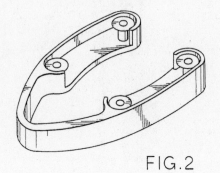

FIG.2

TITLE: TELEPHONE SET
INVENTORS: JOSEPH G. ASCHAUER & JOHN CUCCIO
ASSIGNEE: TIE COMMUNICATIONS

PATENT NUMBER: USD 299,459
PATENT FILED: OCTOBER 14, 1987
PATENT GRANTED: JANUARY 17, 1989

United States Patent [19]

Aschauer et al.

[11] **Patent Number:** **Des. 299,459**

[45] **Date of Patent:** ** **Jan. 17, 1989**

[54] **TELEPHONE SET**

[75] Inventors: **Joseph G. Aschauer**, Newtown; **John Cuccio**, Westport, both of Conn.

[73] Assignee: **TIE Communications, Inc.**, Shelton, Conn.

[**] Term: **14 Years**

[21] Appl. No.: **108,574**

[22] Filed: **Oct. 14, 1987**

[52] **U.S. Cl.** **D14/151;** D14/245

[58] **Field of Search** D14/52, 53, 57, 58, D14/62, 63; 379/440, 419, 420, 428, 433, 436

[56] **References Cited**

U.S. PATENT DOCUMENTS

D. 284,188	6/1986	Kondo et al.	D14/62 X
D. 286,042	10/1986	Fukutani	D14/60
D. 287,012	12/1986	Yanagichi et al.	D14/62 X
D. 287,246	12/1986	Brown et al.	D14/58
D. 287,489	12/1986	Sekiguchi	D14/58 X
D. 287,491	12/1986	Brown et al.	D14/58 X
D. 287,585	1/1987	Brown et al.	D14/62 X
D. 287,852	1/1987	Brown et al.	D14/58
D. 288,810	3/1987	Ando	D14/62 X
D. 289,642	5/1987	Kaku	D14/62 X
D. 293,905	1/1988	Aschauer et al.	D14/62 X

Primary Examiner—Horace B. Fay, Jr.
Attorney, Agent, or Firm—Amster, Rothstein & Ebenstein

[57] **CLAIM**

The ornamental design for telephone set, as shown and described.

DESCRIPTION

FIG. 1 is a front, top and right side isometric view of a telephone set showing our new design;
FIG. 2 is a top plan view thereof;
FIGS. 3 and 4 are respectively right and left side elevational views thereof;
FIGS. 5 and 6 are respectively front and rear elevational views thereof; and
FIG. 7 is a bottom plan view thereof.

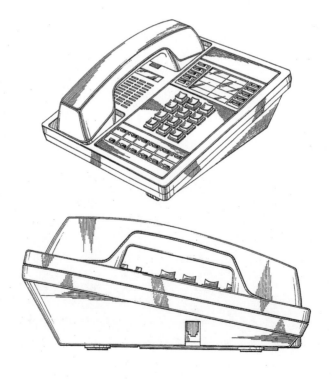

TITLE: COFFEEMAKER
INVENTOR: MICHAEL KNÖCHNER
ASSIGNEE: ROWENTA-WERKE

PATENT NUMBER: USD 299,608
PATENT FILED: NOVEMBER 25,1985
PATENT GRANTED: JANUARY 31,1989

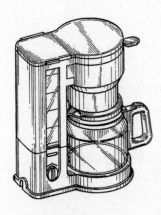

Fig. 1

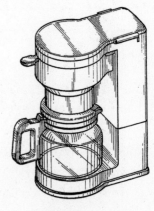

Fig. 2

Fig. 3

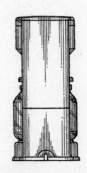

Fig. 4

TITLE: VIDEO GAME CONTROL UNIT
INVENTOR: MASAYUKI YUKAWA
ASSIGNEE: NINTENDO COMPANY

PATENT NUMBER: USD 299,726
PATENT FILED: NOVEMBER 4, 1985
PATENT GRANTED: FEBRUARY 7, 1989

FIG.1

FIG.2

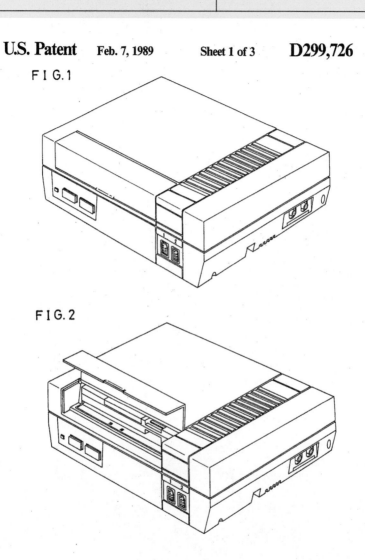

TITLE: SERVICE STATION
INVENTOR: SAUL BASS
ASSIGNEE: THE STANDARD OIL COMPANY

PATENT NUMBER: USD 301,169
PATENT FILED: AUGUST 27, 1986
PATENT GRANTED: MAY 16, 1989

United States Patent [19]

Bass

[11] Patent Number: **Des. 301,169**

[45] Date of Patent: ** May 16, 1989

[54] **SERVICE STATION**

[75] Inventor: **Saul Bass,** Los Angeles, Calif.

[73] Assignee: **The Standard Oil Company,** Cleveland, Ohio

[**] Term: **14 Years**

[21] Appl. No.: **901,244**

[22] Filed: **Aug. 27, 1986**
[52] **U.S. Cl.** **D25/56;** D15/9.2
[58] **Field of Search** D15/9.1–9.3;
D25/1, 4, 56; 52/27, 633, 648; 222/24–28,
144.5, 129, 173, 250–251, 566, 575, 631; 235/1
R, 61 A, 94 R, 94 A; 137/234.6

[56] **References Cited**

U.S. PATENT DOCUMENTS

D. 296,133 6/1988 Baffo .... D15/9.2 X
D. 298,538 11/1988 Baffo et al. D15/9.2

Primary Examiner—Wallace R. Burke
Assistant Examiner—Brian N. Vinson
Attorney, Agent, or Firm—David J. Untener; Larry W. Evans

[57] **CLAIM**

The ornamental design for a service station, as shown and described.

DESCRIPTION

FIG. 1 is a perspective view of a service station showing my new design;
FIG. 2 is a rear elevational view thereof;
FIG. 3 is a front elevational view thereof;
FIG. 4 is a side elevational view thereof, the opposite side being a mirror image of that shown;
FIG. 5 is a top plan view thereof;
FIG. 6 is a bottom plan view thereof;
FIG. 7 is an enlarged perspective view thereof, showing a pump housing element;
FIG. 8 is an enlarged front elevational view thereof, showing a pump housing element;
FIG. 9 is an enlarged side elevational view thereof, showing a pump housing element, the opposite side being a mirror image of that shown;
FIG. 10 is an enlarged horizontal cross-sectional taken along line 10—10 of FIG. 8;
FIG. 11 is an enlarged rear elevational view thereof, showing a pump housing element;
FIG. 12 is an enlarged horizontal cross-sectional view thereof, showing a pump housing element, taken along line 12—12 of FIG. 11;
FIG. 13 is an enlarged perspective view thereof, showing the building element;
FIG. 14 is an enlarged side elevational view thereof, showing the building element;
FIG. 15 is a front elevational view thereof, showing the building element; and
FIG. 16 is an enlarged rear elevational view thereof, showing the building element.
Portions of the service station are omitted from FIGS. 7–16 for clarity of illustration.

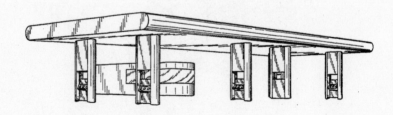

TITLE: KITCHEN SCALE
INVENTOR: RIDO BUSSE
ASSIGNEE: SOEHNLE-WAAGEN

PATENT NUMBER: USD 302,395
PATENT FILED: MARCH 27, 1986
PATENT GRANTED: JULY 25, 1989

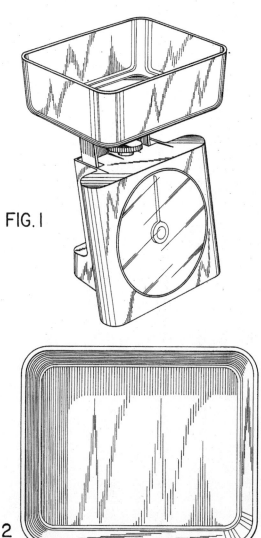

FIG. 1

FIG. 2

TITLE: ADJUSTABLE TABLE LAMP
INVENTOR: MICHELE DE LUCCHI
ASSIGNEE: ARTEMIDE

PATENT NUMBER: USD 302,735
PATENT FILED: JUNE 11, 1987
PATENT GRANTED: AUGUST 8, 1989

United States Patent [19]

De Lucchi

[11] **Patent Number:** **Des. 302,735**

[45] **Date of Patent:** ٭٭* **Aug. 8, 1989**

[54] **ADJUSTABLE TABLE LAMP**

[75] Inventor: **Michele De Lucchi**, Milan, Italy

[73] Assignee: **Artemide S.p.A.,** Milan, Italy

[*] Notice: The portion of the term of this patent subsequent to Aug. 8, 2003 has been disclaimed.

[٭٭] Term: **14 Years**

[21] Appl. No.: **60,584**

[22] Filed: **Jun. 11, 1987**

[30] **Foreign Application Priority Data**

Dec. 19, 1986 [IT] Italy 24153 B/86

[52] **U.S. Cl.** **D26/65**

[58] **Field of Search** D26/60–65; 362/410–414, 269, 270, 275, 287, 418, 419, 427

[56] **References Cited**

U.S. PATENT DOCUMENTS

D. 264,634 5/1982 Okuno D26/65
3,543,019 11/1970 Jacobsen .... 362/413 X
3,694,647 9/1972 Chapman, Jr. et al. 362/411

4,213,172 7/1980 Scottolin et al. 362/413

FOREIGN PATENT DOCUMENTS

117122 7/1946 Sweden 362/427

Primary Examiner—Susan J. Lucas
Attorney, Agent, or Firm—Guido Modiano; Albert Josif

[57] **CLAIM**

The ornamental design for adjustable table lamp, as shown and described.

DESCRIPTION

FIG. 1 is a top, rear, right side perspective view of an adjustable table lamp showing my new design;

FIG. 2 is a right side elevational view thereof on an enlarged scale;

FIG. 3 is a front elevational view thereof on an enlarged scale;

FIG. 4 is a rear elevational view thereof on an enlarged scale;

FIG. 5 is a left side elevational view thereof on an enlarged scale;

FIG. 6 is a top plan view thereof on an enlarged scale;

FIG. 7 is a bottom plan view thereof on an enlarged scale.

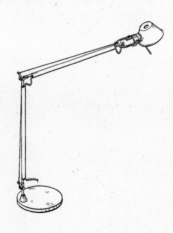

TITLE : TALKING CLOCK
INVENTOR : HIDEKATSU NOMIZU
ASSIGNEE : TWIN BIRD INDUSTRIAL COMPANY

PATENT NUMBER : USD 304,161
PATENT FILED : NOVEMBER 10, 1986
PATENT GRANTED : OCTOBER 24, 1989

United States Patent [19]

Nomizu

[11] **Patent Number: Des. 304,161**

[45] **Date of Patent: ** Oct. 24, 1989**

[54] **TALKING CLOCK**

[75] Inventor: **Hidekatsu Nomizu,** Yoshida, Japan

[73] Assignee: **Twin Bird Industrial Company, Limited,** Niigata, Japan

[**] Term: **14 Years**

[21] Appl. No.: **929,237**

[22] Filed: **Nov. 10, 1986**

[30] **Foreign Application Priority Data**

May 12, 1986 [GB] United Kingdom 1034024
[52] U.S. Cl. **D10/21; D10/2**
[58] Field of Search D10/1–39, D10/122–128; 368/10, 11–12, 63, 75, 211

[56] **References Cited**

U.S. PATENT DOCUMENTS

D. 191,460 10/1961 Ducommun .... D10/21 X

D. 193,521 9/1962 Ducommun .... D10/21 X
D. 250,174 11/1978 Hedgecock .... D10/21 X

OTHER PUBLICATIONS

Gift & Art Buyer–10/55–p. 2–Pyramid Clocks.

Primary Examiner—Nelson C. Holtje
Attorney, Agent, or Firm—Lowe, Price, LeBlanc, Becker & Shur

[57] **CLAIM**

The ornamental design for a talking clock, as shown.

DESCRIPTION

FIG. **1** is a front elevational view of a talking clock showing my new design;
FIG. **2** is a rear elevational view thereof;
FIG. **3** is a right side elevational view thereof, the left side view being a mirror image thereof;
FIG. **4** is a top plan view thereof;
FIG. **5** is a bottom plan view thereof;
FIG. **6** is a top and right-front perspective view thereof.

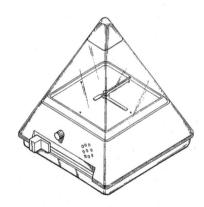

TITLE: RECYCLING CONTAINER
INVENTOR: LOTHAR RUEHLAND
ASSIGNEE: NONE

PATENT NUMBER: USD 304,873
PATENT FILED: NOVEMBER 18, 1987
PATENT GRANTED: NOVEMBER 28, 1989

United States Patent [19]

Ruehland

[11] **Patent Number:** **Des. 304,873**

[45] **Date of Patent:** ** Nov. 28, 1989

[54] **RECYCLING CONTAINER**

[76] Inventor: **Lothar Ruehland,** Grasgarten 34, 3304 Wendeburg/Bortfeld, Fed. Rep. of Germany

[**] Term: **14 Years**

[21] Appl. No.: **122,883**

[22] Filed: **Nov. 18, 1987**

[30] **Foreign Application Priority Data**

May 18, 1987 [DE] Fed. Rep. of Germany .... 36 MR 1394
Oct. 6, 1987 [DE] Fed. Rep. of Germany .... 36 MR 1412
Oct. 6, 1987 [DE] Fed. Rep. of Germany .... 36 MR 1411

[52] **U.S. Cl.** D34/5; D34/1; D34/46

[58] **Field of Search** .... D34/1, 4, 5, 6, 7, 11, D34/46, 40; 220/1 T, 23.4, 23.6, 23.83

[56] **References Cited**

U.S. PATENT DOCUMENTS

2,217,644	10/1940	Conner	220/23.4
2,599,853	6/1952	McClain et al.	220/23.4
2,874,835	2/1959	Poupitch	220/23.4
3,420,367	1/1969	Carmichael	220/23.4
3,759,373	9/1973	Werth et al.	220/23.4

Primary Examiner—Wallace R. Burke
Assistant Examiner—Kay H. Chin
Attorney, Agent, or Firm—Foley & Lardner, Schwartz, Jeffery, Schwaab, Mack, Blumenthal & Evans

[57] **CLAIM**

The ornamental design for a recycling container, as shown and described.

DESCRIPTION

FIG. 1 is a front elevational view of a recycling container showing my new design;
FIG. 2 is a front perspective view thereof;
FIG. 3 is a side elevational view thereof, the opposite side elevational view being a mirror image of that shown;
FIG. 4 is a top plan view thereof;
FIG. 5 is a front elevational view of a second embodiment of the recycling container;
FIG. 6 is a front perspective view of FIG. 5;
FIG. 7 is a side elevational view of FIG. 5, the opposite side elevational view being a mirror image of that shown;
FIG. 8 is a top plan view of FIG. 5;
FIG. 9 is a front elevational view of a third embodiment of the recycling container;
FIG. 10 is a front perspective view of FIG. 9;
FIG. 11 is a side elevational view of FIG. 9, the opposite side elevational view being a mirror image of that shown;
FIG. 12 is a top plan view of FIG. 9;
FIG. 13 is a front elevational view of a fourth embodiment of the recycling container;
FIG. 14 is a front perspective view of FIG. 13;
FIG. 15 is a side elevational view of FIG. 13, the opposite side elevational view being a mirror image of that shown;
FIG. 16 is a top plan view of FIG. 13;
FIG. 17 is a front elevational view of a fifth embodiment of the recycling container;
FIG. 18 is a side elevational view of FIG. 17, the opposite side elevational view being a mirror image of that shown;
FIG. 19 is a top plan view of FIG. 17; and
FIG. 20 is a front perspective view of FIG. 17.

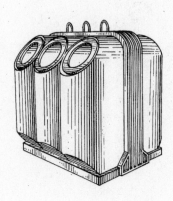

TITLE: VACUUM CLEANER
INVENTOR: JAMES DYSON
ASSIGNEE: IONA APPLIANCES / APPAREILS IONA

PATENT NUMBER: USD 305,269
PATENT FILED: OCTOBER 21, 1987
PATENT GRANTED: DECEMBER 26, 1989

United States Patent [19]

Dyson

[11] **Patent Number: Des. 305,269**

[45] **Date of Patent: ✶✶ Dec. 26, 1989**

[54] **VACUUM CLEANER**

[75] Inventor: **James Dyson**, Bathford, United Kingdom

[73] Assignee: **Iona Appliances Inc./Appareils Iona Inc.**, Welland, Canada

[✶✶] Term: **14 Years**

[21] Appl. No.: **110,957**

[22] Filed: **Oct. 21, 1987**

[30] **Foreign Application Priority Data**

Apr. 21, 1987 [CA] Canada 21-04-87-4
[52] **U.S. Cl.** **D32/22**
[58] **Field of Search** D32/1, 21–22, D32/31–34; 15/320–325, 328–336, 338, 344–345, 346, 350, 353–354, 352

[56] **References Cited**

U.S. PATENT DOCUMENTS

D. 101,322   9/1936   Beitman .
D. 153,974   5/1949   Petersen .
D. 155,903   11/1949   Kelly .

D. 162,633   3/1951   Dreyfuss .
D. 193,264   7/1962   Kelnhofer .
3,755,843   9/1973   Goertzen, III et al. 15/350
4,373,228   2/1983   Dyson 15/350
4,559,665   12/1985   Fitzwater 15/353
4,571,772   2/1986   Dyson 15/335

Primary Examiner—Bruce W. Dunkins
Assistant Examiner—Ruth Takemoto
Attorney, Agent, or Firm—Weldon F. Green

[57] **CLAIM**

The ornamental design for a vacuum cleaner, as shown.

DESCRIPTION

FIG. 1 is a top, front and right side perspective view of a vacuum cleaner showing my new design;
FIG. 2 is a top, rear and left side perspective view thereof;
FIG. 3 is a left side elevational view thereof;
FIG. 4 is a bottom plan view thereof;
FIG. 5 is a top, front and left side perspective view of a second embodiment thereof;
FIG. 6 is a top, rear and right side perspective view thereof;
FIG. 7 is a right side elevational view thereof.

TITLE: MOUSE FOR A COMPUTER
INVENTOR: HARTMUT ESSLINGER
ASSIGNEE: NEXT

PATENT NUMBER: USD 305,331
PATENT FILED: JUNE 30, 1988
PATENT GRANTED: JANUARY 2, 1990

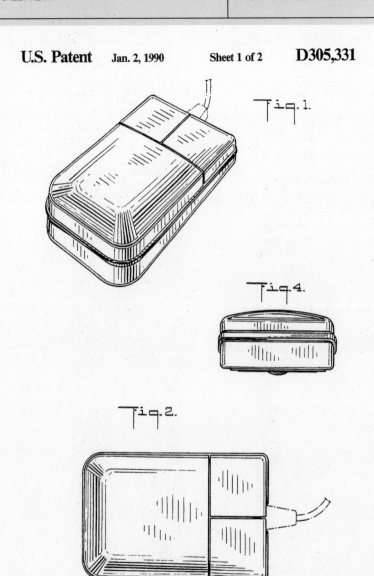

Fig.1.

Fig.4.

Fig.2.

TITLE: HOUSING FOR A PORTABLE HANDSET
TELEPHONE OR SIMILAR ARTICLE
INVENTORS: LEONID SOREN & ALBERT L. NAGELE
ASSIGNEE: MOTOROLA

PATENT NUMBER: USD 305,427
PATENT FILED: OCTOBER 11, 1988
PATENT GRANTED: JANUARY 9, 1990

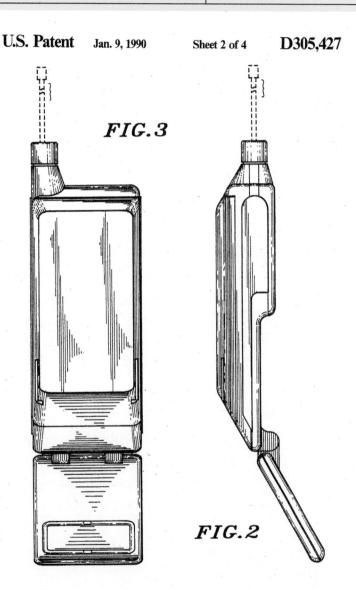

FIG.3

FIG.2

TITLE: COMBINED TAPE RECORDER AND RADIO RECEIVER
INVENTOR: RYOH KASHIWAGI
ASSIGNEE: SONY CORPORATION

PATENT NUMBER: USD 306,588
PATENT FILED: OCTOBER 15, 1987
PATENT GRANTED: MARCH 13, 1990

FIG.1

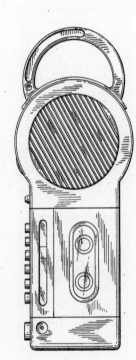

FIG.2

TITLE: JOY STICK CONTROLLER FOR VIDEO GAME
INVENTOR: LANCE N. BARR
ASSIGNEE: NINTENDO OF AMERICA

PATENT NUMBER: USD 307,921
PATENT FILED: OCTOBER 13, 1987
PATENT GRANTED: MAY 15, 1990

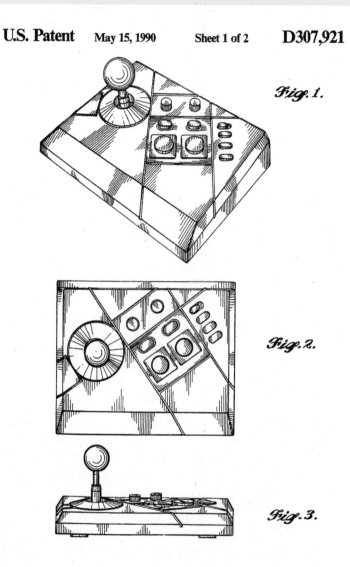

Fig. 1.

Fig. 2.

Fig. 3.

TITLE: CAN OPENER
INVENTOR: FRANZ A. STÖTZER
ASSIGNEE: ROWENTA-WERKE

PATENT NUMBER: USD 308,159
PATENT FILED: MARCH 28, 1988
PATENT GRANTED: MAY 29, 1990

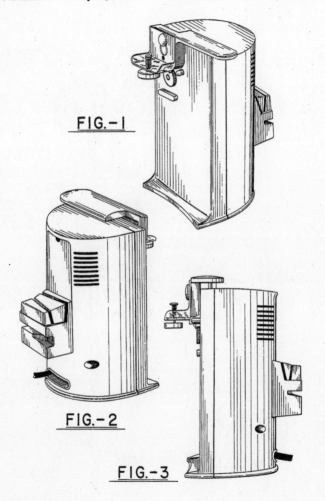

FIG.-1

FIG.-2

FIG.-3

TITLE: TEA KETTLE
INVENTORS: JANE ANCONA & BRUCE ANCONA
ASSIGNEE: M. KAMENSTEIN

PATENT NUMBER: USD 308,314
PATENT FILED: OCTOBER 27, 1988
PATENT GRANTED: JUNE 5, 1990

United States Patent [19]

Ancona et al.

[11] **Patent Number:** **Des. 308,314**

[45] **Date of Patent:** ** **Jun. 5, 1990**

[54] **TEA KETTLE**

[75] Inventors: **Jane Ancona; Bruce Ancona,** both of New York, N.Y.

[73] Assignee: **M. Kamenstein, Inc.,** White Plains, N.Y.

[**] Term: **14 Years**

[21] Appl. No.: **263,342**

[22] Filed: **Oct. 27, 1988**

[52] U.S. Cl. **D7/322;** D7/312

[58] Field of Search D7/321, 322, 312, 300, D7/316–319, 320, 302

[56] **References Cited**

U.S. PATENT DOCUMENTS

D. 95,354	4/1936	Kircher	D7/322
D. 115,928	8/1939	Kircher	D7/322
D. 133,823	9/1942	Schneider	D7/312
D. 157,599	3/1950	John et al.	D7/322
D. 159,307	7/1950	Welden	D7/322
D. 163,725	6/1951	Welden	D7/322
D. 191,005	8/1951	Jepson	D7/322
D. 287,984	1/1987	Thomson et al.	D7/312 X
D. 288,518	3/1987	Lebowitz	D7/322
D. 288,890	3/1987	Lebowitz	D7/322
D. 296,068	6/1988	Yano	D7/322
2,197,141	4/1940	Belden	222/465.1 X
2,670,107	2/1954	Welden	222/471 X
3,130,881	4/1964	Jepson	222/470

OTHER PUBLICATIONS

Design, Jun. 1986, p. 18, "Letting Off Steam", Michael Graves, top right, Stainless Steel Kettle/Bird Shaped Bung, rivets at bottom wall.

HFD, Dec. 28, 1987, p. 51, Zani Tea Kettle, bottom left, hinged spout.

Primary Examiner—Winifred E. Herrmann
Attorney, Agent, or Firm—Henry R. Lerner

[57] **CLAIM**

The ornamental design for a tea kettle, as shown and described.

DESCRIPTION

FIG. 1 is a top, front, and right side perspective view of a tea kettle showing our new design;
FIG. 2 is a top plan view thereof;
FIG. 3 is a left side elevational view thereof, the opposite side being a mirror image;
FIG. 4 is a front elevational view thereof;
FIG. 5 is a rear elevational view thereof; and
FIG. 6 is a bottom plan view thereof.

TITLE: DISPLAY
INVENTOR: ETTORE SOTTSASS
ASSIGNEE: OLIVETTI

PATENT NUMBER: USD 308,362
PATENT FILED: DECEMBER 7, 1987
PATENT GRANTED: JUNE 5, 1990

United States Patent [19]

Sottsass

[11] **Patent Number:** **Des. 308,362**

[45] **Date of Patent:** ** **Jun. 5, 1990**

[54] **DISPLAY**

[75] Inventor: **Ettore Sottsass,** Milan, Italy

[73] Assignee: **Ing. C. Olivetti & C., S.p.A.,** Ivrea,
Italy

[**] Term: **14 Years**

[21] Appl. No.: **129,083**

[22] Filed: **Dec. 7, 1987**

[30] **Foreign Application Priority Data**

Jun. 15, 1987 [IT]   Italy .... 53418/87[U]
[52] **U.S. Cl.** D14/113
[58] **Field of Search** D14/100, 102, 105, 106,
D14/107, 113, 114, 115; 340/700, 706, 711, 712;
341/22, 23; 358/248, 249, 254; 312/7.2, 208;
248/122, 125, 127, 133, 149, 161, 178, 179, 183,
349, 346, 371

[56] **References Cited**

U.S. PATENT DOCUMENTS

D. 276,236   11/1984   Akiyama D14/113

D. 287,013	12/1986	Satherley	D14/106
D. 288,567	3/1987	Moggridge	D14/106
D. 290,704	7/1987	Schaum et al.	D14/113
D. 299,347	1/1989	Landry et al.	D14/113
4,645,153	2/1987	Granzow et al.	248/178

Primary Examiner—Susan J. Lucas
Assistant Examiner—Freda S. Nunn
Attorney, Agent, or Firm—Banner, Birch, McKie &
Beckett

[57] **CLAIM**

The ornamental design for a display, as shown and
described.

DESCRIPTION

FIG. 1 is a front and right side perspective view of a
display showing my new design;
FIG. 2 is a rear and left side perspective view thereof;
FIG. 3 is a left side elevational view thereof;
FIG. 4 is a top plan view thereof;
FIG. 5 is a bottom plan view thereof;
FIG. 6 is a rear elevational view thereof on an enlarged
scale;
FIG. 7 is a right side elevational view thereof.

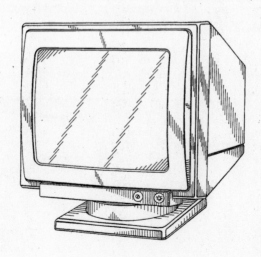

TITLE: KITCHEN SCALE
INVENTOR: RIDO BUSSE
ASSIGNEE: SOEHNLE-WAAGEN

PATENT NUMBER: USD 308,834
PATENT FILED: JANUARY 13, 1987
PATENT GRANTED: JUNE 26, 1990

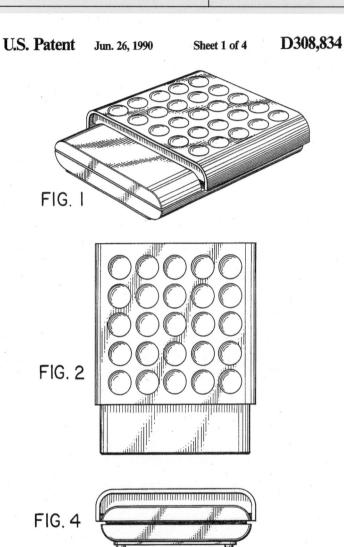

FIG. 1

FIG. 2

FIG. 4

TITLE: SOLAR POWERED LIGHT
INVENTOR: TSENG L. CHIEN
ASSIGNEE: NONE

PATENT NUMBER: USD 309,785
PATENT FILED: DECEMBER 7, 1988
PATENT GRANTED: AUGUST 7, 1990

United States Patent [19]

Chien

[11] **Patent Number: Des. 309,785**

[45] **Date of Patent:** ** **Aug. 7, 1990**

[54] **SOLAR POWERED LIGHT**

[76] Inventor: **Tseng L. Chien,** Suite 8-6, No. 9, San-Min Rd., Taipei, Taiwan

[**] Term: **14 Years**

[21] Appl. No.: **280,993**

[22] Filed: **Dec. 7, 1988**

[52] **U.S. Cl.** **D26/67**

[58] **Field of Search** D26/67–71; 362/431, 183, 432, 362, 267, 410, 147; 136/291

[56] **References Cited**

U.S. PATENT DOCUMENTS

D. 263,340	3/1982	Budnovitch et al.	....	D26/67
3,833,804	9/1974	Vesely	....	362/431 X
4,200,904	4/1980	Doan	....	362/431
4,441,143	4/1984	Richardson, Jr.	....	362/183
4,816,970	3/1989	Garcia, Jr.	....	362/183

OTHER PUBLICATIONS

Home Lighting & Accessories, 3–1985, p. 38, Solar Powered Outdoor Light.

Primary Examiner—Susan J. Lucas
Attorney, Agent, or Firm—Bacon & Thomas

[57] **CLAIM**

The ornamental design for a solar powered light, as shown and described.

DESCRIPTION

FIG. 1 is a top, front perspective view of a solar powered light showing my new design;

FIG. 2 is a front elevation view thereof, the rear being a mirror image;

FIG. 3 is a left side elevational view thereof, the right side being a mirror image;

FIG. 4 is a top plan thereof; and

FIG. 5 is a bottom plan view thereof.

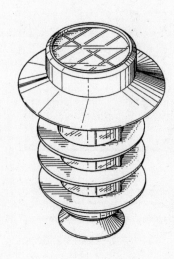

TITLE: CENTRAL PROCESSING UNIT FOR COMPUTER
INVENTOR: HARTMUT ESSLINGER
ASSIGNEE: NEXT

PATENT NUMBER: USD 310,661
PATENT FILED: JUNE 30, 1988
PATENT GRANTED: SEPTEMBER 18, 1990

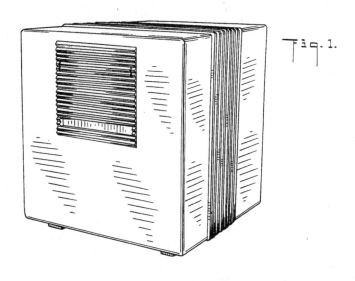

Fig. 1.

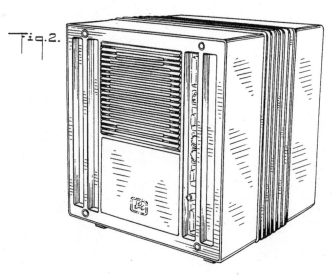

Fig. 2.

TITLE: CLOCK
INVENTOR: RYO MURATA
ASSIGNEE: CASIO COMPUTER COMPANY

PATENT NUMBER: USD 311,141
PATENT FILED: JULY 7, 1987
PATENT GRANTED: OCTOBER 9, 1990

United States Patent [19]

Murata

[11] **Patent Number:** **Des. 311,141**

[45] **Date of Patent:** ** Oct. 9, 1990

[54] **CLOCK**

[75] Inventor: **Ryo Murata**, Tachikawa, Japan

[73] Assignee: **Casio Computer Co., Ltd.**, Tokyo, Japan

[**] Term: **14 Years**

[21] Appl. No.: **70,516**

[22] Filed: **Jul. 7, 1987**
[52] **U.S. Cl.** **D10/15**; D10/21
[58] **Field of Search** D10/1–39, D10/122–132; 368/82–84, 10–11, 63, 239–242, 276–277, 285

[56] **References Cited**

U.S. PATENT DOCUMENTS

D. 234,578	3/1975	Powers	D10/15
D. 245,765	9/1977	Yoshida	D10/15
D. 246,351	11/1977	Yoshida	D10/15
D. 263,124	2/1982	Dennis	D10/15
D. 264,944	6/1982	Palmer	D10/15
D. 267,319	12/1982	Van DeVen	D10/15
D. 304,018	10/1989	Nomizu	D10/26

Primary Examiner—Nelson C. Holtje
Attorney, Agent, or Firm—Frishauf, Holtz, Goodman & Woodward

[57] **CLAIM**

The ornamental design for a clock, as shown and described.

DESCRIPTION

FIG. 1 is a front elevational view of a clock showing my new design;
FIG. 2 is a top plan view thereof;
FIG. 3 is a right side elevational view thereof;
FIG. 4 is a left side elevational view thereof;
FIG. 5 is a bottom plan view thereof;
FIG. 6 is a rear elevational view thereof; and
FIG. 7 is a perspective view thereof.

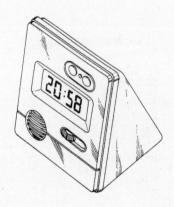

TITLE: TELEPHONE
INVENTORS: MICHAEL GRAVES & ALEXANDER T. F. LEE
ASSIGNEE: MICHAEL GRAVES

PATENT NUMBER: USD 320,206
PATENT FILED: JULY 27, 1990
PATENT GRANTED: SEPTEMBER 24, 1991

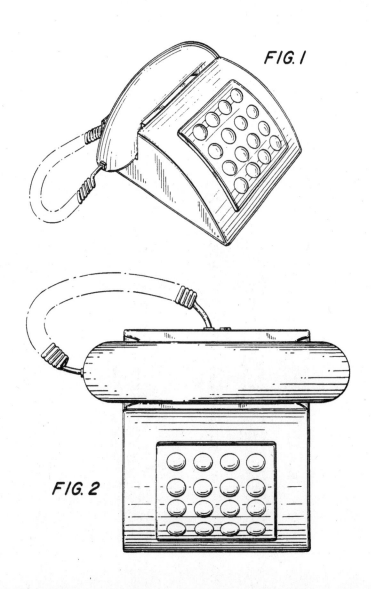

FIG. 1

FIG. 2

TITLE: COMBINED TAPE PLAYER AND RADIO TUNER   PATENT NUMBER: USD 320,208
INVENTORS: ETSURO IKEYAMA & MASAYOSHI TSUCHIYA   PATENT FILED: AUGUST 23, 1989
ASSIGNEE: SONY CORPORATION   PATENT GRANTED: SEPTEMBER 24, 1991

United States Patent [19]

Ikeyama et al.

[11] **Patent Number:** **Des. 320,208**

[45] **Date of Patent:** **** Sep. 24, 1991**

[54] **COMBINED TAPE PLAYER AND RADIO TUNER**

[75] Inventors: **Etsuro Ikeyama; Masayoshi Tsuchiya,** both of Tokyo, Japan

[73] Assignee: **Sony Corporation,** Tokyo, Japan

[**] Term: **14 Years**

[21] Appl. No.: **397,311**

[22] Filed: **Aug. 23, 1989**

[30]   **Foreign Application Priority Data**

Feb. 23, 1989 [JP] Japan 1-6826

[52] **U.S. Cl.** **D14/163; D14/165**
[58] **Field of Search** D14/160–165, D14/167–168, 188, 192, 196; 455/344, 350, 351

[56]   **References Cited**

U.S. PATENT DOCUMENTS

D. 281,877 12/1985 Kurata et al. D14/165
D. 312,638 12/1990 Hino et al. .... D14/161 X

OTHER PUBLICATIONS

Design 470; Feb. 1988; p. 33; top left—Sony Solar--Powered Walkman.
Ski Magazine; 11/88; p. 62; Top right—Sony Walkman.
International Design; Sep./Oct. 1985; p. 63; left center—Sony Sports Walkman.

Primary Examiner—Theodore M. Shooman
Attorney, Agent, or Firm—Lewis H. Eslinger; Jay H. Maioli

[57]   **CLAIM**

The ornamental design for a combined tape player and radio tuner, as shown.

DESCRIPTION

FIG. 1 is a top, front and left-side perspective view of a combined tape player and radio tuner showing our new design;
FIG. 2 is a front elevational view thereof;
FIG. 3 is a rear elevational view thereof;
FIG. 4 is a left-side elevational view thereof;
FIG. 5 is a right-side elevational view thereof;
FIG. 6 is a top plan view thereof; and
FIG. 7 is a bottom plan view thereof.

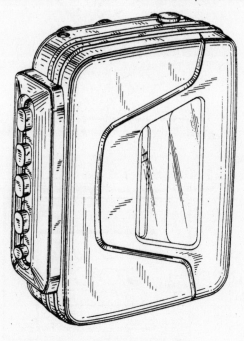

TITLE: PACKAGE FOR A DISPOSABLE CAMERA
INVENTOR: TAKUYA ARAI
ASSIGNEE: FUJI PHOTO FILM COMPANY

PATENT NUMBER: USD 320,937
PATENT FILED: APRIL 6, 1990
PATENT GRANTED: OCTOBER 22, 1991

FIG. 1

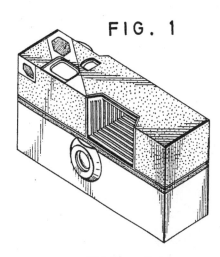

FIG. 2

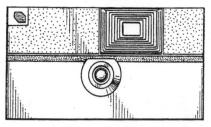

FIG. 3

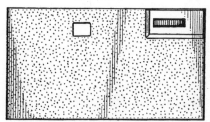

TITLE: TELEPHONE ANSWERING MACHINE
INVENTORS: DANIEL K. HARDEN & JOHN B. HAVENER
ASSIGNEE: AT&T BELL LABORATORIES

PATENT NUMBER: USD 321,348
PATENT FILED: SEPTEMBER 14, 1990
PATENT GRANTED: NOVEMBER 5, 1991

Fig. 1

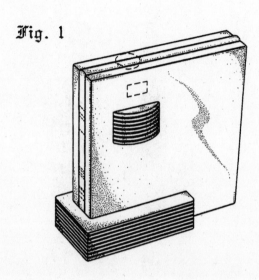

Fig. 2

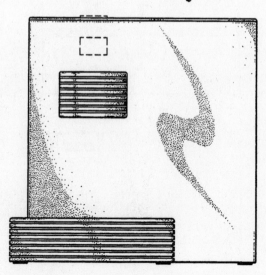

TITLE: HAND-HELD MIXER
INVENTOR: LUDWIG LITTMANN
ASSIGNEE: BRAUN

PATENT NUMBER: USD 321,811
PATENT FILED: OCTOBER 26, 1988
PATENT GRANTED: NOVEMBER 26, 1991

FIG.6

FIG.5

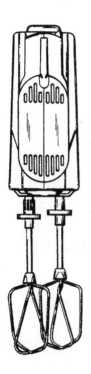

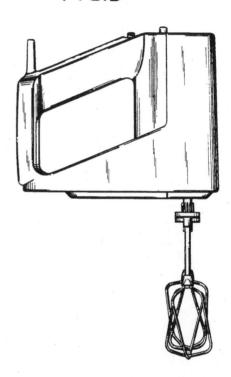

FIG.7

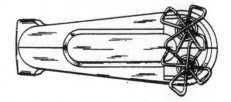

TITLE: GAME BALL CATCHER AND HOLDER
INVENTORS: MARK A. DANESE & MICHAEL E. LAUDE
ASSIGNEE: RALPH LIQUORI

PATENT NUMBER: USD 322,645
PATENT FILED: MAY 3, 1989
PATENT GRANTED: DECEMBER 24, 1991

U.S. Patent   Dec. 24, 1991   **Des. 322,645**

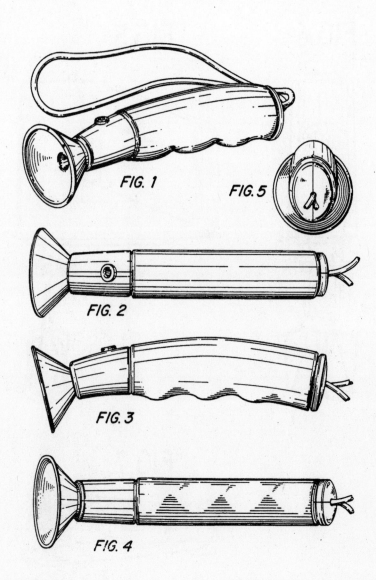

FIG. 1

FIG. 5

FIG. 2

FIG. 3

FIG. 4

TITLE: COMBINED KETTLE AND SIDE TABLES
FOR A BARBECUE GRILL
INVENTORS: JAMES R. PARENT, ET AL.
ASSIGNEE: CLOROX COMPANY

PATENT NUMBER: USD 325,316
PATENT FILED: FEBRUARY 7, 1989
PATENT GRANTED: APRIL 14, 1992

FIGURE 3

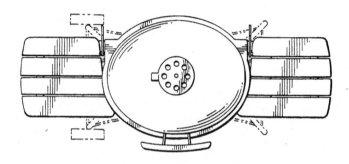

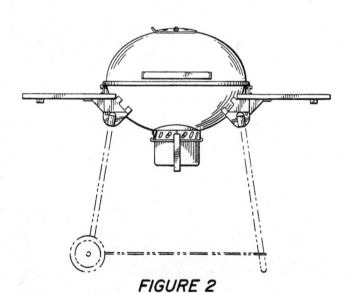

FIGURE 2

TITLE: DISPLAY PAGER
INVENTORS: MAKOTO TAKAHASHI & TOSHIAKI MIZUSHIMA
ASSIGNEE: NEC CORPORATION

PATENT NUMBER: USD 325,913
PATENT FILED: DECEMBER 11, 1990
PATENT GRANTED: MAY 5, 1992

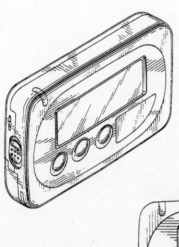

FIG.1

FIG.2

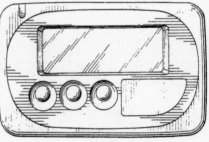

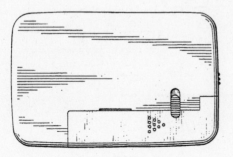

FIG.3

TITLE: TRACKBALL FOR COMPUTER
INVENTORS: STUART ASHMUN, CHARLIE GARTHWAITE,
BRIDGET CAMERON, ALLAN H. STEPHAN, ET AL.
ASSIGNEE: MICROSOFT CORPORATION

PATENT NUMBER: USD 326,261
PATENT FILED: MARCH 8, 1991
PATENT GRANTED: MAY 19, 1992

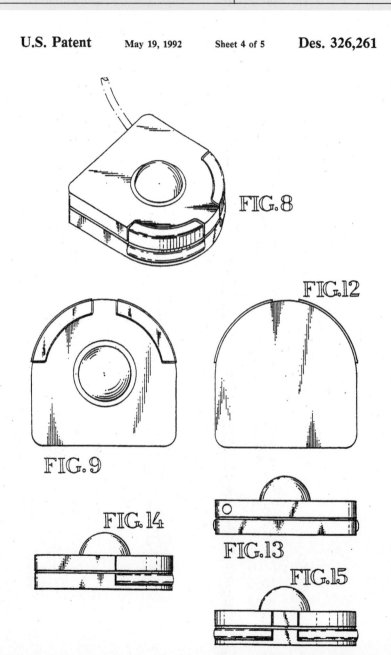

FIG.8

FIG.12

FIG.9

FIG.14

FIG.13

FIG.15

TITLE: ARMCHAIR
INVENTOR: RAYMOND GROSFILLEX
ASSIGNEE: GROSFILLEX

PATENT NUMBER: USD 329,339
PATENT FILED: SEPTEMBER 18, 1989
PATENT GRANTED: SEPTEMBER 15, 1992

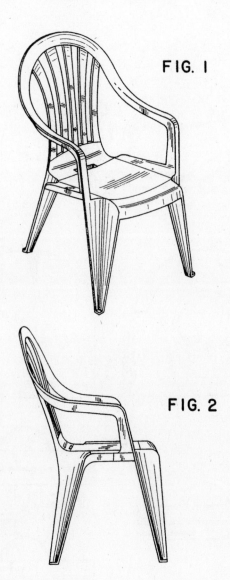

FIG. 1

FIG. 2

TITLE: MUSIC SYSTEM
INVENTOR: DAVID LEWIS
ASSIGNEE: BANG & OLUFSEN

PATENT NUMBER: USD 331,238
PATENT FILED: AUGUST 22, 1990
PATENT GRANTED: NOVEMBER 24, 1992

United States Patent [19]

Lewis

[11] **Patent Number:** **Des. 331,238**

[45] **Date of Patent:** ** Nov. 24, 1992

[54] **MUSIC SYSTEM**

[75] Inventor: **David Lewis**, Copenhagen K, Denmark

[73] Assignee: **Bang & Olufsen A/S**, Struer, Denmark

[**] Term: **14 Years**

[21] Appl. No.: **572,091**

[22] Filed: **Aug. 22, 1990**

[30]   **Foreign Application Priority Data**

Feb. 23, 1990 [DK]   Denmark .... MA 0214 1990
[52] **U.S. Cl.** **D14/168**
[58] **Field of Search** D14/154, 160–172,
D14/188–198, 257, 259, 265, 299, 214; 455/344,
347, 350, 351; 312/7.1

[56]   **References Cited**

U.S. PATENT DOCUMENTS

D. 302,275   7/1989   Jachmann et al. .... D14/160 X

D. 304,943	12/1989	Saunders	D14/162
D. 306,024	2/1990	Eberbach	D14/214
D. 313,598	1/1991	Mori	D14/163

OTHER PUBLICATIONS

HFD, Jan. 5, 1987, p. 88, Bottom left—Home Audio unit.

Primary Examiner—Theodore M. Shooman
Attorney, Agent, or Firm—Darby & Darby

[57]   **CLAIM**

The ornamental design for a music system, as shown and described.

DESCRIPTION

FIG. 1 is a front and right side perspective view of a music system showing my new design;
FIG. 2 is a front perspective view thereof;
FIG. 3 is a rear perspective view thereof;
FIG. 4 is a top perspective view thereof;
FIG. 5 is a bottom perspective view thereof; and,
FIG. 6 is a left side elevational view thereof, the right side being a mirror image.

TITLE: TABLE
INVENTOR: WARD BENNETT
ASSIGNEE: NONE

PATENT NUMBER: USD 331,512
PATENT FILED: SEPTEMBER 5, 1990
PATENT GRANTED: DECEMBER 8, 1992

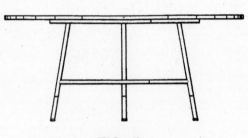

FIG. 6

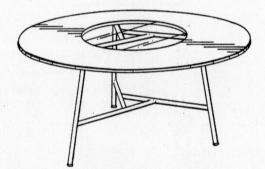

FIG. 7

FIG. 8

TITLE: VEGETABLE PEELER
INVENTOR: TUCKER VIEMEISTER
ASSIGNEE: SMART DESIGN

PATENT NUMBER: USD 332,034
PATENT FILED: JANUARY 22, 1991
PATENT GRANTED: DECEMBER 29, 1992

U.S. Patent   Dec. 29, 1992   Sheet 1 of 2   **Des. 332,034**

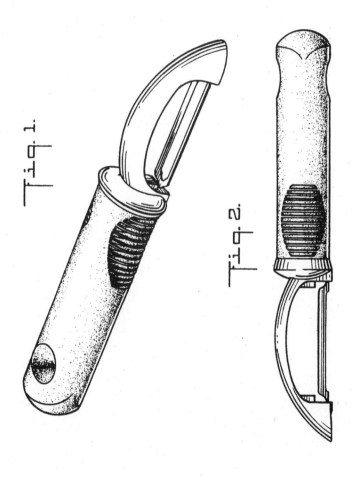

Fig. 1.

Fig. 2.

TITLE: COMBINED DIGITAL CLOCK & SPRING CLIP
INVENTOR: JUNJI HIROMORI
ASSIGNEE: HIROMORI

PATENT NUMBER: USD 333,099
PATENT FILED: OCTOBER 22, 1991
PATENT GRANTED: FEBRUARY 9, 1993

United States Patent [19]

Hiromori

[11] **Patent Number:** **Des. 333,099**

[45] **Date of Patent:** ** **Feb. 9, 1993**

[54] **COMBINED DIGITAL CLOCK AND SPRING CLIP**

[75] Inventor: **Junji Hiromori**, Tokyo, Japan

[73] Assignee: **Hiromori Inc.**, Tokyo, Japan

[**] Term: **14 Years**

[21] Appl. No.: **781,936**

[22] Filed: **Oct. 22, 1991**

[30] **Foreign Application Priority Data**

Jul. 10, 1991 [JP] Japan 20625/1991

[52] **U.S. Cl.** **D10/2**; D10/15;
D10/31; D19/65; D19/96

[58] **Field of Search** D10/2, 15; D19/35, 34,
D19/36, 65, 75, 86, 90, 91, 98, 99, 100; D8/395;
D32/61–63; 24/67 R, 67.1–67.11, 67 P, 511;
368/10

[56] **References Cited**

U.S. PATENT DOCUMENTS

D. 215,223	9/1969	Goldfarb	D21/51
D. 240,270	6/1976	Kawano	D10/15 X
D. 276,313	11/1984	Matthias	D10/15
D. 276,703	12/1984	Au	D10/15 X
D. 292,677	11/1987	Jordi	D19/65 X
D. 295,501	5/1988	Brayford	D10/15 X
D. 312,408	11/1990	Isobe	D10/15
D. 312,657	12/1990	Saffrau	D19/34
D. 313,758	1/1991	Klose	D10/15 X
D. 323,469	1/1992	Saito	D10/15 X

OTHER PUBLICATIONS

Hong Kong Enterprise, Nov. 1987, p. 129 see circled clip right center.

Primary Examiner—Nelson C. Hotje
Assistant Examiner—Martha Thompson
Attorney, Agent, or Firm—Dilworth & Barrese

[57] **CLAIM**

The ornamental design for a combined digital clock and spring clip, as shown and described.

DESCRIPTION

FIG. 1 is a top, right front perspective view of a combined digital clock and spring clip showing my new design;

FIG. 2 is a front elevational view;

FIG. 3 is a rear elevational view;

FIG. 4 is a right side elevational view, the left side being a mirror image thereof;

FIG. 5 is a top plan view;

FIG. 6 is a bottom plan view; and,

FIG. 7 is a cross-sectional view thereof, with the clock mechanism removed for convenience of illustration.

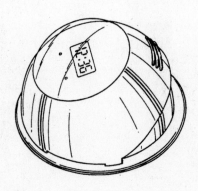

TITLE: MOTORCYCLE
INVENTOR: WILLIAM G. DAVIDSON
ASSIGNEE: HARLEY-DAVIDSON

PATENT NUMBER: USD 333,806
PATENT FILED: MAY 31, 1990
PATENT GRANTED: MARCH 9, 1993

Fig. 2

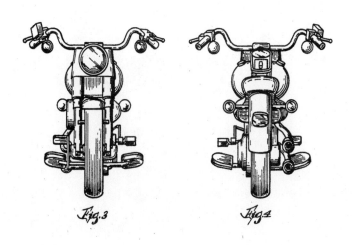

Fig. 3   *Fig. 4*

TITLE: CHAIR
INVENTOR: FRANK O. GEHRY
ASSIGNEE: WESTINGHOUSE ELECTRIC CORPORATION

PATENT NUMBER: USD 334,098
PATENT FILED: SEPTEMBER 24, 1990
PATENT GRANTED: MARCH 23, 1993

United States Patent [19]

Gehry

[11] **Patent Number:** **Des. 334,098**

[45] **Date of Patent:** ** Mar. 23, 1993

[54] **CHAIR**

[75] Inventor: **Frank O. Gehry**, Santa Monica, Calif.

[73] Assignee: **Westinghouse Electric Corp.,**
Pittsburgh, Pa.

[**] Term: **14 Years**

[21] Appl. No.: **587,367**

[22] Filed: **Sep. 24, 1990**

[52] U.S. Cl. **D6/369; D6/373**

[58] Field of Search D6/334, 369, 370, 371,
D6/372, 373, 374, 375, 376, 379, 500, 501, 502;
297/445, 446, 447, 452, 453, 457

[56] **References Cited**

U.S. PATENT DOCUMENTS

D. 12,144	2/1881	Bent .	
D. 151,967	12/1948	Cunningham .	
D. 172,858	8/1954	Yellen	D6/375
D. 238,233	12/1975	Welton	D6/375
D. 249,836	10/1978	Olko .	
D. 266,545	10/1982	Caldwell .	
D. 296,628	7/1988	Glass .	
D. 316,338	4/1991	Frinier	D6/369 X
3,743,353	7/1973	Lupinsky	297/445

3,834,759	9/1974	Panton	297/445
3,950,028	4/1976	Schnepel	297/445
4,210,182	7/1980	Danko	297/446 X
5,040,847	8/1991	Nguyen	297/445 X

OTHER PUBLICATIONS

Identikit Chair Book by Abitare, May, 1985, pp. 90–91, Chair by Aalto at right.

Primary Examiner—Alan P. Douglas
Assistant Examiner—Gary D. Watson
Attorney, Agent, or Firm—B. R. Studebaker

[57] **CLAIM**

The ornamental design for a chair, as shown and described.

DESCRIPTION

FIG. 1 is a right-front perspective view of a chair showing my new design;
FIG. 2 is a front elevational view;
FIG. 3 is a left side elevational view;
FIG. 4 is a top plan view;
FIG. 5 is as bottom plan view; and,
FIG. 6 is a rear elevational view thereof.
The right side of the chair (not shown) is a mirror image of the view of FIG. 3.

TITLE: COMBINED WATER FILTER & CONTAINER
INVENTOR: HANS T. RAUNKJAER
ASSIGNEE: BRITA WASSER-FILTER SYSTEME

PATENT NUMBER: USD 336,760
PATENT FILED: SEPTEMBER 24, 1990
PATENT GRANTED: JUNE 22, 1993

United States Patent [19]

Raunkjaer

[11] **Patent Number: Des. 336,760**

[45] **Date of Patent:** ** **Jun. 22, 1993**

[54] **COMBINED WATER FILTER AND CONTAINER**

[75] Inventor: **Hans T. Raunkjaer,** Mailand, Italy

[73] Assignee: **Brita Wasser-Filter Systeme GmbH,** Fed. Rep. of Germany

[**] Term: **14 Years**

[21] Appl. No.: **587,360**

[22] Filed: **Sep. 24, 1990**

[30]   **Foreign Application Priority Data**

Mar. 24, 1990 [DE] Fed. Rep. of Germany 9002146
[52] **U.S. Cl.** **D23/209;** D7/317
[58] **Field of Search** D23/207-10;
210/97, 198.1, 205-206, 231, 244-246,
257.1-257.2, 258, 260-261, 275, 282, 287-290,
295, 321.6, 321.78, 348, 416.3, 443-449;
D6/300, 316-319, 543

[56]   **References Cited**

U.S. PATENT DOCUMENTS

D. 252,604 8/1979 Harris D7/317
D. 255,531 6/1980 Daenen et al. .... D7/312 X
D. 287,325 12/1986 Schmidt .... D7/318 X
D. 295,888 5/1988 Schulein et al. D23/207
D. 319,368 8/1991 Picozza et al. D7/317
D. 325,146 4/1992 Pedersen .... D7/319 X
3,631,793 1/1972 Bednartz .... 210/348 X
4,776,956 10/1988 Gannaway 210/282
4,969,996 11/1990 Hankammer 210/282

Primary Examiner—Wallace R. Burke
Assistant Examiner—M. H. Tung
Attorney, Agent, or Firm—Austin R. Miller

[57]   **CLAIM**

The ornamental design for a combined water filter and container, as shown and described.

DESCRIPTION

FIG. 1 is a side elevational view of a combined water filter and container, the other side being a mirror image;
FIG. 2 is a front elevational view of a combined water filter and container;
FIG. 3 is a rear elevational view of a combined water filter and container;
FIG. 4 is a top plan view of a combined water filter and container; and,
FIG. 5 is a bottom plan view of the combined water filter and container.

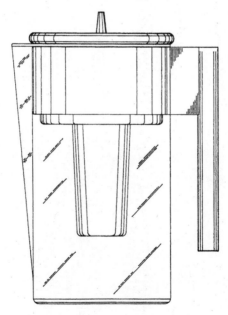

TITLE: DISPOSABLE LAWN CHAIR
INVENTOR: JAKE M. WILLIAMS
ASSIGNEE: NONE

PATENT NUMBER: USD 337,000
PATENT FILED: JUNE 24, 1991
PATENT GRANTED: JULY 6, 1993

United States Patent [19]

Williams

[11] **Patent Number:** **Des. 337,000**

[45] **Date of Patent:** ∗∗ **Jul. 6, 1993**

[54] **DISPOSABLE LAWN CHAIR**

[76] Inventor: **Jake M. Williams,** 4267 Knob's End Ct., Ellicott City, Md. 21043

[∗∗] Term: **14 Years**

[21] Appl. No.: **719,597**

[22] Filed: **Jun. 24, 1991**

[52] U.S. Cl. **D6/368**

[58] **Field of Search** D6/334, 335, 336, 361, D6/368, 374, 375, 500, 501, 502; 297/183, 377, 440, 442

[56] **References Cited**

U.S. PATENT DOCUMENTS

D. 164,619	9/1951	Bargen	D6/375
D. 181,827	12/1957	White	D6/374
D. 219,377	12/1970	Peery	D6/335
D. 244,336	5/1977	Stein	D6/368
D. 248,345	7/1978	Stoddard	D6/368 X
272,273	2/1883	Leavitt, Jr.	297/377
D. 278,004	3/1985	Sigona	D6/361
D. 286,708	11/1986	Heinson	D6/361
D. 299,988	2/1989	Parabita	D6/368
1,842,424	1/1932	Ponten et al.	297/377
2,570,571	10/1951	Leeman	297/377
3,312,503	4/1967	Suzuki	D6/368 X
3,519,307	7/1970	Gittings	297/183 X
3,556,593	1/1971	Speegle	D6/368 X
3,817,574	6/1974	McNab	D6/335 X
4,194,601	3/1980	Yellin	297/377 X
4,556,253	12/1985	Geneve et al.	D6/368 X
4,869,553	9/1989	Powell	297/377
4,926,512	5/1990	Coyle	297/377 X
5,020,854	6/1991	Powell	297/377

Primary Examiner—Alan P. Douglas
Assistant Examiner—Gary D. Watson

[57] **CLAIM**

The ornamental design for a disposable lawn chair, as shown and described.

DESCRIPTION

FIG. **1** is a perspective view of the front;
FIG. **2** is a perspective view of the rear; and,
FIG. **3** is a perspective view of the front with the seat folded up for carrying.

TITLE: FLASHLIGHT
INVENTOR: ANTHONY MAGLICA
ASSIGNEE: MAG INSTRUMENT

PATENT NUMBER: USD 342,333
PATENT FILED: FEBRUARY 11, 1992
PATENT GRANTED: DECEMBER 14, 1993

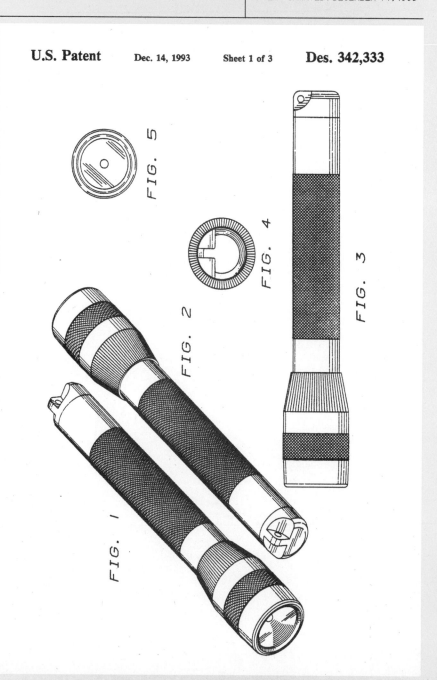

FIG. 5

FIG. 4

FIG. 3

FIG. 2

FIG. 1

TITLE: COMPUTER MOUSE
INVENTORS: DANIEL HARDEN & TINO MELZER
ASSIGNEE: LOGITECH

PATENT NUMBER: USD 343,392
PATENT FILED: SEPTEMBER 24, 1991
PATENT GRANTED: JANUARY 18, 1994

United States Patent [19]

Harden et al.

[11] **Patent Number:** **Des. 343,392**

[45] **Date of Patent:** ** **Jan. 18, 1994**

[54] **COMPUTER MOUSE**

[75] Inventors: **Daniel Harden**, Palo Alto; **Tino Melzer**, San Francisco, both of Calif.

[73] Assignee: **Logitech Inc.**, Fremont, Calif.

[**] Term: **14 Years**

[21] Appl. No.: **764,483**

[22] Filed: **Sep. 24, 1991**

[52] **U.S. Cl.** **D14/114**

[58] **Field of Search** .... 178/18–19; 200/5 R, 5 A, 6 R, 6 A; 213/148 B; 273/148 B; 340/707, 709–710; 74/471 XY; D14/100, 114; D13/158; D21/48, 148, 188; D11/48–49, 82, 158, 134

[56] **References Cited**

U.S. PATENT DOCUMENTS

D. 278,646	4/1985	McCoy	D21/188
D. 287,985	1/1987	Lin	D21/188 X
D. 301,905	6/1989	Havelock	D21/188
D. 305,649	1/1990	Lin	D14/114
D. 308,967	7/1990	Roth	D14/114
5,157,381	10/1992	Cheng	D14/114 X

Primary Examiner—Wallace R. Burke
Assistant Examiner—M. H. Tung
Attorney, Agent, or Firm—James E. Eakin; Janet Kaiser Castaneda

[57] **CLAIM**

The ornamental design for a computer mouse, as shown.

DESCRIPTION

FIG. 1 is a front and right side perspective view in elevation of a computer mouse showing the new design of the present invention;
FIG. 2 is a top plan view thereof;
FIG. 3 is a front elevational view thereof;
FIG. 4 is a rear elevational view thereof;
FIG. 5 is a bottom plan view thereof;
FIG. 6 is a left side elevational view thereof; and,
FIG. 7 is a right side elevational view thereof.

TITLE: PHYSICAL EXERCISER
INVENTORS: ANNE-MARIE BENNSTROM, LESLIE G.
SINCLAIR, GEORGE REYNOLDS & STEPHAN A. SCHWARTZ
ASSIGNEE: V-PARTNERS

PATENT NUMBER: USD 343,882
PATENT FILED: DECEMBER 30, 1991
PATENT GRANTED: FEBRUARY 1, 1994

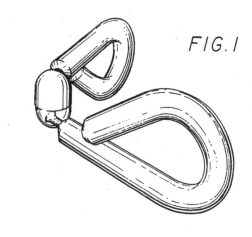

FIG. 1

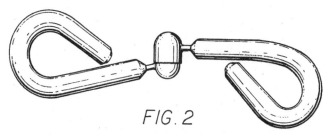

FIG. 2

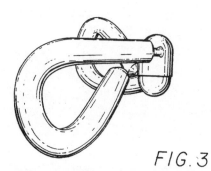

FIG. 3

TITLE: IN-LINE ROLLER-SKATE
INVENTOR: GIUSEPPE CAVASIN
ASSIGNEE: ROCES

PATENT NUMBER: USD 345,405
PATENT FILED: FEBRUARY 20, 1992
PATENT GRANTED: MARCH 22, 1994

FIG.1

FIG.2

TITLE: FACSIMILE MACHINE
INVENTOR: GEORGE SOWDEN
ASSIGNEE: OLIVETTI

PATENT NUMBER: USD 346,163
PATENT FILED: SEPTEMBER 10, 1992
PATENT GRANTED: APRIL 19, 1994

United States Patent [19]

Sowden

[11] **Patent Number:** **Des. 346,163**

[45] **Date of Patent:** ** Apr. 19, 1994

[54] **FACSIMILE MACHINE**

[75] Inventor: **George Sowden**, Milan, Italy

[73] Assignee: **Ing. C. Olivetti & C., S.p.A.,** Ivrea, Italy

[**] Term: **14 Years**

[21] Appl. No.: **941,643**

[22] Filed: **Sep. 10, 1992**

[30] **Foreign Application Priority Data**

Mar. 31, 1992 [IT] Italy T0920 00 0060
[52] **U.S. Cl.** **D14/118**
[58] **Field of Search** 358/400–404; D14/116, 118, 124, 299

[56] **References Cited**

U.S. PATENT DOCUMENTS

D. 304,187 10/1989 Komatsu D14/118

D. 315,341 3/1991 Komatsu D14/118
D. 315,555 3/1991 Komatsu D14/118
D. 316,712 5/1991 Tsukada D14/118

OTHER PUBLICATIONS

The Office, Jul. 1988, p. 125, Left–NEC Nefax 3EX facsimile.

Primary Examiner—Theodore M. Shooman
Attorney, Agent, or Firm—Banner, Birch, McKie & Beckett

[57] **CLAIM**

The ornamental design for a facsimile machine, as shown and described.

DESCRIPTION

FIG. **1** is a top and left perspective view of a facsimile machine showing my new design;
FIG. **2** is a right side elevational view thereof;
FIG. **3** is a rear elevational view thereof; and,
FIG. **4** is a bottom plan view thereof.

TITLE: CHAIR
INVENTORS: WILLIAM E. STUMPF, RODNEY C.
SCHOENFELDER, DONALD CHADWICK & CAROLYN KELLER
ASSIGNEE: HERMAN MILLER

PATENT NUMBER: USD 346,279
PATENT FILED: JUNE 15, 1992
PATENT GRANTED: APRIL 26, 1994

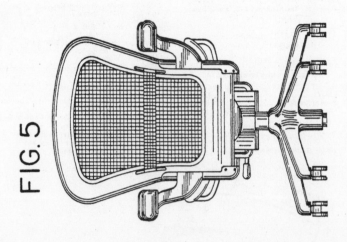

FIG. 5

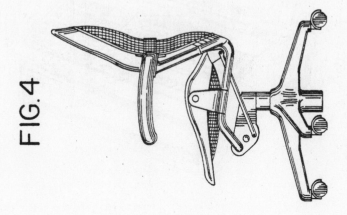

FIG. 4

TITLE: PERSONAL COMPUTER
INVENTORS: YOSHIYUKI MANABE, TOMOYUKI TAKAHASHI
& RICHARD F. SAPPER
ASSIGNEE: INTERNATIONAL BUSINESS MACHINES

PATENT NUMBER: USD 348,049
PATENT FILED: MARCH 27, 1992
PATENT GRANTED: JUNE 21, 1994

United States Patent [19]

Manabe et al.

[11] **Patent Number:** Des. 348,049

[45] **Date of Patent:** ** Jun. 21, 1994

[54] **PERSONAL COMPUTER**

[75] Inventors: **Yoshiyuki Manabe**, Ebina; **Tomoyuki Takahashi**, Fujisawa, both of Japan; **Richard F. Sapper**, Milan, Italy

[73] Assignee: **Internal Business Machines Corporation**, Armonk, N.Y.

[**] Term: **14 Years**

[21] Appl. No.: **859,540**

[22] Filed: **Mar. 27, 1992**

[30] **Foreign Application Priority Data**

Sep. 30, 1991 [JP]   Japan 3-29081

[52] **U.S. Cl.** **D14/100**
[58] **Field of Search** .... 235/145 A, 145 R;
340/700, 706; 341/22, 23; 361/390, 394;
364/708, 709.04; D14/100, 101, 106, 113, 115;
D18/1, 7, 11, 12

[56] **References Cited**

U.S. PATENT DOCUMENTS

D. 290,363 6/1987 Conway et al. D14/113
D. 292,213 10/1987 Nezu et al. D14/113

Primary Examiner—Wallace R. Burke
Assistant Examiner—Freda S. Nunn
Attorney, Agent, or Firm—Bernard D. Bogdon

[57] **CLAIM**

The ornamental design for a personal computer, as shown and described.

DESCRIPTION

FIG. 1 is a perspective view of the personal computer with the front cover closed, showing our new design;
FIG. 2 is a perspective view thereof with the front cover opened;
FIG. 3 is a front elevational view thereof;
FIG. 4 is a rear elevational view thereof;
FIG. 5 is a top plan view thereof;
FIG. 6 is a bottom plan view thereof;
FIG. 7 is a right side elevational view thereof; and,
FIG. 8 is a left side elevational view thereof.

TITLE: PORTABLE ELECTRONIC KEYBOARD
MUSICAL INSTRUMENT
INVENTOR: PRINCE R. NELSON
ASSIGNEE: PAISLEY PARK ENTERPRISES

PATENT NUMBER: USD 349,127
PATENT FILED: JANUARY 16, 1992
PATENT GRANTED: JULY 26, 1994

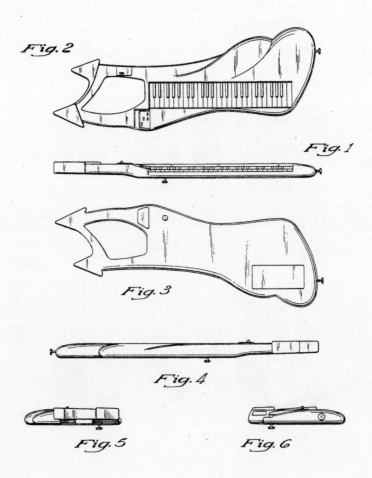

Fig. 2

Fig. 1

Fig. 3

Fig. 4

Fig. 5

Fig. 6

TITLE: COMPUTER MOUSE
INVENTOR: STEVEN T. KANEKO
ASSIGNEE: MICROSOFT CORPORATION

PATENT NUMBER: USD 349,280
PATENT FILED: OCTOBER 6, 1992
PATENT GRANTED: AUGUST 2, 1994

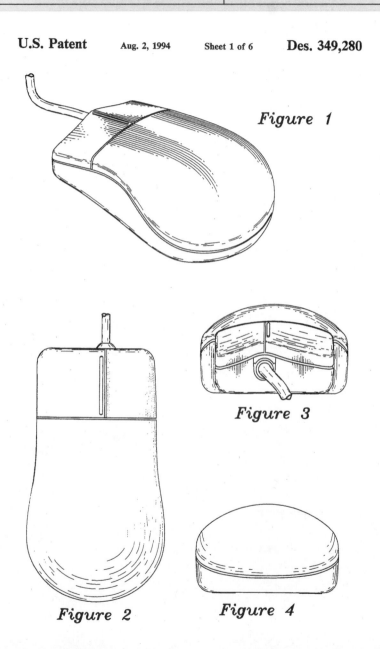

U.S. Patent   Aug. 2, 1994   Sheet 1 of 6   **Des. 349,280**

Figure 1

Figure 3

Figure 2

Figure 4

TITLE: ELECTRIC IRON
INVENTOR: ALVARO CORREA
ASSIGNEE: BLACK & DECKER

PATENT NUMBER: USD 349,986
PATENT FILED: APRIL 10, 1992
PATENT GRANTED: AUGUST 23, 1994

United States Patent [19]

Correa

[11] **Patent Number: Des. 349,986**

[45] **Date of Patent: ** Aug. 23, 1994**

[54] **ELECTRIC IRON**

[75] Inventor: **Alvaro Correa**, Cheshire, Conn.

[73] Assignee: **Black & Decker Inc.**, Newark, Del.

[**] Term: **14 Years**

[21] Appl. No.: **866,914**

[22] Filed: **Apr. 10, 1992**

[52] U.S. Cl. **D32/70**

[58] Field of Search 38/74, 77.1, 77.4, 77.8, 38/77.83, 77.9, 82, 85, 90–93; 219/245, 248, 258; D32/17, 68–72

[56] **References Cited**

U.S. PATENT DOCUMENTS

D. 286,216	10/1986	Pataki	D32/70
D. 291,617	8/1987	Stutzer	D32/70
D. 326,547	5/1992	Osit	D32/70
D. 326,940	6/1992	Barrault	D32/70

2,786,286	3/1957	Brace	38/77.83
4,893,422	1/1990	Mahlich et al.	38/77.8 X
5,120,934	6/1992	Nakada et al.	38/82 X

Primary Examiner—Wallace R. Burke
Assistant Examiner—Lavone D. Tabor
Attorney, Agent, or Firm—Barry E. Deutsch

[57] **CLAIM**

The ornamental design for an electric iron, as shown and described.

DESCRIPTION

FIG. 1 is a perspective view of an electric iron showing my new design;

FIG. 2 is a top plan view thereof;

FIG. 3 is a right side elevational view thereof;

FIG. 4 is a front elevational view thereof;

FIG. 5 is a rear elevational view thereof;

FIG. 6 is a bottom plan view thereof; and,

FIG. 7 is a left side elevational view thereof.

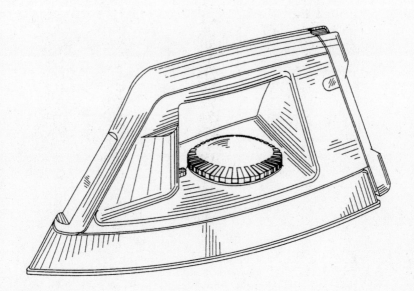

TITLE: COMPOSTING TOILET
INVENTOR: HENRIC SUNDBERG
ASSIGNEE: NONE

PATENT NUMBER: USD 354,340
PATENT FILED: AUGUST 30, 1993
PATENT GRANTED: JANUARY 10, 1995

United States Patent [19]

Sundberg

[11] **Patent Number:** **Des. 354,340**

[45] **Date of Patent:** ** **Jan. 10, 1995**

[54] **COMPOSTING TOILET**

[76] Inventor: **Henric Sundberg,** 5035 North Service Road, Unit C9, Burlington, Ontario, Canada, L7L 5V2

[**] Term: **14 Years**

[21] Appl. No.: **12,294**

[22] Filed: **Aug. 30, 1993**

[30] **Foreign Application Priority Data**

Mar. 11, 1993 [CA] Canada 1103931

[52] **U.S. Cl.** **D23/299**
[58] **Field of Search** D23/295, 299;
4/DIG. 12, 449, 612, 605, 614

[56] **References Cited**

U.S. PATENT DOCUMENTS

D. 193,169	7/1962	Wood	D23/299
D. 255,597	6/1980	Sargent et al.	D23/299
4,196,477	4/1980	Stewart	4/DIG. 12 X
4,521,304	6/1985	Youst	4/DIG. 12 X
5,303,431	4/1994	Johansson	4/DIG. 12 X

Primary Examiner—A. Hugo Word
Assistant Examiner—Eric Watterson

[57] **CLAIM**

The ornamental design for a composting toilet, as shown and described.

DESCRIPTION

FIG. 1 is a front perspective view from the left of the composting toilet;
FIG. 2 is a rear perspective view from the right of the composting toilet; and,
FIG. 3 is a top plan view of the composting toilet. The bottom side is plain and unornamented.

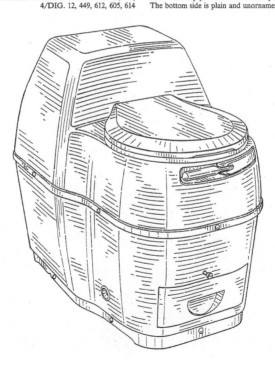

TITLE: PORTABLE COMPUTER
INVENTORS: MICHELE DE LUCCHI & HAGAI SHVADRON
ASSIGNEE: OLIVETTI

PATENT NUMBER: USD 358,375
PATENT FILED: JUNE 29, 1993
PATENT GRANTED: MAY 16, 1995

United States Patent [19]

De Lucchi et al.

[11] **Patent Number:** **Des. 358,375**

[45] **Date of Patent:** ✶✶ **May 16, 1995**

[54] **PORTABLE COMPUTER**

[75] Inventors: **Michele De Lucchi; Hagai Shvadron,** both of Milan, Italy

[73] Assignee: **Ing. C. Olivetti & C. S.p.A.,** Ivrea, Italy

[✶✶] Term: **14 Years**

[21] Appl. No.: **10,065**

[22] Filed: **Jun. 29, 1993**

[30] **Foreign Application Priority Data**

Dec. 28, 1992 [IT] Italy TO920000266
[52] **U.S. Cl.** **D14/106**
[58] **Field of Search** .... D14/100, 101, 106, 113, D14/115; D18/1, 2, 7, 11, 12; 235/145 A, 145 R; 341/22, 23; 345/104, 156, 168, 173, 901–905; 361/679, –686; 364/708.1, 709.04, 709.12; 400/486, 489; 248/918, 225.31

[56] **References Cited**

U.S. PATENT DOCUMENTS

D. 338,456 8/1993 Brunner et al. D14/106

D. 347,214	5/1994	You-Chi	D14/106
4,913,387	4/1990	Tice	248/918
5,253,836	10/1993	Tso	248/225.31
5,287,246	2/1994	Sen	D14/106 X

Primary Examiner—Freda S. Nunn
Attorney, Agent, or Firm—Banner, Birch, McKie & Beckett

[57] **CLAIM**

The ornamental design for a portable computer, as shown and described.

DESCRIPTION

FIG. 1 is a top plan view of a portable computer showing our design;
FIG. 2 is a bottom plan view thereof;
FIG. 3 is a front elevational view thereof;
FIG. 4 is a rear elevational view thereof;
FIG. 5 is a right side elevational view thereof;
FIG. 6 is a left side elevational view thereof;
FIG. 7 is a top front and right side perspective view thereof; and,
FIG. 8 is a reduced top front and right side perspective view thereof shown opened and in an operating position.

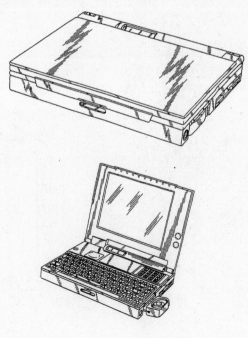

TITLE: DUAL COMPARTMENT AIR FRESHENER
INVENTOR: JOHN MARTIN
ASSIGNEE: S. C. JOHNSON & SON

PATENT NUMBER: USD 359,346
PATENT FILED: JULY 25, 1994
PATENT GRANTED: JUNE 13, 1995

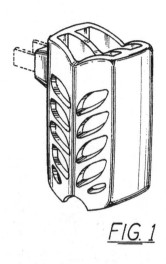

FIG. 1

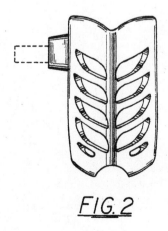

FIG. 2

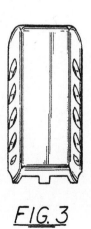

FIG. 3

TITLE: AUTOMATED TELLER MACHINE
INVENTOR: RICHARD B. HALL
ASSIGNEE: INTERBOLD

PATENT NUMBER: USD 360,734
PATENT FILED: MARCH 15, 1994
PATENT GRANTED: JUNE 25, 1995

United States Patent [19]

Hall

[11] **Patent Number:** **Des. 360,734**

[45] **Date of Patent:** ** Jul. 25, 1995

[54] **AUTOMATED TELLER MACHINE**

[75] Inventor: **Richard B. Hall,** North Canton, Ohio

[73] Assignee: **Interbold,** North Canton, Ohio

[**] Term: **14 Years**

[21] Appl. No.: **19,938**

[22] Filed: **Mar. 15, 1994**
[52] U.S. Cl. **D99/28**
[58] Field of Search D99/28, 43; 379/143,
379/144, 155, 153, 419, 420, 330, 340, 428;
235/379, 381; D14/130, 140; D6/481; 109/10,
24.1; 232/1 D, 1 R

[56] **References Cited**

U.S. PATENT DOCUMENTS

D. 263,344 3/1982 McCarthy et al. D99/28

D. 272,291 1/1984 Hauser D99/28
D. 282,114 1/1986 Nishida D99/28
D. 348,263 6/1994 Veeneman D99/28

Primary Examiner—Alan P. Douglas
Assistant Examiner—Jeffry H. Musgrove
Attorney, Agent, or Firm—Ralph E. Jocke

[57] **CLAIM**

The ornamental design for an automated teller machine, as shown and described.

DESCRIPTION

FIG. 1 is a front perspective view of an automated teller machine, showing my new design;
FIG. 2 is a front elevational view thereof; and,
FIG. 3 is a right side elevational view thereof, the left side view being a mirror image thereof.
The rear elevational view is generally plain and unornamented.

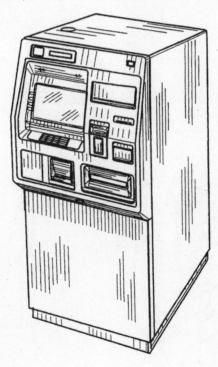

TITLE: BICYCLE
INVENTORS: TIMOTHY J. DIETZ, PAUL S. HANEY
& DEBRA A. OSADA
ASSIGNEE: HUFFY CORPORATION

PATENT NUMBER: USD 362,209
PATENT FILED: FEBRUARY 5, 1993
PATENT GRANTED: SEPTEMBER 12, 1995

United States Patent [19]

Dietz et al.

[11] **Patent Number:** **Des. 362,209**

[45] **Date of Patent:** ** Sep. 12, 1995

[54] **BICYCLE**

[75] Inventors: **Timothy J. Dietz**, Springboro; **Paul S. Haney**, Cincinnati; **Debra A. Osada**, Kettering, all of Ohio

[73] Assignee: **Huffy Corporation**, Miamisburg, Ohio

[**] Term: **14 Years**

[21] Appl. No.: **4,481**

[22] Filed: **Feb. 5, 1993**
[52] **U.S. Cl.** **D12/111**
[58] **Field of Search** D12/111; 280/281.1, 280/288.1, 288.2, 288.3

[56] **References Cited**

U.S. PATENT DOCUMENTS

D. 342,702	12/1993	Camfield et al.	D12/111
D. 343,810	2/1994	Sanford	D12/111
D. 346,138	4/1994	Camfield et al.	D12/111

Primary Examiner—A. Hugo Word
Assistant Examiner—M. Brown
Attorney, Agent, or Firm—Biebel & French

[57] **CLAIM**

The ornamental design for a bicycle, as shown.

DESCRIPTION

FIG. 1 is a perspective view of the bicycle of the present invention;
FIG. 2 is a front elevational view thereof;
FIG. 3 is a rear elevational view thereof;
FIG. 4 is a right side elevational view thereof;
FIG. 5 is a left side elevational view thereof;
FIG. 6 is a top plan view thereof; and,
FIG. 7 is a bottom plan view thereof.

TITLE: ELECTRIC TOASTER
INVENTORS: ALBERTO ALESSI ANGHINI, ALESSANDRO
MENDINI & SEIYA OHTA
ASSIGNEE: U.S. PHILIPS CORPORATION

PATENT NUMBER: USD 362,992
PATENT FILED: AUGUST 4, 1994
PATENT GRANTED: OCTOBER 10, 1995

United States Patent [19]

Alessi Anghini et al.

[11] **Patent Number:** **Des. 362,992**

[45] **Date of Patent:** **∗∗Oct. 10, 1995**

[54] **ELECTRIC TOASTER**

[75] Inventors: **Alberto Alessi Anghini**, Omegna (NO); **Alessandro Mendini**, Milan, both of Italy; **Seiya Ohta**, Hanover, Germany

[73] Assignee: **U.S. Philips Corporation**, New York, N.Y.

[∗∗] Term: **14 Years**

[21] Appl. No.: **26,772**

[22] Filed: **Aug. 4, 1994**

[30] **Foreign Application Priority Data**

Feb. 7, 1994 [CH] Switzerland DM/029.477
[52] **U.S. Cl.** **D7/330**; D7/328
[58] **Field of Search** D7/323, 328–330, D7/390; 99/331, 332, 334, 335, 372, 385, 389

[56] **References Cited**

U.S. PATENT DOCUMENTS

D. 107,552 12/1937 Scharfenberg D7/330

D. 115,630	7/1939	Pavelka, Jr. et al.	D7/330
D. 142,146	8/1945	Pavelka	D7/330
D. 148,936	3/1948	Laylon	D7/330
D. 338,368	8/1993	Naft et al.	D7/328 X

Primary Examiner—Alan P. Douglas
Assistant Examiner—Caron D. Veynar
Attorney, Agent, or Firm—Jack E. Haken

[57] **CLAIM**

The ornamental design for an electric toaster, as shown.

DESCRIPTION

FIG. **1** is a perspective view showing our new design;

FIG. **2** is a front elevational view thereof;

FIG. **3** is a rear elevational view thereof;

FIG. **4** is a right side elevational view thereof;

FIG. **5** is a left side elevational view thereof;

FIG. **6** is a top plan view thereof; and,

FIG. **7** is a bottom plan view thereof.

1 Claim, 3 Drawing Sheets

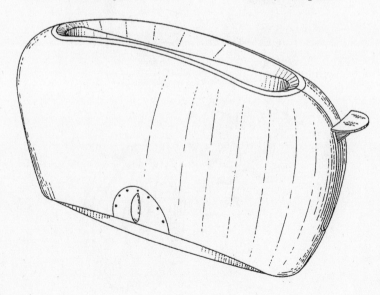

TITLE: SINGLE-LENS REFLEX CAMERA BODY
INVENTORS: GIORGETTO GIUGIARO, JUN AKABANE
& NOBUO HASHIMOTO
ASSIGNEE: NIKON CORPORATION

PATENT NUMBER: USD 363,301
PATENT FILED: AUGUST 1, 1994
PATENT GRANTED: OCTOBER 17, 1995

FIG. 5

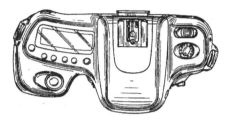

FIG. 6

FIG. 7

TITLE: REMOTE CONTROL
INVENTOR: PHILIPPE STARCK
ASSIGNEE: THOMSON CONSUMER ELECTRONICS

PATENT NUMBER: USD 363,933
PATENT FILED: AUGUST 2, 1994
PATENT GRANTED: NOVEMBER 7, 1995

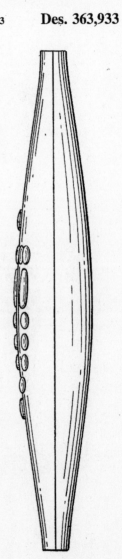

FIG. 2   FIG. 3

TITLE: RIDING MOWER
INVENTORS: HISATO KATO & HIROYUKI OGASAWARA
ASSIGNEE: KUBOTA CORPORATION

PATENT NUMBER: USD 363,939
PATENT FILED: MAY 4, 1994
PATENT GRANTED: NOVEMBER 7, 1995

United States Patent [19]

Kato et al.

[11] **Patent Number:** **Des. 363,939**

[45] **Date of Patent:** ∗∗**Nov. 7, 1995**

[54] **RIDING MOWER**

[75] Inventors: **Hisato Kato; Hiroyuki Ogasawara,** both of Sakai, Japan

[73] Assignee: **Kubota Corporation**, Osaka, Japan

[∗∗] Term: **14 Years**

[21] Appl. No.: **22,395**

[22] Filed: **May 4, 1994**

[30] **Foreign Application Priority Data**

Nov. 9, 1993 [JP] Japan 5-33991

[52] **U.S. Cl.** **D15/15**
[58] **Field of Search** D15/14–17, 23,
D15/26; 56/13.3, 13.4, 15.8, 15.9, 16.1,
16.7, 175, 202, 255, 294, 320.1, 320.2;
180/89.1, 89.2, 900

[56] **References Cited**

U.S. PATENT DOCUMENTS

D. 248,397	7/1978	Cognata et al.	D15/15
D. 297,538	9/1988	Ogasawara et al.	D15/15
D. 310,374	9/1990	Westimayer et al.	D15/15
D. 311,008	10/1990	Durfee et al.	D15/15
D. 314,777	2/1991	Crabtree et al.	D15/15
D. 325,183	4/1992	Nishikawa et al.	D15/15
D. 345,166	3/1994	Kamlukin et al.	D15/15
D. 353,146	12/1994	Yaguchi et al.	D15/15
5,209,314	5/1993	Nishiyama	180/900
5,367,864	11/1994	Ogasawara et al.	180/900

OTHER PUBLICATIONS

Honda Brochure, HT3810 10Hp Lawn Tractor, bottom.
Implement Tractor, Mar. 1989, p. 13 Kubota Lawn Tractor, bottom.

Primary Examiner—Sandra Morris
Attorney, Agent, or Firm—Jordan and Hamburg

[57] **CLAIM**

The ornamental design of a riding mower, as shown and described.

DESCRIPTION

FIG. **1** is a left side view of a riding mower, showing our new design;
FIG. **2** is a right side view thereof;
FIG. **3** is a front view thereof;
FIG. **4** is a rear view thereof;
FIG. **5** is a top plan view thereof; and,
FIG. **6** is a bottom plan view thereof.

1 Claim, 6 Drawing Sheets

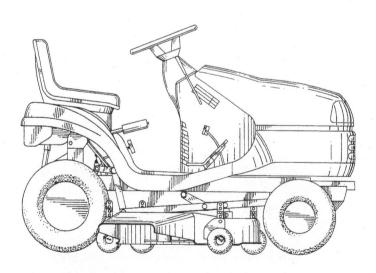

TITLE: DISH BRUSH
INVENTOR: MORISON S. COUSINS
ASSIGNEE: DART INDUSTRIES

PATENT NUMBER: USD 364,506
PATENT FILED: JUNE 3, 1994
PATENT GRANTED: NOVEMBER 28, 1995

United States Patent [19]

Cousins

[11] **Patent Number:** **Des. 364,506**

[45] **Date of Patent:** **∗∗Nov. 28, 1995**

[54] **DISH BRUSH**

[75] Inventor: **Morison S. Cousins**, Winter Park, Fla.

[73] Assignee: **Dart Industries Inc.**, Deerfield, Ill.

[∗∗] Term: **14 Years**

[21] Appl. No.: **23,551**

[22] Filed: **Jun. 3, 1994**

[52] U.S. Cl. **D4/133; D4/118**

[58] **Field of Search** D4/116, 118, 130, D4/132–134, 136, 138; 15/111, 143.1, 159.1, 160, 186–187; 401/268, 270

[56] **References Cited**

U.S. PATENT DOCUMENTS

D. 197,637	3/1964	Vallis .	
D. 231,284	4/1974	Lindbo	D4/133
D. 241,091	8/1976	Ahlstrom et al.	D4/133
D. 249,599	9/1978	Whitaker .	
D. 311,120	10/1990	Cautereels et al. .	
D. 349,193	8/1994	Sloan et al.	D4/118
388,880	9/1888	Kirkland et al. .	
1,706,408	3/1929	Miller .	

3,411,723	11/1968	Kohn .	
4,826,340	5/1989	Rothweiler et al.	401/270 X

Primary Examiner—A. Hugo Word
Assistant Examiner—Lavone D. Tabor
Attorney, Agent, or Firm—John A. Doninger

[57] **CLAIM**

The ornamental design for a dish brush, as shown and described.

DESCRIPTION

FIG. 1 is a top and side perspective view of a dish brush showing my new design;

FIG. 2 is a top plan view thereof;

FIG. 3 is a bottom plan view thereof;

FIG. 4 is a left side elevational view thereof;

FIG. 5 is a right side elevational view thereof;

FIG. 6 is a front elevational view thereof;

FIG. 7 is a rear elevational view thereof;

FIG. 8 is a cross-section view taken on line 8—8 in FIG. 2; and,

FIG. 9 is a cross-section view taken on line 9—9 of FIG. 4.

1 Claim, 5 Drawing Sheets

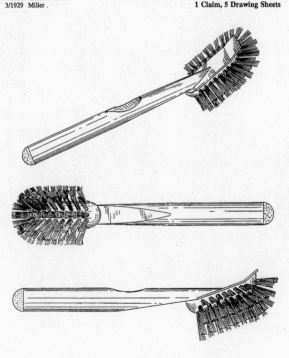

TITLE: ELECTRONIC CALCULATOR
INVENTORS: HIDEAKI YAMABE & TORU SUZUKI
ASSIGNEE: CASIO COMPUTER COMPANY

PATENT NUMBER: USD 364,890
PATENT FILED: FEBRUARY 15, 1995
PATENT GRANTED: DECEMBER 5, 1995

FIG.4

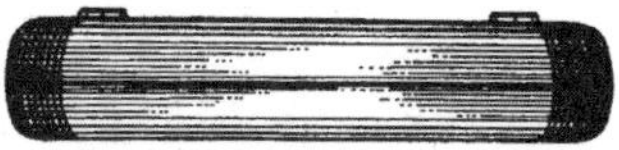

FIG.3 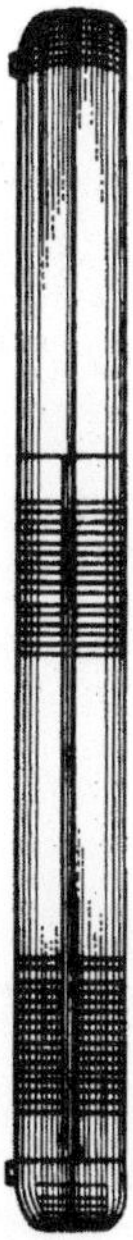   FIG.I   FIG.2

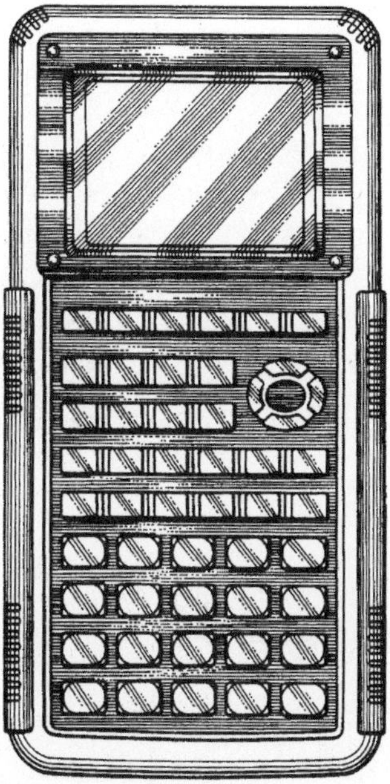

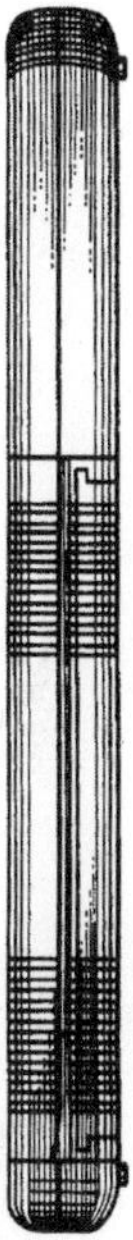

FIG.5

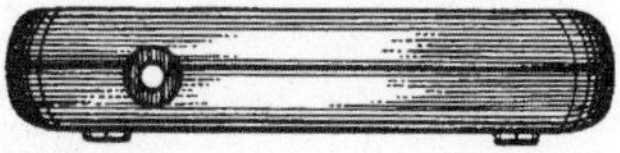

TITLE: ELECTRIC CITRUSPRESS
INVENTORS: ALBERTO ALESSI ANGHINI, ALESSANDRO
MENDINI & SEIYA OHTA
ASSIGNEE: U.S. PHILIPS CORPORATION

PATENT NUMBER: USD 366,398
PATENT FILED: AUGUST 4, 1994
PATENT GRANTED: JANUARY 23, 1996

United States Patent [19]

Alessi Anghini et al.

[11] **Patent Number:** **Des. 366,398**

[45] **Date of Patent:** ****Jan. 23, 1996**

[54] **ELECTRIC CITRUSPRESS**

[75] Inventors: **Alberto Alessi Anghini**, Omegna; **Alessandro Mendini**, Milan, both of Italy; **Seiya Ohta**, Hanover, Germany

[73] Assignee: **U.S. Philips Corporation**, New York, N.Y.

[**] Term: **14 Years**

[21] Appl. No.: **26,771**

[22] Filed: **Aug. 4, 1994**

[30] **Foreign Application Priority Data**

Feb. 7, 1994 [XH] Hague Agreement DMA002421

[52] **U.S. Cl.** **D7/665**

[58] **Field of Search** D7/665, 369, 372–374, D7/381; 99/501–508

[56] **References Cited**

U.S. PATENT DOCUMENTS

D. 153,645 5/1949 Stiles D7/665

D. 193,461 8/1962 Talge D7/665
D. 227,971 7/1973 Weiss D7/665

OTHER PUBLICATIONS

Home Furnishings Daily, Jul. 14, 1975, p. 22 Fruit Juicer.

Primary Examiner—Terry A. Wallace
Attorney, Agent, or Firm—Jack E. Haken

[57] **CLAIM**

The ornamental design for an electric citruspress, as shown.

DESCRIPTION

FIG. 1 is a perspective view of an electric citruspress showing our new design;
FIG. 2 is a front elevational view thereof;
FIG. 3 is a rear elevational view thereof;
FIG. 4 is a right side elevational view thereof;
FIG. 5 is a left side elevational view thereof;
FIG. 6 is a top plan view thereof; and,
FIG. 7 is a bottom plan view thereof.

1 Claim, 7 Drawing Sheets

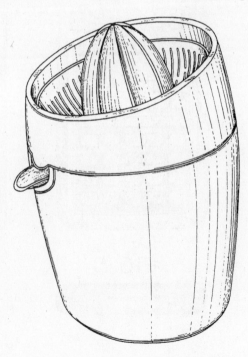

TITLE: HANDHELD COMPUTER HOUSING
INVENTORS: JONATHAN P. IVE & RONALD J. MOLLER
ASSIGNEE: APPLE COMPUTER

PATENT NUMBER: USD 366,463
PATENT FILED: MARCH 2, 1994
PATENT GRANTED: JANUARY 23, 1996

United States Patent [19]

Ive et al.

[11] **Patent Number:** **Des. 366,463**

[45] **Date of Patent:** **Jan. 23, 1996

[54] **HANDHELD COMPUTER HOUSING**

[75] Inventors: **Jonathan P. Ive**, San Francisco; **Ronald J. Moller**, Boulder Creek, both of Calif.

[73] Assignee: **Apple Computer, Inc.**, Cupertino, Calif.

[**] Term: **14 Years**

[21] Appl. No.: **19,471**

[22] Filed: **Mar. 2, 1994**

[52] **U.S. Cl.** **D14/100**; D18/7

[58] **Field of Search** D14/100, 106, D14/115; D18/1, 7, 11, 12; 345/156, 168, 169, 172, 173, 87; 341/22, 23; 364/708.1; 235/454, 462, 472

[56] **References Cited**

U.S. PATENT DOCUMENTS

D. 283,711	5/1986	Deura et al.	D18/7 X
D. 292,706	11/1987	Fischer	D18/7 X
D. 321,865	11/1991	Derocher	D14/100
D. 350,763	9/1994	Matsuda et al.	D18/7

OTHER PUBLICATIONS

Cohen, Raines, "Slimmed–Down MessagePad to Beef up RAM, Recognition," MacWEEK, Feb. 14, 1994, vol. 8, No. 7, pp. 1 & 84.

Primary Examiner—Freda Nunn
Attorney, Agent, or Firm—Hickman & Beyer

[57] **CLAIM**

The ornamental design for a handheld computer housing, as shown and described.

DESCRIPTION

FIG. 1 is a top plan view of a handheld computer housing in accordance with the present design;
FIG. 2 is a rear end elevational view of the computer housing;
FIG. 3 is a bottom plan view of the computer housing;
FIG. 4 is a front end elevational view of the computer housing;
FIG. 5 is a left side elevational view of the computer housing;
FIG. 6 is a right side elevational view of the computer housing with a cover of the housing closed;
FIG. 7 is a side elevational view similar to that of FIG. 6 with the cover open and engaging a support surface;
FIG. 8 is a top perspective view of the housing with the cover closed;
FIG. 9 is a reduced top perspective view of the housing with the cover partially opened; and,
FIG. 10 is a bottom perspective view of the housing with the cover fully opened and latched to the bottom of the case. The broken lines are shown in FIG. 9 for illustrative purposes only and form no part of the claimed design.

1 Claim, 6 Drawing Sheets

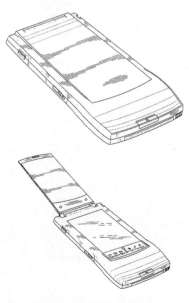

TITLE: GAME MACHINE
INVENTOR: TEIYU GOTO
ASSIGNEE: SONY CORPORATION

PATENT NUMBER: USD 367,895
PATENT FILED: OCTOBER 7, 1994
PATENT GRANTED: MARCH 12, 1996

FIG.8

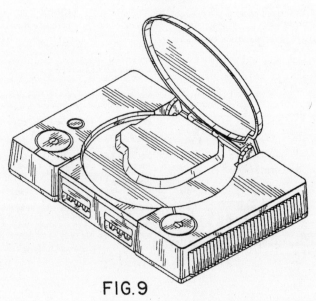

FIG.9

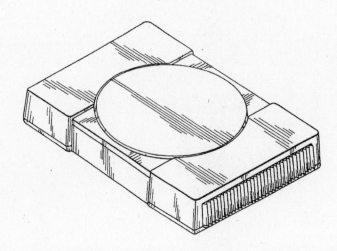

896

TITLE: CYLINDRICAL COMBINED REFRIGERATOR
AND FREEZER
INVENTOR: MATTHEW C. MONTGOMERY
ASSIGNEE: NONE

PATENT NUMBER: USD 368,271
PATENT FILED: APRIL 25, 1995
PATENT GRANTED: MARCH 26, 1996

U.S. Patent　　　　Mar. 26, 1996　　　　**Des. 368,271**

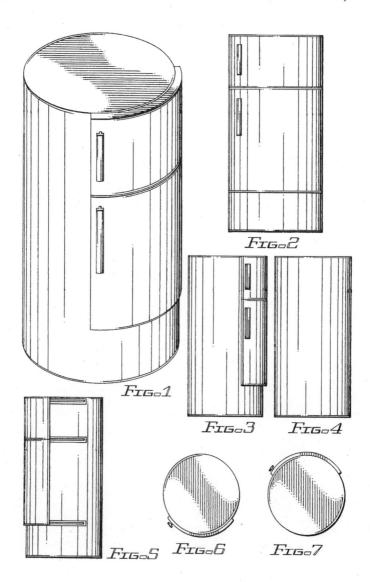

FIG. 1

FIG. 2

FIG. 3

FIG. 4

FIG. 5

FIG. 6

FIG. 7

TITLE: BICYCLE FRAME
INVENTORS: WESTON M. WILCOX, MATTHEW A. RHOADES
& MICHAEL L. ZEIGLE
ASSIGNEE: TREK BICYCLE CORPORATION

PATENT NUMBER: USD 368,678
PATENT FILED: SEPTEMBER 21, 1994
PATENT GRANTED: APRIL 9, 1996

United States Patent [19]

Wilcox et al.

[11]	**Patent Number:** **Des. 368,678**
[45]	**Date of Patent:** ****Apr. 9, 1996**

[54] **BICYCLE FRAME**

[75] Inventors: **Weston M. Wilcox**, Sun Prairie;
Matthew A. Rhoades, Madison;
Michael L. Zeigle, Sun Prairie, all of
Wis.

[73] Assignee: **Trek Bicycle, Corp.**, Waterloo, Wis.

[**] Term: **14 Years**

[21] Appl. No.: **28,727**

[22] Filed: **Sep. 21, 1994**

[52] **U.S. Cl.** **D12/111**

[58] **Field of Search** D12/111; 280/281.1,
280/288.1, 288.2, 288.3

[56] **References Cited**

U.S. PATENT DOCUMENTS

D. 313,381	1/1991	Moeller	D12/111
D. 349,869	4/1994	Burrows et al.	D12/111
5,240,268	8/1993	Allops et al.	D12/111

5,415,423	5/1995	Allsop et al.	D12/111

Primary Examiner—Melody N. Brown
Attorney, Agent, or Firm—David C. Brezina, Lee, Mann,
Smith, McWilliams, Sweeney & Ohlson

[57] **CLAIM**

The ornamental design for a bicycle frame, as shown and
described.

DESCRIPTION

FIG. **1** is a right side elevation view of a bicycle frame
showing our new design, the broken lines are for illustrative
purposes only and form no part of the claimed design;
FIG. **2** is a perspective view of a bicycle frame showign our
new design;
FIG. **3** is a right side elevation view thereof;
FIG. **4** is a top plan view thereof;
FIG. **5** is a bottom plan view thereof;
FIG. **6** is a front end view thereof; and,
FIG. **7** is a back end view thereof.

1 Claim, 3 Drawing Sheets

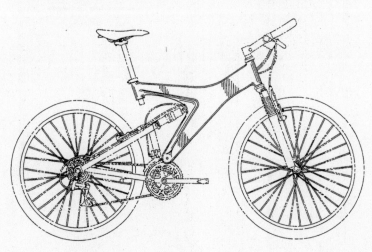

TITLE: HAND HELD ELECTRONIC GAME
INVENTORS: GUMPEI YOKOI, HIDEO NAGATA, KENICHI
SUGINO, NOBORU WAKITANI, YUJI HORI, ET AL.
ASSIGNEE: NINTENDO COMPANY

PATENT NUMBER: USD 383,798
PATENT FILED: JULY 10, 1996
PATENT GRANTED: SEPTEMBER 16, 1997

United States Patent [19]

Yokoi et al.

[11] **Patent Number:** **Des. 383,798**

[45] **Date of Patent:** **∗∗Sep. 16, 1997**

[54] **HAND HELD ELECTRONIC GAME**

[75] Inventors: **Gumpei Yokoi; Hideo Nagata;
Kenichi Sugino; Noboru Wakitani;
Yuji Hori; Norikatsu Furuta**, all of
Higashiyama-ku, Japan

[73] Assignee: **Nintendo Co., Ltd.**, Japan

[∗∗] Term: **14 Years**

[21] Appl. No.: **56,840**

[22] Filed: **Jul. 10, 1996**

[30] **Foreign Application Priority Data**

Mar. 11, 1996 [JP] Japan 8-6685

[51] **LOC (6) Cl.** **21-01**
[52] **U.S. Cl.** **D21/13**
[58] **Field of Search** .... D21/13, 48; 273/148 B;
463/30–35, 43–47; D14/125, 217, 117

[56] **References Cited**

U.S. PATENT DOCUMENTS

D. 310,390	9/1990	Besasie	D21/13
D. 318,884	8/1991	Kojo	D21/13
D. 329,470	9/1992	Kaneko	D21/13
D. 357,507	4/1995	Chen et al.	D21/48 X
D. 361,602	8/1995	Lee	D21/13
D. 367,890	3/1996	Osterhout	D21/13
D. 368,282	3/1996	Lin	D21/13
5,213,327	5/1993	Kitaue	273/148 B
5,325,280	6/1994	Tortola et al.	273/148 B X

OTHER PUBLICATIONS

HongKong Enterprise, Oct. 1994, p. 439.

Primary Examiner—Prabhakar G. Deshmukh
Attorney, Agent, or Firm—Nixon & Vanderhye P.C.

[57] **CLAIM**

The ornamental design for a "hand held electronic game", as shown and described.

DESCRIPTION

FIG. 1 is a top plan view of the hand held electronic game in accordance with my new design;
FIG. 2 is a front elevational view thereof;
FIG. 3 is a rear elevation view thereof;
FIG. 4 is a left side view thereof;
FIG. 5 is a right side view thereof; and,
FIG. 6 is a bottom plan view thereof.

1 Claim, 3 Drawing Sheets

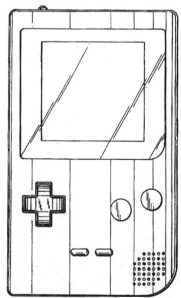

TITLE: AUTOMOBILE BODY
INVENTORS: HARTMUT WARKUSS & GREGORY GUILLAUME
ASSIGNEE: VOLKSWAGEN

PATENT NUMBER: USD 385,220
PATENT FILED: MAY 10, 1996
PATENT GRANTED: OCTOBER 21, 1997

United States Patent [19]

Warkuss et al.

[11] **Patent Number:** **Des. 385,220**

[45] **Date of Patent:** ****Oct. 21, 1997**

[54] **AUTOMOBILE BODY**

[75] Inventors: **Hartmut Warkuss**, Ummern; **Gregory Guillaume**, Brauschweig, both of Germany

[73] Assignee: **Volkswagen AG**, Wolfsburg, Germany

[**] Term: **14 Years**

[21] Appl. No.: **54,271**

[22] Filed: **May 10, 1996**

[30] **Foreign Application Priority Data**

Oct. 25, 1995 [DE] Germany M9508476.2

[51] LOC (6) Cl. **12-08**
[52] U.S. Cl. **D12/90**
[58] Field of Search D12/86, 90–92; 296/185

[56] **References Cited**

U.S. PATENT DOCUMENTS

D. 352,482 11/1994 Cannara et al. D12/90

D. 367,440 2/1996 Mays D12/90

Primary Examiner—Melody N. Brown
Attorney, Agent, or Firm—Watson Cole Stevens Davis, P.L.L.C.

[57] **CLAIM**

The ornamental design for an automobile body, as shown and described.

DESCRIPTION

FIG. 1 is a front perspective view of a new and ornamental design for an automobile body according to the present invention;
FIG. 2 is a left side view of the automobile body of FIG. 1 the right side view being identical;
FIG. 3 is a front view of the automobile body according to the invention;
FIG. 4 is a rear view of the automobile body according to the invention; and,
FIG. 5 is a top view of the automobile body according to the invention, the wheels, mirrors and spoiler shown in dotted lines form no part of the design.

1 Claim, 4 Drawing Sheets

TITLE: CAMERA
INVENTORS: YASUSHI SHIOTANI & MASAKAZU TAKU
ASSIGNEE: CANON KABUSHIKI KAISHA

PATENT NUMBER: USD 386,775
PATENT FILED: JUNE 25, 1996
PATENT GRANTED: NOVEMBER 25, 1997

FIG. 5

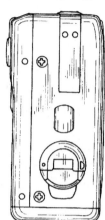

FIG. 6

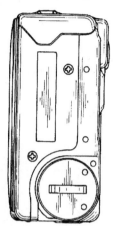

FIG. 7

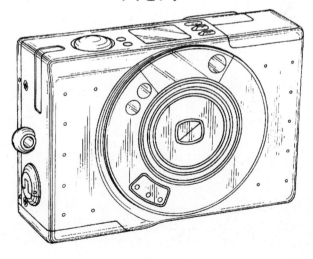

901

TITLE: POCKET-SIZE ORGANIZER
INVENTORS: JEFFREY C. HAWKINS, ROBERT YUJI
HAITANI, MALCOLM SLOAN SMITH & GISELA SCHMOLL
ASSIGNEE: PALM COMPUTING

PATENT NUMBER: USD 397,679
PATENT FILED: NOVEMBER 4, 1996
PATENT GRANTED: SEPTEMBER 1, 1998

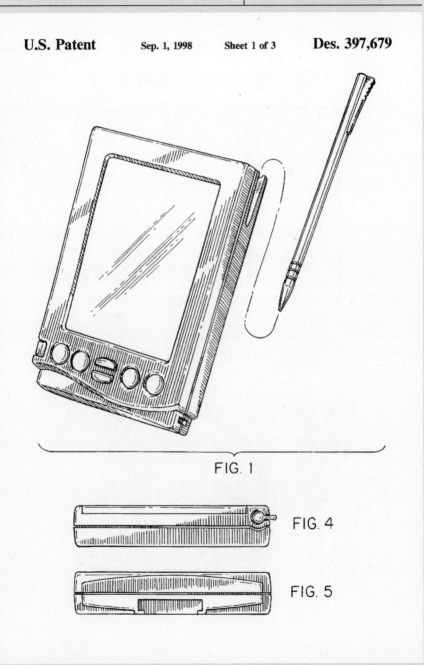

FIG. 1

FIG. 4

FIG. 5

902

TITLE: FAN
INVENTORS: KEVIN E. KELLER, GLEN W. EDIGER,
GARY P. ISRAEL & DUSTAN L. HAHN
ASSIGNEE: VORNADO AIR CIRCULATION SYSTEMS

PATENT NUMBER: USD 398,983
PATENT FILED: AUGUST 8, 1997
PATENT GRANTED: SEPTEMBER 29, 1998

United States Patent [19]

Keller et al.

[11] **Patent Number:** **Des. 398,983**

[45] **Date of Patent:** **∗∗Sep. 29, 1998**

[54] **FAN**

[75] Inventors: **Kevin E. Keller**, Wichita; **Glen W. Ediger**, N. Newton; **Gary P. Israel**, Andover; **Dustan L. Hahn**, Derby, all of Kans.

[73] Assignee: **Vornado Air Circulation Systems, Inc.**, Andover, Kans.

[∗∗] Term: **14 Years**

[21] Appl. No.: **74,622**

[22] Filed: **Aug. 8, 1997**

[51] **LOC (6) Cl.** **23-04**
[52] **U.S. Cl.** **D23/382**; D23/381
[58] **Field of Search** D23/382, 370, D23/381; 416/247, 246; 415/208.1, 211.2, 209.2, 211.1, 213.1

[56] **References Cited**

U.S. PATENT DOCUMENTS

D. 312,124 11/1990 Coup et al.

D. 323,708 2/1992 Wang D23/382
4,927,324 5/1990 Coup et al.

Primary Examiner—Lisa Lichtenstein
Attorney, Agent, or Firm—Stinson, Mag & Fizzell

[57] **CLAIM**

The ornamental design for a fan, as shown.

DESCRIPTION

FIG. 1 is a front and right side perspective view of the fan of the present invention;

FIG. 2 is a left side elevational view of the fan of FIG. 1;

FIG. 3 is a right side elevational view of the fan of FIG. 1;

FIG. 4 is a front elevational view of the fan of FIG. 1;

FIG. 5 is a rear elevational view of the fan of FIG. 1;

FIG. 6 is a top plan view of the fan of FIG. 1; and,

FIG. 7 is a bottom plan view of the fan of FIG. 1.

1 Claim, 4 Drawing Sheets

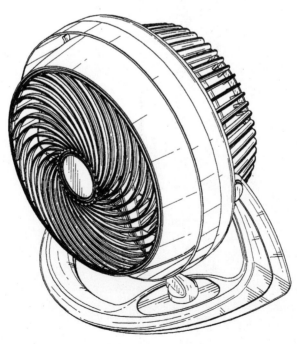

TITLE: COFFEEPOT
INVENTOR: FRANCESCO RANZONI
ASSIGNEE: ALFONSO BIALETTI

PATENT NUMBER: USD 399,384
PATENT FILED: MARCH 5, 1997
PATENT GRANTED: OCTOBER 13, 1998

United States Patent [19]

Ranzoni

[11] **Patent Number:** **Des. 399,384**

[45] **Date of Patent:** ****Oct. 13, 1998**

[54] **COFFEEPOT**

[75] Inventor: **Francesco Ranzoni**, Chiari, Italy

[73] Assignee: **S.p.A. Alfonso Bialetti & C.**, Omegna, Italy

[**] Term: **14 Years**

[21] Appl. No.: **67,560**

[22] Filed: **Mar. 5, 1997**

[51] **LOC (6) Cl.** **07-01**
[52] **U.S. Cl.** **D7/318**; D7/317
[58] **Field of Search** D7/300, 312, 316,
D7/317, 318, 319, 321, 372, 305, 310;
220/475, 756; 222/472

[56] **References Cited**

U.S. PATENT DOCUMENTS

D. 45,331	3/1914	Farr	D7/319 X
D. 191,624	10/1961	Day	D7/319 X
3,935,804	2/1976	Perez	D7/318 X

Primary Examiner—M. N. Pandozzi
Attorney, Agent, or Firm—Sheridan Ross P.C.

[57] **CLAIM**

The design for a "coffeepot," as shown and described.

DESCRIPTION

FIG. 1 shows a perspective view of the coffeepot depicting the new design;
FIG. 2 shows a right side view of the coffeepot depicting the new design;
FIG. 3 shows a front view of the coffeepot depicting the new design;
FIG. 4 shows a left side view of the coffeepot depicting the new design;
FIG. 5 shows a back view of the coffeepot depicting the new design;
FIG. 6 shows a top view of the coffeepot depicting the new design; and,
FIG. 7 shows a bottom view of the coffeepot depicting the new design.

1 Claim, 6 Drawing Sheets

TITLE: MICROWAVE OVEN
INVENTORS: MAKOTO TAKIMOTO, NOBUHIRO FUJII
& TAKASHI MATSUDA
ASSIGNEE: SHARP KABUSHIKI KAISHA

PATENT NUMBER: USD 400,047
PATENT FILED: JUNE 12, 1997
PATENT GRANTED: OCTOBER 27, 1998

United States Patent [19]

Takimoto et al.

[11] **Patent Number:** **Des. 400,047**

[45] **Date of Patent:** ****Oct. 27, 1998**

---

[54] **MICROWAVE OVEN**

[75] Inventors: **Makoto Takimoto**, Nara-ken; **Nobuhiro Fujii**, Osaka-fu; **Takashi Matsuda**, Nara-ken, all of Japan

[73] Assignee: **Sharp Kabushiki Kaisha**, Osaka, Japan

[**] Term: **14 Years**

[21] Appl. No.: **72,195**

[22] Filed: **Jun. 12, 1997**

[30] **Foreign Application Priority Data**

Dec. 12, 1996 [JP] Japan 8-37928

[51] **LOC (6) Cl.** **07-02**
[52] **U.S. Cl.** **D7/351**
[58] **Field of Search** .... D7/350, 351; 126/275 R, 126/275 E, 273 R, 273 A, 19 M, 21 A; 219/756–758, 678, 680

[56] **References Cited**

U.S. PATENT DOCUMENTS

D. 304,150	10/1989	Kubo et al.	D7/351
D. 329,353	9/1992	Yamada .	
D. 334,688	4/1993	Kitae et al. .	
D. 335,064	4/1993	Sugiyama et al. .	
D. 352,636	11/1994	Nakamura .	
D. 353,510	12/1994	Nakamura .	
D. 353,511	12/1994	Saimen .	
D. 353,512	12/1994	Saimen et al. .	
D. 356,006	3/1995	Saimen et al. .	
D. 357,159	4/1995	Mitsui et al. .	
D. 367,991	3/1996	Saimen .	
D. 367,992	3/1996	Saimen .	
D. 368,405	4/1996	Tada .	
D. 368,406	4/1996	Nakamura .	
D. 371,039	6/1996	Matoba et al.	D7/351
D. 373,502	9/1996	Fujii et al. .	
D. 373,925	9/1996	Kim	D7/351
D. 390,411	1/1997	Nakagawa	D7/351
D. 390,412	1/1997	Takimoto	D7/351

Primary Examiner—Ruth McInroy
Attorney, Agent, or Firm—Nixon & Vanderhye

[57] **CLAIM**

The ornamental design for a microwave oven, as shown and described.

DESCRIPTION

FIG. **1** is a top, front and right side perspective view of a microwave oven showing our new design;
FIG. **2** is a top plan view thereof;
FIG. **3** is a front elevational view thereof;
FIG. **4** is a right side elevational view thereof;
FIG. **5** is a left side elevational view thereof;
FIG. **6** is a rear elevational view thereof; and,
FIG. **7** is a bottom plan view thereof.

1 Claim, 4 Drawing Sheets

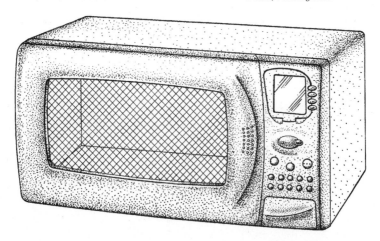

TITLE: VEHICLE BODY
INVENTORS: BRYAN NESBITT, STEVEN W. FERRERIO,
WILLIAM A. DAYTON & K. NEIL WALLING
ASSIGNEE: CHRYSLER CORPORATION

PATENT NUMBER: USD 413,081
PATENT FILED: MARCH 31, 1998
PATENT GRANTED: AUGUST 24, 1999

United States Patent [19]

Nesbitt et al.

[11] **Patent Number:** **Des. 413,081**

[45] **Date of Patent:** ＊＊ **Aug. 24, 1999**

[54] **VEHICLE BODY**

[75] Inventors: **Bryan Nesbitt**, Lake Orion; **Steven W. Ferrerio**, Troy; **William A. Dayton**, Northville; **K. Neil Walling**, Leonard, all of Mich.

[73] Assignee: **Chrysler Corporation**, Auburn Hills, Mich.

[**] Term: **14 Years**

[21] Appl. No.: **29/085,866**

[22] Filed: **Mar. 31, 1998**

[51] LOC (6) Cl. **12-08**

[52] U.S. Cl. **D12/91**

[58] Field of Search D12/91, 90, 92; 296/185

[56] **References Cited**

U.S. PATENT DOCUMENTS

D. 298,521	11/1988	Ui et al.	D12/91
D. 346,990	5/1994	Abbott et al.	D12/91
D. 355,397	2/1995	Verduyn et al.	D12/92
D. 357,648	4/1995	Osawa et al.	D12/91
D. 373,331	9/1996	Ohkuna et al.	D12/91

D. 392,920   3/1998 Verduyn et al. D12/91

OTHER PUBLICATIONS

John Lee, Standard Catalog of Chrysler, 1924–1990, pp. 33, 53.

Primary Examiner—Melody N. Brown
Attorney, Agent, or Firm—Mark P. Calcaterra

[57] **CLAIM**

The ornamental design for an vehicle body, as shown and described.

DESCRIPTION

FIG. 1 is a front perspective view illustrating an automobile body constructed in accordance with the teachings of the present invention.

FIG. 2 is a left side view, it will be understood that the side opposite to that shown is a substantial mirror image thereof.

FIG. 3 is a rear perspective view thereof.

FIG. 4 is a front view thereof; and,

FIG. 5 is a rear view thereof.

It will be understood that the broken line showing of the wheels and tires throughout the drawings is for illustrative purposes only and forms no part of the subject invention.

1 Claim, 4 Drawing Sheets

TITLE: COMPUTER ENCLOSURE
INVENTORS: STEVEN P. JOBS, JONATHAN P. IVE, DANIEL
J. COSTER, CHRISTOPHER J. STRINGER, ET AL.
ASSIGNEE: APPLE COMPUTER

PATENT NUMBER: USD 413,105
PATENT FILED: MAY 6, 1998
PATENT GRANTED: AUGUST 24, 1999

United States Patent [19]

Jobs et al.

[11] **Patent Number:** **Des. 413,105**

[45] **Date of Patent:** ✶✶ **Aug. 24, 1999**

[54] **COMPUTER ENCLOSURE**

[75] Inventors: **Steven P. Jobs**, Palo Alto; **Jonathan P. Ive**; **Daniel J. Coster**, both of San Francisco; **Christopher J. Stringer**, Pacifica; **Daniele De Iuliis**, San Francisco; **Bart K. Andre**, Menlo Park; **Richard P. Howarth**, San Francisco; **Calvin Q. Seid**, Palo Alto; **Douglas B. Satzger**, San Carlos; **Marc J. van de Loo**, Palo Alto, all of Calif.

[73] Assignee: **Apple Computer, Inc.**, Cupertino, Calif.

[**] Term: **14 Years**

[21] Appl. No.: **29/087,642**

[22] Filed: **May 6, 1998**

[51] **LOC (6) Cl.** **14-02**
[52] **U.S. Cl.** **D14/100**; D14/113
[58] **Field of Search** D14/100, 113, D14/114, 126, 102, 105, 125, 106; 345/133, 156, 901–5; 348/180, 184, 325, 739; 248/917–24

[56] **References Cited**

U.S. PATENT DOCUMENTS

D. 314,373 2/1991 Sacherman D14/113

D. 355,167	2/1995	Barbera et al.	D14/100
D. 361,550	8/1995	Mundt et al.	D14/100
D. 370,466	6/1996	Vossoughi	D14/100
D. 370,664	6/1996	Oates	D14/100
D. 370,897	6/1996	Lin	D14/113
D. 379,805	6/1997	Ratzlaff	D14/113
D. 383,444	9/1997	Han	D14/100
D. 398,591	9/1998	Back	D14/113

Primary Examiner—M. H. Tung
Attorney, Agent, or Firm—Nancy R. Simon

[57] **CLAIM**

The ornamental design for a computer enclosure, as shown and described.

DESCRIPTION

FIG. 1 is a front, top, right side perspective view of a computer enclosure, showing our new design;
FIG. 2 is a front view thereof;
FIG. 3 is a right side view thereof;
FIG. 4 is a rear view thereof;
FIG. 5 is a left side view thereof;
FIG. 6 is a top view thereof;
FIG. 7 is a bottom view thereof; and,
FIG. 8 is a right side view of a computer enclosure with a flip stand extended, showing our new design.

1 Claim, 8 Drawing Sheets

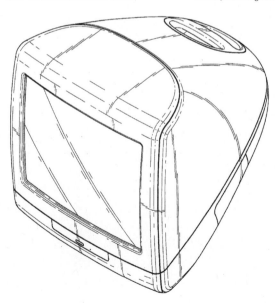

TITLE: RAZOR HANDLE
INVENTOR: KENNETH GRANGE
ASSIGNEE: WARNER-LAMBERT COMPANY

PATENT NUMBER: USD 414,898
PATENT FILED: MAY 1, 1997
PATENT GRANTED: OCTOBER 5, 1999

United States Patent [19]

Grange

[11] **Patent Number:** **Des. 414,898**

[45] **Date of Patent:** ** **Oct. 5, 1999**

[54] **RAZOR HANDLE**

[75] Inventor: **Kenneth Grange**, London, United Kingdom

[73] Assignee: **Warner-Lambert Company**, Morris Plains, N.J.

[**] Term: **14 Years**

[21] Appl. No.: **29/070,179**

[22] Filed: **May 1, 1997**

[51] **LOC (6) Cl.** **28-03**
[52] **U.S. Cl.** **D28/48**
[58] **Field of Search** D28/45–48; 30/32, 30/34.2, 41, 47–51, 62–65, 74.1, 77–81, 526

[56] **References Cited**

U.S. PATENT DOCUMENTS

D. 229,876	1/1974	Glaberson	D28/46
D. 311,784	10/1990	Schwartz	D28/48
D. 355,049	1/1995	Yasui	D28/48
D. 363,141	10/1995	Burout et al.	D28/46
D. 365,419	12/1995	Kamiya	D28/48
D. 386,821	11/1997	Shurtleff et al.	D28/48
D. 392,418	3/1998	Gray	D28/48

3,140,542	7/1964	Craig	30/62
3,203,092	8/1965	Craig	30/62
3,204,338	9/1965	Kruger et al.	30/63
3,252,335	5/1966	Kruger et al.	30/62
3,861,040	1/1975	Dorion, Jr.	30/50 X
3,872,589	3/1975	Braginetz	30/62

Primary Examiner—Ted Shooman
Assistant Examiner—C Tuttle
Attorney, Agent, or Firm—Charles W. Almer

[57] **CLAIM**

The ornamental design for a razor handle, as shown and described.

DESCRIPTION

FIG. 1 is a top, rear and left side perspective view of the razor handle;
FIG. 2 is a bottom, front and right perspective view of the razor handle;
FIG. 3 is a bottom end view of the razor handle;
FIG. 4 is a top end view of the razor handle;
FIG. 5 is a back view of the razor handle;
FIG. 6 is a side view of the razor handle; and,
FIG. 7 is a front view of the razor handle.
The broken line portion of the drawing is for illustrative purposes only and forms no part of the claimed design.

1 Claim, 6 Drawing Sheets

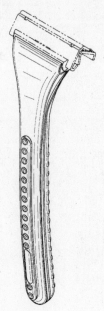
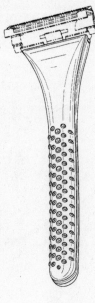

TITLE: TEA KETTLE
INVENTOR: STEPHANE DE BERGEN
ASSIGNEE: LE CREUSET OF AMERICA

PATENT NUMBER: USD 414,979
PATENT FILED: DECEMBER 2, 1998
PATENT GRANTED: OCTOBER 12, 1999

United States Patent [19]

de Bergen

[11] **Patent Number:** **Des. 414,979**

[45] **Date of Patent:** ** **Oct. 12, 1999**

[54] **TEA KETTLE**

[75] Inventor: **Stephane de Bergen**, Villecerf, France

[73] Assignee: **Le Creuset of America, Inc.,** Early Branch, S.C.

[**] Term: **14 Years**

[21] Appl. No.: **29/097,223**

[22] Filed: **Dec. 2, 1998**

[51] **LOC (6) Cl.** **07-01**
[52] **U.S. Cl.** **D7/320**; D7/321
[58] **Field of Search** D7/312, 321, 322, D7/320, 319; 222/470, 475.1, 572; 97/306

[56] **References Cited**

U.S. PATENT DOCUMENTS

D. 43,106	10/1912	Hoffmann	D7/321
D. 59,218	10/1921	Havilland	D7/312
D. 80,412	1/1930	Fairchild	D7/312
D. 279,755	7/1985	Lax	D7/320
D. 283,780	5/1986	Laslo	D7/320
D. 342,640	12/1993	Lebowitz	D7/322
D. 347,139	5/1994	Ancona et al.	D7/322 X
D. 380,337	7/1997	Lien	D7/322

Primary Examiner—M. N. Pandozzi
Attorney, Agent, or Firm—Dority & Manning, P.A.

[57] **CLAIM**

The ornamental design for tea kettle, as shown and described.

DESCRIPTION

FIG. 1 is a side view of a tea kettle according to the present invention. The opposite side is a mirror image.
FIG. 2 is a top view of the tea kettle of FIG. 1.
FIG. 3 is a front view of the tea kettle of FIG. 1.
FIG. 4 is a rear view of the tea kettle of FIG. 1.
FIG. 5 is a bottom view of the tea kettle of FIG. 1; and,
FIG. 6 is an isometric view of the tea kettle of FIG. 1.

1 Claim, 6 Drawing Sheets

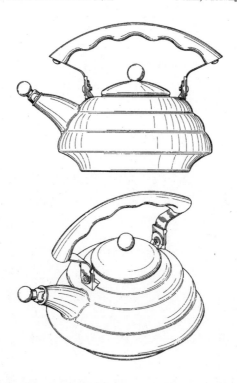

TITLE: MULTIFUNCTIONAL FURNITURE
INVENTOR: VERNER PANTON
ASSIGNEE: NONE

PATENT NUMBER: USD 418,987
PATENT FILED: JUNE 5, 1998
PATENT GRANTED: JANUARY 18, 2000

FIG. 6

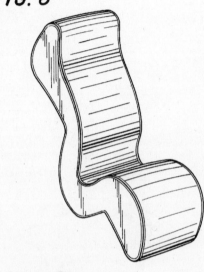

FIG. 7

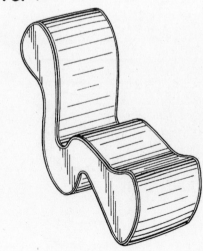

TITLE: TOY
INVENTORS: KOZO KAWAKITA, TAKESHI YAMAGISHI,
HIROSHI OSAWA, KAZUHIRO KATO, ET AL.
SIGNEE: SONY CORPORATION

PATENT NUMBER: USD 431,270
PATENT FILED: JUNE 10, 1999
PATENT GRANTED: SEPTEMBER 26, 2000

FIG. 4

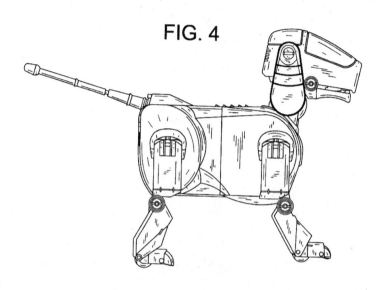

FIG. 5

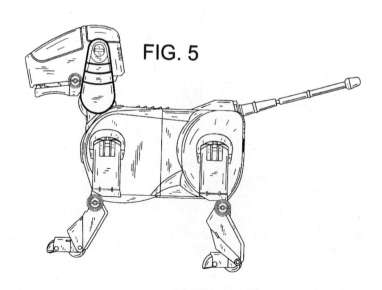

TITLE: MARS ROVER
INVENTORS: DON BICKLER, KENNETH JEWETT,
HOWARD EISEN & LEE SWORD
ASSIGNEE: CALIFORNIA INSTITUTE OF TECHNOLOGY

PATENT NUMBER: USD 437,255
PATENT FILED: APRIL 4, 1996
PATENT GRANTED: FEBRUARY 6, 2001

(12) **United States Design Patent**   (10) **Patent No.:**   **US D437,255 S**

Bickler et al.   (45) **Date of Patent:**   **   **Feb. 6, 2001**

(54) **MARS ROVER**

(75) Inventors: **Don Bickler**, Temple City; **Kenneth Jewett**, North Hollywood; **Howard Eisen**, Los Angeles; **Lee Sword**, Tujunga, all of CA (US)

(73) Assignee: **California Institute of Technology**, Pasadena, CA (US)

(**) Term: **14 Years**

(21) Appl. No.: **29/052,892**

(22) Filed: **Apr. 4, 1996**

(51) **LOC (7) Cl.** **12-13**

(52) **U.S. Cl.** **D12/1**

(58) **Field of Search** D12/1, 2; 181/2.1, 181/2.2, 22; 901/1

(56) **References Cited**

U.S. PATENT DOCUMENTS

3,299,978 * 1/1967 Sponsler .... 180/22 X

3,809,004 * 5/1974 Leonheart .... 180/22 X
5,323,867 * 6/1994 Allard 180/22

* cited by examiner

Primary Examiner—Nelson C. Holtje
(74) *Attorney, Agent, or Firm*—Limbach & Limbach, L.L.P.

(57) **CLAIM**

The ornamental design for a Mars Rover, as shown.

DESCRIPTION

FIG. 1 is a perspective view of the rover showing our new design;
FIG. 2 is another perspective view thereof;
FIG. 3 is a side elevational view thereof (with the other side being a mirror image thereof);
FIG. 4 is a top plan view thereof;
FIG. 5 is an end elevational view thereof;
FIG. 6 is the other end elevational view thereof; and,
FIG. 7 is a bottom plan view thereof.

1 Claim, 7 Drawing Sheets

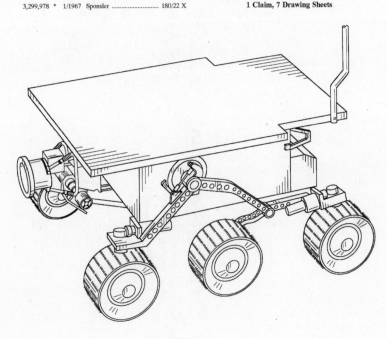

TITLE: DISHWASHER
INVENTOR: HOON JEONG
ASSIGNEE: LG ELECTRONICS

PATENT NUMBER: USD 438,351
PATENT FILED: JUNE 22, 2000
PATENT GRANTED: FEBRUARY 27, 2001

(12) **United States Design Patent**
    Jeong

(10) Patent No.:   **US D438,351 S**
(45) Date of Patent: **   **Feb. 27, 2001**

(54) **DISHWASHER**

(75) Inventor: **Hoon Jeong**, Seoul (KR)

(73) Assignee: **LG Electronics Inc.**, Seoul (KR)

(**) Term: **14 Years**

(21) Appl. No.: **29/125,370**

(22) Filed: **Jun. 22, 2000**

(30)   **Foreign Application Priority Data**

Dec. 22, 1999   (KR) 99-31024

(51) **LOC (7) Cl.** **15-05**
(52) **U.S. Cl.** **D32/2**
(58) **Field of Search** .... D32/2, 3, 25; 134/56 D,
    134/57 D, 57 DL, 58 DL, 93, 257; 312/108,
    109, 138 R; 40/490

(56)   **References Cited**

U.S. PATENT DOCUMENTS

D. 320,487 * 10/1991 Marks et al. D32/3

D. 320,489 * 10/1991 Marks et al. D32/3
D. 423,287 * 4/2000 Marchand D32/25
D. 424,257 * 5/2000 Umeda et al. D32/2
4,732,431 * 3/1988 Mason 312/109

* cited by examiner

Primary Examiner—Mitchell Siegel

(57)   **CLAIM**

The ornamental design for a dishwasher, as shown and described.

DESCRIPTION

FIG. **1** is a perspective view;
FIG. **2** is a front elevational view;
FIG. **3** is a left side elevational view;
FIG. **4** is a right side elevational view;
FIG. **5** is a rear elevational view;
FIG. **6** is a top plan view; and,
FIG. **7** is a bottom plan view.

1 Claim, 4 Drawing Sheets

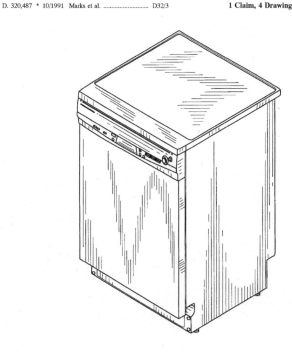

TITLE: TELEVISION SET
INVENTOR: TOSHIYUKI KITA
ASSIGNEE: SHARP KABUSHIKI KAISHA

PATENT NUMBER: USD 439,224
PATENT FILED: JUNE 23, 2000
PATENT GRANTED: MARCH 20, 2001

(12) **United States Design Patent**
Kita

(10) Patent No.: **US D439,224 S**
(45) Date of Patent: ** **Mar. 20, 2001**

(54) **TELEVISION SET**

(75) Inventor: **Toshiyuki Kita**, Osaka-fu (JP)

(73) Assignee: **Sharp Kabushiki Kaisha**, Osaka (JP)

(**) Term: **14 Years**

(21) Appl. No.: **29/125,452**

(22) Filed: **Jun. 23, 2000**

(30) **Foreign Application Priority Data**

Dec. 24, 1999   (JP) 11-35934

(51) LOC (7) Cl. **14-03**
(52) U.S. Cl. **D14/126**
(58) Field of Search D14/125–136,
D14/239, 371, 374–375; 312/7.2; 348/836,
838, 180, 184, 325, 739; 345/905, 104,
133, 156, 168, 87, 173; 341/12

(56) **References Cited**

U.S. PATENT DOCUMENTS

D. 336,645	6/1993	Saito et al. .
D. 337,113	7/1993	Saito et al. .
D. 342,497	12/1993	Saito et al. .
D. 342,501	12/1993	Saeki et al. .
D. 342,509	12/1993	Saito et al. .
D. 351,155	10/1994	Usami et al. .
D. 351,156	10/1994	Usami et al. .
D. 357,244	4/1995	Usami et al. .

D. 357,245	4/1995	Usami et al. .	
D. 357,472	4/1995	Usami et al. .	
D. 369,596	5/1996	Akiyama et al. .	
D. 372,026	7/1996	Akiyama et al. .	
D. 373,583	9/1996	Akiyama et al. .	
D. 392,628	* 3/1998	Hayashi	D14/374
D. 395,453	* 6/1998	Kawasaki et al.	D14/374
D. 407,077	* 3/1999	Shibata	D14/126
D. 412,892	* 8/1999	Lee	D14/126
D. 413,594	* 9/1999	Renk	D14/126
D. 432,101	* 10/2000	Oba	D14/126

* cited by examiner

Primary Examiner—Raphael Barkai
(74) Attorney, Agent, or Firm—Nixon & Vanderhye

(57) **CLAIM**

The ornamental design for a "television set", as shown and described.

DESCRIPTION

FIG. **1** is a top, front and right side perspective view of a television set according to my design;
FIG. **2** is a front elevational view thereof;
FIG. **3** is a rear elevational view thereof;
FIG. **4** is a top plan view thereof;
FIG. **5** is a bottom plan view thereof;
FIG. **6** is a left side elevational view thereof; and,
FIG. **7** is a right side elevational view thereof.

1 Claim, 6 Drawing Sheets

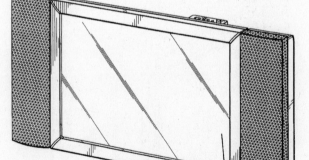

TITLE: CD/DVD JEWEL CASE
INVENTOR: JAY S. DERMAN
ASSIGNEE: NONE

PATENT NUMBER: USD 440,108
PATENT FILED: MARCH 15, 2000
PATENT GRANTED: APRIL 10, 2001

(12) **United States Design Patent**
Derman

(10) **Patent No.:** **US D440,108 S**
(45) **Date of Patent:** ** **Apr. 10, 2001**

(54) **CD/DVD JEWEL CASE**

(76) Inventor: **Jay S. Derman**, P.O. Box 3823, Palos
Verdes, CA (US) 90274-9533

(**) Term: **14 Years**

(21) Appl. No.: **29/120,081**

(22) Filed: **Mar. 15, 2000**

(51) **LOC (7) Cl.** **06-04**
(52) **U.S. Cl.** **D6/632**; D6/407; D6/634;
D6/635
(58) **Field of Search** D3/201; D6/407,
D6/408, 626–635, 124; D14/26, 27; D19/32,
33, 74, 89; D27/340, 360; 40/626, 771,
775, 307; 150/149; 132/312; 206/307, 232,
308.1, 308.3, 309, 311, 312, 313, 387.13,
396, 408, 730, 755; 229/67.1, 68.1, 70–72;
340/572.5

(56) **References Cited**

U.S. PATENT DOCUMENTS

D. 304,880	*	12/1989	Philosophe	D6/634
D. 375,015	*	10/1996	Kobayashi et al.	D6/632
D. 421,870	*	3/2000	Boucard	D6/627
D. 422,445	*	4/2000	Markowitz	D6/632
4,702,369	*	10/1987	Philosophe	206/312
4,736,840	*	4/1988	Deiglmeier	206/308.1
5,253,751	*	10/1993	Wipper	206/756
5,259,498	*	11/1993	Weisburn et al.	206/756
5,377,825	*	1/1995	Sykes et al.	206/232
5,417,324	*	5/1995	Joyce et al.	206/310
5,462,159	*	10/1995	Roth et al.	206/310
5,474,174	*	12/1995	Lin	206/310
5,494,156	*	2/1996	Nies .	

5,513,749	*	5/1996	Simmons	206/308.1
5,515,968	*	5/1996	Taniyama	206/310
5,526,926	*	6/1996	Deja	206/308.1
5,529,182	*	6/1996	Anderson et al.	206/308.1
5,551,559	*	9/1996	Roth et al.	206/308.1
5,660,274	*	8/1997	Chien	206/308.1
5,682,988	*	11/1997	Salisbury	206/303
5,727,680	*	3/1998	Liu	206/308.1
5,772,021	*	6/1998	Bolenbaugh et al.	206/310
5,833,068	*	11/1998	Fantone	206/459.1
5,887,713	*	3/1999	Smith et al.	206/308.1
5,896,985	*	4/1999	Nakasuji	206/308.2
5,944,181	*	8/1999	Lau	206/308.1
6,041,922	*	3/2000	Kollinek	206/308.1

* cited by examiner

Primary Examiner—Celia Murphy
(74) *Attorney, Agent, or Firm*—Monty Koslover

(57) **CLAIM**

The ornamental design for a CD/DVD jewel case, as shown
and described.

DESCRIPTION

FIG. **1** is a top plan view of a CD/DVD jewel case showing
my new design;
FIG. **2** is a bottom plan view thereof;
FIG. **3** is a back side elevation view thereof;
FIG. **4** is a front opening side elevation view thereof;
FIG. **5** is a left side elevation view thereof, the opposite side
elevational view being a mirror image of that shown; and,
FIG. **6** is a perspective view thereof.
The disk shown as broken lines in FIG. **6** is included for
environmental illustration, and forms no part of the claimed
design.

1 Claim, 3 Drawing Sheets

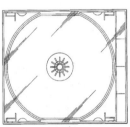

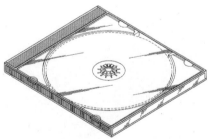

TITLE: CLOCK RADIO RECEIVER
INVENTOR: JOHN GRINKUS
ASSIGNEE: BOSE CORPORATION

PATENT NUMBER: USD 440,957
PATENT FILED: MAY 7, 1993
PATENT GRANTED: APRIL 24, 2001

(12) **United States Design Patent**
Grinkus

(10) Patent No.: **US D440,957 S**
(45) **Date of Patent:** ** **Apr. 24, 2001**

(54) **CLOCK RADIO RECEIVER**

(75) Inventor: **John Grinkus**, Randolph, MA (US)

(73) Assignee: **Bose Corporation**, Framingham, MA (US)

(**) Term: **14 Years**

(21) Appl. No.: **29/008,076**

(22) Filed: **May 7, 1993**

(51) **LOC (7) Cl.** **14-01**
(52) **U.S. Cl.** **D14/170**; D10/2
(58) **Field of Search** D14/155–157, D14/160–163, 170–172, 188, 189, 192, 195; D10/2; 455/344, 345, 347; 312/7.1

(56) **References Cited**

U.S. PATENT DOCUMENTS

D. 204,494 * 4/1966 Adams D14/170
D. 249,148 * 8/1978 Miyamoto D14/171

D. 249,651 * 9/1978 Hirosawa .... D14/171 X
2,510,103 * 6/1950 Griffin .... 312/7.1 X

* cited by examiner

Primary Examiner—Dominic Simone
(74) *Attorney, Agent, or Firm*—Fish & Richardson P.C.

(57) **CLAIM**

The ornamental design for a clock radio receiver, as shown and described.

DESCRIPTION

FIG. 1 is a perspective view of a clock radio receiver showing my new design;
FIG. 2 is a front view thereof;
FIG. 3 is a rear view thereof;
FIG. 4 is a right side view thereof;
FIG. 5 is a left side view thereof;
FIG. 6 is a top view thereof; and,
FIG. 7 is a bottom view thereof.

1 Claim, 5 Drawing Sheets

TITLE: CHAIR
INVENTOR: RON ARAD
ASSIGNEE: PROTONED

PATENT NUMBER: USD 442,378
PATENT FILED: OCTOBER 12, 1999
PATENT GRANTED: MAY 22, 2001

(12) **United States Design Patent**
Arad

(10) Patent No.: **US D442,378 S**
(45) **Date of Patent:** ✱✱ **May 22, 2001**

(54) **CHAIR**

(75) Inventor: **Ron Arad**, London (GB)

(73) Assignee: **Protoned, B.V.,** Amsterdam (NL)

(✱✱) Term: **14 Years**

(21) Appl. No.: **29/112,159**

(22) Filed: **Oct. 12, 1999**

(30) **Foreign Application Priority Data**

Apr. 12, 1999 (XH) DM/047 444

(51) **LOC (7) Cl.** **06-01**
(52) **U.S. Cl.** **D6/366**
(58) **Field of Search** D6/334, 335, 364,
D6/365, 366, 374, 380, 498, 500, 501,
502; 297/445.1, 411.2

(56) **References Cited**

U.S. PATENT DOCUMENTS

D. 158,508	5/1950	Saarinen .
D. 158,509	5/1950	Saarinen .
D. 158,510	5/1950	Saarinen .
D. 168,212	11/1952	Cicchelli .
D. 191,704	11/1961	Stauffer .
D. 193,338	8/1962	Tepper .
D. 196,719 ✱	10/1963	Johnson D6/366
D. 197,643 ✱	3/1964	Kramer D6/366
D. 197,712	3/1964	Fischer, Jr. .
D. 207,840	6/1967	Rodrigo .

D. 213,683	4/1969	Leistikow .
D. 251,942	5/1979	VonHeck .
D. 260,056 ✱	8/1981	Sapper D6/366
D. 260,204 ✱	8/1981	Sapper D6/366
D. 260,334	8/1981	Van Horn .
D. 276,768	12/1984	Enthoven .
D. 351,294	10/1994	Fleishman .
D. 410,799 ✱	6/1999	Meda D6/366
3,078,063 ✱	2/1963	Frankl D6/498
3,142,514 ✱	7/1964	Ginat .... D6/366 X

✱ cited by examiner

*Primary Examiner—*Gary D. Watson
(74) *Attorney, Agent, or Firm—*Selitto, Behr & Kim

(57) **CLAIM**

The ornamental design for a chair, as shown and decribed.

DESCRIPTION

FIG. **1** is a front perspective view of a chair showing my new design;
FIG. **2** is a front elevational view thereof;
FIG. **3** is a rear elevational view thereof;
FIG. **4** is a left side elevational view thereof, the right side being a mirror image thereof;
FIG. **5** is a top plan view thereof;
FIG. **6** is a bottom plan view thereof; and,
FIG. **7** is a front perspective view of a second embodiment of a chair which is essentially identical to the one shown in FIGS. **1–6**, except that it is provided with a caster-like base.

1 Claim, 4 Drawing Sheets

TITLE: HANDSET
INVENTORS: TOM ARBISI & TODD WOOD
ASSIGNEE: NOKIA MOBILE PHONES

PATENT NUMBER: USD 443,866
PATENT FILED: SEPTEMBER 7, 2000
PATENT GRANTED: JUNE 19, 2001

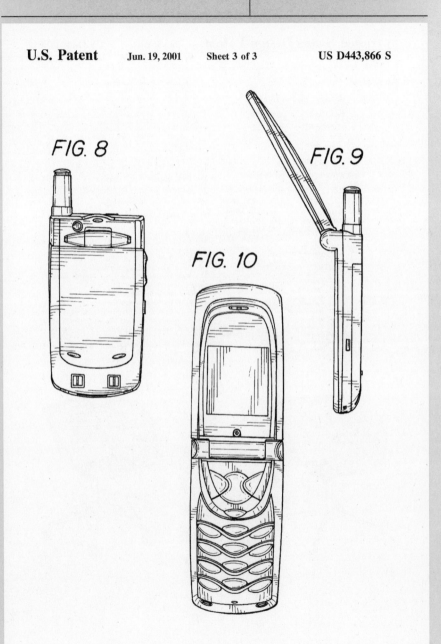

FIG. 8

FIG. 9

FIG. 10

918

TITLE: FOLDING TOOL INCLUDING PLIERS
INVENTOR: BENJAMI C. RIVERA
ASSIGNEE: LEATHERMAN TOOL GROUP

PATENT NUMBER: USD 445,009
PATENT FILED: OCTOBER 31, 2000
PATENT GRANTED: JULY 17, 2001

(12) **United States Design Patent**
Rivera

(10) Patent No.: **US D445,009 S**
(45) Date of Patent: ** **Jul. 17, 2001**

(54) **FOLDING TOOL INCLUDING PLIERS**

(75) Inventor: **Benjamin C. Rivera**, West Linn, OR (US)

(73) Assignee: **Leatherman Tool Group, Inc.**, Portland, OR (US)

(**) Term: **14 Years**

(21) Appl. No.: **29/132,027**

(22) Filed: **Oct. 31, 2000**

(51) **LOC (7) Cl.** **08-05**
(52) **U.S. Cl.** **D8/52**; D8/105
(58) **Field of Search** D8/51, 52, 54, D8/55, 105, 107, 99; 30/34, 143, 153, 155; 7/118, 119, 125, 127, 128, 129, 132, 158, 165, 167, 168; 81/305

(56) **References Cited**

U.S. PATENT DOCUMENTS

D. 380,362	* 7/1997	Rivera	D8/52
D. 384,872	* 10/1997	Yeh	D8/105
D. 385,169	* 10/1997	Rivera	D8/52
D. 392,519	* 3/1998	Hung	D8/5
D. 398,209	9/1998	Rivera	D8/52
D. 398,213	* 9/1998	Rivera	D8/105
D. 401,133	* 11/1998	Gardiner et al.	D8/105
D. 414,092	* 9/1999	Chang	D8/55
D. 423,893	* 5/2000	Mackin et al.	D8/52
D. 426,446	* 6/2000	Chau	D8/105
D. 426,447	* 6/2000	Chau	D8/105
D. 429,616	* 8/2000	Rivera	D8/105

5,029,354	7/1991	Boyd, Jr. et al.	7/118
5,537,750	7/1996	Seber et al.	30/161
5,564,318	10/1996	Pail	81/427.5
5,809,599	* 9/1998	Frazer	7/128
6,014,787	1/2000	Rivera	7/128
6,092,444	7/2000	Hsiao	81/440

OTHER PUBLICATIONS

Hong Kong Enterprise Catalog Mar. 1989 p. 12 Item #FE3998.*
Blade, Jun. 1998, What's New, p. 90.

* cited by examiner

Primary Examiner—Alan P. Douglas
Assistant Examiner—Clare E Heflin
(74) *Attorney, Agent, or Firm*—Chernoff, Vilhauer, McClung & Stenzel, LLP

(57) **CLAIM**

The ornamental design for a folding tool including pliers, as shown and described.

DESCRIPTION

FIG. **1** is an isometric view from the upper left front of a folding tool including pliers, showing my new design;
FIG. **2** is a side elevational view thereof, an elevational view of the opposite side being identical therewith;
FIG. **3** is a top plan view thereof, a bottom plan view thereof being identical therewith;
FIG. **4** is a rear elevational view thereof; and,
FIG. **5** is a front elevational view thereof.

1 Claim, 3 Drawing Sheets

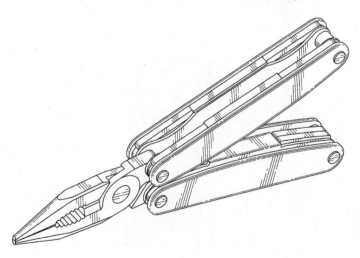

TITLE: CORK EXTRACTOR
INVENTOR: EDWARD KILDUFF
ASSIGNEE: METROKANE

PATENT NUMBER: USD 446,098
PATENT FILED: JANUARY 9, 2001
PATENT GRANTED: AUGUST 7, 2001

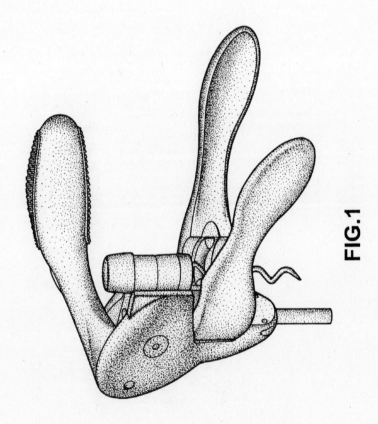

FIG.1

TITLE: INSTANT CAMERA
INVENTOR: KAZUHISA HORIKIRI
ASSIGNEE: FUJI PHOTO FILM COMPANY

PATENT NUMBER: USD 447,503
PATENT FILED: JANUARY 25, 2001
PATENT GRANTED: SEPTEMBER 4, 2001

FIG. 1

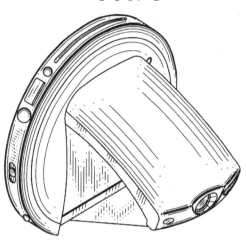

FIG. 2

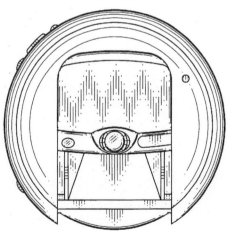

TITLE: RESPIRATORY MASK
INVENTOR: DANIEL T. CHEN
ASSIGNEE: 3M INNOVATIVE PROPERTIES COMPANY

PATENT NUMBER: USD 448,472
PATENT FILED: FEBRUARY 17, 1999
PATENT GRANTED: SEPTEMBER 25, 2001

(12) **United States Design Patent**
Chen

(10) Patent No.: **US D448,472 S**
(45) Date of Patent: ✱✱ *Sep. 25, 2001

(54) **RESPIRATORY MASK**

(75) Inventor: **Daniel T. Chen**, St. Paul, MN (US)

(73) Assignee: **3M Innovative Properties Company**, St. Paul, MN (US)

(*) Notice: This patent is subject to a terminal disclaimer.

(**) Term: **14 Years**

(21) Appl. No.: **29/100,707**

(22) Filed: **Feb. 17, 1999**

(51) LOC (7) Cl. **29-02**
(52) U.S. Cl. **D24/110.1**
(58) Field of Search D24/110.1, 110;
128/205.25, 205.28, 205.29, 206.12, 206.14,
206.13, 206.18, 206.21

(56) **References Cited**

U.S. PATENT DOCUMENTS

D. 326,540	* 5/1992	Scholey	D24/110.1
2,362,382	* 11/1944	Lehmberg	128/206.15
5,012,805	* 5/1991	Muckerheide	128/205.28
5,701,893	* 12/1997	Kern et al.	128/206.24
5,934,275	* 8/1999	Gazzara	128/205.27

FOREIGN PATENT DOCUMENTS

388638	3/1933	(GB) .
871661	6/1961	(GB) .
2103491A	2/1983	(GB) .
WO 96/28216	9/1996	(WO) .
WO 96/28217	9/1996	(WO) .
WO 97/32493	9/1997	(WO) .
WO 97/32494	9/1997	(WO) .

OTHER PUBLICATIONS

Product Literature: "Glendale Respiratory Protection," Glendale Optical Company, Inc.
Product Literature: "Delta Disposable Respirators," Racal Health & Safety, Inc.
Product Literature: "Racal® N95 Respirator & Delta® N95 Respirator," Racal Health & Safety, Inc., (1995).

* cited by examiner

Primary Examiner—Ian Simmons
(74) *Attorney, Agent, or Firm*—Karl G. Hanson; James A. Rogers

(57) **CLAIM**

The ornamental design for a respiratory mask, as shown and described.

DESCRIPTION

FIG. 1 is a perspective view showing the new design for a respiratory mask design.
FIG. 2 is a front view thereof.
FIG. 3 is a top elevational view thereof.
FIG. 4 is a bottom elevational view thereof.
FIG. 5 is a rear elevational view; and,
FIG. 6 is a side elevational view. The left side elevational view is the same as the right side elevational view.
The broken lines showing in FIGS. 1–6 are for illustrative purposes only and forms no part of the claimed design.

1 Claim, 2 Drawing Sheets

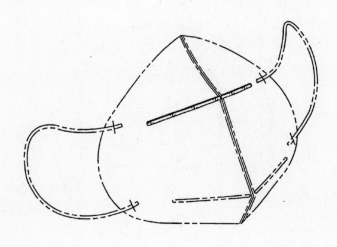

TITLE: COFFEE MAKER
INVENTOR: JØRGEN BODUM
ASSIGNEE: PI-DESIGN

PATENT NUMBER: USD 448,602
PATENT FILED: JANUARY 4, 2001
PATENT GRANTED: OCTOBER 2, 2001

(12) **United States Design Patent**
Bodum

(10) **Patent No.:** **US D448,602 S**
(45) **Date of Patent:** ** Oct. 2, 2001

(54) **COFFEE MAKER**

(75) Inventor: **Jørgen Bodum**, St. Niklausen (CH)

(73) Assignee: **PI-Design AG**, Triengen (CH)

(**) Term: **14 Years**

(21) Appl. No.: **29/135,011**

(22) Filed: **Jan. 4, 2001**

(30) **Foreign Application Priority Data**

Jul. 13, 2000 (DK) .... MA 2000 00729

(51) **LOC (7) Cl.** **07-01**
(52) **U.S. Cl.** **D7/319**; D7/317
(58) **Field of Search** D7/316, 317, 318,
D7/319, 300; 220/759, 278, 758, 755, 718,
719; 222/465.1, 475.1, 156

(56) **References Cited**

U.S. PATENT DOCUMENTS

D. 342,414	*	12/1993	Jorgensen	D7/317
D. 343,333	*	1/1994	Jorgensen	D7/317
D. 372,627	*	8/1996	Ireland	D7/319
D. 377,132	*	1/1997	Jorgensen	D7/318
D. 378,261	*	3/1997	Jorgensen	D7/319
D. 383,638	*	9/1997	Joergensen	D7/319
D. 383,639	*	9/1997	Jorgensen	D7/319
D. 384,539	*	10/1997	Joergensen	D7/318
D. 384,540	*	10/1997	Joergensen	D7/319
D. 386,040	*	11/1997	Joergensen	D7/317
D. 386,351	*	11/1997	Joergensen	D7/319
D. 388,275	*	12/1997	Joergensen	D7/319
D. 401,466	*	11/1998	Joergensen	D7/318
D. 405,641	*	2/1999	Brady	D7/319
D. 405,642	*	2/1999	Toriba	D7/319
D. 410,170	*	5/1999	Sheu	D7/319
D. 413,480	*	9/1999	Joergensen	D7/317
D. 441,248	*	5/2001	Brady	D7/319

* cited by examiner

Primary Examiner—M. N. Pandozzi
(74) *Attorney, Agent, or Firm*—Nath & Associates PLLC;
Gary M. Nath; Marvin C. Berkowitz

(57) **CLAIM**

The ornamental design for a coffee maker, as shown and
described.

DESCRIPTION

FIG. 1 is an oblique perspective view of the coffee maker;
FIG. 2 is a right side view of the coffee maker, as shown in
FIG. 1;
FIG. 3 is a left side view of the coffee maker;
FIG. 4 is a front side view of the coffee maker;
FIG. 5 is a back side view of the coffee maker;
FIG. 6 is a top view of the coffee maker; and,
FIG. 7 is a bottom view of the coffee maker.

1 Claim, 7 Drawing Sheets

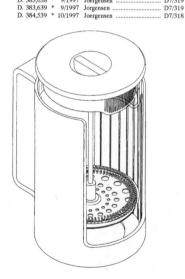

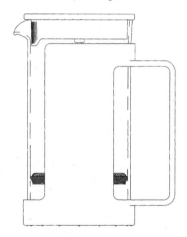

TITLE: CAMERA
INVENTOR: YASUSHI SHIOTANI
ASSIGNEE: CANON KABUSHIKI KAISHA

PATENT NUMBER: USD 448,787
PATENT FILED: JANUARY 17, 2001
PATENT GRANTED: OCTOBER 2, 2001

FIG. 1

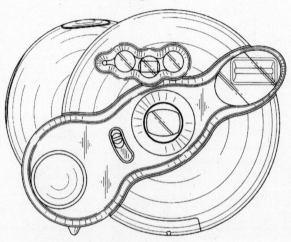

FIG. 2

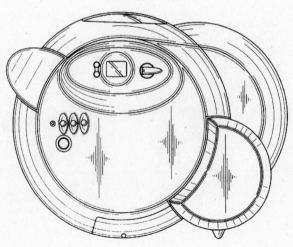

924

TITLE: PORTION OF AN ELECTRONIC HOUSING
INVENTORS: JAMES R. STEWART & HOK-SUM
HORACE LUKE
ASSIGNEE: MICROSOFT CORPORATION.

PATENT NUMBER: USD 452,282
PATENT FILED: JANUARY 11, 2001
PATENT GRANTED: DECEMBER 18, 2001

(12) **United States Design Patent**　(10) Patent No.: 　**US D452,282 S**
Stewart et al.　　　　　　　　　　　(45) **Date of Patent:**　****　Dec. 18, 2001**

(54) **PORTION OF AN ELECTRONIC HOUSING**

(75) Inventors: **James R. Stewart**, Woodinville;
Hok-Sum Horace Luke, Mercer Island,
both of WA (US)

(73) Assignee: **Microsoft Corporation**, Redmond, WA
(US)

(**) Term: **14 Years**

(21) Appl. No.: **29/135,335**

(22) Filed: **Jan. 11, 2001**

(51) **LOC (7) Cl.** **21-01**
(52) **U.S. Cl.** **D21/333**
(58) **Field of Search** D21/324, 328–333;
D14/400, 401, 435, 495; 273/148 B; 463/1,
29–35, 46, 47

(56) **References Cited**

U.S. PATENT DOCUMENTS

D. 362,869	* 10/1995	Oikawa	D21/332
D. 376,822	* 12/1996	Osterhout	D21/329
D. 412,940	8/1999	Kato et al.	.
D. 433,076	* 10/2000	Hayes	D21/333
D. 435,272	* 12/2000	Swanson et al.	D21/328
D. 435,871	* 1/2001	Yu	D21/333
5,192,082	* 3/1993	Inoue et al.	463/46
5,976,018	* 11/1999	Druckman	463/46
6,254,477	* 7/2001	Saski et al.	463/47

OTHER PUBLICATIONS

www.Amazon.com, Color Pictures of Outdoor Trekker
product by V–Tech, 2 pages, (date unknown but prior to Jan.
11, 2001).

Color pictures of Gamecube video game system by Nintendo, from various internet web pages, 3 pages, (date
unknown but prior to Jan. 11, 2001).
Color pictures of Playstation 2 video game system by Sony,
from various internet web pages, 3 pages, (date unknown but
prior to Jan. 11, 2001).

* cited by examiner

Primary Examiner—Prabhakar Deshmukh
(74) *Attorney, Agent, or Firm*—Banner & Witcoff, Ltd.

(57) **CLAIM**

The ornamental design for a portion of an electronic housing, as shown and described.

DESCRIPTION

FIG. **1** is a perspective view of a portion of an electronic
housing showing our new design;

FIG. **2** is a top plan view thereof;

FIG. **3** is a front view thereof;

FIG. **4** is rear view thereof;

FIG. **5** is right side view thereof; and,

FIG. **6** is a left side view thereof.

The broken line showing of the circle within the claimed
design and the remainder of the electronic housing is for
illustrative purposes only and form no part of the claimed
design. The unshaded regions including the region inside of
the unclaimed circle, and the bottom of the electronic
housing form no part of the claimed design.

1 Claim, 3 Drawing Sheets

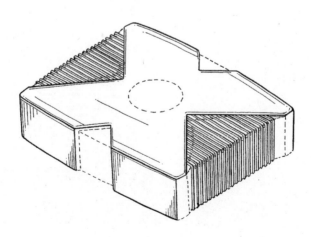

TITLE: SCALE
INVENTORS: NICOLAUS BACHMAYER & WOLFGANG FABIAN
ASSIGNEE: SOEHNLE

PATENT NUMBER: USD 452,660
PATENT FILED: NOVEMBER 14, 2000
PATENT GRANTED: JANUARY 1, 2002

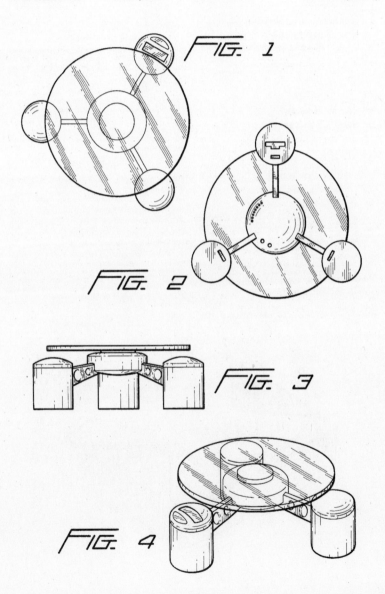

FIG. 1

FIG. 2

FIG. 3

FIG. 4

926

TITLE: DISC PLAYER COMBINED WITH RADIO
RECEIVER AND TAPE RECORDER
INVENTOR: SATOSHI SUZUKI
ASSIGNEE: SONY CORPORATION

PATENT NUMBER: USD 452,963
PATENT FILED: APRIL 27, 2001
PATENT GRANTED: JANUARY 15, 2002

(12) **United States Design Patent** (10) Patent No.: **US D452,963 S**

Suzuki (45) Date of Patent: ** **Jan. 15, 2002**

(54) **DISC PLAYER COMBINED WITH RADIO RECEIVER AND TAPE RECORDER**

(75) Inventor: **Satoshi Suzuki**, Tokyo (JP)

(73) Assignee: **Sony Corporation**, Tokyo (JP)

(**) Term: **14 Years**

(21) Appl. No.: **29/140,909**

(22) Filed: **Apr. 27, 2001**

(51) **LOC (7) Cl.** **14-01**
(52) **U.S. Cl.** **D14/168**
(58) **Field of Search** D14/135–136,
D14/156–157, 160–165, 167–168, 188,
193–198; 455/344, 347–351

(56) **References Cited**

U.S. PATENT DOCUMENTS

D378,590 S	*	3/1997	Zeitman	D14/165
D406,843 S	*	3/1999	Zeitman	D14/162
D420,000 S		2/2000	Yoneda	
D423,501 S	*	4/2000	Kokkinis	D14/168
D426,224 S		6/2000	Yoneda	
D430,551 S		9/2000	Shiono	
D436,103 S		1/2001	Yamada et al.	
D440,550 S		4/2001	Nakano	
D442,160 S		5/2001	Tsuchiya	

D442,574 S   5/2001 Ishii

OTHER PUBLICATIONS

Catalog "MD–CD System", p. 10, Sony Corporation (Nov. 2000).
Home page "CD Radio cassette (CSD–EX150)", 2 pgs., Aiwa (1999–2000).

* cited by examiner

Primary Examiner—Nanda Bondade
(74) *Attorney, Agent, or Firm*—Rader, Fishman & Grauer, PLLC

(57) **CLAIM**

The ornamental design for a disc player combined with radio receiver and tape recorder, as shown and described.

DESCRIPTION

FIG. 1 is a perspective view of a disc player combined with radio receiver and tape recorder showing my new design;
FIG. 2 is a front elevational view thereof;
FIG. 3 is a rear elevational view thereof;
FIG. 4 is a left side elevational view thereof;
FIG. 5 is a right side elevational view thereof;
FIG. 6 is a top plan view thereof; and,
FIG. 7 is a bottom plan view thereof.

1 Claim, 4 Drawing Sheets

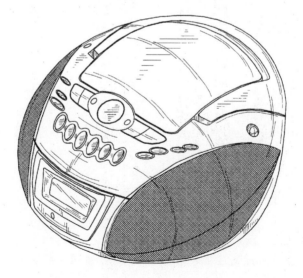

TITLE: PORTION OF A COMPUTER INPUT DEVICE
INVENTORS: ALLEN M. HAN, CHUNGMING YING
& THOMAS W. BROOKS
ASSIGNEE: MICROSOFT CORPORATION

PATENT NUMBER: USD 453,932
PATENT FILED: MARCH 29, 2001
PATENT GRANTED: FEBRUARY 26, 2002

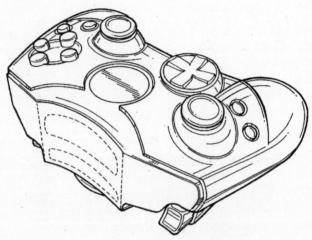

FIG. 1

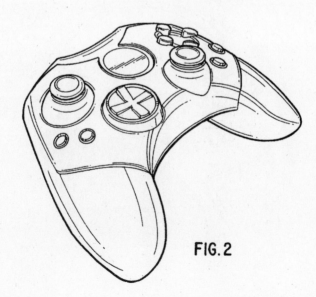

FIG. 2

TITLE: MOUSE
INVENTORS: BARTLEY K. ANDRE, DANIEL J. COSTER,
DANIELE DE IULIIS, RICHARD P. HOWARTH, ET AL.
ASSIGNEE: APPLE COMPUTER

PATENT NUMBER: USD 454,568
PATENT FILED: JULY 17, 2000
PATENT GRANTED: MARCH 19, 2002

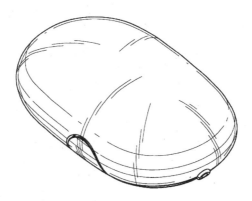

FIG. 1

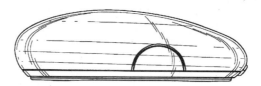

FIG. 2

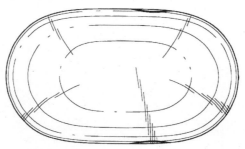

FIG. 3

TITLE: ELECTRIC FAN
INVENTOR: RAVIN G. MELWANI
ASSIGNEE: B.K. REHATEX

PATENT NUMBER: USD 458,673
PATENT FILED: JANUARY 4, 2002
PATENT GRANTED: JUNE 11, 2002

(12) **United States Design Patent** (10) **Patent No.:** **US D458,673 S**

Melwani (45) **Date of Patent:** ** **Jun. 11, 2002**

(54) **ELECTRIC FAN**

(75) Inventor: **Ravin G Melwani**, Hong Kong (HK)

(73) Assignee: **B.K. Rehatex (H.K.) Ltd.**, Kowloon (HK)

(**) Term: **14 Years**

(21) Appl. No.: **29/152,879**

(22) Filed: **Jan. 4, 2002**

(51) **LOC (7) Cl.** **23-04**

(52) **U.S. Cl.** **D23/379**

(58) **Field of Search** .... D23/379, 370, D23/378, 413; 416/246 R, 247 R, 146 R

(56) **References Cited**

U.S. PATENT DOCUMENTS

D99,501 S * 5/1936 Devore D23/379

* cited by examiner

Primary Examiner—Lisa Lichtenstein
(74) Attorney, Agent, or Firm—Leydig, Voit, & Mayer, Ltd.

(57) **CLAIM**

The ornamental design for an electric fan, as shown and described.

DESCRIPTION

FIG. 1 is a front and left side perspective view of an electric fan showing my new design;

FIG. 2 is a front elevational view thereof;

FIG. 3 is a rear elevational view thereof;

FIG. 4 is a left side elevational view thereof;

FIG. 5 is a right side elevational view thereof;

FIG. 6 is a top plan view thereof; and,

FIG. 7 is a bottom plan view thereof.

1 Claim, 7 Drawing Sheets

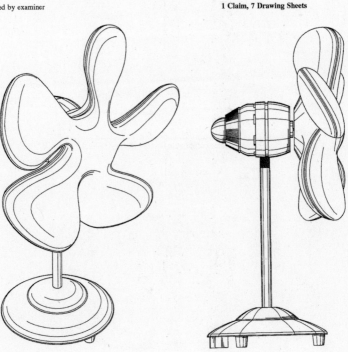

TITLE: REMOTE CONTROLLER FOR TELEVISION SET
INVENTOR: TOSHIYUKI KITA
ASSIGNEE: SHARP KABUSHIKI KAISHA

PATENT NUMBER: USD 458,920
PATENT FILED: JUNE 18, 2001
PATENT GRANTED: JUNE 18, 2002

(12) **United States Design Patent**   (10) **Patent No.:**   **US D458,920 S**
     Kita   (45) **Date of Patent:**   ** **Jun. 18, 2002**

(54) **REMOTE CONTROLLER FOR TELEVISION SET**

(75) Inventor: **Toshiyuki Kita**, Osaka-fu (JP)

(73) Assignee: **Sharp Kabushiki Kaisha**, Osaka (JP)

(**) Term: **14 Years**

(21) Appl. No.: **29/143,538**

(22) Filed: **Jun. 18, 2001**

(30) **Foreign Application Priority Data**

Dec. 18, 2000 (JP) 2000-036180

(51) **LOC (7) Cl.** **14-03**
(52) **U.S. Cl.** **D14/218**
(58) **Field of Search** D14/174, 217,
          D14/218, 167, 168, 191–193, 124, 299;
          D13/168, 162–164; D21/512–517, 566;
          D10/104, 106; 348/114, 734; 455/352–355,
          151.1–151.4

(56)   **References Cited**

              U.S. PATENT DOCUMENTS

D350,962 S   * 9/1994 Reardon et al. D14/218
D377,797 S   * 2/1997 Stropkay et al. D14/218
D381,660 S   * 7/1997 Grewe et al. D14/218
D387,352 S   * 12/1997 Kaneko et al. D14/218
D393,628 S   * 4/1998 Ledbetter et al. D13/168
D396,233 S   * 7/1998 Renk et al. D14/218
D409,201 S   * 5/1999 Barraza et al. D14/218
D429,718 S   * 8/2000 Rudolph D14/218
6,157,319 A * 12/2000 Johns et al. 340/10.31

* cited by examiner

Primary Examiner—Louis S. Zarfas
Assistant Examiner—Deanne Levy
(74) *Attorney, Agent, or Firm*—Nixon & Vanderhye

(57)   **CLAIM**

The ornamental design for a "remote controller for television set", as shown and described.

              DESCRIPTION

FIG. 1 is a front, bottom and right side perspective view of a remote controller for a television set according to my design;

FIG. 2 is a front elevational view thereof;
FIG. 3 is a top plan view thereof;
FIG. 4 is a rear elevational view thereof;
FIG. 5 is a bottom plan view thereof;
FIG. 6 is a right side elevational view thereof; and,
FIG. 7 is a left side elevational view thereof.

              1 Claim, 4 Drawing Sheets

931

TITLE: GAS GRILL
INVENTORS: GEORGE BRAKE & SHAWN MINSHALL
ASSIGNEE: FIESTA GAS GRILLS

PATENT NUMBER: USD 462,564
PATENT FILED: JULY 16, 2001
PATENT GRANTED: SEPTEMBER 10, 2002

(12) **United States Design Patent**
Brake et al.

(10) Patent No.: **US D462,564 S**
(45) Date of Patent: ✳✳ **Sep. 10, 2002**

(54) **GAS GRILL**

(75) Inventors: **George Brake; Shawn Minshall**, both of Dickson, TN (US)

(73) Assignee: **Fiesta Gas Grills, LLC**, Dickson, TN (US)

(✳✳) Term: **14 Years**

(21) Appl. No.: **29/145,110**

(22) Filed: **Jul. 16, 2001**

(51) LOC (7) Cl. **07-02**
(52) U.S. Cl. **D7/334**
(58) Field of Search D7/332–337, 402–405;
126/25 R, 25 A, 25 AA, 29–30, 33, 38,
41 R; 99/421 H, 419, 427, 449

(56) **References Cited**

U.S. PATENT DOCUMENTS

D406,488 S	✳	3/1999	Bates et al.	D7/334
D406,489 S	✳	3/1999	Williams et al.	D7/334
D416,164 S	✳	11/1999	Wagner et al.	D7/334
D426,101 S	✳	6/2000	Pai	D7/334
D426,741 S	✳	6/2000	Pai	D7/334
D437,177 S	✳	2/2001	Giebel et al.	D7/334

✳ cited by examiner

Primary Examiner—Ruth McInroy
(74) *Attorney, Agent, or Firm*—Waddey & Patterson; I. C. Waddey, Jr.

(57) **CLAIM**

What is claimed is the ornamental design for a gas grill, as shown and described.

DESCRIPTION

FIG. 1 is a front perspective view of a gas grill showing our new design;
FIG. 2 is a front elevation view thereof;
FIG. 3 is a back elevation view thereof, the details shown in broken lines are for illustrative purposes only and form no part of the claimed design;
FIG. 4 is a right side elevation view thereof;
FIG. 5 is a left side elevational view thereof;
FIG. 6 is a top plan view thereof; and,
FIG. 7 is a bottom plan view thereof.
The portions of the cart not shown in the drawings (behind the broken lines) or described in the specification form no part of the claimed design.

1 Claim, 5 Drawing Sheets

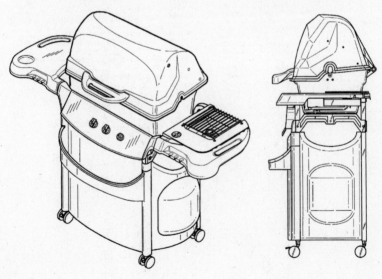

TITLE: TELEPHONE WITH A BASE STATION
INVENTOR: HENRIK SØRIG THOMSEN
ASSIGNEE: BANG & OLUFSEN

PATENT NUMBER: USD 463,388
PATENT FILED: MAY 25, 2001
PATENT GRANTED: SEPTEMBER 24, 2002

(12) **United States Design Patent** (10) Patent No.:   **US D463,388 S**

Thomsen   (45) **Date of Patent:**   ✱✱ **Sep. 24, 2002**

(54) **TELEPHONE WITH A BASE STATION**

(75) Inventor: **Henrik Sørig Thomsen**, Århus C (DK)

(73) Assignee: **Bang & Olufsen A/S**, Struer (DK)

(✱✱) Term: **14 Years**

(21) Appl. No.: **29/142,472**

(22) Filed: **May 25, 2001**

(30)   **Foreign Application Priority Data**

   Mar. 2, 2001 (DK) .... MA 2001 000257

(51) **LOC (7) Cl.** **14-03**
(52) **U.S. Cl.** **D14/148**
(58) **Field of Search** D14/137, 434,
         D14/138, 447, 148, 147, 149–151, 140–142,
         240, 241, 251, 253, 144, 451, 218, 143;
         379/426, 449, 419, 420.04, 428.01, 440,
         454, 455, 446, 430, 433.01–436; 455/500–575,
         90; D13/107, 108, 168; 320/110, 113, 114,
         115; D3/218

(56)   **References Cited**

              U.S. PATENT DOCUMENTS

D211,362 S	✱	6/1968	Janda	D14/147
D234,849 S	✱	4/1975	Tyson et al.	D14/148
D263,045 S	✱	2/1982	Janda et al.	D14/149
D272,064 S	✱	1/1984	Coons et al.	D14/148
D284,468 S	✱	7/1986	Matras	D14/147
D284,762 S	✱	7/1986	Mo	D14/143
D290,118 S	✱	6/1987	Kaufman	D14/147
D291,309 S	✱	8/1987	Kaufman	D14/149
D327,060 S	✱	6/1992	Wachob et al.	D14/138
D353,371 S	✱	12/1994	Delhaes	D14/149
D365,102 S	✱	12/1995	Gioscia	D14/218
5,479,486 A	✱	12/1995	Saji	455/573
D369,163 S	✱	4/1996	Leung et al.	D14/150
D373,124 S	✱	8/1996	Behar et al.	D14/148
D386,495 S	✱	11/1997	Schmoll	D14/149
D389,832 S	✱	1/1998	Chong	D14/150

D401,579 S	✱	11/1998	Benjamin et al.	D14/149
D414,490 S	✱	9/1999	Heinen et al.	D14/148
D424,558 S	✱	5/2000	Hong	D14/143
D430,861 S	✱	9/2000	Lytel	D14/147

✱ cited by examiner

Primary Examiner—Jeffrey Asch
(74) *Attorney, Agent, or Firm*—Darby & Darby

(57)   **CLAIM**

The ornamental design for a telephone with a base station,
as shown and described.

                DESCRIPTION

FIG. 1 is a front perspective view of a telephone in the base
station;
FIG. 2 is a rear perspective view thereof;
FIG. 3 is a left-side view thereof;
FIG. 4 is a right-side view thereof;
FIG. 5 is a front view thereof;
FIG. 6 is a rear view thereof;
FIG. 7 is a top view thereof;
FIG. 8 is a bottom plan view thereof;
FIG. 9 is a front perspective view of the telephone;
FIG. 10 is a rear perspective view thereof;
FIG. 11 is a rear view thereof;
FIG. 12 is a front view thereof;
FIG. 13 is a right-side view thereof;
FIG. 14 is a left-side view thereof;
FIG. 15 is a bottom plan view thereof;
FIG. 16 is top plan view thereof;
FIG. 17 is a front perspective view of the base station;
FIG. 18 is a rear perspective view thereof;
FIG. 19 is a front view thereof, the rear view being the same
as FIG. 6;
FIG. 20 is a right-side view thereof, the left-side view being
a mirror image; and,
FIG. 21 is a top view thereof, the bottom view being the
same as FIG. 8.

                1 Claim, 21 Drawing Sheets

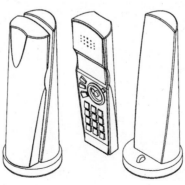

TITLE: LUMINAIRE
INVENTORS: MICHELE DE LUCCHI & GERHARDT REICHERT
ASSIGNEE: DZ LIGHT

PATENT NUMBER: USD 464,762
PATENT FILED: JUNE 19, 2001
PATENT GRANTED: OCTOBER 22, 2002

(12) **United States Design Patent**
De Lucchi et al.

(10) Patent No.: **US D464,762 S**
(45) Date of Patent: **** Oct. 22, 2002**

(54) **LUMINAIRE**

(75) Inventors: **Michele De Lucchi**, Pregnana Milanese (IT); **Gerhardt Reichert**, Pregnana Milanese (IT)

(73) Assignee: **DZ Light GmbH & Co. KG** (DE)

(**) Term: **14 Years**

(21) Appl. No.: **29/143,719**

(22) Filed: **Jun. 19, 2001**

(30) **Foreign Application Priority Data**

Dec. 21, 2000 (XH) DM/054 689

(51) **LOC (7) Cl.** **26-03**
(52) **U.S. Cl.** **D26/106**
(58) **Field of Search** D26/93–112; 362/410–414, 362/153, 153.1, 806, 808

(56) **References Cited**

U.S. PATENT DOCUMENTS

D351,040 S * 9/1994 Lin D26/108

D402,076 S * 12/1998 Chan D26/93

* cited by examiner

Primary Examiner—Alan P. Douglas
Assistant Examiner—Linda Brooks
(74) *Attorney, Agent, or Firm*—Cantor Colburn LLP

(57) **CLAIM**

The ornamental design for a luminaire, as shown and described.

DESCRIPTION

FIG. 1 is a front elevational view of a luminaire, showing my new design;

FIG. 2 is a side elevational view thereof, the opposite side being a mirror image thereof;

FIG. 3 is a rear view thereof; and,

FIG. 4 is a front, side perspective view thereof.

1 Claim, 4 Drawing Sheets

TITLE: BICYCLE
INVENTORS: TAKUJI MASUI, HARTMUT ESSLINGER,
NICO MICHLER & STASCHA OFFENBECK
ASSIGNEE: SHIMANO

PATENT NUMBER: USD 466,055
PATENT FILED: NOVEMBER 9, 2001
PATENT GRANTED: NOVEMBER 26, 2002

(12) **United States Design Patent**   (10) Patent No.:   **US D466,055 S**

Masui et al.   (45) Date of Patent: ** **Nov. 26, 2002**

(54) **BICYCLE**

(75) Inventors: **Takuji Masui**, Sakai (JP); **Hartmut Esslinger**, Altensteig (DE); **Nico Michler**, Baden-Württemberg (DE); **Stascha Offenbeck**, Ottobrunn Bayern (DE)

(73) Assignee: **Shimano Inc.**, Osaka (JP)

(**) Term: **14 Years**

(21) Appl. No.: **29/150,162**

(22) Filed: **Nov. 9, 2001**

(51) **LOC (7) Cl.** 12-11

(52) **U.S. Cl.** **D12/111**

(58) **Field of Search** D12/111; 280/274, 280/275, 281.1, 283, 284, 287, 288.1–288.4

(56)   **References Cited**

U.S. PATENT DOCUMENTS

2,604,179 A * 7/1952 Gilardi 180/225

4,856,801 A * 8/1989 Hollingsworth 280/284
5,226,674 A * 7/1993 Buell et al. 280/284

* cited by examiner

Primary Examiner—Alan P. Douglas
Assistant Examiner—Linda Brooks
(74) *Attorney, Agent, or Firm*—Shinjyu Global IP Counselors, LLP

(57)   **CLAIM**

The ornamental design for a bicycle, as shown and described.

DESCRIPTION

FIG. **1** is a side elevational view of a bicycle in accordance with our new design;

FIG. **2** is a rear side perspective view of the bicycle illustrated in FIG. **1**; and,

FIG. **3** is a front side perspective view of the bicycle illustrated in FIGS. **1** and **2**.

The portions of the bicycle that cannot be seen in FIGS. **1–3** do not form a part of the claimed design.

1 Claim, 3 Drawing Sheets

TITLE: LOUDSPEAKER
INVENTOR: DAVID LEWIS
ASSIGNEE: BANG & OLUFSEN

PATENT NUMBER: USD 466,887
PATENT FILED: MAY 25, 2001
PATENT GRANTED: DECEMBER 10, 2002

(12) **United States Design Patent**

Lewis

(10) **Patent No.:** **US D466,887 S**

(45) **Date of Patent:** ** **Dec. 10, 2002**

(54) **LOUDSPEAKER**

(75) Inventor: **David Lewis**, Copenhagen (DK)

(73) Assignee: **Bang & Olufsen A/S**, Struer (DK)

(**) Term: **14 Years**

(21) Appl. No.: **29/142,473**

(22) Filed: **May 25, 2001**

(30) **Foreign Application Priority Data**

Mar. 2, 2001 (DK) 2001-00258

(51) **LOC (7) Cl.** **14-01**

(52) **U.S. Cl.** **D14/216**

(58) **Field of Search** D14/204, 207–216, D14/221–222; 181/144–145, 147–148, 150, 152–153, 157, 198–199; 381/300–302, 307, 359, 361–364, 386

(56) **References Cited**

U.S. PATENT DOCUMENTS

D210,538 S * 3/1968 Lahti D14/213

D297,233 S	*	8/1988	Livigni	D14/215
5,812,685 A	*	9/1998	Fujita et al.	181/153
D426,230 S	*	6/2000	De Luliis et al.	D14/216
D440,557 S	*	4/2001	Su	D14/215

* cited by examiner

Primary Examiner—Nanda Bondade

(74) *Attorney, Agent, or Firm*—Darby & Darby

(57) **CLAIM**

An ornamental design for a loudspeaker, as shown.

DESCRIPTION

FIG. 1 is a front perspective view of a loudspeaker according to the invention;

FIG. 2 is a rear perspective view thereof;

FIG. 3 is a front view thereof;

FIG. 4 is a rear view thereof;

FIG. 5 is a right-side view thereof;

FIG. 6 is a left-side view thereof;

FIG. 7 is a top plan view thereof; and,

FIG. 8 is a bottom plan view thereof.

1 Claim, 8 Drawing Sheets

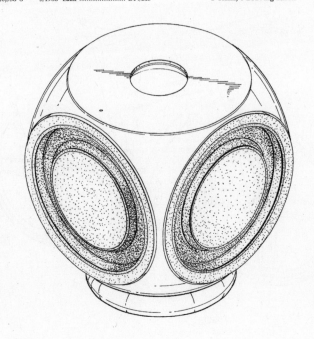

TITLE: MEDIA PLAYER
INVENTORS: BARTLEY K. ANDRE, DANIEL J. COSTER,
DANIELE DE IULIIS, RICHARD P. HOWARTH, ET AL.
ASSIGNEE: APPLE COMPUTER

PATENT NUMBER: USD 469,109
PATENT FILED: OCTOBER 22, 2001
PATENT GRANTED: JANUARY 21, 2003

(12) **United States Design Patent**   (10) Patent No.:   **US D469,109 S**
Andre et al.   (45) Date of Patent: ** **Jan. 21, 2003**

(54) **MEDIA PLAYER**

(75) Inventors: **Bartley K. Andre**, Menlo Park, CA (US); **Daniel J. Coster**, San Francisco, CA (US); **Daniele De Iuliis**, San Francisco, CA (US); **Richard P. Howarth**, San Francisco, CA (US); **Jonathan P. Ive**, San Francisco, CA (US); **Steve Jobs**, Palo Alto, CA (US); **Duncan Robert Kerr**, San Francisco, CA (US); **Matthew Dean Rohrbach**, San Francisco, CA (US); **Douglas B. Satzger**, San Carlos, CA (US); **Calvin Q. Seid**, Palo Alto, CA (US); **Christopher J. Stringer**, Pacifica, CA (US); **Eugene Anthony Whang**, San Francisco, CA (US)

(73) Assignee: **Apple Computer, Inc.**, Cupertino, CA (US)

(**) Term: **14 Years**

(21) Appl. No.: **29/153,169**

(22) Filed: **Oct. 22, 2001**

(51) LOC (7) Cl. **14-03**
(52) U.S. Cl. **D14/496**
(58) Field of Search .... D14/400, 401, D14/435, 454, 474, 496, 483, 217; D21/332, 333; 273/148 B; 463/43–47, 1; 206/308.1, 308.3, 307; 369/2, 24, 25; 370/342, 343, 344

(56) **References Cited**

U.S. PATENT DOCUMENTS

D264,969 S	*	6/1982	McGourty	.... D14/496
4,976,435 A	*	12/1990	Shaford et al.	.... 345/156
5,192,082 A	*	3/1993	Inoue et al.	.... 463/44
5,661,632 A	*	8/1997	Register	.... 345/905
5,964,661 A	*	10/1999	Dodge	.... 463/24
D430,169 S	*	8/2000	Scibora	.... D14/496
D450,713 S	*	11/2001	Masamitsu et al.	.... D14/496
D542,250	*	12/2001	Chan	.... D14/496

* cited by examiner

Primary Examiner—Prabhakar Deshmukh
(74) *Attorney, Agent, or Firm*—Beyer Weaver & Thomas, LLP.

(57) **CLAIM**

We claim the ornamental design for a media player, substantially as shown and described.

DESCRIPTION

FIG. 1 is a perspective view of a media player showing our new design;
FIG. 2 is a front elevational view thereof;
FIG. 3 is a left side elevational view thereof;
FIG. 4 is a right side elevational view thereof;
FIG. 5 is a bottom plan view thereof;
FIG. 6 is a top plan view thereof; and,
FIG. 7 is a rear elevational view thereof.

1 Claim, 5 Drawing Sheets

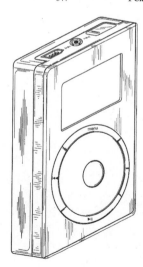

TITLE: INSTANT CAMERA
INVENTOR: NORIKO KATAYAMA
ASSIGNEE: FUJI PHOTO FILM COMPANY

PATENT NUMBER: USD 473,251
PATENT FILED: MAY 15, 2002
PATENT GRANTED: APRIL 15, 2003

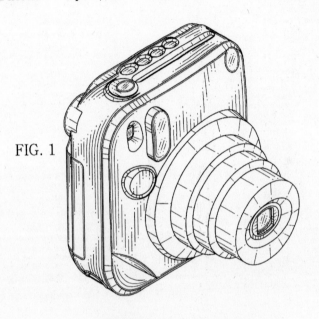

FIG. 1

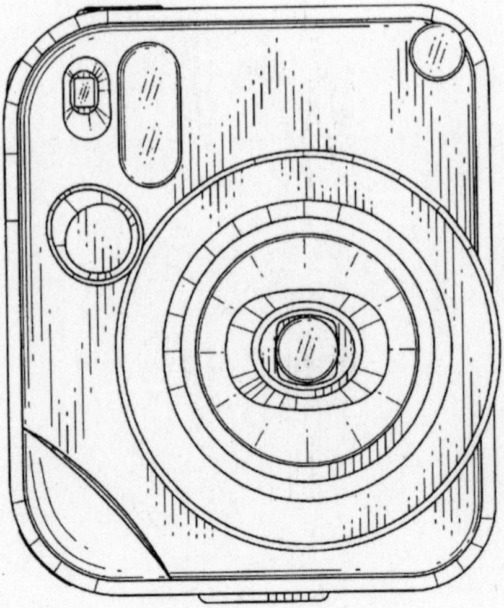

FIG. 2

938

TITLE: HANDHELD ELECTRONIC DEVICE
INVENTOR: JASON T. GRIFFIN
ASSIGNEE: RESEARCH IN MOTION

PATENT NUMBER: USD 479,233
PATENT FILED: JANUARY 8, 2002
PATENT GRANTED: SEPTEMBER 2, 2003

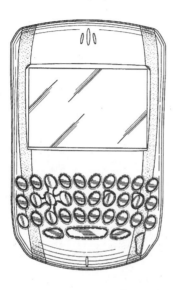

FIG.1

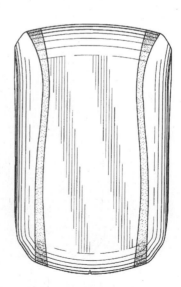

FIG.2

939

TITLE: ELECTRIC FAN HEATER
INVENTOR: TAKEO KOIKE
ASSIGNEE: SHARP KABUSHIKI KAISHA

PATENT NUMBER: USD 479,589
PATENT FILED: JANUARY 27, 2003
PATENT GRANTED: SEPTEMBER 9, 2003

(12) **United States Design Patent**
Koike

(10) **Patent No.:** **US D479,589 S**
(45) **Date of Patent:** ✱✱ **Sep. 9, 2003**

(54) **ELECTRIC FAN HEATER**

(75) Inventor: **Takeo Koike**, Nara-ken (JP)

(73) Assignee: **Sharp Kabushiki Kaisha**, Osaka (JP)

(**) Term: **14 Years**

(21) Appl. No.: **29/174,806**

(22) Filed: **Jan. 27, 2003**

(30) **Foreign Application Priority Data**

Jul. 29, 2002 (JP) 2002-020137

(51) **LOC (7) Cl.** **23-03**
(52) **U.S. Cl.** **D23/336**
(58) **Field of Search** D23/314, 328,
D23/332, 335–8, 340, 341, 370, 377, 380–2;
392/360, 365–9, 373–6; 312/236; 126/110 B,
110 D, 90 A, 92 A

(56) **References Cited**

U.S. PATENT DOCUMENTS

D267,970 S * 2/1983 Gronwick D23/336

D271,132 S	*	10/1983	Boldt et al.	D23/336
D343,231 S	*	1/1994	Lim	D23/336
D346,017 S	*	4/1994	Lim	D23/336
D389,567 S	*	1/1998	Gudefin	D23/381
D468,414 S	*	1/2003	Fok	D23/328

* cited by examiner

Primary Examiner—B. J. Bullock
(74) *Attorney, Agent, or Firm*—Nixon & Vanderhye

(57) **CLAIM**

The ornamental design for an "electric fan heater", as shown and described.

DESCRIPTION

FIG. **1** is a top, front and right side perspective view of an electric fan heater according to my design;
FIG. **2** is a front elevational view thereof;
FIG. **3** is a rear elevational view thereof;
FIG. **4** is a top plan view thereof;
FIG. **5** is a bottom plan view thereof;
FIG. **6** is a right side elevational view thereof; and,
FIG. **7** is a left side elevational view thereof.

1 Claim, 6 Drawing Sheets

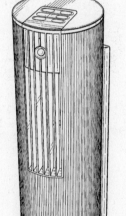

TITLE: SINGLE-LENS REFLEX CAMERA
INVENTORS: YOSHIYUKI MATSUMURA, HIROSHI SANO,
KENNOSUKE CHUJO & HITOSHI TAKAONO
ASSIGNEE: CANON KABUSHIKI KAISHA

PATENT NUMBER: USD 480,743
PATENT FILED: NOVEMBER 4, 2002
PATENT GRANTED: OCTOBER 14, 2003

(12) **United States Design Patent** (10) Patent No.: **US D480,743 S**

Matsumura et al. (45) Date of Patent: ✱✱ **Oct. 14, 2003**

(54) **SINGLE-LENS REFLEX CAMERA**

(75) Inventors: **Yoshiyuki Matsumura**, Yokosuka (JP);
Hiroshi Sano, Yokohama (JP);
Kennosuke Chujo, Tokyo (JP); **Hitoshi
Takaono**, Tokyo (JP)

(73) Assignee: **Canon Kabushiki Kaisha**, Tokyo (JP)

(**) Term: **14 Years**

(21) Appl. No.: **29/170,203**

(22) Filed: **Nov. 4, 2002**

(30)   **Foreign Application Priority Data**

May 7, 2002 (JP) 2002-011913

(51) **LOC (7) Cl.** **16-01**
(52) **U.S. Cl.** **D16/217**
(58) **Field of Search** D16/200–205,
D16/208, 209, 216–218; 396/354–359,
175, 176, 535–541

(56)   **References Cited**

U.S. PATENT DOCUMENTS

D316,720 S	5/1991	Sano	.... D16/202
5,253,003 A	* 10/1993	Fujii et al.	.... 396/175

D363,301 S	*	10/1995	Giugiaro et al.	.... D16/217
D411,218 S	*	6/1999	Kumakura et al.	.... D16/217
D418,530 S	*	1/2000	Tanaka et al.	.... D16/217
D439,922 S	*	4/2001	Kumakura	.... D16/217
D446,235 S		8/2001	Morishita et al.	.... D16/217
D451,940 S	*	12/2001	Haga	.... D16/217

* cited by examiner

Primary Examiner—Adir Aronovich
(74) *Attorney, Agent, or Firm*—Fitzpatrick, Cella, Harper &
Scinto

(57)   **CLAIM**

The ornamental design for a single-lens reflex camera, as
shown and described.

DESCRIPTION

FIG. 1 is a front view of a single-lens reflex camera showing
our new design;
FIG. 2 is a rear view thereof;
FIG. 3 is a top plan view thereof;
FIG. 4 is a bottom plan view thereof;
FIG. 5 is a left side view thereof;
FIG. 6 is a right side view thereof; and,
FIG. 7 is a perspective view thereof.

1 Claim, 4 Drawing Sheets

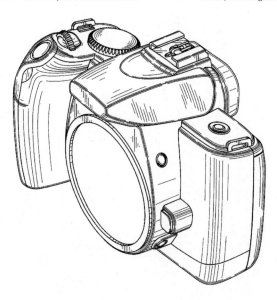

TITLE: COMBINED VIDEO CASSETTE RECORDER
AND DIGITAL DISC PLAYER
INVENTORS: MASAKATSU ITO, TAMOTSU SENDA, ET AL.
ASSIGNEE: MATSUSHITA ELECTRICAL

PATENT NUMBER: USD 481,367
PATENT FILED: SEPTEMBER 9, 2002
PATENT GRANTED: OCTOBER 28, 2003

FIG. 1

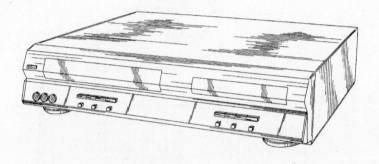

FIG. 2

FIG. 3

TITLE: HANDSET
INVENTOR: MATTHEW SINCLAIR
ASSIGNEE: NOKIA CORPORATION

PATENT NUMBER: USD 481,695
PATENT FILED: JULY 30, 2002
PATENT GRANTED: NOVEMBER 4, 2003

FIG.1

FIG.2   FIG.3   FIG.4

FIG.5

TITLE: ELECTRIC FAN
INVENTOR: PING CHEUNG WONG
ASSIGNEE: IMS INTERNATIONAL

PATENT NUMBER: USD 483,852
PATENT FILED: JANUARY 15, 2003
PATENT GRANTED: DECEMBER 16, 2003

(12) **United States Design Patent**   (10) Patent No.:   **US D483,852 S**
Wong   (45) **Date of Patent:**   ** **Dec. 16, 2003**

(54) **ELECTRIC FAN**

(75) Inventor: **Ping Cheung Wong**, Tsuen Wan (CN)

(73) Assignee: **IMS International Ltd.**, Tsuen Wan
                  (CN)

(**) Term: **14 Years**

(21) Appl. No.: **29/174,290**

(22) Filed: **Jan. 15, 2003**

(30)   **Foreign Application Priority Data**

  Jul. 16, 2002   (CN) 02 3 32152

(51) **LOC (7) Cl.** **23-04**
(52) **U.S. Cl.** **D23/382**
(58) **Field of Search** D23/370, 381,
                 D23/382, 328; 416/244 R, 247 R, 246

(56)   **References Cited**

             U.S. PATENT DOCUMENTS

  D104,064 S   * 4/1937 Hamilton D23/382

D391,357 S   * 2/1998 Chi D23/382

* cited by examiner

Primary Examiner—Lisa Lichtenstein
(74) *Attorney, Agent, or Firm*—Alix, Yale & Ristas, LLP

(57)   **CLAIM**

The ornamental design for an electric fan, as shown and
described.

                DESCRIPTION

FIG. **1** is a front view of the electric fan showing my new
design;
FIG. **2** is a rear view of the electric fan of FIG. **1**;
FIG. **3** is a left side view of the electric fan of FIG. **1**;
FIG. **4** is a right side view of the electric fan of FIG. **1**;
FIG. **5** is a top plan view of the electric fan of FIG. **1**; and,
FIG. **6** is a bottom plan view of the electric fan of FIG. **1**.

1 Claim, 6 Drawing Sheets

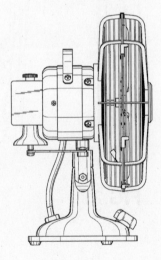

TITLE: STEAM IRON
INVENTOR: JASPER MORRISON
ASSIGNEE: ROWENTA-WERKE

PATENT NUMBER: USD 487,832
PATENT FILED: MAY 28, 2003
PATENT GRANTED: MARCH 23, 2004

(12) **United States Design Patent** (10) Patent No.: **US D487,832 S**

Morrison (45) Date of Patent: ** Mar. 23, 2004

(54) **STEAM IRON**

(75) Inventor: **Jasper Morrison**, London (GB)

(73) Assignee: **Rowenta-Werke GmbH** (DE)

(**) Term: **14 Years**

(21) Appl. No.: **29/182,502**

(22) Filed: **May 28, 2003**

(51) LOC (7) Cl. **07-05**
(52) U.S. Cl. **D32/69**; D32/70
(58) Field of Search D32/68–72; 38/74,
38/75, 77.1, 77.8, 77.9, 88, 90, 93; 219/245–248,
252

(56) **References Cited**

U.S. PATENT DOCUMENTS

4,233,763 A	*	11/1980	McMullen	38/77.83
D323,047 S	*	1/1992	O'Flynn	D32/70
5,901,481 A	*	5/1999	Simmons et al.	38/93
D415,865 S	*	10/1999	Littmann et al.	D32/70
D427,403 S	*	6/2000	Gudefin	D32/70
D443,743 S	*	6/2001	Edwards et al.	D32/70

D459,045 S	*	6/2002	Figur et al.	D32/70
D466,260 S	*	11/2002	Wu	D32/69

* cited by examiner

Primary Examiner—Alan P. Douglas
Assistant Examiner—Lavone D. Tabor
(74) *Attorney, Agent, or Firm*—Ostrolenk, Faber, Gerb & Soffen, LLP

(57) **CLAIM**

I claim the ornamental design for a steam iron, as shown.

DESCRIPTION

FIG. 1 is a front left side perspective view of the steam iron of the present invention;
FIG. 2 is an enlarged left side perspective view thereof;
FIG. 3 is an enlarged front view thereof;
FIG. 4 is an enlarged rear view thereof;
FIG. 5 is an enlarged top view thereof;
FIG. 6 is an enlarged bottom view thereof; and,
FIG. 7 is an enlarged left side view thereof, the right side being a mirror image.

1 Claim, 7 Drawing Sheets

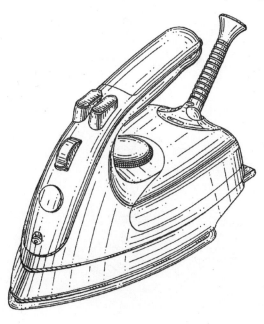

TITLE: COMPUTING DEVICE
INVENTORS: BARTLEY K. ANDRE, DANIEL J. COSTER,
DANIELE DE IULIIS, RICHARD P. HOWARTH, ET AL.
ASSIGNEE: APPLE COMPUTER

PATENT NUMBER: USD 493,785
PATENT FILED: DECEMBER 31, 2002
PATENT GRANTED: AUGUST 3, 2004

(12) **United States Design Patent** (10) Patent No.: **US D493,785 S**

Andre et al. (45) Date of Patent: ** **Aug. 3, 2004**

(54) **COMPUTING DEVICE**

(75) Inventors: **Bartley K. Andre**, Menlo Park, CA
(US); **Daniel J. Coster**, San Francisco,
CA (US); **Daniele De Iuliis**, San
Francisco, CA (US); **Richard P.
Howarth**, San Francisco, CA (US);
Jonathan P. Ive, San Francisco, CA
(US); **Steve Jobs**, Palo Alto, CA (US);
Duncan Robert Kerr, San Francisco,
CA (US); **Matthew Dean Rohrbach**,
San Francisco, CA (US); **Douglas B.
Satzger**, San Carlos, CA (US); **Calvin
Q. Seid**, Palo Alto, CA (US);
Christopher J. Stringer, Pacifica, CA
(US); **Eugene Anthony Whang**, San
Francisco, CA (US)

(73) Assignee: **Apple Computer, Inc.**, Cupertino, CA
(US)

(**) Term: **14 Years**

(21) Appl. No.: **29/173,537**

(22) Filed: **Dec. 31, 2002**

(51) **LOC (7) Cl.** **14-02**

(52) **U.S. Cl.** **D14/318**

(58) **Field of Search** D14/315–322,
D14/327; D18/1, 2, 7; 235/145 A, 145 R;
341/22, 23; 345/104, 156, 168, 169, 173;
361/680–686

(56) **References Cited**

U.S. PATENT DOCUMENTS

D416,238 S * 11/1999 Irie et al. D14/318
D435,549 S * 12/2000 Amano et al. D14/318
D453,756 S * 2/2002 Kamegi D14/318
D463,797 S * 10/2002 Andre et al. D14/327

OTHER PUBLICATIONS

"Apple Announces 14–inch iBook" press release, MacWorld
Expo, San Francisco, Jan. 7, 2002.
Apple iBook, "The most affordable Mac portable ever,"
product information, Apple Computer, Inc., downloaded
from www.apple.com/ibook on Dec. 6, 2002.
Apple iBook Technical Specifications, "This impact–resis-
tant notebook makes a powerful impact," Apple Computer,
Inc., downloaded from www.apple.com/ibook/specs.html on
Dec. 27, 2002.
iBook Photos (for Media and Analysts Only), downloaded
from www.apple.com/ibook on Dec. 6, 2002.

(List continued on next page.)

Primary Examiner—Freda Nunn
(74) *Attorney, Agent, or Firm*—Beyer Weaver & Thomas,
LLP

(57) **CLAIM**

We claim the ornamental design for a computing device,
substantially as shown and described.

DESCRIPTION

FIG. 1 is a perspective view of a computing device while in
an open position in accordance with the present design;
FIG. 2 is a first side view thereof while in an open position;
FIG. 3 is a second side view thereof while in an open
position;
FIG. 4 is a front view thereof while in a closed position;
FIG. 5 is a rear view thereof while in a closed position;
FIG. 6 is a bottom view thereof while in a closed position;
and,
FIG. 7 is a top view thereof while in a closed position.
The broken lines are shown in the views for illustrative
purposes only and form no part of the claimed design.

1 Claim, 5 Drawing Sheets

TITLE: HOUSEHOLD ELECTRIC KETTLE
INVENTOR: JASPER MORRISON
ASSIGNEE: NONE

PATENT NUMBER: USD 498,638
PATENT FILED: NOVEMBER 12, 2003
PATENT GRANTED: NOVEMBER 23, 2004

(12) **United States Design Patent**
Morrison

(10) Patent No.: **US D498,638 S**
(45) Date of Patent: ** Nov. 23, 2004

(54) **HOUSEHOLD ELECTRIC KETTLE**

(76) Inventor: **Jasper Morrison**, 51 Hoxton Sq.,
London N1 6 PB (GB)

(**) Term: **14 Years**

(21) Appl. No.: **29/193,436**

(22) Filed: **Nov. 12, 2003**

(30) **Foreign Application Priority Data**

Sep. 12, 2003 (FR) 03 2709

(51) **LOC (7) Cl.** **07-01**
(52) **U.S. Cl.** **D7/319**; D7/318
(58) **Field of Search** D7/300, 316, 317,
D7/318, 319, 312; D23/207; 215/398; 220/504,
574, 318, 912; 222/196, 131, 465.1, 146.6,
189.07

(56) **References Cited**

U.S. PATENT DOCUMENTS

D220,773 S	*	5/1971	Dilyard	D7/317
D263,105 S	*	2/1982	Okazaki et al.	D7/319
D263,783 S	*	4/1982	Okazaki et al.	D7/317
D270,602 S	*	9/1983	Fritz	D7/319
D285,160 S	*	8/1986	Osit	D7/317
D302,370 S	*	7/1989	Gibert	D7/317
4,967,939 A	*	11/1990	Taylor	222/196
D345,670 S	*	4/1994	Piret	D7/319
D356,004 S	*	3/1995	Van Valkenburg et al.	D7/317
D367,580 S	*	3/1996	Joergensen	D7/318
D368,404 S	*	4/1996	Zive	D7/318
D473,092 S	*	4/2003	Heiberg et al.	D7/319
D475,233 S	*	6/2003	De Visser	D7/317

* cited by examiner

Primary Examiner—M. N. Pandozzi
(74) *Attorney, Agent, or Firm*—Young & Thompson

(57) **CLAIM**

The ornamental design for a household electric kettle, as shown.

DESCRIPTION

FIG. 1 is a top, front and side perspective view of a household electric kettle, showing my new design;
FIG. 2 is a front elevational view thereof;
FIG. 3 is a side elevational view thereof from the left of FIG. 2;
FIG. 4 is a side elevational view thereof from the right of FIG. 2;
FIG. 5 is a rear elevational view thereof;
FIG. 6 is a top plan view thereof; and,
FIG. 7 is a bottom plan view thereof.

1 Claim, 7 Drawing Sheets

TITLE: HOUSING FOR A COMMUNICATION DEVICE
INVENTORS: CHRISTOPHER A. ARNHOLT,
PAUL M. PIERCE & TIM J. SUTHERLAND
ASSIGNEE: MOTOROLA

PATENT NUMBER: USD 500,750
PATENT FILED: MARCH 16, 2004
PATENT GRANTED: JANUARY 11, 2005

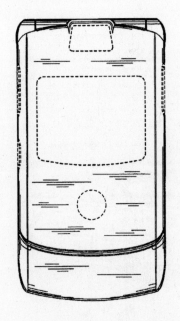

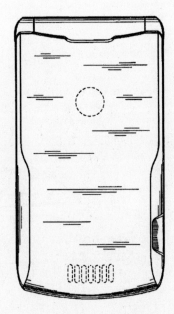

FIG. 2   *FIG. 3*

TITLE: AUTOMOBILE BODY
INVENTORS: MARK D. HALL, MICHAEL R. CASTIGLIONE
JEFF C. GALE & RALPH V. GILLES
ASSIGNEE: DAIMLER CHRYSLER CORPORATION

PATENT NUMBER: USD 510,056
PATENT FILED: OCTOBER 12, 2004
PATENT GRANTED: SEPTEMBER 27, 2005

(12) **United States Design Patent**

Hall et al.

(10) Patent No.: **US D510,056 S**

(45) Date of Patent: ∗∗ **Sep. 27, 2005**

(54) **AUTOMOBILE BODY**

(75) Inventors: **Mark D Hall**, Rochester, MI (US); **Micheal R Castiglione**, Carlsbad, CA (US); **Jeff C Gale**, Rochester, MI (US); **Ralph V Gilles**, Lake Orion, MI (US)

(73) Assignee: **DaimlerChrysler Corporation**, Auburn Hills, MI (US)

(∗∗) Term: **14 Years**

(21) Appl. No.: **29/214,980**

(22) Filed: **Oct. 12, 2004**

(51) LOC (8) Cl. **12-08**

(52) U.S. Cl. **D12/92**

(58) Field of Search D12/90–92, 86; D21/424, 433; 296/185

(56) **References Cited**

U.S. PATENT DOCUMENTS

D453,713 S	∗	2/2002	McMahan et al.	D12/91
D466,053 S	∗	11/2002	O'Connell et al.	D12/91
D466,443 S	∗	12/2002	Faurote et al.	D12/91
D472,850 S	∗	4/2003	Frasher et al.	D12/91
D479,492 S	∗	9/2003	Gale et al.	D12/91
D482,990 S	∗	12/2003	Sims et al.	D12/91
D489,648 S	∗	5/2004	Gale et al.	D12/92
D495,624 S	∗	9/2004	Dolan et al.	D12/91

∗ cited by examiner

Primary Examiner—Melody N. Brown

(74) Attorney, Agent, or Firm—Ralph E. Smith

(57) **CLAIM**

The ornamental design for an automobile body, as shown and described.

DESCRIPTION

FIG. 1 is a front perspective view of an automobile body showing our new design;

FIG. 2 is a side view thereof;

FIG. 3 is a front view thereof;

FIG. 4 is a rear view thereof; and,

FIG. 5 is a rear perspective view thereof.

It will be understood that the dashed lines presented in the drawings are for illustration only, and do not form a part of the claimed design.

1 Claim, 4 Drawing Sheets

TITLE: USB LIGHT HEAD WITH FAN
INVENTOR: SHUI-SHENG CHANG
ASSIGNEE: NONE

PATENT NUMBER: USD 511,017
PATENT FILED: OCTOBER 29, 2003
PATENT GRANTED: OCTOBER 25, 2005

(12) **United States Design Patent**　(10) Patent No.:　　**US D511,017 S**
Chang　　　　　　　　　　　　　　　　　　(45) **Date of Patent:**　∗∗　**Oct. 25, 2005**

(54) **USB LIGHT HEAD WITH FAN**

(76) Inventor: **Shui-Sheng Chang**, 3F, 13, Lane 155, Sec.3, Pechen Road, Shenkeng, Taipei Hsien (TW)

(∗∗) Term: **14 Years**

(21) Appl. No.: **29/192,636**

(22) Filed: **Oct. 29, 2003**

(51) **LOC (8) Cl.** **26-05**

(52) **U.S. Cl.** **D26/51;** D14/432

(58) **Field of Search** D26/51, 60–66; 362/282, 283, 284, 285, 413, 418, 419, 427–428

(56) **References Cited**

U.S. PATENT DOCUMENTS

D381,978 S　∗　8/1997　Nakada et al. D14/432
D498,320 S　∗　11/2004　Leung D26/51

∗ cited by examiner

Primary Examiner—Marcus A. Jackson
(74) *Attorney, Agent, or Firm*—Troxell Law Office, PLLC

(57) **CLAIM**

The ornamental design for USB light head with fan, as shown and described.

DESCRIPTION

FIG. 1 is a top front and left side perspective view of USB light head with fan showing my new design, with the bottom portion broken away for ease of illustration;
FIG. 2 is a front elevational view thereof;
FIG. 3 is a rear elevational view thereof;
FIG. 4 is a left side elevational view thereof;
FIG. 5 is a right side elevational view thereof;
FIG. 6 is a top plan view thereof; and,
FIG. 7 is a bottom plan view thereof; and,
FIG. 8 is a top front and left side perspective view of USB light head with fan embodiment attached a tube and USB plug.

1 Claim, 3 Drawing Sheets

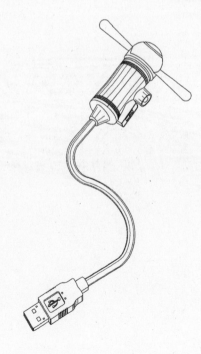

TITLE: STORAGE DEVICE
INVENTORS: ERIC BONE, WESLEY G. BREWER, JEFFREY
ALLEN SALAZAR & GLENN ALWYN WONG
ASSIGNEE: SANDISK CORPORATION

PATENT NUMBER: USD 511,519
PATENT FILED: JUNE 2, 2004
PATENT GRANTED: NOVEMBER 15, 2005

(12) **United States Design Patent** (10) Patent No.: **US D511,519 S**

Bone et al. (45) Date of Patent: ** **Nov. 15, 2005**

(54) **STORAGE DEVICE**

(75) Inventors: **Eric Bone**, San Mateo, CA (US);
Wesley G. Brewer, Menlo Park, CA
(US); **Jeffrey Allen Salazar**, Palo Alto,
CA (US); **Glenn Alwyn Wong**,
Mountain View, CA (US)

(73) Assignee: **SanDisk Corporation**, Sunnyvale, CA
(US)

(**) Term: **14 Years**

(21) Appl. No.: **29/206,851**

(22) Filed: **Jun. 2, 2004**

(51) **LOC (8) Cl.** **14-02**
(52) **U.S. Cl.** **D14/432; D14/435**
(58) **Field of Search** D14/156, 167,
D14/432, 435, 341, 356, 474, 496; 455/45,
344, 346–51, 2.01; 369/75.11, 76; 84/602;
360/55

(56) **References Cited**

U.S. PATENT DOCUMENTS

5,192,082 A	3/1993	Inoue et al.
5,452,180 A	9/1995	Register et al.
5,563,400 A	10/1996	Le Roux
D396,860 S *	8/1998	Yasutomi D14/168
6,122,526 A	9/2000	Parulski et al.
D433,400 S *	11/2000	Boucard D14/160
D446,511 S *	8/2001	Kanno et al. D14/167
D469,109 S	1/2003	Andre et al.
D475,359 S *	6/2003	Hirose D14/167
6,671,567 B1	12/2003	Dwyer et al.
D487,750 S *	3/2004	Dietel et al. D14/474
D488,464 S *	4/2004	Lin et al. D14/242

D489,053 S	*	4/2004 Nakamura	D14/167
D496,944 S		10/2004 Huang	
D498,759 S	*	11/2004 Lewis et al.	D14/436
D499,424 S		12/2004 Bahroocha	
D500,302 S	*	12/2004 Deguchi	D14/167
D500,485 S	*	1/2005 Deguchi	D14/167
D501,485 S		2/2005 Lian et al.	
2004/0074264 A1	*	4/2004 Kung et al.	70/58

* cited by examiner

Primary Examiner—M. H. Tung
(74) *Attorney, Agent, or Firm*—Beyer Weaver & Thomas,
LLP

(57) **CLAIM**

We claim the ornamental design for a storage device, as
shown and described.

DESCRIPTION

This application is related to U.S. Design Application No.
29/206,850 filed concurrently, and entitled "Media Device".
FIG. **1** is a perspective view of a storage device in accordance with the present design, on an enlarged scale.
FIG. **2** is a top view for the storage device in accordance
with the present design.
FIG. **3** is a bottom view for the storage device in accordance
with the present design.
FIG. **4** is a left side view for the storage device in accordance
with the present design.
FIG. **5** is a right side view for the storage device in
accordance with the present design.
FIG. **6** is a front view for the storage device in accordance
with the present design; and,
FIG. **7** is a rear view for the storage device in accordance
with the present design.

1 Claim, 3 Drawing Sheets

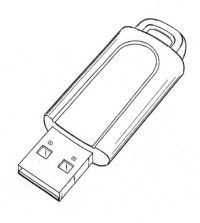

TITLE: PORTABLE FOLDING BICYCLE
INVENTORS: CLIVE MARLES SINCLAIR & ALEXANDER
JOSEPH KALOGROULIS
ASSIGNEE: DAKA RESEARCH

PATENT NUMBER: USD 512,346
PATENT FILED: MAY 21, 2004
PATENT GRANTED: DECEMBER 6, 2005

(12) **United States Design Patent**   (10) Patent No.:   **US D512,346 S**

Sinclair et al.   (45) **Date of Patent:**   ∗∗   **Dec. 6, 2005**

(54) **PORTABLE FOLDING BICYCLE**

(75) Inventors: **Clive Marles Sinclair**, London (GB);
Alexander Joseph Kalogroulis,
Coulsdon (GB)

(73) Assignee: **Daka Research Inc.**, Tortolla (VG)

(∗∗) Term: **14 Years**

(21) Appl. No.: **29/205,879**

(22) Filed: **May 21, 2004**

(51) **LOC (8) Cl.** **12-11**

(52) **U.S. Cl.** **D12/111**

(58) **Field of Search** D12/111; 280/274–278,
280/283–288, 281.1

(56) **References Cited**

U.S. PATENT DOCUMENTS

D306,841 S ∗ 3/1990 Hellestam et al. D12/111

∗ cited by examiner

Primary Examiner—Alan P. Douglas
Assistant Examiner—Linda Brooks
(74) *Attorney, Agent, or Firm*—Curtis L. Harrington

(57)   **CLAIM**

The ornamental design for an portable folding bicycle, as
shown and described.

DESCRIPTION

FIG. 1 is a perspective view of the portable folding bicycle;

FIG. 2 is a right side view;

FIG. 3 is a left side view;

FIG. 4 is a front view;

FIG. 5 is a rear view;

FIG. 6 is a top view; and,

FIG. 7 is a bottom view.

1 Claim, 4 Drawing Sheets

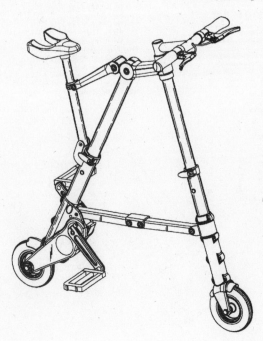

TITLE: PROJECTOR
INVENTORS: ALLEN ZADEH, BLAKE MCELDOWNEY,
JOOST GOODEE, DAVIN STOWALL, ET AL.
ASSIGNEE: HEWLETT-PACKARD DEVELOPMENT COMPANY

PATENT NUMBER: USD 512,736
PATENT FILED: JUNE 7, 2004
PATENT GRANTED: DECEMBER 13, 2005

(12) **United States Design Patent**
Zadeh et al.

(10) Patent No.: **US D512,736 S**
(45) Date of Patent: ** **Dec. 13, 2005**

(54) **PROJECTOR**

(75) Inventors: **Allen Zadeh,** New York, NY (US);
Blake McEldowney, New York, NY
(US); **Joost Goodee,** Palo Alto, CA
(US); **Davin Stowall,** New York, NY
(US); **Sam Lucente,** San Francisco, CA
(US); **Shizunori S. Kobara,** Foster
City, CA (US); **Peter K. Lee,** San Jose,
CA (US)

(73) Assignee: **Hewlett-Packard Development
Company, L.P.,** Houston, TX (US)

(**) Term: **14 Years**

(21) Appl. No.: **29/207,038**

(22) Filed: **Jun. 7, 2004**

(51) **LOC (6) Cl.** **16-02**
(52) **U.S. Cl.** **D16/230**
(58) **Field of Search** D16/205, 208,
D16/213, 221, 225, 230, 231, 234; D21/514;
352/34, 242, 243; 353/119, 122

(56) **References Cited**

U.S. PATENT DOCUMENTS

D428,619 S * 7/2000 Saeki et al. D16/230

D437,607 S	*	2/2001	Takahashi	D16/230
D473,253 S	*	4/2003	Shimamoto	D16/231
D480,409 S	*	10/2003	Wang et al.	D16/230
D482,380 S	*	11/2003	Salvatori et al.	D16/230
D482,715 S	*	11/2003	Schoenert et al.	D16/230
6,830,340 B2	*	12/2004	Olson et al.	353/122

* cited by examiner

Primary Examiner—Adir Aronovich
(74) *Attorney, Agent, or Firm*—Lloyd E. Dakin, Jr.

(57) **CLAIM**

The ornamental design for a projector, as shown and
described.

DESCRIPTION

FIG. **1** is a perspective view of a projector showing the new
design;
FIG. **2** is a front elevation view thereof;
FIG. **3** is a rear elevation view thereof;
FIG. **4** is a left side elevation view thereof;
FIG. **5** is a right side elevation view thereof;
FIG. **6** is a top plan view thereof; and,
FIG. **7** is a bottom plan view thereof.

1 Claim, 3 Drawing Sheets

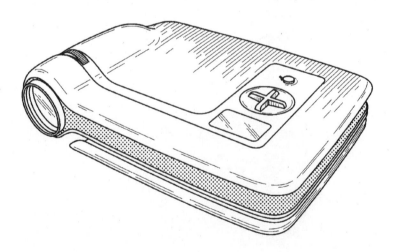

TITLE: SOUND SYSTEM FOR PORTABLE MUSIC PLAYER
INVENTORS: RICHARD J. CARBONE & GUSTAVO
L. FONTANA
ASSIGNEE: BOSE CORPORATION

PATENT NUMBER: USD 514,090
PATENT FILED: JUNE 29, 2004
PATENT GRANTED: JANUARY 31, 2006

(12) **United States Design Patent**   (10) Patent No.: **US D514,090 S**
Carbone et al.   (45) Date of Patent: ** **Jan. 31, 2006**

(54) **SOUND SYSTEM FOR PORTABLE MUSIC PLAYER**

(75) Inventors: **Richard J. Carbone**, Sterling, MA (US); **Gustavo L. Fontana**, Framingham, MA (US)

(73) Assignee: **Bose Corporation**, Framingham, MA (US)

(**) Term: **14 Years**

(21) Appl. No.: **29/208,492**

(22) Filed: **Jun. 29, 2004**

(51) LOC (8) Cl. **14-01**
(52) U.S. Cl. **D14/214**; D14/168
(58) Field of Classification Search D14/204, D14/207, 209–216, 356; 181/143–144, 147–148, 181/150, 157, 198–199, 151, 153; 381/300–302, 381/306, 333, 345, 361–364, 386–388, 332, 381/336
See application file for complete search history.

(56) **References Cited**

U.S. PATENT DOCUMENTS

D188,326	S	*	7/1960	Levy et al.	D14/214
3,143,182	A	*	8/1964	Sears et al.	181/153
3,194,339	A	*	7/1965	Pawlowski	181/146
D369,356	S	*	4/1996	Olson	D14/214
D482,344	S	*	11/2003	Green	D14/214

* cited by examiner

Primary Examiner—Nanda Bondade
(74) Attorney, Agent, or Firm—Fish & Richardson P.C.

(57) **CLAIM**

The ornamental design for a sound system for portable music player, substantially as shown and described.

DESCRIPTION

FIG. 1 is an isometric view of the sound system for portable music player;
FIG. 2 is a front view of the sound system for portable music player;
FIG. 3 is a back view of the sound system for portable music player;
FIG. 4 is a left side view of the sound system for portable music player;
FIG. 5 is a right side view of the sound system for portable music player;
FIG. 6 is a top view of the sound system for portable music player; and,
FIG. 7 is a bottom view of the sound system for portable music player.
The broken line showing on the drawings is for illustrative purposes only and forms no part of the claimed design.

1 Claim, 4 Drawing Sheets

TITLE: ERGONOMIC DISPOSABLE CUP
INVENTORS: STEPHEN ALAN SMITH, KEVIN RAY SMITH,
WARREN GILES WIEDMEYER, ET AL.
ASSIGNEE: SOLO CUP COMPANY

PATENT NUMBER: USD 514,385
PATENT FILED: NOVEMBER 23, 2004
PATENT GRANTED: FEBRUARY 7, 2006

(12) **United States Design Patent** (10) Patent No.: **US D514,385 S**

Smith et al. (45) Date of Patent: ** Feb. 7, 2006

(54) **ERGONOMIC DISPOSABLE CUP**

(75) Inventors: **Stephen Alan Smith**, Naperville, IL (US); **Kevin Ray Smith**, Round Lake Beach, IL (US); **Warren Giles Wiedmeyer**, Trevor, WI (US); **Kimberly Vaile Healy**, Chicago, IL (US); **Randy Golden**, Ada, OK (US); **Rudy DesChamps**, Mahomet, IL (US); **Irshad Khan**, Round Lake Beach, IL (US); **Bryce C. Rutter**, St. Louis, MO (US); **Brian C. Bone**, St. Louis, MO (US); **John H. Loudenslager**, Phoenix, AZ (US); **Jan Rolf Stillerman**, Phoenix, AZ (US)

(73) Assignee: **Solo Cup Company**, Highland Park, IL (US)

(**) Term: **14 Years**

(21) Appl. No.: **29/217,960**

(22) Filed: **Nov. 23, 2004**

Related U.S. Application Data

(60) Division of application No. 29/194,964, filed on Dec. 3, 2003, now Pat. No. Des. 505,830, which is a continuation-in-part of application No. 10/676,807, filed on Oct. 1, 2003.

(51) **LOC (8) Cl.** **07-01**

(52) **U.S. Cl.** **D7/509**; D7/531

(58) **Field of Classification Search** D7/532, D7/531, 523, 507, 509, 392.1, 396, 396.2, D7/629, 615, 530; D9/429, 556, 557; 222/129, 222/465.1; 426/394, 86; 428/36.4; 206/520, 206/519, 217, 514; 366/341; 215/373, 384; 220/705, 676, 738, 671, 675, 669, 694, 735; 229/403, 400, 402, 401; 53/426
See application file for complete search history.

(56) **References Cited**

U.S. PATENT DOCUMENTS

703,125 A 6/1902 Emrich

1,636,174 A 7/1927 Dolan et al.
2,013,243 A 9/1935 Landon

(Continued)

FOREIGN PATENT DOCUMENTS

DE 1 175 564 8/1964
DE 1 216 139 5/1966
DE 44 19 161 A1 12/1995

(Continued)

OTHER PUBLICATIONS

Communication from the European Patent Office transmitting an International Search Report, mailed Nov. 19, 2004, for International Application No. PCT/US2004/009357.

Primary Examiner—M. N. Pandozzi
(74) *Attorney, Agent, or Firm*—Wallenstein Wagner & Rockey, Ltd.

(57) **CLAIM**

We claim the ornamental Design for an ergonomic disposable cup, as shown and described.

DESCRIPTION

FIG. 1 is a perspective view of a first embodiment of the cup of the present invention;
FIG. 2 is a front elevation view of the cup of FIG. 1, with an opposite view being identical thereto;
FIG. 3 is a side elevation view of the cup of FIG. 1, with an opposite view being identical thereto;
FIG. 4 is a top plan view of the cup of FIG. 1;
FIG. 5 is a bottom plan view of the cup of FIG. 1;
FIG. 6 is a perspective view of a second embodiment of the cup of the present invention;
FIG. 7 is a front elevation view of the cup of FIG. 6, with an opposite view being identical thereto;
FIG. 8 is a side elevation view of the cup of FIG. 6, with an opposite view being identical thereto;
FIG. 9 is a top plan view of the cup of FIG. 6; and,
FIG. 10 is a bottom plan view of the cup of FIG. 6.
Broken lines in the Figures form no part of the claimed design.

1 Claim, 6 Drawing Sheets

TITLE: ELECTRIC FAN
INVENTOR: DOMINIC JONES
ASSIGNEE: FOURSTAR GROUP

PATENT NUMBER: USD 515,689
PATENT FILED: SEPTEMBER 26, 2003
PATENT GRANTED: FEBRUARY 21, 2006

(12) **United States Design Patent**　(10) Patent No.: **US D515,689 S**

Jones　　　　　　　　　　　　　　　　　(45) Date of Patent: ✱✱ **Feb. 21, 2006**

(54) **ELECTRIC FAN**

(75) Inventor: **Dominic Jones**, Brighton, MA (US)

(73) Assignee: **Fourstar Group Inc.** (TW)

(✱✱) Term: **14 Years**

(21) Appl. No.: **29/190,864**

(22) Filed: **Sep. 26, 2003**

(51) **LOC (8) Cl.** **23-04**

(52) **U.S. Cl.** **D23/381**

(58) **Field of Classification Search** D23/370,
D23/381, 332, 413; 416/247 R, 246
See application file for complete search history.

(56) **References Cited**

U.S. PATENT DOCUMENTS

D413,685 S ✱ 9/1999 Lasko et al. D23/381
D503,975 S ✱ 4/2005 Jones D23/370

✱ cited by examiner

Primary Examiner—Lisa Lichtenstein
(74) Attorney, Agent, or Firm—Salter & Michaelson

(57) **CLAIM**

The ornamental design for an electric fan, as shown and described.

DESCRIPTION

FIG. 1 is a perspective view of an electric fan showing my new design;
FIG. 2 is a front elevational view thereof;
FIG. 3 is a rear elevational view thereof;
FIG. 4 is a left side elevational view thereof;
FIG. 5 is a right side elevational view thereof;
FIG. 6 is a top plan view thereof; and,
FIG. 7 is a bottom plan view thereof.
The portions shown in broken lines in FIGS. 1 through 6 are for illustration only and form no part of the claimed design.

1 Claim, 4 Drawing Sheets

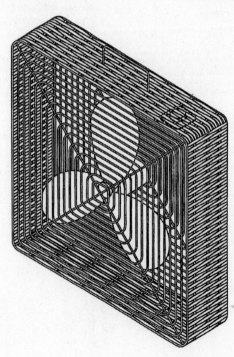

TITLE: SCOOTER
INVENTOR: STEVE SRAMEK
ASSIGNEE: RAZOR USA

PATENT NUMBER: USD 516,132
PATENT FILED: JANUARY 21, 2004
PATENT GRANTED: FEBRUARY 28, 2006

(12) **United States Design Patent**
Sramek

(10) Patent No.: **US D516,132 S**
(45) Date of Patent: ✱✱ **Feb. 28, 2006**

(54) **SCOOTER**

(75) Inventor: **Steve Sramek**, Long Beach, CA (US)

(73) Assignee: **Razor USA LLC**, Cerritos, CA (US)

(✱✱) Term: **14 Years**

(21) Appl. No.: **29/197,886**

(22) Filed: **Jan. 21, 2004**

(51) **LOC (8) Cl.** **21-01**
(52) **U.S. Cl.** **D21/423**
(58) **Field of Classification Search** D21/538,
D21/432, 423; D12/110; 446/440; 180/219–223,
180/227, 181; 280/827, 828, 220, 68.5, 87.021,
280/87.041, 87.042, 87.05; 296/203.1, 78.1
See application file for complete search history.

(56) **References Cited**

U.S. PATENT DOCUMENTS

5,775,452 A	* 7/1998	Patmont	180/181
5,848,660 A	* 12/1998	McGreen	280/87.05
D433,718 S	* 11/2000	McGreen	D21/423
D447,188 S	* 8/2001	Lan	D21/423
6,338,393 B1	* 1/2002	Martin	180/227
D453,804 S	* 2/2002	Robinson	D21/423
D456,460 S	* 4/2002	Tseng	D21/423
6,431,302 B2	* 8/2002	Patmont et al.	180/228
6,481,728 B2	* 11/2002	Chen	280/87.041
D486,532 S	* 2/2004	Christianson	D21/423
D489,771 S	* 5/2004	Laver et al.	D21/423

OTHER PUBLICATIONS

MrToys.com, Jul. 7, 2005,
Razor–electric–scooter–E100.htm.*
Bladez website (www.bladezracing.com) XTR Lite electric
scooter—250 Electric (3 pages).

Bladez website (www.bladezracing.com) Bladez Racing—
Gas Scooters & Electric Scooters (2 pages).

go–ped website (www.Goped.com) The new . . . lighter,
faster, and ultra–low emission (2 pages).

go–ped website (www.Goped.com) "How do you want to
ride?" (2 pages).

go–ped website (www.Goped.com) X25 ridefree (2 pages).

go–ped website (www.Goped.com) Sport & Extreme (1
page).

* cited by examiner

Primary Examiner—Raphael Barkai
(74) Attorney, Agent, or Firm—Knobbe, Martens, Olson &
Bear, LLP

(57) **CLAIM**

The ornamental design for a "scooter," as shown and
described.

DESCRIPTION

FIG. 1 is a perspective view of a preferred embodiment of
a scooter;

FIG. 2 is a top plan view thereof;

FIG. 3 is a bottom plan view thereof;

FIG. 4 is a front elevational view thereof;

FIG. 5 is a rear elevational view thereof;

FIG. 6 is a left side elevational view thereof; and,

FIG. 7 is a right side elevational view thereof.

1 Claim, 4 Drawing Sheets

TITLE: DISPOSABLE BEVERAGE CUP LID
INVENTORS: HEIDI B. SCHWEIGERT, JONATHAN C.
CANNELL & CAROL A. BAKER
ASSIGNEE: STARBUCKS CORPORATION

PATENT NUMBER: USD 516,424
PATENT FILED: NOVEMBER 30, 2004
PATENT GRANTED: MARCH 7, 2006

(12) **United States Design Patent**

Schweigert et al.

(10) Patent No.: **US D516,424 S**

(45) Date of Patent: **∗∗ Mar. 7, 2006**

(54) **DISPOSABLE BEVERAGE CUP LID**

(75) Inventors: **Heidi B. Schweigert**, Seattle, WA (US);
Jonathan C. Cannell, North Bend, WA
(US); **Carol A. Baker**, Seattle, WA
(US)

(73) Assignee: **Starbucks Corporation**, Seattle, WA
(US)

(**) Term: **14 Years**

(21) Appl. No.: **29/218,226**

(22) Filed: **Nov. 30, 2004**

(51) **LOC (8) Cl.** **09-07**
(52) **U.S. Cl.** **D9/447**
(58) **Field of Classification Search** D9/454,
D9/449, 447, 445, 439, 438, 435, 452, 453,
D9/450; D7/638, 511, 510, 392, 392.1; D3/323;
220/270–271, 709, 718, 781, 575, 715, 719;
215/254
See application file for complete search history.

(56) **References Cited**

U.S. PATENT DOCUMENTS

D212,843	S	* 12/1968	Hart et al.	.... D9/452
4,589,569	A	5/1986	Clements	
4,615,459	A	10/1986	Clements	
D287,919	S	1/1987	Clements	
D299,010	S	* 12/1988	Wall	.... D9/454
5,139,163	A	* 8/1992	Diaz	.... D9/438
5,398,843	A	3/1995	Warden et al.	

5,509,568	A	4/1996	Warden et al.	
D379,928	S	6/1997	Freek et al.	
D402,556	S	12/1998	Frye	
D417,845	S	12/1999	Sadlier et al.	
5,996,837	A	* 12/1999	Freek et al.	.... 220/713
D437,223	S	* 2/2001	Coy et al.	.... D9/447
D476,566	S	* 7/2003	Smith et al.	.... D9/447
D476,891	S	7/2003	Clarke et al.	
D480,968	S	* 10/2003	Atkins et al.	.... D9/449
6,824,003	B1	* 11/2004	Wong	.... 220/719
2005/0173443	A1	* 8/2005	Crudgington	.... 220/713

* cited by examiner

Primary Examiner—Robert M. Spear
Assistant Examiner—Susan Bennett Hattan
(74) *Attorney, Agent, or Firm*—Christensen O'Connor
Johnson Kindness PLLC

(57) **CLAIM**

The ornamental design for a disposable beverage cup lid, as
shown and described.

DESCRIPTION

FIG. 1 is a perspective view of the disposable beverage cup
lid of our design;
FIG. 2 is a top view thereof;
FIG. 3 is a bottom view thereof; and
FIG. 4 is a front view thereof;
FIG. 5 is a left side view thereof;
FIG. 6 is a back view thereof; and,
FIG. 7 is a right side view thereof.

1 Claim, 3 Drawing Sheets

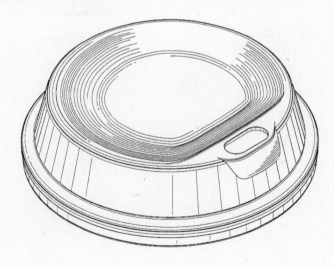

TITLE: LOUDSPEAKER
INVENTORS: HARRI KOSKINEN, MARKKU KULOMÄKI,
ILPO MARTIKAINEN, JARI MÄKINEN & ARLI VARLA
ASSIGNEE: GENELEC

PATENT NUMBER: USD 521,494
PATENT FILED: NOVEMBER 5, 2004
PATENT GRANTED: MAY 23, 2006

(12) **United States Design Patent** (10) Patent No.: **US D521,494 S**

Koskinen et al. (45) Date of Patent: ** **May 23, 2006**

(54) **LOUDSPEAKER**

(75) Inventors: **Harri Koskinen**, Iittala (FI); **Markku Kulomäki**, Iisalmi (FI); **Ilpo Martikainen**, Mäntylahti (FI); **Jari Mäkinen**, Iisalmi (FI); **Ari Varla**, Iisalmi (FI)

(73) Assignee: **Genelec Oy**, Iisalmi (FI)

(**) Term: **14 Years**

(21) Appl. No.: **29/216,546**

(22) Filed: **Nov. 5, 2004**

(30) **Foreign Application Priority Data**

May 7, 2004 (FI) M20040079

(51) **LOC (8) Cl.** **14-01**
(52) **U.S. Cl.** **D14/214**
(58) **Field of Classification Search** D14/204,
D14/207, 209–216, 356; 181/143–144, 147–148,
181/150, 157, 198–199, 151, 153; 381/300–302,
381/306, 333, 345, 361–364, 386–388, 332,
381/336
See application file for complete search history.

(56) **References Cited**

U.S. PATENT DOCUMENTS

5,067,583 A * 11/1991 Hathaway 181/151
D439,238 S * 3/2001 Mackie et al. D14/214
D473,212 S * 4/2003 Nugent et al. D14/214
D500,305 S * 12/2004 Lin et al. D14/215

* cited by examiner

Primary Examiner—Nanda Bondade
(74) *Attorney, Agent, or Firm*—Birch Stewart Kolasch & Birch LLP

(57) **CLAIM**

The ornamental design for a loudspeaker, as shown and described.

DESCRIPTION

FIG. 1 is a front, left, top perspective view of a loudspeaker showing our new design;
FIG. 2 is a back, right, top perspective view thereof;
FIG. 3 is a front elevational view thereof;
FIG. 4 is a rear elevational view thereof;
FIG. 5 is a right side view thereof;
FIG. 6 is a left side view thereof;
FIG. 7 is a top plan view thereof;
FIG. 8 is a front, left, top perspective view of a second embodiment of the present invention thereof;
FIG. 9 is a back, right, top perspective view thereof;
FIG. 10 is a front elevational view thereof;
FIG. 11 is a rear elevational view thereof;
FIG. 12 is a right side view thereof;
FIG. 13 is a left side view thereof;
FIG. 14 is a top plan view thereof;
FIG. 15 is a front, left, top perspective view of a third embodiment of the present invention;
FIG. 16 is a back, right, top perspective view thereof;
FIG. 17 is a front elevational view thereof;
FIG. 18 is a rear elevational view thereof;
FIG. 19 is a right side view thereof;
FIG. 20 is a left side view thereof; and,
FIG. 21 is a top plan view thereof.

1 Claim, 12 Drawing Sheets

TITLE: PACKAGING FOR BEVERAGE CONTAINERS
INVENTORS: FRANCIS FORD COPPOLA
& GUNDOLF PFOTENHAUER
ASSIGNEE: NONE

PATENT NUMBER: USD 524,155
PATENT FILED: FEBRUARY 25, 2005
PATENT GRANTED: JULY 4, 2006

(12) **United States Design Patent** (10) **Patent No.:**   **US D524,155 S**

Coppola et al. (45) **Date of Patent:**   ** Jul. 4, 2006**

(54) **PACKAGING FOR BEVERAGE CONTAINERS**

(76) Inventors: **Francis Ford Coppola**, 687 Carolina St., Rutherford, CA (US) 94107; **Gundolf Pfotenhauer**, 687 Carolina St., New York, NY (US) 94107

(**) Term: **14 Years**

(21) Appl. No.: **29/224,231**

(22) Filed: **Feb. 25, 2005**

(51) **LOC (8) Cl.** **09-03**

(52) **U.S. Cl.** **D9/430**

(58) **Field of Classification Search** .... D9/430–433, D9/414, 418, 420, 423, 419; 206/139, 140, 206/822; 229/100, 110, 116.1, 124, 800, 229/107, 120.02, 108, 45; 220/23.83, 500, 220/501, 507, 509, 62, 62.12, 62.13, DIG. 1, 220/2

See application file for complete search history.

(56)   **References Cited**

U.S. PATENT DOCUMENTS

D349,052 S	*	7/1994	Goldstein et al. D9/430
D372,423 S	*	8/1996	Cook D9/418
D374,619 S	*	10/1996	Cook D9/629
D401,147 S	*	11/1998	Miller D9/431

D402,201 S	*	12/1998	Miller D9/431
5,971,263 A	*	10/1999	Mangano 229/110
D429,429 S	*	8/2000	Murphy D6/455
D436,253 S	*	1/2001	Licari D3/321
6,446,859 B1	*	9/2002	Holladay 229/109
D486,732 S	*	2/2004	Borkoski D9/430
D495,598 S	*	9/2004	Smith D9/430

* cited by examiner

Primary Examiner—Mitchell Siegel
Assistant Examiner—Mark Goodwin
(74) *Attorney, Agent, or Firm*—McDonnell Boehnen Hulbert & Berghoff

(57)   **CLAIM**

The ornamental design for packaging for beverage containers, as shown.

DESCRIPTION

FIG. 1 is a front and top perspective view of packaging for beverage containers showing our new design;
FIG. 2 is a front view thereof;
FIG. 3 is a back view thereof;
FIG. 4 is a left side view thereof;
FIG. 5 is a right side view thereof;
FIG. 6 is a top view thereof; and,
FIG. 7 is a bottom view thereof.

1 Claim, 6 Drawing Sheets

TITLE: TABLE LAMP
INVENTOR: ANTONIO CITTERIO
ASSIGNEE: FLOS

PATENT NUMBER: USD 527,132
PATENT FILED: APRIL 8, 2004
PATENT GRANTED: AUGUST 22, 2006

(12) **United States Design Patent**
Citterio

(10) Patent No.: **US D527,132 S**
(45) **Date of Patent:** ✶✶ **Aug. 22, 2006**

(54) **TABLE LAMP**

(75) Inventor: **Antonio Citterio**, Milan (IT)

(73) Assignee: **Flos S.p.A.**, Bovezzo (IT)

(✶✶) Term: **14 Years**

(21) Appl. No.: **29/203,008**

(22) Filed: **Apr. 8, 2004**

(51) **LOC (8) Cl.** **26-05**
(52) **U.S. Cl.** **D26/65**; D26/107
(58) **Field of Classification Search** D26/61–63,
D26/93, 118, 107, 128; 362/269, 277, 278,
362/282, 285, 287, 288, 410, 413, 418–430,
362/449
See application file for complete search history.

(56) **References Cited**

U.S. PATENT DOCUMENTS

D329,916 S ✶ 9/1992 Copeland D26/63

5,339,233 A ✶ 8/1994 Yang 362/402
D385,646 S ✶ 10/1997 Chan D26/107
D408,570 S ✶ 4/1999 Bird D26/63
D410,298 S ✶ 5/1999 Sherman D26/118
D441,476 S ✶ 5/2001 Mendelsohn et al. D26/63
D469,202 S ✶ 1/2003 Tsai D26/65

✶ cited by examiner

Primary Examiner—Clare E Heflin
(74) *Attorney, Agent, or Firm*—McGlew and Tuttle, P.C.

(57) **CLAIM**

The ornamental design for a table lamp, as shown and described.

DESCRIPTION

FIG. 1 is a perspective view taken from the front and side of my new table lamp design;
FIG. 2 is an elevation view from a side thereof;
FIG. 3 is an elevation view the opposite side thereof; and,
FIG. 4 is an enlarged front view thereof.

1 Claim, 4 Drawing Sheets

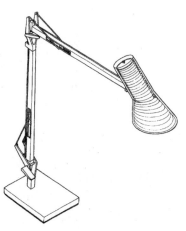

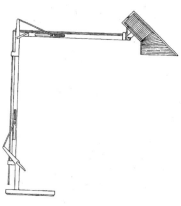

TITLE: PORTABLE COMPUTER HOUSING
INVENTORS: JOHN DAVID SCHULTZ, ROBERT BRUNNER
BENJAMIN PEI-MING CHIA, TOSHIYUKI TANAKA, ET AL.
ASSIGNEE: DELL PRODUCTS

PATENT NUMBER: USD 530,320
PATENT FILED: JULY 21, 2005
PATENT GRANTED: OCTOBER 17, 2006

(12) **United States Design Patent**

Schultz et al.

(10) Patent No.: **US D530,320 S**

(45) Date of Patent: ** **Oct. 17, 2006**

(54) **PORTABLE COMPUTER HOUSING**

(75) Inventors: **John David Schultz**, Austin, TX (US);
Robert Brunner, San Francisco, CA
(US); **Benjamin Pei-Ming Chia**,
Cupertino, CA (US); **Toshiyuki
Tanaka**, Austin, TX (US); **Steven D.
Gluskoter**, Austin, TX (US); **Symon
Whitehorn**, Sausalito, CA (US)

(73) Assignee: **Dell Products L.P.**, Round Rock, TX
(US)

(**) Term: **14 Years**

(21) Appl. No.: **29/234,686**

(22) Filed: **Jul. 21, 2005**

(51) **LOC (8) Cl.** **14-02**

(52) **U.S. Cl.** **D14/315**

(58) **Field of Classification Search** D14/315–328;
D18/1, 2, 7, 11; 235/145 A, 145 R; 341/22,
341/23; 345/104, 156, 168, 169, 173; 361/680–686;
400/486, 489
See application file for complete search history.

(56) **References Cited**

U.S. PATENT DOCUMENTS

5,774,384 A	*	6/1998	Okaya et al.	345/169
D396,703 S	*	8/1998	Han	D14/318
D408,798 S	*	4/1999	Lee et al.	D14/318
D430,868 S	*	9/2000	Cho	D14/315
D490,806 S	*	6/2004	Wang et al.	D14/318
D492,301 S	*	6/2004	Lu	D14/318
D492,677 S		7/2004	Shimizu	D14/318
D498,753 S		11/2004	Yamada	D14/328
D499,726 S	*	12/2004	Kurokawa	D14/318
D502,943 S		3/2005	Ma et al.	D14/318
D504,683 S		5/2005	Kim et al.	D14/315

* cited by examiner

Primary Examiner—Freda S. Nunn

(74) *Attorney, Agent, or Firm*—Hamilton & Terrile, LLP;
Stephen A. Terrile

(57) **CLAIM**

The ornamental design for a portable computer housing, as
shown and described.

DESCRIPTION

FIG. **1** is an angled top frontal perspective view of the
portable computer housing comprising the present invention;

FIG. **2** is a front elevation view thereof;

FIG. **3** is a right side elevation view thereof;

FIG. **4** is a left side elevation view thereof;

FIG. **5** is a back elevation view thereof;

FIG. **6** is a bottom plan view thereof; and,

FIG. **7** is a front perspective view thereof shown in the open
position.

The broken lines are shown in the views for illustrative
purposes only and form no part of the claimed design.

1 Claim, 4 Drawing Sheets

TITLE: BLENDER
INVENTOR: KONSTANTIN GRCIC
ASSIGNEE: SEB

PATENT NUMBER: USD 530,565
PATENT FILED: NOVEMBER 8, 2004
PATENT GRANTED: OCTOBER 24, 2006

(12) **United States Design Patent**   (10) Patent No.:   **US D530,565 S**

Grcic   (45) Date of Patent: ** **Oct. 24, 2006**

(54) **BLENDER**

(75) Inventor: **Konstantin Grcic**, Munich (DE)

(73) Assignee: **SEB S.A.**, Ecully Cedex (FR)

(**) Term: **14 Years**

(21) Appl. No.: **29/216,666**

(22) Filed: **Nov. 8, 2004**

(30)   **Foreign Application Priority Data**

May 6, 2004   (FR) 04 2376

(51) **LOC (8) Cl.** **31-00**
(52) **U.S. Cl.** **D7/378**
(58) **Field of Classification Search** D7/306,
D7/309, 311, 376–386, 412, 413, 415, 509,
D7/523, 529, 530; 99/348, 509–511; 241/30,
241/33, 37.5, 101.01, 101.1, 101.2, 282.2,
241/285.1, 285.2, 301; 366/64, 65, 129, 197–214,
366/219, 241–254, 314, 341, 349
See application file for complete search history.

(56)   **References Cited**

U.S. PATENT DOCUMENTS

D347,966 S	*	6/1994	Doggett	.... D7/378
D387,948 S	*	12/1997	Leverrier	.... D7/378
D396,990 S	*	8/1998	Leverrier	.... D7/378

D404,247 S	*	1/1999	Spagnolo	.... D7/378
D404,607 S	*	1/1999	Huang	.... D7/378
6,092,922 A	*	7/2000	Kett et al.	.... 366/205
D436,288 S	*	1/2001	Thackray	.... D7/386
D451,756 S	*	12/2001	Deros et al.	.... D7/378
D466,759 S	*	12/2002	Moore	.... D7/378
D474,066 S	*	5/2003	Morton et al.	.... D7/386
2005/0122837 A1	*	6/2005	Bravard et al.	.... 366/199

* cited by examiner

Primary Examiner—Caron D. Veynar
Assistant Examiner—Ricky Pham
(74) *Attorney, Agent, or Firm*—Browdy and Neimark, PLLC

(57)   **CLAIM**

The ornamental design for a blender, as shown.

DESCRIPTION

FIG. **1** is a front view of a blender in accordance with the present design;
FIG. **2** is a rear view thereof;
FIG. **3** is a left side view thereof;
FIG. **4** is a right side view thereof;
FIG. **5** is a top plan view thereof;
FIG. **6** is a bottom plan view thereof; and,
FIG. **7** is a perspective view thereof.

1 Claim, 7 Drawing Sheets

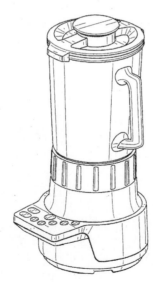

TITLE: MEMORY PACKAGE WITH REMOVABLE CAP
INVENTORS: DAN HARKABI, GIDON ELAZAR,
NEHEMIAH WEINGARTEN, JOSEF GUY HEFETZ, ET AL.
ASSIGNEE: SANDISK CORPORATION

PATENT NUMBER: USD 534,167
PATENT FILED: DECEMBER 14, 2005
PATENT GRANTED: DECEMBER 26, 2006

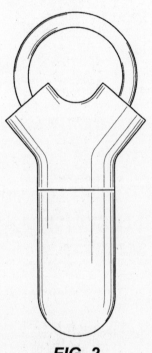

FIG. 2

FIG. 3

FIG. 4

FIG. 5

TITLE: TELEVISION SET
INVENTOR: TOSHIYUKI KITA
ASSIGNEE: SHARP KABUSHIKI KAISHA

PATENT NUMBER: USD 536,678
PATENT FILED: MAY 11, 2005
PATENT GRANTED: FEBRUARY 13, 2007

(12) **United States Design Patent**
   Kita

(10) **Patent No.:**   **US D536,678 S**

(45) **Date of Patent:**   ** Feb. 13, 2007

---

(54) **TELEVISION SET**

(75) Inventor: **Toshiyuki Kita**, Osaka-fu (JP)

(73) Assignee: **Sharp Kabushiki Kaisha**, Osaka (JP)

(**) Term: **14 Years**

(21) Appl. No.: **29/229,686**

(22) Filed: **May 11, 2005**

(30) **Foreign Application Priority Data**

Nov. 11, 2004   (JP) 2004-034355

(51) **LOC (8) Cl.** **14-03**

(52) **U.S. Cl.** **D14/126**

(58) **Field of Classification Search** D14/125–134,
          D14/239, 371, 136, 374–377; 312/7.2; 348/836,
          348/838, 180, 184, 325, 739; 341/12; 248/917–924,
          248/465; 345/104, 133, 156, 168, 87, 173;
          720/605, 669, 600, 655; 369/99, 197; 455/344–347
          See application file for complete search history.

(56)   **References Cited**

U.S. PATENT DOCUMENTS

D371,551 S	*	7/1996	Renk D14/126
D427,169 S		6/2000	Saeki et al.
D429,227 S		8/2000	Shimizu
D431,537 S		10/2000	Saeki et al.
D438,848 S		3/2001	Kita
D439,224 S		3/2001	Kita
D439,225 S		3/2001	Kita
D453,747 S		2/2002	Kita
D453,748 S		2/2002	Kita
D456,370 S		4/2002	Kita
D458,910 S		6/2002	Kita
D462,353 S		9/2002	Kita
D482,339 S	*	11/2003	Yin et al. D14/134
D492,269 S		6/2004	Kita

D496,915 S		10/2004	Kita
D497,351 S		10/2004	Kita
D497,599 S		10/2004	Kita
D499,076 S		11/2004	Kita
D501,186 S		1/2005	Kita
D501,654 S		2/2005	Kita
D502,451 S		3/2005	Kita
D502,931 S		3/2005	Kita
D504,118 S	*	4/2005	Esslinger et al. D14/126
D505,123 S		5/2005	Kita
D505,403 S		5/2005	Kita

OTHER PUBLICATIONS

U.S. Appl. No. 29/207,659, filed Jun. 2004, Kita.
U.S. Appl. No. 29/207,660, filed Jun. 2004, Kita.
U.S. Appl. No. 29/206,962, filed Jun. 2004, Kita.

* cited by examiner

Primary Examiner—Raphael Barkai
(74) *Attorney, Agent, or Firm*—Nixon & Vanderhye, PC

(57)   **CLAIM**

The ornamental design for a "television set," as shown and
described.

        DESCRIPTION

FIG. **1** is a top, front and right side perspective view of a
television set according to my design;
FIG. **2** is a front elevational view thereof;
FIG. **3** is a rear elevational view thereof;
FIG. **4** is a right side elevational view thereof; and
FIG. **5** is a left side elevational view thereof
FIG. **6** is a top plan view thereof;
FIG. **7** is a bottom plan view thereof; and,
FIG. **8** is a top, right side and rear perspective view of the
television set hereof.

        1 Claim, 6 Drawing Sheets

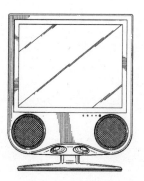

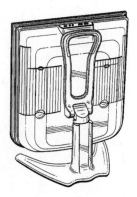

TITLE: HAND DRYING APPARATUS
INVENTORS: JOHN CHURCHILL, JAMES DYSON
& PETER DAVID GAMMACK
ASSIGNEE: DYSON

PATENT NUMBER: USD 542,474
PATENT FILED: DECEMBER 15, 2005
PATENT GRANTED: MAY 8, 2007

(12) **United States Design Patent** (10) **Patent No.:** **US D542,474 S**

Churchill et al. (45) **Date of Patent:** ** May 8, 2007

(54) **HAND DRYING APPARATUS**

(75) Inventors: **John Churchill**, Tetbury (GB); **James Dyson**, Dodington (GB); **Peter David Gammack**, Bath (GB)

(73) Assignee: **Dyson Limited**, Wiltshire (GB)

(**) Term: **14 Years**

(21) Appl. No.: **29/244,805**

(22) Filed: **Dec. 15, 2005**

(51) **LOC (8) Cl.** **28-03**
(52) **U.S. Cl.** **D28/54.1**
(58) **Field of Classification Search** D28/54.1,
D28/58, 12; 392/380, 381; D23/357, 361,
D23/385, 370, 371; 34/266, 201, 202
See application file for complete search history.

(56) **References Cited**

U.S. PATENT DOCUMENTS

D253,244 S	*	10/1979	Aroa	D28/54.1
D254,565 S	*	3/1980	Brown	D23/377
D279,412 S	*	6/1985	Fung	D28/58
D292,625 S	*	11/1987	Fung	D28/58
5,084,984 A	*	2/1992	Duchoud et al.	34/549
D451,247 S	*	11/2001	Khalaj	D28/54.1
D483,152 S	*	12/2003	Martinuzzo et al.	D28/54.1

D533,305 S * 12/2006 Takahashi et al. D28/54.1

* cited by examiner

Primary Examiner—Janice Seeger
Assistant Examiner—Zenia I. Bennett
(74) *Attorney, Agent, or Firm*—Morrison & Foerster LLP

(57) **CLAIM**

We claim the ornamental design for a hand drying apparatus, as shown and described.

DESCRIPTION

FIG. 1 is a perspective view from above, in front and one side of a hand drying apparatus of the design according to this invention.
FIG. 2 is a plan view from above of a hand drying apparatus of the design according to this invention.
FIG. 3 is a view from underneath of a hand drying apparatus of the design according to this invention.
FIG. 4 is a view of one side of a hand drying apparatus of the design according to this invention.
FIG. 5 is a view from the other side of a hand drying apparatus of the design according to this invention.
FIG. 6 is a front view of a hand drying apparatus of the design according to this invention.
FIG. 7 is a rear view of a hand drying apparatus of the design according to this invention.

1 Claim, 7 Drawing Sheets

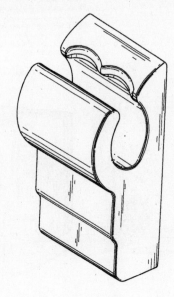

TITLE: HUMAN TRANSPORTER
INVENTORS: SHIH-TAO CHANG & SCOTT WATERS
ASSIGNEE: SEGWAY

PATENT NUMBER: USD 551,592
PATENT FILED: JUNE 30, 2006
PATENT GRANTED: SEPTEMBER 25, 2007

(12) **United States Design Patent**　(10) Patent No.:　　**US D551,592 S**

Chang et al.　　　　　　　　　　　(45) **Date of Patent:**　＊＊ **Sep. 25, 2007**

(54) **HUMAN TRANSPORTER**

(75) Inventors: **Shih-Tao Chang**, Lawrence, MA (US);
　　　　　　　Scott Waters, Hollis, NH (US)

(73) Assignee: **Segway Inc.**, Bedford, NH (US)

(**) Term: **14 Years**

(21) Appl. No.: **29/262,412**

(22) Filed: **Jun. 30, 2006**

(51) **LOC (8) Cl.** **08-14**
(52) **U.S. Cl.** **D12/1**
(58) **Field of Classification Search** D12/85,
　　　　　D12/1, 174, 178–181; 280/93.502, 229, 226;
　　　　　180/21, 8.2, 5.26, 6.5, 7.1, 65.8, 907
　　　See application file for complete search history.

(56) **References Cited**

U.S. PATENT DOCUMENTS

D355,148 S	2/1995	Orsolini	D12/85
6,561,294 B1	5/2003	Kamen et al.	180/21
D489,027 S	4/2004	Waters	D12/174
D489,029 S	4/2004	Waters	D12/186
D489,300 S	5/2004	Chang et al.	D12/186
D493,127 S	7/2004	Waters et al.	D12/174
D493,128 S	7/2004	Waters et al.	D12/174
D494,099 S	8/2004	Maurer et al.	D12/1
6,907,949 B1 *	6/2005	Wang	180/65.5
D507,206 S	7/2005	Wang	D12/1

D528,468 S	9/2006	Arling et al.	D12/1
2005/0134014 A1	6/2005	Xie	

FOREIGN PATENT DOCUMENTS

EP	000323332-0001	6/2005
EP	000323332-0002	6/2005
EP	000323332-0003	6/2005

* cited by examiner

Primary Examiner—Louis S. Zarfas
Assistant Examiner—Anna Dworzecka
(74) *Attorney, Agent, or Firm*—Proskauer Rose LLP

(57) **CLAIM**

The ornamental design for a human transporter, as shown and described.

DESCRIPTION

FIG. **1** shows a front perspective view of a human transporter showing our new design;
FIG. **2** is a front plan view thereof;
FIG. **3** is a top view thereof;
FIG. **4** is a rear plan view thereof;
FIG. **5** is a left side view thereof;
FIG. **6** is a bottom plan view thereof; and,
FIG. **7** is a right side view thereof.
The broken line shown in FIGS. **1–7** are for illustrative purposes only and forms no part of the claimed design.

1 Claim, 3 Drawing Sheets

TITLE: HEADPHONE
INVENTORS: ROBERT BRUNNER & FRANCOIS NGUYEN
ASSIGNEE: NONE

PATENT NUMBER: USD 552,077
PATENT FILED: JUNE 13, 2006
PATENT GRANTED: OCTOBER 2, 2007

(12) **United States Design Patent**   (10) **Patent No.:**   **US D552,077 S**
Brunner et al.   (45) **Date of Patent:**   ** **Oct. 2, 2007**

(54) **HEADPHONE**

(76) Inventors: **Robert Brunner**, 642 Carolina St., San
Francisco, CA (US) 94107; **Francois
Nguyen**, 1830 Ellis St. #C, San
Francisco, CA (US) 94115

(**) Term: **14 Years**

(21) Appl. No.: **29/261,443**

(22) Filed: **Jun. 13, 2006**

(51) **LOC (8) Cl.** **14-01**
(52) **U.S. Cl.** **D14/205**
(58) **Field of Classification Search** D14/188,
D14/192, 205–206, 223; 2/209; 181/129–130;
379/430–431; 381/379, 380, 383, 371, 382;
24/3.1; D29/112
See application file for complete search history.

(56)   **References Cited**

U.S. PATENT DOCUMENTS

3,104,398 A * 9/1963 Palmaer 2/209

(Continued)

Primary Examiner—Paula A. Greene
(74) *Attorney, Agent, or Firm*—Dergosits & Noah LLP

(57)   **CLAIM**

The ornamental design for headphone, as shown.

DESCRIPTION

FIG. 1 is a perspective view of a headphone, according to
one embodiment of the present invention;
FIG. 2 is a front view of the headphone illustrated in FIG.
1, according to one embodiment of the present invention;

FIG. 3 is a back view of the headphone illustrated in FIG. 1,
according to one embodiment of the present invention;
FIG. 4 is a left side view of the headphone illustrated in FIG.
1, according to one embodiment of the present invention;
FIG. 5 is a right side view of the headphone illustrated in
FIG. 1, according to one embodiment of the present invention;
FIG. 6 is a top view of the headphone illustrated in FIG. 1,
according to one embodiment of the present invention;
FIG. 7 is a bottom view of the headphone illustrated in FIG.
1, according to one embodiment of the present invention;
FIG. 8 is a perspective view of a headphone, according to
another embodiment of the present invention;
FIG. 9 is a front view of the headphone illustrated in FIG.
8, according to another embodiment of the present invention;
FIG. 10 is a back view of the headphone illustrated in FIG.
8, according to another embodiment of the present invention;
FIG. 11 is a left side view of the headphone illustrated in
FIG. 8, according to another embodiment of the present
invention;
FIG. 12 is a right side view of the headphone illustrated in
FIG. 8, according to another embodiment of the present
invention;
FIG. 13 is a top view of the headphone illustrated in FIG. 8,
according to another embodiment of the present invention;
and,
FIG. 14 is a bottom view of the headphone illustrated in FIG.
8, according to another embodiment of the present invention.

1 Claim, 8 Drawing Sheets

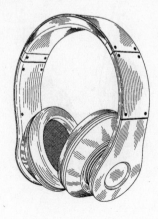

TITLE: COOKING APPARATUS
INVENTORS: MARIO BELLINI & CLAUDIO BELLINI
ASSIGNEE: SMARTECH ITALIA

PATENT NUMBER: USD 555,417
PATENT FILED: JANUARY 15, 2007
PATENT GRANTED: NOVEMBER 20, 2007

(12) **United States Design Patent**　(10) **Patent No.:**　　**US D555,417 S**
　Bellini et al.　　　　　　　　　　　(45) **Date of Patent:**　**** Nov. 20, 2007**

(54) **COOKING APPARATUS**

(75) Inventors: **Mario Bellini**, Milan (IT); **Claudio Bellini**, Milan (IT)

(73) Assignee: **Smartech Italia S.p.A.**, Azzano Decimo (PN) (IT)

(**) Term: **14 Years**

(21) Appl. No.: **29/276,094**

(22) Filed: **Jan. 15, 2007**

(51) **LOC (8) Cl.** **07-02**
(52) **U.S. Cl.** **D7/323**
(58) **Field of Classification Search** D7/323,
　　　D7/332–347, 354–366, 403–404; 126/9 R,
　　　126/9 B, 13, 2, 25 R, 25 B, 26, 29, 37 R–38,
　　　126/39 E, 40–41, 50, 218, 260, 262, 274
　　　See application file for complete search history.

(56) **References Cited**

U.S. PATENT DOCUMENTS

D225,433 S　*　12/1972　Rosenlund D7/360
D233,585 S　*　11/1974　Thomas D7/354
D341,291 S　*　11/1993　Dow, III D7/376

D387,240 S　*　12/1997　Simmonds et al. D7/339

* cited by examiner

Primary Examiner—Catherine R. Oliver
(74) *Attorney, Agent, or Firm*—Polster, Lieder, Woodruff & Lucchesi, L.C.

(57)　　　　　　　**CLAIM**

The ornamental design for cooking apparatus, as shown and described.

DESCRIPTION

FIG. 1 is a front elevational view of the cooking apparatus of the present invention

FIG. 2 is a right side elevational view of thereof;

FIG. 3 is a left side elevational view thereof;

FIG. 4 is a rear elevational view thereof;

FIG. 5 is a top plan view of thereof

FIG. 6 is a bottom plan view of the thereof; and,

FIG. 7 is a front elevational view thereof with an access door being shown in an open position.

1 Claim, 7 Drawing Sheets

TITLE: ROBOT
INVENTORS: THOMAS SWYST & STEPHEN A. HICKEY
ASSIGNEE: IROBOT CORPORATION

PATENT NUMBER: USD 556,961
PATENT FILED: OCTOBER 31, 2006
PATENT GRANTED: DECEMBER 4, 2007

(12) **United States Design Patent** (10) Patent No.: **US D556,961 S**
Swyst et al.   (45) Date of Patent: ** **Dec. 4, 2007**

(54) **ROBOT**

(75) Inventors: **Thomas Swyst**, Arlington, MA (US);
Stephen A. Hickey, Somerville, MA
(US)

(73) Assignee: **iRobot Corporation**, Burlington, MA
(US)

(**) Term: **14 Years**

(21) Appl. No.: **29/250,033**

(22) Filed: **Oct. 31, 2006**

(51) **LOC (8) Cl.** **15-05**
(52) **U.S. Cl.** **D32/21**; D15/199
(58) **Field of Classification Search** D10/106;
D15/199; D32/21, 23–25, 31; 15/319, 327.1,
15/340.1, 340.3; 180/8.2, 169; 901/1
See application file for complete search history.

(56)   **References Cited**

U.S. PATENT DOCUMENTS

D233,213	S	*	10/1974	Anderson D32/31
5,050,264	A	*	9/1991	Breslin 15/327.1
D367,622	S	*	3/1996	DeWitt D10/106
D375,592	S		11/1996	Ljunggren
D422,521	S	*	4/2000	Morrow D10/106
D474,312	S		5/2003	Stephens et al.
D478,697	S	*	8/2003	Song D32/25
D503,251	S		3/2005	Christianson
D524,495	S	*	7/2006	Ljunggren D32/21
D526,753	S	*	8/2006	Tani et al. D32/21
D539,996	S		4/2007	Owens
2005/0217042	A1		10/2005	Reindle
2006/0196003	A1*		9/2006	Song et al. 15/319
2006/0230514	A1*		10/2006	Meincke 4/507
2006/0288519	A1*		12/2006	Jaworski et al. 15/340.1

OTHER PUBLICATIONS

Advertisement - UAMA (Asia) Industrial Co., Ltd., Robot Family
(RV-2, RV-7, RV-9, RV-10, RV-11) (1 page).
Internet Product Advertisement, Global Sources, Matsutek Enter-
prises Co., Ltd. Automatic Recharheable (sic) Vacuum Cleaner, pp.

1-3, Retrieved on Apr. 23, 2007, http://matsutek.manufacturing.
globalsources.com/si/6008801427181/pdf1/Home~vacuum/10. . .
Advertisement - RoboKing Commercial Robot, 4 pages.
Device AA - Commercial Robot, 2 drawings.
Device AB - Commercial Robot, 2 drawings.
Device AC - Commercial Robot, 3 drawings.
Device AD - Commercial Robot, 2 drawings.
Device AE - Commercial Robot, 1 drawing.
Device AF - Commercial Robot, 1 drawing.
Device AG - Commercial Robot, 2 drawings.
Device AH - Commercial Robot, 3 drawings.
Device AI - Commercial Robot, 4 drawings.
Device AJ - Commercial Robot, 1 drawing.
Device AK - Commercial Robot, 1 drawing.
Device AL - Commercial Robot, 1 drawing.
Device AM - Commercial Robot, 1 drawing.
Device AN - Commercial Robot, 4 drawings.
Device AO - Commercial Robot, 2 drawings.
Device AP - Commercial Robot, 1 drawing.

(Continued)

Primary Examiner—Gary D. Watson
Assistant Examiner—Patricia Palasik
(74) Attorney, Agent, or Firm—Fish & Richardson P.C.

(57)   **CLAIM**

The ornamental design for a robot, as shown and described.

DESCRIPTION

FIG. **1** is a perspective view of a robot from the side,
showing our design;

FIG. **2** is a front view of the apparatus thereof;

FIG. **3** is a back view of the apparatus thereof;

FIG. **4** is a left side view of the apparatus thereof;

FIG. **5** is a right side view of the apparatus thereof;

FIG. **6** is a top plan view of the apparatus thereof; and,

FIG. **7** is a bottom plan view of the apparatus thereof.

The broken lines which define the bounds of the claimed
design form no part thereof.

1 Claim, 4 Drawing Sheets

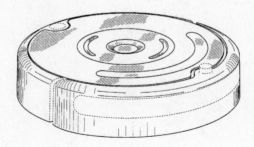

TITLE: ELECTRONIC DEVICE
INVENTORS: BARTLEY K. ANDRE, DANIEL J. COSTER
DANIELE DE IULIIS, RICHARD P. HOWARTH, ET AL.
ASSIGNEE: APPLE

PATENT NUMBER: USD 558,758
PATENT FILED: JANUARY 5, 2007
PATENT GRANTED: JANUARY 1, 2008

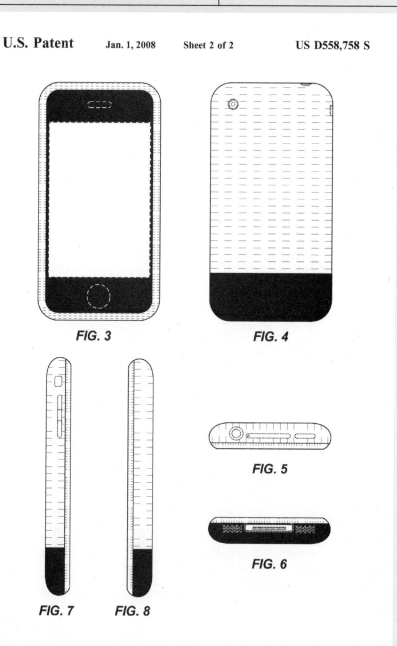

FIG. 3

FIG. 4

FIG. 5

FIG. 6

FIG. 7   FIG. 8

TITLE: HEADSET
INVENTOR: ANDERS HERMANSEN
ASSIGNEE: BANG & OLUFSEN

PATENT NUMBER: USD 560,206
PATENT FILED: DECEMBER 6, 2006
PATENT GRANTED: JANUARY 22, 2008

(12) **United States Design Patent** (10) Patent No.: **US D560,206 S**

Hermansen (45) **Date of Patent:** ** **Jan. 22, 2008**

(54) **HEADSET**

(75) Inventor: **Anders Hermansen**, Copenhagen (DK)

(73) Assignee: **Bang & Olufsen A/S**, Struer (DK)

(**) Term: **14 Years**

(21) Appl. No.: **29/269,686**

(22) Filed: **Dec. 6, 2006**

(51) **LOC (8) Cl.** **14-01**

(52) **U.S. Cl.** **D14/206**

(58) **Field of Classification Search** D14/205–206,
D14/223, 138, 142, 143; 181/129–130, 135;
379/430; 381/370, 374, 375, 376, 378, 379,
381/380, 381; 206/6.1; D24/106; D29/112;
24/457

See application file for complete search history.

(56) **References Cited**

U.S. PATENT DOCUMENTS

720,389	A	*	2/1903	Young 24/457
3,547,219	A	*	12/1970	Bothos 181/135
D318,669	S	*	7/1991	Nakayama D14/205
5,062,526	A	*	11/1991	Rudnick et al. 206/6.1
D331,408	S	*	12/1992	Ellermeier D14/205
D350,354	S	*	9/1994	Nakamura D14/205
D371,558	S	*	7/1996	Yoshizawa D14/205
6,123,168	A	*	9/2000	Berg et al. 181/129
D454,124	S	*	3/2002	Lee D14/206
D464,038	S	*	10/2002	Bebenroth D14/223
D471,176	S	*	3/2003	Suzuki D14/205
D482,674	S	*	11/2003	Rath et al. D14/206
D502,463	S	*	3/2005	Bhakta D14/205

* cited by examiner

Primary Examiner—Paula A. Greene
(74) *Attorney, Agent, or Firm*—Buchanan Ingersoll & Rooney PC

(57) **CLAIM**

The ornamental design for a headset, as shown and described.

DESCRIPTION

FIG. **1** is a front, side perspective view of a headset showing my new design, the headset is shown separately for purposes of illustration;

FIG. **2** is a rear, side perspective view thereof;

FIG. **3** is a front elevational view thereof;

FIG. **4** is a rear elevational view thereof;

FIG. **5** is a right side elevational view thereof;

FIG. **6** is a left side elevational view thereof;

FIG. **7** is a top plan view thereof;

FIG. **8** is a bottom plan view thereof;

FIG. **9** is a front, side perspective view of the charger for the headset of FIG. **1** shown separately for purposes of illustration;

FIG. **10** is a rear, side perspective view thereof;

FIG. **11** is a front elevational view thereof;

FIG. **12** is a rear elevational view thereof;

FIG. **13** is a right side elevational view thereof;

FIG. **14** is a left side elevational view thereof;

FIG. **15** is a top plan view thereof;

FIG. **16** is a bottom plan view thereof;

FIG. **17** is a front, side perspective view of the headset of FIG. **1** shown in position in the charger of FIG. **9**;

FIG. **18** is a rear, side perspective view thereof;

FIG. **19** is a front elevational view thereof;

FIG. **20** is a rear elevational view thereof;

FIG. **21** is a right side elevational view thereof;

FIG. **22** is a left side elevational view thereof;

FIG. **23** is a top plan view thereof; and,

FIG. **24** is a bottom plan view thereof.

1 Claim, 24 Drawing Sheets

TITLE: MEDIA DEVICE
INVENTORS: BARTLEY K. ANDRE, DANIEL J. COSTER
DANIELE DE IULIIS, RICHARD P. HOWARTH, ET AL.
ASSIGNEE: APPLE

PATENT NUMBER: USD 560,228
PATENT FILED: SEPTEMBER 1, 2006
PATENT GRANTED: JANUARY 22, 2008

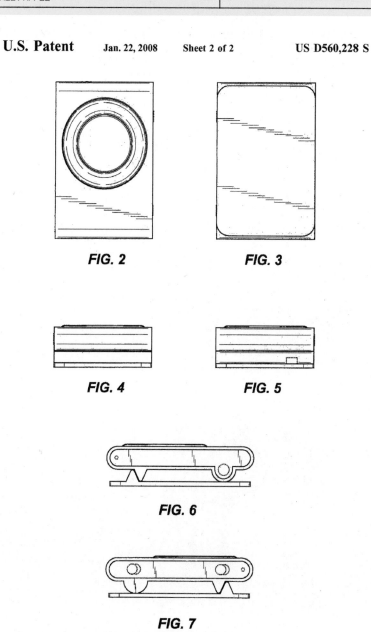

FIG. 2

FIG. 3

FIG. 4

FIG. 5

FIG. 6

FIG. 7

TITLE: FAUCET ASSEMBLY
INVENTORS: FELIX HECK & ANTONIO CITTERIO
ASSIGNEE: HANSGROHE

PATENT NUMBER: USD 560,757
PATENT FILED: JUNE 8, 2006
PATENT GRANTED: JANUARY 29, 2008

(12) **United States Design Patent** (10) Patent No.: **US D560,757 S**

Heck et al.   (45) **Date of Patent: ** **Jan. 29, 2008**

(54) **FAUCET ASSEMBLY**

(75) Inventors: **Felix Heck**, Munich (DE); **Antonio Citterio**, Milan (IT)

(73) Assignee: **Hansgrohe AG** (DE)

(**) Term: **14 Years**

(21) Appl. No.: **29/247,241**

(22) Filed: **Jun. 8, 2006**

(30) **Foreign Application Priority Data**

Dec. 14, 2005   (EP)   000447933-0001

(51) **LOC (8) Cl.** 23-01
(52) **U.S. Cl.** D23/238
(58) **Field of Classification Search** D23/238–250,
D23/253–255; 4/671–678; 137/801, 615
See application file for complete search history.

(56) **References Cited**

U.S. PATENT DOCUMENTS

4,611,626	A	*	9/1986	Logsdon 4/675
D339,410	S	*	9/1993	Gottwald D23/241
D339,629	S	*	9/1993	Gottwald D23/241
D419,643	S	*	1/2000	Gottwald et al. D23/238
D438,597	S	*	3/2001	Gottwald et al. D23/238
D450,808	S	*	11/2001	Gottwald D23/250
D457,222	S	*	5/2002	Gottwald D23/242
D457,223	S	*	5/2002	Gottwald D23/242
D457,224	S	*	5/2002	Gottwald D23/243
D457,225	S	*	5/2002	Gottwald D23/243
D457,226	S	*	5/2002	Gottwald D23/243
D457,602	S	*	5/2002	Gottwald D23/242
D457,603	S	*	5/2002	Lobermeier D23/242
D457,941	S	*	5/2002	Lobermeier D23/242
D458,987	S	*	6/2002	Gottwald D23/242
D464,402	S	*	10/2002	Saraya D23/238
D479,580	S	*	9/2003	Haug et al. D23/238
D485,602	S	*	1/2004	Lee D23/241
D492,390	S	*	6/2004	Fraser et al. D23/241
D493,211	S	*	7/2004	Fraser et al. D23/241
D514,200	S	*	1/2006	Starck D23/238
D531,270	S	*	10/2006	Smith D23/241

* cited by examiner

Primary Examiner—Stella M. Reid
Assistant Examiner—David G Muller
(74) *Attorney, Agent, or Firm*—Leon E. Redman; Lloyd D. Doigan

(57) **CLAIM**

The ornamental design for a faucet assembly, as shown and described.

DESCRIPTION

FIG. 1 is a front perspective view of a faucet assembly showing our design;

FIG. 2 is a top plan view thereof;

FIG. 3 is a front elevational view thereof;

FIG. 4 is a rear elevational view thereof;

FIG. 5 is a bottom plan view thereof;

FIG. 6 is a right side elevational view thereof; and,

FIG. 7 is a left side elevational view thereof.

1 Claim, 5 Drawing Sheets

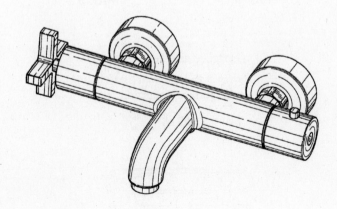

TITLE: PORTION OF A REFRIGERATOR
INVENTORS: ROBERT H. MARTIN, ROBERTO PEZZETTA
KENT ALLEN STEPHEN CROOKSHANKS, ET AL.
ASSIGNEE: ELECTROLUX HOME PRODUCTS

PATENT NUMBER: USD 565,064
PATENT FILED: JULY 26, 2007
PATENT GRANTED: MARCH 25, 2008

(12) **United States Design Patent**   (10) Patent No.:   **US D565,064 S**

Martin et al.   (45) Date of Patent: ** Mar. 25, 2008

---

(54) **PORTION OF A REFRIGERATOR**

(75) Inventors: **Robert H. Martin**, Anderson, SC (US);
Roberto Pezzetta, Porcia (IT); **Kent Allen Stephen Crookshanks**, Anderson, SC (US); **Vittorio Cascianelli**, Anderson, SC (US)

(73) Assignee: **Electrolux Home Products, Inc.**, Cleveland, OH (US)

(**) Term: **14 Years**

(21) Appl. No.: **29/282,675**

(22) Filed: **Jul. 26, 2007**

(51) LOC (8) Cl. **15-07**
(52) U.S. Cl. **D15/91**
(58) **Field of Classification Search** D15/79, D15/80, 81, 85, 88, 91; 312/236, 352, 400–408; 62/3.1, 3.6, 3.63, 3.64, 45.1, 236, 293, 331, 62/352, 371, 400–406, 440, 467, 529, 531
See application file for complete search history.

(56) **References Cited**

U.S. PATENT DOCUMENTS

D496,373	S	*	9/2004	Jang	.... D15/85
D524,832	S	*	7/2006	Kim et al.	.... D15/85
D527,395	S	*	8/2006	Kim	.... D15/85
D527,745	S	*	9/2006	Kim et al.	.... D15/85
D527,748	S	*	9/2006	Kim	.... D15/85
D528,135	S	*	9/2006	Kim et al.	.... D15/85
D544,002	S	*	6/2007	Kim et al.	.... D15/85
D551,260	S	*	9/2007	Kim et al.	.... D15/85
D553,651	S	*	10/2007	Morrison et al.	.... D15/85
D555,177	S	*	11/2007	Yeo et al.	.... D15/85
D555,178	S	*	11/2007	Yeo et al.	.... D15/85
2003/0132689	A1	*	7/2003	Shin	.... 312/405

* cited by examiner

Primary Examiner—Mitchell Siegel
Assistant Examiner—Shanda C. Hill
(74) *Attorney, Agent, or Firm*—Banner & Witcoff, Ltd.

(57)   **CLAIM**

The ornamental design for a portion of a refrigerator, as shown and described.

DESCRIPTION

FIG. 1 is a front perspective view of a portion of a refrigerator showing our new design;

FIG. 2 is a front view thereof;

FIG. 3 is a left side view thereof;

FIG. 4 is a right side view thereof;

FIG. 5 is a top view thereof;

FIG. 6 is a bottom view thereof; and,

FIG. 7 is an enlarged fragmentary view of FIG. 2.

The broken lines shown in the drawing disclosure are for illustrative purposes only and form no part of the claimed design.

1 Claim, 6 Drawing Sheets

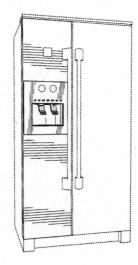

TITLE: WRITING INSTRUMENT
INVENTORS: FRANCK ROLION & FRANCK VADENNE
ASSIGNEE: SOCIETE BIC

PATENT NUMBER: USD 566,176
PATENT FILED: SEPTEMBER 19, 2006
PATENT GRANTED: APRIL 8, 2008

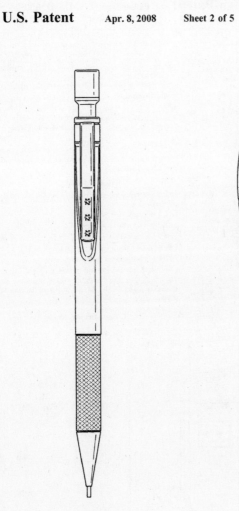

Fig. 2

Fig. 3

TITLE: LAMP
INVENTORS: YVES BÉHAR, JACQUES L. GAGNE
& GEORGE JANOUR
ASSIGNEE: HERMAN MILLER

PATENT NUMBER: USD 569,539
PATENT FILED: MAY 4, 2006
PATENT GRANTED: MAY 20, 2008

(12) **United States Design Patent**   (10) Patent No.:   **US D569,539 S**
Behar et al.   (45) Date of Patent: ** **May 20, 2008**

(54) **LAMP**

(75) Inventors: **Yves Behar**, Oakland, CA (US);
Jacques L. Gagne, Los Gatos, CA
(US); **George Janour**, Santa Cruz, CA
(US)

(73) Assignee: **Herman Miller Inc.**, Zeeland, MI (US)

(**) Term: **14 Years**

(21) Appl. No.: **29/246,701**

(22) Filed: **May 4, 2006**

(51) **LOC (8) Cl.** **26-05**
(52) **U.S. Cl.** **D26/63**
(58) **Field of Classification Search** D26/14,
D26/60–66; 362/410, 413, 414, 418, 419,
362/427, 285, 287, 282, 277, 275, 274, 271,
362/270, 269, 431
See application file for complete search history.

(56)   **References Cited**

U.S. PATENT DOCUMENTS

D122,711	S	*	9/1940	May D26/63
D301,632	S	*	6/1989	Lohrentz D26/61
5,034,863	A	*	7/1991	Huang 362/652
D320,865	S	*	10/1991	Chang D26/108
D329,098	S	*	9/1992	Lu D26/62
D376,440	S	*	12/1996	Chan D26/65

D513,088 S * 12/2005 Baarman et al. D26/106
* cited by examiner

Primary Examiner—Cathron Brooks
Assistant Examiner—Barbara Fox
(74) *Attorney, Agent, or Firm*—Barnes & Thornburg LLP

(57)   **CLAIM**

What is claimed is the ornamental design for a lamp, as
shown and described.

DESCRIPTION

FIG. 1 is a perspective view of a lamp, indicating an arm, a
stem and a base;

FIG. 2 is a left side view of the lamp;

FIG. 3 is a right side view of the lamp;

FIG. 4 is a front view of the lamp;

FIG. 5 is a rear view of the lamp;

FIG. 6 is a top view of the lamp;

FIG. 7 is a bottom view of the lamp; and,

FIG. 8 is an enlarged, fragmentary bottom perspective view
of the lamp as shown in FIGS. 1–7 illustrating a perspective
view of the protrusions on an underside of a portion of the
lamp as shown in FIGS. **2**, **3**, **4**, and **7**.

The broken lines shown in the drawings are for the purpose
of illustrating portions of the lamp and form no part of the
claimed design.

1 Claim, 7 Drawing Sheets

TITLE: TRAIN HEAD
INVENTORS: LIONEL GRAF & XAVIER ALLARD
ASSIGNEE: ALSTOM TRANSPORT

PATENT NUMBER: USD 577,313
PATENT FILED: DECEMBER 20, 2007
PATENT GRANTED: SEPTEMBER 23, 2008

(12) **United States Design Patent**
Graf et al.

(10) **Patent No.:** **US D577,313 S**
(45) **Date of Patent:** ** Sep. 23, 2008

(54) **TRAIN HEAD**

(75) Inventors: **Lionel Graf**, Paris (FR); **Xavier Allard**, Clamart (FR)

(73) Assignee: **Alstom Transport SA**, Levallois-Perret (FR)

(**) Term: **14 Years**

(21) Appl. No.: **29/299,185**

(22) Filed: **Dec. 20, 2007**

(51) **LOC (8) Cl.** **12-03**
(52) **U.S. Cl.** **D12/38**
(58) **Field of Classification Search** D12/36, D12/37, 38, 39, 40, 41, 42, 43, 44, 320, 195, D12/345, 99; 105/329, 342, 345, 356, 463.1; 454/83, 77, 87, 88
See application file for complete search history.

(56) **References Cited**

U.S. PATENT DOCUMENTS

D329,028 S * 9/1992 Malewicki D12/37
D499,047 S * 11/2004 Meissner D12/37

D514,982 S * 2/2006 Meissner D12/37

* cited by examiner

Primary Examiner—Robert M. Spear
Assistant Examiner—Ania K Dworzecka
(74) *Attorney, Agent, or Firm*—Hughes Hubbard & Reed LLP; Ronald Abramson; Peter A. Sullivan

(57) **CLAIM**

The ornamental design for a train head, as shown and described.

DESCRIPTION

FIG. 1 is a perspective view of a train head showing my new design;

FIG. 2 is a right side elevational view thereof, the left side elevational view being a mirror image thereof;

FIG. 3 is a top plan view thereof; and,

FIG. 4 is a front elevational view thereof.

The broken line showing on portions of FIG. 1 is for illustrative purposes only and forms no part of the claimed design.

1 Claim, 4 Drawing Sheets

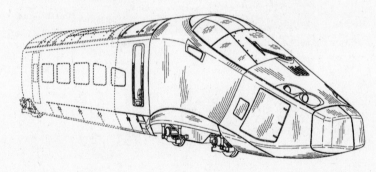

TITLE: COMBINED WATER CLOSET AND PRIVATE PART WASHING DEVICE
INVENTORS: NAOTO FUKASAWA, MASAAKI TAIKA, ET AL.
ASSIGNEE: PANASONIC ELECTRIC WORKS IP CENTER

PATENT NUMBER: USD 583,030
PATENT FILED: APRIL 16, 2007
PATENT GRANTED: DECEMBER 16, 2008

(12) **United States Design Patent**
Kobayashi et al.

(10) Patent No.: **US D583,030 S**
(45) Date of Patent: ** **Dec. 16, 2008**

(54) **COMBINED WATER CLOSET AND PRIVATE PART WASHING DEVICE**

(75) Inventors: **Jiro Kobayashi**, Kadoma (JP); **Masaaki Taika**, Kadoma (JP); **Naoto Fukasawa**, Tokyo (JP)

(73) Assignee: **Panasonic Electric Works IP Center Co., Ltd.**, Osaka (JP)

(**) Term: **14 Years**

(21) Appl. No.: **29/285,960**

(22) Filed: **Apr. 16, 2007**

(30) **Foreign Application Priority Data**

Oct. 16, 2006 (JP) 2006-027818

(51) **LOC (8) Cl.** **23-02**
(52) **U.S. Cl.** **D23/295**
(58) **Field of Classification Search** D23/273–274, D23/295–299, 303, 309; 4/663–664, 300, 4/312, 329, 348, 352–353
See application file for complete search history.

(56) **References Cited**

U.S. PATENT DOCUMENTS

D382,325 S * 8/1997 Kawamura et al. D23/295

D382,947 S * 8/1997 Kawamura et al. D23/295
6,964,068 B2 * 11/2005 Shiraki et al. 4/444

* cited by examiner

Primary Examiner—Robert A Delehanty
(74) *Attorney, Agent, or Firm*—Osha • Liang LLP

(57) **CLAIM**

The ornamental design for a combined water closet and private part washing device, as shown and described.

DESCRIPTION

FIG. **1** is a perspective view of the top, front and left side of a combined water closet and private part washing device showing our new design;

FIG. **2** is a front view thereof;

FIG. **3** is a rear view thereof;

FIG. **4** is the top plan view thereof;

FIG. **5** is a bottom view thereof;

FIG. **6** is a left side view thereof;

FIG. **7** is a right side view thereof; and

FIG. **8** is a reduced perspective view with the lid in open condition; and,

FIG. **9** is a cross section view thereof.

1 Claim, 6 Drawing Sheets

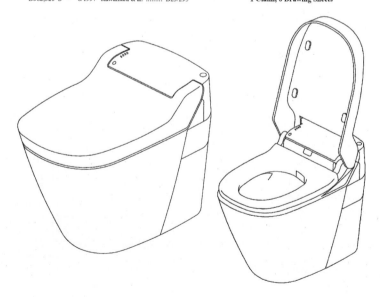

TITLE: HANDSET
INVENTORS: GUOPING WU & ZHIYAN YANG
ASSIGNEE: HUAWEI TECHNOLOGIES COMPANY

PATENT NUMBER: USD 584,708
PATENT FILED: JUNE 1, 2007
PATENT GRANTED: JANUARY 13, 2009

FIG.10

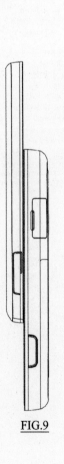

FIG.9

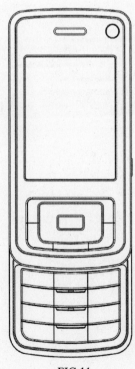

FIG.11

TITLE: SEAT
INVENTOR: PIERRE PAULIN
ASSIGNEE: ROSET

PATENT NUMBER: USD 596,862
PATENT FILED: JULY 14, 2008
PATENT GRANTED: JULY 28, 2009

(12) **United States Design Patent**
Paulin

(10) **Patent No.:** **US D596,862 S**
(45) **Date of Patent:** ✱✱ **Jul. 28, 2009**

(54) **SEAT**

(75) Inventor: **Pierre Paulin**, Saint Roman de Codieres (FR)

(73) Assignee: **Roset S.A.** (FR)

(✱✱) Term: **14 Years**

(21) Appl. No.: **29/321,235**

(22) Filed: **Jul. 14, 2008**

(30) **Foreign Application Priority Data**

Jan. 14, 2008   (FR) 000 857 495-0001

(51) **LOC (9) Cl.** **06-01**
(52) **U.S. Cl.** **D6/334**
(58) **Field of Classification Search** D6/334,
D6/341, 371, 372, 373, 374, 375, 381, 491,
D6/492, 500, 501, 502; 297/232, 233, 239,
297/300.1, 311, 353, 445.1, 446.1, 448.1,
297/448.2, 452.11, DIG. 7, DIG. 8; 5/12.1,
5/12.2

See application file for complete search history.

(56) **References Cited**

U.S. PATENT DOCUMENTS

D183,743	S	✱	10/1958	Howell	D6/334
D244,569	S	✱	6/1977	Laroye	D6/334
D265,027	S	✱	6/1982	Meyers	D6/334
D309,199	S	✱	7/1990	McMahon	D30/118
D395,759	S	✱	7/1998	Smith	D6/334
D429,917	S	✱	8/2000	Hazen et al.	D6/438
D430,420	S	✱	9/2000	Peterson	D6/381
D435,355	S	✱	12/2000	Peterson	D6/334
D435,974	S	✱	1/2001	Hsu et al.	D6/334
D441,205	B1	✱	5/2001	Hsu et al.	D6/334
6,328,385	B1	✱	12/2001	Lau	297/452.41
D552,853	S	✱	10/2007	Goodrick	D6/334
D576,808	S	✱	9/2008	Ton	D6/349
D585,212	S	✱	1/2009	Paulin	D6/381

✱ cited by examiner

Primary Examiner—Sandra Snapp
(74) *Attorney, Agent, or Firm*—Cantor Colburn LLP

(57)   **CLAIM**

I claim, the ornamental design for a seat, as shown and described.

DESCRIPTION

FIG. **1** is a front perspective view of a seat showing my new design;

FIG. **2** is a rear perspective view thereof;

FIG. **3** is a side view thereof;

FIG. **4** is an opposite side view thereof;

FIG. **5** is a top plan view thereof;

FIG. **6** is a rear elevation view thereof; and,

FIG. **7** is a front elevation view thereof.

1 Claim, 7 Drawing Sheets

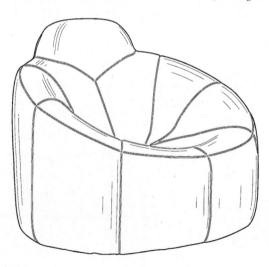

TITLE: SEAT
INVENTOR: PHILIPPE STARCK
ASSIGNEE: CASSINA

PATENT NUMBER: USD 600,458
PATENT FILED: JANUARY 13, 2009
PATENT GRANTED: SEPTEMBER 22, 2009

(12) **United States Design Patent**
Starck

(10) **Patent No.:** **US D600,458 S**
(45) **Date of Patent:** ** **Sep. 22, 2009**

(54) **SEAT**

(75) Inventor: **Philippe Starck**, Paris (FR)

(73) Assignee: **CASSINA S.p.A.**, Meda (Milan) (IT)

(**) Term: **14 Years**

(21) Appl. No.: **29/311,198**

(22) Filed: **Jan. 13, 2009**

(51) **LOC (9) Cl.** **06-01**
(52) **U.S. Cl.** **D6/334**
(58) **Field of Classification Search** D6/334,
D6/336, 338, 349, 352, 363, 374, 375, 380,
D6/381, 491, 492, 500–502; 297/175, 411.2,
297/445.1, 446.1, 446.2, 447.1, 447.2, 448.1,
297/451.2, 452.11, 452.29, 461, 462; 5/12.1,
5/12.2
See application file for complete search history.

(56) **References Cited**

U.S. PATENT DOCUMENTS

D181,945	S	*	1/1958	Saarinen	D6/365
2,989,112	A	*	6/1961	Sonnleitner	156/213
D192,029	S	*	1/1962	Avedon	D6/375
D193,847	S	*	10/1962	Mason	D6/375
D199,621	S	*	11/1964	Johnson	D6/374
D205,939	S	*	10/1966	Leverne	D6/375
D224,856	S	*	10/1972	Charity	D6/372
D226,648	S	*	4/1973	Sobel	D6/375
D237,664	S	*	11/1975	Costable	D6/365
D368,176	S	*	3/1996	Mourgue	D6/381
D440,064	S	*	4/2001	Deacon	D6/375
D518,968	S	*	4/2006	Magnani et al.	D6/375

* cited by examiner

Primary Examiner—Sandra Snapp
(74) *Attorney, Agent, or Firm*—Nixon & Vanderhye P.C.

(57) **CLAIM**

The ornamental design for a seat, as shown and described.

DESCRIPTION

FIG. 1 is a front elevational view of the seat;

FIG. 2 is a rear elevational view thereof;

FIG. 3 is a right elevational view thereof;

FIG. 4 is a left elevational view thereof;

FIG. 5 is a top plan view thereof;

FIG. 6 is a bottom plan view thereof; and,

FIG. 7 is a front, bottom, right side perspective view thereof.

1 Claim, 7 Drawing Sheets

TITLE: TABLE LAMP
INVENTORS: JAY OSGERBY & EDWARD BARBER
ASSIGNEE: FLOS

PATENT NUMBER: USD 600,849
PATENT FILED: SEPTEMBER 28, 2007
PATENT GRANTED: SEPTEMBER 22, 2009

(12) **United States Design Patent**
Osgerby et al.

(10) Patent No.: **US D600,849 S**
(45) Date of Patent: ** **Sep. 22, 2009**

(54) **TABLE LAMP**

(75) Inventors: **Jay Osgerby**, London (GB); **Edward Barber**, London (GB)

(73) Assignee: **FLOS S.p.A.**, Bovezzo, Brescia (IT)

(**) Term: **14 Years**

(21) Appl. No.: **29/295,419**

(22) Filed: **Sep. 28, 2007**

(30) **Foreign Application Priority Data**

Mar. 30, 2007 (EM) 000698774-0001

(51) **LOC (9) Cl.** **26-03**
(52) **U.S. Cl.** **D26/107**
(58) **Field of Classification Search** D26/24, D26/61–67, 93, 102, 104–105, 108–109; 362/509, 516, 523, 186, 217, 255, 257, 277, 362/317, 319, 351, 354, 355, 357, 358, 362, 362/382, 410, 413, 417, 806
See application file for complete search history.

(56) **References Cited**

U.S. PATENT DOCUMENTS

D203,863 S * 2/1966 Neumann D26/107
D251,930 S * 5/1979 Didone D26/107

D450,408 S * 11/2001 Wang D26/109
D468,855 S * 1/2003 Gismondi D26/109
D474,557 S * 5/2003 Eusterbrock D26/107
D538,964 S * 3/2007 Martin D26/109

* cited by examiner

Primary Examiner—Brian N Vinson
(74) *Attorney, Agent, or Firm*—McGlew and Tuttle, P.C.

(57) **CLAIM**

The ornamental design for a table lamp, as shown and described.

DESCRIPTION

FIG. **1** is a top, front, and left side perspective view of a table lamp showing our new design;

FIG. **2** is a front perspective view thereof;

FIG. **3** is a rear perspective view thereof;

FIG. **4** is a top plan view thereof;

FIG. **5** is a bottom plan view thereof;

FIG. **6** is a right side elevational view thereof; and,

FIG. **7** is a left side elevational view thereof.

The broken-line disclosure of elements beneath the angled shade are for illustrative purposes only and understood to form no part of the claimed design.

1 Claim, 7 Drawing Sheets

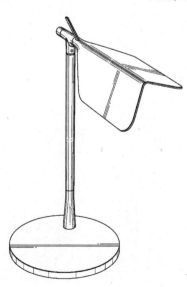

TITLE: SEAT
INVENTOR: MARIO BELLINI
ASSIGNEE: CASSINA

PATENT NUMBER: USD 602,267
PATENT FILED: MARCH 31, 2009
PATENT GRANTED: OCTOBER 20, 2009

(12) **United States Design Patent**
Bellini

(10) **Patent No.:** **US D602,267 S**
(45) **Date of Patent:** ** **Oct. 20, 2009**

(54) **SEAT**

(75) Inventor: **Mario Bellini**, Milan (IT)

(73) Assignee: **Cassina S.p.A.**, Meda (Milan) (IT)

(**) Term: **14 Years**

(21) Appl. No.: **29/311,489**

(22) Filed: **Mar. 31, 2009**

(30) **Foreign Application Priority Data**

Jan. 13, 2009 (WO) DM/071 352

(51) **LOC (9) Cl.** **06-01**
(52) **U.S. Cl.** **D6/334**
(58) **Field of Classification Search** D6/334,
D6/336, 338, 349, 352, 363, 374, 375, 380,
D6/381, 491, 492, 500–502; 297/175, 411.2,
297/445.1, 446.1, 446.2, 447.1, 447.2, 448.1,
297/451.2, 452.11, 452.29, 461, 462; 5/12.1,
5/12.2

See application file for complete search history.

(56) **References Cited**

U.S. PATENT DOCUMENTS

D219,016 S	*	10/1970	Muller	.... D6/375
D256,970 S	*	9/1980	Cassina	.... D6/334
D396,960 S	*	8/1998	Maly	.... D6/334
D409,848 S	*	5/1999	Staubach et al.	.... D6/334
D422,158 S	*	4/2000	Newhouse	.... D6/375

D426,972 S	*	6/2000	Bellini	.... D6/375
D448,942 S	*	10/2001	Mourgue	.... D6/375
D465,100 S	*	11/2002	Savini	.... D6/375
D469,970 S	*	2/2003	Molteni	.... D6/374
D475,212 S	*	6/2003	Savini	.... D6/374
D529,726 S	*	10/2006	Cutler et al.	.... D6/334
D541,068 S	*	4/2007	Foster	.... D6/374
D549,970 S	*	9/2007	Bouroullec et al.	.... D6/334
D555,379 S	*	11/2007	Ziliani	.... D6/375
D563,111 S	*	3/2008	Lievore	.... D6/375
D574,622 S	*	8/2008	Neil	.... D6/374
D580,673 S	*	11/2008	Wright et al.	.... D6/374

* cited by examiner

Primary Examiner—Sandra Snapp
(74) *Attorney, Agent, or Firm*—Nixon & Vanderhye P.C.

(57) **CLAIM**

The ornamental design for a seat, as shown and described.

DESCRIPTION

FIG. **1** is a front elevational view of a seat;

FIG. **2** is a rear elevational view thereof;

FIG. **3** is a left elevational view thereof;

FIG. **4** is a right elevational view thereof;

FIG. **5** is a top plan view thereof;

FIG. **6** is a bottom plan view thereof; and,

FIG. **7** is a front, left, top perspective view thereof.

1 Claim, 7 Drawing Sheets

TITLE: CHAIR
INVENTOR: KONSTANTIN GRCIC
ASSIGNEE: MAGIS

PATENT NUMBER: USD 611,262
PATENT FILED: JULY 24, 2009
PATENT GRANTED: MARCH 9, 2010

(12) **United States Design Patent**　　(10) **Patent No.:**　　　**US D611,262 S**

Grcic　　　　　　　　　　　　　　　(45) **Date of Patent:**　　✱✱　**Mar. 9, 2010**

(54) **CHAIR**

(75) Inventor: **Konstantin Grcic**, Munich (DE)

(73) Assignee: **MAGIS S.p.A.**, Treviso (IT)

(**) Term: **14 Years**

(21) Appl. No.: **29/311,890**

(22) Filed: **Jul. 24, 2009**

(30) **Foreign Application Priority Data**

Mar. 25, 2009　(EM) 001111728-1

(51) **LOC (9) Cl.** **06-01**
(52) **U.S. Cl.** **D6/366**
(58) **Field of Classification Search** D6/334–336,
D6/360, 364, 365, 366, 367, 379, 380, 498,
D6/500–502; 297/344.12, 353, 411.36, 423.1,
297/423.38, 452.19, 452.3
See application file for complete search history.

(56) **References Cited**

U.S. PATENT DOCUMENTS

D76,151	S	*	8/1928	Racz D6/366
D273,729	S	*	5/1984	Pelly et al. D6/366

D274,958 S * 8/1984 Aronowitz et al. D6/360
5,009,467 A * 4/1991 McCoy 297/411.36
D395,173 S * 6/1998 Pate D6/366
D495,508 S * 9/2004 Summers D6/366
D515,831 S * 2/2006 Hosoe D6/360
7,104,606 B2 * 9/2006 Congleton et al. 297/353
D577,229 S * 9/2008 Haaksma D6/500

* cited by examiner

Primary Examiner—Mimosa De
(74) *Attorney, Agent, or Firm*—Hoffman, Wasson & Gitler, P.C.

(57) **CLAIM**

The ornamental design for a chair, as shown, and described.

DESCRIPTION

FIG. **1** is a perspective view of the chair;

FIG. **2** is a front view of the chair;

FIG. **3** is a rear view of the chair;

FIG. **4** is a right side view of the chair; the opposite sides of the chair being identical;

FIG. **5** is a top view of the chair; and,

FIG. **6** is a bottom view of the chair.

1 Claim, 6 Drawing Sheets

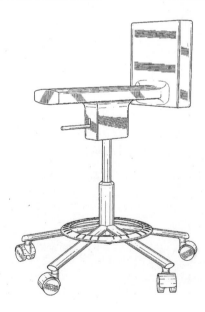

TITLE: REUSABLE PIZZA CONTAINER
INVENTOR: MICHAEL T. SUDIA
ASSIGNEE: NONE

PATENT NUMBER: USD 620,766
PATENT FILED: OCTOBER 23, 2009
PATENT GRANTED: AUGUST 3, 2010

(12) **United States Design Patent**

Sudia

(10) **Patent No.:** **US D620,766 S**

(45) **Date of Patent:** ✶✶ **Aug. 3, 2010**

(54) **REUSABLE PIZZA CONTAINER**

(76) Inventor: **Michael T. Sudia**, 416 Antelope Ridge Way, Danville, CA (US) 94506

(**) Term: **14 Years**

(21) Appl. No.: **29/316,717**

(22) Filed: **Oct. 23, 2009**

(51) **LOC (9) Cl.** **07-07**

(52) **U.S. Cl.** **D7/629**

(58) **Field of Classification Search** D7/629, D7/602, 630, 601; D9/426, 416, 414, 430–432; 229/406, 103.11, 178, 902, 903, 906, 199, 229/120.18, 120.13, 120.17
See application file for complete search history.

(56) **References Cited**

U.S. PATENT DOCUMENTS

4,237,171	A *	12/1980	Laage et al.	426/127
5,385,292	A *	1/1995	Labianca et al.	229/120
6,601,758	B2 *	8/2003	Lizzio	229/120
6,932,267	B2 *	8/2005	Potenza et al.	229/199

* cited by examiner

Primary Examiner—Terry A Wallace

(74) *Attorney, Agent, or Firm*—Bruce H Johnsonbaugh

(57) **CLAIM**

The ornamental design for a reusable pizza container, as shown and described.

DESCRIPTION

FIG. **1** is a perspective view of the reusable pizza container, showing the detachable top in its raised and detached position.

FIG. **2** is a perspective view of the reusable pizza container, showing the lid in its closed position.

FIG. **3** is a top plan view of the container with the lid detached.

FIG. **4** is a front elevational view of the container.

FIG. **5** is a right side elevational view of the container.

FIG. **6** is a bottom plan view of the container.

FIG. **7** is rear elevational view of the container; and,

FIG. **8** is a left side view of the container.

1 Claim, 4 Drawing Sheets

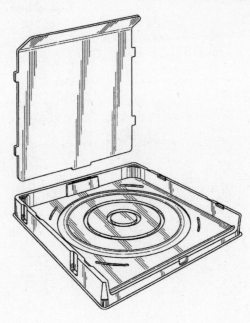

TITLE: CORKSCREW
INVENTORS: JEREMY MORGAN & GARY COOKE
ASSIGNEE: LE CREUSET SAS

PATENT NUMBER: USD 635,424
PATENT FILED: JULY 22, 2010
PATENT GRANTED: APRIL 5, 2011

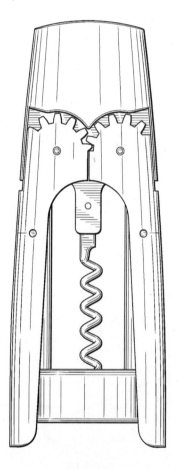

FIG. 2

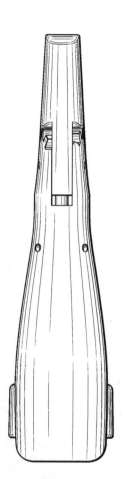

FIG. 3

TITLE: PORTABLE DISPLAY DEVICE
INVENTORS: JODY AKANA, BARTLEY K. ANDRE,
DANIEL J. COSTER, DANIELE DE IULIIS, ET AL.
ASSIGNEE: APPLE

PATENT NUMBER: USD 637,596
PATENT FILED: JANUARY 6, 2010
PATENT GRANTED: MAY 10, 2011

(12) **United States Design Patent**   (10) **Patent No.:**   **US D637,596 S**
Akana et al.   (45) **Date of Patent:**   ** *May 10, 2011

(54) **PORTABLE DISPLAY DEVICE**

(75) Inventors: **Jody Akana**, San Francisco, CA (US);
Bartley K. Andre, Menlo Park, CA
(US); **Daniel J. Coster**, San Francisco,
CA (US); **Daniele De Iuliis**, San
Francisco, CA (US); **Evans Hankey**,
San Francisco, CA (US); **Richard P.
Howarth**, San Francisco, CA (US);
Jonathan P. Ive, San Francisco, CA
(US); **Steve Jobs**, Palo Alto, CA (US);
Duncan Robert Kerr, San Francisco,
CA (US); **Shin Nishibori**, Portola Valley,
CA (US); **Matthew Dean Rohrbach**,
San Francisco, CA (US); **Peter
Russell-Clarke**, San Francisco, CA
(US); **Christopher J. Stringer**,
Woodside, CA (US); **Eugene Antony
Whang**, San Francisco, CA (US); **Rico
Zorkendorfer**, San Francisco, CA (US)

(73) Assignee: **Apple Inc.**, Cupertino, CA (US)

(*) Notice: This patent is subject to a terminal disclaimer.

(**) Term: **14 Years**

(21) Appl. No.: **29/353,311**

(22) Filed: **Jan. 6, 2010**

(51) **LOC (9) Cl.** **14-02**

(52) **U.S. Cl.** **D14/341**

(58) **Field of Classification Search** D14/341–347,
D14/137, 138, 138.1, 138 AA, 138 R, 138 AB,
D14/138 G, 138 A, 496, 426, 429, 129, 130,
D14/420, 439–441, 448, 125, 147, 156, 218,
D14/250, 389, 336, 203.1, 203.3, 203.4, 203.7,
D14/315; D21/324, 329, 330; D10/65, 104;
D18/6–7; 345/169, 901, 905, 156, 157, 168,
345/173; 361/814, 680, 686, 679.27, 679.3;
341/22; 348/168; 379/433.04, 433.07, 433.11,
379/916, 433.01, 433.06
See application file for complete search history.

(56)   **References Cited**

U.S. PATENT DOCUMENTS

D306,583 S * 3/1990 Krolopp et al. D14/137
(Continued)

FOREIGN PATENT DOCUMENTS

CN   200430011774.1   6/2005
(Continued)

OTHER PUBLICATIONS

HP Compaq Tablet PC TC1000-TM5800 1GHz-10.4" TFT, CNET
Reviews, http://reviews.cnet.com/tablet-pcs/hp-compaq-tablet-pc/
4505-1707__7-20627295.html. Downloaded Apr. 20, 2010, 13 pages.

(Continued)

Primary Examiner — Cathron C Brooks
Assistant Examiner — Barbara Fox
(74) *Attorney, Agent, or Firm* — Sterne, Kessler, Goldstein
& Fox PLLC

(57)   **CLAIM**
The ornamental design for a portable display device, as
shown and described.

DESCRIPTION

FIG. 1 is a bottom front perspective view of a portable display
device showing our new design;
FIG. 2 is a bottom rear perspective view thereof;
FIG. 3 is a front view thereof;
FIG. 4 is a rear view thereof;
FIG. 5 is a top plan view thereof;
FIG. 6 is a left side view thereof;
FIG. 7 is a right side view thereof; and,
FIG. 8 is a bottom plan view thereof.
The shade lines in the Figures show contour and not surface
ornamentation.
The broken lines in the figures show portions of the portable
display device which form no part of the claimed design.

1 Claim, 5 Drawing Sheets

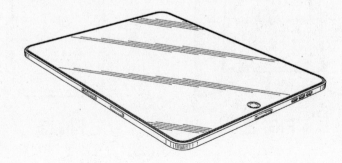

TITLE: FLOOR LAMP
INVENTOR: ZAHA HADID
ASSIGNEE: ARTEMIDE

PATENT NUMBER: USD 638,161
PATENT FILED: OCTOBER 13, 2009
PATENT GRANTED: MAY 17, 2011

(12) **United States Design Patent**　(10) **Patent No.:**　　**US D638,161 S**

Hadid　　　　　　　　　　　　　(45) **Date of Patent:**　✱✱ **May 17, 2011**

(54) **FLOOR LAMP**

(75) Inventor: **Zaha Hadid**, Milan (IT)

(73) Assignee: **Artemide S.p.A.**, Milan (IT)

(✱✱) Term: **14 Years**

(21) Appl. No.: **29/345,238**

(22) Filed: **Oct. 13, 2009**

(51) **LOC (9) Cl.** **26-03**

(52) **U.S. Cl.** **D26/93**

(58) **Field of Classification Search** D26/24,
D26/61–67, 93, 102, 104–105, 108–109;
362/509, 516, 523, 186, 217, 255, 257, 277,
362/317, 319, 351, 354, 355, 357, 358, 362,
362/382, 410, 413, 417, 806

See application file for complete search history.

(56)　　　　　　　**References Cited**

U.S. PATENT DOCUMENTS

D512,171 S	*	11/2005	Opolka	D26/62
D522,158 S	*	5/2006	Lovegrove	D26/61
D566,317 S	*	4/2008	Meda et al.	D26/62
D590,976 S	*	4/2009	Levine	D26/62
D605,800 S	*	12/2009	Hodgson	D26/62
D608,925 S	*	1/2010	Hodgson	D26/62
D614,788 S	*	4/2010	Bourotte	D26/61

* cited by examiner

Primary Examiner — Brian N Vinson
(74) *Attorney, Agent, or Firm* — Ladas & Parry LLP

(57)　　　　　　　　**CLAIM**
I claim the ornamental design for a floor lamp, as shown.

DESCRIPTION

FIG. **1** is a left side view of a floor lamp of my new design;
FIG. **2** is a front view thereof;
FIG. **3** is a right side view thereof;
FIG. **4** is a a top view thereof;
FIG. **5** is a bottom view thereof; and,
FIG. **6** is a perspective view thereof.

1 Claim, 3 Drawing Sheets

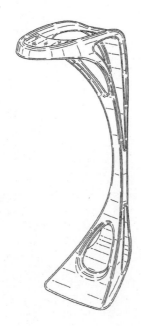

TITLE: TAPE DISPENSER
INVENTORS: KARIM RASHID, SHAELYN D. CRUTCHLEY,
KAYLA A. HAGENS, GERALD E. MUELLER, ET AL.
ASSIGNEE: 3M INNOVATIVE PROPERTIES COMPANY

PATENT NUMBER: USD 638,880
PATENT FILED: AUGUST 24, 2010
PATENT GRANTED: MAY 31, 2011

(12) **United States Design Patent**
Rashid et al.

(10) Patent No.: **US D638,880 S**
(45) **Date of Patent:** ** **May 31, 2011**

(54) **TAPE DISPENSER**

(75) Inventors: **Karim Rashid**, New York, NY (US);
Shaelyn D. Crutchley, St. Paul, MN
(US); **Kayla A. Hagens**, Cottage Grove,
MN (US); **Gerald E. Mueller**, Eagan,
MN (US); **Dominic M. Pitera**,
Woodbury, MN (US)

(73) Assignee: **3M Innovative Properties Company**,
St. Paul, MN (US)

(**) Term: **14 Years**

(21) Appl. No.: **29/368,463**

(22) Filed: **Aug. 24, 2010**

(51) LOC (9) Cl. **08-02**

(52) U.S. Cl. **D19/69**

(58) **Field of Classification Search** D19/36,
D19/70, 69, 68; D13/133, 146; 242/588.6,
242/588.3, 588.2; 225/77, 6, 56, 69, 26,
225/25, 19, 11; 206/411; 156/577, 527,
156/523
See application file for complete search history.

(56) **References Cited**

U.S. PATENT DOCUMENTS

D144,391 S	*	4/1946	Krueger	D19/69
D246,659 S	*	12/1977	Vailati	D19/69
D274,825 S	*	7/1984	Lissoni	D19/69
D293,338 S	*	12/1987	Evenson	D19/67
D400,586 S	*	11/1998	Yuen	D19/73
D480,110 S	*	9/2003	Lin	D19/75
D541,348 S	*	4/2007	Mandel	D19/69
D541,863 S	*	5/2007	Gerules	D19/69
D543,244 S	*	5/2007	Tsuruha	D19/73
D571,405 S	*	6/2008	Boulais	D19/69
D592,249 S	*	5/2009	Chang	D19/69
D614,700 S	*	4/2010	Magid et al.	D19/73

* cited by examiner

Primary Examiner — Austin Murphy
(74) *Attorney, Agent, or Firm* — Lisa P. Fulton

(57) **CLAIM**

The ornamental design for a tape dispenser, as shown and
described.

DESCRIPTION

FIG. **1** is a perspective view of a tape dispenser showing the
new design;
FIG. **2** is a front view thereof;
FIG. **3** is a side view thereof;
FIG. **4** is another side view thereof;
FIG. **5** is a top view thereof;
FIG. **6** is a bottom view thereof; and,
FIG. **7** is a rear view thereof.
The broken line showings of a roll of tape inside the tape
dispenser, a tape cutting area at the front of the tape dispenser,
and a grip pad on the bottom of the tape dispenser are included
for illustrative purposes only and form no part of the claimed
design.

1 Claim, 3 Drawing Sheets

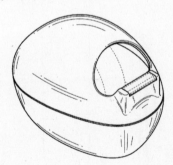
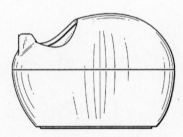

TITLE: INTEGRATED TOILET
INVENTOR: PHILIPPE STARCK
ASSIGNEE: DURAVIT

PATENT NUMBER: USD 639,401
PATENT FILED: AUGUST 3, 2010
PATENT GRANTED: JUNE 7, 2011

(12) **United States Design Patent**
Starck

(10) **Patent No.:** **US D639,401 S**
(45) **Date of Patent:** ⁎⁎ **Jun. 7, 2011**

(54) **INTEGRATED TOILET**

(75) Inventor: **Philippe Starck**, Paris (FR)

(73) Assignee: **Duravit AG**, Hornberg (DE)

(**) Term: **14 Years**

(21) Appl. No.: **29/367,139**

(22) Filed: **Aug. 3, 2010**

(30) **Foreign Application Priority Data**

Feb. 25, 2010 (CN) 2010 3 0119915

(51) **LOC (9) Cl.** **23-02**

(52) **U.S. Cl.** **D23/295**

(58) **Field of Classification Search** D23/295,
D23/309; 4/300, 329, 420, 443–444, DIG. 15
See application file for complete search history.

(56) **References Cited**

U.S. PATENT DOCUMENTS

D586,893 S ⁎ 2/2009 Cummings et al. D23/295
D600,333 S ⁎ 9/2009 Liu D23/295
⁎ cited by examiner

Primary Examiner — Robert A Delehanty
(74) *Attorney, Agent, or Firm* — Faegre & Benson LLP

(57) **CLAIM**

The ornamental design for integrated toilet, as shown and described.

DESCRIPTION

FIG. **1** is a front perspective view.
FIG. **2** is a front view.
FIG. **3** is a back view.
FIG. **4** is a right side view.
FIG. **5** is a left side view.
FIG. **6** is a top view; and,
FIG. **7** is a bottom view.
The broken line showing of the bottom is for illustrative purpose only and forms no part of the claimed design.

1 Claim, 7 Drawing Sheets

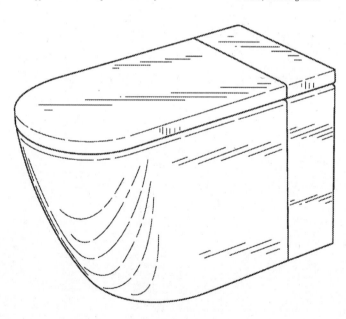

TITLE: CEILING LAMP
INVENTOR: ROSS LOVEGROVE
ASSIGNEE: ARTEMIDE

PATENT NUMBER: USD 644,778
PATENT FILED: OCTOBER 13, 2009
PATENT GRANTED: SEPTEMBER 6, 2011

(12) **United States Design Patent**
Lovegrove

(10) Patent No.: **US D644,778 S**
(45) **Date of Patent:** ** **Sep. 6, 2011**

(54) **CEILING LAMP**

(75) Inventor: **Ross Lovegrove**, Milan (IT)

(73) Assignee: **ARTEMIDE S.p.A.**, Milan (IT)

(**) Term: **14 Years**

(21) Appl. No.: **29/345,235**

(22) Filed: **Oct. 13, 2009**

(30) **Foreign Application Priority Data**

Apr. 10, 2009 (EM) 001120646

(51) **LOC (9) Cl.** **26-03**
(52) **U.S. Cl.** **D26/89**; D26/83
(58) **Field of Classification Search** D26/84–92,
D26/120, 128; 362/147, 404–408, 431, 432
See application file for complete search history.

(56) **References Cited**

U.S. PATENT DOCUMENTS

D46,664 S * 11/1914 Cobb D26/84
D61,360 S * 8/1922 Blackwell D26/88

5,868,490 A * 2/1999 Barthelmess 362/249.16
D541,970 S * 5/2007 Blackman D26/81
D613,448 S * 4/2010 Lovegrove D26/86
D624,230 S * 9/2010 Lovegrove D26/86

* cited by examiner

Primary Examiner — Clare E Heflin
(74) *Attorney, Agent, or Firm* — Ladas & Parry LLP

(57) **CLAIM**

I claim the ornamental design for a ceiling lamp, as shown and described.

DESCRIPTION

FIG. 1 is a left side view of a ceiling lamp of my new design;
FIG. 2 is a rear view thereof;
FIG. 3 is a right side view thereof;
FIG. 4 is a front view thereof;
FIG. 5 is a top view thereof;
FIG. 6 is a bottom view thereof; and,
FIG. 7 is a perspective view thereof.
Features shown in broken lines show environmental structure and form no part of the claimed design.

1 Claim, 7 Drawing Sheets

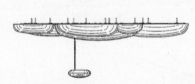

TITLE: CHAIR
INVENTOR: PIERO LISSONI
ASSIGNEE: KARTELL

PATENT NUMBER: USD 645,272
PATENT FILED: APRIL 13, 2010
PATENT GRANTED: SEPTEMBER 20, 2011

(12) **United States Design Patent**
Lissoni

(10) **Patent No.:** **US D645,272 S**
(45) **Date of Patent:** ✱✱ **Sep. 20, 2011**

(54) **CHAIR**

(75) Inventor: **Piero Lissoni**, Milan (IT)

(73) Assignee: **Kartell S.p.A.** (IT)

(✱✱) Term: **14 Years**

(21) Appl. No.: **29/359,585**

(22) Filed: **Apr. 13, 2010**

(51) **LOC (9) Cl.** **06-01**

(52) **U.S. Cl.** **D6/376**; D6/379; D6/380

(58) **Field of Classification Search** D6/334–336,
D6/369, 370, 374, 375, 376, 379, 380, 500–502;
297/411.28, 445.1, 446.1, 452.46, 452.64
See application file for complete search history.

(56) **References Cited**

U.S. PATENT DOCUMENTS

D390,028	S	*	2/1998	Caldwell D6/376
D420,828	S	*	2/2000	Bertoni D6/380
D449,459	S	*	10/2001	Diez Mintegi D6/374
D458,468	S	*	6/2002	Levrangi D6/376
D464,494	S	*	10/2002	Gasca Burges D6/374
D485,084	S	*	1/2004	Bales D6/379
D513,134	S	*	12/2005	Asano et al. D6/380
D557,031	S	*	12/2007	Marin D6/376
D558,477	S	*	1/2008	Nardi D6/376

D572,049 S * 7/2008 Kerr D6/500
* cited by examiner

Primary Examiner — Mimosa De
(74) *Attorney, Agent, or Firm* — Cantor Colburn LLP

(57) **CLAIM**
I claim, the ornamental design for a chair, as shown and described.

DESCRIPTION

FIG. **1** is a front perspective view of a chair, showing my new design;
FIG. **2** is a front elevation view thereof;
FIG. **3** is a rear elevation view thereof;
FIG. **4** is a side elevation view thereof taken from the right of FIG. **2**, the opposite side view being a mirror image hereof;
FIG. **5** is a top plan view thereof;
FIG. **6** is a front perspective view of another embodiment thereof;
FIG. **7** is a front elevation view thereof;
FIG. **8** is a rear elevation view thereof;
FIG. **9** is a side elevation view thereof taken from the right of FIG. **7**, the opposite side view being a mirror image hereof; and,
FIG. **10** is a top view thereof.

1 Claim, 10 Drawing Sheets

TITLE: ARMCHAIR
INVENTOR: NAOTO FUKASAWA
ASSIGNEE: B&B ITALIA

PATENT NUMBER: USD 646,496
PATENT FILED: OCTOBER 18, 2010
PATENT GRANTED: OCTOBER 11, 2011

(12) **United States Design Patent**
Fukasawa

(10) **Patent No.:** **US D646,496 S**
(45) **Date of Patent:** ** **Oct. 11, 2011**

(54) **ARMCHAIR**

(75) Inventor: **Naoto Fukasawa**, Tokyo (JP)

(73) Assignee: **B&B Italia S.p.A.**, Milan (IT)

(**) Term: **14 Years**

(21) Appl. No.: **29/377,199**

(22) Filed: **Oct. 18, 2010**

(51) LOC (9) Cl. **06-01**

(52) **U.S. Cl.** **D6/364**; D6/375

(58) **Field of Classification Search** D6/334–336,
D6/364, 365, 371, 372, 373, 375, 500–502;
297/445.1, 446.1, 451.4, 451.5, 452.12, 452.19

See application file for complete search history.

(56) **References Cited**

U.S. PATENT DOCUMENTS

D222,538	S	*	11/1971	Bernard	D6/364
D222,745	S	*	12/1971	Bernard	D6/364
D226,793	S	*	5/1973	Watamura	D6/364
D252,060	S	*	6/1979	Prevost	D6/375

* cited by examiner

Primary Examiner — Mimosa De
(74) *Attorney, Agent, or Firm* — Mintz, Levin, Cohn, Ferris,
Glovsky Popeo, P.C.

(57) **CLAIM**
The ornamental design for an armchair, as shown and
described.

DESCRIPTION

FIG. **1** is a front view of an armchair;
FIG. **2** is a back view of an armchair; and,
FIG. **3** is a side perspective view of an armchair.
The broken lines shown in the drawing disclosure are for
illustrative purposes only and form no part of the claimed
design.

1 Claim, 3 Drawing Sheets

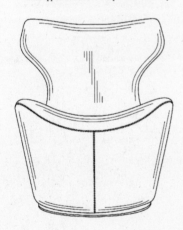

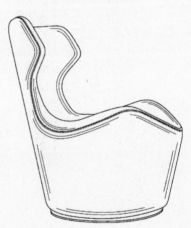

TITLE: WEARABLE DISPLAY DEVICE
INVENTORS: MITCHELL JOSEPH HEINRICH & MAJ
ISABELLE OLSSON
ASSIGNEE: GOOGLE

PATENT NUMBER: USD 659,741
PATENT FILED: OCTOBER 26, 2011
PATENT GRANTED: MAY 15, 2012

(12) **United States Design Patent**　(10) **Patent No.:**　**US D659,741 S**

Heinrich et al.　(45) **Date of Patent:**　⁑ **May 15, 2012**

(54)　**WEARABLE DISPLAY DEVICE**

(75)　Inventors: **Mitchell Joseph Heinrich**, San
　　　　　Francisco, CA (US); **Maj Isabelle
　　　　　Olsson**, San Francisco, CA (US)

(73)　Assignee: **Google Inc.**, Mountain View, CA (US)

(**)　Term:　**14 Years**

(21)　Appl. No.: **29/404,883**

(22)　Filed:　**Oct. 26, 2011**

(51)　**LOC (9) Cl.** **16-06**

(52)　**U.S. Cl.** **D16/309**; D16/335; D16/326

(58)　**Field of Classification Search** D16/101,
　　　　D16/300–342, 900; D29/109–110; D24/110.2;
　　　　351/41, 44, 51–52, 62, 158, 92, 103–123,
　　　　351/140, 153, 45–46; 2/426–432, 447–449,
　　　　2/441, 434–437, 13, 15; D21/483, 659–661;
　　　　　　　　　　　　　　　　　　　　　D14/372

　　　See application file for complete search history.

(56)　　　　　**References Cited**

　　　　　　U.S. PATENT DOCUMENTS

D124,542 S	*	1/1941	Bachmann D9/715
3,701,591 A	*	10/1972	Wichers 351/41
D327,079 S	*	6/1992	Allen D16/309
D616,486 S		5/2010	Carlow et al. D16/325
D647,123 S	*	10/2011	Cho D16/309
D649,177 S	*	11/2011	Cho et al. D16/309
2010/0045928	A1 *	2/2010	Levy 351/158

* cited by examiner

Primary Examiner — Raphael Barkai

(74)　*Attorney, Agent, or Firm* — Lerner, David, Littenberg,
Krumholz & Mentlik, LLP

(57)　　　　　**CLAIM**

The ornamental design for a wearable display device, as
shown and described.

　　　　　DESCRIPTION

FIG. **1** is a front perspective view of a wearable display device
shown in a first embodiment;

FIG. **2** is a front elevation view of the wearable display device
of FIG. **1**;

FIG. **3** is a rear elevation view of the wearable display device
of FIG. **1**;

FIG. **4** is a left side elevation view of the wearable display
device of FIG. **1**;

FIG. **5** is a right side elevation view of the wearable display
device of FIG. **1**;

FIG. **6** is a top plan view of the wearable display device of
FIG. **1**;

FIG. **7** is a bottom plan view of the wearable display device of
FIG. **1**;

FIG. **8** is a front perspective view of a wearable display device
shown in a second embodiment;

FIG. **9** is a front elevation view of the wearable display device
of FIG. **8**;

FIG. **10** is a rear elevation view of the wearable display device
of FIG. **8**;

FIG. **11** is a left side elevation view of the wearable display
device of FIG. **8**;

FIG. **12** is a right side elevation view of the wearable display
device of FIG. **8**;

FIG. **13** is a top plan view of the wearable display device of
FIG. **8**; and,

FIG. **14** is a bottom plan view of the wearable display device
of FIG. **8**.

The appearance of elements presented in broken line format
form no part of the claimed design.

　　　　　1 Claim, 10 Drawing Sheets

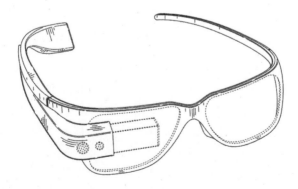

TITLE: FAUCET HANDLE
INVENTOR: ANTONIO CITTERIO
ASSIGNEE: HANSGROHE

PATENT NUMBER: USD 668,745
PATENT FILED: FEBRUARY 24, 2012
PATENT GRANTED: OCTOBER 9, 2012

(12) **United States Design Patent**   (10) Patent No.:   **US D668,745 S**
  Citterio   (45) Date of Patent: ** Oct. 9, 2012**

(54) **FAUCET HANDLE**

(75) Inventor: **Antonio Citterio**, Milan (IT)

(73) Assignee: **Hansgrohe SE**, Schiltach (DE)

(**) Term: **14 Years**

(21) Appl. No.: **29/414,096**

(22) Filed: **Feb. 24, 2012**

(30) **Foreign Application Priority Data**

  Aug. 31, 2011   (EM) 001291447

(51) **LOC (9) Cl.** **23-01**
(52) **U.S. Cl.** **D23/253**
(58) **Field of Classification Search** D23/238–243,
    D23/250, 252–254, 249, 245; 4/675–678;
    137/801
    See application file for complete search history.

(56) **References Cited**

U.S. PATENT DOCUMENTS

D162,678	S	*	3/1951	Muller-Munk D23/254
D199,555	S	*	11/1964	Doman D23/252
D434,476	S	*	11/2000	Meda D23/252
D466,988	S	*	12/2002	Marshall D23/250
D570,963	S	*	6/2008	Hoernig D23/250

OTHER PUBLICATIONS

Brochure—Bonglo, 3 pgs., Bonglo srl, Opaglio, Italy (at least as early as Sep. 28, 2004).
Brochure—Collection, 3 pgs., Carlo Nobili SpA Rubinetterie, Borgomanero, Italy (at least as early as Sep. 29, 2009).

* cited by examiner

Primary Examiner — Robert Delehanty
(74) *Attorney, Agent, or Firm* — Nirav D. Parikh; Lora J. Graentzdoerffer; Edgar A. Zarins

(57) , **CLAIM**
The ornamental design for a faucet handle, as shown and described.

DESCRIPTION

FIG. 1 is a perspective view of a faucet handle showing my design;
FIG. 2 is a front elevational view thereof;
FIG. 3 is a rear elevational view thereof;
FIG. 4 is a left side elevational view thereof; the right side elevational view being a mirror image thereof;
FIG. 5 is a top plan view thereof; and,
FIG. 6 is a bottom plan view thereof.
The broken-line disclosure in the views represents portions of the article in which the claimed design is embodied, but which form no part of the claimed design.

1 Claim, 6 Drawing Sheets

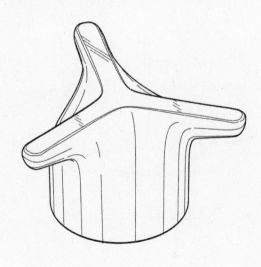

TITLE: ARMCHAIR
INVENTOR: PATRICIA URQUIOLA
ASSIGNEE: B&B ITALIA

PATENT NUMBER: USD 670,098
PATENT FILED: OCTOBER 11, 2011
PATENT GRANTED: NOVEMBER 6, 2012

(12) **United States Design Patent**
Urquiola

(10) **Patent No.:** **US D670,098 S**
(45) **Date of Patent:** ** **Nov. 6, 2012**

(54) **ARMCHAIR**

(75) Inventor: **Patricia Urquiola**, Milan (IT)

(73) Assignee: **B&B Italia S.p.A.**, Milan (IT)

(**) Term: **14 Years**

(21) Appl. No.: **29/403,807**

(22) Filed: **Oct. 11, 2011**

(30) **Foreign Application Priority Data**

Apr. 12, 2011 (EM) 001849415-0003

(51) **LOC (9) Cl.** **06-01**
(52) **U.S. Cl.** **D6/375**
(58) **Field of Classification Search** D6/334–336,
D6/369, 371–373, 374, 375, 376, 379, 380,
D6/500–502; 297/445.1, 446.1, 452.1, 452.12,
297/452.14, 452.19, 452.41
See application file for complete search history.

(56) **References Cited**

U.S. PATENT DOCUMENTS

D175,802	S	*	10/1955	Sherman D6/375
D199,621	S	*	11/1964	Johnson D6/374
3,499,682	A	*	3/1970	Orenstein 297/452.41

D243,895	S	*	4/1977	Powell D6/375
D600,028	S	*	9/2009	Starck D6/334
D600,458	S	*	9/2009	Starck D6/334
D613,956	S	*	4/2010	Jehs et al. D6/375
D627,574	S	*	11/2010	Joly D6/375

* cited by examiner

Primary Examiner — Mimosa De
(74) *Attorney, Agent, or Firm* — Mintz, Levin, Cohn, Ferris, Glovsky and Popeo, P.C.

(57) **CLAIM**
The ornamental design for an armchair, as shown and described.

DESCRIPTION

FIG. 1 is a perspective view of an armchair.
FIG. 2 is a front view of an armchair.
FIG. 3 is a side view of an armchair.
FIG. 4 is a side view of an armchair.
FIG. 5 is a back view of an armchair.
FIG. 6 is a top view of an armchair; and,
FIG. 7 is a bottom view of an armchair.
The broken lines shown in the drawing disclosure are for illustrative purposes only and form no part of the claimed design.

1 Claim, 7 Drawing Sheets

TITLE: COMBINED AUDIO PLAYER & CLOCK RADIO
INVENTORS: XIAOFENG SONG & ZHONGSHENG HONG
ASSIGNEE: SONY CORPORATION

PATENT NUMBER: USD 671,521
PATENT FILED: JUNE 30, 2010
PATENT GRANTED: NOVEMBER 27, 2012

(12) **United States Design Patent**
Song et al.

(10) **Patent No.:** **US D671,521 S**
(45) **Date of Patent:** ** Nov. 27, 2012

(54) **COMBINED AUDIO PLAYER AND CLOCK RADIO**

(75) Inventors: **Xiaofeng Song**, Shanghai (CN);
Zhongsheng Hong, Shanghai (CN)

(73) Assignee: **Sony Corporation**, Tokyo (JP)

(**) Term: **14 Years**

(21) Appl. No.: **29/347,867**

(22) Filed: **Jun. 30, 2010**

(30) **Foreign Application Priority Data**

Dec. 30, 2009 (CN) 2009 3 0385964

(51) **LOC (9) Cl.** **14-01**
(52) **U.S. Cl.** **D14/168**
(58) **Field of Classification Search** D14/156,
D14/160–165, 170, 171, 168, 188, 193–198;
D10/1, 2, 15, 128; 455/91, 95, 128, 344–351;
369/6–12, 75.11, 75.21, 77.11, 77.21
See application file for complete search history.

(56) **References Cited**

U.S. PATENT DOCUMENTS

D241,977	S	*	10/1976	Makino et al. D14/171
D430,135	S	*	8/2000	Isonaga D14/168
D449,589	S		10/2001	Ishibashi et al.
D450,063	S	*	11/2001	Bentley D15/13
D454,856	S	*	3/2002	Kobayashi D14/168
D499,715	S		12/2004	Zeitman
D525,536	S	*	7/2006	Chan D10/2

D532,817	S		11/2006	Ishii
D533,864	S	*	12/2006	Yokoyama D14/168
D542,772	S		5/2007	Shimizu
7,239,237	B2	*	7/2007	Hess 340/539.1
D549,212	S	*	8/2007	Wada D14/171
D556,185	S		11/2007	Motoishi
D560,657	S	*	1/2008	Langberg et al. D14/214
D565,536	S		4/2008	Obata
D581,392	S		11/2008	Zheng
D599,322	S		9/2009	Zheng
D601,998	S		10/2009	Zheng
7,710,831	B2	*	5/2010	Driska 368/10
8,194,507	B2	*	6/2012	Mills 368/83
8,195,114	B2	*	6/2012	Krampf et al. 455/154.1

* cited by examiner

Primary Examiner — Prabhakar Deshmukh
(74) *Attorney, Agent, or Firm* — Rader, Fishman & Grauer PLLC

(57) **CLAIM**

The ornamental design for a combined audio player and clock radio, as shown.

DESCRIPTION

FIG. **1** is a perspective view of a combined audio payer and clock radio showing our new design;
FIG. **2** is a front elevational view thereof;
FIG. **3** is a rear elevational view thereof;
FIG. **4** is a left side elevational view thereof;
FIG. **5** is a right side elevational view thereof;
FIG. **6** is a top plan view thereof; and,
FIG. **7** is a bottom plan view thereof.

1 Claim, 7 Drawing Sheets

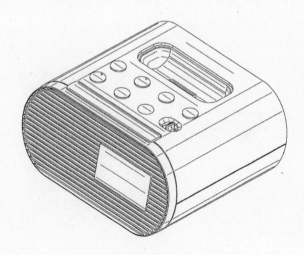

TITLE: ELECTRIC POWERED HANDCYCLE
INVENTORS: MICHAEL SHANE LOFGREN & BRIAN
CHARLES STEWART
ASSIGNEE: NONE

PATENT NUMBER: USD 680,913
PATENT FILED: APRIL 24, 2012
PATENT GRANTED: APRIL 30, 2013

(12) **United States Design Patent**
Lofgren et al.

(10) Patent No.: **US D680,913 S**
(45) Date of Patent: ✱✱ **Apr. 30, 2013**

(54) **ELECTRIC POWERED HANDCYCLE**

(76) Inventors: **Michael Shane Lofgren**, Tualatin, OR
(US); **Brian Charles Stewart**, Oregon
City, OR (US)

(✱✱) Term: **14 Years**

(21) Appl. No.: **29/418,947**

(22) Filed: **Apr. 24, 2012**

(51) LOC (9) Cl. **12-11**
(52) U.S. Cl.
USPC **D12/112**
(58) **Field of Classification Search** D12/112,
D12/111, 114; 280/274–280, 282–288, 288.1–288.4;
180/65.1, 65.29, 68.5, 210, 216, 220, 331,
180/205.1, 206.1, 207.3; D15/1, 3; D13/103,
D13/158, 184; 429/163, 176
See application file for complete search history.

(56) **References Cited**

U.S. PATENT DOCUMENTS

5,853,062	A	✱ 12/1998	Hulett	180/206.4
D434,349	S	✱ 11/2000	Currie et al.	D12/111
D438,825	S	✱ 3/2001	Tsuboi et al.	D12/114
D550,592	S	✱ 9/2007	Wu	D12/114
D613,312	S	✱ 4/2010	Lopp	D15/1
D626,038	S	✱ 10/2010	Li	D12/112
D637,528	S	✱ 5/2011	Tanaka et al.	D12/114
8,047,320	B2	✱ 11/2011	Hadley	180/206.5

✱ cited by examiner

Primary Examiner — Susan M Lee
Assistant Examiner — Linda G Brooks

(57) **CLAIM**
The ornamental design for an electric powered handcycle, as
shown.

DESCRIPTION

FIG. **1A** is an isometric view of an electric powered hand-
cycle showing my new design;
FIG. **2** is a bottom view thereof;
FIG. **3** is a right side elevation view thereof; and,
FIG. **4** is a left side elevation view thereof.
The broken lines illustrating a rider form no part of the
claimed design.

1 Claim, 4 Drawing Sheets

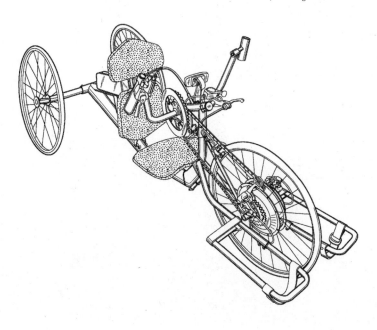

TITLE: VEHICLE
INVENTORS: ELON REEVE MUSK, FRANZ VON HOLZHAUSEN,
BERNARD LEE & DAVID TADASHI IMAI
ASSIGNEE: TESLA MOTORS

PATENT NUMBER: USD 683,268
PATENT FILED: FEBRUARY 8, 2012
PATENT GRANTED: MAY 28, 2013

(12) **United States Design Patent**
Musk et al.

(10) **Patent No.:**   **US D683,268 S**
(45) **Date of Patent:**   ** **May 28, 2013**

(54) **VEHICLE**

(75) Inventors: **Elon Reeve Musk**, Los Angeles, CA
(US); **Franz von Holzhausen**, Malibu,
CA (US); **Bernard Lee**, Aliso Viejo, CA
(US); **David Tadashi Imai**, Los Angeles,
CA (US)

(73) Assignee: **Tesla Motors, Inc.**, Palo Alto, CA (US)

(**) Term: **14 Years**

(21) Appl. No.: **29/412,833**

(22) Filed: **Feb. 8, 2012**

(51) LOC (9) Cl. **12-08**

(52) U.S. Cl.
USPC **D12/92**

(58) **Field of Classification Search**
USPC D12/86, 90–92; D21/424, 433, 434;
296/181.1, 181.5
See application file for complete search history.

(56) **References Cited**

U.S. PATENT DOCUMENTS

D629,718 S * 12/2010 Reichman et al. D12/92
D635,059 S * 3/2011 Futschik et al. D12/92
D676,789 S * 2/2013 Song et al. D12/92

* cited by examiner

Primary Examiner — Melody Brown
(74) *Attorney, Agent, or Firm* — Patent Law Office of David
G. Beck

(57)   **CLAIM**
The ornamental design for a vehicle, as shown and described.

DESCRIPTION

FIG. 1 is a front and side perspective view of an automobile
and/or toy replica thereof showing our new design;
FIG. 2 is a rear and side view thereof;
FIG. 3 is a side elevational view thereof;
FIG. 4 is an opposite side elevational view thereof;
FIG. 5 is a front elevational view thereof;
FIG. 6 is a rear elevational view thereof; and,
FIG. 7 is a top plan view thereof.
The broken lines are for illustrative purposes and form no part
of the claimed design.

1 Claim, 7 Drawing Sheets

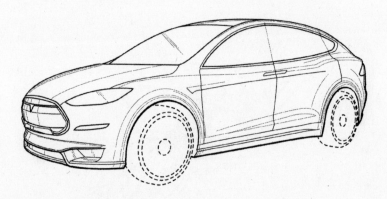

TITLE: VEHICLE CHARGER
INVENTORS: YVES ALBERT BÉHAR, JOSHUA TREE
MORENSTEIN, MATTHEW JOHN MALONE, ET AL.
ASSIGNEE: GENERAL ELECTRIC COMPANY

PATENT NUMBER: USD 688,199
PATENT FILED: JANUARY 13, 2011
PATENT GRANTED: AUGUST 20, 2013

(12) **United States Design Patent**
Behar et al.

(10) Patent No.: **US D688,199 S**
(45) Date of Patent: ** **Aug. 20, 2013**

(54) **VEHICLE CHARGER**

(75) Inventors: **Yves Albert Behar**, San Francisco, CA (US); **Joshua Tree Morenstein**, San Francisco, CA (US); **Matthew John Malone**, Astoria, NY (US); **Jennifer Yoko Olson**, Brooklyn, NY (US); **Pichaya Puttorngul**, New York, NY (US); **Matthew David Swinton**, Brooklyn, NY (US)

(73) Assignee: **General Electric Company**, Schenectady, NY (US)

(**) Term: **14 Years**

(21) Appl. No.: 29/383,179

(22) Filed: **Jan. 13, 2011**

(51) **LOC (9) Cl.** **13-02**
(52) **U.S. Cl.**
USPC **D13/107**
(58) **Field of Classification Search**
USPC D13/107–110, 118–119, 184, 199; D14/251, 253, 432, 434; 320/103–115
See application file for complete search history.

(56) **References Cited**

U.S. PATENT DOCUMENTS

D237,718	S	*	11/1975	Bozich	D13/139.5
D270,831	S	*	10/1983	Jensen	D13/139.5
5,461,299	A	*	10/1995	Bruni	320/108
D434,001	S	*	11/2000	Sayger	D13/139.5
6,362,594	B2	*	3/2002	Kajiura	320/104
D597,937	S	*	8/2009	Haw et al.	D13/107
D608,731	S	*	1/2010	Amit	D13/107
D608,733	S	*	1/2010	Smith	D13/107
D613,683	S	*	4/2010	Baxter et al.	D13/107
D618,168	S	*	6/2010	Baxter et al.	D13/107
D628,960	S	*	12/2010	Shimizu et al.	D13/107
D629,747	S	*	12/2010	Rajakaruna	D13/107
D639,733	S	*	6/2011	Liu et al.	D13/107
D641,316	S	*	7/2011	Schneiderat	D13/107
2010/0320966	A1	*	12/2010	Baxter et al.	320/109
2011/0140656	A1	*	6/2011	Starr et al.	320/109
2011/0145141	A1	*	6/2011	Blain	705/39
2011/0174875	A1	*	7/2011	Wurzer	235/380

* cited by examiner

Primary Examiner — Rosemary K Tarcza
(74) *Attorney, Agent, or Firm* — Cantor Colburn LLP

(57) **CLAIM**
We claim, the ornamental design for a vehicle charger, as shown and described.

DESCRIPTION

FIG. 1 is a perspective view of a first embodiment the invention;
FIG. 2 is a front view of the embodiment of FIG. 1;
FIG. 3 is a rear view of the embodiment of FIG. 1;
FIG. 4 is a side view of the embodiment of FIG. 1, the opposite side being a mirror image thereof;
FIG. 5 is a top view of the embodiment of FIG. 1; and,
FIG. 6 is a bottom view of the embodiment of FIG. 1.
The phantom lines shown in FIG. 1-FIG. 6 are environmental and not part of the claimed design.
The color and shading of the vehicle charger forms no part of the claimed design, the vehicle charger according to the claimed design may be any color or combination of colors.
The surface treatment of the vehicle charger forms no part of the claimed design, the vehicle charger of the claimed design may have any surface treatment.
References to "side", "top", "front", "rear" and "bottom" in the figure descriptions are not meant to require certain in-use orientation; a vehicle charger according to the claimed design may be used in any orientation.

1 Claim, 6 Drawing Sheets

TITLE: PHOTOVOLTAIC DEVICE
INVENTORS: FABRIZIO MOZZARDI & MAURIZIO MOZZARDI
ASSIGNEE: NONE

PATENT NUMBER: USD 688,621
PATENT FILED: DECEMBER 4, 2012
PATENT GRANTED: AUGUST 27, 2013

(12) **United States Design Patent**
Mozzardi et al.

(10) **Patent No.:** **US D688,621 S**
(45) **Date of Patent:** ** **Aug. 27, 2013**

(54) **PHOTOVOLTAIC DEVICE**

(71) Applicants: **Fabrizio Mozzardi**, Lanciano (IT);
Maurizio Mozzardi, Lanciano (IT)

(72) Inventors: **Fabrizio Mozzardi**, Lanciano (IT);
Maurizio Mozzardi, Lanciano (IT)

(**) Term: **14 Years**

(21) Appl. No.: **29/438,827**

(22) Filed: **Dec. 4, 2012**

(30) **Foreign Application Priority Data**

Jun. 6, 2012 (WO) DM/078793

(51) **LOC (9) Cl.** **13-02**

(52) **U.S. Cl.**
USPC **D13/102**

(58) **Field of Classification Search**
USPC D13/102, 101, 184, 199; D26/113;
126/569, 571, 578, 580, 609, 610, 611, 612,
126/634, 640, 643, 652, 658, 680–685, 689,
126/699; 136/206, 243–252, 256, 257, 260,
136/261; 351/203
See application file for complete search history.

(56) **References Cited**

U.S. PATENT DOCUMENTS

D309,789	S	*	8/1990	Luce	D26/68
D311,722	S	*	10/1990	Cheng	D13/102
D420,973	S	*	2/2000	Kalarney	D13/102
6,058,930	A	*	5/2000	Shingleton	126/600
D494,536	S	*	8/2004	Pu	D13/102
D543,500	S	*	5/2007	Parness et al.	D13/102
D555,084	S	*	11/2007	Sharma et al.	D13/102
D600,200	S	*	9/2009	Dimov et al.	D13/102
D600,201	S	*	9/2009	Dallaire	D13/102
D610,536	S	*	2/2010	Brumels	D13/102
D618,166	S	*	6/2010	Sanoner	D13/102
D624,491	S	*	9/2010	Xuan	D13/102
D641,315	S	*	7/2011	Rock	D13/102

* cited by examiner

Primary Examiner — Derrick Holland

(57) **CLAIM**
The ornamental design for a photovoltaic device, as shown and described.

DESCRIPTION

FIG. **1** is a perspective view of a photovoltaic device showing our new design.
FIG. **2** is a rear view thereof.
FIG. **3** is a top view thereof.
FIG. **4** is a front view thereof.
FIG. **5** is a right side view thereof.
FIG. **6** is a left side view thereof; and,
FIG. **7** is a bottom view thereof.

1 Claim, 7 Drawing Sheets

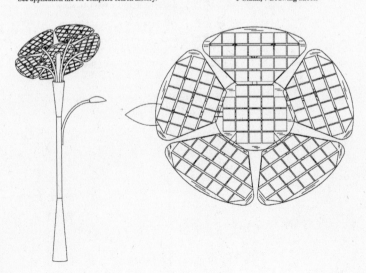

TITLE: DIGITAL CAMERA
INVENTORS: TATSUYA UEMACHI, TAKASHI UMEHARA
& AKIRA NOJIMA
ASSIGNEE: NIKON CORPORATION

PATENT NUMBER: USD 692,044
PATENT FILED: MARCH 28, 2013
PATENT GRANTED: OCTOBER 22, 2013

(12) **United States Design Patent**
Uemachi et al.

(10) Patent No.: **US D692,044 S**

(45) Date of Patent: ** Oct. 22, 2013

(54) **DIGITAL CAMERA**

(71) Applicant: **Nikon Corporation**, Tokyo (JP)

(72) Inventors: **Tatsuya Uemachi**, Kanagawa pref. (JP);
Takashi Umehara, Tokyo (JP); **Akira
Nojima**, Tokyo (JP)

(73) Assignee: **Nikon Corporation**, Tokyo (JP)

(**) Term: **14 Years**

(21) Appl. No.: **29/451,227**

(22) Filed: **Mar. 28, 2013**

Related U.S. Application Data

(63) Continuation of application No. 29/415,360, filed on
Mar. 9, 2012, now Pat. No. Des. 682,906.

(30) **Foreign Application Priority Data**

Sep. 20, 2011 (JP) 2011-021395

(51) **LOC (9) Cl.** **16-05**
(52) **U.S. Cl.**
USPC **D16/219**
(58) **Field of Classification Search**
USPC D16/200, 202, 204, 218, 219;
348/373–376; 358/909.1; 396/535,
396/540, 541
See application file for complete search history.

(56) **References Cited**

U.S. PATENT DOCUMENTS

D243,007 S	1/1977	Uellenberg
D251,975 S	5/1979	Kramer et al.
D257,434 S	10/1980	Conner et al.
D257,850 S	1/1981	Matsumoto
D257,982 S	1/1981	Maitani
D463,810 S *	10/2002	Suzuki et al. D16/202

D555,689 S	11/2007	Yoo et al.
D556,230 S *	11/2007	Hanafusa et al. D16/202
D557,311 S *	12/2007	Hanafusa et al. D16/219

(Continued)

FOREIGN PATENT DOCUMENTS

JP	D1077250 S	7/2000
JP	D1432563 S	1/2012

(Continued)

OTHER PUBLICATIONS

[No Author Listed] Model "D-LUX 4 Safari" Leica Limited, Olive
Paint. DC Watch. Jun. 25, 2009. Accessed online at http://dc.watch.
impress.co.jp/docs/news/20090625_296613.html Last accessed
Feb. 14, 2013.

(Continued)

Primary Examiner — Adir Aronovich

(74) *Attorney, Agent, or Firm* — Wolf, Greenfield & Sacks,
P.C.; Randy J. Pritzker

(57) **CLAIM**

The ornamental design for a digital camera, as shown and
described.

DESCRIPTION

FIG. 1 is a front perspective view of a digital camera showing
our new design;
FIG. 2 is a rear perspective view thereof;
FIG. 3 is a front elevational view thereof;
FIG. 4 is a rear elevational view thereof;
FIG. 5 is a top plan view thereof;
FIG. 6 is a bottom plan view thereof;
FIG. 7 is a right side elevational view thereof; and,
FIG. 8 is a left side elevational view thereof.
The features shown in broken lines in the drawings depict
environmental subject matter only and form no part of the
claimed design.

1 Claim, 5 Drawing Sheets

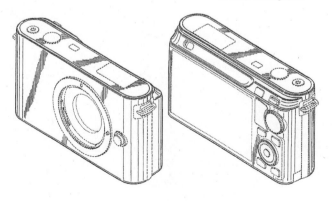

TITLE: PEN
INVENTOR: MARC NEWSON
ASSIGNEE: HERMES SELLIER
(SOCIETE PAR ACTIONS SIMPLIFIEE)

PATENT NUMBER: USD 692,485
PATENT FILED: MAY 31, 2012
PATENT GRANTED: OCTOBER 29, 2013

(12) **United States Design Patent** (10) **Patent No.:** **US D692,485 S**

Newson (45) **Date of Patent:** ** **Oct. 29, 2013**

(54) **PEN**

(75) Inventor: **Marc Newson**, London (GB)

(73) Assignee: **Hermes Sellier (Societe par Actions Simplifiee)**, Paris (FR)

(**) Term: **14 Years**

(21) Appl. No.: **29/423,409**

(22) Filed: **May 31, 2012**

(30) **Foreign Application Priority Data**

Dec. 2, 2011 (WO) DM/077 237

(51) **LOC (9) Cl.** **19-06**
(52) **U.S. Cl.**
USPC **D19/51**
(58) **Field of Classification Search**
USPC D14/411; D19/35, 36, 41–51, 53–58;
24/11 F, 11 P, 11 R; 401/52, 99–109,
401/192, 195, 196
See application file for complete search history.

(56) **References Cited**

U.S. PATENT DOCUMENTS

D116,098 S	*	8/1939	Parker	D19/51
D146,806 S	*	5/1947	Moholy-Nagy	D19/51
2,608,953 A	*	9/1952	Kollsman	401/35
2,669,223 A	*	2/1954	Miessner	401/183
2,669,224 A	*	2/1954	Miessner	15/447
D178,033 S	*	6/1956	Young et al.	D19/51
D472,240 S	*	3/2003	Seog	D14/411
D500,790 S	*	1/2005	Jaakkola	D19/43
D589,556 S	*	3/2009	Keda	D19/45
D641,409 S	*	7/2011	Wang et al.	D19/50
D647,964 S	*	11/2011	Wang et al.	D19/50
D667,828 S	*	9/2012	Park	D14/411
D669,128 S	*	10/2012	Zhang	D19/50

* cited by examiner

Primary Examiner — Elizabeth Albert
(74) *Attorney, Agent, or Firm* — Foley & Lardner LLP

(57) **CLAIM**

I claim the ornamental design for a pen, as shown and described.

DESCRIPTION

FIG. 1 is a front elevation view of a pen showing my new design with the nib retracted;
FIG. 2 is a rear elevation view of FIG. 1;
FIG. 3 is a right side elevation view of FIG. 1;
FIG. 4 is a left side elevation view of FIG. 1;
FIG. 5 is a top plan view of FIG. 1;
FIG. 6 is a bottom plan view of FIG. 1;
FIG. 7 is a front, bottom perspective view of FIG. 1;
FIG. 8 is a front, top perspective view of FIG. 1;
FIG. 9 is a front elevation view of FIG. 1 with the nib extended;
FIG. 10 is a rear elevation view of FIG. 9;
FIG. 11 is a right side elevation view of FIG. 9;
FIG. 12 is a left side elevation view of FIG. 9;
FIG. 13 is a top plan view of FIG. 9;
FIG. 14 is a bottom plan view of FIG. 9;
FIG. 15 is a front, bottom perspective view of FIG. 9; and,
FIG. 16 is an enlarged perspective detail view of a portion of FIG. 15.
The broken lines in FIGS. 15 and 16 are included for the purpose of identifying the detail view and form no part of the claimed design.

1 Claim, 14 Drawing Sheets

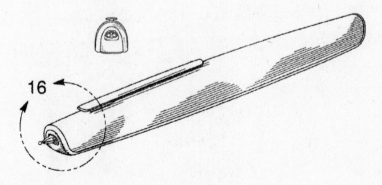

16

TITLE: MOTORBIKE
INVENTOR: PHILIPPE STARCK
ASSIGNEE: NONE

PATENT NUMBER: USD 694,672
PATENT FILED: SEPTEMBER 6, 2012
PATENT GRANTED: DECEMBER 3, 2013

(12) **United States Design Patent**
Starck

(10) Patent No.: **US D694,672 S**
(45) **Date of Patent:** ✱✱ Dec. 3, 2013

(54) **MOTORBIKE**

(76) Inventor: **Philippe Starck**, Paris (FR)

(✱✱) Term: **14 Years**

(21) Appl. No.: **29/431,357**

(22) Filed: **Sep. 6, 2012**

(30) **Foreign Application Priority Data**

Mar. 12, 2012 (FR) 002006981

(51) **LOC (9) Cl.** **12-11**
(52) **U.S. Cl.**
USPC **D12/110**
(58) **Field of Classification Search**
USPC D12/110; 180/218–220, 206.1–206.8,
180/207.3, 65.1, 65.6–65.8
See application file for complete search history.

(56) **References Cited**

U.S. PATENT DOCUMENTS

D477,254 S ✱ 7/2003 Kim et al. D12/110
6,631,774 B2 ✱ 10/2003 Hayashi 180/65.1
D591,203 S ✱ 4/2009 Martin D12/110
D653,590 S ✱ 2/2012 Patterson et al. D12/110
2006/0000655 A1 ✱ 1/2006 Schless 180/220

OTHER PUBLICATIONS

Cycle World Nov. 2010, electric motorcycle on p. 8.✱

✱ cited by examiner

Primary Examiner — Susan M Lee
Assistant Examiner — Linda Brooks
(74) *Attorney, Agent, or Firm* — Blue Filament Law PLLC;
Avery N. Goldstein

(57) **CLAIM**
The ornamental design for a motorbike, as shown and
described.

DESCRIPTION

FIG. **1** is a front, upper perspective view of the inventive
motorbike;
FIG. **2** is a rear, upper perspective view of the motorbike
depicted in FIG. 1;
FIG. **3** is a right side view of the motorbike depicted in FIG.
1;
FIG. **4** is a left side view of the motorbike depicted in FIG. 1;
FIG. **5** is a front view of the motorbike depicted in FIG. 1;
FIG. **6** is a rear view of the motorbike depicted in FIG. 1; and,
FIG. **7** is a top view of the motorbike depicted in FIG. 1.

1 Claim, 3 Drawing Sheets

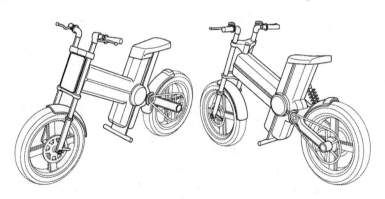

TITLE: SPEAKER HOUSING
INVENTORS: BRANKO LUKIC, STEVEN RYUTARO TAKAYAMA, DAVID YIM, DENIS O'KEEFFE, ET AL.
ASSIGNEE: LOGITECH EUROPE

PATENT NUMBER: USD 706,743
PATENT FILED: NOVEMBER 20, 2012
PATENT GRANTED: JUNE 10, 2014

(12) **United States Design Patent**
Lukic et al.

(10) Patent No.: **US D706,743 S**
(45) Date of Patent: ** **Jun. 10, 2014**

(54) **SPEAKER HOUSING**

(71) Applicant: **Logitech Europe S.A.**, Morges (CH)

(72) Inventors: **Branko Lukic**, Menlo Park, CA (US); **Steven Ryutaro Takayama**, Atherton, CA (US); **David Yim**, Vancouver, WA (US); **Denis O'Keeffe**, Cork (IR); **Neil O'Connell**, Portland, OR (US); **Steve McGarry**, Vancouver, WA (US); **Chris LaBrutto**, Fremont, CA (US)

(73) Assignee: **Logitech Europe S.A.**, Lausanne (CH)

(**) Term: **14 Years**

(21) Appl. No.: **29/437,807**

(22) Filed: **Nov. 20, 2012**

(51) **LOC (10) Cl.** **14-01**
(52) **U.S. Cl.**
    USPC **D14/204**
(58) **Field of Classification Search**
    USPC D14/204, 210–216, 203, 207, 209.1,
        D14/177; D13/184; 181/147, 148, 150, 151,
        181/152, 153, 157, 198, 199; 381/300–303,
        381/306, 332, 333, 336, 345, 361–364,
        381/386–388
    See application file for complete search history.

(56)   **References Cited**

              U.S. PATENT DOCUMENTS

4,325,455	A		4/1982	Kirkpatrick
4,503,292	A		3/1985	Johnson et al.
4,936,410	A		6/1990	Howell
D344,951	S	*	3/1994	Christie D14/216
D349,499	S	*	8/1994	Collins D14/216
5,400,413	A		3/1995	Kindel
5,412,162	A		5/1995	Kindel
5,674,076	A	*	10/1997	Billings et al. 434/365
5,762,194	A	*	6/1998	Clegg 206/449
D402,660	S	*	12/1998	Swansey D14/216

D421,262	S	*	2/2000	Warren D14/214
6,096,160	A		8/2000	Kadomura
6,186,269	B1	*	2/2001	Vollmer et al. 181/144
6,345,685	B1	*	2/2002	Wells et al. 181/153
6,431,308	B1	*	8/2002	Vollmer et al. 181/144
D483,350	S	*	12/2003	Chen D14/216
6,973,994	B2	*	12/2005	Mackin et al. 181/156
D513,746	S	*	1/2006	Allen D14/216
D551,656	S	*	9/2007	Ritsher et al. D14/216
D555,636	S	*	11/2007	Chen et al. D14/216

(Continued)

OTHER PUBLICATIONS

A Bluetooth speaker for the great outdoors, Posting date May 21, 2013, © CBS Interactive Inc. All rights reserved [online], [site visited on Dec. 16, 2013], <http://reviews.cnet.com/portable-speakers/logitech-ue-boom-blue/4505-11313_7-35765418.html>.*

(Continued)

Primary Examiner — Deanna L Pratt
Assistant Examiner — Harold Blackwell, II
(74) *Attorney, Agent, or Firm* — Kilpatrick Townsend & Stockton LLP

(57)   **CLAIM**
The ornamental design for speaker housing, as shown and described.

              DESCRIPTION

FIG. **1** is a perspective view of a speaker housing showing my new design;
FIG. **2** is another perspective view;
FIG. **3**. is another perspective view;
FIG. **4** is a bottom elevation view;
FIG. **5** is a top elevation view;
FIG. **6** is a front elevation view;
FIG. **7** is a back elevation view;
FIG. **8** is a right side elevation view; and,
FIG. **9** is a left side elevation view.

1 Claim, 8 Drawing Sheets

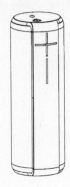

TITLE: PORTABLE AUDIO SYSTEM
INVENTORS: DAVID J. FUSTINO
& RICHARD J. CARBONE
ASSIGNEE: BOSE CORPORATION

PATENT NUMBER: USD 708,228
PATENT FILED: MAY 20, 2013
PATENT GRANTED: JULY 1, 2014

(12) **United States Design Patent**
Fustino et al.

(10) Patent No.: **US D708,228 S**
(45) Date of Patent: ** **Jul. 1, 2014**

(54) **PORTABLE AUDIO SYSTEM**

(71) Applicants: **David J. Fustino**, Framingham, MA (US); **Richard J. Carbone**, Sterling, MA (US)

(72) Inventors: **David J. Fustino**, Framingham, MA (US); **Richard J. Carbone**, Sterling, MA (US)

(73) Assignee: **Bose Corporation**, Framingham, MA (US)

(**) Term: **14 Years**

(21) Appl. No.: **29/455,310**

(22) Filed: **May 20, 2013**

(51) **LOC (10) Cl.** **14-03**

(52) **U.S. Cl.**
USPC **D14/496**; D14/203.1

(58) **Field of Classification Search**
USPC .... D14/496, 401, 435, 474, 483, 217, 137, D14/138, 160, 168, 356, 203.1–203.8, 507; 345/156, 169, 173–179, 905; 715/727–729, 864; 710/1, 5, 8; 713/1, 713/600; 455/1.1, 1.7, 73, 344–347, 93, 95, 455/3.01–3.06, 550.1, 573.1; 370/342–344; 369/1, 2, 6–12; 463/43–47; 273/148 B
See application file for complete search history.

(56) **References Cited**

U.S. PATENT DOCUMENTS

4,676,619	A	*	6/1987	Woolley 396/432
5,471,659	A	*	11/1995	Wong 455/132
5,867,774	A	*	2/1999	Summers et al. 455/575.1
6,328,570	B1	*	12/2001	Ng .... 434/307 A
7,090,582	B2	*	8/2006	Danieli et al. 463/35
D551,679	S	*	9/2007	Hayes D14/496
D558,788	S	*	1/2008	Yu et al. D14/496
D571,822	S	*	6/2008	Madonna et al. D14/496
D596,196	S	*	7/2009	Laituri et al. D14/496
D600,251	S	*	9/2009	Poandl D14/496
D614,200	S	*	4/2010	Skurdal D14/496
D618,252	S	*	6/2010	Bradford et al. D14/496
D648,743	S	*	11/2011	Chang D14/496

* cited by examiner

Primary Examiner — Prabhakar Deshmukh
(74) *Attorney, Agent, or Firm* — Bose Corporation

(57) **CLAIM**
The ornamental design for a portable audio system, substantially as shown and described.

DESCRIPTION

FIG. **1** is a perspective view of a portable audio system as seen from the front, top and side;
FIG. **2** is a perspective view thereof as seen from the back, bottom and opposite side;
FIG. **3** is a front view thereof;
FIG. **4** is a back view thereof;
FIG. **5** is a top view thereof;
FIG. **6** is a bottom view thereof;
FIG. **7** is a side view thereof; and,
FIG. **8** is an opposite side view thereof.
The dotted line portions of the drawings represent environmental structure only and form no part of the claimed design.

1 Claim, 7 Drawing Sheets

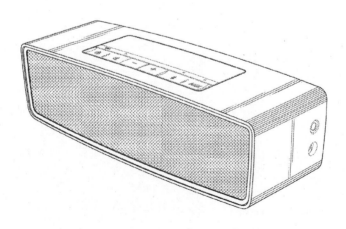

TITLE: LAMP
INVENTORS: ISSY MIYAKE, SACHIKO YAMAMOTO,
MANABU KIKUCHI, SEN KAWAHARA, ET AL.
ASSIGNEE: ARTEMIDE

PATENT NUMBER: USD 708,383
PATENT FILED: NOVEMBER 21, 2012
PATENT GRANTED: JULY 1, 2014

(12) **United States Design Patent** (10) **Patent No.:**   **US D708,383 S**
Miyake et al.   (45) **Date of Patent:** ∗∗   **Jul. 1, 2014**

(54) **LAMP**

(71) Applicant: **Artemide S.p.A.**, Milan (IT)

(72) Inventors: **Issey Miyake**, Tokyo (JP); **Sachiko Yamamoto**, Tokyo (JP); **Manabu Kikuchi**, Tokyo (JP); **Sen Kawahara**, Tokyo (JP); **Yuki Itakura**, Tokyo (JP); **Yusuke Takahashi**, Tokyo (JP); **Noritoshi Shionoya**, Tokyo (JP)

(73) Assignee: **Artemide S.p.A.**, Milan (IT)

(∗∗) Term: **14 Years**

(21) Appl. No.: **29/437,948**

(22) Filed: **Nov. 21, 2012**

(30)   **Foreign Application Priority Data**

May 23, 2012   (IT) 002046243

(51) **LOC (10) Cl.** **26-03**
(52) **U.S. Cl.**
     USPC **D26/88**; D26/118; D26/128
(58) **Field of Classification Search**
     USPC D26/72, 73, 81, 84, 88, 90, 118, D26/127–137; 362/147, 404–408, 351, 360, 362/361
     See application file for complete search history.

(56)   **References Cited**

U.S. PATENT DOCUMENTS

D39,902	S	∗	3/1909	Marlow D99/37
D44,086	S	∗	5/1913	Cravath D26/128
D48,309	S	∗	12/1915	Cravath D26/128
D51,021	S	∗	7/1917	Mohr D26/90
D76,437	S	∗	9/1928	Vande Genachte D26/130
D78,956	S	∗	7/1929	Zweig D26/86
D80,293	S	∗	1/1930	Silverman D26/130
D80,794	S	∗	3/1930	Kramer D26/90
D80,827	S	∗	4/1930	Beyer D26/130
D82,497	S	∗	11/1930	Haas D26/134
1,868,692	A	∗	7/1932	Bruckmann 362/357
D95,521	S	∗	5/1935	Laxer D26/136
D96,921	S	∗	9/1935	Laxer D26/136
D176,921	S	∗	2/1956	Koepke D26/130
D197,859	S	∗	3/1964	Harper D26/152
3,895,229	A	∗	7/1975	Strom 362/351
D237,003	S	∗	9/1975	Jabandideh D26/104
D240,852	S	∗	8/1976	Jacobsen D26/86
D257,643	S	∗	12/1980	Zurcher D26/85
D274,475	S	∗	6/1984	Caldwell D26/110
4,562,521	A	∗	12/1985	Noguchi 362/433
D402,393	S	∗	12/1998	Kuo D26/118
D468,475	S	∗	1/2003	De Lucchi D26/90
D480,171	S	∗	9/2003	Alduby D26/118
D528,695	S	∗	9/2006	Salatto-Rose D26/93
D537,185	S	∗	2/2007	Gehry D26/72

(Continued)

Primary Examiner — Clare E Heflin
(74) *Attorney, Agent, or Firm* — Venable LLP; Robert Kinberg

(57)   **CLAIM**
We claim the ornamental design for a lamp, as shown and described.

DESCRIPTION

FIG. **1** is a perspective view of a lamp, according to an embodiment of the invention;
FIG. **2** is a left side view of the lamp, according to FIG. **3**;
FIG. **3** is a front view of the lamp, according to FIG. **1**;
FIG. **4** is a right side view of the lamp, according to FIG. **3**;
FIG. **5** is a rear view of the lamp, according to FIG. **3**;
FIG. **6** is a bottom view of the lamp, according to FIG. **3**; and,
FIG. **7** is a top view of the lamp, according to FIG. **3**.

1 Claim, 7 Drawing Sheets

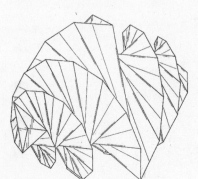
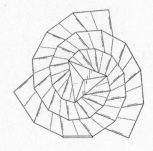

TITLE: HAIR DRYER
INVENTORS: JAMES DYSON, PETER DAVID GAMMACK,
STEPHEN BENJAMIN COURTNEY, ET AL.
ASSIGNEE: DYSON TECHNOLOGY

PATENT NUMBER: USD 715,996
PATENT FILED: MARCH 25, 2014
PATENT GRANTED: OCTOBER 21, 2014

(12) **United States Design Patent**
Dyson et al.

(10) **Patent No.:** **US D715,996 S**
(45) **Date of Patent:** ✶✶ **Oct. 21, 2014**

(54) **HAIR DRYER**

(71) Applicant: **Dyson Technology Limited**, Wiltshire (GB)

(72) Inventors: **James Dyson**, Bristol (GB); **Peter David Gammack**, Swindon (GB); **Stephen Benjamin Courtney**, Bath (GB); **Patrick Joseph William Moloney**, Swindon (GB); **Edward Sebert Maurice Shelton**, Swindon (GB)

(73) Assignee: **Dyson Technology Limited**, Malmesbury, Wiltshire (GB)

(**) Term: **14 Years**

(21) Appl. No.: **29/485,993**

(22) Filed: **Mar. 25, 2014**

(30) **Foreign Application Priority Data**

Sep. 26, 2013 (EM) 001384796-0003

(51) **LOC (10) Cl.** 28-03
(52) **U.S. Cl.**
CPC *A45D 20/12* (2013.01)
USPC **D28/13**
(58) **Field of Classification Search**
CPC A45D 20/12
USPC D28/12–19; 34/96–101; 392/380–385; 219/222; D23/238–243
See application file for complete search history.

(56) **References Cited**

U.S. PATENT DOCUMENTS

4,350,872 A	9/1982	Meywald et al.	
4,596,921 A	6/1986	Hersh et al.	
4,767,914 A	8/1988	Glucksman	
5,133,043 A	7/1992	Baugh	
D350,413 S	* 9/1994	Feil	D28/13
D352,365 S	* 11/1994	Hansen et al.	D28/13
5,378,882 A	1/1995	Gong et al.	
5,546,674 A	8/1996	Lange et al.	
5,572,800 A	11/1996	West	
5,598,640 A	2/1997	Schepisi	
5,681,630 A	10/1997	Smick et al.	
5,875,562 A	3/1999	Fogarty	
6,203,349 B1	3/2001	Nakazawa	
6,751,886 B2	* 6/2004	Chang et al.	34/96
6,889,445 B1	* 5/2005	Varona et al.	34/97
D550,813 S	* 9/2007	Lammel et al.	D23/238

(Continued)

FOREIGN PATENT DOCUMENTS

CH	588 835	6/1977
CN	200973446	11/2007

(Continued)

OTHER PUBLICATIONS

Reba, I. (1966). "Applications of the Coanda Effect," Scientific American 214:84-92.

Primary Examiner — Zenia Bennett
(74) *Attorney, Agent, or Firm* — Morrison & Foerster LLP

(57) **CLAIM**

We claim the ornamental design for a hair dryer, as shown and described.

DESCRIPTION

FIG. **1** is a rear perspective view of a hair dryer showing our new design;
FIG. **2** is a front perspective view thereof;
FIG. **3** is a rear view thereof;
FIG. **4** is a front view thereof;
FIG. **5** is a side view thereof;
FIG. **6** is a top view thereof; and,
FIG. **7** is a bottom view thereof.

1 Claim, 6 Drawing Sheets

TITLE: AUDIO/VIDEO PLAYER CASE
INVENTORS: NEIL YOUNG & MIKE NUTTALL
ASSIGNEE: IVANHOE

PATENT NUMBER: USD 718,750
PATENT FILED: MARCH 14, 2013
PATENT GRANTED: DECEMBER 2, 2014

(12) **United States Design Patent**
Young et al.

(10) **Patent No.:** **US D718,750 S**
(45) **Date of Patent:** ** **Dec. 2, 2014**

(54) **AUDIO/VIDEO PLAYER CASE**

(71) Applicants: **Neil Young**, Irvine, CA (US); **Mike Nuttall**, Portola Valley, CA (US)

(72) Inventors: **Neil Young**, Irvine, CA (US); **Mike Nuttall**, Portola Valley, CA (US)

(73) Assignee: **Ivanhoe (DE) Inc.**, Woodland Hills, CA (US)

(**) Term: **14 Years**

(21) Appl. No.: **29/449,149**

(22) Filed: **Mar. 14, 2013**

(51) **LOC (10) Cl.** **14-01**
(52) **U.S. Cl.**
USPC **D14/238.1**; D14/203.7; D14/496
(58) **Field of Classification Search**
USPC D14/248, 250–253, 440, 203.1–203.7,
D14/168, 474, 496, 181, 511, 224.1, 238.12,
D14/160; D3/201, 218, 169, 301, 273;
D21/332, 333, 324; 361/670.55,
361/679.56; 379/426; 455/575.1, 575.8;
206/305, 320; 273/148 B; 461/1,
461/29–36, 46, 47
See application file for complete search history.

(56) **References Cited**

U.S. PATENT DOCUMENTS

D194,821 S	*	3/1963	Watke	D19/21
3,198,339 A	*	8/1965	Stolarz	211/50
D251,082 S	*	2/1979	Petrie	D3/247
5,738,218 A	*	4/1998	Gonzales	206/583
5,916,665 A	*	6/1999	Fischer et al.	428/195.1
6,301,825 B1	*	10/2001	Doreian	43/57.1
6,324,292 B1	*	11/2001	Mitsuhashi et al.	381/349
D599,781 S	*	9/2009	Lee et al.	D14/205
D677,668 S	*	3/2013	Phillips et al.	D14/440
D685,342 S	*	7/2013	Cetera et al.	D14/203.4
D692,434 S	*	10/2013	Kim	D14/440
D694,245 S	*	11/2013	Sanz	D14/440
D698,776 S	*	2/2014	Fathollahi	D14/250

* cited by examiner

Primary Examiner — Prabhakar Deshmukh
(74) *Attorney, Agent, or Firm* — Perkins Coie, LLP

(57) **CLAIM**
The ornamental design for an audio-video player case, as shown and described.

DESCRIPTION

FIG. **1** is a perspective view of front and top an audio-video player case showing my new design;
FIG. **2** is a rear and bottom perspective view thereof;
FIG. **3** is a front elevation thereof;
FIG. **4** is atop plan view thereof; and,
FIG. **5** is a bottom plan view thereof.

1 Claim, 2 Drawing Sheets

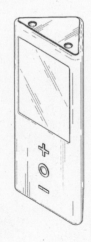

TITLE: CHANDELIER HAVING ARMS
INVENTOR: MARCEL WANDERS
ASSIGNEE: MOOOI

PATENT NUMBER: USD 719,697
PATENT FILED: OCTOBER 4, 2013
PATENT GRANTED: DECEMBER 16, 2014

(12) **United States Design Patent**
Wanders

(10) Patent No.: **US D719,697 S**
(45) **Date of Patent:** ∗∗ **Dec. 16, 2014**

(54) **CHANDELIER HAVING ARMS**

(71) Applicant: **Moooi B.V.**, Breda (NL)

(72) Inventor: **Marcel Wanders**, Amsterdam (NL)

(73) Assignee: **Moooi B.V.**, Breda, ZL (NL)

(∗∗) Term: **14 Years**

(21) Appl. No.: **29/469,008**

(22) Filed: **Oct. 4, 2013**

(30) **Foreign Application Priority Data**

Apr. 4, 2013 (EP) 002214056-0007

(51) **LOC (10) Cl.** **26-03**
(52) **U.S. Cl.**
USPC **D26/81**; D26/88
(58) **Field of Classification Search**
USPC D26/73, 80–84, 86, 88, 90, 91;
362/147, 404–408, 431, 432
See application file for complete search history.

(56) **References Cited**

U.S. PATENT DOCUMENTS

D37,856 S	∗	2/1906	Losli	D26/91
D79,814 S	∗	11/1929	Hoch	D26/81
D82,415 S	∗	11/1930	Bohl	D26/81
D100,939 S	∗	8/1936	D'Aschbach	D11/121
D179,086 S	∗	10/1956	Kelly	D26/86
D181,554 S	∗	11/1957	Stiffel	D26/81
3,018,362 A	∗	1/1962	Joyce	362/566
3,113,679 A	∗	12/1963	Smith	211/118
D415,302 S	∗	10/1999	Porter et al.	D26/81
D545,998 S	∗	7/2007	Mazzie, Jr.	D26/144
D570,526 S	∗	6/2008	Cenedese	D26/88
D635,709 S	∗	4/2011	Federico et al.	D26/84
D647,661 S	∗	10/2011	Steenhoudt	D26/84
D663,884 S	∗	7/2012	Baylar	D26/88
D667,158 S	∗	9/2012	Fisher et al.	D26/80
D683,896 S	∗	6/2013	Yando	D26/144
D704,882 S	∗	5/2014	Wanders	D26/82
D713,086 S	∗	9/2014	Clark	D26/81

∗ cited by examiner

Primary Examiner — Clare E Heflin
(74) *Attorney, Agent, or Firm* — Andrew Rush; PCT Law Group, PLLC

(57) **CLAIM**

The ornamental design for a chandelier having arms, as shown and described.

DESCRIPTION

FIG. **1** is a top perspective view of a chandelier having arms showing my new design;
FIG. **2** is a front view thereof;
FIG. **3** is a back view thereof;
FIG. **4** is a left side view thereof;
FIG. **5** is a right side view thereof; and,
FIG. **6** is a bottom view thereof.

1 Claim, 6 Drawing Sheets

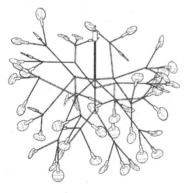

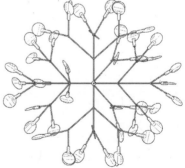

TITLE: FAN
INVENTORS: JAMES DYSON, DAVID DOS REIS,
ADAM JAMES BATES, ARRAN GEORGE SMITH, ET AL.
ASSIGNEE: DYSON TECHNOLOGY

PATENT NUMBER: USD 728,769
PATENT FILED: JANUARY 30, 2014
PATENT GRANTED: MAY 5, 2015

(12) **United States Design Patent**
Dyson et al.

(10) Patent No.: **US D728,769 S**
(45) Date of Patent: ** **May 5, 2015**

(54) **FAN**

(71) Applicant: **Dyson Technology Limited**, Wiltshire (GB)

(72) Inventors: **James Dyson**, Bristol (GB); **David Dos Reis**, Bristol (GB); **Adam James Bates**, Oxford (GB); **Arran George Smith**, Bristol (GB); **Thomas Richard Mogridge**, Bristol (GB); **Roy Edward Poulton**, Swindon (GB); **Joseph Eric Hodgetts**, Bristol (GB); **David Robert Sunderland**, Bristol (GB)

(73) Assignee: **Dyson Technology Limited**, Malmesbury, Wiltshire (GB)

(**) Term: **14 Years**

(21) Appl. No.: **29/480,896**

(22) Filed: **Jan. 30, 2014**

(30) **Foreign Application Priority Data**

Aug. 1, 2013 (EM) 001379531-0001

(51) **LOC (10) Cl.** **23-04**

(52) **U.S. Cl.**
USPC **D23/370**; D23/378; D23/342

(58) **Field of Classification Search**
USPC D23/336, 342, 370–379, 411, 499;
D6/309; 415/90, 110, 119, 126, 148,
415/182.1, 183, 207, 208.1, 208.2, 211.2,
415/230; 416/100, 244 R, 246, 247 R;
261/28, 31, 116; 417/84, 177, 198,
417/313, 423.1, 234; 137/338; 392/361,
392/365, 367
See application file for complete search history.

(56) **References Cited**

U.S. PATENT DOCUMENTS

284,962 A   9/1883   Huston

1,357,261 A   11/1920   Svoboda
(Continued)

FOREIGN PATENT DOCUMENTS

BE   560119   8/1957
CA   1055344   5/1979
(Continued)

OTHER PUBLICATIONS

Pisenic Bladeless Fan (16 Inches with Remote Control, Bladeless Fan Air Conditioner 110v, Air Multiplier Table Fans, Green). Amazon.com [online PDF] 4 pages. Posted May 11, 2013[retrieved on Sep. 2, 2014]. Retrieved from Internet: <http://www.amazon.com/Pisenic-Bladeless-Control-Conditioner-Multiplier/dp/B007VCI78M/ref=pd_rhf_se_p_imgnr_3/>.*
(Continued)

Primary Examiner — Susan Bennett Hattan
Assistant Examiner — Marie Fast Horse
(74) *Attorney, Agent, or Firm* — Morrison & Foerster LLP

(57) **CLAIM**

We claim the ornamental design for a fan, as shown and described.

DESCRIPTION

FIG. **1** is a perspective view of a fan showing our new design;
FIG. **2** is a front view thereof;
FIG. **3** is a rear view thereof;
FIG. **4** is a side view thereof;
FIG. **5** is a side view of the opposite side of FIG. **4**;
FIG. **6** is a top view thereof; and,
FIG. **7** is a bottom view thereof.
The broken lines in the drawings consisting of even dashes depict portions of the fan that form no part of the claimed design. The broken lines consisting of uneven dashes depict the bounds of the claim.

1 Claim, 6 Drawing Sheets

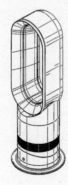

TITLE: TELEVISION
INVENTORS: SCOTT MCMANIGAL & GLEN KIM
ASSIGNEE: VIZIO

PATENT NUMBER: USD 729,755
PATENT FILED: SEPTEMBER 23, 2014
PATENT GRANTED: MAY 19, 2015

(12) **United States Design Patent** (10) Patent No.: **US D729,755 S**
McManigal et al. (45) **Date of Patent:** ** **May 19, 2015**

(54) **TELEVISION**

(71) Applicants: **Scott McManigal**, Irvine, CA (US);
Glen Kim, Irvine, CA (US)

(72) Inventors: **Scott McManigal**, Irvine, CA (US);
Glen Kim, Irvine, CA (US)

(73) Assignee: **Vizio Inc.**, Irvine, CA (US)

(**) Term: **14 Years**

(21) Appl. No.: **29/503,136**

(22) Filed: **Sep. 23, 2014**

(51) LOC (10) Cl. **14-03**

(52) **U.S. Cl.**
USPC **D14/126**

(58) **Field of Classification Search**
CPC ... G06F 1/1601; G06F 1/1643; H05K 5/0004;
H05K 5/0017; H05K 5/02; H05K 5/0217
USPC D14/125–134, 239, 371, 136, 374–377,
D14/440, 450, 448, 336, 342, 159; 312/7.2;
348/836, 838, 180, 184, 325, 739;
248/917–924, 465; 345/104, 133, 156,
345/168, 87, 173; D21/329, 515, 577, 622,
D21/333, 433, 448, 452, 450, 331, 505;
D10/15, 26; 446/484, 175, 356;
D6/477, 479, 300; D24/185; D34/14
See application file for complete search history.

(56) **References Cited**

U.S. PATENT DOCUMENTS

D489,342	S	*	5/2004	Campbell et al. D14/130
D543,960	S	*	6/2007	Bloem D14/126
D680,106	S	*	4/2013	Hwangbo et al. D14/239
D700,187	S	*	2/2014	Lee D14/451
D708,596	S	*	7/2014	Park ....,...................... D14/126
D716,244	S	*	10/2014	Kim et al. D14/126
D719,119	S	*	12/2014	Park et al. D14/126

* cited by examiner

Primary Examiner — Raphael Barkai
(74) *Attorney, Agent, or Firm* — Law Office of Scott C. Harris, Inc.

(57) **CLAIM**
We claim the ornamental design for a television, as shown and described.

DESCRIPTION

FIG. **1** shows a front perspective view of the television;
FIG. **2** shows a front view of the television;
FIG. **3** shows a rear view of the television;
FIG. **4** shows a first side view of the television;
FIG. **5** shows a second side view of the television;
FIG. **6** shows a top view of the television; and,
FIG. **7** shows a bottom view of the television.
The portions of the graphical user interface shown in broken lines form no part of the claimed design.

1 Claim, 5 Drawing Sheets

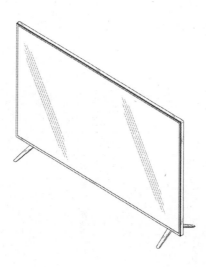

TITLE: ARMCHAIR
INVENTOR: DONATELLA VERSACE
ASSIGNEE: GIANNI VERSACE

PATENT NUMBER: USD 731,195
PATENT FILED: OCTOBER 8, 2013
PATENT GRANTED: JUNE 9, 2015

(12) **United States Design Patent**
Versace

(10) **Patent No.:** **US D731,195 S**
(45) **Date of Patent:** ** **Jun. 9, 2015**

(54) **ARMCHAIR**

(71) Applicant: **GIANNI VERSACE S.p.A.**, Milan (IT)

(72) Inventor: **Donatella Versace**, Milan (IT)

(73) Assignee: **Gianni Versace S.p.A.**, Milan (IT)

(**) Term: **14 Years**

(21) Appl. No.: **29/469,178**

(22) Filed: **Oct. 8, 2013**

(30) **Foreign Application Priority Data**

Apr. 8, 2013 (EM) 002215855

(51) **LOC (10) Cl.** **06-01**
(52) **U.S. Cl.**
USPC **D6/371**
(58) **Field of Classification Search**
USPC D6/334–336, 371, 372, 373, 374, 375,
D6/379, 380, 716, 716.1, 716.2, 716.3,
D6/716.4
CPC A47C 4/03; A47C 4/02; A47C 4/025;
A47C 4/028; A47C 5/046
See application file for complete search history.

(56) **References Cited**

U.S. PATENT DOCUMENTS

D101,570	S	*	10/1936	Vavrik	D6/379
D222,450	S	*	10/1971	Brook	D6/373
D243,727	S	*	3/1977	Blanco	D6/373
D246,685	S	*	12/1977	Blodee	D6/379
D269,830	S	*	7/1983	Nijhuis	D6/373
D293,519	S	*	1/1988	Conn	D6/373
D336,792	S	*	6/1993	White, Jr.	D6/379
D517,823	S	*	3/2006	Sterner	D6/372

* cited by examiner

Primary Examiner — Mimosa De
(74) *Attorney, Agent, or Firm* — Meunier Carlin & Curfman LLC

(57) **CLAIM**
An ornamental design for an armchair, as shown and described.

DESCRIPTION

FIG. **1** is a front perspective view of one embodiment of the armchair.
FIG. **2** is a front view of the embodiment depicted in FIG. **1**.
FIG. **3** is a back view of the embodiment depicted in FIG. **1**.
FIG. **4** is a right side view of the embodiment depicted in FIG. **1**.
FIG. **5** is a left side view of the embodiment depicted in FIG. **1**.
FIG. **6** is a top view of the embodiment depicted in FIG. **1**; and,
FIG. **7** is a bottom view of the embodiment depicted in FIG. **1**.
The broken lines showing elements of the armchair in the above-described Figures are for illustrative purposes and form no part of the claimed design.

1 Claim, 7 Drawing Sheets

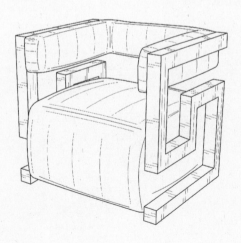

TITLE: SPEAKER
INVENTORS: YVES ALBERT BÉHAR & GABRIEL J. LAMB
ASSIGNEE: ALPHCOM

PATENT NUMBER: USD 731,462
PATENT FILED: SEPTEMBER 9, 2013
PATENT GRANTED: JUNE 9, 2015

(12) **United States Design Patent**
Behar et al.

(10) Patent No.: **US D731,462 S**
(45) Date of Patent: ✳✳ **Jun. 9, 2015**

(54) **SPEAKER**

(71) Applicant: **ALIPHCOM**, San Francisco, CA (US)

(72) Inventors: **Yves Albert Behar**, San Francisco, CA (US); **Gabriel J. Lamb**, San Francisco, CA (US)

(73) Assignee: **ALIPHCOM**, San Francisco, CA (US)

(✳✳) Term: **14 Years**

(21) Appl. No.: **29/466,536**

(22) Filed: **Sep. 9, 2013**

Related U.S. Application Data

(63) Continuation-in-part of application No. 29/445,283, filed on Feb. 8, 2013, now Pat. No. Des. 698,757, which is a continuation of application No. 29/413,571, filed on Feb. 16, 2012, now Pat. No. Des. 678,864.

(51) LOC (10) Cl. **14-03**
(52) U.S. Cl.
USPC **D14/214**
(58) **Field of Classification Search**
USPC D14/167, 168, 170–172, 188, 194–196, D14/204, 207, 209.1, 210–216, 219, 221, D14/222, 224, 496; 181/143, 144, 147, 148, 181/150, 153, 157, 198, 199; 381/300–303, 381/306, 332, 333, 336, 345, 361–364, 381/386–388; 369/6–12
See application file for complete search history.

(56) **References Cited**

U.S. PATENT DOCUMENTS

D228,389 S	✳	9/1973	Schneider	D14/214
D401,932 S	✳	12/1998	Deguchi	D14/165
D489,707 S		5/2004	Kobayashi	
D526,643 S	✳	8/2006	Ishizaki	D14/214
D531,986 S		11/2006	Azumi et al.	
D546,318 S		7/2007	Yoon et al.	
D547,748 S	✳	7/2007	Tsuge	D14/211
D568,289 S		5/2008	Solland	
D589,939 S		4/2009	Hsu	
D597,064 S	✳	7/2009	Machida	D14/167
D597,529 S		8/2009	Tan et al.	
D622,699 S	✳	8/2010	Jiang et al.	D14/209.1
D632,675 S	✳	2/2011	Behar et al.	D14/223

(Continued)

OTHER PUBLICATIONS

Notice of Allowance from related U.S. Appl. No. 29/378,325 dated May 10, 2011.

(Continued)

Primary Examiner — Keli L Hill
(74) *Attorney, Agent, or Firm* — Kilpatrick Townsend & Stockton LLP

(57) **CLAIM**
The ornamental design for a speaker, as shown and described.

DESCRIPTION

FIG. 1 is a perspective view of a speaker, showing our new design;
FIG. 2 is a front elevational view thereof;
FIG. 3 is a right side elevational view thereof;
FIG. 4 is a left side elevational view thereof;
FIG. 5 is a top plan view thereof; and,
FIG. 6 is a bottom plan view thereof.
The submitted drawings show some additional solid lines on the speaker; some of these solid lines are not meant to convey actual solidly drawn lines, such as actual surface markings or ornamentation, on the speaker. As is generally recognized by persons skilled in the art of preparing digital drawings, such solid lines are meant to convey the boundaries for curved surfaces on the speaker.
The broken lines shown are included for the purpose of illustrating portions of the speaker that form no part of the claim. JAWBONE is a registered trademark of AliphCom dba Jawbone and does not form part of the claimed design.

1 Claim, 4 Drawing Sheets

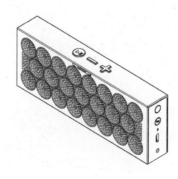

TITLE: AUTONOMOUS VEHICLE EXTERIOR
INVENTORS: YOOJUNG AHN, PHILIPP HABAN, JARED S.
GROSS, JONAS DE MOE, BENJAMIN W. JULIAN, ET AL.
ASSIGNEE: GOOGLE

PATENT NUMBER: USD 734,211
PATENT FILED: MAY 23, 2014
PATENT GRANTED: JULY 14, 2015

(12) **United States Design Patent**
 Ahn et al.

(10) Patent No.: **US D734,211 S**
(45) Date of Patent: ** **Jul. 14, 2015**

(54) **AUTONOMOUS VEHICLE EXTERIOR**

(71) Applicant: **Google Inc.**, Mountain View, CA (US)

(72) Inventors: **YooJung Ahn**, Mountain View, CA
(US); **Philipp Haban**, San Francisco,
CA (US); **Jared S. Gross**, Belmont, CA
(US); **Jonas De Moe**, Mountain View,
CA (US); **Benjamin W. Julian**, San
Francisco, CA (US); **Albert Shane**,
Berkeley, CA (US)

(73) Assignee: **Google Inc.**, Mountain View, CA (US)

(**) Term: **14 Years**

(21) Appl. No.: **29/491,722**

(22) Filed: **May 23, 2014**

(51) **LOC (10) Cl.** 12-08
(52) **U.S. Cl.**
 USPC **D12/86**; D12/90
(58) **Field of Classification Search**
 USPC D12/86, 90–92, 82, 1, 7, 14, 190;
 D21/424, 433, 434, 548; 296/181.1,
 296/181.5, 185.1
 CPC B62D 31/003; B62D 29/043; B62D 31/00;
 B62D 35/00; B62D 25/06; B62D 25/08
 See application file for complete search history.

(56) **References Cited**

U.S. PATENT DOCUMENTS

D411,814 S * 7/1999 Chibuka et al. D12/90
D418,471 S   1/2000 Gabath
D447,191 S * 8/2001 Hoelzel et al. D21/433
D459,764 S * 7/2002 Hoelzel et al. D21/433
D467,849 S   12/2002 Murkett
6,530,251 B1   3/2003 Dimig
D472,863 S   4/2003 Carroll

(Continued)

OTHER PUBLICATIONS

McFadden, Colin-Druce, "Autonomous car concept swaps steering
wheel for gesture controls", <http://www.dvice.com/2014-3-12/au-
tonomous-car-concept-swaps-steering-wheel-gesture-controls>,
Mar. 12, 2014.

(Continued)

Primary Examiner — Cathron Brooks
Assistant Examiner — Clese Moore, Jr.
(74) *Attorney, Agent, or Firm* — Lerner, David, Littenberg,
Krumholz & Mentlik, LLP

(57) **CLAIM**

The ornamental design for an autonomous vehicle exterior, as
shown and described.

DESCRIPTION

The present application is related to copending application
Ser. No. 29/491,723, entitled Autonomous Vehicle Door, to
application Ser. No. 29/491,717, entitled Tire Rim, to application Ser. No. 29/491,734, entitled Autonomous Vehicle
Headlamp, to application Ser. No. 29/491,730, entitled
Autonomous Vehicle Taillamp, to application Ser. No.
29/491,726, entitled Autonomous Vehicle Wing Assembly,
and to application Ser. No. 29/491,727, entitled Autonomous
Vehicle Rear Vent/Reflector, each of which is filed concur-
rently herewith, the entire disclosures of which are incorpo-
rated by reference herein.
FIG. 1 is a front perspective view of an autonomous vehicle
exterior according to a first embodiment of our design;
FIG. 2 is a front elevation view thereof;
FIG. 3 is a back elevation view thereof;
FIG. 4 is a right side elevation view thereof;
FIG. 5 is a left side elevation view thereof;
FIG. 6 is a top plan view thereof; and,
FIG. 7 is a bottom plan view thereof.
The broken lines shown illustrate portions of the autonomous
vehicle exterior that form no part of the claimed design.

1 Claim, 7 Drawing Sheets

TITLE: CARD READER
INVENTORS: TRENT WEBER & ELLIOT SATHER
ASSIGNEE: SQUARE

PATENT NUMBER: USD 740,819
PATENT FILED: APRIL 14, 2014
PATENT GRANTED: OCTOBER 13, 2015

(12) **United States Design Patent**
Weber et al.

(10) **Patent No.:** **US D740,819 S**

(45) **Date of Patent:** ✶✶ **Oct. 13, 2015**

(54) **CARD READER**

(71) Applicant: **Square, Inc.**, San Francisco, CA (US)

(72) Inventors: **Trent Weber**, San Francisco, CA (US);
Elliot Sather, San Francisco, CA (US)

(73) Assignee: **Square, Inc.**, San Francisco, CA (US)

(**) Term: **14 Years**

(21) Appl. No.: **29/487,975**

(22) Filed: **Apr. 14, 2014**

(51) **LOC (10) Cl.** **14-02**

(52) **U.S. Cl.**
USPC **D14/385**

(58) **Field of Classification Search**
USPC D14/356–358, 383–385, 420, 426, 427,
D14/432–439, 447, 453, 454, 217, 253,
D14/299; D13/107, 108, 133, 146, 147,
D13/152, 154, 156, 158, 162, 162.1, 168,
D13/173, 177, 102; 235/441, 451, 492, 380,
235/439, 375; 361/679.31, 600, 679.01,
361/679.02
CPC ... G06Q 20/347; G06Q 20/322; G06Q 40/02;
G06Q 30/06; G07F 7/0886
See application file for complete search history.

(56) **References Cited**

U.S. PATENT DOCUMENTS

D417,442	S	*	12/1999	Butts et al. D14/385
D477,321	S	*	7/2003	Baughman D14/385
D590,828	S	*	4/2009	Sherrod et al. D14/385
D607,000	S	*	12/2009	Cheng et al. D14/385
D653,664	S	*	2/2012	Turnbull et al. D14/385
D675,618	S	*	2/2013	Behar et al. D14/385
D680,537	S	*	4/2013	Miller et al. D14/385
D686,208	S	*	7/2013	Miller et al. D14/385
D700,606	S	*	3/2014	Lo D14/385
D706,266	S	*	6/2014	Rotsaert D14/385
D711,876	S	*	8/2014	McWilliam et al. D14/385
D725,655	S	*	3/2015	Debaigue et al. D14/385
D728,568	S	*	5/2015	Debaigue et al. D14/385
2012/0118959	A1	*	5/2012	Sather et al. 235/449
2012/0132712	A1	*	5/2012	Babu et al. 235/449

* cited by examiner

Primary Examiner — Austin Murphy

(74) *Attorney, Agent, or Firm* — Novak Druce Connolly
Bove + Quigg LLP

(57) **CLAIM**
We claim the ornamental design for a card reader, as shown
and described.

DESCRIPTION

FIG. **1** is a perspective view of a card reader;
FIG. **2** is a top plan view thereof;
FIG. **3** is a bottom plan view thereof;
FIG. **4** is a right side elevational view thereof;
FIG. **5** is a left side elevational view thereof;
FIG. **6** is a front elevational view thereof;
FIG. **7** is a rear elevational view thereof;
FIG. **8** is a cross-sectional view thereof taken along axis **8-8**
from FIG. **2**; and,
FIG. **9** is a cross-sectional view thereof taken along axis **9-9**
from FIG. **2**.
Cross-sectional views opposite those of FIGS. **8** and **9** are
mirror images, and are therefore not shown. Broken lines are
used to illustrate unclaimed portions of the card reader; broken lines form no part of the claimed design.

1 Claim, 9 Drawing Sheets

TITLE: CHAIR
INVENTOR: JASPER MORRISON
ASSIGNEE: VITRA PATENTE

PATENT NUMBER: USD 741,615
PATENT FILED: AUGUST 4, 2014
PATENT GRANTED: OCTOBER 27, 2015

(12) **United States Design Patent**
Morrison

(10) Patent No.: **US D741,615 S**
(45) Date of Patent: ** Oct. 27, 2015

(54) **CHAIR**

(71) Applicant: **Vitra Patente AG**, Birsfelden (GB)

(72) Inventor: **Jasper Morrison**, London (GB)

(73) Assignee: **VITRA PATENTE AG**, Birsfelden (CH)

(**) Term: **14 Years**

(21) Appl. No.: **29/498,409**

(22) Filed: **Aug. 4, 2014**

(30) **Foreign Application Priority Data**

Feb. 4, 2014 (DM) 082882

(51) **LOC (10) Cl.** **06-01**
(52) **U.S. Cl.**
USPC **D6/375**
(58) **Field of Classification Search**
USPC D6/334–336, 371–373, 374, 375, 379,
D6/380, 716, 716.1, 716.2, 716.3, 716.4
CPC A47C 3/04; A47C 4/02; A47C 4/03;
A47C 5/12; A47C 3/12; B60N 2/686
See application file for complete search history.

(56) **References Cited**

U.S. PATENT DOCUMENTS

2,845,699	A	* 8/1958	Woodard	A47C 3/12
3,521,929	A	* 7/1970	Pearson	A47C 3/12
3,565,486	A	* 2/1971	Channon	A47C 3/12
D417,795	S	* 12/1999	Rashid	D6/375
D525,446	S	* 7/2006	Farber	D6/375
D546,089	S	7/2007	Ebenestelli	
D555,380	S	* 11/2007	Farber	D6/375

D602,276	S	10/2009	Neil	
D647,316	S	* 10/2011	Kim	D6/375
D686,831	S	* 7/2013	Lemson et al.	D6/375
D726,468	S	4/2015	McKenna et al.	
D729,564	S	5/2015	Robins et al.	

* cited by examiner

Primary Examiner — Mimosa De
(74) *Attorney, Agent, or Firm* — Dorsey & Whitney LLP

(57) **CLAIM**
The ornamental design for chair, as shown and described.

DESCRIPTION

FIG. **1** shows a front, right perspective view of an embodiment of a chair;
FIG. **2** shows a front view thereof;
FIG. **3** shows a rear view thereof;
FIG. **4** shows a right-side view thereof;
FIG. **5** shows a left-side view thereof;
FIG. **6** shows a top view thereof;
FIG. **7** shows a bottom view thereof;
FIG. **8** shows a front, right perspective view of another embodiment of a chair;
FIG. **9** shows a front view thereof;
FIG. **10** shows a rear view thereof;
FIG. **11** shows a right-side view thereof;
FIG. **12** shows a left-side view thereof;
FIG. **13** shows a top-view thereof; and,
FIG. **14** shows a bottom view thereof.
The broken lines illustrate environmental structure and form no part of the claimed design.

1 Claim, 14 Drawing Sheets

1018

TITLE: WEARABLE FITNESS BAND SYSTEM
INVENTORS: KENNETH S.M. LING, ALEXANDER JOSEPH RINGROSE, PATRICK JAMES MARKAN, GAD AMIT, ET AL.
ASSIGNEE: FITBIT

PATENT NUMBER: USD 759,516
PATENT FILED: MARCH 20, 2015
PATENT GRANTED: JUNE 21, 2016

(12) **United States Design Patent**   (10) Patent No.:   **US D759,516 S**

Ling et al.   (45) Date of Patent: ** **Jun. 21, 2016**

(54) **WEARABLE FITNESS BAND SYSTEM**

(71) Applicant: **Fitbit, Inc.**, San Francisco, CA (US)

(72) Inventors: **Kenneth S. M. Ling**, San Francisco, CA (US); **Alexander Joseph Ringrose**, Oakland, CA (US); **Patrick James Markan**, San Francisco, CA (US); **Gad Amit**, San Mateo, CA (US); **Daniel J. Clifton**, San Francisco, CA (US); **Erik Keith Askin**, San Francisco, CA (US)

(73) Assignee: **Fitbit, Inc.**, San Francisco, CA (US)

(**) Term: **14 Years**

(21) Appl. No.: **29/521,264**

(22) Filed: **Mar. 20, 2015**

Related U.S. Application Data

(63) Continuation-in-part of application No. 29/520,607, filed on Mar. 16, 2015.

(51) **LOC (10) Cl.** **10-04**

(52) **U.S. Cl.**
USPC **D10/70**; D10/30; D10/65; D10/78; D10/98; D24/167; D14/344

(58) **Field of Classification Search**
USPC .... D10/30–39, 65, 70, 78, 97; D11/3; D14/138 R, 203.5, 203.6, 341, 344, D14/347; D24/167, 168
CPC A44C 5/00–5/16; G04B 37/00–37/228; G04B 45/0069; G04B 47/04; G04B 19/00–19/34; G04B 21/12; G04B 23/12; G04B 47/00–47/068; G01C 17/00; G01C 21/00–21/3697
See application file for complete search history.

(56)   **References Cited**

U.S. PATENT DOCUMENTS

D141,753 S   7/1945   Ou Bois
D272,759 S   2/1984   Koziol

(Continued)

OTHER PUBLICATIONS

U.S. Appl. No. 29/497,740, filed Jul. 28, 2014, Park et al.
(Continued)

Primary Examiner — Antoine D Davis
(74) *Attorney, Agent, or Firm* — Weaver Austin Villeneuve & Sampson LLP

(57)   **CLAIM**
We claim the ornamental design for a wearable fitness band system, as shown and described.

DESCRIPTION

FIG. 1 is a top view of a wearable fitness band system.
FIG. 2 is a bottom view of the wearable fitness band system of FIG. 1.
FIG. 3 is a front view of the wearable fitness band system of FIG. 1.
FIG. 4 is a back view of the wearable fitness band system of FIG. 1.
FIG. 5 is a side view of the wearable fitness band system of FIG. 1; the wearable fitness band system of FIG. 1 is symmetric, so only one side view is shown.
FIG. 6 is an isometric view of the wearable fitness band system of FIG. 1; and,
FIG. 7 is an isometric view of the wearable fitness band system of FIG. 1 in a band-closed configuration, such as is formed when the ends of the band are pinned together as shown; the band portions of the wearable fitness band system are made from a flexible material, allowing them to be flexed into the configuration shown in order to be worn.
Stipple shading is used in the accompanying Figures to convey surface contouring, not texture. The case portion in between the two band portions may have a transparent or translucent window that allows a display within the case portion to be seen by the wearer; the window may be smoked or tinted to obscure the internal components housed within the case portion (although permitting light from a display within the case portion to be transmitted through the window). This window is not stipple shaded in the accompanying pictures, but is rendered with diagonal line hatching to indicate transparency.
The logos, e.g., "Fitbit" (visible in FIG. 3), and text, e.g., "L/G" (visible on the inside of the wristband in FIG. 6), shown do not form part of the claimed design and are indicated using dotted lines and an absence of shading in order to show that they are unclaimed environmental subject matter.

1 Claim, 4 Drawing Sheets

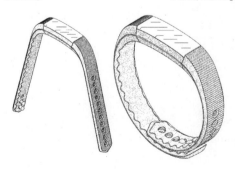

TITLE: CEILING LAMP
INVENTOR: TOM DIXON
ASSIGNEE: TOM DIXON

PATENT NUMBER: USD 760,938
PATENT FILED: NOVEMBER 3, 2014
PATENT GRANTED: JULY 5, 2016

(12) **United States Design Patent**
Dixon

(10) **Patent No.:** **US D760,938 S**
(45) **Date of Patent:** ** **Jul. 5, 2016**

(54) **CEILING LAMP**

(71) Applicant: **Tom Dixon Limited**, London (GB)

(72) Inventor: **Tom Dixon**, London (GB)

(73) Assignee: **TOM DIXON LIMITED**, London (GB)

(**) Term: **14 Years**

(21) Appl. No.: **29/508,043**

(22) Filed: **Nov. 3, 2014**

(30) **Foreign Application Priority Data**

May 1, 2014 (EM) 002456798-0006

(51) **LOC (10) Cl.** **26-03**
(52) **U.S. Cl.**
USPC **D26/81**
(58) **Field of Classification Search**
USPC D26/72, 80–84, 88–91, 118, 143, 144;
362/147, 404–408, 249.02
CPC F21S 8/028; F21S 8/036; F21S 8/04;
F21S 8/043; F21S 8/046; F21S 8/06; F21S
8/061; F21S 8/063; F21S 8/065; F21S 8/068;
F21V 21/03
See application file for complete search history.

(56) **References Cited**

U.S. PATENT DOCUMENTS

4,161,021 A	* 7/1979	George, Jr.	H01K 7/06
			362/235
D348,321 S	* 6/1994	Segill	D26/81
D348,322 S	* 6/1994	Segill	D26/81
D538,460 S	* 3/2007	Rugee	D26/84
D703,366 S	* 4/2014	Crosby	D26/85
D703,860 S	* 4/2014	Crosby	D26/88
D719,698 S	* 12/2014	Mollaghaffari	D26/81
D729,430 S	* 5/2015	Poulton	D26/88

* cited by examiner

Primary Examiner — Clare E Heflin
(74) *Attorney, Agent, or Firm* — Soroker Agmon Nordman

(57) **CLAIM**
The ornamental design for a ceiling lamp, as shown and described.

DESCRIPTION

FIG. **1** is a perspective view of the ceiling lamp showing my new design with the support member shown broken away for ease of illustration only;
FIG. **2** is a side view thereof;
FIG. **3** is a front view thereof;
FIG. **4** is a bottom view thereof; and,
FIG. **5** is a top view thereof.
The broken lines shown on the drawings depict portions of the ceiling lamp that form no part of the claimed design.

1 Claim, 5 Drawing Sheets

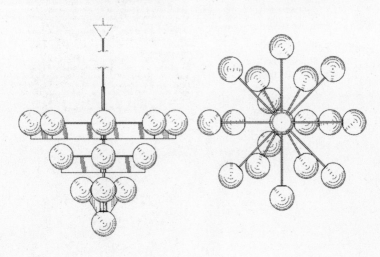

TITLE: LOUDSPEAKER
INVENTORS: FRANCESCO PELLISARI & RON ARAD
ASSIGNEE: FRANCESCO PELLISARI

PATENT NUMBER: USD 770,415
PATENT FILED: JUNE 29, 2015
PATENT GRANTED: NOVEMBER 1, 2016

(12) **United States Design Patent**   (10) Patent No.:   **US D770,415 S**
Pellisari et al.   (45) Date of Patent: ** Nov. 1, 2016**

(54) **LOUDSPEAKER**

(71) Applicant: **Francesco Pellisari**, Sawston (GB)

(72) Inventors: **Francesco Pellisari**, Sawston (GB);
Ron Arad, London (GB)

(73) Assignee: **Francesco Pellisari**, Sawston (GB)

(**) Term: **15 Years**

(21) Appl. No.: **29/531,654**

(22) Filed: **Jun. 29, 2015**

(30)   **Foreign Application Priority Data**

Dec. 29, 2014   (EM) 002606608-0003

(51) **LOC (10) Cl.** **14-03**
(52) **U.S. Cl.**
USPC **D14/216**
(58) **Field of Classification Search**
USPC D14/167, 168, 170–172, 188, 194–196,
D14/204, 207, 209.1, 210–216, 219, 221,
D14/222, 224, 239, 496; 181/143, 144, 147,
181/148, 150, 153, 157, 198, 199;
381/300–303, 306, 332, 333, 336, 345,
381/361–364, 386–388; 369/6–12
CPC ... B60R 11/0217; G06F 1/1688; G10K 9/22;
G10K 11/004; H03F 1/327; H04M 1/03;
H04M 1/035; H04N 5/642; H04N 21/4852;
H04R 1/02; H04R 1/06; H04R 1/021; H04R
1/025; H04R 1/026; H04R 1/028; H04R
1/105; H04R 1/323; H04R 1/403; H04R
1/2803; H04R 1/2834; H04R 5/02; H04R
7/20; H04R 9/06; H04R 9/025; H04R

2201/021; H04R 2400/00; H04R 2400/07;
H04R 2499/11; H04R 2499/13; H04R
2499/15; H04S 3/00; H04S 7/30
See application file for complete search history.

(56)   **References Cited**

U.S. PATENT DOCUMENTS

D319,243 S	*	8/1991	Yamakawa	D14/215
D626,939 S	*	11/2010	Chen	D14/216
D647,508 S	*	10/2011	Lee	D14/216
D701,831 S	*	4/2014	Park	D13/108
D726,151 S	*	4/2015	Wong	D14/215
D736,183 S	*	8/2015	Kim	D14/216
D743,941 S	*	11/2015	Patsis	D14/216

* cited by examiner

Primary Examiner — Keli L Hill
(74) *Attorney, Agent, or Firm* — Reising Ethington P.C.

(57)   **CLAIM**
The ornamental design for a loudspeaker, as shown and
described.

DESCRIPTION

FIG. **1** is a perspective view of the loudspeaker;
FIG. **2** is a front view of the loudspeaker;
FIG. **3** is a rear view of the loudspeaker; and,
FIG. **4** is a left side view of the loudspeaker, the top and
bottom views being the same and the right side being a
mirror image thereof.
The broken lines shown in the drawings represent unclaimed
portions of the design and form no part thereof.

1 Claim, 2 Drawing Sheets

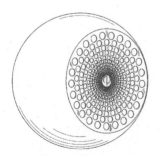

TITLE: AUDIO INPUT/OUTPUT DEVICE
INVENTORS: HEINZ-DOMINIK LANGHAMMER, GILES DAVID
MATTHEW MCWILLIAM, MARC RENE WALLISER, ET AL.
ASSIGNEE: AMAZON TECHNOLOGIES

PATENT NUMBER: USD 771,141
PATENT FILED: MAY 22, 2015
PATENT GRANTED: NOVEMBER 8, 2016

(12) **United States Design Patent** (10) Patent No.: **US D771,141 S**

Langhammer et al. (45) **Date of Patent:** ** Nov. 8, 2016

(54) **AUDIO INPUT/OUTPUT DEVICE**

(71) Applicant: **Amazon Technologies, Inc.**, Seattle, WA (US)

(72) Inventors: **Heinz-Dominik Langhammer**, San Francisco, CA (US); **Giles David Matthew McWilliam**, San Francisco, CA (US); **Marc Rene Walliser**, San Francisco, CA (US); **Christopher Green**, San Francisco, CA (US)

(73) Assignee: **Amazon Technologies, Inc.**, Seattle, WA (US)

(**) Term: **15 Years**

(21) Appl. No.: **29/527,977**

(22) Filed: **May 22, 2015**

(51) **LOC (10) Cl.** **14-03**

(52) **U.S. Cl.**
USPC **D14/496**

(58) **Field of Classification Search**
USPC D14/496, 401, 435, 474, 483, 217, 137,
D14/138, 160, 168, 356, 203.1–203.8, 507;
345/156, 169, 173–179, 905;
715/727–729, 864; 710/1, 5, 8; 713/1,
713/600; 455/1.1, 1.7, 73, 344–347, 93, 95,
455/3.01–3.06, 550.1, 573.1; 370/342–344;
369/1, 2, 6–12; 463/43–47; 273/148 B
CPC A63F 13/00; A63F 11/00; A63F
2300/8047; G06F 17/00
See application file for complete search history.

(56) **References Cited**

U.S. PATENT DOCUMENTS

5,893,798 A	*	4/1999	Stambolic A63F 9/24 463/37
5,914,707 A	*	6/1999	Kono G06K 19/08 345/173
7,209,648 B2	*	4/2007	Barber H04N 9/7921 348/E5.108

7,303,476 B2	*	12/2007	Blanco A63F 13/10 463/43
D609,718 S	*	2/2010	Chang D14/203.3
D616,416 S	*	5/2010	Lin D14/189
D686,186 S	*	7/2013	Kaneko D14/168
D687,017 S	*	7/2013	Ashcraft D14/216

(Continued)

OTHER PUBLICATIONS

The Canadian Office Action mailed Feb. 2, 2016 for Canadian design application No. 165036, a counterpart foreign application of Design U.S. Appl. No. 29/527,977, 4 pages.

(Continued)

Primary Examiner — Prabhakar Deshmukh
(74) *Attorney, Agent, or Firm* — Lee & Hayes, PLLC

(57) **CLAIM**

The ornamental design for an audio input/output device, as shown and described.

DESCRIPTION

FIG. 1 is a perspective view of an audio input/output device taken from above;
FIG. 2 is another perspective view of the audio input/output device of FIG. 1 taken from below;
FIG. 3 is a front view of the audio input/output device of FIG. 1;
FIG. 4 is a left-side view of the audio input/output device of FIG. 1;
FIG. 5 is a back view of the audio input/output device of FIG. 1;
FIG. 6 is a right-side view of the audio input/output device of FIG. 1;
FIG. 7 is a top view of the audio input/output device of FIG. 1; and,
FIG. 8 is a bottom view of the audio input/output device of FIG. 1.
The broken lines are directed to unclaimed portions and form no part of the claimed design.

1 Claim, 7 Drawing Sheets

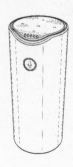

TITLE: AUDIO INPUT/OUTPUT DEVICE
INVENTORS: HEINZ-DOMINIK LANGHAMMER, GILES DAVID
MATTHEW MCWILLIAM, MARC RENE WALLISER, ET AL.
ASSIGNEE: AMAZON TECHNOLOGIES

PATENT NUMBER: USD 771,142
PATENT FILED: AUGUST 27, 2015
PATENT GRANTED: NOVEMBER 8, 2016

(12) **United States Design Patent**
Langhammer et al.

(10) Patent No.: **US D771,142 S**
(45) **Date of Patent:** ✶✶ **Nov. 8, 2016**

(54) **AUDIO INPUT/OUTPUT DEVICE**

(71) Applicant: **Amazon Technologies, Inc.**, Seattle, WA (US)

(72) Inventors: **Heinz-Dominik Langhammer**, San Francisco, CA (US); **Giles David Matthew McWilliam**, San Francisco, CA (US); **Marc Rene Walliser**, San Francisco, CA (US); **Christopher Green**, San Francisco, CA (US)

(73) Assignee: **Amazon Technologies, Inc.**, Seattle, WA (US)

(**) Term: **15 Years**

(21) Appl. No.: **29/537,679**

(22) Filed: **Aug. 27, 2015**

(51) LOC (10) Cl. **14-03**

(52) **U.S. Cl.**
USPC **D14/496; D14/203.6**

(58) **Field of Classification Search**
USPC ...... D14/496, 401, 435, 474, 483, 217, 137, D14/138, 160, 168, 356, 203.1–203.8, 507; 345/156, 169, 173–179, 905; 715/727–729, 864; 710/1, 5, 8; 713/1, 713/600; 455/1.1, 1.7, 73, 344–347, 93, 95, 455/3.01–3.06, 550.1, 573.1; 370/342–344; 369/1, 2, 6–12; 463/43–47; 273/148 B
CPC A63F 13/00; A63F 11/00; A63F 2300/8047; G06F 17/00
See application file for complete search history.

(56) **References Cited**

U.S. PATENT DOCUMENTS

D514,122 S	*	1/2006	Rodarte D14/203.6
D554,614 S	*	11/2007	Lin D14/509
D582,394 S	*	12/2008	Hong D14/216
D609,718 S	*	2/2010	Chang D14/203.3
D613,270 S	*	4/2010	Cooper D13/123

D626,147 S	*	10/2010	Goddard D14/496
8,090,418 B2	*	1/2012	Thiel H04B 1/385 455/575.2
D662,949 S	*	7/2012	Otero D14/203.1
8,315,046 B2	*	11/2012	Cooper H04R 1/1041 248/639
D744,541 S	*	12/2015	Langhammer D14/203.1

(Continued)

OTHER PUBLICATIONS

The Canadian Office Action mailed May 10, 2016 for Canadian Design Application No. 166740, a counterpart foreign design application of Design U.S. Appl. No. 29/537,679, 2 pages.

(Continued)

Primary Examiner — Prabhakar Deshmukh
(74) *Attorney, Agent, or Firm* — Lee & Hayes, PLLC

(57) **CLAIM**
The ornamental design for an audio input/output device, as shown and described.

DESCRIPTION

FIG. **1** is a first perspective view of an audio input/output device, taken from the front.
FIG. **2** is a second perspective view of the audio input/output device of FIG. **1**, taken from the bottom-back.
FIG. **3** is a top view of the audio input/output device of FIG. **1**.
FIG. **4** is a bottom view of the audio input/output device of FIG. **1**.
FIG. **5** is a front view of the audio input/output device of FIG. **1**.
FIG. **6** is a back view of the audio input/output device of FIG. **1**; and,
FIG. **7** is a left-side view of the audio input/output device of FIG. **1**, the right-side view being a mirror image of the left-side view.
The broken lines in the drawings are for illustrative purposes only and form no part of the claimed design.

1 Claim, 6 Drawing Sheets

TITLE: PEN
INVENTOR: MARC ANDREW NEWSON
ASSIGNEE: MONTBLANC-SIMPLO

PATENT NUMBER: USD 774,139
PATENT FILED: JUNE 4, 2015
PATENT GRANTED: DECEMBER 13, 2016

(12) **United States Design Patent**　(10) **Patent No.:**　　**US D774,139 S**

Newson　　　　　　　　　　　　　(45) **Date of Patent:**　****** **Dec. 13, 2016**

(54) **PEN**

(71) Applicant: **Montblanc-Simplo GmbH**, Hamburg (DE)

(72) Inventor: **Marc Andrew Newson**, London (GB)

(73) Assignee: **Montblanc-Simplo GmbH**, Hamburg (DE)

(**) Term: **15 Years**

(21) Appl. No.: **29/529,211**

(22) Filed: **Jun. 4, 2015**

(30) **Foreign Application Priority Data**

Dec. 5, 2014 (WO) 857436301

(51) **LOC (10) Cl.** **19-06**
(52) **U.S. Cl.**
USPC **D19/164**
(58) **Field of Classification Search**
USPC D14/411; D19/115–204
CPC B43K 5/005; B43K 5/16; B43K 7/00;
B43K 7/10; B43K 7/12; B43K
8/02; B43K 8/022; B43K 8/024; B43K
8/04
See application file for complete search history.

(56) **References Cited**

U.S. PATENT DOCUMENTS

1,244,974 A *	10/1917	Gerdom	B43K 1/08
			401/216
D113,633 S *	3/1939	Kahn	D19/184
D121,406 S *	7/1940	Whitehouse	D19/169
D150,320 S *	7/1948	Starr	D19/168
2,457,217 A *	12/1948	Ernst	B43K 27/08
			401/172

D162,213 S *	2/1951	Nelson et al.	D19/168
2,640,297 A *	6/1953	Adams	A63H 37/00
			446/28
D234,471 S *	3/1975	Carre	D19/168
D254,315 S *	2/1980	Carre	D19/164
D260,101 S *	8/1981	Gomez	D19/168
D261,009 S *	9/1981	Gomez	D19/168
4,308,879 A *	1/1982	Thornbloom	A45D 40/18
			132/317
D263,482 S *	3/1982	Carre	D19/168
D309,156 S *	7/1990	Kuwabara	D19/115
D329,461 S *	9/1992	Katami	D19/168
D377,193 S *	1/1997	Takemura	D19/135
5,676,480 A *	10/1997	Tosto	A45D 19/02
			132/108
D403,706 S *	1/1999	Fukami	D19/170
D408,448 S *	4/1999	Rebien	D19/170
D409,241 S *	5/1999	Melnick	D19/164
D545,898 S *	7/2007	Iwasaki	D19/163
D555,726 S *	11/2007	Huff	D19/166

(Continued)

Primary Examiner — Elizabeth Albert
(74) *Attorney, Agent, or Firm* — Taft Stettinius & Hollister LLP

(57) **CLAIM**

The ornamental design for a pen, as shown and described.

DESCRIPTION

FIG. 1 is a front side view of a pen of the present invention.
FIG. 2 is a rear side view of the pen of FIG. 1.
FIG. 3 is a top view of the pen of FIG. 1.
FIG. 4 is a bottom view of the pen of FIG. 1.
FIG. 5 is a left side view of the pen of FIG. 1.
FIG. 6 is a right side view of the pen of FIG. 1.
FIG. 7 is a front left-side perspective view of the pen of FIG. 1; and,
FIG. 8 is a front right-side perspective view of the pen of FIG. 1.

1 Claim, 8 Drawing Sheets

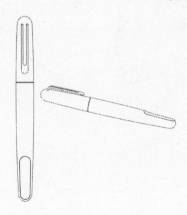

TITLE: LAMP
INVENTOR: OKI SATO
ASSIGNEE: LOUIS POULSEN

PATENT NUMBER: USD 776,319
PATENT FILED: MAY 26, 2015
PATENT GRANTED: JANUARY 10, 2017

(12) **United States Design Patent**   (10) Patent No.: **US D776,319 S**
Sato   (45) Date of Patent: ✸✸ **Jan. 10, 2017**

(54) **LAMP**

(71) Applicant: **Louis Poulsen A/S**, Copenhagen K (DK)

(72) Inventor: **Oki Sato**, Tokyo (JP)

(73) Assignee: **Louis Poulsen A/S**, Copenhagen (DK)

(**) Term: **15 Years**

(21) Appl. No.: **29/528,140**

(22) Filed: **May 26, 2015**

(30)   **Foreign Application Priority Data**

Nov. 26, 2014   (EM) 002585711

(51) **LOC (10) Cl.** **26-03**
(52) **U.S. Cl.**
USPC **D26/63**
(58) **Field of Classification Search**
USPC D26/1, 24, 61, 63, 65, 85, 93, 106, 107
CPC F21V 21/14; F21V 15/01; F21V 14/02;
F21V 21/30; F21V 21/00; F21V
14/00; F21S 8/00; F21S 8/003; F21S
8/043; F21Y 2105/001
See application file for complete search history.

(56)   **References Cited**

U.S. PATENT DOCUMENTS

D310,886 S * 9/1990 Gismondi D26/65
D330,266 S * 10/1992 Lin D26/65

D588,737 S * 3/2009 Fu D26/63
D599,930 S * 9/2009 Huang D26/63
D628,729 S * 12/2010 Citterio D26/65
D690,858 S * 10/2013 Citterio D26/63
D744,683 S * 12/2015 Fukasawa D26/63

* cited by examiner

Primary Examiner — Brian N Vinson
(74) *Attorney, Agent, or Firm* — Flener IP Law, LLC;
Zareefa B. Flener

(57)   **CLAIM**

An ornamental design for a lamp, as shown and described.

DESCRIPTION

FIG. **1** is a front perspective view of a lamp showing our design;
FIG. **2** is a left side elevational view thereof;
FIG. **3** is a right side elevational view thereof;
FIG. **4** is a front elevational view thereof;
FIG. **5** is a rear elevational view thereof;
FIG. **6** is a top plan view thereof;
FIG. **7** is a bottom plan view thereof; and,
FIG. **8** is a rear perspective view thereof.
The broken lines shown in the drawings represent unclaimed portions of the lamp and form no part of the lamp.

1 Claim, 6 Drawing Sheets

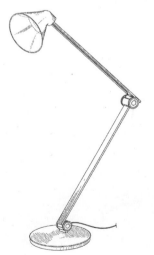

TITLE: LAMP
INVENTOR: KARIM RASHID
ASSIGNEE: FONTANAARTE

PATENT NUMBER: USD 776,860
PATENT FILED: OCTOBER 13, 2015
PATENT GRANTED: JANUARY 17, 2017

(12) **United States Design Patent**
Rashid

(10) Patent No.: **US D776,860 S**

(45) Date of Patent: ** **Jan. 17, 2017**

(54) **LAMP**

(71) Applicant: **FONTANAARTE S.p.A.**, Corsico, Milan (IT)

(72) Inventor: **Karim Rashid**, New York, NY (US)

(73) Assignee: **FONTANAARTE S.p.A.** (IT)

(**) Term: **15 Years**

(21) Appl. No.: **29/542,317**

(22) Filed: **Oct. 13, 2015**

(30) **Foreign Application Priority Data**

Apr. 10, 2015 (IT) MI2015O0060

(51) **LOC (10) Cl.** **26-03**
(52) **U.S. Cl.**
USPC **D26/107**
(58) **Field of Classification Search**
USPC D26/1, 24, 93, 104, 106, 107, 109, 110, D26/62
CPC F21S 6/00; F21S 6/043; F21S 8/08; F21V 21/00; F21V 21/02; F21W 2121/00; F21W 2131/30
See application file for complete search history.

(56) **References Cited**

U.S. PATENT DOCUMENTS

D368,549 S * 4/1996 Huang D26/107
D401,377 S * 11/1998 Eusterbrock D26/107

D673,716 S	*	1/2013	Huang	D26/93
D683,887 S	*	6/2013	Sabernig	D26/93
D728,845 S	*	5/2015	Huang	D26/107
D734,528 S	*	7/2015	Douglas	D26/107
D759,289 S	*	6/2016	Newhouse	D26/107

* cited by examiner

Primary Examiner — Brian N Vinson
(74) *Attorney, Agent, or Firm* — Saidman DesignLaw Group, LLC

(57) **CLAIM**

The ornamental design for a lamp, as shown and described.

DESCRIPTION

FIG. 1 is a perspective view of a lamp showing my new design, the following figures showing various positions thereof;
FIG. 2 is another perspective view thereof;
FIG. 3 is a front view thereof;
FIG. 4 is a rear view thereof;
FIG. 5 is a left side view thereof, the right side view being a mirror image;
FIG. 6 is a top view thereof; and,
FIG. 7 is a bottom view thereof.
The drawings include CAD lines that represent contour and not surface decoration.

1 Claim, 7 Drawing Sheets

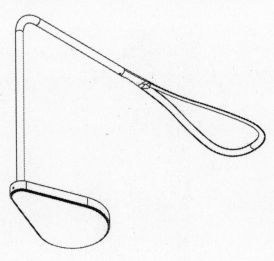

TITLE: INSTANT CAMERA
INVENTOR: HARUKA IKEGAME
ASSIGNEE: FUJIFILM CORPORATION

PATENT NUMBER: USD 779,577
PATENT FILED: AUGUST 27, 2015
PATENT GRANTED: FEBRUARY 21, 2017

(12) **United States Design Patent**   (10) **Patent No.:**   **US D779,577 S**

Ikegame   (45) **Date of Patent:**   ✱✱ **Feb. 21, 2017**

(54) **INSTANT CAMERA**

(71) Applicant: **FUJIFILM Corporation**, Tokyo (JP)

(72) Inventor: **Haruka Ikegame**, Tokyo (JP)

(73) Assignee: **FUJIFILM Corporation**, Tokyo (JP)

(**) Term: **15 Years**

(21) Appl. No.: **29/537,581**

(22) Filed: **Aug. 27, 2015**

(30) **Foreign Application Priority Data**

Feb. 27, 2015   (JP) 2015-004178

(51) **LOC (10) Cl.** **16-01**
(52) **U.S. Cl.**
USPC **D16/218**; D16/211
(58) **Field of Classification Search**
USPC D16/202, 208, 209, 210, 211, 218, 219,
D16/220, 237
CPC G03B 5/02; G03B 7/102; G03B 17/04;
G03B 17/18; G03B 17/48; G03B 17/50;
G03B 17/52
See application file for complete search history.

(56) **References Cited**

U.S. PATENT DOCUMENTS

D447,504 S	*	9/2001	Horikiri D16/218
D456,437 S	*	4/2002	Omino D16/202
D457,543 S	*	5/2002	Petravic D16/200
D463,472 S	*	9/2002	Horikiri D16/218
D472,258 S	*	3/2003	Yin D16/202
D473,251 S	*	4/2003	Katayama D16/218
D484,523 S	*	12/2003	Senda D16/218
6,712,531 B2	*	3/2004	Takagi G03B 17/04
			396/349
6,847,783 B2	*	1/2005	Sasaki G03B 17/52
			116/213

D582,954 S	*	12/2008	Imai D16/202
D594,047 S	*	6/2009	Lee D16/202
D662,962 S	*	7/2012	Inoue D16/219
D662,963 S	*	7/2012	Muraki D16/219
D697,122 S	*	1/2014	Ikegame D16/218
D709,543 S	*	7/2014	Isozaki D16/218

(Continued)

OTHER PUBLICATIONS

"Polaroid MIO", posted at http://on-and-on.ocnk.net/, Dec. 26, 2011, [site visited Aug. 9, 2016]. Available from Internet: <http://on-and-on.ocnk.net/product/4389>.*

(Continued)

Primary Examiner — Celia Murphy
Assistant Examiner — John M Otte
(74) *Attorney, Agent, or Firm* — Young & Thompson

(57) **CLAIM**

The ornamental design for an instant camera, as shown and described.

DESCRIPTION

FIG. **1** is a top, front and right side perspective view of an instant camera showing my new design;
FIG. **2** is a top, rear and right side perspective view thereof;
FIG. **3** is a front elevational view thereof;
FIG. **4** is a rear elevational view thereof;
FIG. **5** is a top plan view thereof;
FIG. **6** is a bottom plan view thereof;
FIG. **7** is a left side elevational view thereof;
FIG. **8** is a right side elevational view thereof; and,
FIG. **9** is a top, front and right side perspective view thereof with a lens barrel protruded.
The portions of the article shown in broken line form no part of the claimed design.

1 Claim, 8 Drawing Sheets

TITLE: HANDSET
INVENTOR: JASPER MORRISON
ASSIGNEE: PUNKT TRONICS

PATENT NUMBER: USD 793,986
PATENT FILED: OCTOBER 19, 2015
PATENT GRANTED: AUGUST 8, 2017

(12) **United States Design Patent** (10) Patent No.:   **US D793,986 S**
Morrison   (45) **Date of Patent:**   **   **Aug. 8, 2017**

(54) **HANDSET**

(71) Applicant: **PUNKT TRONICS AG**, Lugano (CH)

(72) Inventor: **Jasper Morrison**, London (GB)

(73) Assignee: **PUNKT TRONICS AG**, Lugano (CH)

(**) Term: **15 Years**

(21) Appl. No.: **35/500,650**

(22) Filed: **Oct. 19, 2015**

(80) **Hague Agreement Data**

Int. Filing Date: **Oct. 19, 2015**
Int. Reg. No.: **DM/089406**
Int. Reg. Date: **Oct. 19, 2015**
Int. Reg. Pub. Date: **Feb. 26, 2016**

(51) LOC (10) Cl. **14-03**
(52) U.S. Cl.
USPC .... **D14/138 AA**
(58) **Field of Classification Search**
USPC .... D14/137, 138 G, 138 R, 138 AA, 147,
D14/191, 203.1–203.8, 218, 247, 248,
D14/496; D13/168; D18/7; 455/566,
455/575.1, 575.3, 575.4
CPC G06F 1/626; G06F 3/0488; H04M 1/04;
H04M 1/0202; H04M 1/0266; H04M
1/72519; H04M 2250/12; H04M 2250/22;
H04W 4/12
See application file for complete search history.

(56) **References Cited**

U.S. PATENT DOCUMENTS

D370,222	S	*	5/1996	Kajita .... D14/138 AA
D623,160	S	*	9/2010	Garn .... D14/138 AA
D662,073	S	*	6/2012	Tsai .... D14/138 AA
D665,374	S	*	8/2012	Park .... D14/138 AA
D690,695	S	*	10/2013	Butterworth D14/218
D720,326	S	*	12/2014	Chao .... D14/138 AA
D733,087	S	*	6/2015	Park .... D14/138 G
9,059,505	B1	*	6/2015	Asrani H01Q 9/145
D743,386	S	*	11/2015	Im D14/248
2004/0033478	A1	*	2/2004	Knowles G07C 13/00 434/350

* cited by examiner

Primary Examiner — Keli L Hill
(74) *Attorney, Agent, or Firm* — Young & Thompson

(57) **CLAIM**

The ornamental design for a handset, as shown and described.

DESCRIPTION

1. Handset
1.1 is a rear elevation view.
1.2 is a rear perspective view.
1.3 is a front elevation view.
1.4 is a side elevation view.
1.5 is an opposite side elevation view.
1.6 is a top plan view.
1.7 is a bottom plan view.

1 Claim, 7 Drawing Sheets

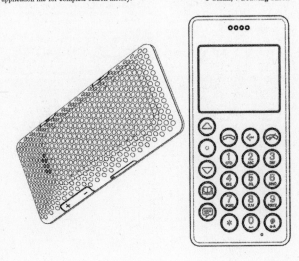

TITLE: DOMESTIC SODA-WATER PREPARING DEVICE
INVENTORS: EYAL SHMUELI, AMIT AVIGDOR,
HAGAI HARDUFF, DORON KROM & ODED GOV
ASSIGNEE: SODASTREAM INDUSTRIES

PATENT NUMBER: USD 799,879
PATENT FILED: MAY 11, 2016
PATENT GRANTED: OCTOBER 17, 2017

(12) **United States Design Patent**   (10) Patent No.:   **US D799,879 S**
Shmueli et al.   (45) Date of Patent: ** Oct. 17, 2017

(54) **DOMESTIC SODA-WATER PREPARING DEVICE**

(71) Applicant: **SodaStream Industries Ltd**, Air Port City (IL)

(72) Inventors: **Eyal Shmueli**, Reut (IL); **Amit Avigdor**, Nitzanei Oz (IL); **Hagai Harduff**, Binyamina (IL); **Doron Krom**, Zichron Yaacov (IL); **Oded Gov**, Tel Aviv (IL)

(73) Assignee: **SODASTREAM INDUSTRIES LTD.**, Air Port City (IL)

(**) Term: **15 Years**

(21) Appl. No.: **29/564,200**

(22) Filed: **May 11, 2016**

(30) **Foreign Application Priority Data**

Feb. 23, 2016   (CA) 167128

(51) **LOC (10) Cl.** **07-01**
(52) **U.S. Cl.**
      USPC **D7/306**; D7/311
(58) **Field of Classification Search**
      USPC D7/305–311, 313, 589; D15/82;
                    222/129.1, 146.6; 99/295
      CPC A47J 31/44; A47J 31/4403; A47J 31/46;
                    A47J 31/4482; A47J 31/369; A47J
                    31/407; A47J 31/30; A47J 31/20; A47J
                    4/025; A47J 31/002; B67D 1/36; B67D
                    2210/0065; B67D 1/0864; B67D 3/0061
      See application file for complete search history.

(56) **References Cited**

U.S. PATENT DOCUMENTS

D408,494 S	4/1999	Parise
D442,010 S	5/2001	Collin et al.
D515,347 S	2/2006	Reuss et al.
D600,493 S	9/2009	Pino et al.
D608,129 S *	1/2010	Spear D7/306
D610,388 S *	2/2010	Hazan D7/306
D658,423 S	5/2012	Curtis et al.
D679,933 S *	4/2013	Bruno D7/306

(Continued)

FOREIGN PATENT DOCUMENTS

CL	200800107	7/2007
CL	201100803	10/2010

(Continued)

OTHER PUBLICATIONS

Notice of Allowance for Taiwanese Patent Application No. 105303784, mailed Dec. 8, 2016.

(Continued)

Primary Examiner — Marianne Pandozzi
(74) *Attorney, Agent, or Firm* — Pearl Cohen Zedek Latzer Baratz LLP

(57) **CLAIM**

The ornamental design for a domestic soda-water preparing device, as shown and described.

DESCRIPTION

FIG. **1** is a top, front, right side perspective of the domestic soda-water preparing device;
FIG. **2** is a top, back, left side perspective view thereof;
FIG. **3** is a front elevation view thereof;
FIG. **4** is a back elevation view thereof;
FIG. **5** is a right side elevation view thereof;
FIG. **6** is a left side elevation view thereof;
FIG. **7** is a top plan view thereof; and,
FIG. **8** is a bottom plan view thereof.
The broken lines in the drawing depict portions of the domestic soda-water preparing device that form no part of the claimed design.

1 Claim, 8 Drawing Sheets

TITLE: TRIPLE ENDED SPINNER TOY
INVENTOR: DAVID ALLEN PAVELSKY
ASSIGNEE: NONE

PATENT NUMBER: USD 801,440
PATENT FILED: NOVEMBER 29, 2016
PATENT GRANTED: OCTOBER 31, 2017

(12) **United States Design Patent**   (10) Patent No.:   **US D801,440 S**

Pavelsky   (45) Date of Patent: ** **Oct. 31, 2017**

(54) **TRIPLE ENDED SPINNER TOY**

(71) Applicant: **David Allen Pavelsky**, Killeen, TX (US)

(72) Inventor: **David Allen Pavelsky**, Killeen, TX (US)

(**) Term: **15 Years**

(21) Appl. No.: **29/585,885**

(22) Filed: **Nov. 29, 2016**

(51) **LOC (10) Cl.** **21-01**

(52) **U.S. Cl.**
USPC **D21/455**; D21/398

(58) **Field of Classification Search**
USPC D21/398, 436, 437, 441, 443, 444,
D21/460–464, 455, 458, 459; 446/46–48,
446/236–266
CPC ... A63H 1/00–1/32; A63H 5/00; A63H 27/12;
A63H 33/00; A63H 33/02; A63H 33/18;
A63H 33/185; A63H 33/22; A63B 5/00;
A63B 5/08; A63B 5/10
See application file for complete search history.

(56)   **References Cited**

U.S. PATENT DOCUMENTS

D27,044 S	*	5/1897	Quinn	D21/455
D137,980 S	*	5/1944	Hoffman	D21/443
3,533,185 A	*	10/1970	Kanbar	A63B 23/16
				446/266
D312,480 S	*	11/1990	Darnell	D21/437
5,045,011 A	*	9/1991	Lovik	A63H 33/18
				273/114
5,490,678 A	*	2/1996	Darnell	A63B 65/08
				473/590
5,655,777 A	*	8/1997	Neading	A63B 65/08
				473/594
D683,798 S	*	6/2013	Goldman	D21/398
2001/0002353 A1	*	5/2001	Moore	A63B 65/08
				446/236
2012/0135666 A1	*	5/2012	Rosenzweig	A63H 33/22
				446/242

FOREIGN PATENT DOCUMENTS

EM	003812536-0001	*	3/2017	
EM	004028488-0001	*	6/2017	
WO	WO-2015176022 A2	*	11/2015	A63B 65/00

* cited by examiner

Primary Examiner — Catherine A Tuttle
(74) *Attorney, Agent, or Firm* — Plager Schack LLP

(57)   **CLAIM**

The ornamental design for a triple ended spinner toy, as shown and described.

DESCRIPTION

FIG. 1 is a front perspective view of the triple ended spinner toy.
FIG. 2 is a top view of the triple ended spinner toy.
FIG. 3 is a bottom view of the triple ended spinner toy.
FIG. 4 is a left side view of the triple ended spinner toy.
FIG. 5 is a right side view of the triple ended spinner toy.
FIG. 6 is a front view of the triple ended spinner toy; and,
FIG. 7 is a rear view of the triple ended spinner toy.

1 Claim, 5 Drawing Sheets

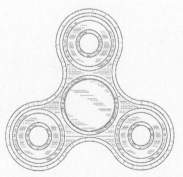

TITLE: HOVERBOARD
INVENTORS: DIANXUAN ZHANG & DENGJIN ZHOU
ASSIGNEE: SHENZHEN CHITADO TECHNOLOGY COMPANY

PATENT NUMBER: USD 808,857
PATENT FILED: JANUARY 10, 2017
PATENT GRANTED: JANUARY 30, 2018

(12) **United States Design Patent**   (10) Patent No.:   **US D808,857 S**
Zhang et al.   (45) Date of Patent: ** Jan. 30, 2018

(54) **HOVERBOARD**

(71) Applicant: **Shenzhen Chitado Technology CO., LTD.**, Shenzhen, Guangdong (CN)

(72) Inventors: **Dianxuan Zhang**, Guangdong (CN); **Dengjin Zhou**, Guangdong (CN)

(73) Assignee: **Shenzhen Chitado technology CO., LTD.** (CN)

(**) Term: **15 Years**

(21) Appl. No.: **29/590,451**

(22) Filed: **Jan. 10, 2017**

(51) LOC (11) Cl. **12-14**
(52) U.S. Cl.
USPC **D12/1**
(58) Field of Classification Search
USPC D12/1, 5; D21/419, 421, 423, 426, 662, D21/760, 765, 766, 769, 771, 776, 803
CPC B62K 3/007; B62K 17/00; B62K 2202/00; B62K 11/007; B62D 51/001; B62D 51/02; B62D 61/00; B62D 37/00; A63C 17/0033; A63C 17/01; A63C 17/016; A63C 2203/40; A63C 17/12; A63C 17/08; B60N 2/002; B60G 17/019
See application file for complete search history.

(56) **References Cited**

U.S. PATENT DOCUMENTS

D737,723 S   *   9/2015   Ying D12/1
D738,256 S   *   9/2015   Ying D12/1
D778,782 S   *   2/2017   Chen D12/1
D780,626 S   *   3/2017   Li D12/1
D784,195 S   *   4/2017   Ying D12/1
D784,198 S   *   4/2017   Zhu D12/1
D785,112 S   *   4/2017   Ying D21/760
D785,113 S   *   4/2017   Ying D21/760
D785,736 S   *   5/2017   Ying D21/760
D786,130 S   *   5/2017   Huang D12/1
D786,994 S   *   5/2017   Chen D21/760
D786,995 S   *   5/2017   Ying D21/760
9,688,340 B1 * 6/2017   Kroymann B62K 13/04
2013/0238231 A1* 9/2013 Chen B62K 11/007
                                                        701/124
2016/0129963 A1* 5/2016 Ying B62D 51/001
                                                        180/6.5
2016/0325803 A1* 11/2016 Waxman B62M 7/12
2017/0144718 A1* 5/2017 Tinaphong B62K 11/007
2017/0240240 A1* 8/2017 Kroymann B62K 13/04

* cited by examiner

Primary Examiner — T. Chase Nelson
Assistant Examiner — Ania Aman

(57)   **CLAIM**
The ornamental design for a hoverboard, as shown and described.

DESCRIPTION

FIG. 1 is a front view of the hoverboard showing our new design;
FIG. 2 is a back view thereof;
FIG. 3 is a top view thereof;
FIG. 4 is a bottom view thereof;
FIG. 5 is a left side view thereof;
FIG. 6 is a right side view thereof;
FIG. 7 is a perspective view thereof; and,
FIG. 8 is another perspective view thereof.

1 Claim, 8 Drawing Sheets

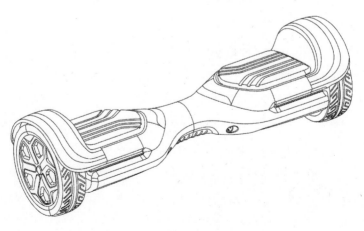

TITLE: VAPORIZER DEVICE WITH CARTRIDGE
INVENTORS: ADAM BOWEN, JAMES MONSEES
STEVEN CHRISTENSEN, JOSHUA MORENSTEIN, ET AL.
ASSIGNEE: JUUL LABS

PATENT NUMBER: USD 825,102
PATENT FILED: JULY 28, 2016
PATENT GRANTED: AUGUST 7, 2018

(12) **United States Design Patent** (10) Patent No.: **US D825,102 S**

Bowen et al. (45) **Date of Patent:** ** **Aug. 7, 2018**

(54) **VAPORIZER DEVICE WITH CARTRIDGE**

(71) Applicant: **JUUL LABS, INC.**, San Francisco, CA (US)

(72) Inventors: **Adam Bowen**, San Francisco, CA (US); **James Monsees**, San Francisco, CA (US); **Steven Christensen**, San Francisco, CA (US); **Joshua Morenstein**, San Francisco, CA (US); **Christopher Nicholas HibmaCronan**, Oakland, CA (US)

(73) Assignee: **JUUL Labs, Inc.**, San Francisco, CA (US)

(**) Term: **15 Years**

(21) Appl. No.: **35/001,169**

(22) Filed: **Jul. 28, 2016**

(80) **Hague Agreement Data**

    Int. Filing Date: **Mar. 11, 2016**
    Int. Reg. No.: **DM/092570**
    Int. Reg. Date: **Jul. 28, 2016**
    Int. Reg. Pub. Date: **Feb. 3, 2017**

(51) **LOC (11) Cl.** **27-02**

(52) **U.S. Cl.**
    USPC **D27/167**

(58) **Field of Classification Search**
    USPC D27/102, 105, 106, 110–112
    CPC A24F 19/0064; A24F 15/18; A24F 13/20;
            A24F 13/18; A24F 23/00; A24F 19/0085;
            A24F 19/14; A24F 13/14; A24F 19/00;
            B65D 5/18; B65D 5/0209
    See application file for complete search history.

(56) **References Cited**

U.S. PATENT DOCUMENTS

374,584 A	12/1887	Cook
576,653 A	2/1897	Bowlby
595,070 A	12/1897	Oldenbusch
720,007 A	2/1903	Dexter
799,844 A	9/1905	Fuller
968,160 A	8/1910	Johnson
969,076 A	8/1910	Pender
1,067,531 A	7/1913	MacGregor
1,163,183 A	12/1915	Stoll
1,299,162 A	4/1919	Fisher
1,505,748 A	8/1924	Louis
1,552,877 A	9/1925	Phillipps et al.
1,632,335 A	6/1927	Hiering
1,706,244 A	3/1929	Louis
1,845,340 A	2/1932	Ritz
1,972,118 A	9/1934	McDill
1,998,683 A	4/1935	Montgomery
2,031,363 A	2/1936	Elof
2,039,559 A	5/1936	Segal
2,104,266 A	1/1938	McCormick
2,159,698 A	5/1939	Harris et al.
2,177,636 A	10/1939	Coffelt et al.
2,195,260 A	3/1940	Rasener
2,231,909 A	2/1941	Hempal
2,327,120 A	8/1943	McCoon
D142,178 S	8/1945	Becwar
2,460,427 A	2/1949	Musselman et al.
2,483,304 A	9/1949	Rudolf
2,502,561 A	4/1950	Ludwig
2,765,949 A	10/1956	Swan
2,830,597 A	4/1958	Kummli
2,860,638 A	11/1958	Bartolomeo
2,897,958 A	8/1959	Tarleton et al.
2,935,987 A	5/1960	Ackerbauer
3,085,145 A	4/1963	Wray
3,146,937 A	9/1964	Joseph
3,258,015 A	6/1966	Ellis et al.
3,271,719 A	9/1966	Ovshinsky
3,292,634 A	12/1966	Beucler
D207,887 S	6/1967	Parsisson
3,373,915 A	3/1968	Anderson et al.
3,420,360 A	1/1969	Young
3,443,827 A	5/1969	Acker et al.
3,456,645 A	7/1969	Brock
3,479,561 A	11/1969	Janning
3,567,014 A	3/1971	Feigelman
3,675,661 A	7/1972	Weaver
3,707,017 A	12/1972	Paquette
3,792,704 A	2/1974	Parker
3,815,597 A	6/1974	Goettelman
3,861,523 A	1/1975	Fountain et al.
3,941,300 A	3/1976	Troth
4,020,853 A	5/1977	Nuttall
4,049,005 A	9/1977	Hernandez et al.
4,066,088 A	1/1978	Ensor

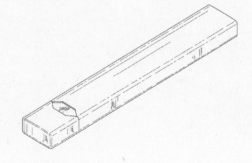

TITLE: PORTABLE COMPUTER
INVENTORS: FUMIYOSHI SUETAKE, KUMPEI FUJITA
& MASATO IBUKI
ASSIGNEE: NINTENDO COMPANY

PATENT NUMBER: USD 833,531
PATENT FILED: MAY 24, 2018
PATENT GRANTED: NOVEMBER 13, 2018

(12) **United States Design Patent** (10) Patent No.: **US D833,531 S**
Suetake et al. (45) Date of Patent: ** Nov. 13, 2018

(54) **PORTABLE COMPUTER**

(71) Applicant: **NINTENDO CO., LTD.**, Kyoto (JP)

(72) Inventors: **Fumiyoshi Suetake**, Kyoto (JP);
Kumpei Fujita, Kyoto (JP); **Masato Ibuki**, Kyoto (JP)

(73) Assignee: **Nintendo Co., Ltd.**, Kyoto (JP)

(**) Term: **15 Years**

(21) Appl. No.: **29/648,865**

(22) Filed: **May 24, 2018**

Related U.S. Application Data

(62) Division of application No. 29/613,796, filed on Aug. 14, 2017.

(30) **Foreign Application Priority Data**

Apr. 6, 2017	(JP)	2017-007368
Apr. 6, 2017	(JP)	2017-007369

(51) **LOC (11) Cl.** **21-01**
(52) **U.S. Cl.**
USPC **D21/330**; D14/345
(58) **Field of Classification Search**
USPC .... D14/341–347, 125–134, 137, 138 R,
D14/138 AA, 138 AB, 138 C, 138 G, 147,
(Continued)

(56) **References Cited**

U.S. PATENT DOCUMENTS

D275,971 S	10/1984	Yokoi
D452,280 S	12/2001	Ota

(Continued)

OTHER PUBLICATIONS

Nintendo DSi Was Originally a Monster With Two DS Slots, posted Feb. 20, 2009, [retrieved Aug. 29, 2018]. Retrieved from Internet, <URL: https://gizmodo.com/5157578/nintendo-dsi-was-originally-a-monster-with-two-ds-slots >.*

(Continued)

Primary Examiner — Barbara Fox
Assistant Examiner — Kristin E Reed
(74) *Attorney, Agent, or Firm* — Nixon & Vanderhye PC

(57) **CLAIM**

The ornamental design for a portable computer, as shown and described.

DESCRIPTION

FIG. **1** is a front view of a portable computer showing our new design;
FIG. **2** is a top view thereof;
FIG. **3** is a back view thereof;
FIG. **4** is a bottom view thereof;
FIG. **5** is a right view thereof;
FIG. **6** is a left view thereof;
FIG. **7** is a front side perspective view thereof;
FIG. **8** is a back side perspective view thereof;
FIG. **9** is a front view showing a closed state thereof;
FIG. **10** is a top view showing a closed state thereof;
FIG. **11** is a back view showing a closed state thereof;
FIG. **12** is a bottom view showing a closed state thereof;
FIG. **13** is a right view showing a closed state thereof;
FIG. **14** is a left view showing a closed state thereof;
FIG. **15** is a front side perspective view showing a closed state thereof; and,
FIG. **16** is a back side perspective view showing a closed state thereof.
The broken lines shown in the drawings depict portions of the portable computer that form no part of the claimed design.

1 Claim, 16 Drawing Sheets

TITLE: AUTOMATED TRANSACTION MACHINE
INVENTORS: DONALD NELSON, DAHAE YI,
SERGIO DE OLIVEIRA & SCOTT DAILEY
ASSIGNEE: DIEBOLD NIXDORF

PATENT NUMBER: USD 867,715
PATENT FILED: JANUARY 28, 2019
PATENT GRANTED: NOVEMBER 19, 2019

(12) **United States Design Patent** (10) Patent No.: **US D867,715 S**

Nelson et al.   (45) **Date of Patent:**   ** **Nov. 19, 2019**

(54) **AUTOMATED TRANSACTION MACHINE**

(71) Applicant: **Diebold Nixdorf Incorporated**, North Canton, OH (US)

(72) Inventors: **Donald Nelson**, Akron, OH (US); **Dahae Yi**, Akron, OH (US); **Sergio de Oliveira**, Massillon, OH (US); **Scott Dailey**, Ann Arbor, MI (US)

(73) Assignee: **Diebold Nixdorf, Incorporated**, North Canton, OH (US)

(**) Term: **15 Years**

(21) Appl. No.: **29/678,380**

(22) Filed: **Jan. 28, 2019**

Related U.S. Application Data

(63) Continuation of application No. 29/601,422, filed on Apr. 21, 2017, now Pat. No. Des. 839,529, which is a continuation of application No. 29/581,847, filed on Oct. 21, 2016, now abandoned, and a continuation of

(Continued)

(51) **LOC (12) Cl.** **99-00**

(52) **U.S. Cl.**
USPC **D99/28**

(58) **Field of Classification Search**
USPC .... D99/28, 34, 35, 36, 43, 99; D14/300–302, 305, 307, 900–902; D18/3.1–3.3, 4.1–4.6, 12.1–12.3; D21/324, 325, 329, 369, 370; 101/66; 109/1 R, 1 V, 2, 23, 24.1, 25, 58, 58.5, 109/66; 446/8–13; 705/16, 17, 18, 42, 705/43, 44, 45; 235/51, 379, 380, 381, 235/382, 382.5, 386; 206/0.8, 0.81, 206/0.815, 0.82, 0.84
CPC .. G06Q 20/10; G06Q 20/108; G06Q 20/1085; G06Q 20/18; G07D 1/00; G07D 1/02; G07D 1/04; G07D 1/06; G07D 11/00; G07D 9/002; G07D 9/04; G07F 19/20; G07F 19/201; G07F 19/202; G07F

19/203; G07F 19/204; G07F 19/105; G07F 19/21; G07F 19/00; G07F 7/04; G07F 5/00; G07F 1/00; E05G 7/001; E05G 1/006; A63H 33/00; A63H 33/005
See application file for complete search history.

(56) **References Cited**

U.S. PATENT DOCUMENTS

D395,129 S	*	6/1998	Johnson	D14/130
D415,330 S	*	10/1999	King	D14/900
D419,277 S	*	1/2000	Ishii	D99/28

(Continued)

Primary Examiner — Elizabeth J Oswecki

(74) *Attorney, Agent, or Firm* — Black, McCuskey, Souers & Arbaugh, LPA

(57) **CLAIM**

The ornamental design for an automated transaction machine, as shown and described.

DESCRIPTION

FIG. 1 is a perspective view of an automated transaction machine showing our new design.
FIG. 2 is a front view of the automated transaction machine of FIG. 1.
FIG. 3 is a rear view of the automated transaction machine of FIG. 1.
FIG. 4 is a left view of the automated transaction machine of FIG. 1.
FIG. 5 is a right view of the automated transaction machine of FIG. 1.
FIG. 6 is a top view of the automated transaction machine of FIG. 1; and,
FIG. 7 is a bottom view of the automated transaction machine of FIG. 1.
The broken lines shown in the drawings represent portions of the automated transaction machine that form no part of the claimed design.

1 Claim, 7 Drawing Sheets

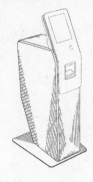

TITLE: REUSABLE SEALABLE SANDWICH BAG
INVENTORS: REBECCA M. FINELL
& JOSHUA J. NELSON
ASSIGNEE: ZIP TOP

PATENT NUMBER: USD 873,084
PATENT FILED: JULY 24, 2019
PATENT GRANTED: JANUARY 21, 2020

(12) **United States Design Patent**   (10) Patent No.:   **US D873,084 S**
Finell et al.   (45) Date of Patent: ** **Jan. 21, 2020**

(54) **REUSABLE SEALABLE SANDWICH BAG**

(71) Applicant: **ZIP TOP, LLC**, Austin, TX (US)

(72) Inventors: **Rebecca M. Finell**, Austin, TX (US);
Joshua J. Nelson, Mesa, AZ (US)

(73) Assignee: **ZIP TOP, LLC**, Austin, TX (US)

(**) Term: **15 Years**

(21) Appl. No.: **29/699,301**

(22) Filed: **Jul. 24, 2019**

Related U.S. Application Data

(63) Continuation-in-part of application No. 29/618,099,
filed on Sep. 19, 2017.

(51) **LOC (12) Cl.** **07-07**
(52) **U.S. Cl.**
USPC **D7/602**
(58) **Field of Classification Search**
USPC D7/601, 602; D9/430; 426/85
CPC A47G 19/02; A47G 19/025
See application file for complete search history.

(56) **References Cited**

U.S. PATENT DOCUMENTS

1,002,346 A	9/1911	Weeks	229/400
2,012,113 A	8/1935	Thompson	215/363
2,117,738 A *	5/1938	Metzger	B65D 35/00
			383/209
2,165,277 A	7/1939	Herman	229/405
2,589,967 A	3/1952	Sawyer	215/372
2,861,716 A	11/1958	Kramer	215/228
3,354,601 A	11/1967	Schneider	493/196
3,799,914 A *	3/1974	Schmitt et al.	B65D 75/008
			426/85
3,844,525 A	10/1974	Parmett	249/127
D285,515 S	9/1986	Papciak	D24/119
4,655,862 A	4/1987	Christoff et al.	156/66
D291,659 S	9/1987	Powell	D7/507

(Continued)

FOREIGN PATENT DOCUMENTS

JP	D140735 S	11/2010	
JP	D1454613 S	11/2012	
WO	2016/140746 A1	9/1916	.... G01F 19/00

OTHER PUBLICATIONS

U.S. Non-Final Office Action, U.S. Appl. No. 15/910,757, 21 pages,
dated Oct. 2, 2018.

(Continued)

Primary Examiner — Cynthia R Underwood
(74) *Attorney, Agent, or Firm* — Slayden Grubert Beard
PLLC

(57)   **CLAIM**

The ornamental design for a reusable sealable sandwich bag,
as shown and described.

DESCRIPTION

FIG. 1 illustrates a perspective top/front view of a reusable
sealable sandwich bag, showing the new, original and ornamental design, wherein the sandwich bag is open and
unsealed.
FIG. 2 shows a front view of the reusable sealable sandwich
bag shown in FIG. 1.
FIG. 3 shows a back view of the reusable sealable sandwich
bag shown in FIGS. 1-2.
FIG. 4 shows a left side view of the reusable sealable
sandwich bag shown in FIGS. 1-3.
FIG. 5 illustrates a right side view of the reusable sealable
sandwich bag shown in FIGS. 1-4.
FIG. 6 shows a top view of the reusable sealable sandwich
bag shown in FIGS. 1-5; and,
FIG. 7 shows a bottom view of the reusable sealable
sandwich bag shown in FIGS. 1-6.

1 Claim, 4 Drawing Sheets

TITLE: BUS
INVENTOR: FRANCK LAMANNA
ASSIGNEE: NONE

PATENT NUMBER: USD 878,245
PATENT FILED: JUNE 19, 2018
PATENT GRANTED: MARCH 17, 2020

(12) **United States Design Patent**　(10) **Patent No.:**　　**US D878,245 S**
Lamanna　　　　　　　　　　　　　　(45) **Date of Patent:**　** **Mar. 17, 2020**

(54) **BUS**

(71) Applicant: **ALSTOM APTIS**, Duppigheim (FR)

(72) Inventor: **Franck Lamanna**, Marlenheim (FR)

(**) Term: **15 Years**

(21) Appl. No.: **35/505,782**

(22) Filed: **Jun. 19, 2018**

(80) **Hague Agreement Data**

Int. Filing Date: **Jun. 19, 2018**
Int. Reg. No.: **DM/102926**
Int. Reg. Date: **Jun. 19, 2018**
Int. Reg. Pub. Date: Oct. 5, 2018

(51) **LOC (12) Cl.** **12-08**

(52) **U.S. Cl.**
USPC **D12/84**

(58) **Field of Classification Search**
USPC D12/82, 84, 86, 92, 100
CPC B62D 23/00; B62D 25/00; B62D 31/02;
B62D 31/04; B62D 53/062; B62D 65/00;
B60G 2202/152; B60G 2300/14; B60P
3/007; B21D 53/88
See application file for complete search history.

(56) **References Cited**

U.S. PATENT DOCUMENTS

D248,033 S	*	5/1978	James	D12/84
D254,609 S	*	4/1980	Neal	D12/84
D255,340 S	*	6/1980	Flesche	D12/84
D257,141 S	*	9/1980	Flesche	D12/84
D268,997 S	*	5/1983	Dubernard	D12/84
D302,802 S	*	8/1989	Manning	D12/84
D305,623 S	*	1/1990	Gallitzendoerfer	D12/84
D345,120 S	*	3/1994	Normand, Jr.	D12/84
D376,562 S	*	12/1996	Sealy	D12/84
5,669,307 A	*	9/1997	Cichy	B61B 1/02
				104/28
D442,888 S	*	5/2001	Papke	D12/84
D503,126 S	*	3/2005	Papke	D12/84
D531,933 S	*	11/2006	Delamour	D12/84
D537,755 S	*	3/2007	Toth	D12/84
D617,236 S	*	6/2010	Counts	D12/84
D637,520 S	*	5/2011	Kerr	D12/84
D642,092 S	*	7/2011	Wiens	D12/84
D704,595 S	*	5/2014	Streicher	D12/84
D714,187 S	*	9/2014	Lian	D12/84
D717,210 S	*	11/2014	Wang	D12/84
D718,659 S	*	12/2014	Lin	D12/84
D721,297 S	*	1/2015	Zhang	D12/84
D721,298 S	*	1/2015	Li	D12/84
2009/0224570 A1	*	9/2009	Haswell	B62D 31/04
				296/178
2012/0161469 A1	*	6/2012	Kerr	B62D 31/02
				296/178

* cited by examiner

Primary Examiner — Darlington Ly

(57) **CLAIM**

The ornamental design for a bus, as shown and described.

DESCRIPTION

FIG. **1.1** is a front and right side perspective view of a bus,
in accordance with the present design;
FIG. **1.2** is a front elevation view thereof;
FIG. **1.3** is a right side elevation view thereof;
FIG. **1.4** is a front and left side perspective view thereof;
FIG. **1.5** is a rear and left side perspective view thereof;
FIG. **1.6** is a rear elevation view thereof;
FIG. **1.7** is a left side elevation view thereof;
FIG. **1.8** is a rear and right side perspective view thereof; and
FIG. **1.9** is a top plan view thereof.

1 Claim, 9 Drawing Sheets

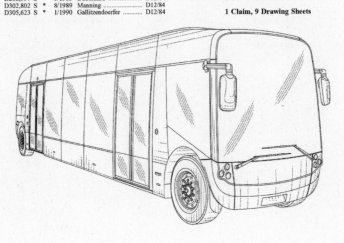

TITLE: DRONE
INVENTOR: JUN ZHOU
ASSIGNEE: GUANGDONG SHIJI TECHNOLOGY COMPANY

PATENT NUMBER: USD 881,067
PATENT FILED: MARCH 8, 2019
PATENT GRANTED: APRIL 14, 2020

(12) **United States Design Patent** (10) Patent No.: **US D881,067 S**
   Zhou   (45) **Date of Patent:** ** Apr. 14, 2020

(54) **DRONE**

(71) Applicant: **Jun Zhou**, Shantou (CN)

(72) Inventor: **Jun Zhou**, Shantou (CN)

(73) Assignee: **GUANGDONG SHIJI TECHNOLOGY CO., LTD.**, Shantou (CN)

(**) Term: **15 Years**

(21) Appl. No.: **29/682,832**

(22) Filed: **Mar. 8, 2019**

(30) **Foreign Application Priority Data**

   Jan. 23, 2019   (CN) 2019 3 0037898

(51) **LOC (12) Cl.** **12-07**
(52) **U.S. Cl.**
   USPC **D12/16.1**
(58) **Field of Classification Search**
   USPC D12/1, 2, 3, 4, 16.1, 319–345;
                                                      D21/437–455
   CPC B64C 29/0033; B64C 2201/021; B64C
               29/02; B64C 2201/088; B64C 2201/104;
                                            B64C 2201/141
   See application file for complete search history.

(56) **References Cited**

U.S. PATENT DOCUMENTS

D628,658	S	*	12/2010	Wurm D21/442
D710,454	S	*	8/2014	Barajas D12/16.1
D741,779	S	*	10/2015	Hsiao D12/16.1
D768,539	S	*	10/2016	Lee D12/16.1
D772,991	S	*	11/2016	Caubel D12/16.1
D793,486	S	*	8/2017	Lee D21/453
D795,741	S	*	8/2017	Li D12/16.1
D795,742	S	*	8/2017	Li D12/16.1

D795,743	S	*	8/2017	Li D12/16.1
D795,967	S	*	8/2017	Haley D12/16.1
D797,602	S	*	9/2017	Li D12/16.1
D798,961	S	*	10/2017	Li D21/441
D803,098	S	*	11/2017	Lee D12/16.1
D803,328	S	*	11/2017	Lee D21/441
D805,431	S	*	12/2017	Li D12/16.1
D806,606	S	*	1/2018	Morrison D12/16.1
D813,723	S	*	3/2018	Ahn D12/16.1
D813,724	S	*	3/2018	Hu D12/16.1
D814,970	S	*	4/2018	Chen D12/16.1
D814,971	S	*	4/2018	Huang D12/16.1
D816,546	S	*	5/2018	Wang D12/16.1
D817,850	S	*	5/2018	Xiao D12/328
D818,872	S	*	5/2018	Ho D12/16.1
D818,874	S	*	5/2018	Tian D12/16.1
D819,749	S	*	6/2018	Caubel D21/449
D830,896	S	*	10/2018	Lutterodt D12/16.1
D843,267	S	*	3/2019	Gao D12/16.1
D849,154	S	*	5/2019	Zhao D21/436
D850,978	S	*	6/2019	Gao D12/16.1
10,317,915	B2	*	6/2019	Tankersley G05D 1/0094

(Continued)

Primary Examiner — Marissa J Cash

(57) **CLAIM**

The ornamental design for a drone, as shown and described.

DESCRIPTION

FIG. 1 is a front perspective view of the drone showing my new design;
FIG. 2 is a rear perspective view thereof;
FIG. 3 is a front elevational view thereof;
FIG. 4 is a rear elevational view thereof;
FIG. 5 is a left side elevational view thereof;
FIG. 6 is a right side elevational view thereof;
FIG. 7 is a top plan view thereof;
FIG. 8 is a bottom plan view thereof; and,
FIG. 9 is a perspective view thereof, showing the drone in packed shape.

1 Claim, 8 Drawing Sheets

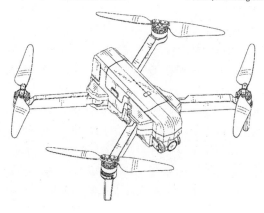

TITLE: ROBOT FOR GUIDING PEOPLE
INVENTORS: JINSU KIM, TAEWOO YOO, YOUSOOK EUN
& SOONHO JUNG
ASSIGNEE: LG ELECTRONICS & INCHEON AIRPORT

PATENT NUMBER: USD 881,249
PATENT FILED: AUGUST 6, 2018
PATENT GRANTED: APRIL 14, 2020

(12) **United States Design Patent**   (10) Patent No.:   **US D881,249 S**
        Kim et al.   (45) **Date of Patent:**   ∗∗ **Apr. 14, 2020**

(54) **ROBOT FOR GUIDING PEOPLE**

(71) Applicants: **LG ELECTRONICS INC.**, Seoul
           (KR); **INCHEON INTERNATIONAL
           AIRPORT CORPORATION**, Incheon
           (KR)

(72) Inventors: **Jinsu Kim**, Seoul (KR); **Taewoo Yoo**,
           Seoul (KR); **Yousook Eun**, Seoul (KR);
           Soonho Jung, Seoul (KR)

(73) Assignees: **LG ELECTRONICS INC.**, Seoul
           (KR); **INCHEON INTERNATIONAL
           AIRPORT CORPORATION**, Incheon
           (KR)

(∗∗) Term: **15 Years**

(21) Appl. No.: **29/659,107**

(22) Filed: **Aug. 6, 2018**

(51) **LOC (12) Cl.** **15-99**

(52) **U.S. Cl.**
      USPC **D15/199**

(58) **Field of Classification Search**
      USPC D15/199; D21/578–583, 621, 622;
                                                              D32/21
      CPC B25J 5/007; B60B 19/006; B62D 57/024;
                          H01F 7/0221; Y10S 901/01
      See application file for complete search history.

(56) **References Cited**

U.S. PATENT DOCUMENTS

D549,756	S	*	8/2007	Park	D15/199
D579,035	S	*	10/2008	Kim	B25J 11/008
					D15/199
D614,251	S	*	4/2010	Chung	D15/199
D635,603	S	*	4/2011	Paz Rodriguez	D15/199
D644,256	S	*	8/2011	Kitano	D15/199
D672,408	S	*	12/2012	Ohler	D15/199
D685,438	S	*	7/2013	Fan	D15/199

D701,256	S	*	3/2014	Song	D15/199
D710,953	S	*	8/2014	Katsutani	D15/199
D719,620	S	*	12/2014	Clerc	B25J 5/007
					D15/199
D725,166	S	*	3/2015	Paik	D15/199
D761,894	S	*	7/2016	Ho	D15/199
D793,145	S	*	8/2017	Huang	D15/199
D806,805	S	*	1/2018	Takahashi	D21/578
D809,040	S	*	1/2018	Webb, II	D15/199
D810,167	S	*	2/2018	Yang	D15/199
D811,458	S	*	2/2018	Wang	D15/199
D813,281	S	*	3/2018	Kittmann	D15/199
D813,285	S	*	3/2018	Wei	D15/199
D817,375	S	*	5/2018	Deyle	D15/199
D822,740	S	*	7/2018	Tsai	D15/199
D822,770	S	*	7/2018	Hsiao	D21/578
D823,917	S	*	7/2018	Bernazeau	D15/199
D825,010	S	*	8/2018	Osentoski	D21/578
D830,438	S	*	10/2018	Haddadin	D15/199
D835,693	S	*	12/2018	Lee	D15/199

(Continued)

Primary Examiner.— Patricia A Palasik
(74) *Attorney, Agent, or Firm* — Birch, Stewart, Kolasch
& Birch, LLP

(57)   **CLAIM**

The ornamental design for a robot for guiding people, as
shown and described.

DESCRIPTION

FIG. 1 is a front perspective view of a robot for guiding
people showing our new design;
FIG. 2 is a front view thereof;
FIG. 3 is a rear view thereof;
FIG. 4 is a left side view thereof where the right side view
is a mirror image;
FIG. 5 is a top plan view thereof; and,
FIG. 6 is a bottom plan view thereof.
The broken lines depict portions of the robot for guiding
people that form no part of the claimed design.

1 Claim, 6 Drawing Sheets

TITLE: RESPIRATORY MASK
INVENTOR: PAMELA GABRIEL
ASSIGNEE: SMARTMASK

PATENT NUMBER: USD 885,559
PATENT FILED: MARCH 4, 2019
PATENT GRANTED: MAY 26, 2020

(12) **United States Design Patent**   (10) **Patent No.:**   **US D885,559 S**
Gabriel   (45) **Date of Patent:**   ✱✱ **May 26, 2020**

(54) **RESPIRATORY MASK**

(71) Applicant: **The SmartMask LLC**, Greenwich, CT (US)

(72) Inventor: **Pamela Gabriel**, Greenwich, CT (US)

(73) Assignee: **The SmartMask LLC**, Greenwich, CT (US)

(✱✱) Term: **15 Years**

(21) Appl. No.: **29/682,231**

(22) Filed: **Mar. 4, 2019**

(51) **LOC (12) Cl.** **29-02**
(52) **U.S. Cl.**
     USPC **D24/110.1; D29/108**
(58) **Field of Classification Search**
     USPC D24/110, 110.1–110.4, 127, 162, 164;
                 D29/102, 107, 108, 110, 129
     CPC A62B 18/006; A62B 18/045; A62B 18/08;
              A62B 18/04; A62B 17/04; A62B 18/10;
              A62B 23/025; A62B 23/02; A62B 18/02;
              A62B 18/025; A62B 7/10; A62B 9/02;
              A62B 18/00; A42B 3/288; A42B 3/225;
              A42B 3/286; A61M 16/06; A61M
              16/0622; A63B 23/18
     See application file for complete search history.

(56) **References Cited**

U.S. PATENT DOCUMENTS

2,281,181	A	4/1942	Clarke
2,362,382	A *	11/1944	Lehmberg A41D 13/1146
			128/206.15
D243,128	S *	1/1977	Morgan D29/108
D277,520	S *	2/1985	Gregory D24/110.1
4,520,509	A	6/1985	Ward
4,641,379	A *	2/1987	Martin A41D 13/1161
			128/206.28
D340,317	S *	10/1993	Cole D24/110.1

5,419,318	A	5/1995	Tayebi
5,467,765	A	11/1995	Maturaporn
5,561,863	A	10/1996	Carlson, II
5,717,991	A	2/1998	Nozaki et al.
5,819,731	A	10/1998	Dyrud et al.
6,176,576	B1	1/2001	Green et al.
7,044,131	B2	5/2006	Griesbach, III et al.
7,313,246	B2	12/2007	Miller et al.
7,488,068	B2	2/2009	Welchel et al.
7,620,429	B1	11/2009	Frerking et al.
7,836,887	B1	11/2010	Kling
D665,903	S *	8/2012	Sullivan, Jr. D24/110.1
8,240,302	B1	8/2012	Tayebi et al.
8,939,769	B2	1/2015	Yoo et al.
9,036,847	B2	5/2015	Han et al.
9,457,207	B2 *	10/2016	Waterford A62B 18/082
9,643,048	B1 *	5/2017	Danford A61M 16/20
9,707,444	B1 *	7/2017	Danford A63B 23/18
D811,581	S *	2/2018	Danford D24/110.1
D820,974	S *	6/2018	Danford D24/110.1

(Continued)

Primary Examiner — Lilyana Bekic

(74) *Attorney, Agent, or Firm* — St. Onge Steward Johnston & Reens LLC

(57) **CLAIM**

The ornamental design for a respiratory mask, as shown and described.

DESCRIPTION

FIG. **1** is a front perspective view of a respiratory mask showing my new design;
FIG. **2** is a front elevational view thereof;
FIG. **3** is a right side elevational view thereof;
FIG. **4** is a rear elevational view thereof;
FIG. **5** is a left side elevational view thereof;
FIG. **6** is a top plan view thereof; and,
FIG. **7** is a bottom plan view thereof.
The broken lines in the drawings depict portions of the respiratory mask that form no part of the claimed design.

1 Claim, 7 Drawing Sheets

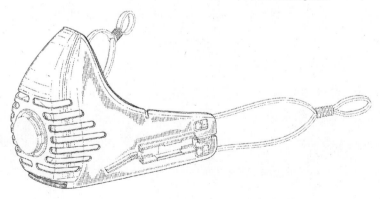

This directory is designed to give readers an overview of the enormous typological range of design patents featured in this volume. This collection of patents falls into a number of typological categories and feature objects designed for various aspects of everyday life including designs for the home, the workplace, designs seen on the streets, and in the stores, buildings and gas stations of towns and cities, and for travel of all kinds. The directory lists the patents under a primary category, and subsequently a secondary category. For example under the primary category of Drink Preparation, you will then find, in alphabetical order, sub-categories to do with the preparation of hot and cold drinks such as bottle openers, cocktail shakers, kettles, ice cube trays, and tea pots.

This directory is designed to give readers an overview of the extraordinary range of gifted designers, referred to as "Inventors" on patent documents, featured in the preceding pages. As well as some of the biggest names in twentieth and twenty-first century product design, including Arne Jacobsen, Henry Dreyfuss, Charles Eames, Dieter Rams, Eero Saarinen, Florence Knoll, Raymond Loewy, Ettore Sottsass, and Philippe Starck, this volume also introduces readers to designers whose names are largely unknown, though their work is familiar to many of us through the everyday items that form an integral part of our lives.

This directory is designed to give readers an overview of the companies and brands (referred to in patent documents as "Assignees") that commissioned so many of the designs featured in the preceding pages. Many of these have been household names for many decades – for example Casio, Coca-Cola, and Chrysler – but some brands had their heyday in the early years of the twentieth century before giving way to new ideas and new technologies, while still others were victims of the ravages of economic instability and other vagaries of the modern world.

3M INNOVATIVE PROPERTIES
COMPANY 922, 990

A

A. AHLSTROM OSAKEYHTIO . . . 750
A. C. GILBERT COMPANY 91,
250, 281, 352
A.S. BECK SHOE CORPORATION . . 166
ACE MFG. COMPANY 210
ACME SHEAR COMPANY, THE . . 315
AGFA ANSCO CORPORATION . . . 179
AKTIEBOLAGET ELEKTROLUX . . 544
AKTIEBOLAGET GUSTAVSBERGS
FABRIKER 744, 756
AKTIEBOLAGET GYLLING &
COMPANY 585
ALFA ROMEO SOCIETÀ 488
ALFONSO BIALETTI 904
ALFRED B. MARX & GEORGE E.
MARX 40
ALKO 692
ALPHICOM 1015
ALSTOM TRANSPORT 978
ALUMINUM COOKING UTENSIL
COMPANY 177, 183
ALVEY-FERGUSON COMPANY 73
AMANA REFRIGERATION 528
AMAZON TECHNOLOGIES 1022, 1023
AMERICAN CAN COMPANY 301
AMERICAN FLOOR SURFACING
MACHINE COMPANY 358
AMERICAN MACHINE & FOUNDRY
COMPANY 582
AMERICAN OPTICAL COMPANY 437
AMERICAN RADIATOR & STANDARD
SANITARY CORPORATION . . . 523
AMERICAN TELEPHONE &
TELEGRAPH COMPANY 112, 117
AMERICAN NATIONAL COMPANY . . . 230
AMI 552
ANIMAL TRAP COMPANY OF
AMERICA 408
ANSCO PHOTOPRODUCTS 131
APPLE 971, 973, 988
APPLE COMPUTER 801, 816,
895, 907, 929, 937, 946
ART METAL WORKS 266
ART METAL-KNOLL CORPORATION . . 667
ARTEMIDE 840,
989, 992, 1008
ASKO OSAKEYHTIO 674
ASSOCIATED ELECTRICAL
INDUSTRIES 609
AT&T BELL LABORATORIES . . . 858
ATARI 772, 806
ATLANTA STOVE WORKS 60
AUTO-MERCHANDISING COMPANY
OF PITTSBURGH 59
AUTOMATIC CANTEEN COMPANY OF
AMERICA 621
AVCO MANUFACTURING
CORPORATION 434, 443,
444, 480, 519

B

B.K. REHATEX 930
B&B ITALIA 994, 997
BANG & OLUFSEN 865,
933, 936, 972
BANK SOUTH CORPORATION . . . 828
BARD-PARKER COMPANY 475
BAYERISCHE MOTOREN WERKE . . . .
580, 606, 775
BELDING-HALL COMPANY 52
BELL & HOWELL COMPANY 530
BELL TELEPHONE LABORATORIES . .
162, 163, 227, 294, 415,
592, 638, 657, 664
BELMONT RADIO CORPORATION . . . 357
BENDIX HOME APPLIANCES . . 269, 414
BERNARD ROBERTS 495
BERT M. MORRIS COMPANY . . . 366
BIC 976
BIRTMAN ELECTRIC COMPANY 418
BLACK & DECKER 787, 882
BOEING AIRPLANE COMPANY 181, 257
BOEING COMPANY 663
BOHN ALUMINUM & BRASS
CORPORATION 354
BORDEN COMPANY 954
BOSE CORPORATION . . 343, 916, 1007
BOSTON PENCIL POINTER
COMPANY 88
BOWSER 603
BRAUN 652,
661, 678, 680, 682, 706,
708, 714, 782, 786, 859
BRAUN ESPANOLA 805
BRIGGS MANUFACTURING
COMPANY 233, 237, 331
BRIONVEGA 832
BRISTOL-MYERS COMPANY 326
BRITA WASSER-FILTER SYSTEME . . 871
BRUNSWICK-BALKE-COLLENDER
COMPANY 142, 283
BURNS-POLLOCK   ELECTRIC
MANUFACTURING COMPANY . . 104
BY THE NUMBERS 635

C

C. JOSEPH LAMY 794
CALIFORNIA INSTITUTE OF
TECHNOLOGY 912
CALKINS APPLIANCE
CORPORATION 367
CALORIC APPLIANCE
CORPORATION 604
CANON KABUSHIKI KAISHA . . 703,
901, 924, 941
CARRIER CORPORATION 421
CARTER'S INK COMPANY 68, 288, 605
CASIO COMPUTER COMPANY . . 854, 893
CASSINA 818,
894, 982
CHARAK FURNITURE COMPANY . . 591

BOOKS

BAKER, ERIC & JANE MARTIN. "GREAT INVENTIONS, GOOD INTENTIONS: AN ILLUSTRATED HISTORY OF AMERICAN DESIGN PATENTS." SAN FRANCISCO: CHRONICLE BOOKS, 1990.

BECK, JAMES AND VICTORIA K. MATRANGA, ET. AL. "AMERICA AT HOME: A CELEBRATION OF TWENTIETH-CENTURY HOUSEWARES"

BIRD, MATTHEW. "USING DIGITAL TOOLS TO WORK AROUND THE CANON," IN KAUFMANN-BUHLER, VICTORIA PASS & CHRISTOPHER WILSON. "DESIGN HISTORY BEYOND THE CANON." LONDON: BLOOMSBURY VISUAL ARTS, 2019.

"CHAIR: 500 DESIGNS THAT MATTER". LONDON: PHAIDON PRESS, 2018.

DREYFUSS, HENRY. "DESIGNING FOR PEOPLE." NEW YORK: SIMON & SCHUSTER, 1955.

FIELL, CHARLOTTE & PETER FIELL. "INDUSTRIAL DESIGN A-Z." COLOGNE: TASCHEN GMBH, 2000.

FLINCHUM, RUSSELL. "HENRY DREYFUSS: INDUSTRIAL DESIGNER." NEW YORK: RIZZOLI INTERNATIONAL, 1997.

GORMAN, CARMA. "THE INDUSTRIAL DESIGN READER." NEW YORK: ALLWORTH PRESS, 2003.

HESKETT, JOHN. "INDUSTRIAL DESIGN." LONDON: THAMES & HUDSON, 1980.

"INDUSTRIAL DESIGN IN AMERICA 1954." NEW YORK: SOCIETY OF INDUSTRIAL DESIGNERS, 1954.

LIPPINCOTT, J. GORDON. "DESIGN FOR BUSINESS." CHICAGO: PAUL THEOBALD, 1947.

LOEWY, RAYMOND. "INDUSTRIAL DESIGN." WOODSTOCK: THE OVERLOOK PRESS, 1979.

MEIKLE, JEFFREY. "TWENTIETH CENTURY LIMITED: INDUSTRIAL DESIGN IN AMERICA 1925–1939." PHILADELPHIA: TEMPLE UNIVERSITY PRESS, 1980.

"PHAIDON DESIGN CLASSICS." LONDON: PHAIDON PRESS, 2006.

PRINCE, KEVIN. "THE ART OF THE PATENT." SAN JUAN CAPISTRANO: GLASSKO PRESS, 2011.

PULOS, ARTHUR J. "THE AMERICAN DESIGN ADVENTURE." CAMBRIDGE: THE MIT PRESS, 1988.

PULOS, ARTHUR J. "THE AMERICAN DESIGN ETHIC: HISTORY OF INDUSTRIAL DESIGN." CAMBRIDGE: THE MIT PRESS, 1983.

RADZINSKY, HARRY. "MAKING PATENT DRAWINGS." NEW YORK: THE MACMILLAN CO., 1946.

"REPORT OF THE COMMISSIONER OF PATENTS TO CONGRESS." WASHINGTON: GOVERNMENT PRINTING OFFICE (MULTIPLE VOLUMES).

SHOEMAKER, WILLIAM D. "PATENTS FOR DESIGNS." WASHINGTON: H.D. WILLIAMS CO., 1929.

"STATISTICAL ABSTRACTS OF THE UNITED STATES." WASHINGTON: GOVERNMENT PRINTING OFFICE, (MULTIPLE VOLUMES).

SYMONS, WILLIAM L. "THE LAW OF PATENTS FOR DESIGNS." WASHINGTON: JOHN BYRNE & CO., 1914.

TEAGUE, WALTER DORWIN. "DESIGN THIS DAY." NEW YORK: HARCOURT, BRACE & CO., 1940.

"THE DESIGN BOOK." LONDON: PHAIDON PRESS, 2013.

"U.S. INDUSTRIAL DESIGN 1949-1950." NEW YORK: THE STUDIO PUBLICATIONS INC., 1950.

"U.S. INDUSTRIAL DESIGN 1951." NEW YORK: THE STUDIO PUBLICATIONS INC., 1951.

VAN DOREN, HAROLD. "INDUSTRIAL DESIGN: A PRACTICAL GUIDE." NEW YORK: MCGRAW-HILL BOOK CO. INC., 1940.

WRIGHT, MILTON. "INVENTIONS AND PATENTS: THEIR DEVELOPMENT & PROMOTION." NEW YORK: MCGRAW-HILL BOOK CO. INC., 1927.

PERIODICALS

AD
ADVERTISING ARTS
COMMERCIAL ART & INDUSTRY
DESIGN & PAPER
DESIGN QUARTERLY
INDUSTRIAL ARTS
INDUSTRIAL DESIGN
INTERIORS
PM
THE STUDIO

"BOTH FISH & FOWL." FORTUNE, FEBRUARY 1934.

BURSTEIN, SARAH. "THE PATENTED DESIGN." 83 TENNESSEE LAW REVIEW J. 161 (2015).

BURSTEIN, SARAH. "THE ARTICLE OF MANUFACTURE IN 1887." 31 BERKELEY TECHNOLOGY LAW JOURNAL, J. 1 (2017).

COOK, LISA D. "VIOLENCE AND ECONOMIC ACTIVITY: EVIDENCE FROM AFRICAN AMERICAN PATENTS, 1870-1940." JOURNAL OF ECONOMIC GROWTH, JUNE 2014.

DU MONT, JASON J. & MARK D. JANIS. "THE ORIGINS OF DESIGN PATENT PROTECTION." 88 INDIANA LAW JOURNAL J. 837 (2013).

GORMAN, CARMA. "THE ROLE OF TRADEMARK LAW IN THE HISTORY OF US VISUAL IDENTITY." JOURNAL OF DESIGN HISTORY, AUGUST 2017.

ACT OF CONGRESS AUG. 29, 1842, CH. 263, § 3, 5 STAT. 543, 543-44 (1842).

ACT OF CONGRESS MAY 9, 1902 CH. 783, 32 STAT. 193, 193. (AMENDING REV. STAT. 4929).

ACT OF CONGRESS JULY 19, 1952, CH. 950, 66 STAT. 805.

ONLINE RESOURCES

PATENTS.GOOGLE.COM
FREEPATENTSONLINE.COM
U.S. PATENT & TRADEMARK OFFICE. MANUAL OF PATENT EXAMINING PROCEDURE (9TH ED., REV. JUL. 2015, NOV. 2015), AVAILABLE AT USPTO. GOV/PATENT/LAWS-AND-REGULATIONS/MANUAL-PATENT-EXAMINING-PROCEDURE

AUTHOR'S ACKNOWLEDGMENTS
The author wishes to acknowledge this
book's debt to the following persons
without whom this project simply could not
have been undertaken. To Virginia McLeod
at Phaidon, who saw potential in this idea,
collaborated on the grueling selection
process and talked me off the ledge on
more than one occasion, I offer my deep-
est gratitude. Nancy Green helped shape
the concept from the proposal stage.
Matthew Bird at the Rhode Island School
of Design offered everything from inspira-
tion to proof reading. Carma Gorman of the
University of Texas at Austin and Victoria Matranga of the Industrial Designers
Society of America fielded all variety of
barely intelligible inquiries from someone
they'd never met. To friends and family for
their support throughout, and especially
to Pamela Anderson at the U.S. National
Archives and Records Administration, Henry
Cittone, Chris Katopis at the U.S. Patent
Office, Scott Keeley, Alex Magoun, Kevin
Prince, Danielle Shapiro, Allen Shifrin, and
Kyle Supley, my heartfelt thanks; I could
not have done this without you.

PUBLISHER'S ACKNOWLEDGMENTS
The publisher would like to extend
special thanks to Caitlin Arnell Argles,
Clive Burroughs, Vishwa Kaushal, Anthony
Naughton, and Ana Teodoro for their
invaluable contributions to this book.

IMAGE CREDITS
Every reasonable effort has been made
to acknowledge the ownership of copyright
for drawings included in this volume.
Any errors that may have occurred are
inadvertent, and will be corrected in
subsequent editions provided notification
is sent in writing to the publisher.

NOTES
[1] Dreyfuss, "Designing for People," 219.
[2] Lippincott, "Design for Industry," 199.
[3] Cook, "Violence and Economic Activity," 222.

Phaidon Press Limited
2 Cooperage Yard
London E15 2QR

Phaidon Press Inc.
65 Bleecker Street
New York, NY 10012

phaidon.com

First published 2021
© 2021 Phaidon Press Limited

ISBN 978 1 83866 256 1

A CIP catalogue record for this book
is available from the British Library and
the Library of Congress.

COMMISSIONING EDITOR ...... Virginia McLeod

PRODUCTION CONTROLLER .... Lily Rodgers

DESIGN .... João Mota

PRINTED IN ITALY